ESSAYS ON MEXICO, CENTRAL AND SOUTH AMERICA

Scholarly Debates from the 1950s to the 1990s

Series Editor

JORGE I. DOMÍNGUEZ

Harvard University

A GARLAND SERIES

Series Contents

VOLUME

1

ECONOMIC STRATEGIES AND POLICIES IN LATIN AMERICA

Edited with an introduction by

JORGE I. DOMÍNGUEZ

GARLAND PUBLISHING, INC.
New York & London
1994

Library of Congress Cataloging-in-Publication Data

Economic strategies and policies in Latin America / edited, with an introduction, by Jorge I. Domínguez.
p. cm. — (Essays on Mexico, Central and South America ; v. 1)
ISBN 0–8153–1485–X (alk. paper)
1. Latin America—Economic policy. 2. Latin America—Economic conditions—1945– I. Domínguez, Jorge I., 1945– . II. Series.
HC125.E376 1994
338.98—dc20 93–43066
CIP

Printed on acid-free, 250-year-life paper
Manufactured in the United States of America

Contents

INTRODUCTION

Economists have debated Latin America's economic strategies at two moments since the second world war. The first debate, often characterized as between monetarists and structuralists, flourished from the late 1950s to the early 1970s. It focused on the strengths and weaknesses of a strategy of import-substituting industrialization (ISI). The second debate has unfolded since the early 1980s. It focuses on policies of economic stabilization to control inflation, and on exchange rates, trade regimes and, especially, a strategic orientation toward reliance upon markets in order to foster economic growth.

The central figure in the first debate was Raúl Prebisch. He sought to promote industrialization; he was deeply skeptical that the application of new technologies in primary exporting sectors would be an engine for growth. He argued that there were serious disparities in the income elasticity of demand for primary products (low) and for manufactures (high); as a result, the terms of trade of primary exporters deteriorated inexorably. "The only way" to correct these deleterious effects was to foster industrialization by means of substituting for imports. This should be done through tariff protection, not through devaluation, because the latter forces the adjustment of the entire price system, whereas protection limits the adjustment just to certain branches of industry. Prebisch symbolized one important wing of structuralist economic analysis.

One critic was Arnold Harberger. He argued that trade barriers lowered economic activity and reduced national income. He criticized ISI for generating higher rates of inflation, and the disincentive to savings from negative real rates of interest that were being used to foster industrialization. He argued on behalf of low uniform tariff rates to reduce distortions within and across economic sectors. He believed that technological changes could accelerate the growth rate and argued, therefore, for investments in education and training to improve the quality of the labor supply.

Dudley Seers presented a clear exposition of a structuralist argument that already featured a critique of ISI. His starting diagnosis was the same as Prebisch's: the income elasticity of demands for Latin America's primary exports was low. He also believed that the ISI strategy was appropriate though he criticized its lack of balance, that is, it favored consumer goods industries. He argued that ISI had succeeded in transforming the economies of those countries that had pursued it. Growth rates, and especially the growth rates of manufacturing, had been very high. He disagreed with those who blamed the slow growth of exports on ISI, claiming that only in Argentina between 1945 and 1952 did "bad policy" have a "major adverse influence on total exports." Structural rigidities in the primary goods sectors, not ISI, were a major cause of inflation: as urban incomes and urban consumer demand for food rose, agriculture was unable to supply food, and thus prices rose.

Nathaniel Leff and Antonio Delfim Netto illustrate the tempered enthusiasm for ISI. ISI generated very high growth rates; indeed, its main problem was its excessive success. As incomes rise, the demand for imports rises as well, offsetting the balance of payments gains of the ISI effort. Their prescription was to fine-tune ISI by fostering the inflow of public capital—a harbinger of subsequent international indebtedness. Netto would become the architect of Brazil's economic policies from the late 1960s to the early 1980s.

By the mid-1960s, as David Felix argues, structuralists seemed ascendant. As structuralists had forecast, a series of monetarist-inspired stabilization programs could not be sustained. Though Felix calls himself a "structuralist in spirit," he echoes the monetarists' reply that some of these adjustment programs had been ill-conceived because they had failed to take sufficiently into account the severe distortions already created by ISI in the structure of consumer demand and in the capacity to import. He recapitulates the debate, with special attention to the cases of Argentina and Chile.

By the late 1960s, the enthusiasm for ISI had begun to wane. Albert Hirschman's influential article called attention to the reemergence of Latin American *fracasomanía,* namely, the belief that Latin Americans could do nothing right. ISI in Latin America had imported techniques, not the process of learning; thus the transformative effects of industrialization were weaker than expected. The government had to play a stronger and longer role in protecting industries than expected. Entrepreneurship seemed weak, and too dependent on foreign firms and immigrants. Industrial costs were high, exports were low, job creation was limited, and the deficit on the balance of payments current account typically high. Hirschman did not think, however, that ISI had become exhausted. He pointed to the forward and backward linkage effects of industrialization, which continued to provide economic dynamism, and to the potential for further industrial growth as domestic markets grew. Moreover, he argued inflation and over-valued exchange rates were not so bad, for they amounted to "an indirect rather than a direct squeeze of political and socially powerful groups"—a politically useful, hidden tax on the powerful.

Werner Baer, too, reflected the mixed feelings about ISI. It was hard to imagine, he noted, how economies could grow without industrialization; he emphasized that ISI made sense particularly in a large country such as Brazil—though not in a small country such as Chile. But Baer also called attention to ISI's inefficient allocation of resources, its indiscriminate and across-the-board industrial protection, and its lack of economies of scale.

The Central American countries came late to the ISI strategies but, as Edelberto Torres-Rivas and Victor Bulmer-Thomas show, they followed it along the lines of their predecessors with two differences. First, because the domestic markets in Central American countries are so small, the Central American Common Market was launched in the early 1960s. Second, agricultural export sectors remained economically and politically dominant. As Bulmer-Thomas notes, long-term growth rates were quite good. The common market stopped working effectively in 1969, however, when El Salvador and Honduras went to war with each other. By the end of the 1970s, commodity prices collapsed, launching Central America into a severe economic depression from which it has yet to recover fully. Bulmer-Thomas calls attention to an important explanation for Central American agribusiness export growth: driving peasants off the land. As a result, the more the export economy grew, the greater the problem of land dispossession and rural unemployment, and the greater the social instability—a cauldron for revolution.

By the late 1970s, the "real world" had changed. First in Chile, and then in Argentina, governments adopted policies to constrain inflation, reduce industrial protection, and rely more fully upon markets. These strategies, in turn, generated new scholarly debates.

Carlos Díaz-Alejandro welcomed various aspects of financial liberalization in southern cone countries, in particular freeing domestic capital markets from government-induced distortions. By the early 1980s, he also observed that these strategies failed spectacularly, leading to extremely high government intervention in financial markets in Argentina and Chile. The problem was that central banks in both countries were ideologically dogmatic in their faith in free markets and deliberately neglected financial market regulation. They permitted the co-mingling of financial and non-financial firms, which led to concentrated economic power, subsidized interest rates, and eventually cascading bankruptcies. In their love of markets, these governments forgot the role of states in providing market rules.

Sebastian Edwards celebrates several of the important accomplishments of Chilean economic policy in the 1970s, especially the reduction of inflation, and the liberalization of trade and finance. He also criticizes the Chilean government's policy mistakes and inconsistencies, in particular the combination of backward wage indexation—as inflation dropped, indexing wages to the inflation level of the previous month automatically raised real wages—and a fixed exchange rate. He agrees with Díaz-Alejandro that insufficient financial regulation may have permitted too large an inflow of foreign funds (in part to supplement a very low domestic savings rate), which also led to peso appreciation, and the loss of competitiveness of the tradeables sector. To remain afloat, the latter searched for loans that it could not repay, leading eventually to a financial crash and large currency devaluation.

Mario Blejer and Adrienne Cheasty summarize the comparative experience, mainly in Argentina, Brazil, and Israel, all of which introduced "shock" stabilization programs in 1985–86, which sought to reduce inflation rates drastically. The programs featured a mix of policies, including wage and price freezes. These policies failed, they argue, because they were not accompanied by the necessary fiscal and monetary policies. They created shortages, bottlenecks, and losses of efficiency. They could not be administered effectively. Statist approaches to inflation reduction did not work.

On the other hand, Bolivia broke its hyperinflation of 1984–85 in orthodox fashion. Interest rates were raised, monetary growth was curtailed dramatically, government expenditures and especially consumer subsidies were cut, and taxes were raised. Bolivia remains in terrible shape, Manuel Pastor notes, but its weak state, and its dire inflationary situation, may have left it with no options but the program it adopted successfully.

A subtle theme throughout the debate begun in the late 1970s focused on the proper role of the state in regulating markets. The concluding articles touch most directly on this issue and, in effect, frame the evolving debate in the 1990s.

Rudiger Dornbusch and Sebastian Edwards develop a devastating critique of what they call "macroeconomic populism," which, they argue, characterized the policies of Salvador Allende in Chile and Alan García in Peru. This failed policy approach emphasizes growth and income distribution and deemphasizes the risks of inflation and deficit finance, external constraints, and the reaction of economic agents to statist policies.

In his article on trade liberalization, Dornbusch argues vigorously for such policies though, in so doing, he calls attention to the need for government officials to act to foster such markets against the protectionist wishes of both bureaucrats and previously protected business firms. His argument, it might be said, requires the state to make markets free.

Helen Shapiro and Lance Taylor are more convinced defenders of the state's role in fostering economic growth. They argue that the state has had a role historically in launching accelerated growth, and that it still can. They focus on such issues as country size, the fiscal and managerial capacities of the state, the role of the state in fostering technological learning, and related issues, to insist on the utility of a wider array of state strategies in markets than some neoclassical economists might allow.

Albert Fishlow, finally, summarizes decades of scholarly analysis of states and markets, noting the retreat of ISI and of statist ideologies but also the newer critiques of *laissez-faire*. Modern micro-economic theory, he argues, has focused on incomplete markets, imperfect information, strategic interactions, principal-agent problems, transaction costs, and bounded rationality. Rent-seeking agents, after all, are often "private" firms milking the bloated state; they resist the markets and they abuse the state: to leave them "free to act" is counter-productive for markets and for policy.

A strong state, it seems, is needed to make markets free and to keep them free, to supply the public goods needed for economy and society, to invest in schools and thus in the acquisition and spread of learning and technologies, and to shape the investments for increased domestic savings. In their search for the market, the economists rediscovered the state.

Economic Strategies and Policies in Latin America

THE FUNDAMENTALS OF ECONOMIC PROGRESS IN UNDERDEVELOPED COUNTRIES

USING THE RESOURCES AT HAND MORE EFFECTIVELY[1]

By ARNOLD C. HARBERGER
University of Chicago

In this paper I attempt to explore the possible results of eliminating misallocations of resources in economies like Chile, Brazil, and Argentina. In Section I, a static framework is adopted; the conclusion is reached that reallocating existing resources, while maintaining the existing production functions in each line of activity, would raise national welfare by no more than 15 per cent. Section II focuses on the rate of growth; here it is concluded that policies aimed at eliminating "distortions" in the price mechanism can raise the long-term rate of growth of national income, but not spectacularly. It is argued that spectacular advances in the growth rate will come, if at all, from improvement in the quality of the labor force and from an increased pace of technical advance.

I

The principal sources of misallocation in the countries in question are: (*a*) a rapid rate of inflation, (*b*) a rate of interest on bank loans below the rate of inflation and hence negative in real terms, (*c*) substantial barriers to foreign trade, through a number of different devices, (*d*) considerable monopoly, usually in protected industries, (*e*) a sluggish and disequilibrated labor market, in which "equivalent" labor may get as little as two-thirds or three-fourths the average wage in some sectors (e.g., agriculture), and as much as one and one-fourth or one and one-half times the average wage in others (e.g., the large foreign-owned enterprises), and (*f*) a system of taxes and tax evasion which in various ways draws resources into a pattern in which the value of marginal product of similar resources differs quite substantially among activities and sectors. To try to estimate precisely the welfare costs of each type of distortion would at the present stage be hopelessly difficult. I have contented myself with trying to overestimate the welfare costs of each of two broad categories of distortions: external and internal. I try to overestimate in the sense that at the many places where more-or-less arbitrary assumptions were necessary, I have leaned toward those leading to a higher rather than a lower estimate of welfare cost. I divide

[1] This and all other footnotes appear at the end of this paper.

the internal from the external distortions because it is convenient to attempt to measure their costs in somewhat different ways.

To estimate the welfare costs of trade restrictions, I utilize the concept of an equivalent tariff. There must exist some rate of ad valorem duty on all imports which would restrict imports to their present overall level. I judge this rate to be around 50 per cent in the case of Chile.[2] This judgment is based on the fact that most of the protected industries could maintain present levels of output with this amount of protection. A few industries would have to curtail output if given only 50 per cent protection, but counterbalancing them would be a number of industries for which 50 per cent protection would be more than they currently enjoy, and which would expand output at the expense of imports if given such protection.

Assuming, then, that a 50 per cent tariff would restrict trade about as much as the present restrictions, we proceed to estimate the welfare costs of such a tariff. The foreign trade sector is sufficiently small (some 10 per cent of national income) that we can employ Marshallian methods without serious error. Initially, I assume that Chile has no influence over the world price of either her exports or her imports. With a 50 per cent tariff, the marginal dollar's worth of exports will buy import goods worth $1.50 internally; on the first dollar's worth of expanded exports, accordingly, the net gain is $.50. On the last unit of expanded trade following the elimination of the tariff, the net gain would be zero. Our measure of the welfare cost of a 50 per cent tariff is thus a triangle whose altitude is $.50 and whose base is the number of dollars by which exports (and imports) under free trade would exceed their levels under the tariff. I assume that trade would not more than double as a result of the introduction of free trade. The base of the triangle in question is thus taken to be not more than the present dollar value of exports, which amounts, in the countries in question, to some 10 per cent of the national income; and the area of the triangle, which is our measure of the welfare gain which would result from eliminating present restrictions, is estimated to be no more than 2½ per cent of the national income.

Why is it reasonable to suppose that trade would not more than double as a consequence of removing a 50 per cent tariff? Let us consider an example in which the freeing of trade leads to a 20 per cent rise in the relative price of the dollar. Internal prices of export-type goods thus rise 20 per cent. Internal prices of import-type goods, which would have fallen from index 150 to index 100 as a result of the tariff repeal if the exchange rate had remained unchanged, actually end up at 120, having fallen in the net by 20 per cent. In these circumstances a doubling of trade would reflect elasticities of import demand and export supply equal to 5. Neither a commodity-by-commodity approach, asking where one might expect additional imports or exports to appear as a result of price changes in, say, the Chilean economy, nor an examination of how imports and exports appear to have responded to price changes in the past suggests that the elasticities in question are as high as this.[3]

Two considerations would operate to modify our estimate that trade restrictions might cost the Chilean economy up to 2½ per cent of its national income. The first is that an across-the-board tariff at 50 per cent for all commodities tends to have less welfare cost than a set of different tariffs whose average rate is 50 per cent, since the welfare cost of a tariff varies with the square of the rate. This consideration, which would lead us to raise our estimate of the welfare costs of restrictions, is unlikely to be serious except in the cases of a few commodities (e.g., automobiles) on which the present restrictions operate with extreme severity, and which account for only a very small fraction of total trade. The second consideration is that to the extent that Chile has some monopoly power in the markets for its exports, the expansion of trade should optimally stop somewhat short of the free-trade point. This would lead us to lower our estimate, but again probably not to a serious extent. The only plausible instances of monopoly power are in copper and nitrates, and even here Chile's power to influence world market prices is probably quite small, especially in the longer run relevant to this discussion.

In estimating the welfare costs of "internal" distortions, I have chosen to focus on the basic resources: labor and capital. By comparing their actual distribution among sectors with that which would emerge in an optimum situation, we get an idea of the quantity distortions prevailing in the economy. Alternatively, by comparing the values of the marginal product produced by given resources in different sectors, we get an idea of the price distortions in the economy. This device is highly convenient for a problem as complicated as ours. A sector can have "too little" labor because of monopoly power of its producers, or because its output is subject to excise taxation, or because of an artificially high wage rate; yet the welfare costs of having a given amount less labor than the optimum are to a first approximation the same, regardless of the cause. Viewed from the price distortion side, the story is the same. The welfare costs of a given sector's having a marginal productivity of capital 10 per cent above the level which would equalize net rates of return in all sectors do not in the first instance depend on the reason why too little capital is used in the sector.

Needless to say, a focus as broad as ours requires a general-equilibrium approach. I have chosen to divide the economy into ten sectors producing equal values of product and to use initially as my measure of welfare a utility index of the Cobb-Douglas form:

$$U = X_1^{1/10} X_2^{1/10} X_3^{1/10} X_4^{1/10} X_5^{1/10} X_6^{1/10} X_7^{1/10} X_8^{1/10} X_9^{1/10} X_{10}^{1/10}$$

This index has the property that it says people are y per cent better off in any instance in which each of the goods and services they use has increased by y per cent. It furthermore implies a unit of elasticity of demand for the product of each of the sectors; in the case given, 10 per cent of the national income is spent on the product of each of the sectors regardless of the relative price structure. This assumption will be defended later, as will the arbitrary division into ten sectors.

Within each sector, I assume a production function of the form $X_i = L_i^{1/2} K_i^{1/2}$, where X_i is the output of the sector (measured in value-added terms), and L_i and K_i the quantities of labor and capital it uses. This function implies that if labor and capital were paid the value of their marginal product, half of the value added of each sector would go to each. These production functions can be substituted into the utility function to express utility directly as a function of the allocation of resources. Thus:

$$U = L_1^{1/20} K_1^{1/20} L_2^{1/20} K_2^{1/20} \cdots \quad \cdots \quad \cdots L_{10}^{1/20} K_{10}^{1/20} .$$

If labor in any sector were paid the value of its marginal product, it would receive 1/20 of the national income; thus in a competitive optimum situation labor would be equally distributed among the sectors. The same goes for capital. If we set the available amounts of labor and capital at 1,000 each, we conclude that the optimal allocation would be 100 of each factor in each sector.

We are now in a position to impose a set of distortions on this model economy. Table 1 shows a possible allocation of labor, different from the optimum, together with indices of the value of marginal product of labor in each sector.

TABLE 1

Sector	1	2	3	4	5	6	7	8	9	10
Quantity of labor...........	33⅓	50	75	90	100	100	110	125	150	166⅔
Marginal productivity of labor	300	200	133⅓	111	100	100	91	80	66⅔	60

In this case, sector 1 has only a third of the optimum quantity of labor, while sector 10 has two-thirds "too much." The marginal product of labor in sector 1 is five times that in sector 10, and that in sector 2 more than three times that in sector 10. I feel quite confident that the situation depicted in Table 1 is substantially more distorted than that actually prevailing in the labor market in Chile. Wages for labor of equivalent quality there may differ by a factor of two, but probably not much more and not in a very large fraction of the total market. The example thus allows for substantial effects from other influences, such as monopoly and taxes, which would cause differences between wages and the value of marginal product, and might make for more variance among sectors in marginal productivity than there is in wages.[4]

Under the optimum distribution of labor and capital (100 units of each factor in each sector), our welfare index would be 100; if capital were allocated optimally but labor were distributed as in Table 1, the welfare index would be 95. If labor were distributed as in Table 1, and capital likewise, the welfare index would be 91.[5] I believe that this last case allows for distortions in both the labor and capital markets which are more extreme than any likely distortions in the actual Chilean economy. My conclusion is accordingly that eliminating the internal, intersectoral distortions in the Chilean economy would raise the level of welfare by probably no more than 10 per cent.

I now turn to a brief defense of the assumptions underlying the above model, followed by an indication of how sensitive the result obtained is to changes in the assumptions.

The elasticity of demand for each sector's product was assumed to be unity. I take this to be a reasonable central value for the range of price elasticities that have been reliably estimated in demand studies. The price elasticity of demand for food appears to be about $-.4$, and this is almost surely at the low end of the scale; at the other extreme, price elasticities for housing and for refrigerators appear to be in the range between -1 and -2. Higher elasticities have been measured only in cases where the good in question has been so narrowly defined as to exclude an obvious close substitute.[6] I define my sectors as sets of products such that for no member of a set is there an obvious close substitute outside the set; thus guarding almost by definition against extremely high sector elasticities. On this definition there would be many more sectors than ten, but the sectors can then be reaggregated, putting those with similar resource distortions in one group.

The elasticity of substitution between labor and capital was assumed to be unity. In the absence of strong empirical evidence on this point, I defend my assumption by assuming alternatively very low (say .25) and very high (say 4.0) values for the elasticity of substitution. If capital were a very poor substitute for labor, the marginal product of capital would fall rapidly as extra capital was absorbed; we should have to conclude that Chile's capacity to absorb capital profitably was quite severely limited. On the other hand, if capital and labor were extremely good substitutes, the idea of Chile being seriously short of capital would make little sense. Labor, production-wise, could do practically the same jobs as capital would, and even adding greatly to the stock of capital relative to labor would have little effect on real wages. Even elasticities as low as .5 or as high as 2.0 appear to me to have implausible implications as to the consequences of a doubling of the capital stock in a country like Chile.[7]

The result obtained is only mildly sensitive to some of the assumptions made. It is, for example, not necessary that all the demand elasticities be unity, but only that they average to unity, in order to yield roughly the same result, provided that the sectoral demand elasticities are not highly correlated with the sectoral distortions. A similar situation prevails in the case of the sectoral elasticities of substitution between labor and capital. The result is quite insensitive to the division of the product of each sector between labor and capital; indeed it is mathematically invariant to changes in the exponents of the Cobb-Douglas function in the set of cases where the exponents are the same in all sectors.

The sensitivity to changes in the average demand elasticity and average substitution elasticity is a bit curious, because if we keep the price distortions the same as assumed earlier and reduce the amount of substitution in the model, the quantity distortions have to be reduced; while if we keep the quantity distortions the same as earlier and reduce the amount of substitution, the price distortions have to be increased. The welfare costs of a set of price distortions vary directly with the elasticities assumed, while the costs of a set of quantity distortions vary inversely with the elasticities. Thus, saying that the average demand elasticity and the average substitution elasticity "ought" to have been assumed to be $\frac{1}{2}$ rather than unity does not get one very far; one must decide whether to maintain the old set of price distortions or the old set of quantity distortions in the new situation in order to know whether the new elasticity assumption will cut our earlier estimate in half or double it. If, however, one is prepared to say that neither more extreme price distortions nor more extreme quantity distortions than those assumed are likely to prevail in the Chilean economy, then no changes in the assumed average elasticities can yield a higher estimate of welfare cost.

The principal sensitivity of the estimate is to the extreme distortions assumed. If, for sector 5 in Table 1, we had assumed the same quantity and price distortions as for sector 1, and if for sector 6 we had assumed the same quantity and price distortions as for sector 10, and if a similar augmentation of extreme distortions were made in the case of capital, our welfare index would have been 86 rather than 91. I feel reasonably confident that the assumed distortions are sufficiently extreme but indicate this sensitivity in the event that the judgments of others may differ.

Thus far we have not considered the possibility of distortions within sectors. Here I shall allow for 30 per cent of the national income to be affected by such distortions. Within this 30 per cent, I allow for one-half of each set of close substitutes to be priced 50 per cent "too high" relative to the other half of the set, and I allow for the cross-elasticities of demand between the two halves of each set to be 5 (to my knowledge, no reliable estimate of this high a cross-elasticity has yet appeared). These extreme allowances lead to an estimate of the welfare cost of within-sector distortions equal to 3 per cent of the national income. (The derivation of this result will be provided on request.)

In summary, I have estimated that the welfare costs of external distortions are less than 2½ per cent of the national income, the welfare costs of internal distortions among sectors less than 10 per cent of the national income, and the welfare costs of within-sector distortions less than 3 per cent of the national income. I reach the judgment that eliminating resource misallocations while maintaining existing production functions might raise the level of national welfare by some 15 per cent, but probably not more.

II

Section I suggests that policies to improve resource allocation in economies like Chile may have effects which are substantial but would probably not lead to spectacular changes in the level of living. In this section we test the possibility that better allocation policies might lead to a substantial increase in the rate of growth of national income; thus having a spectacular dynamic effect on living standards.

The percentage rate of growth, g, of national income can be expressed as follows:

$$g = s_L l + im + r + q_L + t,$$

where s_L is the share of labor in the national income, l the percentage rate of growth of the (employed) labor force, i the fraction of national income devoted to net investment, m a weighted average of the net marginal productivities of capital in the various segments of the economy, r the contribution to the rate of income growth of reallocations of the resources of the economy, q_L the contribution of improvements in the quality of the labor force, and t the contribution of technological advance. I shall consider each of the five components of the rate of growth in turn, defining it in more detail, indicating its possible order of magnitude, and attempting to judge its sensitivity to improved allocation policies.

The contribution of labor force growth to income growth is measured by $s_L l$. If the aggregate employed labor force grows at 2 per cent per year, we estimate its potential contribution to national income by assuming that the new entrants have a similar quality distribution as the existing labor force and that they distribute themselves among industries and activities in the same proportions as the existing labor force. Taking the wage rate in each activity as our indicator of marginal productivity, we estimate the dollar contribution of this year's labor force growth to be 2 per cent of last year's aggregate wage bill. Expressing this as a percentage of last year's national income yields $s_L l$. In Chile the labor force has grown at around 2 per cent or slightly more per annum and the share of labor in the national income has been a little over one-half. Hence we reach the conclusion that labor force growth contributes slightly more than 1 per cent per annum to the rate of income growth. Presumably neither the share of labor in the national income nor the rate of growth of the labor force would be affected by improved allocation policies.

The contribution of increased capital can be measured analogously with that of labor, yielding an expression $s_K k$, where s_K is the share of capital in the national income and k is the percentage rate of growth of the capital stock. Improved allocation policies would presumably not influence the share of capital but might influence the rate of growth of the capital stock through their effect on savings. Eliminating inflation would be the principal mechanism through which savings might be influenced; presumably voluntary savings would increase with less inflation, but "forced" savings would decline. To get an idea of the present magnitude of $s_K k$, it is convenient to express s_K as mK/Y, and k as I/K, where K is capital stock, I is net investment, and Y is national income. Thus $s_K k$ is equal to mI/Y, or im, which appeared in the formula given earlier. Net investment in Chile appears to have averaged somewhat less than 5 per cent of the national income in recent years, and the marginal productivity of capital (in real terms) appears to be somewhere between 10 and 20 per cent. The contribution of net investment to the rate of income growth thus probably lies between $\frac{1}{2}$ and 1 per cent per year. My judgment is that the low level of income of Chile would itself prevent net domestic investment from reaching a figure as high as 7 per cent of the national income; hence I conclude that even in the event that the stopping of inflation leads to greater savings and investment, the resulting increase in the rate of income growth would be small, probably less than $\frac{1}{2}$ per cent per year.[8]

In isolating the influence of increased labor and capital, we hypothetically held the distribution of each resource among industries and activities constant. The actual distribution will of course typically change over time, making for increases in national income if resources have moved from less productive to more productive uses, and for decreases in income if the opposite sort of movement has occurred. The potential increase of up to 15 per cent in national welfare, which we estimated in Section I might result from policies leading to improved resource allocation, would be reflected in r, the reallocation component of the growth rate. Since the job of reallocation clearly takes time, the whole gain would not be reflected in the income growth of a single year but would presumably be spread over several years, contributing, say, 1 or 2 per cent to the annual growth rate for a series of years. Once this process of adjustment was completed, there would presumably be no further significant influence of improved policies on the reallocation component of the growth rate.[9]

Improved quality of labor makes a contribution q_L to the growth rate, which could be measured with reasonable accuracy if we had statistics on the distribution of the labor force by stable and well-defined quality categories. In the absence of such data, let me note (*a*) that policies to improve resource allocation would presumably have no direct effect on the improvement of labor quality; (*b*) that improvement in labor quality at present appears to contribute only a relatively small component to the rate of income growth in Chile; and (*c*) that additional expenditures on technical training and education in Chile might have substantial effects on the growth rate.[10]

The contribution of technical advance to the rate of growth of income works via changes in production functions which reduce unit costs (or improve quality for given cost). These changes can be organizational or technical, and may or may not entail additional net expenditures on capital equipment. We do not have measures of the contribution of technical advance to the rate of economic growth in Chile, but, as in the case of improvement in the quality of labor, we infer from the low rate of per capita income growth that the contribution of technical advance has been small. I would not expect policies leading toward better resource allocation to have a substantial effect upon t, the contribution of technical advance to the growth rate. Incentives to reduce costs are just as strong in the present distorted price structure as they would be in an optimal one. Possibly, however, the elimination of inflation would produce a minor increment in t, because rapid inflation blurs people's perceptions of the relative price structure and may prevent them from being aware of some of the possibilities of reducing real costs.

I conclude from this evaluation of the possibilities of increase in the different components of the growth rate that policies aimed at improving resource allocation might help somewhat but would probably not provide the spectacular "take off" into economic development which most countries in Chile's position hope for. I would think of improved allocation policies as being an important component of any well-planned effort at achieving such a take off but not as the key factor. In the case of Chile, the potential gain of up to 15 per cent in national income, indicated in Section I as the static effect of improved resource allocation, would probably add a per cent or two to the growth rate over a period of years. As the reallocation of resources neared completion, the contribution of r to the growth rate would fall back to its normal low level, but there might be some longer term influence of improved allocation policies on the growth rate via the increased saving and the increased precision of cost calculations which might result from stopping or greatly reducing inflation.

If there is any key factor at all for achieving rapid development, I believe it is technical advance. The possibilities of increasing the rate of saving are quite limited in poor countries, as are the possibilities of reducing the rate of population growth. The limited changes in these factors that seem plausible would not have a drastic effect on the growth rate of income. Technical advance, on the other hand, seems to be capable of contributing substantially to the growth rate for fairly long periods. According to Kendrick's estimates, technical advance (i.e., real cost reduction) in U.S. manufacturing went on at an average rate of over 3 per cent per year from 1919 to 1929 and at an average rate of over 2 per cent per year from 1929 to 1937.[11] Brazil, in spite of being poorer than Chile and in spite of having equally severe distortions in internal resource allocation, has enjoyed a growth rate of between 2 and 3 per cent per year in per capita real income in recent years, as compared with Chile's rate of close to zero. I find the only plausible source of this difference to be a differential rate of technical progress.

One way of viewing technical advance which may help rationalize its variations as among time periods and places is to treat it as a process of adaptation to possibilities. Let Z be the maximum income that could be produced with a country's existing resources if the best techniques possible with today's level of scientific knowledge were used. Define G $(=(Z-Y)/Y)$ as the percentage gap between today's income and its potential, Z. Let A be the coefficient of adaptation, telling the fraction of previously unutilized possibilities which are put to use in a year. If G were 50 per cent, indicating a potentiality of raising income levels by 50 per cent, and A were 2 per cent, then technical advance would contribute 1 per cent to the rate of income growth this year, the formula being $t = AG$.

Even the most casual observation suggests that the percentage gap between actual and potential use of existing resources is much greater in Chile than it has been in the United States—probably easily twice as big. If Chile were to achieve a coefficient of adaptation equal to that of the United States, she would thus probably obtain a level of t two or more times as high as prevails in the U.S. The long-term average level of t for the whole U.S. economy appears to have been somewhere between 1.0 and 1.5 per cent per year.[12] We are thus suggesting that raising the Chilean coefficient of adaptation to the U.S. level might lead to a rate of technical advance of 2 or 3 per cent per year. This would give Chile a rate of per capita income growth comparable to those which Brazil and Mexico appear to have had in recent years.

The disturbing thing about focusing on the rate of technical advance and on the coefficient of adaptation is the possibility that these key factors may be largely beyond the influence of policy decisions. An energetic and acquisitive society is likely to have a high coefficient of adaptation, but it is hard to see how public policy can create such a society. Furthermore, as Kendrick's work shows, even in a given society the rate of technical advance is subject to substantial fluctuations, for which no satisfactory explanation has yet appeared. Yet there are surely ways in which public policy can accelerate the rate at which available knowledge is applied to use resources more efficiently. This can be done in part by promoting the international flow of technical knowledge (e.g., fostering foreign direct investment or co-operative technical arrangements between domestic and foreign firms and technical training of nationals abroad) and in part by spreading knowledge internally.

In the Chilean case, I would emphasize the possibilities to be achieved from spreading technical knowledge internally. The rewards given by the market to engineers, technically trained managers, agronomists, and other technicians themselves justify the investment in their training at a rate of real return which compares favorably with the best returns on investment in physical capital equipment. Yet these are the very people who make it their business to reduce costs, and the benefits of cost reduction accrue largely to the general public. Between the reward of these cost-reducers and their real social productivity we probably find divergences far more extreme than those which occur between private and social benefits in any other significant area of the economy. So long as the rate of private return on investment in technical training remains at or near the normal rate of return on capital, we have evidence that the social rate of return must be much higher, and an indication that public policy efforts to expand the supply of technically trained people have a high place on the list of policies to promote economic development.[13]

FOOTNOTES:

[1] This paper summarizes the main lines of a more extensive study done at the Centro de Investigaciones Economicas of the Catholic University of Chile. Space limitations have made it necessary to eliminate much of the supporting argument at several points. The author will provide further information on request.

[2] My own experience has been largely with the Chilean economy. I have the feeling and several knowledgeable experts have assured me that the situations of Argentina and Brazil are roughly similar to Chile in the matters treated in this section.

[3] A 20 per cent fall in the internal prices of imports and a 20 per cent rise in the internal prices of exports represent only one of the possible sets of price changes that might result from eliminating a 50 per cent tariff. If the exchange rate rose by 35 per cent, there would be a 35 per cent rise in the internal price level of exports, but only a 10 per cent fall in the internal price level of imports. In this case a doubling of trade would entail an elasticity of export supply of roughly 3, and an elasticity of import demand of 10. If the exchange rate rose only by 5 per cent, there would be a 30 per cent fall in import prices, and a 5 per cent rise in export prices, requiring elasticities of around 3 for import demand and around 20 for export supply in order to produce a doubling of trade. In all of these cases at least one of the elasticities necessary for a doubling of trade is implausibly high. In arriving at my judgments as to the elasticity of import demand, I have in mind that the relevant elasticity is long run and should take into account the curtailment of domestic production of import-type goods following a reduction in their internal price. Suppose that at present the total demand for import-type goods is 100, and that it is supplied half by domestic production and half by imports. A doubling of imports could then emerge if domestic production were cut from 50 to 25, while total demand expanded from 100 to 125. I believe that it is pressing towards the limits of plausibility to assume that this result would come from a price change as small as 20 per cent. It might quite plausibly result from a price reduction of a third, but then the rise in export prices would not be sufficient to generate the necessary doubling of the level of exports.

[4] The much-discussed case of zero marginal productivity of labor in agriculture does not exist in the economies of southern South America. The bulk of the agricultural labor force in these countries is voluntarily hired by entrepreneurs who are free to adjust the size of their labor force over time, in accordance with their notions of profit possibilities. It may indeed be possible in these countries to reduce the agricultural labor supply and at the same time maintain or increase output, but these possibilities entail either adding to the capital employed in agriculture and/or changing the production functions along which entrepreneurs are operating. This analysis takes the production functions currently "in use" as given, and measures the marginal product of any resource on the basis of given amounts of co-operating resources. I take sectors 1 and 2, where labor's marginal productivity is low relative to the rest of the economy, to represent agriculture in the Chilean case. Note that in our example these sectors account for almost a third of the labor force.

[5] I assume here not that the same sector will have one-third the optimum amount of capital as has one-third the optimum amount of labor, etc., but only that there be one sector with one-third the optimum amount of capital, another with one-half, etc. In our example, the result is invariant with respect to shifts in the location of distortions, so long as the percentages of the labor force and capital stock subject to given amounts of distortion remain unchanged.

[6] The elasticity for prime beef, holding the price of choice beef constant, or that for Fords, holding the price of Chevrolets constant, would surely be greater than 2, but the elasticities of beef of all types, and for automobiles as a group, appear from existing studies to be substantially less than 2. Likewise, there is evidence that elasticities of import demand are sometimes greater than 2, but not that elasticities of demand for import-type goods (imports and their domestic substitutes) are as high as 2.

[7] Assuming that initially capital gets half the national income and has a marginal net productivity of 20 per cent, a doubling of the capital stock while keeping the labor force constant would lead to a fall of capital's marginal productivity to 17 per cent in the case of an elasticity of substitution of 2, to 14 per cent if the elasticity were 1, and to 8 per cent if the elasticity were one-half. Wages would rise only a little more than 20 per cent in response to the doubled capital stock if the elasticity were 2; they would rise by 50 per cent if the elasticity were 1, and by 90 per cent if it were one-half. These calculations assume a perpetual capital stock; if depreciation is allowed for, the implied changes in the net marginal productivity become even more markedly different under the alternative elasticity assumptions. In the calculations, arc elasticities were evaluated at the midpoint of the range of each variable.

[8] Foreign investment does not help to raise the per capita income of the host country

to the extent that the marginal product of the investment accrues to foreigners. The host country gains to the extent that part of the return on the foreign capital can be siphoned off, principally by taxes, and also through such technical advances as may be embodied in the foreign investment. Technical advance will be considered separately below. For the moment I shall write off as negligible the amount that could be siphoned off by the government out of the return on such extra foreign investment as might be made as a result of improved allocation policies.

[9] There is always some reallocation being called for, because of the changes in tastes and technology that steadily take place. However, the amount of reallocation newly called for in any given year would be only a small fraction of the total amount needed to move from the present highly distorted situation to an optimum. The normal contribution of r to the growth rate would thus probably be quite small once the transition toward an optimal allocation was substantially completed. This small contribution might be lower than the present normal contribution of r, because at present some of the reallocation which takes place is in response to price or wage disequilibria, which presumably would be smaller (or absent) in an optimal situation. On the other hand, some of the reallocation which now occurs may actually take resources from uses of higher to uses of lower marginal productivity (e.g., because of a subsidy on the latter uses). Such negative contributions to r would presumably not occur under a set of optimal policies.

[10] Statement *b* is based on the fact that over the last five or so years the rate of income growth has been at about the same rate as the rate of growth of population and can be largely explained on the basis of the incremental capital and labor that have been fed into the productive machine. There is thus little room for a substantial contribution from q_L. Because of Chile's high rate of population growth, relatively large expenditures on education and training are necessary in order to keep the average quality of the labor force constant, counteracting, so to speak, a potential decline in labor quality. Statement *c* is based on the fact that a year of technical training will raise an unskilled laborer's earning power by 50 per cent or more, while four years of technical university training will about treble a high school graduate's earning capacity. The rate of return on investment in technical training is in the neighborhood of 20 per cent per year, in real terms; this counts both foregone earnings and costs of providing instruction as components of the sum "invested."

[11] John W. Kendrick, "Productivity Trends: Capital and Labor," *Rev. of Econ. and Statis.*, Aug., 1956, p. 254. Kendrick's measure was essentially of $(q_L + t)$. He netted out of the observed growth the effects of added labor and capital, assuming that labor quality remained unchanged. Effects of reallocations were largely removed by his measuring growth rates for thirty-three industry groups separately. Kendrick's median measure for the 1919-29 period was 3.9 per cent per year and for the 1929-37 period 2.6 per cent per year. I use somewhat lower figures to make allowance for possible improvement in labor quality.

[12] Kendrick, *op. cit.*, estimates $(r + q_L + t)$ for the U.S. private domestic economy to have averaged 1.7 per cent per year from 1899 to 1953. A figure of about 1.6 per cent is estimated by Abramovitz in "Resource and Output Trends in the United States since 1870," *A.E.A. Papers and Proceedings*, May, 1956, p. 8 (Table 1, Row 18). My lower figures attempt to make plausible allowance for the contributions of r and q_L.

[13] Most of the physical investment projects which are justified on the basis of external economies have a private rate of return well below the normal rate; in addition, many of the external economies alleged to exist in these cases turn out on close examination to be questionable or of small magnitude. I feel that public investment in technical training represents a more advantageous use of public funds than a goodly fraction of the physical investments which have been carried out in Latin America either by the state or through direct or indirect subsidies.

In terms of the breakdown of the growth rate given earlier, the training of engineers, managers, etc., presents a problem. Should it be classified as contributing to q_L or to t? In principle the increment in quality of labor as measured by improvement in productivity along existing production functions belongs in q_L, while the effect of shifting production functions belongs in t. Faced with the need of making a practical choice, I would allocate the increment in market earning power of the people trained to q_L, and the excess of their total social productivity over their earnings to t. The issue is, however, in any case not substantive.

INTERNATIONAL TRADE AND PAYMENTS IN AN ERA OF COEXISTENCE

COMMERCIAL POLICY IN THE UNDERDEVELOPED COUNTRIES

By Raúl Prebisch*

United Nations Economic Commission for Latin America

I. *Industrialization*

Historically, the spread of technical progress has been uneven, and this has contributed to the division of the world economy into industrial centers and peripheral countries engaged in primary production, with consequent differences in income growth. We are now at a transitional stage, in which this division is being gradually weakened, but it may take rather a long time to disappear. As the spread of technical progress into the periphery—limited originally to exports of primary commodities and related activities—is advancing more and more into other sectors, it brings with it the need for industrialization.

Indeed, industrialization is an inescapable part of the process of change accompanying a gradual improvement in per capita income. In response to differences in the income elasticities of demand and in rates of increase in productivity, the active population is tending to shift—chiefly through the distribution of its increment—from occupations with a relatively low income elasticity of demand—principally primary production—to industry and other activities where this is relatively high.

This process has characterized the development of the industrial centers and is now advancing into the periphery. Industrialization of the centers is not a matter of dispute: it seems quite obvious that industrial countries should continue to industrialize. On the other hand, industrialization of the periphery has always been a controversial subject, not only in the centers, but also in the peripheral countries themselves. Although the opposition is receding, there are still some who consider industrialization to be a harmful diversion of productive resources from primary activities. Those who promote industrialization

* I am indebted for valuable criticism and constructive suggestions to: Professor Hollis B. Chenery, Stanford University, and to my Deputy at the Economic Commission for Latin America, Mr. Louis N. Swenson, as well as to Dr. Hans Singer and Mr. Sidney Dell, of the United Nations Department of Economic and Social Affairs. I am further pleased to place on record here the coincidence of ideas of this paper with the main lines of argument in Dr. Singer's paper on "Industrialization—The Other Side of the Coin," presented at the recent ECAFE Working Party on "The Role of Industrialization in Economic Development," which was received after this one had been written.

of the periphery are still credited with odd or ill-founded motives: the belief that industry makes nations weathy while agriculture is a source of poverty; animosity towards the countryside, reasons of prestige, or the desire to achieve self-sufficiency or to imitate the centers.

Let the peripheral countries increase productivity in their primary activities through much-needed technical progress and thus expand their exports. Their rate of development will then be accelerated on a sound basis. So runs the argument.

Technical progress in export activities of these peripheral countries has undoubtedly been a great stimulus to their growth. But if this process is extended to other primary activities for internal consumption, where productivity is usually very low, and industry is not developed to absorb redundant manpower, then the inevitable outcome will be more disguised unemployment or downright unemployment.

Thus the plea for technical advance in primary production as an alternative to industrialization in order to improve standards of living defeats its own purpose, as some of the fruits of such technical advance will usually be transferred from the peripheral countries to the outer world, unless it is buttressed by a vigorous process of industrialization and increasing productivity in industry. The greater the inelasticity of demand for peripheral exports, the larger the proportion of the fruits that is so transferred.

Industry and technical advance in primary production are thus complementary aspects of the same process. And in this process industry plays a dynamic role, not only in inducing technical progress in primary and other activities, but in the new attitudes fostered by industrial development.

As in the centers, industrial development at the periphery responds to the same disparities in income elasticity as regards internal demand; and in addition to that, to the effects of similar disparities in foreign trade. It is a well-established fact that the income elasticity of demand for imports of Latin American primary commodities by the centers is generally lower than the income elasticity of demand for Latin-American imports of industrial products from these centers. This difference is frequently accentuated by measures to protect primary commodities in the centers, whereas, as will be shown later, it is reduced by protection in peripheral countries, provided this is established between certain limits.

Let us take one instance: the case of Argentina. This country has followed the very mistaken policy of trying to stimulate industrialization to the detriment of agriculture, instead of promoting a balanced growth of both. In the recent ECLA study prepared at the request of the Argentine government, we examined a series of measures that might considerably increase exports through mechanization and other technical advances in agriculture. But even so, exports would only grow at the rate of 1.1 for every 1 per cent of growth of income, while the demand for imports was estimated with a coefficient of income-elasticity of 1.4 per cent, given the projected rate of income growth up to 1967 as compared with 1955. Similarly high elasticities for imports have been found in ECLA's studies for Brazil, Mexico, Colombia, and Peru.

In other words, in addition to the need for industrialization arising from the internal growth of Argentine income, there is the further need, because of the disparities between exports and imports just described, for substituting domestic production for imports of industrial goods.

The other aspect of this process is to be found in manpower figures. Indeed, the active population employed in agriculture in Argentina in 1955 represented 26 per cent of the total. Although this is rather a low figure for Latin America and exports are supposed to grow at a very high rate, we have estimated that, in the period considered, due to technical progress only about 10 per cent of the increment of active population will be absorbed in agriculture, whereas industry will have to absorb some 47 per cent of it.

Import substitution (defined here as an increase in the proportion of goods that is supplied from domestic sources and not necessarily as a reduction in the ratio of imports to total income) is the only way to correct the effects on peripheral growth of disparities in foreign trade elasticity. Let us take a numerical example to clarify this aspect of our problem. For the sake of simplicity, we shall assume that there is only one center and a periphery, having equal rates of population growth. Assuming that the center's rate of income growth is 3 per cent yearly and the income elasticity of demand for imports of primary commodities is 0.80 and that there is no import substitution, then the rate of growth of these imports will be 2.40 per cent (3 per cent × 0.80 per cent) per year.

Suppose now that at the periphery income elasticity of demand for industrial goods from the center is 1.30. If, in a balanced development process, the rate of growth of these imports is to be no higher than that of exports, then peripheral income cannot increase faster than 1.84 per cent per year. This is the rate which, combined with that coefficient of elasticity, gives the limit of import growth—that is to say a rate of 2.40 per cent, the same as that for exports.

Should peripheral income grow at a rate, say, similar to the 3 per cent of the center, its demands for imports of industrial products would grow at the rate of 3.90 per cent (3 per cent × 1.3 per cent) while exports of primary commodities would increase at the rate of only 2.40 per cent. To bridge the gap between these two rates, either the rate of increase of demand for imports would have to fall by 1.50 per cent, by means of import substitution, or industrial exports would have to be added to the primary ones, or a combination of the two.

We have assumed the same rates of population growth at the center and periphery. If the rate is higher at the latter, as is the case in Latin America, industrialization has to be intensified in order to have the same per capita rate of income growth as the center. This is particularly necessary if the present differences in per capita income are to be gradually narrowed down.

We have seen that import substitution tends to correct the disparity in income elasticities of demand for imports and for exports. This does not mean that industrialization is not necessary in the exceptional cases —at least in Latin America—where there is no such disparity. It has been shown that industrialization also responds to internal disparities of demand. If exports of a particular country grow faster than its demand for imports, industry will still have to grow, but its contribution towards meeting total demand for industrial goods will decline while that of imports will increase. By contrast, when demand for imports tends to grow at a faster rate than exports, import substitution is necessary to correct this disparity, and then imports constitute a declining proportion of total demand for industrial goods.

On the other hand, a country whose exports grow at a very fast rate and constitute a relatively high component of its aggregate product is in a better position than others to accelerate its rate of economic growth; but this acceleration may induce a rate of increase in the demand for imports higher than the increase in exports, requiring import substitution to correct the disparity.

The acceleration of the rate of growth will be the more necessary if exports absorb only a small fraction of the increment of population. This is the peculiar case of Venezuela, where fast growing oil exports constitute 32 per cent of its total product, whereas they employ only 2.6 per cent of the total active population.

II. *Protection*

In the changing pattern of employment associated with the process of development, a declining proportion of the continuously increasing active population is needed for the growth of existing activities for the internal market, due to improvements in productivity. Therefore a part of the growing manpower is not required in these existing activities. Moreover, there is manpower that for the same reason is not needed to produce the present level of exports. All this redundant manpower has to be employed in the expansion of these exports and in new branches of industries for substitution purposes, as well as in other new activities. These new forms of employment are geared to internal and external demand elasticities and to different rates of increase in productivity.

In other words, in a dynamic economy redundant manpower is continually emerging as a result of technical progress, and it tends to be absorbed to meet the increasing demand generated by that very same technical progress.

In addition, there is a second form of manpower that has to be so absorbed. There are indeed vast numbers of marginal workers of low productivity rendering poorly paid personal services, as well as people engaged in other forms of precarious employment or disguised unemployment of a precapitalist character who should be moved to new jobs.

In the process of growth, at every level of per capita income, a certain proportion of this manpower is made available for transfer to other forms of employment, through shifts in demand as well as through technical changes in production.

For the sake of brevity, we will use the term "surplus manpower" to describe both these sources of labor and we will confine ourselves to that part of the surplus to be transferred to exports or new branches of industry for import substitution.

Redundant manpower as such does not produce any income and the real measure of the fruits of technical progress is the increment that accrues to the community when such manpower is transferred to new forms of employment. In addition to this increment, there is the net increase in income obtained by transferring available manpower from these precapitalist forms of employment of very low productivity to exports or industrial activities of much higher productivity.

Let us first clarify one important point. Industrial costs higher than import prices do not necessarily mean that an industry is not economic for a country as is sometimes assumed.[1] Of course the smaller the difference the better.

The problem has to be considered from another angle. It is not really a question of comparing industrial costs with import prices but of comparing the increment of income obtained in the expansion of industry with that which could have been obtained in export activities had the same productive resources been employed there.

I am afraid that it is not possible to arrive at the optimum solution of this problem if market forces are left unrestricted. The classical mechanism of the free play of market forces, either in its original form of wage adjustments or in its contemporary version of price adjustments

[1] This was the assumption made by the Currie Mission on the iron and steel industry in Colombia, in the report presented to the International Bank some years ago.

through exchange rate movements, does not bring about that optimum solution. On the contrary, the periphery transfers to the outer world a greater part of the fruits of increased productivity than if the market forces had been contained at a certain point, either through customs protection or some other form of interference in the process.

Let us see briefly how exchange depreciation would work. Depreciation itself is considered as an outcome of market forces. If disparities in elasticities cause the demand for imports to grow faster than exports, let the exchange rate depreciate and find its own equilibrium level, when the surplus manpower will be fully absorbed.

As regards the absorption of manpower in exports, internal price increases due to exchange depreciation will bring higher profits and stimulate expanded production and exports. It is conceivable that this increase in exports could happen without any, or only a very small, decline in external prices. This, however, would mean a very high elasticity for export demand, which is quite unrealistic in the light of Latin-American experience. Income elasticity is generally low and so is price elasticity. Consequently, only a part—and not a very large one—of the surplus manpower can be employed in exports at given prices, and beyond that limit prices decline.

On the other hand, higher import prices will now make attractive those new branches of industries which were not so before because their costs were higher than import prices.

In this process, competitive equilibrium will be reached at a point where returns for export producers will equalize those for these new industries. However, this is not the optimum point for the periphery. Indeed, the marginal increment of income, arising out of successive increments of employment in export activities, has been falling faster than prices. And it can be demonstrated (see appendix) that, at the equilibrium point, except in very extreme cases, the marginal increment of income in those activities is lower than in industrial ones. It may even be negative if elasticity is very low.

Therefore, the optimum solution is attained before competitive equilibrium at a point where marginal increments are the same in both activities. In other words, the maximum gain for the periphery as a whole falls short of the equilibrium position where marginal costs and marginal revenues are equated.

The best solution for the periphery would be to stop the increase of exports beyond that optimum point of maximum gain. Some advocates of exchange rate adjustment to correct the disparity in foreign trade elasticities recommend that an export tax be imposed, high enough to deprive exporters of the profit incentive for continuing to expand production.

By and large, an export tax of this kind means a clear interference with market forces and acts in the same way as a protective duty on imports. If this import duty is levied at the optimum point, where marginal increments of income are equal, it will divert manpower to industrial activities and hence curtail employment in exports, just as the export tax does. (Throughout this process I have assumed constant costs, in order to avoid unnecessary complication.)

Again, if an export tax has an effect similar to protection, I have strong doubts about the advisability of exchange rate adjustments as an instrument to correct foreign trade disparities in demand elasticities. The main appeal of depreciation as compared with protection is that it leaves private initiative rather than government agencies to decide which branches of industry will be profitable substitutes for imports. But this could also be achieved through a uniform protective duty.

Protection (or subsidies) seems a more direct and simple solution, as it limits the adjustment to those new branches of industries that should be developed within a given period of time. To obtain the same result, depreciation forces the adjustment of the whole price system. In my view, a policy of depreciation or devaluation should be used only to correct an externally overvalued currency and not as an instrument for effecting structural changes in the economy.[2] A selective protection policy is a preferable instrument, notwithstanding the obstacles that have to be overcome in practice; and if it is applied gradually, higher import prices, affecting a relatively small proportion of imports each time, could be absorbed by general increments of productivity without affecting the price level of the entire economy, provided that protection has not been exaggerated to shelter inefficiency.

In any event, this is not relevant to our main line of argument. What is highly relevant is that the cost of spontaneous industrialization—by the unrestricted play of market forces through exchange depreciation—is a transfer abroad of part of the increment in real income derived from the employment of the surplus manpower, and that this transfer could be reduced or avoided by protection, subsidies, an export tax, or other forms of interference.

We have explained before that this increment of income represented the fruits of increased productivity. Therefore, the periphery transfers part of these fruits through the unrestricted play of market forces, in order to employ the surplus manpower whenever exports must increase beyond the limit at which external prices remain constant.

The classical mechanism in its original form of wage adjustment works, in the last instance, in the same way as its new version of ex-

[2] The difference is really between present and future equilibrium prices.

change rate depreciation. In both cases the level of wages in foreign currency has to drop in order to bring industrial costs down to a level competitive with imports, both expressed in foreign currency.

Setting aside other aspects of the classical mechanism, it is essentially the pressure of the surplus manpower which in this mechanism forces the fall in wages (in domestic as well as foreign currency, since it is assumed that there is monetary stability). This fall makes new industries attractive and stimulates exports, with the consequent price decline. All this is based on quite unrealistic assumptions concerning labor mobility and willingness to accept nominal wage reductions, whereas the mechanism of exchange depreciation does not require these assumptions. As a result of depreciation, the level of wages falls in foreign currency and, at the same time, this is accompanied by the fall of external prices. This is compatible with imperfect labor mobility and different levels of wages, and so is more realistic than the old classical mechanism.

Wage reduction does not mean a corresponding fall in real wages. In the classical mechanism the nominal fall is supposed to be largely offset by the fall in the level of prices, except in new branches of industry where costs are higher than import prices.

In the depreciation version, the level of real wages is restored through wage adjustments compensating for the effect of higher import prices on the cost of living. Of course, since imports constitute merely a fraction of the cost of living, wages need to increase less than import prices do. If in the process of adjustment wages rise more than the cost of living, the protective effects of depreciation are lost and a new depreciation might then be necessary.

In other words, internally there is no change except that real costs in new branches of industry will be higher than in existing ones. But externally the fall of wages in export activities, as a counterpart to the fall in prices (both in foreign currency), reflects the process of transfer of real income through the deterioration in the terms of trade.

In order to clarify this transfer process, we have to introduce concepts of the physical productivity ratio (henceforth called the "productivity ratio") and wage ratio. The productivity ratio expresses the relationship of physical productivity per man between the periphery and the center. There is a wide range of such ratios. For instance, exports of primary commodities at the periphery may have a range of, say, from 3 times the productivity at the center to only 0.50; and these exports of less relative productivity will be made if the level of wages is proportionately lower. So if the level is only half that at the centers, those export activities having only half the productivity of the center will be developed; while those having a higher productivity ratio will tend to transfer part of the difference to the center through the free play of market forces. (To avoid complications, I have not included land rental, since it cannot be transferred.)

There is a similar range of industrial productivity ratios. Industries having a ratio of 0.50 or higher at the periphery could develop without protection, but those having less, say 0.40, would need it. We have seen that if these marginal industries are necessary for the full employment of the surplus manpower, the free play of the market forces will bring a wage deterioration, in terms of foreign currency, so far as this is necessary to offset the lower productivity ratio as compared with export activities (another way of expressing costs higher than import prices). Thus, to make marginal industries competitive, wages in foreign currency must decline so as to reduce the wage ratio from 0.50 to 0.40 and this process is accompanied by the decline of export prices. This is the case of transfer of real income that we have seen before.

Let us take now the other case. Let us assume that technical progress in exports advances in such a way that the productivity ratio of marginal export activities is increased from 0.50 to 0.70, without any increase in the industrial productivity ratio, which is also 0.50 at the margin. In this case, also, it will be the differential productivity of exports in relation to industry which tends to be transferred.

We may simplify the two cases in a broad generalization: Whenever the productivity ratio in exports is higher than in the marginal industries needed to employ the full surplus manpower, the real income corresponding to the difference in productivity will tend to be transferred abroad in the unrestricted play of market forces. This occurs either when the surplus manpower has to be employed in industrial branches where the productivity ratio is lower than in exports of primary commodities, or when the latter improves faster than does the ratio of industrial productivity. Therefore, it would be a very mistaken policy to advocate technical progress in primary activities without a parallel policy of industrialization. The higher the technical progress in those activities, the greater is the surplus of manpower. If this surplus is absorbed only in relatively small proportions by export activities—as is usually the case—industrial development is even more necessary because, as we have seen before, without it the fruits of technical progress in primary activities will be lost wholly or in part. We have also seen that to a certain extent this transfer is avoided by protection. But protection by itself does not increase productivity. On the contrary, if excessive, it tends to weaken the incentive to produce. Therefore, in order to maintain at the periphery the major fruits of technical progress in primary activities and especially in exports, similar progress has to be made in industrial activities in order to improve their productivity and increase the level of wages in foreign currency. This will allow a parallel increase in wages for export activities; thus preventing a corresponding transfer of real income.

The need for technical progress in industrial activities has been duly emphasized in the infant industries argument. As productivity improves, protection may decrease until it is completely eliminated. This argument seems to overlook the need for helping exports to retain the fruits of technical progress. Indeed, if industrial productivity increases and wages do not rise proportionately, due to reduction or elimination of protection, exports will transfer their differential productivity.

Let us revert to our previous example to clarify this matter. If the productivity ratio in marginal exports is 0.50 and the wage ratio is the same and industries have to be developed with a productivity ratio of 0.40, then the difference must be offset by protection. Now, if technical progress at the periphery increases the productivity ratio of the marginal industries to 0.50, protection will no longer be needed. But then the wage ratio will continue to be 0.50. If, on the contrary, protection is maintained, the wage ratio will have increased in accordance with the productivity ratio and in this way, if exports also increase their productivity ratio, the periphery will retain the fruits of this increase up to the new level of wages.

Furthermore, when higher productivity is translated into higher wages rather than into lower protection, there is the additional advantage of forcing similar increases in productivity in other activities lagging behind. But all this requires a very cautious and selective policy of protection and does not conflict with the possibility and advisability of reducing and eventually eliminating protection in those industries having a faster rate of technical progress.

In all the reasoning of this section we have, for the sake of simplicity, considered a center and a periphery as a whole. But there are great differences between the centers. Secondary centers, as distinct from the main ones, may have some problems similar to those of the peripheral countries, when in order to fully employ their surplus manpower they have to engage in activities where costs are higher than import prices. This raises problems which, although interesting, are outside the scope of this paper.

On the other hand, there are also great differences between peripheral countries. A peripheral country might advantageously employ the whole increment of its manpower in increasing exports without industrialization, provided that too many others do not do the same. But we are considering the general need of the peripheral countries for industrialization.

III. *Terms of Trade*

In the last instance, the pressure upon export prices and the corresponding tendency towards deterioration in the terms of trade in the peripheral process of growth subject to the unrestricted play of market forces is the result of disparities in income elasticity of demand and the uneven form in which technical progress has spread into the world economy, bringing very great disparities in technological densities. That is to say, the amount of technological knowledge as well as the real aptitude for using it in production.

Let us imagine a world without such disparities. In it we will not find any tendency to deterioration. Let us assume that there is a country A which is prevailingly industrial and a country B which is prevailingly primary. The wage rate is the same and trade is in equilibrium at a point where marginal productivity is the same in both countries. Then the productivity ratio at that margin is 1.0 and the wage ratio is the same. The productivity ratio is such that in A there is a full range of activities, principally industrial, where productivity is, say, up to three times as high as that of B. And in B there is another range of activities, principally primary, where productivity is also up to three times that of A. Therefore, there are no technological disparities. Neither are there any disparities of elasticities and the demand for goods is equally divided between primary commodities and industrial products. Finally, population and per capita income grow at the same rates in both countries.

Given these assumptions, there is no reason for a deterioration in the terms of trade working against primary production. Indeed, demand for primary products grows at the same pace as industrial demand, and consequently, the given increment of manpower at B does not need to be diverted from primary production, where the productivity ratio is favorable to B, to industry, where the productivity ratio is unfavorable for the same country.

Furthermore, as technological density is the same and productivity improves at the same rate in A and B, there is no differential productivity from this source to be transferred from the one country to the other.

Let us assume now that income elasticity of demand for industrial products is higher than for primary commodities, without any other change in the remaining assumptions.

If country B is unable or unwilling to send to A manpower which would increase the latter's rate of industrialization, it has no other way out than to decrease the proportion of manpower in primary activities in favor of industry, through a different distribution of the increment than was formerly the case.

Here comes the important aspect. In B, manpower is transferred from primary occupations with a favorable productivity ratio to industrial occupations with an unfavorable ratio. Consequently the pressure of the surplus manpower will force employment down on the productivity ratio curve from 1.00 to say 0.80, with the wage ratio falling correspondingly at the new competitive equilibrium point. In the process of this adjustment to 0.80 of the wage ratio, export prices will fall, transferring income to country A. The contrary happens in country A. In response to a higher rate of industrial demand, manpower will flow from primary production to industry, where the productivity ratio is more favorable, thus improving the wage ratio.

Note that, according to our original assumption, the rate of increase of productivity is the same in both countries. Yet wages will increase less than productivity in the primary producing country due to the downward pressure of the surplus manpower, while they will increase more than productivity in the industrial country due to the pressure upwards.

This tendency to deterioration will be accentuated if, in addition to disparities in elasticity, we introduce disparities in technological densities. Suppose that in country B the export productivity ratio continues to be the same as in primary activities in our original assumption in relation to A but that the industrial productivity ratio is much lower than in the previous case. Thus in country B one of the important characteristics of a peripheral country appears.

It is obvious that if the industrial productivity ratio is more unfavorable than before, the level of wages has to drop more steeply in country B, hence increasing the transfer of real income to country A. Therefore, the combination of disparities in income elasticities of demand and in technological densities put the periphery in a weaker position vis-à-vis the center, as regards the terms of trade.

The center is in a better position to retain the fruits of its general increase in productivity because the increment in manpower does not need, as in the periphery, to press on occupations with a lower productivity ratio to the detriment of the wage level. In other words, general improvements in productivity tend to be fully reflected in the increment of the wage rate at the center, while at the periphery a part of the fruits of these improvements is transferred through the fall of export prices and the corresponding deterioration in the terms of trade.

In addition to this tendency, if productivity for export increases faster than marginal productivity of industry, then the fall of export prices will also tend to be more severe. The same may happen at the center, but the greater degree of technological homogeneity suggests that this phenomenon is likely to be less intense than at the periphery.

Furthermore, protection at the center gives additional force to the peripheral tendency towards a deterioration in the terms of trade. If there is free play of market forces at the center, some marginal primary activities there might disappear because of competition from increased peripheral exports at lower prices. But if these marginal activities are protected at the center, the possibility of increasing exports in the periphery will be less, and consequently a greater part of the surplus manpower will have to seek employment in industrial activities with a lower marginal productivity ratio, which would entail a further decrease of the wage level in foreign currency, with a further deterioration in the terms of trade.

This tendency of the terms of trade at the periphery to deteriorate in a process of spontaneous growth may be offset by compensatory forces in the free play of the market. One of these forces is of a Ricardian character. Even if wages deteriorate in foreign currency, the terms of trade may improve for the periphery if growing demand for some products prompts a resort to agricultural or mining land with lower returns. The other is connected with the center. Technical progress in some export activities at the center may advance faster than general productivity, resulting in a transfer of differential productivity of the same type as at the periphery although, probably, much less intense due to greater technological homogeneity at the center.

Interference with market forces may also counteract the tendency to deterioration. As we have explained, this is the effect of protective duties or export taxes. Combinations to restrict or eliminate competition in export activities may have similar effects, provided that not all of the profits are transferred abroad. Moreover, labor union action to increase wages in export activities may maintain the terms of trade, and, last but not least, international action to defend primary commodities may have this same effect.

On the other hand, a policy to reduce or eliminate primary protection at the center may, through the expansion of peripheral exports, absorb a greater part of the increment of manpower at the periphery, so alleviating the tendency towards deterioration of the terms of trade.

All this is very tentative but it offers a working hypothesis for inquiring into the past. A higher rate of increase of productivity in export than in domestic activities, coupled with a rather weak industrialization process, may in the past have been powerful forces contributing to the deterioration in the terms of trade for some products. Further deterioration may occur in the future if efforts are concentrated on technical improvements in primary production without a vigorous development of industries and their technical advance, accompanied by a cautious policy of interference with the free play of international market forces to support the prices of important primary commodities.

IV. *Reciprocity*

Protection has different meanings in the peripheral countries and in the industrial centers. In the former it is, up to a certain point, the instrument for correcting the effects of the disparity in income elasticity of demand for exports of primary commodities and for imports of industrial goods and does not hamper the rate of growth of world trade. In the industrial centers, by contrast, protection of primary production accentuates this disparity and tends to depress peripheral development and to decrease the rate of growth of world trade.

The reduction or elimination of such protection at the centers has an implicit element of reciprocity, since the resultant increase in exports of primary commodities from the periphery will be followed by a corresponding increase in its imports of industrial goods, in response to their high income elasticity of demand, and there is no need for any reduction or elimination of duties to obtain this result.

The traditional form of reciprocity, under which peripheral countries are asked to grant duty concessions similar to those introduced by the centers, does not take into account this implicit element of reciprocity.

Moreover, these reciprocal duty concessions may have an unfavorable influence on the periphery's rate of growth. The development process requires a continual change in the composition of imports. These changes usually start with the decline in the proportion of imports of light consumer goods in favor of imports of basic material, capital goods, and durables. At more advanced stages of industrialization, when import substitution of these light consumer goods has been nearly completed, new changes relating to the other categories of goods are necessary, so that by reducing or eliminating imports of some of them it is possible to increase imports responding to the needs of the development process. Now, if these duty concessions interfere with these changes, then the increased peripheral capacity to import resulting from duty concessions at the centers instead of helping to attain a higher rate of growth might be accompanied by a real decline in the rate of industrial development. This might be a very harmful use of the increase in the periphery's capacity to import deriving from such duty concessions at the centers. What is needed is a policy to encourage these changes in composition in order to accelerate the rate of economic growth, so that imports are adapted to the need for greater technical progress in primary production and for more intense industrial development.

I do not mean to suggest that existing duties and restrictions at the periphery should be untouchable. Far from it. Instead of the ideal of a rational and selective policy, there has frequently been shortsighted expediency and sheer improvisation. And in some cases indiscriminate or massive protection has gone far beyond the optimum point, to the serious detriment of exports and world trade. Therefore, although the periphery cannot influence the centers in a positive way, it may have a definite negative influence. The centers can actively stimulate the rate of growth of peripheral countries through trade and investment, but the latter cannot influence in a similar way the rate of growth of the centers and bring about any increase in their demand for primary products. However, if the periphery develops industry through protection beyond the optimum point, to the detriment of imports from the centers, this may have an unfavorable consequence on the center's rate of growth.

Under the conditions just described, protection at the periphery, instead of merely correcting disparities of income elasticity in relation to the centers, creates new disparities in the opposite sense and the centers are forced to adopt defensive protective measures to maintain their own rates of growth.

Of course, duty concessions granted by the centers afford a good opportunity of inducing peripheral countries to correct these anomalies. But much more is needed: a definite readjustment of commercial policy based on the clear recognition that, instead of trying to crystallize the existing pattern of peripheral imports, an effort should be made to help promote those changes in composition which are indispensable for fostering the rate of economic development.

All the foregoing requires a long-term outlook that may jeopardize short-term private trading interests. However, this would not be the first time that fundamental policy considerations have prevailed over those short-term interests, however legitimate they may be.

The centrally planned economies have, in this respect, a better means of adjusting their imports and exports to the needs of developing economies. And it is to be hoped that these countries, since they have long-term plans, will disclose projections of their probable demand for primary commodities, so as to enable producing countries to base their policy decisions on sounder foundations than they have been able to do to date.

V. *Multilateral Trade*

Multilateral trade is the result not so much of adherence to a principle as of the trade policy of the most important countries. In this respect, the most significant behavior is that of the principal dynamic center of the world; that is to say, the center which because of its magnitude and technological progress has a greater influence on the rate of growth (as well as on the short-run fluctuations) of the other centers and of the periphery of world economy.

If the principal center, through the high level of its own imports, creates a great import capacity for its products in countries in the rest of the world, these countries may not only have a relatively high coefficient of imports (in relation to their income) from the center, but also from each other. World trade then constitutes a relatively high proportion of world income and multilateralism flourishes.

But if the principal center has a low level of imports, the countries in the rest of the world are forced to reduce their coefficient of imports from the center, and under the multilateral trade principle they are also forced to restrict imports from each other, as they cannot discriminate against the principal center.

Of course, every country, great or small, which has no disparities in foreign trade elasticities to correct and which resorts to protectionism has an unfavorable influence on world trade. But the greater the country the larger is its influence and the greater its responsibility.

Far-reaching changes have occurred in the pattern of world trade. In the nineteenth century, under the aegis of the United Kingdom as the world's principal dynamic center, trade developed at a very fast rate. The center's import coefficient was very high, which made it easy for the other countries of the world to have a high coefficient, too, not only with the center, but also with each other.

Moreover, the principal center's import coefficient increased continuously throughout almost the entire century, offsetting in the peripheral countries the effects of the lower income-demand elasticity for their primary commodities.

By contrast, the United States has always been a country of relatively low import coefficients, because of its natural resources and protectionist policy. Furthermore, this coefficient has been continually dropping. Nevertheless, at the time of British trade hegemony this decline had no apparent effects on world trade. Indeed, the extraordinary rate of growth of the United States economy tended to compensate for these effects, and its imports from the rest of the world grew at a very fast pace. On the other hand, this rate of growth, so much higher than that of the rest of the world, considerably enhanced the relative importance of the United States in world economy, transforming it eventually into the principal dynamic center.

A principal center with a relatively low level of imports from the rest of the world in relation to the latter's income necessarily exerts a powerful influence on the pattern of world trade. This influence began to be felt as the rate of growth of the United States economy was gradually losing its nineteenth-century impetus, due to the decline in the rate of population increase, while at the same time this country was increasing its competitiveness on world markets.

This process reached a crisis with the great world depression. A further compression of the United States import coefficient and a rather lengthy pause in the growth of the economy have had a considerable impact on world trade and economy. And the world suffered considerable hardship in adapting to these events at the new dynamic center.

Bilateral trade emerged. It was a precarious and largely unsuccessful attempt to maintain trade among other countries, while imports from the United States were adjusted to the capacity to import. Multilateralism and the gold standard were destroyed and can only be restored—on a new basis—once structural changes in world trade and payments have been finally adapted to the new dynamic center with its very low import coefficient.

The long overdue formation of common markets in Europe—based on preferences—means that that inorganic bilateral reaction is being transformed into a rational policy of restricted multilateralism, with intense trade between its members and a coefficient of imports from the principal center geared to the capacity to import generated by it. Let us hope that the coefficient of imports from the rest of the world will not be unnecessarily forced down.

Destruction of world multilateralism and the decline in the relative importance of world trade has had serious consequences for the Latin-American countries. Their capacity to import is very low indeed in relation to their needs, given the present structure of production. This has been one of the major obstacles retarding the pace of industrial growth. Furthermore, it has forced countries to increase the proportion of domestic industrial production within total industrial demand through a more intense process of import substitution than would have been advisable under more favorable conditions of world trade.

On the other hand, this process of industrialization has been carried out without destroying the old pattern according to which each of the Latin-American countries is orientated in its trade towards the industrial centers, with very weak mutual trade. Trade between Latin-Amer-can countries forms only 10 per cent of their total foreign trade, and industrial exports are relatively very small by contrast with countries such as Italy, Japan, and others with similar income levels. All this has resulted in the splitting of the industrialization process into as many watertight compartments as there are countries, without the advantages of specialization and the economies of scale.

The response to this should be the enlargement of national markets through the gradual establishment of a common market. But the common market, just as in Europe, cannot be established on the basis of the principle of universal multilateralism. Preferential treatment is needed inside the area to promote specialization in industrial products and primary commodities. European countries need preferences between them mainly to restore a pattern of very intensive mutual trade, which has been impaired in the way we have seen, whereas Latin America needs preferences to develop new forms of reciprocal trade, mainly in industrial products, that practically did not exist before.

Latin-American protectionism and preferences, if kept within reasonable limits inside a common market, will not hamper world trade. Imports from the centers will continue to depend on Latin-American exports to them—a clearly passive situation. The only changes—and these will be very important indeed—will take place in import composition, and through them countries will specialize in industrial products as well as agricultural ones. Without the common market, there will be a continued tendency by each country to try to produce everything—say from automobiles to machinery—under the sheltering wing of very high protection.

These are not the only considerations making the common market appear imperative. Paradoxically enough, the more advanced Latin-American countries are tending to become more externally vulnerable because of the form that industrialization has taken. In the process of import substitution, accentuated by adverse trade conditions, they have compressed their import requirements to a series of goods absolutely essential for the maintenance and growth of their economy and have lost the margin for the further reduction in imports which they had when they imported consumer goods. Thus an unfavorable fluctuation in exports tends to have critical effects on economic development far more so than when, as in former times, vulnerability was more on the demand side. The common market by diversifying trade within the area can gradually correct this situation. This is without detriment to the possibilities of developing industrial exports to countries outside the region that the common market may foster through the reduction of industrial costs.

The favorable attitude shown by the United States government, as well as others, towards the formation of a Latin-American common market is most encouraging and may be a very important element in the framing of a commercial policy geared to the need for accelerating the rate of Latin-American development.

A vigorous policy of industrialization is required as an inevitable complement to technical progress in primary production. In this connection, the decisive support given by the United States government (through the Export-Import Bank) to the establishment of the iron and steel industry in some Latin-American countries is a noteworthy step in the right direction. Its significance lies in the fact that not only was a positive stand taken as regards heavy industry in the region, which has been and still is the subject of considerable controversy, but that financial and technical support were given to Latin-American entrepreneurs. While the contribution of foreign enterprises to development is highly valuable, it is essential for the promotion and consolidation of free enterprise to encourage the ability and initiative of the Latin-American entrepreneur as well.

Industrialization needs a dynamic policy of protection, which should be continually adapted so as to introduce new changes in import composition as the economy develops and disparities in the income elasticity of demand play their role. Trade treaties should not try to crystallize existing situations but should be flexible enough to promote these changes in import composition in an orderly, selective, and rational way.

As for the common market, there is no fixed blueprint. Help is needed within the GATT and other bodies to explore new paths in accordance with Latin-American conditions and potentialities.

In all the foregoing, there is ample room for new forms of reciprocity. Duty concessions by the centers, apart from their influence on a sound protection policy in Latin-American countries, may become a very useful instrument for inducing measures of trade liberalization and economic integration between these countries. And the gradual relaxation or elimination of the preference given to certain imports from the United States in some Latin-American countries may serve this purpose very effectively.

APPENDIX

Let us see how the process of spontaneous industrialization might operate according to the classical mechanism, assuming that there is free mobility of labor and unrestricted competition. We are concerned here only with the alternative employment of the surplus manpower in export production and industrial activities: for the sake of simplicity, other aspects will be overlooked. For this same reason, we have resorted to a simplified diagram (Figure 1) in order to illustrate our point.

In this diagram, the surplus manpower to be employed in both activities over a given period of time is represented by the axis *OP*. Growth of income at the center and its income elasticity of demand

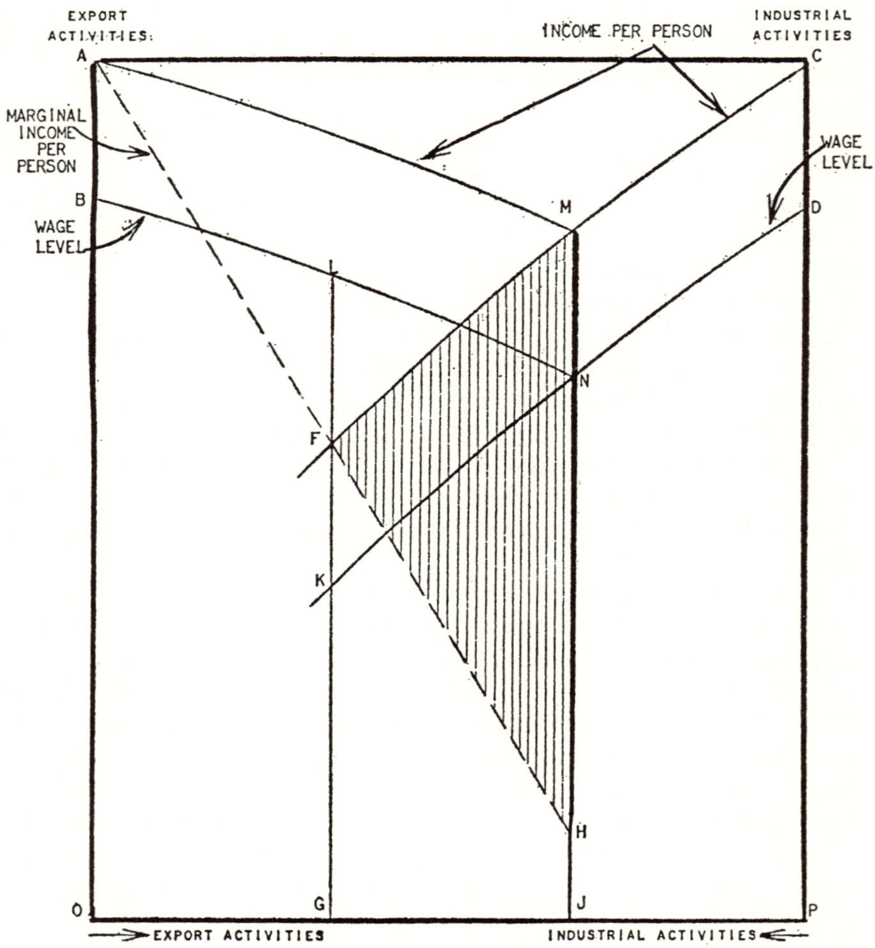

FIGURE 1

will determine up to what point additional production for export at the periphery could be sold at constant prices. This is assumed to be point *O*. From *O* towards *P*, beyond this point of constant prices, successive increments of employment are added to export activities; and in the opposite direction, from *P* towards *O*, successive increments of employment are added to industrial activities in new branches of production.

Furthermore, we assume, for the time being, that real income per person employed in export activities, represented by *AO*, is the same as *CP* in industrial activities at the beginning of the process, and that real wages, *BO* and *DP*, respectively, are also the same.

As increments of employment are added in export activities beyond the point of constant prices, the fall in prices exerts a downward pressure on per capita income along the line *AM*, and wages accordingly decline in a parallel manner along the line *BN*. Constant unit profits have been assumed in order not to complicate our reasoning. Given the high mobility of labor, the decline of wages in exports permeates into industry.

Let us see what happens there. At point *P* industrial costs are competitive with import prices. But new branches of industry have costs higher than import prices and per capita income there is lower than at that point *P*. As wages fall, those branches with the smaller difference between cost and import prices will be first affected, followed by others with inferior productivity, measured by the decline of the curve *CF* of per capita income (corresponding to a declining productivity ratio with the center).

In this way, per capita income in export activities falls correspondingly with the decline in prices; the same thing happens in industrial activities due to higher costs of successive new branches of industry. *H* is an equilibrium point at which the surplus manpower is distributed between the two activities.

Meanwhile marginal income per person has been declining faster than income per person employed in export activities, along the line *AH;* and at the equilibrium point it is represented by *HJ*, which is much smaller than *NJ;* that is to say, marginal income in industrial activities. Indeed, after employment in export activities has proceeded beyond point *G*, marginal income per person in these activities has been lower than in industry.

Income per person employed in export activities is the result of successive increments of employment leading to constant increments of physical exports, at diminishing prices.

Marginal income per person, on the other hand, is the result of every addition of income per person to previous export income, less the transfer of part of this latter due to the fall of prices. It so happens that, while per capita income continually diminishes, that transfer of income to the outer world becomes steadily greater due to the fact that the fall in prices affects increasing aggregate physical exports.

In this way, marginal income declines faster than per capita income and may even be negative if, after a certain point, employment in export activities continues to augment, thus reducing instead of increasing the aggregate export income.

In industry, marginal income per person is the same as per capita income, from the point of view of the economy as a whole. Indeed, there is no such transfer of real income to the outer world as in the case of exports. The fall of wages has brought also a decline of prices in existing industries; but this involves a purely internal transfer, whereas in export activities there is an external loss of income which reduces the increment of income due to the employment of the surplus manpower.

This transfer could have been reduced if the surplus manpower in exports had been stopped at point *G,* where the marginal income per person from exports is equal to marginal income in industry. It is true that if employment in the latter had been extended from *J* to *G,* marginal income per person there (as well as per capita income) would have continued to decline, due to higher costs as compared with import prices. But even so, the aggregate marginal income thus generated by industry, represented by the area *FGJM,* is greater than that which would have been generated by exports, represented by the area *FGJH,* if employment increments had proceeded up to *J.* The difference between the two areas, *FHM,* is the net loss due to the spontaneous process of industrialization.

The optimum solution is to stop exports at point *F,* where their marginal income per person is the same as in industry. This is the point of maximum increment of real income derived from the employment of the surplus manpower; before or beyond that point, the increment will be less. However, at this point wages in exports, *GL,* are above the level that could make it attractive to invest in extending employment up to this point *G.* Therefore it would be necessary at this optimum point to levy import duties high enough to allow industry to pay the same level of wages as exports. In other branches to the right of *G,* which have better productivity, the need for protection would be less.

The real magnitude of the outward transfer of income depends chiefly on the income and price elasticities of demand for exports and the difference between internal costs of industrial production and import prices. The larger this difference and the lower the elasticities, the higher is the transfer of real income to the outer world.

We have assumed equality of income per person in exports and industry at the beginning of the process. To abandon this assumption does not modify our reasoning, except in cases where per capita income in exports and the price and income elasticity of demand of these are so high that marginal income per person is still greater than the rate of wages at the equilibrium point (*N*). It does not seem that this case is typical in Latin America. It is true that in some mineral exports per capita income is relatively high, due to a great proportion of land rent, but elasticities are not high and furthermore these activities absorb only a relatively small part of manpower; thus employment of a substantial proportion of its increment in increasing exports may reduce prices in such a way that marginal increments of income might decrease at a very fast rate and intersect marginal increments of income in industry much before the equilibrium point.

A THEORY OF INFLATION AND GROWTH IN UNDER-DEVELOPED ECONOMIES BASED ON THE EXPERIENCE OF LATIN AMERICA

By DUDLEY SEERS

THE August 1961 issue of *Oxford Economic Papers* contains an interesting paper by Mr. G. Maynard[1] describing two features of the inflationary process in Argentina and Chile in the period 1946–55—fluctuations in exports and stagnant agricultural supplies. It is argued that the experience of these countries is relevant to Latin America as a whole. Let me say at the outset that Mr. Maynard has drawn attention to two important factors, and that it is good to see an economist from outside the region discounting the purely monetary explanation of Latin American inflation.

However, I think that the way in which he puts these points, and the emphasis he places on them, are rather misleading, particularly when they are generalized to cover the whole of Latin America. The mistakes which (in my opinion) he makes are not uncommon ones. So I shall start by criticizing one or two aspects of his argument, and by drawing attention to some gaps. After that, I shall put forward a theoretical model of the inflationary process in an exporter of primary products, indicate very briefly how well this theoretical model fits actual Latin American experience, and finally suggest what are in my view the lessons of theoretical and practical importance to be drawn from this experience.[2] At the end of the paper there is a note on the 'structuralist' school of Latin American economists, whose approach is essentially similar to what is followed here.

A. Some Criticisms of Mr. Maynard's Paper

To start with, Mr. Maynard's remarks seem more applicable to the case of Chile than Argentina. The Argentine economic system is better able to absorb the shocks of short-period fluctuations in exports than the Chilean;

[1] 'Inflation and Growth: Some lessons to be drawn from Latin American experience.'

[2] In the discussion that follows I have drawn heavily on work on this subject in the Economic Commission for Latin America (ECLA), and on many discussions there, both individual and group. The question of acknowledgement is somewhat embarrassing, since I ought to list twenty to thirty names of colleagues in ECLA, and outside consultants, who have contributed in various ways to my education in Latin American economics. However, two people, with whom I worked particularly closely from mid-1959 to mid-1961, were the Chilean economists Osvaldo Sunkel and Anibal Pinto. Without committing them to the formulation put forward here, I would like to stress that they have each contributed more than I did to the general theoretical explanation. I have also benefited from the views of a number of economists at Yale, including Werner Baer, Carlos Diaz-Alejandro, and Joseph Grunwald, as well as from discussions after I had put forward this thesis at the Economics Club in Geneva, the Department of Applied Economics at Cambridge and Professor Kennedy's seminar at the University College of the West Indies.

for one reason, fiscal revenues are much less dependent on foreign trade, and for another, unsold exports can be more easily absorbed into the domestic economy. (Copper and nitrates are both highly inedible!)

Moreover, while the agricultural problem did, in the case of Chile, show itself in inadequate food supplies (and thus exert an upward pressure on wages and prices, as he describes), the mechanism was different in Argentina. The Argentine consumer was protected from the consequences of agricultural stagnation, by price policies which discouraged exports. The effect, as in Chile, was certainly to increase inflationary tendencies, but this was brought about by an aggravation of the import 'bottleneck', not by turning the internal terms of trade against manufacturing; during the period Mr. Maynard is dealing with, they swung the other way in fact, as he mentions at one point. So the stagnation of agricultural output in Argentina after 1945 was due partly to a fall in relative prices. After 1955 Argentine economic policy consisted largely of a tremendous and painful effort to re-establish the pre-Peron relative price structure, but for some reason the writer has largely ignored the very interesting developments of the past few years.

The other criticisms I have of Mr. Maynard's remarks are more substantial. In the first place, the *trend* in exports is more important than their *fluctuation*, when analysing inflation, as will be seen from the discussion below. This is especially true in the two cases he mentions. Neither in Argentina nor in Chile did the purchasing power of exports (i.e. the value of exports deflated by an import price index) ever regain the level of 1929, or anywhere near it, and in neither country was the upward trend in the 1950's very marked. This has meant a chronic and growing shortage of imports, exerting a chronic and growing pressure on the price level.

Secondly, I do not agree with Mr. Maynard's reference to 'excessive' industrialization, a mistaken judgement due I think to this failure to consider trends in foreign trade. His theoretical model shows that in a closed economy there will be an upward pressure on food prices if industrial output grows much faster than agricultural output, but any closed-economy model has little significance for Latin America. If imports consist largely of manufactures, and cannot, for whatever reason, be increased, growth requires rapid industrial expansion. Moreover, by working with only two categories of manufactures, capital goods and consumer goods, he misses the significance of intermediate products. The main criticism one can levy against industrialization in Argentina and Chile, as in several other countries of Latin America, was not that it was 'excessive' as a whole, but that it was unbalanced. Lagging output of several major products has been a brake on economic growth, e.g. chemicals in Chile, and steel and paper in Argentina. This has meant that imports continued to be heavy in these lines. (Until the middle of the 1950's Chile was also still importing steel and pulp for paper.) In fact, in Chile the ratio of manufacturing to domestic product has only risen slightly since the war, and in Argentina there has been no net industrialization in this sense. One must, however, allow for a possible downward bias in indexes of industrial production which would affect this ratio (in view of the way in which it is calculated).

Thirdly, the scope of his analysis is much too restricted. He ignores the effect of lagging supplies in other sectors—notably energy and transport. The electricity shortages in Greater Buenos Aires in the latter half of the 1950's, for example, acted as an evident brake on industrial expansion and played a big role in the Argentinian inflationary process. So did the delays in rail freight services, and (because of its effects on the balance of payments) the slowness in developing petroleum resources.

I do not feel, therefore, that Mr. Maynard has drawn the right lessons from Latin American experience. Yet the recent history of this region does seem rich in lessons relevant to the whole problem of the growth of under-developed economies (and possibly developed economies too). I shall try to sketch briefly what I think these lessons are. The reader will appreciate that, since I am dealing with developments in twenty countries over the past three decades, I can only deal very summarily with this experience here.[1] (The special, though important, case of revolutionary Cuba will be left out.)

B. A General Theory of Inflation and Growth

Let us make the following assumptions about an economy:

Static assumptions about the structure of production and trade

S1. Exports of a few primary products form a significant proportion of GDP (over 5 per cent.).

S2. There is little or no capacity for producing various types of manufactures, especially engineering products, so that manufactures amount to a significant proportion of imports.

Static assumptions about factors of production

S3. Land distribution is very unequal; a high proportion is in partially cultivated *latifundia*.

S4. A large proportion of the labour force consists of unskilled and under-employed workers in country districts.

[1] A more extensive summary was distributed as a document for the 1961 session of ECLA (United Nations: E/CN.12/563), and a revised version will shortly appear in the *Economic Bulletin for Latin America* (ECLA). The whole study, which is being published by ECLA, consists of a regional analysis and chapters showing in greater detail how the experience of Argentina, Brazil, and Chile fits this analysis. (There is also a paper on Mexico.) A statistical appendix contains the main series for population, national product, prices, exports, and imports for the period 1929–58 (in so far as data are available).

S5. The capital market is imperfectly competitive.

S6. The supply of enterprise is inelastic.

Static assumptions about institutions

S7. Manufacturing organization is highly monopolistic.

S8. Wage-earners have some political and industrial power.

S9. Public administration is of limited efficiency, especially in collection of direct taxes.

A static assumption about patterns of consumption

S10. Income-elasticities of demand differ greatly as between various commodities.

Dynamic assumptions

D1. The population is growing.

D2. The economic aspirations of the population are rising.

D3. There is population migration towards the cities.

D4. Consumer credit facilities are spreading.

D5. Tastes are changing (of those with given income and place of work) under the influence of foreign example.[1]

Symbols[2]

Y = Gross domestic product.
G = Purchases of manufactured consumer goods.
I = *per capita* product.
X = Total exports.
X^* = Total exports *plus* net capital inflows.[3]
M = Total imports.
P = Population.
I' = Minimum tolerable *per capita* product.
Y' = Minimum tolerable gross domestic product.
m = Fraction of G which is imported.
t = Time.

Version I of the Model (m is constant)

Let us suppose we set this model in motion by assuming a steady rise in GDP. We expect the structure of demand to change, because of assumptions S10, D3, D4, and D5. There will be an additional reason, that the income distribution is likely to become more unequal if growth takes place in an economy where there is surplus labour (S4), direct taxes are low (S9), and manufacturing grows relative to GDP (see below). We can in

[1] This is strictly different from S10 which refers to the slopes of expenditure–income functions, assuming a given set of tastes (as well as given geographical distribution of population and given credit institutions).

[2] All variables expressed in capital letters are measured as index numbers.

[3] Net of capital outflows and profit remittances.

particular expect the demand for manufactured consumer goods G to grow more quickly than income, i.e. $(dG/dt) > (dY/dt)$. This is the world-wide experience, and will be reinforced in the circumstances postulated, since propensities to consume manufactures are always higher amongst the rich than the poor, and amongst the urban than the rural population; consumer credit is not normally available for primary products or services; and the foreign examples which are persuasive are those of consumption of motor-cars, household appliances, &c.

Let us suppose that the proportion of the value of manufactured consumer goods imported is constant at m, so that total imports of finished consumer goods are mG. It follows at once that $[d(mG)/dt] > (dY/dt)$. Since in fact income elasticities of demand are particularly high for engineering products, and these are least easily manufactured at home (assumption S2), the inequality is likely to be considerable. This model also implies that domestic production of manufactured consumer goods rises faster than GDP,[1] so (over the long run) imports of intermediate products and capital goods will also increase more quickly than GDP unless something very odd happens to capital-output ratios. But imports consist mostly of manufactures (S2), and there is no reason no expect other types of imports to grow more slowly than GDP, therefore total imports (M) will also grow faster than GDP, i.e. $(dM/dt) > (dY/dt)$.

Ignoring international capital flows for the present, so that trade is balanced ($X = M$), this can be translated into the statement that the national product will grow more slowly than exports, $(dY/dt) < (dX/dt)$. This is the condition for dynamic equilibrium in economic terms.

Whether an adequate rate of economic growth is possible depends therefore on export performance. If exports are climbing fast enough, the changing pattern of demand can be accommodated by imports of various types rising as necessary to avoid shortages appearing.

But what is an 'adequate' rate of growth? This depends on how fast the population is growing (D1) and how rapidly aspirations are rising (D2). The former can be measured: the latter can be defined as dI'/dt, the minimum long-run rate of growth of *per capita* output compatible with lack of social upheaval.[2] This is admittedly a vague concept, but I think that its use will be justified in the discussion that follows. $I' \times P = Y'$, the minimum tolerable GDP. Therefore,

$$\frac{dY'}{dt} = \frac{dP}{dt} + \frac{dI'}{dt}. \tag{1}$$

[1] I exclude processed foodstuffs from the definition of manufactured consumer goods.

[2] Upheaval could result not only from poverty but also from unemployment. This brings in additional variables, such as labour participation rates, and I prefer to use *per capita* output as the determinant of political stability. (If *per capita* output is rising fast enough, unemployment will dwindle.) Naturally, unrest can also occur for non-economic reasons.

But the condition for social equilibrium is $(dY/dt) \not< (dY'/dt)$.

So the condition for full dynamic equilibrium, economic *and* social, is:

$$\frac{dX}{dt} > \frac{dP}{dt} + \frac{dI'}{dt}. \tag{2}$$

In words, the rate of expansion of exports (in percentage terms) must exceed the rate of growth of the population by a substantial margin.

Suppose that exports have been rising at an 'adequate' pace, on this definition, but that this pace slows down. Then on the model developed here (which I shall call Version I), the rate of economic growth will fall, and will cease to be politically tolerable (in the long run).

Version II of the Model (m declines)

Here, however, we can introduce a major variant in the model. If the proportion of manufactures which is imported, m, falls, then the following is possible:

$$\frac{dM}{dt} < \frac{dY}{dt} \quad \text{so that} \quad \frac{dY}{dt} > \frac{dX}{dt}.$$

Under what conditions can such a fall occur? The ratio m can be reduced to certain levels in almost any economy: if this ratio is currently much higher, the domestic product will be able to grow more rapidly than imports for a time. But there is, for technical reasons, a lower limit to m for each economy, set by the sizes of market required for various manufacturing processes. This limiting size is quite small for (say) shirt-making, but much larger for motor-car manufacture. The actual market in any country for any product will be determined by the size of population, the level of *per capita* income, and the degree of equality in income distribution. These three variables therefore set minimum values to m (not rigid minima, but levels at which further industrialization rapidly becomes very costly).

Let us now concentrate on what happens in economies which meet the problem by industrialization, so that their products can keep growing more rapidly than the trend in exports would permit. It should be recognized at once that the decline in m is associated with the rate of urbanization. This has two consequences. One is that an urban proletariat appears, with significant political power. This proletariat (having fixed monetary commitments) cannot tolerate persistent chronic unemployment; so as m falls, dI'/dt is raised, and therefore dY'/dt . . . see (1). Secondly, urbanization is one of the factors causing a rapid growth of demand for manufactures, and since it is likely that industrialization also accelerates changes in taste and in income distribution, the pattern of demand is altered more rapidly in this variant, causing the gap $[(dG/dt)-(dY/dt)]$ to widen. Therefore in two respects the over-all socio-economic problem becomes more severe.[1]

[1] As against this, urbanization may eventually reduce the rate of population growth.

One might think that since the last development would only slow down the fall in m, dM/dt would, nevertheless, be lower than dY/dt. But this may in fact not be so. The immediate effect of accelerated industrialization is to cause imports of capital goods to rise more quickly than before. It is true that, for any given industry, this extra foreign exchange requirement soon ceases, and one gets the benefit of import substitution. But, in the first place, the saving of imports is not as big as it seems because there will be new demands for imports of materials, intermediate products, and spare parts, and these imports will now rise more quickly.

Moreover, individual acts of import substitution must be seen as part of a continuing process. Each year a start is made on new industries, involving fresh requirements of imported capital goods; and progress in substitution means entering into types of production which are more and more capital-intensive. Furthermore, as industrialization proceeds, demands mount quickly for electric power, internal transport, communications, water supply, &c., which again raises the requirements for imported capital goods[1] and which causes imports of fuel to increase more rapidly than Y (in the case of countries without their own petroleum).

It is true that in the end, by the time a country is making its own equipment, import substitution will bring some reduction in the propensity to import, but this may not be achieved for two or three decades.

This gives us the first clue on the structural causes of inflation during a process of import substitution. Pressure is maintained on the exchange rate, and periodic devaluation is likely, particularly since import and exchange controls are not effective (S9).

There are other influences at work too. Because of the difficulties in obtaining labour, capital, and enterprise for the new industries (S4, S5, and S6), factor costs per unit of output are high. The monopolistic system of organization (S7) means that the new industries are probably created as monopolies or as branches of existing monopolies: this is particularly likely for new, protected industries. The scale of output is likely to be too small in most cases to enable full use to be made of equipment, which also implies high costs. Bureaucratic delays (e.g. in customs clearance or getting building permits) and the need for bribery may further add to cost (S9). So the import substitutes are almost certain to be more expensive than the goods they replace. Upward pressures will also be felt on factor costs in other industries, partly because of the example set by the newcomers, and partly because skilled labour, managers, and entrepreneurs will become scarce (S4 and S6).

[1] The transport system has to be transformed, since it has been developed to serve the purposes of foreign trade, and freight facilities between inland centres of population may be very poor.

Moreover, it is unlikely that the extra needs for facilities such as transport, energy, &c., will have been anticipated, so strains will occur, such as delays in freight, waiting for telephone installation, and load-shedding by electric generators. This raises costs throughout the economy.

The foreign exchange implications of the needs for investment have already been mentioned; but in addition the rate of saving has to rise not only to finance the construction of new factories and of the new power stations and transport systems, but also to pay for the accelerated expansion of the cities where the new industries are situated. There may be some increase in savings because of the unavailability of imported durables, but the likely effect is to upset the previous balance between voluntary savings and investment, so that local excess demand in various sectors will be increased by global inflationary pressures.

Once the price rise gets under way, there will be familiar cumulative tendencies as each class attempts to protect itself from the rise in prices. Wage increases become general (S8); prices of foodstuffs rise because of inelastic supply in agriculture (S3); and those of manufactures in response to climbing costs (S7). The salary increase in the civil service and public utilities creates further problems. Since tax revenues are inflexible anyway, due to the failure to collect direct taxes, a budget deficit tends to open up. And those responsible for the price policies of public utilities face a dilemma. If they raise prices, this aggravates the general price rise and causes political troubles. But if they keep their charges unchanged, they risk aggravating symptoms of overloading, and they face a growing deficit in their accounts, which increases global inflationary pressures.

At a later stage, long-term productive investment becomes discouraged in favour of more speculative uses of capital, such as hoarding inventories, buying foreign exchange, and building apartments and shops for the higher income groups. This aggravates structural problems of supply. Personal saving becomes discouraged too, and the whole burden of closing *ex post* the global imbalance between savings and investment falls on corporate profits. In due course exports are penalized (especially if the exchange rate is kept overvalued in order to check price rises), and this makes the original problem, the foreign exchange shortage, more acute.

Monetary Implications

It is true that some expansion in the supply of money is a necessary condition for this process to go very far[1] (though one must expect some elasticity in the velocity of circulation). A restrictive monetary policy would, however, only permit the necessary rate of growth to be combined with price stability if the price rises due to the influences mentioned above were offset

[1] More strictly an expansion in the supply of money faster than that of real GDP.

by price falls in other sectors. Since the upward pressures are strong, and cover wide areas of the economy (through rising prices of imports, skilled labour, &c.), and unskilled wage-earners and existing firms are assumed to have some defensive strength, this is very unlikely. Moreover, it is hard to see by what means the necessary rise in investment can be achieved if the money supply is not increased quite rapidly.

The consequence of a strict monetary policy would be to keep Y linked to X. In fact the first version of this model was essentially an orthodox-money or 'gold standard' model, and this version only obtains price stability at the cost of almost complete dependence on exports.

One should add that the working of the model may be substantially modified by a rising inflow of capital. Provided this is growing faster than profit remittances, it enables imports to grow faster than exports, and thus changes the equilibrium condition (2) to

$$\frac{dX^*}{dt} > \frac{dP}{dt} + \frac{dI'}{dt},$$

where X^* refers to exports *plus* net capital inflows.[1] (Conversely, of course, a change from an inflow to an outflow of capital, or rising remittances of profits when foreign capital investment is constant, aggravates any basic disequilibria.) As well as thus affording relief to structural pressures, an increasing inflow of capital also, of course, helps close any global imbalance between *ex ante* savings and investment, or—from another point of view—permits investment to rise without a big monetary expansion.[2]

Other Possible Processes

There are other possible ways in which inflation could develop. Suppose that an economy is in dynamic equilibrium (in the sense that exports, and thus imports, are rising fast enough to enable the structure of supply to be adapted smoothly to the changing structure of demand) but that output in one important sector suddenly starts to grow much more slowly or stops growing altogether. Then structural problems of supply will emerge, as before, if the total rate of growth does not slow down. Imports of the commodity concerned may rise more rapidly (or fall more slowly) than hitherto, causing a shortage of foreign exchange, or else there will be unsatisfied demands in internal markets, leading to rising prices.[3] The danger of a lag in agriculture is an obvious one (see assumption S3), and

[1] This is close to the concept 'capacity to import', used in many ECLA documents. Capital inflows are net of outflows and profit remittances.

[2] But fluctuating capital flows, which must be expected if foreign firms own a substantial proportion of property, play havoc with monetary policy.

[3] In the case of a sector producing for export, a slowing down in its growth would have the same effect as a weakening in commodity markets.

could lead rather directly to wage increases because of the importance of food to wage-earners. (This is where Mr. Maynard's case of lagging agricultural output comes in.[1])

Similarly, imbalances will arise if attempts are made to accelerate over-all growth without accelerating growth in each major sector, unless the pace of export expansion also quickens. This process could be started if the population increase accelerated, or aspirations started to rise more quickly, lifting dY'/dt to a higher level.

It is in theory quite possible for a growing economy to be afflicted by both a chronic foreign exchange crisis and an agricultural problem which would, of course, greatly increase the difficulty of avoiding inflation on Version II of the model. (On Version I the rate of growth would be lower for any given rate of expansion of exports.) In fact, if the expansion of exports is fast enough, internal sectoral lags can be of but limited effect—tensions arise only because in some cases it takes time to increase supplies (e.g. electric power) or freight is relatively expensive (e.g. bulk foodstuffs).

Theoretically, of course, price rises could also start for internal reasons, for example due to the emergence of a budget deficit unconnected with trade fluctuations. This would reduce exports by raising costs and by simultaneously encouraging local consumption of exportable supplies.[2] The result would be a shortage of foreign exchange which would lead to the same structural problems as occur when an exchange crisis is due to purely external influences, or to sectoral lags.

C. Evidence from Latin American Experience

The Assumptions

The first question is how valid are the assumptions of this model for Latin America? A very slight acquaintance with the region suffices to show that the assumptions are valid to different degrees in different countries, though it will be evident from the foregoing that by no means all of the assumptions are necessary ones for the model.

In most of the region the picture presented by assumptions (S3–S6) on the factors of production seems broadly correct. The majority of countries still show the effects of the land grants to the officers of the Conquest, which imposed an alien property-owning class on an Indian population; the remainder still reflect the slave-owning plantocracies. Large fractions of

[1] It is also possible for fluctuations in exports to set in motion price inflation (Mr. Maynard's other case) even if these fluctuations are around a trend which is itself satisfactory. There is no space to develop a short-period model here.

[2] The vulnerability of exports to local inflation depends largely on the importance of local costs in the selling price and on the possibilities of absorbing internally more of the export commodity. Exports of foodstuffs and raw textiles are likely to be most affected, whereas those of petroleum, metal ores, and beverages are least vulnerable.

the labour force work as tenants or farm labourers or smallholders, at considerable distances from the main urban centres, and receive little education. They are illiterate (sometimes not even speaking Spanish). The upper class consists of large landowners, often absentees. In such a society the field from which industrial entrepreneurs can be drawn is limited, and the values of such a society do not encourage industrial enterprise. Capital markets function badly in countries of this type. Banks are either foreign-owned or dominated by a few local families who receive preferential treatment in loans; stock markets are non-existent or relatively underdeveloped; financial intermediaries (such as insurance companies) play a very limited role. The most highly integrated countries, in a social or economic sense, are Argentina and Uruguay, where the supply of factors, whether from the point of view of the economy as a whole or individual sectors, is much more elastic. At the other extreme are the unindustrialized, racially and socially fragmented countries of the Caribbean and Central America (though not so much Mexico, which has experienced a number of revolutions and land reforms) and also Bolivia, Ecuador, and Paraguay.

In assessing assumptions S1 and S2, let us take the position in 1929, when Version II started to operate. (Its very operation has modified the picture in the meantime.) Only Argentina had a big manufacturing sector then, though there was also significant manufacturing activity in (southern) Brazil, Mexico, Chile, Colombia, and Uruguay. Imports of manufactures were, however, everywhere economically important, and accounted for the great majority of imports, even in Argentina; they were financed by exports of a small number of primary products (often a single commodity). S1 is still true throughout the region; S2 applies everywhere except in Brazil, Argentina, Mexico, Chile, and Columbia (and even in these cases imports of manufactures have been only limited in recent years by using vigorous controls).

The extent to which the institutional assumptions are valid show more variety. Almost everywhere manufacturing is monopolistically (or oligopolistically) organized, but labour organization is correlated with industrialization (being strongest in Argentina), and so possibly is the efficiency of public administration, though more weakly.

On patterns of consumption there is little information. Changes can be seen in Venezuela during the 1950's,[1] and these were so big that they form powerful supporting evidence.[2]

[1] See *Memoria del Banco Central, seriatim* (Carácas).

[2] A comparison of consumption patterns in Panama in 1946 and 1956, where *per capita* incomes showed little change, suggests that the pattern of consumption could change with time, even in a stagnant economy. (Assumptions D3 to D5 can hold simply because of the passage of time.) See *Economic Development of Panama* (ECLA).

There is no lack of evidence on population increase and urbanization.[1] But on the climbing economic aspirations of the population, growth of consumer credit facilities, and changing tastes, I can only say that these are obvious to anyone who has lived in the region.

Countries without Strong Import Substitution (Version I)

In any long-term analysis of the region's economic development it is necessary to split the area into two groups. One group consists of eleven countries—Venezuela, Cuba, Guatemala, the Dominican Republic, Ecuador, Costa Rica, El Salvador, Nicaragua, Panama, Haiti, and Honduras; these all maintained in the years 1929–58 what can be called a dollar-exchange standard, with a consistently high dollar (or gold) backing for the local currency, and little exchange control.[2] They conform to Version I of the model.

So far as one can judge from statistics available, which are poor and which do not go back earlier than 1945 (except for Venezuela, Ecuador, and Honduras), the long-period growth rate of these countries has been highly correlated with export performance.[3] This appears to have been true for shorter periods too; there was some slowing down in both in the 1950's.[4] In Ecuador, for example, it can clearly be seen that the growth rate of the whole economy slowed down after 1955 when the export boom slackened.[5]

The import coefficient generally shows a gradual upward tendency. The governments concerned made only sparing use of import quotas and tariffs during this period; the application of trade controls was in fact restricted by various reciprocal trade agreements with the United States. In any event, in nearly all these economies the minimum value of m (proportion of manufactures imported) was high. Inflation appears to have been moderate throughout the past three decades (with the exception of brief bursts in Ecuador and Nicaragua). It followed the course of United States price movements, apart from the war years, when the typical equilibrating mechanism of the dollar-exchange standard was impaired by shortage of imports. Price rises in all cases slowed down after 1951. Most members of this group had in 1958 the same exchange rate *vis-à-vis* the United States dollar as in 1929 (and the Venezuelan bolívar had actually appreciated.)

[1] e.g. *A Preliminary Study of the Demographic Situation in Latin America* (ECLA).

[2] Sterling-exchange standard economies, such as Jamaica and Trinidad, showed similar patterns of economic behaviour in a number of important respects.

[3] The statistics needed to document these statements will be found in the ECLA report mentioned above.

[4] Though it should be borne in mind that the methods of national income estimation sometimes encourage this correlation.

[5] See the historical section in *Plan Inmediato de Desarrollo*, Tomo I, Junta Nacional de Planificación, Quito.

The way in which these economies operated is of considerable interest theoretically; in less open economies, calculations of elasticities may be vitiated by the operation of import controls, repeated devaluations, &c. Statistics are particularly weak for most of these eleven countries, but nearly all types of imports climbed at least as quickly as domestic products from 1950 to 1958 (data do not permit me to go back much further, and in any case imports were subject to special influences of one kind or another in the 1940's). Price movements were not such as to encourage imports (in fact in Venezuela internal prices seem to have risen less than United States prices), and this was a period when liberalization of trade was by no means being increased. Study of the experience of Ecuador, El Salvador, and Venezuela, where national income data are relatively less weak, shows that there is some tendency for imports of consumer goods to rise more rapidly than consumption, imports of capital goods than capital investment, and for imports of industrial materials to keep pace, at least, with manufacturing output.[1]

The eleven countries listed above were politically better able than the remaining republics of Latin America to face stagnation or declines in domestic incomes, such as is involved for countries on the dollar-exchange standard if their exports stagnate or decline. Profits of foreign companies in export industries absorb a high proportion of export fluctuations, a big fraction of the labour force is in the subsistence sector (or can return to it), and the working classes have little political power. However, a glance at the list of these eleven countries indicates the political tensions that can arise in primary-producing countries which achieve price stability by maintaining restrictive monetary institutions and which neglect industrialization. It would be naïve to ascribe political developments in Cuba entirely to the fact that *per capita* exports and *per capita* income changed little during the period between 1947 and 1958, but it would be just as naïve to deny all connexion between stagnation and revolution.[2] When the petroleum boom subsided after 1957, the Venezuelan Government did not feel able to avoid increasing its expenditures (in view of the already heavy unemployment in Caracas), and growth has continued, but, despite big foreign loans, it has been accompanied by devaluation, import controls, higher tariffs, a reduction of currency backing, and rising prices, so that Venezuela is ceasing to be on the dollar-exchange standard.

In the past few years equilibrium in these countries has been undermined from several directions. In terms of condition (2), the rate of population

[1] Peru, although its behaviour was not typical of this group for most of the past three decades, did have a free import régime for most of the 1950's, and shows similar tendencies. In this case, however, relative prices moved in favour of imports.

[2] *Per capita* real incomes in Cuba had, in fact, shown little net change over the entire period from 1903 to 1947 (*Report on Cuba*, International Bank, p. 40).

growth has accelerated, while the upward trend in economic aspirations has soared since the Cuban revolution. Yet at the same time, commodity markets have weakened and the influx of private capital has declined. Consequently, despite increasing recourse to foreign assistance, political tensions are mounting.

Other Countries (Version II)

The other nine countries (Mexico and the rest of South America) show a much greater variety of experience. They have, however, all followed less orthodox monetary policies than the eleven mentioned above. They have also all experienced faster rises in income than in exports in the past three decades (with the possible exceptions of the smaller countries, for which data are not available). On the other hand, they have all experienced moderate-to-fast inflation which continued (in most cases accelerated) when export markets weakened in the 1950's. In each quinquennium, almost without exception, every member of this group has experienced more rapid inflation than any member of the other group. It should be added that they have had more incentive to attempt to stimulate growth, since they contain large urban working-classes which need employment to avoid starvation and eviction from their dwellings; but these economies also enjoy greater physical possibilities for compensatory finance, having developed larger manufacturing sectors already by the 1920's, and possessing markets large enough to permit considerable industrialization.

(The two exceptions to the last sentence were Bolivia and Paraguay, which are small economies, still very backward economically. The attempt to push import substitution inevitably brings them up against the barrier of the limit to m. It is notable that during the period 1945–55 their inflations were the fastest ever experienced by any Latin American country.[1] In the following discussion these two cases will be ignored.)

The counterpart of this is that these countries have achieved, over the past three decades, big structural changes. An outstanding example is Brazil, where the share of manufacturing in GDP rose from about 12 per cent. in 1939–40 to over 25 per cent. in 1959–60, most of the change occurring in the 1950's. Brazil now has its own vehicle-manufacturing industries as well as plants for making electrical equipment. The 'programme of targets' has ensured that investment has continued in the basic sectors of the economy (largely through government finance, domestic and foreign). Priority has been given to this investment despite the growing acuteness of the foreign exchange problem—the ratio of imports to domestic product fell from about 17 per cent. in 1928–9 to about 7 per cent. in 1958–9.[2] The

[1] They had also been engaged in the war of the Chaco.

[2] Comparing imports of goods with output of goods *and* services in both cases.

very difficulty of obtaining imports has encouraged investment (again partly foreign) in private manufacturing. So economic growth has continued, despite rapid inflation, and the rise in real output and employment has in fact moderated pressures for increases in nominal incomes, as well as helping ease the shortages that are always tending to emerge.[1]

There is no place here to describe, even in such a summary manner, the processes of inflation in the other countries of this group, since in each case it shows somewhat unique characteristics. One or two individual features are perhaps worth mentioning, however. Mexico and Peru have had a more satisfactory experience with their exports (including tourism), and have had to make a relatively smaller structural change in the sense used here. In both these countries, inflation has been more moderate, prices about doubling in the 1950's, and showing no significant tendency to accelerate during this decade. In Argentina and Chile (and also in Colombia) the long-run inelasticity of agricultural supplies has been an additional major inflationary force, acting in the ways described at the beginning of this paper.[2] (In Mexico there appears to be some connexion between earlier land reforms and recent economic progress, since in general its food output has risen at a satisfactory rate.) In the same two countries, petroleum exploration has until recently been inadequate, and the failure to eliminate petroleum imports has (as in Brazil) greatly aggravated structural problems. In these two countries, therefore, inflation could arise despite relatively slow growth; in fact this very stagnation meant that all groups struggled hard to achieve rises in income, so as to avoid declines in standards of consumption, and cumulative forces have proved persistent.[3]

How much has the long-term weakness in Latin American exports, and thus inflation, been due to policy mistakes rather than to external causes?[4] This is very much a matter of opinion, but the only case where bad policy clearly has been a major adverse influence on total exports was Argentina in the years 1945 to 1952. Up to 1945, partly because of its more highly developed industrial base, and partly because it could eat its own exports, Argentina had been able to survive the depression and the war with stable prices and a moderate growth rate, meanwhile accumulating reserves of

[1] However, Brazil has only managed to maintain its imports, even at the low levels of recent years, by running down reserves and accumulating very heavy short-term debts; it would be wrong to conclude that this country has as yet by any means solved its basic problems. For a further discussion see the chapter on Brazil in the ECLA study on inflation, and also 'Inflation and Economic Growth—An Interpretation of the Brazilian Case', by W. Baer, in a forthcoming issue of *Economic Development and Cultural Change*.

[2] Jamaica is a case where agricultural stagnation appears to have set off a mild inflation despite booming exports.

[3] See the chapters on Argentina and Chile in the ECLA study.

[4] This is the question forcefully posed by Roberto Campos in a critique of structuralism, 'Two Views on Inflation in Latin America' (a paper in *Latin American Issues*, edited by Albert Hirschman). Cf. Chapter IV of the ECLA study, analysing policy experience.

foreign exchange. It then adopted a set of price, wage, and fiscal policies which simultaneously diverted exports to the home consumer and hampered agriculture, and yet the government failed to modernize the somewhat archaic capital in basic industries.

In other cases, Latin American exports roughly followed world-market experience.[1] There was certainly some discouragement of exports (e.g. by discriminatory exchange rates in Brazil), but to a considerable extent markets lost by one member of the region were picked up by another, and it is impossible to believe that the region's exports as a whole could have been more than trebled between 1929 and 1958; this is what would have been needed for exports to have kept pace with the total output of Latin America, thus averting the need for structural change and enabling all countries to maintain Version I of this model, and yet to achieve their actual growth rates.

The main general criticism that can be levied against financial policy is that, through price controls and subsidies, shortages in key sectors have often been aggravated. Especially noteworthy have been the failure to charge realistic prices for electricity or for passenger transport, and the actual stimulation of petroleum consumption through these two errors, and also by allowing favourable exchange rates for imports of petroleum.

In any case, whatever the origin of inflation in an underdeveloped country, a structural misfit soon develops between supply and demand through the process described above.[2] Consequently, from the standpoint of policy, to decide on the initial cause is rather an academic question; even if this has been monetary mismanagement, it would not follow that a sound financial policy would be a satisfactory cure.

It is interesting to note that the stabilization policies which have been pursued recently, by nearly every member of this group, have not enabled rapid growth to be reconciled with price stability, although large foreign loans were provided in conjunction with (indeed, conditional upon) the adoption of these policies, enabling imports to be increased. There were big initial declines in output, especially in construction.[3] In every case (except perhaps Peru) this sharp setback in output was only recovered, in *per capita* terms, with difficulty and after some delay. Price inflation has reappeared,

[1] See A. Maizels, 'The Effect of Industrialisation on Exports of Primary-Producing Economies' (*Kyklos*, 1961–1). Even Argentina would have been affected anyway by the long-term problems of marketing temperate-zone products in Europe, caused by protection of European farmers, preferential United Kingdom tariffs for Australia and New Zealand, and subsidized United States exports.

[2] In the ECLA study distortions were mostly picked out by comparing changes in supply in Version-II countries with changes in supply of the same groups of commodities in Venezuela and Ecuador.

[3] This is itself a very serious *long-term* loss for a developing economy. It violates common sense when an economy which badly needs schools, houses, roads, &c., leaves large sections of the construction industry unemployed.

even when there is still persistent and obvious unemployment of resources in various sectors. This is a sure sign of basic structural imbalance, as is the continued rigidity in the composition of imports.

It is scarcely possible to claim that policy weaknesses were the central cause of inflation. To support this, it would be necessary to explain the fundamentally different experiences of different countries in terms of levels of national competence, which would be hard to sustain in an area where power has been in the hands of people who show certain obvious cultural similarities. It would also be necessary to explain why inflation accelerated (or decelerated) in several different countries in the same periods, and this would require rather elaborate psychological cycles.[1] While not denying the significance of policy mistakes, a sufficient explanation of the main lines of the experience of the twenty republics since 1929 can be obtained by referring to the non-monetary factors already outlined.

Policy Implications

The reduction of price distortion is a constructive feature of several stabilization plans,[2] but a basic and lasting cure can come only through the internal structural changes needed to enable growth to continue smoothly with further substitution for imported manufactures (especially equipment). This ultimately implies economic integration to create the markets for advanced products, and thus to make possible further reductions in m.

A pre-condition of the structural change involved, as well of making the economy sufficiently flexible during the interval until it has been achieved (so that it can cope with adverse trends and fluctuations in foreign trade) is increased factor mobility. This in turn implies the need for land reform, educational advance, and new fiscal systems, to break down the existing social structures, which are based on highly unequal distribution of property, restricted educational opportunity, and regressive tax systems. Whether such changes are possible, and how they are to be achieved, politically and administratively, lie outside the scope of this paper.[3]

[1] The question is always one of the degree of credibility of a theory. It is still intellectually possible to argue that the earth is the centre of the solar system, but it requires rather complex hypotheses to explain how this is consistent with the observed movements of the system's members, and most scientists prefer to follow the principle of making the fewest and simplest hypotheses consistent with the evidence.

[2] It should not be inferred that the 'realistic' price structure which results is by any means what is needed, merely that the previous structure of prices was in most cases even less helpful.

[3] The 'Alliance for Progress' of the United States Government is a large-scale programme of capital inflow ($20 billion over ten years) conditional on these changes being made. It remains to be seen whether the United States Government holds to these conditions in political crises (especially if there is a danger of a Castrophile Government appearing); whether it is feasible to impose these conditions from outside, even with the best will in the world; whether Latin American governments will really (as distinct from verbally) co-operate in programmes which are uncongenial to their main sources of support; whether

What is analytically important is that the criticism of past policy cannot have much meaning unless one specifies what social and economic characteristics are considered to have been unchangeable data. Similarly, any policy for achieving dynamic equilibrium in the future has to be based on specified assumptions about which characteristics of the socio-economic structure are to be altered, and on an assessment of what the total effect of such changes will be.

D. The Lessons from Latin American Experience

What in brief occurred in Latin America was that the great depression, and subsequent vicissitudes in commodity markets, population trends, and political developments, set the countries of Latin America a task of adjustment, involving further industrialization and the creation of integrated, diversified economies. For this task they were in every way unprepared—economically, politically, administratively, and socially. The inflations that developed in some countries are one symptom of the failure to carry out the needed adjustments; other symptoms are stagnation, chronic reliance on foreign aid, and increasingly frequent political upheavals.

We can now see why Latin America has suffered more in these ways than other regions. One reason is that the increase in its commodity exports has been slower, at least since 1950, than for other primary producing areas. This is partly because the region's exports consist largely of foodstuffs, for which the income-elasticity of demand is not high (coffee, sugar, bananas); but also partly because its exports are directed towards North America, and economic growth there has been slower than in western Europe; and partly because discrimination against Latin American products has been increasing with the start of the European Common Market and the increased protection of United States mineral producers (petroleum and non-ferrous metals). Secondly, its rate of population growth has risen to over 2½ per cent. a year, which is the highest rate of any region in the world. Thirdly, economic aspirations are probably rising more quickly here: the 'demonstration effect' is stimulated by the widespread exhibition of films, television programmes, radio programmes, &c., originating in the United States (as well as by reports of travellers), and recently the Cuban revolution has further accelerated the rise of expectations. In addition, several Latin American countries have now reached difficult stages of industrialization, particularly the creation of heavy industries, without as yet getting much benefit in the form of saving imports of capital goods or exporting manufactures. Others are too small to be able to carry out much import substitu-

Congress will provide year after year the financial resources needed; and what will be the consequences of initial social reforms. (A rolling stone can be enough to start an avalanche.) Another important query is the behaviour of private capital, both foreign and Latin American.

tion. Some might add that Latin American administrations are particularly incompetent to face these problems because of their archaic social structures, though this is a matter of speculation (there is strong competition for the title of the least competent administration in the world!).

The most important lessons to be drawn from the experience of Latin America seem to me therefore as follows:

(1) Methodology. It is a mistake to treat underdeveloped economies as if they were developed when one is analysing economic trends. It is particularly mistaken to apply 'global' methods of analysis, whether monetary or income, devised for developed countries,[1] or to omit social factors.

It is also not very helpful to attempt to attribute inflation in Latin America either to 'cost' or to 'demand' pressures; inflation can only be understood as a whole process which incorporates both aspects.

One has to distinguish analytically between countries which pursue orthodox monetary policies for long periods, and those with managed currencies. They operate in quite different ways.

(2) Substance. It is meaningless to set up a hypothesis that inflation helps or hinders growth. Growth and inflation are interrelated but not in any simple way. In Latin America there are examples of growth and inflation (Brazil), stagnation and inflation (Argentina), growth and stability (pre-1958 Venezuela), stagnation and stability (pre-1959 Cuba).

Inflation can continue for decades without ever developing into a galloping inflation like the classic twentieth-century inflations of Germany, Hungary, and China. Latin American experience implies that necessary conditions for galloping inflation are heavy physical damage and/or strong unions.[2] (Latin American trade unions are relatively weak, by comparison with European unions, in resisting a decline in real wages.) While a long experience with inflation breeds distrust in the currency, it also breeds confidence that the inflation will not explode. Chile has had inflation for about a century, without it ever causing a complete financial collapse.

There is an inherent and ever-present risk of inflation in developing economies which export primary products, because of the active or potential need for structural change. So long as exports are booming it is possible to grow rapidly without inflation and without industrialization. But every commodity market weakens one day (even for petroleum), and if growth has to continue then, if only because of population increase, structural change has to occur. It is difficult to achieve this without inflation in an

[1] See a paper by Thomas Balogh in *Economic Bulletin for Latin America* (ECLA), Jan. 1961, on the way in which monopolistic elements make global analyses of a neo-classical type quite inappropriate to underdeveloped countries.

[2] It is interesting to note that the two countries which come closest to runaway inflation, Bolivia and Paraguay, were the only two which were heavily engaged in war in this period.

underdeveloped country. A suggestive parallel is with the structural changes needed in developed countries which have to convert themselves from a peace to a war economy, or vice versa (though one must also allow for the lack of administrative experience in an underdeveloped economy, the immobility of factors, &c.).

(3) Policy. Policy measures devised for developed economies are not necessarily, or usually, transferable to economies which are fundamentally different.

The essence of a fundamental stabilization policy is a long-term development programme to achieve the structural changes which are needed. Any other sort of stabilization policy is a palliative.

It is dangerous to insist, as the International Monetary Fund does, on indiscriminate policies of financial restraint. The result is a serious check to growth, and there is no reason to expect the resultant level and pattern of investment to be compatible with development needs. In addition, monopolistic tendencies are aggravated and the distribution of income is made more unequal (restricting the possibilities of further import substitution).

The proponents of *any* major economic policy measure in an underdeveloped economy are under an obligation to show how this measure will stimulate growth.

Even policies of restraint in the developed countries aggravate inflationary tensions overseas because they act as a brake on purchases of primary products.

Foreign borrowing will give a developing economy the room to manœuvre it requires to carry out structural change without great tensions. (Whether this is worthwhile, in view of the political strings which are always attached to loans, in one way or another, is outside the scope of this paper.)

APPENDIX

A Note on the Structuralist School

THIS paper is broadly 'structuralist' in its approach.[1] The Latin American school of 'structuralists' is very little known in the United Kingdom or indeed anywhere outside the region. Yet its theories form an original and (in my view) stimulating

[1] What is meant by the word 'structure' in this connexion? There is some confusion on this point, since members of this school refer to the 'structures' of income, demand, output, industry, exports, imports, administration, politics, society, &c. Broadly speaking the more leftist structuralists mean by the word *all* these things, because each of them is considered in some way an impediment to economic growth and the achievement of a more egualitarian society. The conclusion may be drawn that social revolution is a necessary condition for an adequate rate of economic growth. On the other hand, the more conservative adherents usually put the main, if not the exclusive, emphasis on the structures of production and trade, since they are naturally less inclined to stress the need for social change. (In Marxist terms they are 'commodity fetishists'.)

contribution to the field of economic growth. It must be the first indigenous school of economics in an underdeveloped area. Since economic growth is becoming increasingly fashionable as a subject, and since the weakness in commodity markets, the population boom, and rising economic ambitions appear chronic, the school could acquire in the 1960's an international interest comparable to that of Keynesian economics during the slump-ridden decade of the 1930's.[1] These are the leading general references (apart from the ECLA study already mentioned):

JUAN NOYOLA, 'El desarrollo economico y la inflación en Méjico y otros paises latinoamericanos', *Investigación Económica*, 1956, No. 4. A seminal study in which inflation is treated as merely one type of disequilibrium.

OSVALDO SUNKEL, 'La inflación chileña: Un enfoque heterodoxo', *El Trimestre Económico*, Oct.–Dec., 1958; available in English in *International Economic Papers*, No. 10. The first comprehensive statement of structuralism. See also a paper 'Some Aspects of the Chilean Inflation' in the *Economic Bulletin for Latin America* (ECLA), Jan. 1956, generally attributed to the same author.

ANÍBAL PINTO, *Ni establilidad ni desarrollo — la política del Fondo Monetario.* A polemical attack on the policies advocated by the Klein–Saks Mission, and later by the IMF. Sr. Pinto has been described as 'the Pope of the Structuralists'. A more extensive historical treatment of Chile's experience is in the same author's *Chile, un caso de desarrollo frustrado.*

ALBERT HIRSCHMAN. Chapter IX of *The Strategy of Economic Development.* Inflation is described as the consequence of sectoral imbalances, though on many issues Hirschman would part company with the structuralists.

JOSEPH GRUNWALD, 'The Structuralist School on Price Stability and Development: The Chilean Case', in *Latin American Issues* (ed. Hirschman). A critical evaluation by a United States economist who is broadly sympathetic to the structuralist position, and who is Director of the Economics Institute of the University of Chile. This paper contains (on p. 97) an extended bibliography on inflation and growth in Chile. A pamphlet written by Mr. Grunwald in 1955 (*Chile y la inflación*) is of some historical interest as an early reference to 'structural' tensions.

DAVID FELIX, 'An Alternative View of the Monetarist–Structuralist Controversy', also in *Latin American Issues.* A brief summary of the structuralist position, which the author largely accepts. See also 'Structural Imbalances, Social Conflict and Inflation', by Mr. Felix in *Economic Development and Cultural Change*, Jan. 1960.

CHARLES SCHULTZE, *Recent Inflation in the United States* (Study paper for the Joint Economic Committee of Congress, 1959). This does not refer to Latin American experience, but puts forward independently a point of view in many respects similar, suggesting that it is possible to construct a theory of growth and price movements sufficiently general to cover both developed and underdeveloped countries.

Various elements of the structuralist theory have been developed in the work of past and present ECLA economists (apart from those already named) as Raúl Prebisch, Celso Furtado, Pedro Vuskovic, Jose Antonio Mayobre, Victor Urquidi, Pedro Mendive, Manuel Balboa, Hugo Trivelli, and Jorge Alcazar, among many who have participated in ECLA's development studies and the work of advisory groups on economic policy.[2] These elements include a pessimistic appraisal of the

[1] 'Structuralism' has other affinities with Keynesian economics. It is essentially anti-monetarist, and it is on the whole more easily accepted by the Left than the Right. It, too, can inspire a good deal of enthusiasm, especially among the young. It differs, of course, in being mainly long-period, and in disparaging global techniques of analysis, which even the extensions of Keynesian analysis into the dynamic field (associated with the names of Domar, Harrod, and Mrs. Robinson) maintained.

[2] Visitors to ECLA in recent years who have had some influence in the same direction,

long-term trends in primary-product markets; emphasis on the dependence on imports of manufactures; attention to sectoral 'bottlenecks'; implied criticism of the social structure, especially land tenure, &c. I should add that Noyola and Sunkel have both been ECLA staff members (and worked together), and Pinto has worked with ECLA from time to time. (Pinto and Sunkel are still with ECLA.)

As a fundamentally Latin body, ECLA has been concerned all along with the need for a planned attempt to make Latin American economies less dependent on foreign trade, and this made them look at structural weaknesses. It was soon obvious that traditional theory, classical or Keynesian (even in their 'neo' forms) was little help, and that new theoretical explanations were needed. It was a coincidence that brought ECLA and Dr. Prebisch after the war to Santiago, the capital of a country which has suffered from the most severe structural problems, and where several able and vocal economists were already thinking along these lines. But such geographical coincidences often explain how a school is created by cross-fertilization, and how it achieves the formulation of a new and wide-ranging set of ideas.

If one wants to look more deeply into the origins of structuralism, the name that comes first to mind is that of Leontief, with his emphasis on structural relations between industries. The attention focused by input–output analysis on intermediate products and services has proved suggestive for ECLA's development programming, and has led to the realization of the dangers of overstraining basic industries during economic growth. On the demand side, one must mention Nurkse (and thus indirectly Veblen and Duesenberry). The French economist, Henri Aujac, is widely quoted by structuralists, because of his explanation of the way in which the general attempt to avoid a decline in real income causes an initial inflationary impulse to be maintained.[1] Marx must also be counted amongst the intellectual progenitors of structuralism, in view of the emphasis of Marxists on social factors in consumption, production, and policy formation.

Any historical account would be incomplete if it did not also mention the stimulus given to the structuralists by the appearance of the IMF as a major force in the region, inducing governments to balance the budgets of themselves and their public corporations, to restrict private credit, to prevent general wage increases, and to maintain unified and fixed exchange rates.[2] The tacit assumption is that if financial order is established, exports will benefit, private foreign capital will be attracted, and growth will occur spontaneously. Since (at least until recently) United States government agencies and other potential lenders have made the provision of capital dependent on the conclusion of an agreement with IMF, under which governments undertook to adopt this type of policy, the pressure on governments in this direction has been very powerful. Moreover, nearly every government has had to turn to the IMF for help. As a consequence, the profession in the region has been involved in a major debate between 'structuralist' and 'monetarist' positions, which has, as always occurs in strong polemics, led to theoretical developments, supported more or less appropriately by empirical research, on both sides.[3]

though one would not necessarily call them 'structuralists', have included Thomas Balogh, Hollis Chenery, Nicholas Kaldor, Julio Olivera, Nancy Ruggles, Richard Ruggles, and Jan Tinbergen. I am very well aware that these lists of names could easily be twice or three times as long, and apologize to those omitted.

[1] 'Une hypothèse de travail; L'inflation, conséquence monetaire du comportement des groupes sociaux', *Économie Appliquée* (Apr./June 1950); and in *International Economic Papers*, No. 4.

[2] An unkind critic of the Fund might point out that Cuba is perhaps the only country in the western hemisphere which has any prospect or even intention of carrying out this set of policies in its entirety! However, the peso is unlikely to become convertible.

[3] In Chile and Peru, the Klein–Saks Missions, which took positions close to those of the IMF, had a similar effect.

Whilst Chilean experience has been of great importance as an illustration, as can be seen from the bibliography,[1] I do *not* myself feel that the structuralist theory should be considered primarily relevant to Chile (the reader of the references cited above will, however, see that one of the few points on which Campos, Felix, and Grunwald are all in agreement is precisely that the theory fits best the case of Chile). In some forms of the theory, particularly if the stagnation of agriculture is heavily emphasized, this might be true, but I personally believe that, as outlined above, the theory is sufficiently general to cover all Latin American countries, perhaps all underdeveloped countries. This is because the assumptions appear generally valid, and the experience of the region since 1929 seems broadly consistent with the model in one or other of its versions.

Economic Growth Center, Yale University

[1] I omitted many other Chilean economists from the above bibliography, such as Jorge Ahumada, Luis Escobar, Felipe Herrera, and Flavian Levine, simply because I did not want to give too much emphasis to Chile. See also the article by Nicholas Kaldor in *El Trimestre Económico* (Apr.–June, 1959).

Monetarists, Structuralists, and Import-Substituting Industrialization: A Critical Appraisal

DAVID FELIX
Washington University

THE MONETARIST-STRUCTURALIST debate is more than the Latin American version of the international dispute concerning the efficacy of monetary controls in stabilizing the price level. It also involves a deep disagreement over the ability of the price mechanism to bring about a socially acceptable rate of growth and distribution of income in the Latin American context. Finally, the temperature of the polemics tends to be heated by mutual accusations of political bias to a higher degree than is characteristic of professional debates elsewhere. The interweaving of these three issues accounts for some of the murkiness of the monetarist-structuralist debate. This paper deals, however, with only the first two issues.

The practical focus of the debate has been whether the package of policies—credit constraints, devaluation, the elimination of exchange and price controls, and related measures—invoked in a number of Latin American countries in recent years to halt inflation would succeed, and, if so, whether success would be at the expense of economic growth. These programs have generally been undertaken under the aegis of the International Monetary Fund. In fact the IMF has insisted, as a condition for granting stand-by credits, on setting exact limits to the rate of credit expansion, unification of the exchange rate, and complementary measures.[1] It is evident that the IMF's ability to impose terms has depended in good part on the willingness of U.S. governmental lending agencies, with their more ample resources, to make the granting of credits contingent on an IMF agreement being reached. Such collaboration was the rule during the Eisenhower administration, but under Kennedy's Alliance for Progress the two suppliers of credit have tended at times to part company, and as a result the IMF's leverage has been weakened.

It is by now evident that the stabilization programs have been largely unsuccessful, particularly in the larger Latin American countries. In Argentina, after a period of exchange rate stability between May, 1959 and March, 1962 and of near price stability between January, 1960 and March, 1961 (there was an 8 percent rise in the cost of living in this period), the dam broke, and by 1962 accelerating inflation and exchange depreciation were again underway. A similar, if as yet less dramatic, denouement also occurred in 1962 for the Chilean stabilization program.[2] In neither country, moreover, was there a sustained rise in the growth rate during the stabilization period. Uruguay is at this writing still maintaining its exchange rate, but without the price stability and export expansion needed for long-run support. Peru, with moderate inflation and a stable exchange rate anchored in expanding exports, is apparently the one important victory in the array of partial or total defeats.

Events seem, then, to have given the debating cup to the structuralists. But was this because the stabilization programs miscalculated political limits, or because they were economically misconceived? Would the Argentine and Chilean programs have succeeded if the authorities could have held on a bit longer or turned the screws a bit tighter? It is the contention of this paper that the basic fault lay elsewhere, that the programs were simply not reallocating resources in the *directions* needed to create viable growing economies. This seems to have been due

[1] For tactical reasons, the specific terms of the agreements are not publicized, so that it is not possible, except on the basis of "inside knowledge," to know the precise range of commitments nor the degree of flexibility permitted in carrying out the commitments. It is clear, however, that as the going got more sticky, the authorities tended to push credit expansion beyond agreed-upon limits and to fudge on other commitments, and that the IMF was often forced to accede, albeit reluctantly.

[2] The Chilean effort has had two phases. The first stabilization plan (the so-called Klein-Saks program, after the Washington consulting firm which drew up the plan and advised the Chilean government) was instituted in late 1955, and was patently running down by 1958. A second effort followed in December, 1958 under a new presidential regime. The Argentine program was begun in January, 1959.

to excessive confidence in the efficacy of the price mechanism and to a failure to take account of the adverse effect of the import-substituting pattern of industrialization followed by Argentina and Chile on the structure of consumer demand and on the capacity to import. The first defect has been a central part of the structuralist critique, but the second has not.[3] This paper is, thus, also a partial critique of standard structuralism. It is, however, structuralist in spirit, and its policy suggestions share the greater catholicity in the choice of policy instruments which is characteristic of this school of thought.

THE IMF STABILIZATION PROGRAMS AND THEIR RATIONALE

Two features of the IMF-sponsored stabilization programs should be emphasized at the outset. The first is that credit tightening was only one of a composite set of measures designed to achieve exchange and price stability and to stimulate the rate of growth. The second is that the programs were premised on the explicit awareness that supply rigidities were retarding the growth rate. These rigidities were, however, considered in large part the consequence rather than the cause of inflation. That is, they could in effect be classified into two types: "distortions," engendered by price expectations built up during the long inflation, and supply inelasticities which were the result of "distortions" in the structure of relative prices due to controls.

The first type refers to inflated business inventories, luxury construction, and similar manifestations alleged to be associated with inflationary expectations. In fact, it is not at all easy to sort out behavior due to inflationary expectations from that related to more enduring socioeconomic determinants. Inventorying in poorly integrated economies relying heavily on long distance imports is bound to take a larger share of investment than in advanced economies.[4] Babylonian excesses have been more conspicuous in Caracas, where there was until recently virtually no inflation and easy importation of more mobile forms of conspicuous consumption, than in the residential and commercial construction in and about Santiago or Buenos Aires, where neither condition has prevailed. It is not clear how much the stabilization programs hoped to alter such behavior, although attacks on luxury housing, of course, made good public relations material for the programs.[5]

The second type of "distortion" referred primarily to overvalued exchange rates, underpriced public services, and underpriced agricultural prices. That is, an inadequate capacity to import, power and transport bottlenecks, and a poor growth rate of agricultural output were explicity recognized, just as in structuralist analysis, to be key points of strangulation. The "over- and under-pricing" viewpoint, however, assumed that there was an attainable set of equilibrium prices which would remove these bottlenecks.

In reality, it was much less a matter of removing price controls, despite some loose usage, than of trying to change the relative position of controlled prices. This was obvious for public utility and transport rates. But the same also was true of the exchange rate. For while the full goal of the programs was the establishment of a single stable rate in place of multiple rates, to be held by orthodox pegging operations, in actuality it was only the form rather than the substance of exchange control which changed. After the initial devaluation and formal unification of the rate there was less stress on quantitative import controls. But the shifting of goods between a permitted and a prohibited list of imports in order to protect industry and to meet

[3] *Inflation and Growth*, the valuable five-volume mimeographed study prepared by the Economic Commission for Latin America for the Rio Conference on Inflation and Growth, in particular the sections on the Argentine economy (Vol. IV) and the Chilean economy (Vol. V).

[4] A. S. Shaalan finds that in 1953-59 underdeveloped countries put twice as large a percentage of their gross investment in inventories (exclusive of agricultural surpluses) than did advanced countries. In addition, he finds an *inverse* correlation in his sample group of underdeveloped countries between the average rate of inflation and the percentage of inventory accumulation in gross domestic investment. He does, however, find a positive correlation for some Latin American countries, including Chile, between rises in the rate of inflation and increases in the inventory percentage of gross investment. ("The Impact of Inflation on the Composition of Private Domestic Investment," *International Monetary Fund, Staff Papers*, Vol. IX (July, 1962), pp. 243-63.)

The latter relationship for Chile is supported by a recent analysis of the asset structure of a sample of large Chilean firms, which also indicates that inventories rose more when the rate of inflation rose. *See* Instituto de Economía, Universidad de Chile, *Formación de Capital en Las Empresas Industriales* (Santiago, 1961), p. 124, Table III.

[5] Construction fell drastically during the Klein-Saks period in Chile, generating high rates of unemployment among construction workers. The drop, however, was due in good part to cutbacks in public works and the general slowdown of economic activity. There was a similar decline in construction during the first year of the Argentine stabilization program, which seems also to have been due in large part to similar causes. In the second Chilean effort, construction rose at the outset from the extremely depressed 1958 level as a result, in part, of a more active public works program.

foreign exchange pressures was one of the important tools of foreign exchange policy. In place of a formal structure of multiple rates, import deposits and other temporary surcharges and direct controls on invisible transfers were also varied in a discriminatory manner to achieve the same two objectives. In Argentina, in addition, export taxes were selectively reduced on occasion to encourage exporting, although reduction was limited by the importance of these taxes in the federal budget.[6] Only when these methods failed, and exchange reserves plus the availability of new stabilization credits were patently inadequate, was the exchange rate allowed to fall once more. Severe and unexpected declines in international prices for the major exports did complicate the effort of the Klein-Saks program of Chile to attain an "equilibrium" exchange rate. Copper prices fell from an average of $0.44 per lb. in 1955 to a low of $0.247 in 1958. But no such declines disturbed the other two efforts. During the second Chilean effort, begun at the end of 1958, copper prices rose moderately, the average for the three subsequent years being slightly below $0.30 with little annual variation.[7] Moreover, annual export volume of the foreign-owned mining sector in 1959-61 averaged 10 percent higher than in 1955-58. Similarly, Argentine export prices and terms of trade were moderately higher during 1959-62 than in the previous three years.

Apart from special difficulties in the Klein-Saks effort to stave off falling copper prices, the common problem for these stabilization attempts was to limit the general rise of domestic prices in the private sector while bringing about a relative rise of agricultural prices, as well as of controlled prices, sufficient to remove the critical bottlenecks in supply.[8]

The first part of this problem was met primarily by efforts to restrict the expansion of credit to the private sector and monetary wages. In Chile, during the Klein-Saks period the rise in money wages was held down by utilizing the already existing pattern of legislated annual wage adjustments, but restricting the increases to a fraction of the previous year's rise in the cost of living. This policy, however, ran into increasing opposition, so that the fraction was back to unity in 1958. The subsequent Chilean stabilization effort also began with a fractional adjustment in 1959, with the fraction forced upward in subsequent years by labor unrest and political pressures. In Argentina the principal device used seems to have been a tougher policy toward unions on the part of the government. However, this, too, ran into increasingly heavy sledding.[9]

The second part of the problem would, it was hoped, be solved by an elastic response of the private sector to more profitable opportunities to export and to increase agricultural production, to be supplemented by a greater inflow of private foreign investment which more stable prices and exchange rates would hopefully induce. The transportation and energy bottlenecks would, it was recognized, take more time to resolve, since they required heavy investments by the public sector. While these could be met in part by long-term loans from the IBRD and other foreign sources, the noninflationary financing of such investments would also require a substantial current account surplus in the public sector through cutbacks in current expenditures and increases in tax revenues, as well as higher rates for

[6] They were the third most important source of tax revenue. Compare Bank of London and South America, *Quarterly Review*, January, 1961, pp. 116-22.

[7] London price for electrolytic copper. *See* Banco Central de Chile, *Boletín Mensual*, April, 1962.

[8] The stress put by protagonists on the favorable effects which the removal of domestic price controls in the private sector would have on the structure of relative prices is difficult to fathom. In the first place, such controls as were applied were weakly enforced. At most they had a short-run delaying effect, which in shortage economies subject to severe speculative flurries is probably justifiable.

Secondly, they did not alter the direction of movement of relative prices which excess demand conditions suggested would take place. In Chile, for example, agricultural prices rose 1.32 times more than industrial prices during the pre-stabilization period 1940-55. During the subsequent six years of progressive decontrol, it was industrial prices which, interestingly enough, rose the more rapidly. (See ECLA, *op. cit.*, Vol. V, p. 57; and for the more recent period the components of the wholesale price index in Banco Central de Chile, *Boletín Mensual*, April, 1962). In Argentina also, except for the short period in the late 1940's when a strong effort was made to hold agricultural prices, they rose in 1949-59 almost 1.5 times more than industrial prices, with the relationship reversing direction in 1960 and 1961. (See ECLA, *op. cit.*, Vol. IV, pp. 44, 53.)

Thirdly, after formal decontrol the governments continued to use informal pressures to restrain price increases. In Chile, for example, the government decreed decontrol but threatened to restore controls unless industrialists held the line on prices. To check retail price increases, consumer committees were organized to publicize establishments guilty of raising prices. Probably these methods were about as effective as the previous price controls in restraining price increases.

[9] According to an informed observer, while labor relations in Argentina had shown "remarkable stability" in the "face of a substantial reduction in real wages in 1959 and 1960," there were significant signs by the end of 1960 of "a more militant attitude of trade unions indicating that the working classes are not prepared to accept any further reductions in their standard of living." (Bank of London and South America, *Quarterly Review*, January, 1961, p. 113.)

public services.[10] Thus fiscal reform and a cutback of current budgetary expenditures were key elements in the stabilization programs. However, to bridge the interval required to achieve such reforms and to promote the expansion of the private sector, short-term credits were obtained from the IMF, various U.S. and European governmental agencies, and foreign banks. These were to meet budget deficits in a noninflationary manner as well as to amplify imports and sustain capital formation during the critical adjustment period.[11]

Tactics differed on how rapidly to attempt the relative price changes and the retrenchment of governmental current expenditure. The Klein-Saks program took the most gradual approach, perhaps as much because of governmental foot-dragging as from the original intent of the program advisors. The second Chilean effort tried to make many of the adjustments more speedily; the exchange rate adjustment in 1959 was particularly abrupt. The Argentine effort was the most abrupt of all, setting off a spiral of prices and wages in 1959 during which wholesale prices rose 145 percent and real wages fell by about 25 percent.[12] The last two efforts, however, were each followed by about three years of exchange rate stability and a shorter period of near price stability, while the Klein-Saks effort, bedeviled by falling copper prices, never achieved even this brief triumph. Nevertheless, since all three efforts ultimately failed, the most evident lesson to be drawn seems to be that differences in timing were probably unimportant in explaining the ultimate failure of the efforts.

REASONS FOR THE FAILURE OF THE STABILIZATION PROGRAMS

Why did the programs fail? It is quite arbitrary to single out any one of the propagating factors, to use ECLA'S terminology, as responsible. The collapse of exchange rate stability in all three cases did set off a more rapid price rise. But in each program the exchange rate came to be held up by drawing on foreign credits and exchange reserves long after rising prices had already wiped out the initial cost-price gap created by devaluation.[13] The rise in domestic prices, in turn, can be attributed alternatively to wage pressures or to budget deficits which forced an expansion of the money supply and thus permitted the upward adjustment of wages and prices. But, since wages had substantially lagged behind prices during the earlier phase of the stabilization efforts, it seems uncharitable to blame the workers for resisting further cuts in real wages. Similarly, rising prices and the disappointingly low rate of growth of output and employment undoubtedly made it more difficult to cut back public employment or to resist raising badly lagging public salaries. Hence one of the key elements in the failure to create a current account surplus was the inability to slow markedly the increase of current expenditure. In particular, initial gains in public transport and utilities tended to be lost through rising operating costs.

The failure significantly to increase tax revenues can be less easily dismissed in this manner. A larger tax bite would not have generated widespread destitution among the Argentine or Chilean higher income classes, particularly during a period when their relative and absolute position had significantly if temporarily, improved. However, given the slow longer-run growth of income in the private sector, resistance to increased taxation was understandably sharpened. Moreover, the substantial increase in taxes needed for stabilization would probably have led initially to a further curtailing of private construction, reduced employment in some of the more sumptuary domestic industries, and an increase in the relative importance of the public sector which would run counter to the economic philosophy of

[10]A relatively quick response was achieved in Argentina in removing the heavy drain on foreign exchange from petroleum imports. The state petroleum agency was authorized to open up oil reserves to foreign firms, who were guaranteed remunerative prices for all their output and liberal profit transfer rights. Domestic oil production rose rapidly as a result, so that Argentina by 1961 was largely self-sufficient in crude petroleum. However, the longer-run gain in foreign exchange savings from the reduced outlay on the import of petroleum products is being partly offset by the substantial profit transfers which the foreign contracts entail. In point of fact, many of the contracts were made in 1958 before the formal initiation of the stabilization effort, but they were clearly consistent with the economic philosophy motivating the stabilization program.

[11] They are the main reason why the Chilean balance of payments deficit on current accounts, which was negligible during the early 1950's, rose to 27 percent of gross capital formation during the Klein-Saks period (1956-58) and to 22 percent in 1959-60. *See* UN, *Yearbook of National Accounts Statistics*, 1961, section on Chilean accounts.

[12] ECLA, *op. cit.*, Vol. IV, p. 41; Vol. III, p. 126.

[13] The exchange picture is currently most critical for Argentina. Despite a number of earlier debt renegotiation agreements, the short-term external debt obligations (five years or less maturity) of the central bank and government were reported in Fall, 1962 as follows:

the managers of the stabilization program.[14] Hence, despite the commitment of the programs to budget balancing (apart from foreign loans for capital expenditures), there was a general dragging of feet on tax questions.

How does one break through this circle? Leaving the tax question to one side for the moment, the most promising entry is via the slow growth achieved during the stabilization efforts. Actually, growth declined markedly from the pre-stabilization rates only during the Klein-Saks period, and even in this case the decline had already set in during the preceding quinquennium. In the second Chilean effort, the growth rate in 1959-61 was about equal to that of the Klein-Saks period, while in Argentina output and employment fell absolutely in 1959, recovered in 1960-61, with the average over the three years only slightly below the sluggish rates prevailing in the preceding decade. What this meant, however, was that in none of these cases did the economy respond to the apparent opportunities opened up by the wage lag, devaluation, and foreign credits, either with increased exports or with a sustained rise in domestic output.[15]

The General Structuralist Explanation

The failure of the programs to overcome the sluggishness of the postwar Argentine and Chilean economies strengthens the view that the major rigidities are deeper-rooted than had been assumed by the monetarists, and were causes rather than results of inflation. Of these, two are singled out by the structuralists as, in effect, primordial: the slow growth of agricultural output and the limping capacity to import. The first is attributed primarily to institutional defects in agriculture, the second to unfavorable trends in world primary products markets.[16] The consequences of these two rigidities on output and inflation can be rather summarily treated, since their analysis is by now a familiar feature of economic development literature in Latin America and elsewhere.[17]

Briefly, in a closed economy, with money wages and industrial prices rigid downward, prices will rise if the growth of per capita income times the income elasticity of demand for food exceeds the rate of growth of food production per capita. Since the income elasticity of demand for food in poor countries is likely to be quite high—on the order of 0.5-0.6—a slow rate of growth of food production per capita (in Chile the rate has been negative over the past 25 years) limits the noninflationary increase in aggregate output per capita to perhaps twice the rate of growth of food output per capita. There is, moreover, a redistributive effect if the noninflationary limit set by the food supply is exceeded, since food outlays take up a larger share of working-class than of upper-class budgets. Thus money wages are likely to react to rising food prices, generating a wage-price

---

1962	$ 277,200,000
1963	384,500,000
1964	459,700,000
1965	318,500,000
1966	246,500,000
Total	$1,686,400,000 (U.S. dollars)

In addition the external debt of the private sector, chiefly short-term, was reported as $283,700,000, while the long-term external debt (maturity of over five years) was reported as $751,600,000. (Bank of London and South America, *Quarterly Review*, October, 1962, p. 216.) This is even more serious in the light of the fall of central bank gold and foreign exchange reserves from a high of $705 million in the first quarter of 1961 to $215 million in the third quarter of 1962, and average annual exports in recent years of $1,000,000,000. Moreover, profit transfers from the foreign petroleum contracts and the increased inflow of private direct investment in 1958-61 are now generating an additional service demand for foreign exchange.

[14] This was particularly the case in Argentina, where *smithianismus* had gotten a new lease on life as a reaction to the Perón era. In Chile, however, there has been a marked shift in emphasis to public investment since 1960. This seems to have been due partly to the disappointingly slow growth of the private sector, but it was also impelled by reconstruction needs resulting from the earthquake of May, 1960. The change of heart, however, has not yet affected tax policy.

[15] The moderate increase in exports in the foreign-owned mining sector in Chile during the second stabilization effort had relatively little to do with the stabilization programs. The firms of this sector are not required to return their foreign exchange receipts to the central bank or government except as needed for local outlays on labor and materials or to pay taxes. Local nontax outlays have averaged less than 30 percent of sales in the postwar period, so that devaluation can only have a modest effect on production costs of these firms. Moreover, as taxes, which since 1955 have been levied on profits, take up a larger percentage of sales receipts, the modest gains from lowered production costs as a result of devaluation are partly offset by increased tax payments.

[16] However, in the case of Argentina, whose exports are predominantly agricultural, the inadequate capacity to import in the 1950's has been related to agricultural supply rigidities as well as to the unfavorable trend in world agricultural prices. See ECLA, *op. cit.*, Vol. IV, pp. 10-21.

[17] The food-price relationship is explored in considerable detail in Geoffrey Maynard, *Economic Development and the Price Level* (London; Macmillan & Co., 1962). See in particular Chapter III. The other is part of the well-known Prebisch thesis. Both are elaborated upon in ECLA, *Inflation and Growth.*

spiral. In other words, excess demand inflation in the agricultural sector becomes cost inflation for the rest of the economy.

Opening the model to bring in the capacity to import makes it more realistic, since underdeveloped economies depend on imports for some of their consumer goods including food, much of their industrial materials and fuels, and most of their capital goods. With the income elasticity of demand for imports greater than unity, cost pressures are felt via import shortages and rising import prices when the capacity to import grows less rapidly than domestic output. These shortages and rising prices, however, also provide opportunities for import-substituting industries to develop, although this development will be associated with a rising price level.

The model now becomes more complex and can take off in various directions, depending on the relative growth of food output and the capacity to import, the nature of the labor market and wage pressures, the rate of growth of productivity in industry, etc. For example, if we separate the industrial enterprise sector from the household sector, it will be noted that the redistribution effect of substituting domestic production for consumer imports works against the higher income households in whose budgets such consumables take up a larger share than in working-class budgets. The extent to which this is compensated for by profits received as owners of industrial enterprise depends on wage and productivity trends in the industrial sector and on the dividend policy of corporate enterprises. For example, in Argentina and Chile real wages in corporate industry prior to the stabilization efforts seem to have risen at least as fast as man-hour productivity,[18] although workers in smaller enterprises and in services fared much worse. Profits of the Chilean corporate sector tended downward in the 1950's, and firms resorted to progressively higher profit retention to finance inventory and fixed capital formation.[19] The fact that household savings turned negative in Chile during the 1940-55 inflation may, therefore, be due at least in part to the redistribution effect of import-substituting industrialization, rather than to the supposed depressing effect of inflation as such on the propensity of households to save.

Thus, whereas in the closed model there is a strong presumption that the share of wages will fall and the aggregate savings rate will rise as a result of inflation, in the open model there is no firm basis for such a presumption. In point of fact, the wage share was quite stable in Chile during the 1940-55 inflation, tending downward only during the subsequent stabilization period.[20] In Argentina there was a remarkably large rise in the wage share during the late 1940's, the share subsequently sagging somewhat and then falling rapidly in 1959 to the early postwar level. In both countries the savings rate declined in the 1950's.

Industrial growth, however, may still proceed fairly rapidly despite unaccommodating wage movements, as long as there is a large margin of consumer imports to be compressed and foreign exchange to be diverted to import-substituting industries at subsidized rates. Thus inflation and exchange discrimination in favor of industry may for a time raise the growth rate of the economy beyond what would occur from a policy of monetary constraints designed to keep the rate of growth from upsetting price and exchange rate stability. But as consumer imports contract toward an incompressible minimum, the ability to divert foreign exchange to the industrial sector falls correspondingly, although such diversions to new industries may still occur at the expense of the older ones. And since inflation is unable progressively to depress the wage share, industrial capital formation and economic growth decline. This is the stage which Argentina and Chile had reached by the 1950's, according to structuralist analysis, and since the two primordial rigidities have continued to prevail during the stabilization periods, the rate of growth has remained low.

The structuralist model is, in fact, more richly embellished with sociopolitical propositions than the above skeletal statement. Other constraints are also recognized as coming into play during the inflationary spiral; for example chronic infrastructure bottlenecks due to lagging transport and energy prices and cuts in public investment in order to restrain mounting budget deficits. Such constraints are judged, however, to be largely derivatives of the two basic rigidities. That is, the apparently greater confusion and contretemps in Argentine and Chilean

[18] For Argentina, see ECLA, *op. cit.*, Vol. III, p. 130, graph 2. The short period fluctuations in the relationship have been quite substantial, so that it is possible to claim an up or down trend, depending on the choice of dates for measuring the trend.

[19] Instituto de Economía, *op. cit.*, *pp.* 110-11, 166-69.

[20] The reference is to the Klein-Saks period. I have not seen any income shares data for the more recent period.

policy than in the policies of some other Latin American countries is related to two essentially sociological observations. One is the plausible proposition that growth with a lagging capacity to import puts more severe pressure for rapid adjustment not only on the economic structure but also in the administrative and policy-making machinery. The second, rather paradoxical, proposition is that the more industrialized and technologically advanced Latin American economies with their correspondingly greater urbanization adjust less easily to economic shocks than do the less developed countries. Thus the greater success of the recent stabilization effort in Peru is attributed in large part to a comparatively favorable capacity to import, which in turn put less pressure on the economy to industrialize.[21]

Import-Substituting Industrialization and Structural Rigidities

Has the sluggishness of agricultural supply and of the capacity to import been, in fact, grounded in institutional or exogenous forces? In the case of Chilean agriculture, the evidence that this is so appears convincing enough. That is, neither the trend in relative prices, nor agricultural taxation, nor the evidence on agricultural profits suggest a situation which should have depressed a reasonably responsive, technologically alert agricultural sector.[22] Argentine evidence is not as clear cut. Government price fixing, which depressed relative agricultural prices by 25 percent in 1946-49, undoubtedly damaged agricultural output. However, the sluggish supply response to the rise of about 50 percent in relative prices during the subsequent 13 years plausibly suggest institutional deficiencies.[23]

The capacity to import presents, however, a more complex picture. Granted that world excess capacity in minerals, coupled with import restrictions by a number of leading industrial powers, have held down earnings from Chile's mineral exports. Granted that a somewhat similar situation has prevailed for Argentina's agricultural exports.[24] Granted also that in the circumstances a lavish resort to devaluation or to greater concessions to foreign mineral investors might be only a beg from my neighbor policy which would evoke mutually damaging reponses from other depressed primary exporters. What remains to be explained is why Argentina and Chile, with their sizeable industrial sectors, have been unable to become significant industrial exporters both prior to and during stabilization efforts. This calls for closer analysis of the import-substituting industrialization pattern. But since what follows is not based on research in depth, careful economic analyses of Latin American industries being still rather sparse, the discussion will perforce be in rather general terms. To the extent that it is valid, however, the analysis may fit other industrializing economies of Latin America—Brazil, for example—as well as Argentina and Chile.

In form the import-substituting pattern recapitulates the conventional pattern of capitalist industrialization. That is, the initial industries are generally consumer goods or building materials producers with a relatively simple technology and a low capital requirement per worker and per unit of output. They are then followed by consumer goods industries requiring a more sophisticated technology and larger capital outlay, shading subsequently into industries producing relatively complex consumer durables, steel, engineering, and chemical products.

The patterns diverge, however, in two important respects. The first is that, in contrast to European, North American, or even Japanese industrialization, Latin American countries have lacked an extensive structure of handicraft industries from which to draw skilled labor and entrepreneurial talent. The development of such a structure was inhibited by the highly stratified two-class society which characterized most Latin American countries prior to World War I, in

[21] ECLA, *op. cit.*, Vol. III, pp. xiv–xv. The assumption that Peru's favorable capacity to import in recent years has been due more to exogenous factors than to astute monetary and exchange rate policies is by no means implausible. In the foreign-owned mineral industries—most notably in copper—and the partially foreign-owned fishing industry, investments to expand capacity were under way some years before the stabilization effort in 1959. They came to completion fortuitously when the stabilization effort was under way.

[22] Supplementing the data referred to in the ECLA *Inflation and Growth* study is a recent calculation of Chilean agricultural production over the longer run which indicates that the average annual increase in 1921–40 was 1.9 percent, or only slightly in excess of the rate of population growth. In the period of 1941–57, the annual increase fell to 1.7 percent, while the population growth rate rose to over 2 percent per annum. See Tom E. Davis, "The Growth of Output Employment, Capital Stock and Real Wages in Basic Sectors of the Chilean Economy," in *Hearings before the Sub-Committee on Inter-American Relationships, Joint Economic Committee*, 87th Cong., 2nd sess. (Washington, D.C.; Government Printing Office, 1962), p. 104, Table 1.

[23] Compare ECLA, *op. cit.*, Vol. IV, pp. 11, 17–22.

[24] In actuality, the slow growth of agricultural output and relatively favorable home prices have also depressed the volume of Argentine exports in the postwar period.

particular by the absence of a middle class of farmers and merchants to provide an extensive market for such industries. Argentina, it should be noted parenthetically, is a partial exception, since much of its population was of recent European, albeit of largely poor peasant origin. The industrialization efforts, therefore, have been forced to draw on a particularly inexperienced stock of human inputs. To a varying degree, deficiencies in entrepreneurship and capital accumulation have been compensated for by foreign firms which have established branches and subsidiaries, in good part to avoid a threatened loss of the local market due to import restrictions, and by government-financed industries when capital outlays have been too large to interest private investors. But at the same time the highly protected monopolistic market environment which has been created to induce private investment lessens pressure on industrial firms to increase productive efficiency. To this must be added the notorious lag of Latin American education in developing trade and technical schools to augment the supply of industrial and scientific skills. The consequence has been that even with modern plants and low wages, domestic industries tend to have considerably higher unit costs than foreign equivalents.[25]

The second major difference is that widening of the industrial spectrum has taken place more rapidly than had been characteristic of the conventional pattern of capitalist industrialization. The pace has been more rapid the more sluggish the capacity to import, for then the saving of foreign exchange by encouraging import-replacing industries became high policy. This has also tended to give the industrialization pattern a bias toward producing middle class products, such as consumer durables, since it is the less essential imports which have been restricted most severely. But even when efforts are made to check this bias, policy still tends to favor the allocation of foreign exchange and tax concessions to establish new industries which would save foreign exchange, as against the modernization and expansion of existing industries.

Two significant consequences have followed from this precocious widening of the industrial spectrum. Firstly, it has meant a rapid movement toward the production of technologically sophisticated products in which complex economy of scale factors are especially critical determinants of production costs, even though the domestic market has often been inadequate to exploit such economies. These scale economies relate not merely to the size of individual plants, but also to the size of the intricate complex of feeder firms. Thus, whereas in advanced economies with larger domestic markets supplemented by exports, the market size and level of organizational competence permit complex flow production within and between plants, the smaller markets and lower organizational competence in Latin America has meant batch production, lags in supply, larger inventories, and other cost elevating deficiencies. Secondly, output curves have tended to be kinked, rising rapidly when exports are being replaced, but flattening out when further growth of demand has been grounded in the growth of domestic income. Profits have also followed this kinked pattern. Thus industries have moved rapidly from high profit and growth to precocious "maturity," at which point they fall back to monopolistic quiescence with lower profit rates, a reduced level of investment, and aging plant and equipment.

The inability of even the more industrialized Latin American countries to develop export markets follows from the general pattern described. The initial cost disadvantage stemming from the lack of skills and deficient organization could, taken by itself, be overcome in time, particularly in industries of lesser technological sophistication with relatively low capital-output ratios. Precisely because the initial skill differential vis-à-vis older foreign competitors is great, the learning curve in Latin American countries is likely to slope more steeply, despite the absence of internal competitive pressures. This, plus a slower growth of real wages relative to foreign competitors, plus devaluation, might bring down costs in such industries to a profitable exporting level. Of course, even this possibility could well be thwarted by the effect on wages of relatively rising food prices. For the relevant wage relationship is real wages in terms of industrial product, and the latter would rise more rapidly than real wages as such when the industrial terms of trade are worsening.

But even if these adverse terms of trade do not completely thwart the narrowing of the cost gap, the added effect of the relative aging of the capital stock in industries with export potential may well do so. For one of the convincing generalizations emerging from contemporary analysis of productivity is that

[25] For a detailed appraisal of the factors involved in one important industry, see ECLA, *Labor Productivity of the Cotton Textile Industry in Five Latin American Countries* (New York, 1951).

its growth is positively correlated with the growth of capacity because this results in a stock of plant and equipment which is more *au courant* with the latest technological developments in the industry. This is due not merely to a more rapid addition of capacity, but also to a more rapid rate of replacement. The combined effect of an inadequate growth of food production and of the import-substitution pattern followed in Latin America may, therefore, create a continual state of dynamic cost disadvantage.

The argument can be developed more formally. Whether or not an import-substituting industry reaches exporting efficiency depends on the interplay of at least four sets of forces: (1) the effect on the industry's productivity of the growth of other industries; (2) the effect on its productivity of its own growth in output; (3) the growth in productivity of competitors abroad, (4) wage and exchange rates trends.

The first set of forces, the external economy-diseconomy problem, may for our purposes be disposed of quickly. If the establishment of new industries always lowers unit costs in existing industries, then the rapid widening of the industrial spectrum would be broadly justifiable, and the case against continuing import-substituting industrialization much the weaker. But, clearly, industries also compete for scarce resources. Indeed, deepening shortages of foreign exchange (imports) and public services have, as already indicated, been a major cause of the slackening of industrial growth in recent years in Argentina and Chile. Between specific subclusters of industries, complementary relations in production may perhaps outweigh the competitive ones,[26] but this would still mean that the choice of industries to encourage can critically affect a country's ability to become an industrial exporter.

The other sets of forces are combined in Diagram 1 which, after a necessary if tedious explication of its components, will be used to illustrate how the interplay of these sets of forces can render import-substituting industries incapable of exporting.[27]

DIAGRAM 1

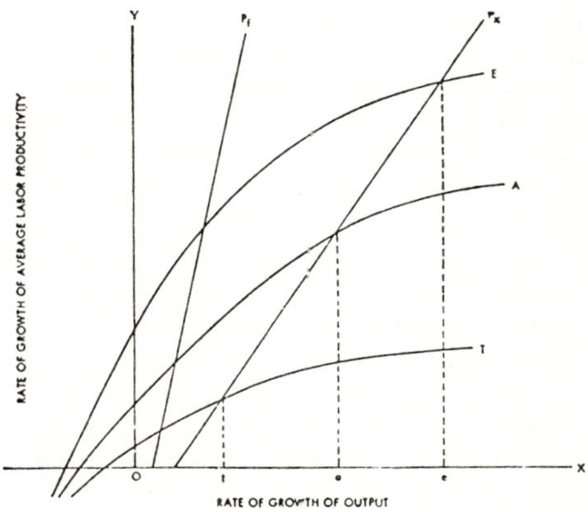

The T (textiles?), A (automotive?) and E (electronic?) industries are selected to represent industries in different portions of the industrial gamut created by import-substitution. They broadly represent an ordering in terms of increasing technical sophistication and probably, also, in terms of recency of establishment, although the last is incidental to the argument. The ordering is assumed capable of being extended to other industries, so that we may imagine an array of curves filling the space around those actually depicted. The *Pf*-line represents the annual rates of increase in labor productivity in the equivalent exporting foreign industries. For our purposes this is simply exogenous information. The line slants to the right because the evidence suggests that in recent years the productivity increases have been higher the more technically sophisticated the industry.[28]

The *Px*-line is the export-efficiency line. Starting from current levels of output, let us provisionally take both the exchange rate and the differences between domestic and foreign wages and between

[26] The *pôles de croissance* theory of François Perroux is built on this notion of complementary clusters. "Note sur la notion de pôle de croissance," *Economie Appliquée*, January–June, 1955, pp. 309–20.

On the other hand, the view attributed to Nurkse (perhaps wrongly) that complementarity in demand insures that the external effects between industries are positive, is analytically incorrect. See Marcus Fleming, "External Economies and the Doctrine of Balanced Growth," *Economic Journal*, June, 1955, pp. 241–56.

[27] This is a revised version of a diagram in the original draft of this paper presented at the Rio conference. I am grateful to the Quantitative Seminar of the London School of Economics for useful criticisms which caused me to reconstruct the diagram. Far from the revised version being the responsibility of the seminar, however, its members would probably resent such an implication.

[28] For a bit of evidence on this, *see* UN, *World Economic Survey*, 1961, Tables 2–13.

other factor prices also as given. Let us fix the time interval at the end of which the industrial sector is to become capable of exporting. There will then be a point on each industry curve representing the rate of increase in its output and productivity necessary to allow it to export. The *Px*-line connects such points. As drawn, no industry is initially capable of exporting—approximately the current situation in Latin America.

The curves are derived by combining four functional relations between industry output and productivity. A fifth is incorporated in the *Px*-line.

The first relation we call the Salter effect.[29] New technology is incorporated in any industry mainly through gross investment in currently most advanced equipment. Since plant and equipment is durable, each industry, soon after its founding, comes to consist of layers of plant and equipment of different vintages, the older the vintage the less efficient the equipment. Consequently, the faster the growth of output, the younger will be the age structure of the industry's plant and equipment and the larger the growth of average productivity of its capital and labor. Higher rates of growth of output will hasten both the expansion of capacity and the obsolescence rate for old equipment. The relationship between growth of output and productivity is curvilinear, approximately as in Diagram 1, rather than linear, for reasons which should be apparent to the reader.

The curves array themselves approximately as indicated in the diagram because of a second relationship, the economy of scale effect. It is generally accepted that Latin American industries suffer in varying degrees from inadequate scale of output. The productivity effect of this is depicted in rather oversimplified form by Diagram 2, where current rates of output are taken as given. The diagram assumes that the more sophisticated Latin American industries suffer most from inadequate scale of operations. This is more likely to be true if by scale we refer not to individual plants alone but, as already mentioned earlier, to industrial complexes. It should then follow that the industries which are further from optimum operations will have the higher rate of increase in productivity for a given increase in the output rate, because the economy of scale effect will be reinforcing the Salter effect the more strongly.[30]

DIAGRAM 2

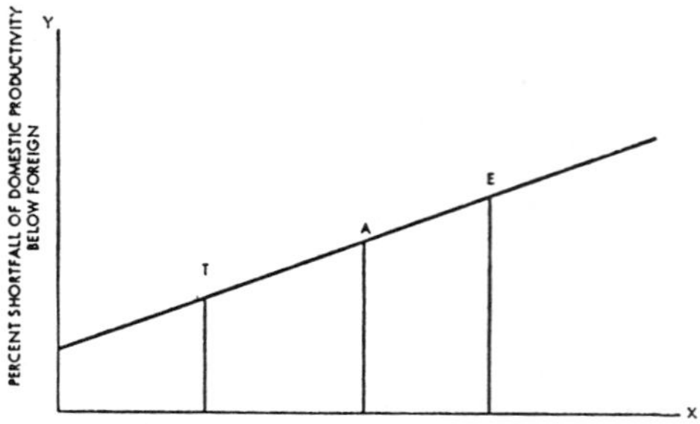

The third relationship, the learning effect, simply shifts the industry curves upward. This effect says that with a given plant, equipment, labor force, and rate of output, productivity will rise over time because production experience will increase labor skills and the coordination of operations. The effect is likely to be greater for the more technologically sophisticated industries, and the curves in Diagram 1 are drawn this way.[31]

The fourth is between the degree of utilization of plant and equipment and productivity. The extension of the curves to the left-hand quadrant of Diagram 1 indicates that productivity increases as output falls below the full capacity level.

Finally, industrial efficiency may be enhanced for technological borrowers, such as Latin American countries, if they can lower unit costs by adapting imported technology to their lower wages and higher capital costs. The consequence of effectively substituting labor for capital is to increase total productivity, but to lower labor productivity. Such substitution would therefore lessen the increase in output per head and the corresponding rate of

[29] After W. E. G. Salter, who first made important use of a major fact about capital structures which had been ignored by capital theory. *See* his *Productivity and Technical Change* (Cambridge: Cambridge University Press, 1960).

[30] For a perfect ordering, it is necessary for the downward sloping section of all long-run industry cost curves to have approximately the same slope. This is unlikely to be the case, although how far off the mark such an assumption is cannot be assessed directly, since we have limited information on the shape of such curves. It can, however, be assessed indirectly by testing our model's prediction that, for example, the industries in Argentina or Chile with the highest increases in productivity per given increase in output also have the greatest shortfall in productivity levels relative to foreign competitors. This prediction depends on the legitimacy of arraying the industry curves as in Diagram 1 and the array is derived from the economy-of-scale ordering in Diagram 2.

[31] This is also an oversimplification. The learning-by-repetition influence on the efficiency of a given plant, equipment, and labor force should peter out in time. Correcting for this should, however, strengthen rather than weaken the main conclusions derived from Diagram 1.

increase in output required to attain export efficiency. The *Px*-line and the industry curves may thus be expressed in terms of labor productivity, as in Diagram 1.[32] The more sophisticated, however, the imported technology, the less the ability of Latin American countries, with their limited engineering and managerial cadres, effectively to make such adaptations. Empirically, this should show up for each country in smaller differences between the capital-labor ratios at home and abroad per given plant, the more sophisticated the industry. That is, the capital-labor ratio for T-type industries should be lower than in foreign equivalents by a greater percentage than for A- and E-type industries, a hypothesis which I believe is broadly valid, and should at any rate be testable.[33] The *Px*-line, therefore, slants further to the right than the *Pf*-line, because it is given an added tilt by the declining ability to substitute labor for capital as we move from the less to the more sophisticated sections of the industrial spectrum.

We may now, at long last, manipulate Diagram 1 to indicate a number of conclusions concerning import-substituting industrialization.

1. Despite higher rates of increase in output per head, the more sophisticated industries will require greater sustained rates of increase in output to reach export efficiency than the T-type industries; $Oe > Oa > Ot$. Under the import-substituting pattern of industrialization, interindustry differences in the levels and rates of growth of labor productivity are misleading indicators of comparative industrial efficiency.

2. The shorter the time interval in which it is desired, say for balance-of-payments reasons, to become an industrial exporter, the greater will be the rate of increase in industrial output. That is, if the time period is cut from x to $x/2$, the *Px*-line shifts to the right.

3. Widening the difference between foreign and domestic industrial wages can reduce the needed rates of output growth, that is, it can shift the *Px*-line to the left. The effectiveness of such a policy is, however, limited by three considerations. The first arises from the linkage between industrial wages and food prices. If food prices are chronically rising by more than industrial prices, as has been the case in Argentina and Chile, the fall in wage costs per unit of industrial product may be much smaller than the widening of differences between domestic and foreign real wages. The second is that if industrial wage costs are reduced by a sufficient cut in wages, consumer demand would shift from T-type consumables to sophisticated A- and E-type consumer goods. The implication of this for the failure of the Argentine and Chilean stabilization programs is discussed in the following section. The third is that if it is necessary to depress industrial output and employment in order to force down real wages, productivity falls. That is, we move into the left-hand quadrant of Diagram 1. Although the *Px*-line may have been moved to the left by the fall in wages, the output and productivity gap which has to be bridged in order to reach export efficiency can remain as wide as ever.

4. Devaluation as a means of promoting industrial exporting is also subject to at least two constraints germane to the model. The first is that if the redistributive effect of devaluation is toward greater income inequality, the shift in consumer demand will be toward A- and E-type goods. This point is elaborated below. Secondly, the ability of devaluation to shift the *Px*-line leftward is limited by the degree to which higher price of imports feeds back on industrial costs. The degree appears to be substantial, because the import-substituting pattern relies heavily on Professor Hirschman's strategy of establishing industries and letting the backward linkages come along later. Hence, the industrial sector develops with a heavy dependence on imported materials, fuels, and parts.[34]

5. The extension of import-substituting to capital goods establishes new industries which are likely to be in the A- and E-range of the industrial spectrum. Whether the *Px*-line shifts to the right or left depends on whether the higher price of such goods to in-

[32] The Salter, economy of scale, and learning effects presumably influence total productivity, that is, both capital and labor efficiency, proportionately. Hence, the resulting curves should be the same whether expressed in labor or total productivity.

[33] Alternatively, a possible definition of that sexy but imprecise concept, technological sophistication, could be concocted in terms of ratios between capital-labor ratios at home and abroad. This, however, might be giving too many hostages to stochasticism.

[34] This has been brought out in a number of recent ECLA studies of the growing "rigidity" of imports in the more industrialized Latin American countries.

Due to the monopolistic character of Latin American industry increases in costs are also passed along rapidly, and even anticipated. Wage demands may then set off a wage-price spiral which can wipe out in short order the gain from devaluation. This is clearly a serious problem for economic policy. The points made under 4, however, concern not the speed of adjustment of money incomes but whether devaluation can shift resources so as to facilitate industrial exporting.

dustrial users is offset by more ready availability and, hence, lower inventory costs. There is no a priori reason for assuming that the extension will improve the prospects for industrial exporting. It depends on which industries are established and what their economy of scale shortfall might be.

6. Economy of scale deficiencies are obviously less of a problem the larger the domestic market. Hence the industry curve array should be narrower for Argentina than for Chile, and somewhat narrower for Brazil than for Argentina.

The general presumption is that economies which have pushed import-substituting industrialization in the context of stagnating agriculture to the extent to which Argentina and Chile have, tend to box themselves in. As industrial growth slows down when imports become less compressible, the industrial sector, for reasons suggested by the above analysis, is unable to revive its momentum by exporting. Clearly the analysis needs to be tested more carefully against the facts than I have been able to do. The model, however, provides us not only with a plausible set of reasons for the incontrovertible fact that neither Argentina nor Chile (nor Brazil) has been able to become an industrial exporter, but also, I believe, with a useful agenda for empirical research on this problem.

Import-Substituting Industrialization and the Failure of the Stabilization Programs

The analysis also helps explain why, despite the fall in real wages, devaluation, and foreign credits, the IMF stabilization programs failed to promote a breakthrough to industrial exporting. Basically it was because the programs worked against the reallocation of resources needed for such a breakthrough. There appear to be three major reasons for this.

The first is that the reduction of real wages and the wage share tended to divert investment in the industrial sector excessively and indiscriminately to consumer and capital goods industries in the A- and E-portions of the industrial gamut. This resulted partly from the fact that the less-sophisticated consumer goods industries at the T-end of the gamut are generally industries whose demand depends more heavily on wage income.[35] The resulting stagnation of T-industry demand was further accentuated by sharp changes in relative prices for manufactures consumed by the nonwage households whose real income position had improved. Recall that import-substituting industrialization and the restrictions of sumptuary imports when the capacity to import is tight tend to raise drastically the prices of goods which are more important in the budgets of nonwage than wage households. The most glaring examples in Argentina and Chile in the 1950's were, of course, automobiles, which because of import restrictions sold for five to six times their price in the United States or Europe. But price disparities of a significant, if less spectacular, degree existed for most consumer durables, even when domestic production or assembly was the main source of supply. Some of the greater supply of foreign exchange made possible by stabilization credits was used to increase imports of consumer durables and luxury goods. A much larger share was used to import equipment and supplies for new durable consumer goods industries and to enlarge the output of existing ones. The particularly high income elasticity of demand for such goods among nonwage households combined with the fall in their relative prices to divert a major share of the increased nonwage income to industries producing these products. In turn, this stimulated the demand of domestic suppliers to these industries and encouraged their expansion. Parenthetically, the falling wage share may also help to explain why, contrary to the expectations of the program, the removal of price controls was followed by a fall in relative agricultural prices.[36]

Secondly, most of the augmented inflow of foreign manufacturing investment during the stabilization periods[37] also went into A- and E-type industries. This was due not only to the increased demand for such products from the income distribution changes described above; it was also related to the special characteristics of such investment in Latin America. This investment tends to be limited-risk investment designed to obtain or keep a foothold in the local market when direct exporting is blocked by import restrictions, hence is made despite the fact that local

[35] However, since they are also industries with lower capital-labor ratios, they should reap the greater cost benefits from lower wages. Offsetting this is the fact that they tend to be less dependent on imported inputs and thus benefit less from a greater availability of foreign exchange. The argument in the text is, therefore, essentially an empirical judgment that the cost advantages which might have accrued to the T-industries from the stabilization programs were not enough to offset the disadvantages stemming from the shifts in consumer demand.

[36] See footnote 9. The greater impact of devaluation on industrial costs was probably the other main factor.

[37] The inflow, however, was negligible in Chile during the Klein-Saks period.

costs of production are often substantially higher.[38] It is limited-risk investment because, to the maximum degree commensurate with local regulations, foreign manufacturing firms seek to rely on imported parts and other imports, and to finance operations from local borrowing and retained profits. The gains to the parent firms tend to come from the sale of goods and services to their Latin American subsidiaries as much as from the profits of these subsidiaries. Thus, despite the fact that profit rates of U.S. branches and subsidiaries in Latin America declined progressively in the 1950's[39] and from 1951 on have averaged much less than the profit rate after taxes earned in U.S. manufacturing, the annual inflow of such investment rose until 1958. The flow of such investment tends, therefore, to be heavily influenced by the prospective availability of foreign exchange for importing and, to a lesser extent, for the transfer of profits. But it reacts only slowly to changes in the rate of profit earned by branches and subsidiaries.[40] The greater availability of foreign exchange during the earlier phases of the stabilization effort attracted, therefore, an increased volume of manufacturing investment which went into the partial domestic production of sophisticated products. The most notorious example was, of course, the Argentine automotive industry. Between December, 1958 and November, 1961, Argentine authorities approved automotive investment plans submitted by foreign firms to the amount of $97 million (U.S.). This resulted, by 1961, in the establishment of 22 automotive firms, wholly or partly foreign-owned, in a country with an estimated market potential for motor vehicles in the half-decade ahead of at the most 150 to 200 thousand units per annum. In 1961 alone, the industry imported $153 million in parts, supplies, and equipment, or about 16 percent of that year's imports, in order to produce 136,000 units.[41] An additional volume of imports, impossible to quantify without an input-output table, was consumed by the steel industry and domestic-parts manufacturers in order to fill orders for the automotive industry. While there were no such spectacular examples in Chile, an accumulation of small-scale partial production of sophisticated consumer goods, including automotive assembly, took place, to which foreign investors contributed.[42]

The third reason is that the policy of tighter credit diverted private finance to A- and E-type firms. When credit is tight, the activities of firms with higher rates of profits are usually less affected, since they are better able to finance internally through retained earnings and also have superior credit ratings. This seems to have been true in both Argentina and Chile.[43] Moreover, since credit was tightened primarily by imposing global limits on bank lending to the private sector, a nonbank lending market emerged in each country with extremely high interest rates, in which the more profitable operations could obtain marginal funds but which was too costly for less profitable firms.[44] It is difficult to assess the quantitative importance of these diversions, although their direction seems clear enough. During the earlier phases of the stabilization programs, when budget deficits were largely met by foreign credits, the squeeze on the private sector as a whole does not seem to have been very severe. But, as the net inflow of foreign credits fell off, a larger portion of government budgets had to be financed by central bank borrowing. To keep within the credit limits agreed upon with the IMF, loans to the private sector were restricted more severely, chiefly by raising marginal reserve ratios of the commercial banks. The effect was felt most acutely, evidently, by less profitable firms. In Argentina, in particular, this led

[38] For a more detailed discussion of this characteristic, see *United States Business and Labor in Latin America*, prepared at the request of the Subcommittee on American Republic Affairs, Committee on Foreign Relations, U.S. Senate, 86th Cong. (Washington, D.C.: Government Printing Office, 1960), Chapters I–III.

[39] *Ibid.*, p. 12, Table 9.

[40] In contrast to investment in extractive industries for export. *Ibid.*, pp. 13–15, Charts 1–3.

[41] Bank of London and South America, *Quarterly Review*, July, 1962, pp. 124–30.

[42] There was a particularly heavy concentration of such new industries in the northernmost province of Tarapacá. In order to offset the decline of the nitrate industry, ports in this province were given free importing privileges. It became highly profitable, therefore, to locate industrial activity in these ports, even though the market (the central provinces) was located 1300 miles to the south.

[43] For Argentina, see Bank of London and South America, *Quarterly Report*, July, 1962, p. 148. For Chile, some rather indirect evidence is indicated in Instituto de Economía, *Formación de Capital*. The latter shows that while domestic loans financed a decreasing percentage of gross capital formation for the sample of corporations studied, the firms with the most rapid growth of real assets had both the highest rate of retained profits and received a higher rate of loans as a percentage of profits. In addition, see some general remarks in ECLA, *op. cit.*, Vol. III, pp. 86–103.

[44] Interest rates in the nonbank credit markets in Chile during the Klein-Saks period and in Argentina during the recent stabilization period ranged to well over 40 percent per annum. For Argentina, see Bank of London and South America, *Quarterly Review* January, 1962, pp. 25–26. The most important single use of the high interest credit in Argentina was to finance motorcar sales.

to a serious credit crisis in June, 1962, during which the central bank had to undertake the emergency rediscounting of industrial paper to enable firms to meet wages and other current commitments.[45]

TABLE 1

	Argentina 1952=100		*Chile* 1953=100	
	Manufacturing Production	*Manufacturing Employment*	*Manufacturing Production*	*Manufacturing Employment*
1957	..	..	103.7	95.7
1958	123.7	95.7	106.9	91.8
1959	107.4	91.6	122.1	93.4
1960	109.5	84.2	119.3	96.9
1961	120.1	81.6	127.5	102.6

Sources: Argentina: Dirección Nacional de Estadística y Censos, *Boletín Mensual de Estadística*, January, 1961; March, 1962. Chile: Banco Central de Chile, *Boletín Mensual*, April, 1962.

In sum, the effect of the IMF stabilization policies on the industrial sector was mainly to shift an excessive proportion of resources to A- and E-type industries. The cul-de-sac into which the industrial sector had worked itself prior to the stabilization efforts was made a bit roomier, but no breakthrough to exporting occurred because the stabilization policies, rather than directing resources to industries with export potential, continued the pattern of precocious widening of the industrial spectrum. Even the apparent gain in labor and productivity for the industrial sector as a whole was partly illusion. (see Table 1) For, while tighter credit probably did force an increase in efficiency, part of the apparent gain in productivity seems to have been merely due to a shift in output toward industries with higher capital/labor ratios made possible by greater capital imports.[46]

TABLE 2

Argentina 1952 = 100	*Vehicles and Nonelectrical Machinery*		*Electrical Products and Machinery*		*Rubber Products*		*Food and Drink*		*Textiles*		*Leather*	
	O	P	O	P	O	P	O	P	O	P	O	P
1958	99	102	128	109	123	103	133	121	102	122	90	101
1959	80	97	123	115	119	105	114	115	81	117	70	98
1960	103	111	136	116	144	114	110	123	85	116	66	107
1961	109	123	122	105	199	140	115	131	90	122	73	110

Chile 1953=100	*Metal Products Other Than Machinery*		*Electrical Products*		*Chemicals*		*Rubber Products*		*Food Products*		*Textiles*		*Leather*	
	O	P	O	P	O	P	O	P	O	P	O	P	O	P
1957	118	108	111	101	112	101	93	89	103	106	93	106	103	104
1958	124	112	104	118	122	109	99	106	99	102	93	112	103	110
1959	149	132	106	131	121	106	134	140	107	110	107	127	103	122
1960	155	130	112	134	126	109	147	139	111	93	95	121	90	91
1961	195	149	115	139	134	114	161	150	114	84	103	122	102	123

O=Output.
P=Labor productivity (Man-hour output in Argentina; per worker output in Chile).
Source: See footnote 41.

[45] Earlier in the same year, the Minister of Economy had appealed to the automotive industry to obtain foreign funds for retail financing in order to relieve pressure on the local credit market. (Bank of London and South America, *Fortnightly Review*, March 24, 1962, p. 233.)

[46] Two-digit industry classes are too gross to be very illuminating about output and productivity trends. Moreover, it is not clear how well the data gatherers make allowance for new products in these classes. (The small rise in output of the Argentine vehicle and nonelectric machinery class does not seem to conform with the information on automotive expansion.) For what they are worth, the sectoral data in Table 2 are offered.

The need for drastic measures to slow inflation and stimulate growth in Argentina and Chile has been obvious beyond question. One cannot but conclude, however, that the IMF-type programs were based on a misappraisal of where some of the leading difficulties lay, as well as on an erroneous normative perspective. The contention that under quite restrictive assumptions a free market economy will allocate resources with optimum efficiency simply does not support the corollary that the performance of a half-free economy will necessarily be improved merely by making it 60 percent free. Yet it is this sort of reasoning, buttressed by an uncritical faith in the benefits of private foreign investment, rather than detailed analysis of the structure of the Argentine and Chilean economies, which seems to have guided much of the stabilization programs.

POLICY IMPLICATIONS

If the analysis of this paper is broadly correct, Argentina and Chile have reached another major impasse in their frustrating climb to self-sustaining growth, similar to that of the 1930's. Then, the decline and stagnation of their primary export markets made clear that the economic growth of Argentina and Chile could no longer be supported primarily by a handful of primary exports for which substantial Ricardian rents provided by nature offset the technological backwardness of the economy. The impasse, temporarily overcome by import-substituting industrialization, has now reappeared in a new guise. Import-substituting industrialization has also proved inadequate to elevate the economy to growth-sustaining efficiency. Continued agricultural backwardness, inadequate investment in public overhead capital, and precocious widening of the industrial spectrum have combined with a fall in the external terms of trade to bring Argentina and Chile to their present impasse. How is this to be overcome?

Firstly, the preceding analysis underlines—if such emphasis is still needed—the necessity to accelerate agricultural development by agricultural reforms and related measures and to augment substantially public investment in education, transport, and power. The attempt to outflank technological backwardness by import-substituting industrialization without such ancillary measures has failed. Nevertheless, the attempt has given Argentina and Chile a substantial heritage of industrial skills and experience which should now be utilized to supplement their primary exports. Indeed, the viability of their economies required this, for the growth of their traditional exports is hardly likely alone to support their import needs, even under optimistic projections of world primary market trends. In brief, they must also turn to industrial exporting. But the existing demand structure as well as ingrained industrial habits stand in the way of a simple market solution to the problem of restructuring their industrial sector. What are required, therefore, are more direct and drastic measures, conceived in the spirit of Mrs. Robinson's dictum that the "task is not merely to study the coefficients but to change them." More specifically, the following lines of policy are suggested:

1. Taxation should be used to alter the structure of consumer demand. It is not sufficient to raise taxes in order to finance more public investment. The tax incidence must also fall much more heavily than is now the case on consumer durables and other sumptuary items of consumption, whether imported or domestically produced, with the object of curtailing new investment in such products. This requires some combination of heavy indirect taxes on A- and E-type consumables and augmented and progressive taxation of *personal* income.

2. A larger share of industrial investment must be directed to T-type industries with good export potential. This implies cost and market studies to identify such industries and input-output studies to estimate the direct and indirect demand for foreign exchange of alternative industrial investments. Given such information, exchange and capital issues controls, tax concessions, and public funds will probably have to be used to help proportion industrial investment so as to maximize net foreign exchange availability and to direct entrepreneurial perspectives outward rather than toward the domestic market. Since the required scope and rigor of such measures would vary inversely with the buoyancy of traditional exports, the authorities should link these measures to medium-term projections of traditional exports. Similarly, government outlays on power, transport, manpower training, and industrial research should be channelled to facilitate the industrial exporting effort.

3. Foreign manufacturing investment must also be screened with the same criterion in mind. The authorities must not be seduced by the appearance of direct exchange saving, or by the fact that such investments may not compete with existing industries, into overlooking possible indirect defects of such investments in augmenting the demand for foreign exchange and stimulating low priority complementary investment.

4. Foreign technical assistance should be sought to assist in modernizing promising T-industries.

5. Vigorous efforts should be made to get the United States and Europe to open their markets to T-exports from Latin America.

In short, the emphasis, particularly while the exchange crisis resulting from stagnating markets for primary exports lasts, must be on export promoting industrialization. The focus, however, should be on raising promising industries to long run exporting efficiency, not on indiscriminately subsidizing industrial exports.

Let me finally anticipate three lines of criticism.

The first is that world demand for T-industry products has generally risen less rapidly than for A- and E-industry products. While this is not necessarily the case for all items, it is broadly true for the general class of less sophisticated industrial products. Yet it is also true that world demand for such products has expanded more rapidly in recent years than for primary products. Moreover, in more advanced industrial economies the rapid rise of A- and E-industries has been pulling up real wages and labor costs in T-industries, so that imports have been progressively supplementing and even replacing domestic production of many T-type items. Coupled with this is the growing middle-class taste in these countries for exotics, which also favors the demand for technologically less-sophisticated industrial imports. To hasten the gradual process in the advanced countries of substituting imports for domestic output of T-products undoubtedly requires further liberalizing of the import restrictions against T-imports.[47] What is disturbing is that while the industrially more advanced Latin American countries are pressing hard for the removal of import restrictions against primary products, they have shown little interest in measures which would promote industrial exports to hard-currency markets.[48]

The second objection is that the Argentine and Chilean governments have been singularly inept in administering controls. This is, however, a *tu quoque* argument, for neither has the private sector been notably efficient. More importantly, the objection tends to confuse the essential issue. As indicated in the preceding discussion, a strong measure of discriminatory controls in Argentina and Chile is unavoidable. The quest, for example, for an equilibrium exchange rate proved to be chimerical. Exchange controls took on different guises in the stabilization periods, but have shared the major weakness of earlier efforts; namely, they attempted to check immediate symptoms without central guidance on allocation priorities from a general development program. It would be far the wiser course to recognize the inevitability of discriminatory controls and to concentrate more fruitfully on relating them to a coherent development strategy, of which the promotion of industrial exports should surely be a major component.

A third objection is that the stricture against excessive A- and E-type investment overlooks that the feedback on industrial skills and managerial experience is greater from such industries than from T-industries. There is some merit to this criticism, although one should not overlook the favorable feedback on cost and quality control and marketing skills which would derive from exporting T-products. The basic problem is to determine the point at which the educational gain from establishing A- and E-industries is being purchased at too great a cost in short-run resource misallocation. If we use the growth rate as a rough guide, it seems reasonably evident from the critical plight of the Argentine and Chilean economies in the past decade that they have gone beyond the point, and need now to find more economic ways of picking up industrial skills and experience.

Growth economics is not able, of course, to indicate any single right path to maximizing the long-run growth rate, although it can indicate some of the

[47] The Alliance for Progress could well devote some of its efforts to promoting such liberalization and to encouraging the industrial export potential of the relatively industrialized countries of Latin America. The benefit to their balance of payments and to their industrial confidence might lessen the danger of the Alliance becoming little more than a supplier of stabilization credits to demoralized economies. Such funds could be used to better mutual advantage even if partly spent in the United States to ease the transfer of resources out of industries adversely affected by the liberalization of entry to Latin American industrial exports.

[48] The Latin American Free Trade Association is not an exception to this statement, since at present it is largely an effort to extend import-substituting industrialization in A- and E-type goods to the entire region. This is not necessarily a criticism, although it is clear that the limited amount of intraregional trade, the timidity of the Montevideo Treaty, and the difficulties of compensating the less developed members of the LAFTA for the burden of diverting their imports of A- and E- goods to higher-priced Brazilian, Argentine, or Chilean production makes it likely that expansion of intraregional trade in industrial products will be slow. It does not provide, therefore, a sufficiently persuasive argument for foregoing the effort to develop hard-currency industrial exports. The LAFTA consultation machinery, on the other hand, could be used to co-ordinate plans for developing T-type exports, so as to avoid needlessly competitive efforts.

necessary conditions for mounting each path successfully. There is, for example, the path formalized by the turnpike theorem and illustrated, perhaps, by the Soviet Union. That path would indeed call for an intensification of A- and E- investment in capital goods, heavy outlays on education and technical training, compression of real wages and consumption whenever necessary to offset bottlenecks and misallocations in the capital goods sector, and other hard, painful measures. It is possible that by taking this dangerous, long, and tortuous detour the turnpike to rapid economic growth can be reached. I doubt that Latin Americans, who are notoriously wild drivers, are capable of managing the difficult detour. But even if they are tempted, they should at least realize that the Russian people did not make it over the detour to the turnpike in Zils and Moskvitches or outfitted with household durables. If one prefers a less distant payoff in such goods, then one had better choose an easier, if perhaps ultimately slower, road to travel. But even on this road it is possible to break down from the weight of excess baggage, or to tip over from a badly unbalanced load.

Reprinted with permission of the publisher, author, and the Yale University Economic Growth Center, from: *Inflation and Growth in Latin America,* edited by Werner Baer and Isaac Kerstenetzky, Homewood, Ill.: Richard D. Irwin, Inc.. 1964.

Import Substitution, Foreign Investment, and International Disequilibrium in Brazil[1]

By Nathaniel H. Leff

and

*Antonio Delfim Netto**

I

Underdeveloped countries attempting to promote economic development may find their growth prospects constrained by inadequate supply of foreign exchange for imports. This may occur for several reasons. First, exchange rate devaluations may lag behind the country's internal rate of inflation, so that some exports are priced out of the world market at the same time as prices of imports are cheapened relative to domestic goods. Economic development may also divert factors and products from the export sector to supply growing domestic demand.[2] Finally, demand for the country's export products may be relatively inelastic so that export receipts cannot grow as rapidly as the projected rate of growth of income and imports. In such circumstances, a balance of payments problem[3] develops, and the monetary authorities may resort to quantitative import controls and selective exchange rate devaluations in order to equate the demand and supply of foreign exchange.

As a more long-run solution to the balance of payments

* Dr Leff is Research Associate at Harvard University and Dr Netto is Professor Catedratico at Universidade de Sao Paulo. Each reached the conclusions of this paper independently, and the present work is the result of equal collaboration in its presentation.

problem, two other policies may be adopted. First, import-substitution may be promoted as a means of saving foreign exchange presently demanded for given commodity imports. In a second policy approach to the same problem, either independently or under pressure from advanced countries, the government may attempt to increase the inflow of foreign private capital. Such investment comes with a double recommendation from the viewpoint of the balance of payments. First, it constitutes a net addition to foreign exchange receipts. Secondly, by increasing the capital and other resources of the underdeveloped country, it permits a greater import-substitution effort than would otherwise be possible.

In post-war Brazil, both of these policies have been introduced with considerable vigor. Massive import substitution programs have been implemented so that most products previously imported are now produced domestically. Import-substitution has been carried out on so large a scale that the import-substitution industries have become the leading sector in the economy's growth.[4] At the same time, policy affecting foreign capital was changed, and by the end of the 1950's, new foreign capital inflow amounted to more than 100 million dollars annually, apart from re-investments. Nevertheless, a chronic balance of payments problem has persisted.

The present paper attempts to explain this apparent paradox by analysing the balance of payments effects of import-substitution and increasing foreign investment. Our discussion suggests that although these policies may be highly successful from the viewpoint of income creation and growth, they are unlikely to solve the balance of payments problem. For reasons we discuss, just *because* of these dynamic income creating effects, import substitution is not likely to end the balance of payments problem. As income has grown rapidly, so has the demand for imports, swallowing the additional foreign exchange resources made available by government policy. The implication is that public capital may have to be called upon to ease the international disequilibrium of many underdeveloped countries.

II

The following sequential model can be used to depict the national income and balance of payments effects, in real terms, of an import substitution program involving mobilization of domestic and foreign investment resources.

In this economy consumption in the period t is a function of income in the same period.

(1) $C_t = cY$

The investment function has two components. The first is a function of national income in the previous year, (bY_{t-1}). The second part reflects the effort at import substitution, as investments are realized each period to cover a percentage, w, of the balance of payments deficit of the previous period. This two-component investment function is a faithful representation of investment behavior in post-war Brazil. On the one hand, investment has been allocated to the existing, 'vegetative' industries, in accordance with the growth of domestic income and demand. On the other hand, both domestic and foreign investors, stimulated by the government, have directed their investments towards import substitution, as indicated by the deficit. If the percentage of the deficit which investors attempt to cover is w, and the output-capital ratio is a, then the volume of these investments is determined by $\left(\frac{w}{a}\right)B_{t-1}$. Furthermore, if a portion k of these investments are realized in the form of imported equipment, and the rest, (1-k) is spent within the economy, then we can describe this investment as $(1\text{-}k)\left(\frac{w}{a}\right)B_{t-1}$. The complete investment function is:

(2) $I_t = bY_{t-1} + (1\text{-}k)\left(\frac{w}{a}\right)B_{t-1},\ t \geqslant 2.$[5]

By assumption, exports remain at their initial level, i.e.,

(3) $X_t = X_1$.

Imports into the economy are a function of national income in the same period (mY_t), and of the volume of import substitution in the previous period, (wB_{t-1}) Hence we have:

(4) $M_t = mY_t - wB_{t-1}$, with $t \geqslant 2$.

We can express the participation of foreign capital as

220

follows: let h be the total amount of foreign investments. Of this, k enters the economy in the form of imported equipment, and (h-k) enters as a net addition of foreign monetary resources. By assumption, there is no K, foreign capital, invested in the initial period, but as the process continues, we have:

$$K_1 = 0$$
$$K_2 = h\left(\frac{w}{a}\right)B_1$$
$$K_3 = h\left(\frac{w}{a}\right)(B_1 + B_2)$$
$$\text{(5) } K_t = h\left(\frac{w}{a}\right)(B_1 + B_2 \ldots + B_{t-1}) \text{ with } t \geqslant 2.$$

Profit remittances are, in each period, a percentage g of the foreign capital invested in the previous period, or gK_{t-1}

$$\text{(6) } R_t = g_{t-1}K, \text{ with } t \geqslant 2.$$

At equilibrium income, resources of the economy will equal resource utilizations, giving the situation portrayed in Table 1.

TABLE 1

Resources	
Y_t,	National Income
$(mY_t - wB_{t-1})$,	Imports
These resources must balance with:	
cY_t,	Consumption
$bY_{t-1} + \left(\frac{w}{a}\right)B_{t-1}$,	Investment
X_1,	Exports

We can describe this national income process as:

$$\text{(7) } Y_t = \frac{b\,Y_{t-1} + \frac{w}{a}(1\text{-}k + a)\,B_{t-1} + X_1,\ t \geqslant 2}{1 - c + m}$$

The balance of payments deficit can be written as:

$$\text{(8) } B_t = X_1 - R_t - mY_t + wB_{t-1} + (h\text{-}k)\,\frac{w}{a}\,B_{t-1},\ t \geqslant 2$$

Substituting the following values in (5), (6), (7), and (8):[6] c=0.86; b=0.16; a=0.45; h=0.60; k=0.45; m=0.10;

w=0.33; g=0.10, we can fill in Table 2. This shows the balance of payments and national income effects, over time, of an intensive effort at import substitution, using both foreign and domestic resources.

TABLE 2

1	2	3	4	5	6	7	8
			Investments		*Imports*		
Period	*Income*	*Consumption*	*Income Induced*	*Balance of Payments Induced*	*Income Induced*	*Import Substitution*	*Exports*
1	1000.00	860.00	160.00	—	100.00	—	80.00
2	1061.76	913.11	160.00	8.15	106.18	— 6.67	80.00
3	1094.57	941.33	169.88	7.04	109.46	— 5.76	80.00
4	1133.05	974.42	175.13	9.24	113.31	— 7.56	80.00
5	1165.56	1002.38	181.29	10.14	116.56	— 8.30	80.00
6	1197.32	1029.70	186.49	11.47	119.73	— 9.39	80.00

	(9)	(10)	(11)	(12)	(13)
	Foreign Capital Monetary Investment	*Kt Total Foreign Capital Invested*	*Rt Profit Remittances*	*Balance of Payments*	$-\sum_{i=1}^{t=1} Bt$
1	—	—	—	— 20.00	—
2	2.22	8.88	—	— 17.29	20.00
3	1.92	16.57	— 0.89	— 22.67	37.29
4	2.52	26.65	— 1.66	— 24.89	59.96
5	2.77	37.71	— 2.67	— 28.16	84.85
6	3.13	50.22	— 3.77	— 30.98	113.01

Table 2 depicts an economy with an initial balance of payments deficit of 20.2 % of its GNP. To correct this deficit, an import-substitution program, complemented by foreign investment resources, is initiated. We assume that the technical difficulties of producing domestically goods that had previously been imported are overcome. Assuming compensatory foreign credits, and a fixed exchange rate,[7] however, the actual evolution of the international balance is as shown in column (12). As we see, a balance of payments problem persists. Indeed, the deficit is larger at the end of the sequence than it was at the beginning.

Table 2 pictures an economy that is making great strides forward, without attaining the goal that it set itself — improvement of the foreign balance. As column (2) indicates, national income is growing relatively rapidly, with an increase of some 20 % after five periods of activity.

Moreover, in its successful enterprise of producing locally goods which were formerly imported, the economy has saved great amounts of foreign exchange. Column (13) shows the large cumulative balance of payments deficit which has been partially overcome. Nevertheless, as column (12) indicates, a severe balance of payments problem remains. Despite these intensive efforts at import substitution, the international disequilibrium has persisted. We can summarize the conclusions of our model, as evidenced in the calculations of Table 2.

1. The model indicates clearly that in conditions such as in post-war Brazil, the process of import substitution cannot be expected to end the deficits in an underdeveloped country's balance of payments. On the contrary, to the extent that investments for this purpose are successful from the viewpoint of raising income, they may generate a larger deficit, at a higher income level.

2. The balance of payments deficit continues primarily because the income creation effect on increased imports heavily outweighs the import substitution effect shown in column (7). That is, imports stimulated by higher national income more than offset the foreign exchange saved by domestic production of goods formerly imported.

3. Profit remittances to foreign private investors who have invested for import substitution have only a negligible weight in the new balance of payments deficit in this model. The income creation effect is the overwhelming factor at work.

4. Import substitution, with or without foreign resources, has had very dynamic effects on national income creation. If the effort devoted to import substitution is large enough, it can function as the leading sector in an underdeveloped country's growth.

Having recapitulated these conclusions of our model, let us now proceed to their analysis.

III

The principal reason for the continuing balance of payments deficit is the income creation effect generated by increased investment for import substitution and creating additional demand for new imports. We can discuss this effect in terms of its two components: the relatively high magnitude of Y, and the value of m, the marginal propensity to import.

The income creating effect is so great because of the great expansionary effects of investment for import-substitution. Because of the high value of the import-substitution investment multiplier in Brazilian conditions and in our model, additional domestic or foreign investment for import substitution has unusually dynamic multiplier effects on national income. The high value of the multiplier, in turn, can be discussed in terms of the marginal propensity to spend, and the low value of the leakage created by the marginal propensity to import.

The relatively high marginal propensity to spend reflects the high real consumption and investment parameters characteristic of Brazil, an economy with high rates of growth and inflation. The marginal propensities to consume and to invest are so high indeed that they can be maintained only by running a balance of payments deficit. As in the case of most of the other underdeveloped countries, whose consumption functions were studied by Yang,[8] the propensity to consume is high, and the marginal is higher than the average. As the same time, in the investment boom and inflationary conditions that have characterized post-war Brazil, available savings have been absorbed into investment.

We should also note that the explosive impact of the multiplier is not lessened by any leakages into taxation. On the contrary, in Brazil, the government has usually run a budget deficit, so that the government sector has constituted an additional source of expenditure rather than a leakage.[9]

Furthermore, for political reasons, the government has not shown any tendency to implement monetary or fiscal policies that would reduce other investment to compensate for the additional import-substitution investment, and lower the multiplier effect. Even if this were administratively possible, it has conflicted with a political goal of increasing investment and growth to the maximum. Throughout the period 1945-1963, all anti-inflationary efforts, whether put forward by domestic proponents of greater monetary and fiscal orthodoxy, or by the International Monetary

Fund, have come to naught. Consequently, the high aggregate expenditure and multiplier effect that we noted have persisted.

The multiplier's value is also increased by the relatively low value of the marginal propensity to import. A high import coefficient would permit some of the potentially explosive impact of an increase in spending to drain out of the economy, through an increase in imports. Using the comparative data collected by Professor Kuznets,[10] however, we can see that the Brazilian import coefficient is not high, relative to that of other, more developed countries.

TABLE 3

IMPORT COEFFICIENTS OF SELECTED COUNTRIES (M/Y)

	M/Y
United Kingdom, 1945-52	0.18
France, 1946-51	0.15
The Netherlands, 1950-54	0.35
Denmark, 1950-54	0.25
Norway, 1950-54	0.22
Sweden, 1950-54	0.17
Italy, 1949-54	0.13
Canada, 1950-54	0.15
Japan, 1950-54	0.12
Australia, 1947/48-1959/60	0.16
BRAZIL, 1953-61	0.08

This circumstance is due to the Brazilian economy's difficulty in earning foreign exchange, which forcibly limits the volume of imports. In our context, this 'external strangulation' means that imports do relatively little to restrict the expansive effect of an increase in spending, and that the multiplier is so powerful that even with the relatively low *aggregate* investment coefficient of our system, an increase in investment for import substitution is enough to produce the dynamic income growth of our model.

These sharp increases in national income have generated balance of payments deficits as they have interacted with a marginal propensity to import which, after a point, has not declined in the course of the import-substitution process. We emphasize this point because it is sometimes missed in static discussions of import substitution. As the data in Table 4 show, however, even an import substitution process as intensive as Brazil's in the middle and late 1950's has not brought about a decline in the import coefficient.

Because of this circumstance, our model uses a stable value for the marginal propensity to import, even in the midst of a large-scale import-substitution effort.

TABLE 4[11]

IMPORT COEFFICIENT $\left(\frac{M}{Y}\right)$, BRAZIL, 1954-63

	%
1954	9.0
1955	8.2
1956	7.2
1957	7.8
1958	7.5
1959	8.6
1960	8.6
1961	8.6
1962	9.6
1963	8.3

The relative stability of the import coefficient is all the more surprising if we bear in mind that throughout this period, the government made a strong effort, with an impressive array of policy tools — differential exchange rates, import licensing, and prohibitive tariffs for many products — to restrict imports as much as possible. As we note in Table 3, however, compared to many other countries, the Brazilian import coefficient is already relatively low, so that the possibilities for further constriction were not great. Furthermore, increasing difficulties were encountered in the course of the government's effort to prevent the propensity to import from expressing itself. As more and more products were taken off the import list, the remaining imports were goods of low elasticity of substitution in consumption, for which the elasticity of substitution as between imports and potential domestic supply was also very low. A good example is the case of crude petroleum products. To cut back imports drastically, it was feared, would have bottleneck effects on output and growth. For lack of sufficient domestic crude petroleum reserves, moreover, not much could be done to increase domestic production. Similar problems were encountered for other products remaining on the import list. Consequently, the import coefficient in the Brazilian economy, and hence in our model, has remained relatively stable despite serious efforts at constricting it.

The stability of the import coefficient despite successful, massive import substitution may seem paradoxical. The process becomes clearer, however, if we remember that behind the relatively stable m's are increasingly rising Y's. What happened is that income has moved to increasingly higher levels, with corresponding changes in the structure of final demand. As income rises, new consumption and investment goods have been required. Part of these are supplied locally, and part are imported, in a constantly evolving *qualitative* change in the structure of imports. Hence, as income increases — in the case of Brazil, partly *because* of import substitution — the propensity to import remains fairly stable, masking a great change in the list of goods imported.

Furthermore, for an economy like Brazil's, there is another reason for the relative constancy of the import coefficient, determined by upward and downward boundaries. On the upward side, imports are limited by the inelastic supply of foreign exchange generated by its traditional exports. On the downward side, m is limited by the bottleneck effect that too restricted a supply of imports would have on the growth of the rest of the economy. If m reaches given low levels, it restricts the magnitude of Y, so that m does not decline.

Furthermore, because of the conditions affecting the demand for imports into Brazil, the marginal propensity to import is likely to be higher than the average. Consequently, the demand for additional imports generated by the increased income created by import substitution investment is much greater than suggested by the average import coefficients of Table 4.

In Brazilian conditions, the marginal propensity to import, m, means something very different than it does in economies with more ample foreign exchange supply. In other economies, imports are determined by the level of income, relative prices of domestic and imported products, and the exchange rate, subject to the constraint that imports be less than or equal the supply of foreign exchange. In such conditions, the marginal propensity to import can be considered a function of national income. In Brazil, however, the constraint imposed by the availability of foreign exchange intervenes long before the desired level of imports is reached. Given the pattern of consumer tastes and comparative costs, especially with an overvalued exchange rate,[12] within a considerable range, imports would be much higher were it not for the foreign exchange availability constraint. Consequently, the import coefficient, M/Y, is simply the ratio of foreign exchange receipts to national income.[13] That is, the 'average propensity to import' is actually nothing more than FE/Y. For the same reasons, in the relevant range, the effects of income levels and relative prices are unimportant, and the 'marginal propensity to import' becomes simply $\Delta FE/\Delta Y$, as greater availability of foreign exchange would result in an equal increase in imports. In such conditions, the 'marginal propensity to import' is significantly higher than 'the average.' In consequence, any foreign exchange saved by import substitution or made available by foreign capital inflow is swallowed up by the previous excess demand for imports.

These considerations explain why our model maintains a constant value for m, in the midst of a wholesale effort at import substitution. Acting together with the high value of the multiplier, explained above, it produces the explosive income creation effect, generating increased demand for imports, and maintaining the Brazilian economy in chronic balance of payments deficit.

Having analyzed why this is the case in Brazil, let us now consider the extent to which the model can be generalized to other economies.

IV

As we have seen, the essence of our model is the extremely powerful multiplier, which produces a sharp increase in national income following the investment for import substitution. Interacting with the marginal propensity to import which remains stable during the process, the higher income level produces an increased demand for imports that offsets the balance of payments gains of the import substitution effort.

The vital components for this process exist in most underdeveloped countries, especially in the relatively more advanced ones. A high marginal propensity to spend is common to most such countries. Furthermore, many of these countries face inelastic demand for their exports – the circumstance that may have set them on the path of import substitution in the first place. Consequently, they also have the relatively low marginal propensity to import, with its concomitant effects for a very high multiplier. Finally, we can expect that the marginal propensity to import will not decline in most underdeveloped economies, once they have passed a given phase.[14]

We suggest, therefore, that the conditions of many underdeveloped countries approximate those of our model, and its conclusions have a validity going beyond the Brazilian experience: import substitution cannot be relied upon to end the international disequilibrium of most underdeveloped countries.

In the case of foreign investment, however, another factor may intervene to help the balance of payments situation. If a foreign investment boom is touched off, with one foreign investment following another, the influx of *new* investments may be large enough to offset the negative balance of payments effects of the earlier investments.

Earlier investments, with their dynamic income creating effects, enlarge the market, and generate external economies of supply. Consequently, on both the demand and on the supply side, one wave of foreign investment makes the economy more attractive to subsequent foreign investors.

When considering the balance of payments effects of such a cumulative foreign private investment boom, however, we should distinguish two cases.

In the first, the values of the system are such that subsequent investments do not cover the deficit aggravated by the earlier ones. Here the balance of payments situation resembles a snowball rolling downhill at an accelerated rate. Each new investment merely makes the deficit worse at the same time as its splendid income creation effects attract new investments to aggravate the balance of payments situation.

In the second case, subsequent investments *are* large enough to cover the deficit generated by the earlier investments. We can call this case the man-on-the-bicycle: although pleasant at the moment, it is inherently unstable and dangerous. Any economic or political event that might impede the flow of the new, larger investments needed to cover the aggravated deficit turns the situation into a catastrophe. In either case — snowball or man-on-the-bicycle — the *balance of payments* effects of such a cumulative private foreign investment boom may be negative for the underdeveloped country.

It is also worth pointing out that there is very little that the government of the underdeveloped country can do in the face of such a situation. The standard measure of limiting foreign investment to 'productive investments,' or to enterprises that will earn or save foreign exchange will not help. They are already built into our model. Restriction of profit remittances 'to a reasonable level' — i.e. more reasonable than what we have already assumed — will only make things worse. Any policies attempting to control foreign investment are likely to have sharply counter-productive effects. By affecting the investment climate, they will reduce the inflow of subsequent net investment. This is aside from the probable result of stimulating efforts to repatriate capital *already* invested.

The model also helps to explain why a government previously considered favorable toward private capital inflow may suddenly turn hostile to foreign investors. Such a country may have made what it considers substantial concessions to foreign investors in order to secure their help in import substitution and the improvement of its balance of payments. Instead of an improvement, however, it finds that its international accounts remain in persistent — if not aggravated — deficit.

These factors also aid in understanding why some governments have implemented policies to benefit from private foreign investment while others have adopted measures depriving themselves of its income creating effects. For example, Australia and Mexico have had commodity or invisible exports large enough to service the balance of payments effects of large foreign investments. Consequently, the government could take an enlightened approach.[15] In a country like Brazil, where export receipts have not increased sufficiently to cover the new deficit, the economic and political pressures on the government have been of an entirely different order.

V

This leads us to the policy implications of our model. As we have seen, neither foreign private investment nor intensive domestic efforts at import substitution can be expected to end the international disequilibrium of underdeveloped economies like Brazil. On the contrary, to the extent that they are successful from the viewpoint of raising income, they may well generate a larger deficit, at the higher income level.

We should also consider the possibility that the present demand for imports pressing upon available foreign exchange resources in chronic balance of payments crises is a transitory phenomenon. Present imports, this argument might run, are unusually and temporarily large as underdeveloped countries install domestic productive capacity that will lessen their future demand for imports.

We should emphasize, however, that the present import coefficients for Brazil and the other Latin American countries that we considered are by no means unusually high. On the contrary, comparing the Brazilian and Latin American coefficients of Tables 4 and 5 with those of the advanced countries in Table 3, we see that the coefficients for the advanced countries are generally considerably higher.[16] Moreover, a good part of present imports are raw materials for *current* consumption and production needs. If income is to *grow*, even higher levels of imports of raw materials and capital goods will be required. Hence, there can be no question either of present 'abnormally' high levels of imports, or of imports which can be expected to diminish with economic growth. Present import levels are 'transitionally' high only if income is not to reach higher levels. This is only begging the question of the prospects for sustained income growth under present balance of payment constraints.

Furthermore, as discussed above, the marginal propensity to import is likely to be much higher than the average coefficients in Table 4. Hence if anything, the present level of imports is *low*, in that if foreign exchange were available, imports would rise far above their present levels. Finally, the experience of the advanced countries gives no reason to expect that import coefficients will decline in the course of the structural changes involved in the development process.[17]

The implication is that public capital flows must be called upon if the chronic balance of payments deficits of under-developed countries are not to hamper their efforts at economic growth.

[1] We are grateful to Gustav Papanek, Gordon Smith, and Professor Arthur Smithies for helpful comments on an earlier draft of this paper. We bear the sole responsibility for remaining deficiencies.

[2] Cf. e.g. B. Cohen, 'The Stagnation of Indian Exports', *Quarterly Journal of Economics*, 1964.

[3] In Professor Machlup's sense of a 'programmatic' gap between desired and actual imports. Cf. F. Machlup, 'Three Concepts of the Balance of Payments', *Economic Journal*, 1950.

[4] For a detailed sectoral tableau of the extent of import substitution in post-war Brazil, see 'Auge y Declinacion del Processo de Sustitucion de Importaciones en el Brasil', *Boletim Economico de America Latina*, Marzo de 1964 (United Nations, New York), especially Table 25, p. 39.

[5] It should be noted that consumption is a function of income in the cu rent period while investment is lagged one period. On the former point, cf. C. Y. Yang, 'International Comparisons of Consumption Functions', *Review of Economics and Statistics*, August, 1964, especially Table 1, p. 280, for a demonstration of the short-term adjustability of consumption to current income in a number of under-developed countries. Investment, on the other hand. is lagged one period, as investors need this time to form and carry out their investment projects.

[6] These values are suggested from Brazilian experience in the period 1958-1960, and are derived from the following sources:

a is derived from Tables X and XI, p. 11, XII *Exposicao Sobre O Programa de Reaparelhamento Economico* (Annual Report of the National Development Bank) Rio de Janeiro, 1964.

c and *b* were calculated by Tarcisio Arantes of the National Development Bank (BNDE) from material supplied by the Fundaco Getulio Vargas.

m is derived from Chapter one, *Programa de Acado do Economica do Governo Revolucionario* (Preliminary Version, Rio de Janeiro, 1964).

g is determined institutionally, by the law governing profit remittances.

h and *k* were derived from direct interviews with foreign firms in Brazil.

[7] Because of price inelasticity of demand for the country's major export, coffee, of which it is the major supplier and price leader in the world market, the monetary authorities believe that foreign exchange receipts are maximized with an overvalued exchange rate.

[8] C. Y. Yang, 'An International Comparison of Consumption Functions,' *Review of Economics and Statistics*, August, 1964, Table 3, pp. 282 and 283. One can also argue on *a priori* grounds in favour of an average propensity to save larger than the marginal. First, because of the increasing disutility of saving, and secondly in an economy where the decision to save is closely linked to the decision to invest, in terms of a declining marginal return to capital.

[9] The direction of this government expenditure is beyond the scope of the present study, and is being treated separately by one of the present authors. We should point out, however, that the average propensity of the govern-

ment to spend on fixed capital formation has been relatively high, even excluding the construction of Brasilia. In the period 1947-1960, it averaged 19.9 %, rising sharply towards the end of the period. Perhaps more significant, the marginal propensity was even higher, averaging 25.5 %. (Data on government fixed capital formation are from Statistical Appendix II of Werner Baer's *Industrialization and Economic Development in Brazil.* Data on annual government expenditure are from *Revista Brasileira de Economia,* Marzo de 1962).

10 Data for all countries except Brazil and Australia are from Simon Kuznets, *Aspectos Cuantitativos del Desarrollo Economico,* Mexico, 1959, pp. 116-118. The coefficient for Australia was calculated from Tables 271 and 274 of N. G. Butlin, *Australian Domestic Product, Investment and Foreign Borrowing, 1861-1938/39,* Cambridge University Press, 1962. Data for Brazil are from Table 4, p. 16, 'Auge y Declinacion...' *op. cit.*

11 Table III-2, *Plano de Acao Economica ao Governo Revolucionario* (Preliminary Version), Rio de Janeiro, 1964.

12 Overvalued for reasons we mentioned in footnote 7, above.

13 Actually, of exports plus capital inflow. Since private capital inflow depends on debt servicing capacity, however, it too depends ultimately on export receipts.

14 The following data show the evolution of the import coefficient in several Latin American countries which have implemented large-scale import-substitution programs in the post-war period. As we see, despite continuing efforts in this direction, the import coefficients have not declined very much.

TABLE 5

IMPORT COEFFICIENTS (M/Y) (PERCENT)

Periods	*Argentine*	*Chile*	*Columbia*	*Mexico*
1945-1949	11.6	19.6	12.6	14.4
1950-1954	9.1	14.3	13.6	12.5
1955-1961	9.2	16.4	10.9	11.6
1960	9.9	18.5	10.6	11.8
1961	10.9	22.8	10.7	11.0

Source: *The Economic Development of Latin America in the Post War Period,* United Nations, New York, 1964. Tables 87, 113, 95.

Professor Kuznets (*Economic Growth,* 1959, pp. 101-103) has also demonstrated the remarkable stability of the import coefficient of several advanced countries (France, United Kingdom, Sweden, Denmark, Netherlands, Italy, and Japan) in the course of their long run development. In time series going back far into the 19th century, the import coefficient declined only in the depression years with low income levels, and increased institutional barriers to trade.

Richard Cooper has provided a thoughtful analysis for this relative constancy of import coefficients in the midst of great structural changes and vastly higher income levels in 'Growth and Trade'. *Journal of Economic History,* December, 1964.

15 This may, however, lead to possible other problems. Cf. Edith Penrose, 'Foreign Investment and the Growth of the Firm', *Economic Journal,* June, 1956.

16 Kuznets, *op. cit.*, gives further figures for other advanced countries which with the exception of the United States, are all considerably above those for Brazil and the other Latin American countries cited.

17 Cf. the references to Kuznets and to Cooper cited in footnote 14 above.

THE
QUARTERLY JOURNAL
OF ECONOMICS

Vol. LXXXII February 1968 No. 1

THE POLITICAL ECONOMY OF IMPORT-SUBSTITUTING INDUSTRIALIZATION IN LATIN AMERICA *

Albert O. Hirschman

Introduction: Disenchantment with Industrialization in Latin America

Not long ago, industrialization ranked high among the policy prescriptions which were expected to lead Latin America and other underdeveloped areas out of their state of economic, social and political backwardness. In the last few years, however, considerable disenchantment with this particular solution of the development problem has set in. The present paper will survey some characteristics of "import-substituting industrialization" (ISI) in an attempt to appraise its evolution and the principal difficulties it has encountered. Some purely economic aspects of the problem will be discussed, but particular attention has been directed to interrelations with social and political life. The ease with which such inter-

* A preliminary version of this paper formed the subject of public lectures given in the summer of 1967 at Rio de Janeiro under the auspices of the Sociedade Brasileira de Instrucção and at Bogotá under those of Colombia's National Planning Department and Harvard's Development Advisory Service. I am grateful to Christopher Clague, Gottfried Haberler, Nathan Rosenberg, Henry Rosovsky, Daniel Schydlovsky, Judith Tendler, and Raymond Vernon for detailed comments.

relations could be suggested — mostly in the form of tentative and untested hypotheses — indicates serious neglect by social scientists of a fertile terrain.

To set the stage for our inquiry it is useful to illustrate, through quotes from Latin America's most prominent economists, the change in attitude toward industrialization as a cure of the area's ills. In his well-known "manifesto" of 1949 Raúl Prebisch said:

> Formerly, before the great depression, development in the Latin-American countries was stimulated from abroad by the constant increase of exports. There is no reason to suppose, at least at present, that this will again occur to the same extent, except under very exceptional circumstances. These countries no longer have an alternative between vigorous growth along those lines and internal expansion through industrialization. Industrialization has become the most important means of expansion.[1]

Thirteen years later, Prebisch wrote another basic paper on Latin America, in a sense his farewell message to his Latin American friends upon assuming his new post as Secretary-General of the United Nations Conference on Trade and Development. Here industrialization is presented in a rather different light:

> An industrial structure virtually isolated from the outside world thus grew up in our countries . . . The criterion by which the choice was determined was based not on considerations of economic expediency, but on immediate feasibility, whatever the cost of production . . . tariffs have been carried to such a pitch that they are undoubtedly — on an average — the highest in the world. It is not uncommon to find tariff duties of over 500 per cent.
>
> As is well known, the proliferation of industries of every kind in a closed market has deprived the Latin American countries of the advantages of specialization and economies of scale, and owing to the protection afforded by excessive tariff duties and restrictions, a healthy form of internal competition has failed to develop, to the detriment of efficient production.[2]

If we take a look at the writings of Celso Furtado, the shift in the climate of opinion stands out even more starkly. In 1960, after a decade or more of rapid industrial advance, Furtado celebrated the resulting "transfer of decision centers" from abroad to Brazil in almost lyrical terms:

> By now the Brazilian economy could count on its own dynamic element: industrial investments supported by the internal market. Growth quickly became two-dimensional. Each new impulse forward would mean an increasing structural diversification, higher productivity levels, a larger mass of resources

1. *The Economic Development of Latin America and Its Principal Problems* (New York: United Nations, 1950), p. 6.
2. *Towards a Dynamic Development Policy for Latin America* (New York: United Nations, 1963) p. 71.

for investment, a quicker expansion of the internal market, and the possibility of such impulses being permanently surpassed.[3]

Only six years later, after Brazil had suffered a series of political and economic setbacks, a disillusioned Furtado wrote:

> In Latin America . . . there is a general consciousness of living through a period of decline. . . . The phase of 'easy' development, through increasing exports of primary products *or through import substitution* has everywhere been exhausted.[4]

Considering these two pairs of quotes one could easily conclude that we have here an instance of the acceleration of history. The phase of export-propelled growth (*crecimiento hacia afuera*) in Latin America lasted roughly from the middle of the nineteenth century until the Great Depression; and it took another twenty years, from 1929 to the Prebisch manifesto of 1949, before the end-of-export-propelled-growth became official Latin American doctrine. Then came the next phase of Latin American growth, *crecimiento hacia adentro* or growth via the domestic market. It gathered strength during the Depression and World War II, flourished briefly in both theory and practice during the fifties and was pronounced either dead or a dud in the sixties. It looks, therefore, as though the acceleration of technical progress in the developed countries were matched in the underdeveloped ones by an increasingly rapid accumulation of failures in growth experiences!

As will be seen, there may be considerable exaggeration in the announced failure of import-substituting industrialization just as, in spite of the supposed demise of export-propelled growth, Venezuela, Ecuador, Peru, and Central America achieved notable economic gains in the two postwar decades through rapidly growing exports of petroleum, bananas, fishmeal, and cotton, respectively. While *fracasomania*, or the insistence on having experienced yet another failure, certainly has its share in the severity of the recent judgments on industrialization, the widespread criticism of ISI — in Pakistan and India very similar problems are being discussed — indicates that there is real substance to the concern that is being expressed. But the rapidity of the reversal in the climate of opinion

3. Celso Furtado, "The Brazilian Economy in the Middle of the Twentieth Century," Industrial Conference on Science in the Advancement of New States, Israel, 1960 (mimeo), p. 5.

4. "U.S. Hegemony and the Future of Latin America," *The World Today*, Vol. 22 (Sept. 1966), p. 375. My italics. — Detailed critiques of the ISI process in Latin America can be found in two influential articles: "The Growth and Decline of Import Substitution in Brazil," and Santiago Macario, "Protectionism and Industrialization in Latin America," both in *Economic Bulletin for Latin America, IX* (Mar. 1964), 1–61 and 62–102.

makes one rather suspect that ISI had, *from its very onset*, both positive and negative aspects, with the latter simply coming into view a few years after the former. Our inquiry will therefore start out with a brief survey of the principal characteristics which set off ISI from other types of industrialization.

I. Four Impulses of Import-Substituting Industrialization (ISI)

Wars and depressions have historically no doubt been most important in bringing industries to countries of the "periphery" which up to then had firmly remained in the nonindustrial category. The crucial role of the two World Wars and of the Great Depression in undermining acceptance of traditional ideas about the international division of labor between advanced and backward countries is well known.[5] But industrialization has not only been the response to sudden deprivation of imports; it has taken place in many erstwhile nonindustrial countries as a result of the gradual expansion of an economy that grows along the export-propelled path. As incomes and markets expand in such a country and some thresholds at which domestic production becomes profitable are crossed, industries come into being without the need of external shocks or governmental intervention — a process I have described as "import-swallowing"[6] and which has been perhaps more aptly termed industrialization through "final demand linkage," as distinct from the continuation of the process via backward and forward linkage effects.[7] Gradual import substitution in response to the growth of domestic markets accounts for the widespread establishment of industries which have substantial locational advantages because of the weightiness of the product (cement, beer) and of

5. Apparently even earlier crises had positive effects on industrial growth in Latin America. The following quote is instructive: "There is no ill wind that does not blow some good . . . the crisis the country is going through is tremendous — and yet this is a perfect wind for national industry. Many of our industries have had a more or less vigorous protection through customs duties. But all of this would not have been enough had it not been for the crisis of 1875 which gave the impulse to industry and for that of 1890 which strengthened and diffused it." Quoted from *El Nacional* in Adolfo Dorfman, *Desarrollo industrial en la Argentina* (Rosario, 1941), p. 11. My translation.

6. *The Strategy of Economic Development* (New Haven: Yale University Press, 1958), Chap. 7.

7. See Melville H. Watkins, "A Staple Theory of Economic Growth," *Canadian Journal of Economics and Political Science*, Vol. 29 (May 1963), pp. 141–58, and Richard E. Caves, "Vent-for-Surplus Models of Trade and Growth" in *Trade, Growth and the Balance of Payments*, Essays in honor of Gottfried Haberler (Chicago: Rand-McNally, 1965), pp. 95–115.

those whose market is large even at low per capita incomes such as textiles.

Over the past two decades import-substituting industrialization has, of course, no longer been exclusively a matter of natural market forces reacting to either gradual growth of income or to cataclysmic events, such as wars and depressions. It has been undertaken in many countries as a matter of deliberate development policy, carried out no longer just by means of protective duties, but through a wide array of credit and fiscal policy devices, through pressures on foreign importing firms to set up manufacturing operations as well as through direct action: the establishment of state-owned industries or, increasingly, of development corporations or banks which are then entrusted with the promotion of specific ventures.

It is useful to keep in mind these distinct origins of ISI — wars, balance-of-payments difficulties, growth of the domestic market (as a result of export growth) and official development policy — in focusing on the distinctive characteristics of the process.

Clearly, there is not just *one* ISI process. An industrialization that takes place in the midst and as a result of export growth has a wholly different *Gestalt* from one that feeds on foreign exchange deprivation. For example, in the latter situation it seems much more likely that inflationary developments will accompany the industrialization process than in the former. Or, to proceed to one of the alleged — and often criticized — characteristics of the industrialization process itself, namely its tendency to concentrate on nonessential, luxury-type goods. This tendency to give importance to what is unimportant will be present only when the primary impulse to industrialization arises out of unexpected balance-of-payments difficulties which are fought routinely by the imposition of quantitative import controls. The controls will aim at permitting continued supply of the more essential goods traditionally imported at the cost of shutting out nonessentials and will thus cause domestic production of the latter to become especially profitable.

It is easy, however, to make too much of this situation. Of the four motive forces behind ISI — balance-of-payments difficulties, wars, gradual growth of income, and deliberate development policy — only the first leads to a bias in favor of nonessential industries. The last, deliberate development policy, is likely to produce exactly the opposite bias; and the remaining two causes are neutral with respect to the luxury character of the industry. Wars cause interruption of, or hazards for, *all* international commodity flows, essential or nonessential, and therefore provide a general unbiased stimulus to domestic production of previously imported goods. The same is true for the stimulus emanating from the gradual growth of markets. It seems likely, therefore, that the role of nonessential goods within the total ISI process has been exaggerated by the "new" critics who, in stressing this role, sound almost like the old-line Latin American laissez-faire advocates who were forever inveighing against the introduction of "exotic" industries into their countries.

II. Characteristics of the Initial Phase of ISI

Industrialization by tightly separated stages

No matter what its original impulse, ISI starts predominantly with the manufacture of finished consumer goods that were previously imported and then moves on, more or less rapidly and successfully, to the "higher stages" of manufacture, that is, to intermediate goods and machinery, through backward linkage effects. The process can and does start here and there with capital or even intermediate goods insofar as such goods are imported prior to any industrialization because they are needed in connection with agricultural or transportation activities. Machetes, coffee hulling machines, trucks and fertilizers are examples. In the textile industry, the crushing superiority of machine spinning over hand spinning, combined with a lesser advantage of machinery in weaving, has made sometimes for the installation of spinning mills ahead of weaving mills, especially in countries where a strong handweaving tradition had not been previously destroyed by textile imports from the industrial leaders.

But the bulk of new industries are in the consumer goods sector and as they are undertaken in accordance with known processes, on the basis of imported inputs and machines, industrialization via import substitution becomes a *highly sequential*, or *tightly staged*, affair. Herein lies perhaps its principal difference from industrialization in the advanced countries. This aspect is so familiar and seemingly inevitable that it has not received quite the attention it deserves. It is the basic reason for which the ISI process is far smoother, less disruptive, but also far less learning-intensive than had been the case for industrialization in Europe, North America, and Japan.

This is not the place for renewing the discussion over the advantages or drawbacks of an early or late start in industrialization.

Suffice it to point out, however, that those who have stressed the advantages of a late start have often had in mind the ability of newcomers to jump with both feet into a newly emerging dynamic industrial sector (as Germany did with chemicals) instead of remaining bogged down in sectors that had long passed their prime (as England in textiles and railways construction). But the "late latecomers" with whom we are concerned here are not apt to jump in this fashion. Industrialization is here at first wholly a matter of imitation and importation of tried and tested processes. Consider by way of contrast the following description of the establishment of new industries in advanced countries:

> Young industries are often strangers to the established economic system. They require new kinds or qualities of materials and hence make their own; they must overcome technical problems in the use of their products and cannot wait for potential users to overcome them; they must persuade customers to abandon other commodities and find specialized merchants to undertake the task. These young industries must design their specialized equipment and often manufacture it. . . .[8]

Not much of this travail occurs when a new industry is introduced into the "late late" starting countries. It is in this connection that one must be on guard against studies purporting to show that the history of industrialization is substantially the same in all countries, working its way from light consumer goods industries, to heavy and capital goods industries, and eventually to consumer durables. The apparently similar pattern of the earlier and "late late" industrializers in this respect conceal an essential qualitative difference. Even when the earlier industrializers were predominantly in the light consumer goods stage (from the point of view of labor force or value added), they were already producing *their own* capital goods, if only by artisan methods. As Marx wrote: "There were mules and steam-engines before there were any labourers whose exclusive occupation it was to make mules and steam-engines; just as men wore clothes before there were tailors." [9] But the "late late" industrializers will *import*, rather than make, their clothes until such time as they are able to set up a tailor in business all by himself. This situation forecloses, of course, for a considerable time any fundamental adaptation of technology to the characteristics of the importing countries, such as the relative abundance of labor

8. George Stigler, "The Division of Labor is Limited by the Extent of the Market," *Journal of Political Economy*, LIX (June 1951), 190.

9. *Kapital*, I, (Wien-Berlin, 1932), 399. This passage and the previous one by Stigler were brought to my attention by Nathan Rosenberg's article "Capital Goods, Technology, and Economic Growth," *Oxford Economic Papers*, Vol. 15 (Nov. 1963), pp. 223–24.

in relation to capital. Whether and to what extent such an adaptation is desirable is an idle question under these circumstances; given the sequential pattern of industrialization, there is remarkably little choice. ISI thus brings in complex technology, but without the sustained technological experimentation and concomitant training in innovation which are characteristic of the pioneer industrial countries.

"Late" vs. "late late" industrialization

The "late late" industrialization sketched so far may be contrasted not only with that of the presently advanced industrial countries in general, but particularly with that of the so-called latecomers among them. The "late" industrialization of countries like Germany, Italy and Russia has been depicted by Gerschenkron through the following propositions:

1. The more backward a country's economy, the more likely was its industrialization to start discontinuously as a sudden great spurt proceeding at a relatively high rate of growth of manufacturing output.
2. The more backward a country's economy, the more pronounced was the stress in its industrialization on bigness of both plant and enterprise.
3. The more backward a country's economy, the greater was the stress upon producers' goods as against consumers' goods.
4. The more backward a country's economy, the heavier was the pressure upon the levels of consumption of the population.
5. The more backward a country's economy, the greater was the part played by special institutional factors designed to increase the supply of capital to the nascent industries and, in addition, to provide them with less decentralized and better informed entrepreneurial guidance; the more backward the country, the more pronounced was the coerciveness and comprehensiveness of those factors.
6. The more backward a country, the less likely was its agriculture to play any active role by offering to the growing industries the advantages of an expanding industrial market based in turn on the rising productivity of agricultural labor.[1]

Of these six characteristics only the last one applies unconditionally to the late late industrializers. Special institutions designed to supply capital and entrepreneurial guidance (point 5), became important in most of Latin America after the ISI process had already been underway as a result of private, decentralized initiative for a considerable time. As to the remaining four points, almost the opposite could be said to hold for our late latecomers. Their industrialization started with relatively small plants adminis-

1. Alexander Gerschenkron, *Economic Backwardness in Historical Perspective* (Cambridge, Mass.: Harvard University Press, 1962), pp. 343–44.

tering "last touches" to a host of imported inputs, concentrated on consumer rather than producer goods, and often was specifically designed to improve the levels of consumption of populations who were suddenly cut off, as a result of war or balance-of-payments crises, from imported consumer goods to which they had become accustomed. Even though the rates at which new plants were built and at which their output expanded were often respectable, the process thus lacked some of the essential characteristics of Gerschenkron's "great spurt."

As a result, late late industrialization shows little of the inspiring, if convulsive *élan* that was characteristic of the late industrializers such as Germany, Russia and Japan. This is perhaps the basic reason for the feelings of disappointment experienced by Latin American observers who had looked to industrialization for a thorough transformation and modernization of their societies.

Naturally, the difference between the two types of industrialization must not be overdrawn. At least one experience in Latin America, that of Brazil during the fifties, came fairly close to the picture drawn by Gerschenkron: sustained and rapid progress of steel, chemical and capital goods industries during this decade was here combined with a "special institutional factor designed to increase supply of capital," namely inflation, and even with the flowering of a "developmentalist" (*desenvolvimentista*) ideology.[2] But what looked like the hopeful beginning of a "Brazilian economic miracle" was thrown into disarray by the political crises and related economic and social setbacks of the sixties. The gloom that pervades the Latin American mood at present stems precisely from the convergence of frustrations over the unexciting character of late late industrialization in *most* Latin American countries with the despair felt over the stumblings of the *one* country whose advance had assumed the more inspiring characteristics of the "great spurt."

The sources of entrepreneurship

A number of important characteristics of late late industrialization remain to be surveyed. What has been said so far permits, first of all, some discussion of the sources of entrepreneurship. As in-

2. While not included in the six points cited above, support by a vigorous movement of ideas has been stressed elsewhere by Gerschenkron as a characteristic of late industrialization. See, for example, *op. cit.*, pp. 22–26. For a survey of developmentalist-nationalist ideas in Brazil during the fifties, see Frank Bonilla, "A National Ideology for Development: Brazil" in K. H. Silvert (ed.), *Expectant Peoples: Nationalism and Development* (New York: Random, 1963) pp. 232–64.

dustry is started primarily to substitute imports, those engaged in the foreign trade sector are likely to play a substantial role in the process. This is the reason for the industrial prominence of (a) the former importers of Lebanese, Jewish, Italian, German, etc. origin, and (b) of the large foreign firms intent on maintaining their market and therefore turning from exporters into manufacturers. Once again, however, it is useful to distinguish between an industrialization which is brought underway under conditions of expanding income from exports and one that is ignited by deprivation of previously available imports (due to war or balance-of-payments troubles). Only in the latter situation are local importers and foreign exporting firms likely to be the main promoters of industrial enterprise. When foreign exchange income is expanding, one may rather expect industrial opportunities to be exploited by indigenous entrepreneurship. Under such conditions, the importing interests are apt to be well satisfied with their lot and activity; industrial development will run clearly counter to their short-run interests, especially when it requires the imposition of even a moderate level of protection. Some evidence in support of our distinction may be cited: in both Brazil and Colombia, coffee booms in the late nineteenth and early twentieth centuries, respectively, gave rise to periods of industrial expansion led by domestic entrepreneurs who were in no way tied to the importing interests.[3] The latter, on the other hand, were prominent in these and other Latin American countries during the high pressure drives toward import substitution which marked the World Wars and the Great Depression.

The importance of foreigners, of minorities or generally speaking, of non-elite-status groups in the total industrialization process has on occasion been held responsible for the fact that industrial interests do not wield in Latin America the political influence and social prestige which have been theirs in the older industrial countries. Insofar as the phenomenon is real, it can also be explained by the *kind* of industries most characteristic of the first phases of import-substituting industrialization: opinions of the owners of soft-drink bottling plants or of cosmetic or pharmaceutical industries are unlikely to command as much attention as those of steel and machinery manufacturers. In addition, the industrialists of the leading industrial countries always gained considerable influence by virtue of being exporters; as such they achieved prestige abroad,

3. Warren Dean, "The Planter as Entrepreneur: The Case of São Paulo," *The Hispanic American Historical Review*, XLVI (May 1966), 138–52; Luis Ospina Vásquez, *Industria y próteccion en Colombia (1810–1930)*, (Medellín: E. S. F., 1955), Chap. 8.

acquired contacts and gathered information — all accomplishments that were highly prized by their governments. This source of influence is quite unavailable to the import-substituting industrialists who are usually aiming only at supplying the domestic market.[4]

The exuberant phase of ISI and its political consequences

A final characteristic of the early phases of import — substituting industrialization is the growth pattern of the newly established industries. It has been suggested that

> output curves in newly established import-substituting industries have tended to be kinked, rising rapidly when exports are being replaced, but flattening out when further growth of demand has been grounded in the growth of domestic income. Profits have also followed this kinked pattern. Thus industries have moved rapidly from high profit and growth to precocious maturity, at which point they fall back to monopolistic quiescence with lower profit rates, a reduced level of investment, and aging plant and equipment.[5]

The extent to which the kinked pattern of output growth is really a fact rather than an inference from the nature of import-substitution remains to be established. After all, newly established industries have to overcome initial production and organization problems, they encounter some sales resistance due to preference for the imported product so that the early portion of their sales data may still approximate the logistic curve which has given a good fit for the time shape of the expansion of many industries in the advanced countries.[6] Nevertheless, it is probably legitimate to speak of a particularly "easy" phase of import substitution when the manufacturing process is entirely based on imported materials and machinery while importation of the article is firmly and effectively shut out by controls. Under such conditions, the early experience of the new manufacturers is likely to be most gratifying.

4. The proposition that the comparative *lack* of political power of the industrialists can be explained by the *lack* of industrial exports becomes perhaps more convincing when one states its positive counterpart: namely that the continuing political influence of the land-owning interests throughout the period of industrialization in Latin America is explained by the continuing almost total dependence of the capacity to import on exports of primary products. This point is made for Brazil in Francisco C. Weffort, "Estado y masas en el Brasil," *Revista Latinoamericana de Sociologia*, I (Mar. 1965), 53–71.

5. David Felix, "Monetarists. Structuralists and Import-Substituting Industrialization:" in W. Baer and I. Kerstenetzky (eds.), *Inflation and Growth in Latin America* (Homewood, Illinois: Irwin, 1964), p. 384.

6. Simon S. Kuznets, *Secular Movements in Production and Prices* (Boston: Houghton Mifflin, 1930). Arthur F. Burns, *Production Trends in the United States since 1870* (New York: National Bureau of Economic Research, 1934).

It is this phase of import substitution that gives rise to the often noted exuberance and boom atmosphere during which demand is easily overestimated. In any event, low duties or preferential exchange rates for machinery imports make for lavish orders. As a result, the new industry is likely to find itself saddled with excess capacity as soon as it reaches the kink.[7]

It is tempting to speculate about the psychological-political consequences of this pattern of industrialization. Progressive Latin Americans had long hoped that industry would introduce new, much needed disciplines into the behavior of their governments. The very nature of industrial operations — their precision, the need for exact timing, punctuality, reliability, predictability and all-around rationality — was expected to infuse these same qualities into policymaking and perhaps even into the political process itself. This sort of inference was based on the nature — or supposed nature — of industrial operations at the plant level. It disregarded, however, the larger financial and economic aspects of the process which had, of course, a much more direct and determining impact on politics. Thus the ease with which new industries were installed in spite of dire warnings and often in the midst of war and depression, the rapid growth they experienced and the handsome profits they realized during the first phases made import-substituting industry appear as a new incarnation of some primary product that would suddenly erupt with an old-fashioned world market boom. Little wonder, then, that the hoped for achievement of rationality in economic policymaking and in the political process in general failed to occur. On the contrary, the "exuberant" phase of import-substitution was accompanied by flamboyant public policies which badly overestimated the tolerance of the economy for a variety of ventures, be they income redistribution by fiat, the building of a new capital, or other extravaganzas. Here we can do no more than touch upon these matters; but it may be conjectured that in their very different ways, Perón, Kubitschek, Rojas Pinilla and Pérez Jiménez could all be considered victims of the delusions of economic invulnerability fostered by the surprising early successes and rapid penetration of industry into a supposedly hostile environment.

7. Even if expansion plans of competing firms are known all around and there is no excessive optimism, demand tends to be overestimated for two special reasons: with protection the price of the domestically produced product is going to be higher than that of the imported one; and market studies based on import statistics often overestimate the domestic market for the new domestic industry also because the statistics usually include a fair volume of specialty products which the domestic industry is unable to supply.

III. The Alleged Exhaustion of Import Substitution

Then, suddenly, the honeymoon was over and the recriminations began. Import-substituting industrialization was officially added, as we have seen, to the long list of certified *fracasos* in Latin American policymaking. We shall now attempt to sort out and evaluate some of the elements in this reversal of opinion.

Three principal accusations have been leveled against the industrialization process as it has appeared in Latin America:

(1) Import-substituting industrialization is apt to get "stuck" after its first successes, due to the "exhaustion of easy import substitution opportunities"; it leaves the economy with a few relatively high-cost industrial establishments and with a far more vulnerable balance of payments since imports consist now of semifinished materials, spare parts and machinery indispensably required for maintaining and increasing production and employment.

(2) Import-substituting industry is affected by seemingly congenital inability to move into export markets.

(3) The new industries are making an inadequate contribution to the solution of the unemployment problem.

In the following we shall concentrate on the first two critiques; the third cannot be adequately discussed within the limits of the present essay.

A naive and a seminaive exhaustion model

The argument on ISI getting stuck is put forward in several forms. Most frequently and crudely, the assertion is made that the process faces "exhaustion" after a certain period during which the "easy" import substitution opportunities are taken up. Exhaustion evokes the image of a natural resource available in strictly limited quantities which is being depleted; and we must ask now to what extent the image is sensible. One model which could underly the exhaustion concept is an exceedingly simple one: at any one point of time, a country imports commodities $A, B, C \ldots$; the annual import volumes of these commodities are $M_A, M_B, M_C, \ldots$ Next, one assumes the existence of economies of scale such that the minimum economic sizes of plants which are to produce these various goods can be unequivocally defined. If the annual capacities of such plants are designated by $P_A, P_B, P_C, \ldots$ then import substitution opportunities are limited to those products (say, A, C, $E, \ldots$) for which imports (the M's) exceed the minimum economic sizes (the P's).

This would be a truly naive model rationalizing the exhaustion concept, and it is perhaps too much of a caricature of what the critics of import substitution have in mind. The more sophisticated among them, at least, do realize that the first steps of ISI open up new opportunities for the establishment of domestic manufactures through both income and backward linkage effects. In the first place, the domestic production of *A, C,* and *E* creates new incomes which may enlarge the market for a number of additional final demand goods to the point where their domestic production becomes, in turn, feasible. Secondly, domestic production of *A, C,* and *E,* which is *ex hypothesi* set up on the basis of imported inputs, opens up new opportunities for the establishment of domestic manufacturing facilities turning out these inputs.

The income effect is likely to result in a convergent series of new investment opportunities. Thus it postpones exhaustion in relation to the naive model, but does not overcome it. When backward linkage effects are taken into account, however, the exhaustion concept tends to evaporate unless it is bolstered by some additional assumptions.

Again a rather naive, let us call it "seminaive," exhaustion model could be built up as follows. Industry *A* requires imported inputs $a_1, a_2, a_3, \ldots a_i \ldots$; industry *C* inputs $c_1, c_2, c_3, \ldots c_i \ldots$ and so on. It seems plausible that imports of any individual input, such as $M_{a_1}, M_{a_2}, M_{a_3}, \ldots M_{a_i} \ldots$ should be smaller than M_A had been before domestic production of *A* started. On the other hand, it could be surmised (and frequently is unquestioningly assumed) that minimum economic plant size *increases* as one ascends to "higher" stages of production. If this is so, then we have $P_{a_i} > P_A$ while $M_{a_i} < M_A$. Under these circumstances the chances that imports will exceed the minimum economic sizes for any large number of imported inputs for *A, C* and *E* decrease rapidly as one ascends via backward linkage toward the higher stages of production.

Criticism of the seminaive model: the importance of policy

I believe that something like this seminaive model is indeed in the minds of those who speak of exhaustion. For this reason it is useful to spell it out, for as soon as that is done, it is easy to perceive where such an exhaustion model goes wrong and what are, therefore, the requirements of an industrialization process that would "beat" exhaustion.[8]

8. One way of staving off the exhaustion predicted by the naive or semi-

Two modifications of the model serve to make it look both more realistic and less exhaustion-prone. In the first place, some of the inputs needed for the initial import-substitution industries are likely to be identically the same (steel, paper, glass are needed as intermediate inputs in a wide variety of final demand products). As a result of this *product convergence* of industrial processes the a_i's are not always distinct from the c_i's and e_i's, so that imports of a number of intermediate goods may well be larger than the previous imports of final demand goods.

Secondly, it is of course not necessarily true that minimum economic plant size increases regularly as one ascends toward the higher stages of production. I am not aware of any systematic study relating to this point. But it is well known, for example, that automobile assembly plants deal with a number of suppliers and subcontractors for many needed components, just as a single steel plant will draw for its supply of coal on several mines. Large capacity plants do characterize the technology of a few important intermediate and basic products; but at every stage — particularly in the machinery and equipment industries which, in a sense, represent the "highest" stage of production — small and medium-sized establishments are also to be found.[9]

If we put these two considerations together, one particularly favorable possibility appears: minimum economic size could providentially be, and in fact often is, large in those industries for whose products (steel, glass, paper) the convergence phenomenon is important. But even apart from such a happy coincidence, the preceding considerations make the exhaustion concept lose the physical and predictable definiteness it had assumed with the previous models. It appears instead that the difficulties that may well dog the back-

naive model would be to enlarge total market size, either for *all* products through the amalgamation of several national markets, or for *some* products particularly important for industrial progress, through appropriate income redistribution within a given national market. Accordingly the formation of common markets and a redistribution of income which would result in larger domestic markets for mass-produced articles have held an important place in the discussions that arose after the "exuberant" phase of ISI was over. There can be no doubt that the creation of a larger market through either or both of these moves would contribute much to dynamic industrial growth. But we wish to argue here that they are not the only available instruments or, in other words, that market size is not as rigid and definite a barrier as the exhaustion thesis claims.

9. For striking evidence on the smallness of the typical machine tool firm in the United States and on low concentration ratios in the industry, see Murray Brown and Nathan Rosenberg, "Prologue to a Study of Patent and Other Factors in the Machine Tool Industry," *The Patent, Trademark and Copyright Journal of Research and Education*, IV (Spring 1960), 42–46. One reason for this situation is that capital/labor ratios are typically low in the machinery industry.

ward linkage process are to a considerable extent a matter of *economic environments and policies,* instead of being determined exclusively by objective quantities such as market and minimum economic plant sizes.

We have a few more words to say on the latter topics before we turn to the economic and sociopolitical reasons for which the backward linkage process may or may not get stuck. It must be recognized that one implication of the above considerations is to stress even more the importance of market size. In the seminaive exhaustion model, market size sets definite limits to the number of industries which a given country can set up. With increasing market size, an additional number of industries, *all* of larger size than could be accommodated previously, become possible. But if one gives up the idea that minimum economic size and stage of production are closely correlated, the advantages of market size can become larger rather than smaller, for a larger market permits the installation not only of an industry requiring that market, but, *in its wake,* of a host of other plants supplying that industry; the required market size of these plants may be much smaller, but they could not be established without the prior establishment of the industry requiring the larger market and which might therefore be called the "bottleneck industry."

These considerations make us understand better the tremendous importance of market size (so well illustrated by the exceptional achievements in Latin America of Mexico and Brazil) if the backward linkage process is to be vigorous. But they also lead to some interesting policy conclusions: with the seminaive model, the industrialization process is bound to stop at a given point. It can be likened to the ascent of a mountain which gets steeper all the time; the country is the mountain climber and the larger it (or rather its market) is, the higher up the mountain it gets. If this were really so, there would not be much point in pushing it up a bit higher through special incentives or promotion of public enterprise, and any infant industry protection should be uniform. But if we abandon the seminaive model, the mountain alters its shape; at one point its slope does become forbiddingly steep, but then it flattens to turn up again only much later. Under those conditions it becomes exceedingly important to climb the forbidding portion (the bottleneck industry) of the mountain as then the traveling can be continued with ease for some time. In other words, the existence of the bottleneck industries is a powerful argument for special protection, or direct promotion, and even better, for efforts to export the portion of the industry's output that cannot be accommodated by the domestic market. In any event, public policy is very much back in the saddle with this view of the industrialization process.

A further remark along similar lines. The phenomenon of product convergence can also be utilized to help a country negotiate the steeper slopes of its bottleneck industries. When an intermediate product industry faces inadequate domestic demand and cannot therefore be established on an economic scale, it is possible to canvas possibilities for setting up industries which might generate additional demands for the bottleneck industry's output. While this may be difficult in practice, the argument leads to a counsel of caution in policies directed against so-called "nonessential" industries: the demands for intermediate products emanating from these industries can be very precious in permitting *essential* intermediate product industries to be established.

IV. Economic, Political and Technological Determinants of Backward Linkage

While the preceding considerations ended up by stressing the importance of policy, they were still focused on the *mechanism* of industrialization through backward linkages. We must now address ourselves directly to the political economy of the process.

The importance of market size and of an adequate supply of foreign exchange in setting some limits to the process is undoubted; nevertheless, the industrialization processes of countries which are not too dissimilar with respect to these constraints still displays considerable variation so that curiosity is aroused about the role of other factors, such as the behavior of private industrialists and of public authorities.

As is well known by now, the setting up of an industry based on imported inputs has two contradictory effects: it becomes possible, and in some to be defined ways attractive, to set up industries producing inputs for the initial industry; but at the same time, the very establishment of that industry sets up resistances against backward linkage investments. Several reasons for such resistances had already been noted in my *Strategy of Economic Development*:

> The industrialist who has worked hitherto with imported materials will often be hostile to the establishment of domestic industries producing these materials. First, he fears, often with good reason, that the domestic product will not be of as good and uniform quality as the imported one. Secondly, he feels that he might become dependent on a single domestic supplier when he could previously shop around the world. Thirdly, he is concerned about domestic

competition becoming more active once the basic ingredients are produced within the country. Finally, his location may be wrong once the source of supply of the materials he uses is thoroughly altered. For all these reasons, the interests of the converting, finishing, and mixing industries are often opposed to the establishment of domestic sources of supply for the products that they convert, finish, or mix.[1]

Another powerful factor making for resistance has since received much attention: high tariff protection for the initial industry combined with low or zero tariffs or preferential exchange rate treatment for the industry's inputs.[2] The greater the difference between the level of protection accorded to the import-substituting industry and that applying to its imported inputs, the more will the profit margin of the industry depend *on preventing* domestic production of the inputs. For it is a fair assumption that the backward linkage industries would, once established, be eligible for a level of protection similar to that benefiting the initial import-substituting industry, and it is at least doubtful whether the initial industry can obtain a compensatory tariff increase for its own output or, in general, whether the resulting increase in costs can be passed on to the consumers without loss in sales volume.

For those various reasons, the newly established industries may not act at all as the entering wedge of a broad industrialization drive. The high customs duties on their outputs, combined with low (or negative) duties on their inputs, could almost be seen as a plot on the part of the existing powerholders to corrupt or buy off the new industrialists, to reduce them to a sinecured, inefficient, and unenterprising group that can in no way threaten the existing social structure. Indeed, like the workers' aristocracy in Lenin's theory of imperialism, these pampered industrialists might go over to the enemy — that is, make common cause with agrarian and trading interests which had long been opposed to the introduction of "exotic" industries.

The possibility that the industrialists who first appear in non-

1. *Op. cit.*, p. 118. I am quoting myself here because the critics of ISI have sometimes taken me to task for having overrated the power and automaticity of the backward linkage process.

2. See, for example, Santiago Macario, *op. cit.*, and R. Soligo and J. J. Stern, "Tariff Protection, Import Substitution and Investment Efficiency" in *Pakistan Development Review*, V (Summer 1965), 249–270. A general critique of import substitution on the grounds that the concentration on, and strong protection of, consumers goods it usually implies make for misallocation of resources, for obstacles to further industrial growth, and for a bias in favor of consumption is in John H. Power, "Import Substitution as an Industrialization Strategy" (mimeo.), Jan. 1966.

industrial countries may not be all that much in favor of dynamic industrial development leads to an interesting sociopolitical puzzle. Sociologists and political scientists have frequently deplored the weakness of the middle class and particularly of the industrialists in Latin America, its lack of self-assertion and its failure to influence public affairs. Earlier we have tried to account for this phenomenon by some characteristics of late late industrialization. But at this point, one begins to wonder whether it would really be a good thing if the new industrialists were much more self-assertive and powerful than they are — perhaps they would then really be able to choke off further industrialization, something which generally they have not been able to do! Considering what we have called the tightly staged character of late late industrialization it may in fact be preferable for the governments of the late late industrializing countries to be run by *tecnicos*, by groups of planner-technicians, rather than by the new industrialists themselves. It has been in fact due to the regulations issued by the *tecnicos* of the Kubitschek administration that backward linkage was *enforced* rapidly in the Brazilian automotive industry in the late fifties. In Mexico, on the other hand, assembly plants had existed for decades without any progress being made toward the local manufacture of motors and parts until measures similar to those in Brazil were adopted in the sixties. Thus the resistance of the initial industrialists to backward linkage combine with other already noted characteristics of late late industrialization to enhance the potential contribution of public policy to the process.[3]

But we dare not rely on such policies emerging simply because they are needed and because we issue a call for them. Could the resistance to backward linkage be overcome otherwise than by state action? While the resistances of the new industrialists are perfectly rational, one cannot but feel that they are based on a myopic, excessively short-run view of the development process. In this manner, we can supply a concrete justification for the view of a Brazilian sociologist according to which the traditional Western, Puritan-ethnic-imbued, rational, profit-maximizing businessman is not really the type that is most needed in the situation of Latin America; what is required, he feels, are entrepreneurs who can identify themselves with the general developmental aspirations of their society, be it

3. That a policy of forcing backward linkage investments has problems and pitfalls of its own is shown in Leland L. Johnson, "Problems of Import Substitution: The Chilean Automobile Industry," *Economic Development and Cultural Change*, XV (Jan. 1967), 202–16.

even at the expense of some rationality in their everyday business operations.[4]

But, once again, one cannot rest content with issuing a call for the *desenvolvimentista* entrepreneur; it would be more useful to be able to explain his appearance or nonappearance by a series of economic and social factors. This will be our next task. While it is true that backward linkage meets with certain resistances and obstacles, we have yet to inquire about the existence of other forces working in the opposite direction, that is, in the direction of making backward linkage work. This appraisal of the comparative strengths of forces and counterforces is probably the key to understanding why industrialization has been more vigorous and continuous in some developing countries than in others — long before they ran up against any barriers of market size.

As is the case for the start of late late industrialization, so will the continuation of the process through backward linkage be strongly influenced by the industrializing country's balance of payments. The opposition of the initial industrialists to backward linkage investments is likely to be considerably reduced if they occasionally experience curtailments, due to foreign exchange shortages, in the flow of imported inputs; on the other hand, the backward linkage investments require availability of foreign exchange for the importation of machinery. Consequently it is likely that some alternation of foreign exchange stringency and abundance would be optimal from the point of view of generating both the motivation and the resources required for the process. I have previously made this point[5] and considerable attention has been paid to the foreign exchange constraint.[6] Hence, it will be more useful to focus here on other forces affecting the process. There surely exist many situations in which some backward linkage investments are neither impossible in the light of foreign exchange availabilities, nor wholly compelled because of previous searing experience with foreign exchange shortages. We are interested here in the conditions that make for vigorous continuation of industrialization in these situations.

In line with our previous arguments, we posit a certain level of resistance of the new industrialists to the manufacturing of currently imported inputs. The resistance, while rational on the part

4. Fernando H. Cardoso, "The Industrial Elite" in S. M. Lipset and A. Solari (eds.), *Elites in Latin America* (New York: Oxford University Press, 1967), pp. 96–99.

5. *Strategy, op. cit.*, pp. 173–76.

6. See, for example, Carlos F. Diaz-Alejandro, "On the Import Intensity of Import Substitution," *Kyklos*, XVIII (1965), 495–511.

of the initial industrialists, is undesirable from the point of view of the economy in the sense that profitable production of some inputs is assumed to be possible provided some average or normal level of protection is extended to them. In other words, there is room for, but resistance against, further industrialization along reasonably efficient lines of comparative advantage. We now inquire what conditions other than balance-of-payments developments could make this resistance weaken or disappear.

The principal point to be made here is very simple: the resistance is almost wholly premised on the supposition that manufacturing in the higher stages of production is going to be undertaken by entrepreneurs *other* than the already established initial industrialists (or other than members of his immediate family). For if he himself undertakes it, most of the listed objections to the expansion of manufacturing via backward linkage fall to the ground. Thus, the fear of unreliability and poor quality of the domestic article should abate and the fear of domination by a monopoly supplier will disappear entirely. True, domestically produced inputs may have to be purchased at a higher price than was paid for the previously imported product which was perhaps obtained duty free or bought at some preferential exchange rate. But even if the increase in input costs that comes with domestic manufacture cannot be passed on, vertical integration would take the sting out of it; for the decrease of profits in one operation of an integrated industrial concern does not seriously matter if that decrease is compensated by the emergence of profits in another, newly established operation. To realize such profits the industrialist who contemplates the manufacture of hitherto imported inputs will usually have to obtain for those inputs some "normal" level of protection. It must be assumed, therefore, that he does not consider existing customs duties and exchange rate preferences as unchanging parameters immune to his will and influence; the opposite assumption is sometimes made in the literature on import substitution (with pessimistic consequences for the prospects of ISI), but it is manifestly unrealistic for most investment decisions.

If the disposition of the initial industrialists *themselves* to move farther back into the industrial structure is an important element in overcoming obstacles to the backward linkage process, a brief inquiry into the factors making for a disposition of this sort is in order.

The economist can contribute a *general* reason for which backward linkage investments are likely to be carried on by the new industrialists themselves: the mere fact that they have been earning profits and are therefore presumably looking for new investment opportunities. Once the new industries have reached the point at which imports have been wholly substituted so that horizontal expansion is no longer profitable, vertical expansion into the "higher stages" of production may well offer the best available and, in any event, the most obvious outlet for investment funds that have accumulated as a result of the profitable operation of the existing industries. The availability of profits from the first phase of import substitution thus provides a generalized incentive for the successful import-substituting industrialist to plunge once again, naturally after appropriate modification of the tariff and exchange rate policies affecting the products whose manufacture is to be undertaken. The likelihood that the new industrialist will look in this particular direction, is increased by two interrelated factors: one, by the special difficulty of moving into export markets, to be commented on in the next section; and secondly by what we have called the sequential or "tightly staged" character of late late industrialization. The industrialist manufacturing a final demand good during earlier cycles of industrialization was likely to call into life domestic producers of inputs and of the required machinery; therefore, once he was no longer able to expand his domestic sales volume, he found the higher stages already *occupied* by others and was therefore impelled to look elsewhere, including to exports, for further expansion. The situation is very different when production is undertaken wholly on the basis of imported inputs.

The availability of profits and resulting search for new profitable investment opportunities act, as has been said, as a general counterweight to the hostility toward backward linkage investments on the part of new industrialists. Whether or not this counterweight will outweigh the hostility is difficult to say. Under the worst of circumstances the combination of the two forces may result in a dog-in-the-manger situation: the new industrialists are able to prevent others from entering the backward linkage arena, but are not sufficiently motivated to enter it themselves.

To carry the analysis a bit further and to account for the different degrees of strength which the backward linkage dynamic has displayed in different countries, it is tempting to make a brief foray into the realm of sociology. The eagerness of an industrialist to move into related fields of activity instead of being satisfied with his existing operation based on imported inputs, may, for example, be reinforced if he has the feeling that his sons are locked into his own class and career. If an industrialist's sons are able and eager to enter the professions or the government, there is no need for father to think about finding new industries for the sons to expand into and to manage (preferably one for each son so they won't fight). But if industrialists look down on government and the professions, or if the latter look down upon the former, or, as happens frequently, if dislike and disdain are mutual, or simply, if the social distance between the industrialists and other groups is considerable, then the advantage of providing jobs for the family may fully compensate for the inconveniences, headaches, and even for minor monetary sacrifices that may be entailed by backward linkage investments. It appears once again, although from a rather different angle, that it is perhaps not a bad thing for the initial entrepreneurs to belong to a group of immigrants or of some other outsiders, with no immediate prospects of joining the established upper class or of moving into politics or the professions.

Social distance is bred by geographical distance. For this reason, one might expect that an industrialization process which, at least in its beginnings, is strongly identified with one or several centers other than the national capital stands a better chance to spill over vigorously from one industry to another than one which has its base in the capital city itself. The importance of having a somewhat isolated, inbred and self-consciously proud industrial center during the early stages of industrialization is demonstrated by the roles played by São Paulo, Monterrey, and Medellín. No similar pioneering center outside the capital city arose in Chile and Argentina, and it is perhaps not a coincidence that these two countries have provided the critics of the ISI process with far better examples of its alleged irrationality and propensity to exhaustion than Brazil, Mexico, and Colombia.

A final subject of speculation is the differential impact of technology on the comparative strength of the linkage process in different industries. When a backward linkage effect points to an industry which is technologically quite distinct from the one requiring the input, the input-utilizing industrialist is less likely to be attracted to the input-producing industry than if the latter is closely related to processes and techniques with which the industrialist is already familiar. For example, the backward (and forward) linkage dynamic may show more spontaneous vigor in the "inbred" metalworking and chemical industries than in, say, the textile industry whose inputs come in large part from technological strangers such as, precisely, the chemical industry. Thus the backward linkage dynamic may be held back at some point simply by "technological strangeness." This point is of particular importance for the machinery industry since machinery is usually a technological stranger to the industry in which it is utilized. An inquiry into the technological determinants of the differential propensity of different industries toward linkage investments could be of considerable value. To identify and then to remove this sort of bottleneck should be a principal task of public agencies concerned with industrial development.

The purpose of the preceding observations was to convince the reader that there is far more to the vigor or weakness which late late industrialization displays in various countries than minimum economic size of plants, market size and even foreign exchange availabilities. We have left the naive and seminaive exhaustion models far behind and have instead generated a highly complex "field" of forces and counterforces. If the reader feels a bit confused, we have achieved our purpose: for essentially we wished to show that the process is not nearly so straightforward and constrained as it has recently been made to look, and that it depends far more on public and private acts of volition than has sometimes been granted as well as on numerous economic, sociological and technological factors which remain to be investigated.

V. The Inability to Export Manufactures: "Structural" Causes and Remedies

It is hardly necessary to stress how desirable it would be for our late late industrializing countries to become exporters of the outputs of their new industries:

(a) Through exports they would overcome whatever obstacles of market size limit their growth or prevent their establishment.

(b) Through exports they would loosen the balance-of-payments constraint which may otherwise prevent capacity operation of existing industries as well as establishment of new industries.

(c) Finally, by competing in world markets, industries would be forced to attain and maintain high standards of efficiency and product quality and would thereby acquire defenses against oligopolistic collusion and decay to which they often succumb in highly protected, small local markets.

Unfortunately, the intensity with which one would wish for exports of manufacturers from the late late industrializers is matched by the solidity of the arguments which appear to foreclose any real prospects of success in this direction.

Once again, the arguments are familiar: The new industries have been set up exclusively to substitute imports, without any export horizon on the part of either the industrialists themselves or the government; the foreign branch plants and subsidiaries, which have taken an important part in the process, often are under specific instructions not to compete abroad with the products of the parent company; even more decisive than these obstacles deriving from attitudes and institutions, is the fact that the new industries, set up behind tariff walls, usually suffer from high production costs in countries that are, moreover, permanently subject to strong inflationary pressures — hence there is no real possibility of these industries competing successfully in international markets even if they were disposed to do so.

These are weighty arguments and they seem to meet the test of a satisfactory explanation in that they put one's mind to rest. But do they?

After all, there are many industries which started out producing for the home market and eventually spilled over into foreign markets. Prior, successful acceptance of a manufactured commodity in the home market has even been considered to be a prerequisite for successful exporting.[7]

Secondly, foreign firms have been known to be quite adaptable in their manufacturing and export policies. Just as they have been coaxed by national policies to produce or procure domestically a larger proportion of their inputs, so they could be induced to engage on export drives.

Finally, even the most impressive explanation of the inability to export — the cost disadvantage of new industries set up under tariff protection — loses some of its persuasiveness when one remembers that protection of industries in Germany and the United States has not prevented considerable success of those protected industries in world markets. Industrialization of the nineteenth century latecomers was in fact frequently accompanied by both tariff protection and a vigorous export drive which threatened the previous dominant position of the old established industrial countries in a number of important markets. Again, the behavior of the late late industrializers could not be more different and it now begins to appear that we may be in need of some further, perhaps more funda-

7. S.B. Linder., *An Essay on Trade and Transformation* (New York: Wiley, 1961), pp. 87 ff.

mental explanations of the inability to export that afflicts them. While such a "structuralist" strategy of problem-solving may show the problem to be even more deeply rooted than had been thought, it can also uncover new, hitherto unsuspected ways of attacking it.[8]

One additional explanation of the difficulty of exporting has already been given in the preceding section. It was asserted that in view of the sequential character of industrialization, late late industrialists looking for new profitable business opportunities will frequently have the option between investing in backward linkage industries and expanding into export markets, whereas late industrialists had primarily the latter course open to them since the backward linkage industries were already in existence. Little wonder, then, that the late late industrialists decide to stay cozily at home much longer than the late industrialists who were under a far greater compulsion to make the plunge into foreign markets if they were going to expand. It would therefore be unrealistic to expect an industry to become an exporter before it has truly taken root in the country through a variety of the more obvious backward linkage investments. And the expeditious undertaking of these investments is therefore desirable not only per se, but also as a necessary way-station to the opening of the export phase.

Another structural reason for the inability to export derives from the circumstances under which resources have been channeled into the industrial sector in many Latin-American countries. Industrial investments became attractive not only because of customs protection, but additionally because of the combination of internal inflation, overvaluation of the currency, and exchange controls. In effect, maintaining an overvalued exchange rate meant that the exporters of traditional primary products would receive a smaller real income than with an equilibrium or undervalued exchange rate. At the same time, the overvalued exchange rate permitted the acquisition at favorable prices (in domestic currency) of those imports that were let in by the control authorities. And since machinery and essential industrial materials enjoyed preferential status, the overvalued exchange rate acted in effect as a mechanism to transfer income from the traditional export sector to the new industries.[9]

8. A general plea for "structuralist" analysis of Latin America economic problems along with a good bibliography is to be found in Osvaldo Sunkel, "El trasfondo estructural de los problemas del desarrollo latinoamericano," *Trimestre Economico*, XXXIV (Jan.–Mar. 1967), 11–58. For an interpretation of structuralism as a strategy for problem-solving, see my *Journeys Toward Progress* (New York: Twentieth Century Fund, 1963) pp. 210–16 and 231–35.

9. Alexandre Kafka, "The Theoretical Interpretation of Latin American

At the same time, however, the overvalued exchange rate acted as a bar to exports from these industries. This probably was not a serious drawback and certainly was not felt as such during the earlier stages of import-substituting industrialization when exports on the part of the nascent industries were not a real prospect. But as a vigorous industrial establishment grew up in various countries one may well ask the question why a different institutional arrangement was not chosen. For example, why not tax the export sector, subsidize the new industries and do away with the overvalued exchange rate so that industrial exports are encouraged? To ask this question is to answer it: in most Latin American countries such a course would have been politically impossible. The power of the groups tied to the primary export sector would hardly have permitted so direct an assault, as is attested by the strong, permanent and occasionally successful pressures that were exerted against the indirect squeeze of the sector which Latin American monetary authorities had more or less inadvertently stumbled on. The great advantage of the inflation-cum-overvaluation arrangement was in fact not only that it resulted in an indirect rather than direct squeeze of politically and socially powerful groups, but that this mechanism was an *unintended* and, for a long time, an *unnoticed* by-product of a course of action which had the perfectly respectable objective of "defending the national currency against depreciation." [1]

Viewed in this way, the inability to export manufactures appears as the price which had to be paid for building up an industrial sector under adverse sociopolitical conditions. Should we then perhaps be simply gratified that industrialization was contrived at all, and be happy to pay the price? Not necessarily. As industrialization proceeded, the desirability of the overvaluation device became increasingly questionable *from the point of view of industry itself.* For overvaluation not only impeded exports, but interfered, in ways already analyzed, with the vigorous exploitation of the backward linkage dynamic. Moreover, in several countries, industries became sufficiently vigorous and integrated so that the help stemming from the procurement of a few imported inputs at bargain prices (via

Economic Development," in H. S. Ellis (ed.), *Economic Development in Latin America* (New York: St. Martin's Press, 1961), p. 21, and Celso Furtado, "Industrialization and Inflation," *International Economic Papers*, XII (1967), 101–19.

1. The policy originated, ironically enough, in an attempt to *defend* the export interests, e.g., in the case of Brazil, to maintain the cruzeiro price of coffee in the face of falling world market prices during the Great Depression. This policy led to an increase in the money supply, and thereby caused domestic inflationary pressures which would eventually result in the inflation-cum-overvaluation arrangement. Cf. Furtado, *ibid.*, p. 103.

the overvalued exchange rate) was bound to be more than offset, for an increasing number of firms, by the loss of potential profits that could have been realized through exports at a nonovervalued rate of exchange. It could thus be suggested that, at a certain point, overvaluation of the currency turned from a stimulus to industrial progress into a drag on it.

It appears that the much advertised noncompetitiveness of Latin American industry may be rooted more in the failure to modify institutions than in any inability to bring down real costs. The question then arises why the industrial interests have not vigorously pressed for institutional arrangements — export subsidies, preferential exchange rates, or more radically, an exchange rate that is undervalued rather than overvalued — that would make exporting profitable. Are there some grounds on which industrialists could be basically *reluctant* to commit substantial resources to an export drive?

This question leads to a third structural reason for — or speculation about — the difficulties of exporting. It has to do, once again, with the distribution of power in Latin American societies. To stage an export drive, an industrialist must frequently make special investments in research, design and packaging; he must assemble a specialized sales force, delegate considerable authority, launch an entirely different advertising campaign; in short, he incurs special risks and new overhead costs which will be recoverable only over a comparatively long period of successful exporting. Therefore, an industrialist will consider exporting only when he can be sure either that the basic institutions and policies which vitally affect his foreign operations are highly stable or, as a minimum, that his interests will be given the most serious attention when these institutions and policies are altered.

In effect, we have just spelled out a "prerequisite" for a determined and successful export drive for manufactures: to undertake such a drive with all its risks and special costs, the industrialist class must feel reasonably sure that it can control certain crucial fiscal and monetary policies of its government. Differently put: only a cohesive, vocal, and highly influential national bourgeoisie is likely to carry industrialization beyond relatively safe import-substitution to the risky export-oriented stage. It will be noted that this assertion — the industrialists do not export because they are not influential — completes the second half of a vicious circle whose first half, given on pages 10–11, asserted that the ISI industrialists are lacking in influence because they are not "conquering foreign markets." Obviously we should not take inordinate pride in having fashioned a new vicious circle or in having identified a new prerequisite to the economic progress of the developing countries. Rather, we shall consider in a moment ways of breaking out of the circle and of doing without the prerequisite or of finding, à la Gerschenkron, a substitute for it. But we must nevertheless pause at this point in our reasoning and take notice that conditions for a strong export drive by the private sector are highly unfavorable in Latin America: in no country of that continent do the industrialists feel securely in control of vital economic policies affecting them. Policymakers positively cultivate unpredictability and distance from interest groups; at the same time, they are highly manipulative. Changes in fiscal, monetary, and foreign exchange policies are therefore frequent while communication about these changes with the affected interest groups is infrequent. These are the sociopolitical traits that account, perhaps more fundamentally than the cost-price structure of the new industries, for their poor export performance.

Having uncovered ever more cogent reasons for the inability to export, have we encountered by the same token a "fundamental" remedy? One way of staking such a claim would be to expect that, as a result of our analysis, Latin America will change the nature of its politics and that its powerholders will henceforth become less manipulative and more communicative. Unfortunately analysis is not likely to act as so powerful a solvent. But is it really necessary to wait until a trusting and intimate relationship between the industrialists and the policymakers emerges or is it conceivable that countries which find it difficult to establish such a relationship could travel an alternative road?

A radical reaction to the problem would be for the state itself to take over the foreign merchandising function. The spectacle of the state rendering difficult or impossible the performance of an important function by the private sector and then taking over that function because the private sector is ostensibly falling down on the job, is by no means uncommon. If this course of action has not been taken so far for the export of manufactures, one reason is that the importance of this function is only beginning to be appreciated. Also, state enterprise is hardly likely to be at its best in selling a wide variety of manufactures in foreign markets; for, by its nature, this task requires levels of initiative, flexibility, risk-taking and decentralized decisionmaking which it has been difficult for state enterprise to attain.

A less radical and more promising solution would be for the state simply to take an active role in promoting exports by private enterprise. As already mentioned in connection with exports from foreign-owned branch plants and subsidiaries, the state could very well tie the granting of tax and other incentives to the attainment of export targets in a manner analogous to that with which backward linkage has been enforced in the Brazilian automobile industry. From the point of view of the industrialists, such a policy would have the advantage that one sector of the bureaucracy would become committed to the export drive and could then be relied on to do battle with those sectors whose policies interfere with the success of the drive.

Quite a different solution consists in leaving alone, at first, the obstacles to exporting that derive from the actions of one's own government and in concentrating instead on those that are caused by other governments. This is in fact what is being attempted at present through the United Nations Conference on Trade and Development and its campaign for preferences for the manufactures of developing countries in the markets of developed countries. Perhaps this request can be viewed more sympathetically than it has been if it is considered as a *compensation* to the exporters of the newly industrializing countries for some of the extra burdens they must bear because of the policies and frequent policy changes of their own governments. In this reasoning, one may also discern a hope that such preferences would be temporary: once exports in volume would have been achieved, the first half of the vicious circle we have identified — industrialists are not influential because they do not export, and they do not export because they are not influential — would have been shattered. There would then be hope that government policies would become more finely attuned to the needs of the exporting industrialists who might therefore dispense in due course with the special privileges obtained from *other* governments.

The need for common markets among developing countries can also be better appreciated from this perspective. The common markets would not only provide preferential treatment for the industrialists of the participating countries; for these mutual arrangements to be durable, monetary and foreign exchange policies would have to become more uniform and stable than they have been; and such a development would be even more important than the customs preferences themselves in promoting exports from the common market countries, *not only to each other, but also to third* countries.

It is, however, precisely the prospect of less freedom of movement in monetary and foreign exchange policies which makes national governments so skittish about entering effective common market commitments.

Finally our problem could be alleviated by developments in the structure of international trade in manufactures. According to some observers, countries of recent industrialization should be acquiring a comparative advantage in certain types of highly *standardized* industrial products.[2] To sell such goods abroad may not be possible, in a number of lines, without special international market and firm connections, but it does not require either expensive advertisement campaigns or any special adaptation to foreign tastes and conditions. As a result, the overhead cost of exporting would be cut and the risks deriving from the instability or unpredictability of official economic policies would be correspondingly reduced.

Conclusion

In the preceding pages an attempt has been made to describe the varieties and characteristic features of import-substituting industrialization, and to derive from them sociopolitical consequences which in turn affect the process. Among the characteristics of ISI the possibility of proceeding sequentially, in tightly separated stages, because of the availability of imported inputs and machinery, plays, as was shown, a particularly commanding and complex role, direct and indirect, positive and negative.

Thus, the sequential or staged character of the process is responsible not only for the ease with which it can be brought underway, but also for the lack of training in technological innovation and for the resistances to both backward linkage investments and to exporting that are being encountered. The most important consequence of sequentiality, however, is the fact that it has become possible for industrialization to penetrate into Latin America and elsewhere among the late latecomers without requiring the fundamental social and political changes which it wrought among the pioneer industrial countries and also among the earlier group of latecomers. The repercussions of this situation on the industrialization process itself are ambivalent: on the one hand, the lack of political power of the new industrialists means, as we have just seen, that exporting meets with political and institutional, rather than purely economic, obstacles; on the other hand, this very lack of power neutralizes in

2. Raymond Vernon, "International Investment and International Trade in the Product Cycle," this *Journal*, LXXX (May 1966), 202–07.

various ways some of the possible adverse effects of sequentiality, for example, the resistance of the new industrialists to backward linkage.

In addition, the fact that import-substituting industrialization can be accommodated relatively easily in the existing social and political environment is probably responsible for the widespread disappointment with the process. Industrialization was expected to change the social order and all it did was to supply manufactures! Hence one is only too ready to read evidence of total failure into any trouble it encounters.

This paper has by no means denied the various difficulties which the ISI process is apt to experience; in fact, they have on occasion been shown to be more deepseated than had been thought. At the same time, our exploration of the characteristics of the process has made it possible to discern avenues toward continued industrial growth that remain open to the late latecomers.

Harvard University

IMPORT SUBSTITUTION AND INDUSTRIALIZATION IN LATIN AMERICA: EXPERIENCES AND INTERPRETATIONS*

Werner Baer, Vanderbilt University

THROUGHOUT MOST OF THE FIFTIES AND SIXTIES MANY LATIN AMERICAN GOVERNMENTS adopted Import Substitution Industrialization (ISI) as their principal method to achieve economic growth and socio-economic modernization. By the opening of the Seventies, however, there is considerable doubt about ISI's success in solving the region's development problems. In many countries the possibilities for further import-substitution had disappeared. Industrial growth had slowed, job opportunities in industry for Latin America's rapidly growing urban population were scarce, income distribution had in many countries either remained unchanged or had become more concentrated than in the early post-World War II years, and most industrial goods produced within the region were priced so high that export possibilities were severely limited.

Considerable debate has taken place among economists and policymakers over the merits of ISI as a strategy for economic development, the performance of ISI in various countries, over the nature of post-ISI problems which these countries have faced, and over policies to deal with these post-ISI problems.

In this review article I shall first describe the nature of ISI in Latin America, its occurrence prior to World War II, and its development in the decades of the Fifties and Sixties. I shall then review the problems which developed as ISI reached maturity and review various analyses developed to explain these problems. Finally, I shall examine various strategies which have been suggested for the post-ISI period.

THE NATURE OF ISI IN LATIN AMERICA

ISI is an attempt by economically less-developed countries to break out of the world division of labor which had emerged in the nineteenth century and the early part of the twentieth century. Under this division, Latin America (and most areas of Asia and Africa) specialized in the export of food and raw materials, while importing manufactured goods from Europe and the United States. Import substitution consists of establishing domestic production facilities to manufacture goods which were formerly imported. It follows that all countries which industrialized after Great Britain, went through a stage of ISI; that is, all passed through a stage where the larger part of investment in industries was undertaken to replace imports. ISI would

* The author wishes to thank David Felix, Andrea Maneschi, Carlos M. Pelaez, William Steel, and William O. Thweatt for many useful suggestions.

come to a close when most investment was channeled towards the construction of capacity to produce for new incremental demand.

The ISI wave in Europe and the United States occurred in the middle and second half of the nineteenth century.[1] It is a well-known fact that in this early ISI process governments played an active role in encouraging and protecting the development of infant industries. Another characteristic of nineteenth century ISI is its "national" character. Although in some countries finance for infrastructure investment was obtained from abroad, industries were for the most part in domestic hands, while the design of machines and skilled manpower to run them were often imported from England in the early industrialization period.

Once Western Europe and the United States had undergone their initial industrializations, import substitution did not come entirely to an end. However, it ceased being mainly a mechanism of industrialization, and became in the twentieth century part of a continuing process of growth and of a changing pattern of industrial specialization among economically advanced countries.[2]

There are various historical reasons why the countries of Africa, Asia and Latin America did not undergo ISI at the time of, or right after, the European ISI's. Colonial policies of European countries provide much of the explanation for the former two cases, while socio-economic structure helps explain the Latin American case. The presence of attractive external markets for the region's primary exports, which benefited the elites, meant that there was little political desire to change the structure of the economies. Also in the nineteenth century and early part of the twentieth century, Latin American countries did not have the entrepreneurial classes, labor force, infrastructure, market size, or administrative capacity to cope with an extensive industrialization process. Also in the case of some countries, like Brazil, European powers had enough leverage to force governments to maintain free trade policies, thus in effect blocking any possibility of ISI.[3]

ISI BEFORE AND DURING THE SECOND WORLD WAR

Latin America was not completely devoid of manufacturing activities prior to World War I. It has by now been well documented that in the latter part of the nineteenth century workshops and small factories in textiles and food products industries had developed in some parts of Argentina, Brazil, Mexico and other larger countries. Also, machine tools and spare parts workshops developed to service railroads, sugar refining mills, etc.[4] These activities were usually started by importers of equipment. There were some isolated attempts to raise tariffs both to protect incipient industries and to stimulate the creation of new ones.[5] It would be mistaken, however, to speak of "industrialization" prior to World War I. The bulk of manufactured goods consumed in Latin America were either imported or produced by small domestic workshops, while exports consisted almost entirely of primary products.[6] Except for Argentina, the population was primarily rural, and the primary export sector was the pacesetter of economic activity, while workshops and small industries were appendages to general economic activity.

It should be noted, however, that on the eve of World War I the primary export sector with its complementary activities in services (banking, merchandizing, government) and social infrastructure (communication, transportation, etc.) had in many Latin American countries created a fairly substantial middle class which consumed large quantities of imported manufactured consumer goods.

ISI INDUCED FROM ABROAD

World War I, the Great Depression of the Thirties and World War II induced pronounced spurts of ISI in most larger Latin American countries.[7] The interruption of shipping and the decline of non-military production in Europe and the United States during World War I created severe shortages of imported manufactured goods in Latin America, raised relative prices of such goods, and increased profitability of ISI investment. Textiles, food products, and various other light consumer goods industries were the principal fields of ISI in that period. In the Twenties many of these newly created ISI industries stagnated because of renewed U. S. and European competition and the general refusal of policy makers to protect infant industries of recent vintage. It was generally thought that World War I had been an aberration from the natural order of things, which was reflected in the world division of labor of the nineteenth century. Hence policy makers were reluctant to tamper with a movement back to "normalcy."[8]

The depression of the Thirties resulted in renewed shortages of imported goods. The fall of foreign exchange receipts from exports forced most countries of the region drastically to curtail imports. The decline resulted at first in increased use of productive capacity which had been underutilized in the Twenties, and later in the creation of new industrial capacity.[9] As in World War I, the depression-induced ISI occurred primarily in light consumer goods industries, although in some cases, especially Brazil,[10] steel and capital goods industries were developed on a relatively small scale.

World War II had a stimulating effect on ISI industries: shortages of foreign manufactured goods led to full utilization of industrial capacity;[11] some investment in new capacity occurred when capital goods could be imported; and even some textile products were exported by Argentina, Brazil, and Mexico.

ISI IN THE FIFTIES AND SIXTIES

But it was only after World War II that ISI became a deliberate policy tool for economic development. Most of the larger countries of Latin America implicitly or explicitly accepted the ECLA analysis of the hopelessness of gearing their economies towards the traditional world division of labor.[12] Continued reliance on the export of food and primary products was thought to be precarious because of the instability of such exports, which would not be conducive to long term development because of the relatively slow growth of world demand for such products.[13] It was thought that ISI would introduce a dynamic element into the Latin American economies and increase their rates of growth. The latter were deemed essential to deal with the population explosion of the region and to meet the demands of the increasingly urban population for the ways of life of the masses in more advanced countries. It was also thought that ISI would bring greater economic independence to Latin American countries: self-sufficiency in manufactured goods would place Latin American economies less at the mercy of the world economy.

The principal policy instruments used to promote and intensify ISI were: protective tariffs and/or exchange controls; special preferences for domestic and foreign firms importing capital goods for new industries; preferential import exchange rates for industrial raw materials, fuels and intermediate goods; cheap loans by government development banks for favored industries; the construction by governments of infrastructure especially designed to complement industries; and the direct participation of government in certain industries, especially the heavier industries, such as steel, where neither domestic nor foreign private capital was willing or able to invest.[14]

The promotion of ISI industries was indiscriminate, that is, there were not attempts to concentrate on industrial sectors which might have had a potential comparative advantage. In some countries ISI occurred for considerable periods of time in consumer goods industries only. A concise summary is given by David Felix: ". . . the initial industries are generally consumer goods or building materials producers with a relatively simple technology and a low capital requirement per worker and per unit of output. They are then followed by consumer goods industries requiring a more sophisticated technology and larger capital outlay, shading subsequently into industries producing relatively complex consumer durables, steel, engineering and chemical products."[15] This description is especially relevant in the cases of countries such as Argentina, Chile, Venezuela. In other countries, especially Brazil, the government was anxious to promote maximum vertical integration, i.e., to promote both final consumer goods industries and intermediate and capital goods sectors.

In some cases, where the initial thrust of ISI was on final consumer goods industries, a built-in resistance to backward vertical integration developed.[16] That is, firms which established themselves in the first ISI period pressured governments not to develop domestic intermediate and capital goods industries, since these would produce inputs at substantially higher prices than imported inputs. However, as the areas for further ISI declined, most countries pressed on with backward integration efforts.

An important feature of Latin American ISI in the Fifties and Sixties was the participation of foreign capital. Although its proportion of total savings was often substantially below 10 per cent, it was instrumental in setting up key manufacturing industries by transferring know-how and organizational capabilities. This was also true in infrastructure investments and heavy industries owned by governments, which depended on foreign financing and technical aid.[17]

THE RESULTS OF ISI

Tables 1 through 5 present a summary of the impact of ISI on the principal economies of the region and on the Latin American economy as a whole. In Table 1 we have various measures of the changes in the percentage distribution of the Gross Domestic Product. It should be noted that for countries where the data are available,

TABLE 1

Changes in the Structure of the Economies of Selected Countries
(Percentage Distribution of Gross Domestic Product According to Principal Sectors)

ARGENTINA

	1960 Prices		1937 Prices	
	1927–9	1963–5	1927–9	1963–5
Agriculture	27.4	17.1	30.5	18.4
Oil & Mining	0.3	1.5	0.6	3.5
Manufacturing	23.6	33.7	13.4	18.6
Construction	4.2	3.6	3.1	2.6

Source: Díaz-Alejandro, *Essays.*

BRAZIL

	Current Prices					1953 Prices			
	1939	1947	1953	1960	1968	1947	1953	1960	1968
Agriculture	25.8	27.6	26.1	22.6	17.9	30.0	26.1	22.2	20.5
Industry	19.4	19.8	23.7	25.2	28.0	20.6	23.7	28.0	29.3
Other	54.8	52.6	50.2	52.2	54.1	49.4	50.2	49.8	50.2

Source: Fundação Getulio Vargas, Centro de Contas Nacionais.

MEXICO

	Current Prices					
	1900	1910	1930	1940	1950	1960
Rural	34.6	27.9	25.9	24.3	22.5	18.9
Extractive	6.4	9.1	13.5	8.5	5.7	5.4
Commerce & Transp.	23.4	23.4	23.4	28.5	31.0	30.6
Mfg., Construc. & Elec.	13.2	13.7	16.7	22.6	24.5	27.7

Source: Reynolds, *Mexican Economy.*

LATIN AMERICA

	Current Prices		Annual Rates of Growth		
	1950	1967	1950–60	1960–67	1950–67
Produc. of Goods	52.4	52.3	4.9	4.6	4.8
Agriculture	25.2	20.5	3.5	3.5	3.5
Mining	4.1	4.4	6.1	4.1	5.3
Manufacturing	19.6	24.1	6.2	5.8	6.0
Construction	3.5	3.3	4.6	4.1	4.4
Basic Services	7.2	8.3	5.5	5.7	5.6
Other Services	40.4	39.4	4.8	4.4	4.6
Commerce & Finance	18.0	18.8	5.1	4.9	5.0
Misc. Services	22.4	20.6	4.5	3.9	4.2
Total	100.0	100.0	4.9	4.6	4.8

Source: Naciones Unidas, CEPAL, *Estudio económico de América Latina, 1968* (New York, 1969), p. 18.

TABLE 2

a) *Distribution of Economically Active Population*
(per cent distribution)

ARGENTINA

	1925–9	1960–1
Rural Sector	35.7	21.7
Oil and Mining	0.3	0.6
Manufacutring	22.0	26.0
Construction	5.5	6.0
Public Utilities	0.5	0.8
Transport	4.6	5.7
Communications	0.5	1.0
Commerce, Finance and Housing	13.6	14.3
Government Services	4.6	10.4
Other Services	12.6	13.6

Source: Díaz-Alejandro, *Essay.*

BRAZIL

	1940	1950	1960
Primary	71.0	64.4	58.5
Secondary	8.9	12.9	12.7
Tertiary	20.1	22.7	28.8
Total	100.0	100.0	100.0

Source: Various Brazilian Demographic Censuses.

MEXICO

	1910	1940	1950	1960
Agriculture	67.1	65.4	58.3	54.1
Mining	1.9	1.7	1.2	1.2
Mfg., Construc. & Power	13.1	11.0	14.8	17.7
Services	17.8	21.9	25.7	27.0
Total	100.0	100.0	100.0	100.0

Source: Reynolds, *Mexican Economy.*

LATIN AMERICA

	1950	1960	1965	1969
Agriculture	53.4	47.2	44.5	42.2
Mining	1.1	1.0	1.0	1.0
Manufacturing	14.4	14.4	14.0	13.8
(artisan)	(7.5)	(6.8)	(6.4)	(6.1)
Construction	3.8	4.1	3.9	4.5
Basic Services	4.2	5.1	5.3	5.5
Other Services	23.1	28.2	31.3	33.0
(commerce & finance)	(7.8)	(9.0)	(9.5)	(10.1)
Total	100.0	100.0	100.0	100.0

Source: CEPAL, 1969.

b) *Growth of Employment by Sectors and Population Growth*
(yearly rates of growth)

	Employment Growth			Population Growth	
	1950–60	1960–69		1950–60	1960–69
Agriculture	1.3	1.5	Total	2.8	2.9
Manufacturing	2.6	2.3	Urban	4.8	4.4
(artisan)	(1.5)	(1.6)	Rural	1.4	1.4
Mining	2.0	2.2			
Construction	3.2	4.0			
Basic Services	4.6	3.4			
Other Services	4.7	4.6			

Source: CEPAL, 1968.

industry already represented a significant proportion of GDP in the earlier decades of the century.[18] However, as mentioned earlier, these industries consisted to a large extent of small workshops; in 1950 still over half of the work force in manufacturing was engaged in artisan-type of activities (see Table 2a). By the Sixties, industry had become the dominant sector in Argentina, Brazil, Mexico, and Chile. The annual rates of growth of various sectors shown in Table 1 indicate the extent to which industry was the pace setter in the post-World War II decades. We shall comment later on the other tables.

CRITIQUES OF ISI

Let us now turn to the various critiques which have been made of Latin American ISI. The critics can be divided into two groups which I shall designate as the "market critics" and the "structural critics." Although some arguments are common to both sets of critics, there is a certain philosophic-analytical similarity of the views within each camp which seem to justify the division I have made.

a) The Market Critics

Many economists in this category view Latin America's ISI as an inefficient way of using resources to develop the region's countries.[19] The more conservative economists believe that since world production can be best be maximized by having each country (or area of the world) specialize in the sectors where it has the greatest comparative advantage, Latin America should have continued to specialize in the

TABLE 3

a) *Real Rate of Growth (annual) by Sectors for Latin America and Selected Countries*

	1955–60	1960–65	1955–60	1960–65	1955–60	1960–65
	Latin America		Argentina		Brazil	
Agriculture	2.7	4.8	—0.4	2.1	3.7	6.9
Manufacturing	6.6	5.6	3.8	4.1	10.3	4.9
Construction	4.2	5.9	4.3	2.0	7.2	2.8
	Chile		Mexico		Colombia	
Agriculture	2.3	3.1	3.0	3.9	3.5	3.0
Manufacturing	3.2	6.7	8.1	8.0	6.1	5.9
Construction	1.4	4.6	8.1	5.9	—0.2	1.9

Source: Naciones Unidas, *Estudio económico de América Latina, 1965.*

b) *Latin America: Growth Rates of the Total Gross Domestic Product and of Industrial Product (Annual Cumulative Rates)*

	Total Product	Industrial Product
1940–50	5.0	6.8
1950–60	4.7	6.3
1960–68	4.5	5.4

Source: United Nations, *Economic Bulletin for Latin America,* Second Half of 1969.

TABLE 4

a) *Growth of Urban Population and Industrial Employment*
(Average Annual Rates of Growth: 1950–60)

	Urban Population	Industrial Employment
Argentina	3.0	1.7
Brazil	6.5	2.6
Mexico	5.6	4.8

Source: Table in Little, Scitovsky, and Scott, *Industry and Trade*, p. 84.

b) *Growth of Industrial Product and Industrial Employment*
(Annual Growth Rates: 1950–68)

	Industrial Product	Industrial Employment
Argentina	4.5	2.2
Brazil	7.3	2.2
Colombia	6.2	2.4
Chile	4.6	2.2
Peru	7.8	3.4
Mexico	6.7	4.7
Latin America	6.0	2.8

Source: Raúl Prebisch, *Transformación y desarrollo: la gran tarea de América Latina,* (Washington, D.C., 1970), p. 45.

production of primary products. This specialization would have maximized world output and made possible a higher income level in all parts of the world.

Because of the declining share of food and primary products in world trade, more moderate critics recognize the need for some ISI.[20] But they criticize the indiscriminate way in which ISI was carried on, that is, by across-the-board promotion of industries without regard even to potential comparative advantage. The Latin American ISI strategies are seen as drives towards national self-sufficiency in total disregard of the advantages of an international division of labor along newer lines. This emphasis on autarky is seen as prejudicial to rapid economic growth for a number of reasons.

Given small markets, limited capital, and a dearth of skilled manpower, autarkic industrial growth leads to the development of inefficient and high-cost industries. The situation becomes especially pronounced in industries having high fixed costs. These industries require large-scale output in order to bring costs down to levels prevailing in more advanced industrial countries. Outstanding examples are the steel and automobile industries which have been established in most of the larger Latin American countries. In the case of automobiles, the situation was worsened because a large number of these countries permitted the establishment of many firms, thus completely eliminating the possibilities of economies of large scale production. In the late Sixties, the annual output of cars and trucks in eight Latin American countries was 600,000, which was produced by ninety firms (an average of 6,700 per firm).[21] The situation is well summarized by Scitovsky: "Protection usually confines the protected manufacturer to the domestic market and so inhibits the exploitation of

TABLE 5

a) *Latin America's Participation in World Trade*
(Latin America's Exports as a Per Cent of World Exports)

1948—10.9%	1960—7.0%
1950—10.6%	1964—6.4%
1957— 7.8%	1968—5.0%

Source: *Regional Integration and the Trade of Latin America,* Committee for Economic Development, Jan. 1968; and *International Trade, 1968,* GATT.

b) *Changes in Latin America's Import Coefficients*
(Value of Imports of Goods and Services as a Per Cent of GDP)

	1928	1938	1948–9	1957–8	1962	1960*	1967*
Argentina	17.8	12.1	11.2	5.8	7.1	8.0	6.6
Brazil	11.3	6.2	6.6	5.8	4.5	7.8	5.6
Chile	31.2	14.9	11.5	9.5	11.3	15.7	15.7
Colombia	18.0	11.0	10.6	8.2	8.8	12.2	8.8
Mexico	14.2	7.0	8.5	7.8	6.8	7.8	7.8
Peru			9.6	16.1	13.6	19.0	28.1
Latin America			10.2	9.9	8.7	10.0	9.9

Source: Joseph Grunwald and Philip Musgrove, *Natural Resources in Latin American Development* (Baltimore, 1970), p. 20.
* CEPAL, 1968.

c) *Imports as a Percentage of Total Supplies by Categories*

	Consumers' Goods	Intermediate Goods	Capital Goods
Brazil			
1949	9.0	25.9	63.7
1955	2.9	17.9	43.2
1959	1.9	11.7	32.9
1964	1.3	6.6	9.8
Mexico			
1950	2.4	13.2	66.5
1955	2.3	n.a.	63.4
1960	1.3	10.4	54.9
1965	n.a.	9.9	59.8

Source: Little, Scitovsky, and Scott, *Industry and Trade,* p. 60.

economies of scale, especially in small countries and in industries where scale economies are important and call for very large-scale operations. Moreover, governments anxious to secure the benefits of competition often encourage many firms to enter industry in order to create domestic competition where protectionist policies have suspended foreign competition." The result, however, is contrary to what is aimed for, since such government policy ". . . restricts the scope for economies of scale yet further and often leads to the emergence of too many firms, each with too small an output capacity, and frequently with too small a market to utilize fully even that capacity."[22]

In the last few years the concept of "effective protection" has been used by numerous economists to analyze distortions which have arisen during the ISI process. Nominal tariff rates measure only the percentage by which prices of protected goods exceed their world prices. This amount is also the difference by which domestic substitutes can exceed the international price. The "effective" tariff or rate of protection ". . . shows the percentage by which the value added at a stage of fabrication in domestic industry can exceed what this would be in the absence of protection; in other words, it shows by what percentage the sum of wages, profits, and depreciation allowances, payable by domestic firms can, thanks to protection, exceed what this sum would be if the same firms were fully exposed to foreign competition."[23] Thus, if a product uses a considerable amount of imported inputs on which there is no tariff or on which the tariff rate is lower than the tariff on the finished product, protection is higher than is indicated by the nominal tariff, since the margin available for domestic value added is larger than the difference indicated by the tariff. In a number of Latin American countries the effective tariff on consumer goods was found to be much higher than for intermediate or capital goods.[24] Such high levels of effective protection eliminate incentives to increase production efficiency and make it difficult to bring the cost of production to international levels.

The stress on autarky—on maximizing internal vertical industrial integration (promoting not only final goods production, but also intermediate and capital goods)—impedes growth because resources are not used in sectors where they will produce the highest possible output. Had Latin American countries specialized in only a few products with the greatest potential comparative advantage, and exported a large surplus while importing other goods, total output available would have been higher and these nations would have grown more rapidly than they actually did. As it happened, autarky was practiced in each country, and no attempt was made until the late Sixties to at least promote ISI on a regional basis; in other words, to promote a complementary industrial structure within Latin America.

A study by Baranson of automobile industries in developing countries (which includes information on Argentina, Brazil, and Mexico) illustrates many of the problems of autarkic development. He contrasts the proliferation of automobile firms in developing countries with the quest by European producers for increased exports and consolidation with competitors, both inside and outside their countries, in order to keep down unit cost.[25] He finds that among the main deficiencies are ". . . underdeveloped supplier capacities, inadequate quality control systems, and a dearth of qualified technicians and managers. By creating a 'sellers' market', protection and import substitution tend to undermine quality."[26] Thus, Baranson found that many ". . . basic materials that are considered standard stock in open economies often must be procured locally or specially ordered in small batches at considerably higher cost or at inferior quality. . . . Lack of uniformity in raw materials and semi-finished goods such as castings and forgings creates special problems in milling and machining to required specifications. In high-volume production, precision and uniformity are built into automated equipment. Developing countries with limited markets are much more dependent upon the very machine labor skills in which they are deficient." Also, considering the many parts which go into an automobile, Baranson found that outside plant procurement averages about 60 per cent by value in advanced economies, while in countries like Mexico and Brazil this factor amounts to only 40 per cent. Such a condition further reduces the possibility of economies of large scale production.[27] As a result, Baranson found that factory costs in Argentina, Brazil, and Mexico were about 60 per cent to 150 per cent higher than in the United States.[28]

Similar problems were found in many other industries. A study of the manufacture of heavy electrical equipment in developing countries found that in Argentina ". . . excessive diversification, unused capacity, large inventories because of import controls, and difficulties in obtaining outside finance explain the high price level. . . ."[29] ECLA has also provided numerous illustrations of the problems discussed above. It found that in 1964, ". . . the paper industry (excluding newsprint) had 292 plants of which only 25 had a capacity of 100 tons daily, which is considered the minimum economic size. In the chemical industry, too, there are a great many instances in which there is a wide gap between the plant sizes most frequently found in the region and the sizes constructed in the industrialized countries."[30]

Some economists have been concerned about the domestic resource cost involved in the type of ISI which has been promoted in Latin America. They have stressed the need to calculate for various industries the value of domestic resources required to save a unit of foreign exchange. The rate of transformation between domestic and foreign resources thus obtained should be compared to the appropriate exchange rate.[31] The higher the former is over the latter, the greater presumably is the "waste" of resources; that is, if domestic resources had been used for export purposes, the foreign exchange earned would have fetched more goods than the goods produced by using the resources domestically.[32]

Policies employed to stimulate industries have often been prejudicial to the functioning of the more traditional agricultural sector. The allocation of investment resources (credit) to new industries has often meant that few resources were available to increase agricultural efficiency. Overvalued exchange rates, which favored industries by providing cheap imported inputs, hurt agriculture by making its goods less competitive on the international market and/or by making it less profitable to export agricultural products. Finally, the combination of higher industrial prices caused by protection and by price control of agricultural goods, turned the internal terms of trade against agriculture. All these factors hurt agricultural production and exports. Argentina is probably the outstanding example of ISI occurring to the detriment of agriculture and agricultural exports.[33]

Critics have also pointed to the detrimental results of neglecting exports during the heyday of ISI. Some stress the negative effects of ISI policies on the production and exportation of traditional goods, while others emphasize the failure to diversify the export structure in accordance with the changing internal economic structure which ISI brought about. While, as was mentioned earlier, the contribution of industry to GDP became dominant in the years after World War II, the commodity composition of Latin America's exports remained almost unchanged. For example, in the late Sixties, over 90 per cent of Argentina and Brazil's exports still consisted of traditional primary and food products, while about three-quarters of Mexico's exports consisted of such products. Until the Sixties, little efforts were made by Latin American countries to stimulate non-traditional exports. And while in the early Sixties the development of the Latin American Common Market, the Central American Common Market, the introduction of drawbacks and rebates on domestic taxes for export efforts in some countries (Argentina, Mexico, Colombia) represented attempts to stimulate non-traditional exports, the net effects by the late Sixties were still slight.

The neglect of exports during the ISI period in Latin America, that is, the failure to stimulate traditional exports and to diversify the export structure, could have serious consequences. The original advocates of ISI had hoped that their policy would lead Latin American countries to greater self-sufficiency and would make their economies more independent of the vicissitudes of international trade. It appears, however, that there is a lower limit to the import coefficient (import/GDP ratio) for most economies, as becomes clear by examining Table 5(b). While ISI was taking place, not only was the import coefficient reduced,[34] but the commodity composition of imports changed. An increasingly larger proportion of imports consisted of raw materials, semi-finished products, and capital goods. These represented the inputs of the ISI industries which were not available domestically, and were thus the principal reason for the increasing downward stickiness of the import coefficient.[35]

It is thus ironic that the net result of ISI has been to place Latin American countries in a new and more dangerous dependency relationship with the more advanced industrial countries than ever before. In former times, a decline in export receipts acted as a stimulus to ISI. Under the circumstances, a decline in export receipts not counterbalanced by capital inflows can result in forced import curtailments which, in turn, could cause an industrial recession. Such results have been experienced by Argentina and Colombia, and other countries face the same danger.

To guard against such a situation, Latin American countries would have to make increasing efforts to diversify exports. Such actions, however, assume that they are able to compete in the international market. Considering the high cost structure of many Latin American ISI industries, the many bureaucratic obstacles exporters have faced, and the lack of an adequate credit mechanism to export manufactured goods, export diversification is not an easy task.[37]

b) Structural Critics

Since World War II, most Latin American countries have experienced a population explosion. Annual population growth for the entire region increased from 1.9 per cent to over 2.8 per cent in the late Fifties and Sixties. During the same period, migration from the countryside to the cities increased dramatically. One may see in Table 2(b) that the urban population growth rate in the post-World War II period was over three times as large as the rural growth rate. The same table also shows that the rate of labor absorption in industry was substantially smaller than the rate of growth of urban population. In Table 2(a), it is clear that after two decades of industrialization, the proportion of the labor force employed in manufacturing industry in Latin America as a whole actually declined somewhat, and that almost half of these workers were still engaged in artisan workshops. In some of the individual countries shown, the proportion rose a few points, but very modestly compared to the changes in the contribution of industry to GDP. The failure of ISI to create direct employment opportunities has worried both "structural" and "market" critics.[38]

The latter blame the low labor absorption rate on price distortions. Most countries used certain types of subsidies to capital in order to stimulate industrialization. In a number of countries, domestic and foreign firms were given special exchange rate privileges to import capital equipment. Development banks gave cheap credit (often at negative real rates of interest) to help finance investment in favored industries. At the same time, wages in industry were relatively high because of labor legislation which had been introduced in the Thirties and Forties in such countries as Argentina, Brazil, and Chile. Thus, there were no incentives to adopt labor-intensive techniques of production. On the contrary, the relative price structure of capital and labor was such as to actually stimulate the search for and adoption of capital-intensive techniques.[39]

The structural critics of ISI worry about low labor absorption rates not only because of the services social problems of urban unemployment or underemployment which result, but also because of their implication for income distribution. With an unequal distribution of income, a fiscal system which does not redistribute income, and a leading growth sector (industry) whose incremental capital/labor ratio is high (usually substantially higher than the economy's average capital/labor ratio), the tendency will be for income to become even more concentrated than before. The evidence available for Latin American countries tends to confirm this trend.[40]

Because of the concentration of income, the growth of demand for industrial products may not be sufficient to maintain the initial ISI momentum. What makes this situation worse is the lumpiness of many ISI industries. Because of indivisibilities, many industries were forced to build substantially ahead of demand. Thus, the existence of excess capacity which is not being rapidly filled by growing demand dampens the incentive to invest.[41]

This situation could, of course, be avoided by various types of redistributive policies of governments—redistribution by income groups, by sectors of the economy, and by regions. Progressive tax measures and/or appropriate wage policies could be used to redistribute incomes among social groups; government credit and fiscal policies could redirect resources to neglected sectors (such as agriculture, housing, road building) and geographical regions.

Potential domestic demand for industrial products exists in most Latin American countries because the ISI process occurred in an unbalanced fashion. We have already mentioned the trends towards the concentration of income which could be reversed by appropriate policies and thus result in considerable demand expansion. However, there were other imbalances. As ISI proceeded, such sectors as agriculture, low income housing, transportation, and other infrastructure facilities were often neglected, threatening countries with severe bottlenecks. In the larger countries, ISI resulted in a strong regional concentration of industry and income, especially in Brazil, Mexico, and Argentina. Although such regional concentration made sense when taking into account external economies to firms settling close to suppliers, to decent infrastructure facilities, and to skilled labor supplies, etc.,[42] it was of a self-reinforcing nature. Increasing regional concentration of wealth presented many countries with the political need to redistribute income on a regional basis. All these forces make it possible to generate new demand through government policies.[43]

Georgescu-Roegen, however, called attention to a problem which might arise from post-ISI redistribution efforts.[44] The profile of the productive structure which resulted from the ISI process reflects the demand profile which existed at the time when the process was started. This demand profile was based on a distribution of income which, in most cases, was quite unequal. Efforts to change the distribution of income in the post-ISI era in order to achieve greater social justice, increase aggregate demand, diminish inter-sectoral and/or inter-regional imbalances, will change the demand profile. Such changes could result in a substantial amount of imbalance or lack of synchronization between the country's productive and demand profiles. The degree of such imbalance depends, of course, on the flexibility of various productive sectors. For example, to what extent can the productive facilities of the consumer goods and capital goods industries be converted from producing luxury goods to producing mass consumption goods?

The greater the inflexibility of the country's productive structure, the greater the "structural-lock" dilemma of the country. Thus, the full use of the existing productive capacity would imply the necessity for the type of income distribution which would produce the requisite demand profile, i.e., a very unequal distribution of income.[45] The alternative, a more egalitarian distribution of income, might imply considerable capacity in a number of industries.[46]

This "structural lock" dilemma should be set off, however, against the import constraint problem. It has been claimed that high income inequality encourages a more import-intensive demand profile. That is, higher income groups consume technically more sophisticated goods which have relatively high direct and indirect import requirements. Thus, although a greater degree of income concentration could avoid a "structural lock" problem, it could lead to stagnation caused by import constraints.[47]

EVALUATION AND OUTLOOK FOR THE FUTURE

In my general attitude towards the critiques which I have summarized, I fully subscribe to the views of Bergsman and Candal in their evaluation of the Brazilian ISI experience: "Hindsight makes it easy to point out specific mistakes, even to suggest some modifications in policy that clearly would have avoided the greatest inefficiencies. It is much harder to compare actual results with those that might have come from some totally different policy that would not have included industrialization.[48]

It is clear that in most, if not all, Latin American countries, industrialization was carried out on too wide a spectrum, given limited capital and human resources and very narrow markets. Also, excessively high effective protection did not lead resources into fields which would have the highest possible potential comparative advantage, and protection gave a comfortable enough profit margin to all inside the market to neglect the search for greater efficiency. However, outright condemnation of inefficiencies has to be qualified. For political reasons, ISI within the context of a larger Latin American Common Market was not feasible in the immediate postwar period. A more specialized export-oriented ISI not only depended on the possibilities of Latin American economic integration, but also on the willingness of the United States and Europe to accept Latin American manufactured imports. If one admits that an international division of labor can no longer be based on nineteenth century lines (given the relative decline of primary products in world trade), one has to expect structural changes in both the developing and the developed parts of the world. For example, one would expect the United States and Europe to accept a decline in the textile industry in order to make room for such imports from the Third World. Given the unwillingness to do this, one should temper one's condemnation of Latin American countries for not being more selective in their choice of industries.[49] This does not excuse the proliferation of many firms in small markets (e.g., automobiles) which produced unnecessary high costs.

Many economists have the bad habit of generalizing from limited experience and evidence. This is especially true in the ISI discussions. The development of an integrated industrial structure might not make much sense in a small country like Chile, while it does make some sense in a country like Brazil. Although an elegant argument about industrialization having been promoted at the expense of agriculture can be made with empirical evidence from Argentina, it would be difficult to apply this argument to the Brazilian case. Coffee output was not sacrificed for the sake of industrialization.[50]

The explanation of the labor-absorption problem in terms of factor price distortion is based on good deductive reasoning in economic theory, but there is little empirical evidence to back the explanation. In some industries the technological choices are limited.[51] In most Latin American automobile industries the equipment installed was second hand and thus the assembly line operations are technologically substantially behind the more automated plants in Europe and the United States. The equipment in most of Latin America's textile industries is so old that various missions have recommended a thoroughgoing modernization in order to make these industries profitable and competitive. There exists, of course, the possibility of placing greater efforts in discovering more labor-intensive techniques, which might be achieved if Latin American countries would increase the resources earmarked for scientific and technological research. Only 0.5 per cent of Latin America's GNP goes into such efforts, as compared to over 3 per cent for the United States.[52] It remains doubtful, however, whether price distortions explain Latin America's labor absorption problem.

Although the argument about the necessity for export diversification is well taken, the pontification of many economists concerning the past neglect of industrial exports is open to some criticisms. It seems that many forget that a large number of the key manufacturing industries of Latin America were constructed by or with the aid of foreign capital. The chief attraction of the latter was the promise of a growing protected market. It might have been rather difficult to convince firms to establish themselves in Brazil, Argentina, and other countries on the condition that from the beginning 40 to 50 per cent of the output should be exported. Had there been a genuine interest by domestic and foreign firms to export manufactured goods, I suspect that the bureaucratic and exchange rate obstacles to such exports might have fallen earlier.

It could also be asserted that the high-cost structure of Latin America's industries makes export diversification difficult. Here, of course, there might be a dilemma. If the high-cost structure is in large part caused by the narrow market which raises unit costs, only increased sales could reduce the latter. And thus we might face an interesting chicken-egg problem. But even if this could be resolved through subsidies, exports of manufactured goods would still have to face non-price competitive factors such as credit terms, brand names, delivery terms, marketing organizations, etc. Since the importance of price vs. non-price competition in the international trade of manufactured and capital goods has never been firmly established, it is difficult to claim that the high cost structure is one of the principal barriers to export diversification. We have already mentioned the political problem of penetrating European and American markets.

Since most economists' intellectual energies in the last few decades have been spent worrying about the efficient allocation of resources, it is natural that those economists who have devoted their attention to developing countries should have spent most of their time examining and recommending how factors of production are or should be allocated. Relatively little thought was given to the fact that concern about development should include concern about the development of factors of production, not just their allocation. The many "inefficiencies" might prevent a developing country undergoing ISI from realizing its maximum crude growth rate in the short-run. This cost has to be weighed against the modernization or development which ISI brings about.[53] Little work along these lines, that is, on the measurement of changes in the quality of factors of production, has been done in Latin America or in other parts of the developing world.

FUTURE POLICIES

By the late Sixties many Latin American countries were taking measures to eliminate some of the grosser distortions which ISI had brought along. In a number of countries the tariff level was brought down (e. g., Brazil, Argentina). This was not done to encourage more imports, but to decrease the level of effective protection and monopoly profits and thus give an incentive to firms to rationalize their operations. Measures were taken in such countries as Brazil, Argentina, and Peru to reduce the number of automobile firms and thus encourage lower cost production by scale economies.

There has been a constant effort by ECLA and the Inter-American Development Bank to push for greater economic integration via the Latin American Common Market. It is hoped that such integration would increase and diversify the exports of individual countries and that there would also result a rationalization of production throughout the continent by making the Latin American economies more complementary to each other. Besides trade in finished goods, attempts have been made to encourage "complementation agreements," in which there would be a division of labor along vertical lines (for example, the Chilean automobile industry specializing in the production of certain parts which would be assembled in Brazil).[54] Unfortunately this process has not made as much progress as its advocates had hoped. It seems that a division of labor within Latin America would not necessarily result in national economic structures which would be to the liking of individual countries.[55]

The problem of post-ISI stagnation, i.e., the finding of a new dynamic source of growth, has preoccupied many Latin American governments as the decade of the Seventies opened. In Brazil the government of President Emilio Medici has stated that its principal aim would be to develop a "program of social integration" which would increase the labor force participation in the national product, to develop the internal frontier of Amazonia, and to begin a gigantic road building program which would more effectively link various regions of the country and better link farming areas to markets. Peru is currently experiencing some drastic social reforms—land reform, programs of worker profit-sharing schemes, etc. The new Mexican president has also emphasized the need for income redistribution.

It remains to be seen if a redistribution of income and a growth of industrial exports will provide the same dynamism to the Latin American economies as the period of ISI.[56] Turning from the demand to the supply side, one should also consider the effects of high population growth rates and social equity policies on the capital/output ratio. The latter will probably be much higher than in the past, which means that the growth produced by each unit of investment will be lower than in the past. Thus many economies in the future might have to balance the conflicting claims arising from the need for higher saving to attain growth rates similar to those in the ISI days, and the pressures for more egalitarian socio-economic policies which tend to depress the capacity to save.

The employment problem will probably be the most difficult to cope with. At this writing it is doubtful that industry will be able to absorb a substantially larger proportion of the economically active population. Can the service sector effectively make use of the burgeoning urban masses? Can agrarian reforms be instituted in such a manner as to absorb manpower, or will agricultural modernization of necessity have to result in an increased expulsion of labor from the countryside? Even if there is no food problem, is there any possible economic structure in Latin America which will effectively employ all those who are employable? Or is the only solution to the dilemma the development of a population policy? These are probably the most interesting questions which economists doing relevant work in Latin America will have to struggle with in the Seventies.

NOTES

1. For an interesting analysis of continental Europe's emulation of England's industrial develop-

ment during the nineteenth century, see David S. Landes, "Technological Change and Development in Western Europe, 1750–1914," In: *The Cambridge Economic History of Europe,* H. J. Habakkuk and M. Postan, eds., VI: 274–601 (Cambridge, England, 1966). The description Landes gives of the effects of the Napoleonic wars sounds quite familiar to contemporary students of import substitution: "To be sure, war and isolation had some favourable effects. . . . Technology, for example, was stimulated by the need to create substitutes for overseas imports. . . . The trouble was that not all of these wartime anomalies were ready to disappear once peace returned. For every substitute that died quietly . . . another remained as a vested interest. . . . Thus mechanized textile manufacture in central Europe, essentially a product of wartime shortages, made a strong effort to convert monetary advantage into permanent privilege, with some success . . ." (373).

2. The importance of trade relations, i.e., division of labor, among industrialized countries is demonstrated by the following data on trade among these countries as a proportion of world trade:

1953—31.7% 1960—42.3% 1965—46.8% 1968—49.3%

(Source: Annual Reports of GATT—*International Trade.*)

For perceptive explanations of changes in trade specialization among developed countries, see Raymond Vernon, "International Investment and International Trade in the Product Cycle," *The Quarterly Journal of Economics* (QJE) (May 1966); Albert O. Hirschman, *National Power and the Structure of Foreign Trade* (Berkeley and Los Angeles, 1945; reprinted 1969).

3. Stanley Stein and Barbara Stein, *The Colonial Heritage of Latin America* (New York, 1970), have succinctly summarized the main obstacles to earlier industrialization in Latin America:

> Ex-colonies, then and now, cannot readily shed the economic legacy of centuries of colonialism, they cannot rapidly close the gap between backwardness and modernity, between primitive and advanced technology, between low and high levels of income, saving, and investment, between literacy and illiteracy, between obscurantism and enlightenment, between closed and open society. . . . It is not surprising, then, that Latin America did not begin to modernize its economy through industrialization until a century after independence. Under these circumstances the major consequence of the anti-colonial movements in Latin America between 1810 and 1824, the crushing of the ties of the transatlantic empire led . . . to neo-colonialism. . . . We can see how the economic growth of Latin America through diversification and industrialization could not occur while colonial patterns of production, capital accumulation and investment, income distribution and expenditure survived (136).
>
> The backwardness of the Iberian metropolises in capital and technology opened the way to English entrepeneurs. Their textiles and hardware undersold those of their competitors; their capital resources facilitated long-term operations including the payment of high import duties; they extended their credits to Latin American merchants at half the interest rate of their competitors . . . (154).

In his research on the economic history of Brazil, Carlos M. Pelaez has found substantial evidence to show that in the period 1898–1945 the effects of coffee and monetary policies were more to blame for the retardation of industrialization than the neo-colonial influence of European countries and the U.S.

4. Warren Dean, *The Industrialization of São Paulo, 1880–1945* (Austin, Texas, 1969); Carlos F. Díaz-Alejandro, *Essays on the Economic History of the Argentine Republic.* chs. 1–3 (New Haven, 1970); Clark W. Reynolds, *The Mexican Economy: Twentieth Century Structure and Growth,* ch. 5 (New Haven, 1970).

5. Dean, *Industrialization*, ch. 5; Díaz-Alejandro, *Essays*, ch. 4.

6. Comisión Económica para la América Latina de los Naciones Unidas (CEPAL), *El proceso de industrialización en América Latina*, 14–17 (New York, 1965).

7. For some case studies, see: Díaz-Alejandro, *Essays*, chs. 1–3; Celso Furtado, *The Economic Growth of Brazil*, chs. 30 and 31 (Berkeley and Los Angeles, 1963); Werner Baer, *Industrialization and Economic Development in Brazil*, ch. 2 (Homewood, Illinois, 1965); Carlos M. Pelaez, "Acêrca de politica governamental, da grande depressão e da industrialização do Brasil," *Revista Brasileira de Economia* (RBE) (1969); Markos Mamalakis, *Growth and Structure of the Chilean Economy: 1840–1968*, chs. 2 and 6 (forthcoming); Oscar E. Muñoz, "An Essay on the Process of Industrialization in Chile since 1914," *Yale Economic Essays* (1968); CEPAL, *El proceso de industrializacion* . . ., 17–37.

8. Reviewing the experience of Argentina during the first three decades of the twentieth century, Díaz-Alejandro, *Essays*, ch. 3, states that, ". . . contrasted with later periods, the growth of manufacturing during 1900–29 may be explained primarily by the expansion of exports and domestic demand, with a relatively small contribution by import substitution."

9. In the case of Brazil this alteration has been documented in two studies: Annibal V. Villela, *Fontes de crescimento da economia Brasileira* (mimeographed, 1970) I: 406 and II: 218; Carlos M. Pelaez, "A balança comercial, a grande depressão e a industrilização Brasileira," RBE (1968), 15–47.

10. Baer, *The Development of the Brazilian Steel Industry, ch.* 4 (Nashville, Tennessee, 1969); Pelaez, "O desenvolvimento da industria do aço no Brasil," RBE (1970) 191–217; Nathaniel H. Leff, *The Brazilian Capital Goods Industry, 1929–1964*, 8–20 (Cambridge, Mass., 1968). According to Don Huddle's calculations, "Postwar Brazilian Industrialization: Growth Patterns, Inflation, and Sources of Stagnation," In: *The Shaping of Modern Brazil*, Eric N. Baklanoff, ed., 96 (Baton Rouge, Louisiana, 1969), ISI in Brazil ". . . had already been carried very far by 1939. Thus continued across the board import substitution between 1939 and 1963 was necessarily somewhat limited."

11. In a quantitative analysis of five Latin American countries, Henry J. Bruton "Productivity Growth in Latin America," *American Economic Review* (AER), 57: 1110 (1967), found that as a result of being forced to use domestic capacity to the fullest extent, firms had to ". . . find ways to use their existing capital stock with increasing effectiveness. Improvisation and adaptation of existing equipment were common, and one can find many examples of ingeniously and indigenously devised machines producing various items for household and business use. . . . The war then not only provided 'protection' from foreign competition, but also helped to create an environment within which entrepreneurs had incentives to use available resources with increasing effectiveness."

12. The initial position of the Economic Commission for Latin America (ECLA) was contained in *The Economic Development of Latin America and its Principal Problems* (United Nations, 1950); and an elaboration of these views appeared in Raúl Prebisch's "Commercial Policy in the Underdeveloped Countries," AER, 49: 251–273 (1959). There exists a vast literature attacking and defending the Prebisch-ECLA position. See, for instance: Baer, "The Economics of Prebisch and ECLA," *Economic Development and Cultural Change* (EDCC) 10: 169–182 (1962); June Flanders, "Prebisch on Protectionism: An Evaluation," *Economic Journal* (EJ) 74: 305–326 (1964); Gottfried Haberler, "Terms of Trade and Economic Development," In: *Economic Development for Latin America*, Howard S. Ellis and Henry C. Wallich, eds., 275–297 (New York, 1961). An ECLA-type model which avoids the controversial terms of trade arguments, yet builds a similar case for industrialization can be found in Dudley Seers, "A Model of Comparative Rates of Growth in the World Economy," EJ 62: 45–78 (1962).

13. See, for example, the projections for world trade found in Bela Belassa, *Trade Prospects for Developing Countries* (Homewood, Ill., 1964) and UNCTAD, *Trade Prospects and Capital Needs of Developing Countries* (New York, 1968).

14. For policies followed in individual countries, see Díaz-Alejandro, *Essays*; Baer, *Industrialization,* ch. 3; Joel Bergsman, *Brazil, Industrialization and Trade Policies,* chs. 3 and 4 (New York, 1970); Reynolds, *The Mexican Economy,* ch. 7; Timothy King, *Mexico: Industrialization and Trade Policies Since 1940,* chs. 3–5 (New York, 1970); Mamalakis, *Growth and Structure*, chs. 6 and 7 (forthcoming); CEPAL, *El proceso de industrializacion . . .* ,ch. III.

15. David Felix, "Monetarists, Structuralists, and Import-Substituting Industrialization: A Critical Appraisal," In: *Inflation and Growth in Latin America,* Werner Baer and Isaac Kerstenetzky, eds., 383 (Homewood, 1964; 2nd printing, New Haven, 1970).

16. Albert O. Hirschman, "The Political Economy of Import-Substituting Industrialization in Latin America," QJE, 82: 17–24 (1968).

17. For example, all automobile plants were built and run by foreign firms. Almost all government steel mills in Latin America were built with foreign financing and planned and constructed under the supervision of foreign consulting firms. For some interesting comparative data on the macroeconomic impact of foreign financing, see I. Little, T. Scitovsky, and M. Scott, *Industry and Trade in Some Developing Countries: A Comparative Study,* 47–59 (New York, 1970).

18. It has been argued by a number of economists that even if measured in constant prices, taking a base year where relative prices of manufactured goods were not at their highest, the contribution of manufacturing is exaggerated. Some have tried to measure the contribution of the sector by valuing manufactured products at world prices. But even such deflation of industry's contributions do not erase the basic trends. Little, Scitovsky, and Scott, *Industry and Trade*, 7.

19. The region's countries vary substantially as to potential for ISI. However, most of the market critics whose views are summarized here have dealt with the larger Latin American countries.

20. The growth of manufactures as a proportion of world trade was quite spectacular in the forty years, 1928–68, as shown by the following data:
1928—39%; 1938—40%; 1953—45%; 1960—54%; 1968—67%.
Richard N. Cooper, *The Economics of Interdependence* (New York, 1968); GATT, *International Trade 1968.*
It should also be noted that in the post-World War II period, Third World countries have drastically lost their shares in world trade. Their share of world exports declined from 34 per cent in 1950 to 19 per cent in 1968; see various annual reports of GATT, *International Trade.* Finally, it should be noted in Table 5(a) that in the twenty year period 1948–68, Latin America's share in world trade declined from 10.9 per cent to 5.0 per cent.

21. Tibor Scitovsky, "Prospects for Latin American Industrialization within the Framework of Economic Integration," In: *The Process of Industrialization in Latin America,* 43 (Washington, D.C., 1969). The average number might be somewhat misleading. For example, in Brazil, Volkswagen produces more than half the passenger cars, thus benefitting more from scale economies than most other plants. See Bergsman, *Brazil,* 120–130. For an interesting case study of the Chilean automobile industry, which was characterized by a small market being served by twenty firms operating more than one thousand miles away from the principal market, see Leland J. Johnson, "Problems of Import Substitution: The Chilean Automobile Industry," EDCC 15: 202–216 (1967).

22. Scitovsky, "Prospects," 42.

23. Little, Scitovsky, and Scott, *Industry and Trade*, 39.

24. It has been estimated that effective protection for manufactured products in Brazil in 1966 was 254 percent as compared with product protection of 99 percent. Bergsman, *Brazil*, 42; for other countries see Little, Scitovsky, and Scott, *Industry and Trade*, 174.

25. Jack Baranson, *Automotive Industries in Developing Countries*, 15 (Baltimore, 1969).

26. Baranson, *Automotive Industries*, 22.

27. Baranson, *Automotive Industries*, 25–26.

28. Baranson, *Automotive Industries*, 28. He also found that Brazil's costs as compared to those of Argentina are lower because the former's market is larger, the industry is older, and many producers have written off capital costs for machines which are still in good working order, and Brazilians have had a longer period to develop suppliers, improve quality, and reduce costs (39). It is of interest to mention some specific numbers cited by Baranson: he found that in Argentina materials and parts averaged 3.3 times the U.S. cost level; administrative and selling costs are twice as high in Mexico as in the U.S.; special tooling amortization is almost three times as expensive per vehicle in Brazil and Mexico as in the U.S. (39). A yet unpublished study of the Brazilian automobile industry by José Almeida, of the Fundação Getúlio Vargas, presents similar conclusions. One of the principal reasons for the high cost of Brazilian automobiles was found to be the extreme autarky of the industry. The domestic content of Brazilian vehicles amounts to 98 percent. Decreasing this content to a level of 50 percent to 60 percent would substantially lower costs.

29. Ayhan Cilingiroglu, *Manufacture of Heavy Electrical Equipment in Developing Countries*, 31 (Baltimore, 1969).

30. "Industrial Development in Latin America," *Economic Bulletin for Latin America*, 13 (1969).

31. For a thorough discussion of problems in defining the appropriate exchange rate and the domestic resource cost, see William F. Steel, "Import Substitution Policy in Ghana in the 1960's," 53–80 (unpublished Ph.D. dissertation, MIT, 1970).

32. The theoretical literature on this topic is rather lengthy. See, for instance, Bela Balassa and Daniel M. Schydlowsky, "Effective Tariffs, Domestic Cost of Foreign Exchange, and the Equilibrium Exchange Rate," *The Journal of Political Economy* (JPE), 76: 348–360 (1968). For an application of such a criterion to measure the efficiency of an industry in Latin America, see Baer, *Brazilian Steel Industry*, 146–151.

33. See Díaz-Alejandro, *Essays*, ch. 6; also, "An Interpretation of Argentine Economic Growth Since 1930," Part I, *Journal of Development Studies* (JDS), 3: 25–28 (1966).

34. A recent article by Samuel A. Morley and Gordon W. Smith, "On the Measurement of Import Substitution," AER, 60: 728–735 (1970), challenges the usual measurements of import substitution. These underestimate ISI if imports are replaced without induced rises in imported inputs. The authors develop a formula for appropriate corrections.

35. This situation has been well described by David Felix, "The Dilemma of Import Substitution—Argentina," In: *Development Policy: Theory and Practice*, Gustav F. Papanek, ed., 60–61 (Cambridge, Mass., 1968): "As the consumer-goods phase of ISI is succeeded by a predominantly capital- and intermediate-goods phase, three sets of forces close in on the strategy. The import mix shifts predominantly to one of fuels, industrial materials, essential food-stuffs, and capital goods required by the industrial sector. The capital intensity of import-substituting projects rises, resulting in a rising import content of investment and

causing the level of investment to be more severely constrained by the capacity to import. The projects tend to require increasingly large markets in order to reach minimum efficient scale, so that the ability of ISI to induce investment is progressively weakened by the thin domestic markets of even the larger Latin American countries." See also Díaz-Alejandro, "On the Import Intensity of Import Substitution," *Kyklos*, 18: 495–511 (1965), who stresses the fact that rapid ISI raises income before investments mature, resulting in an increase in imports. See also Maria Conceição Tavares, "Auge y declinación del proceso de substitución de importaciones en el Brasil," *Boletín Económico de America Latina*, 9: 1–59 (1964).

36. John Sheahan, "Imports, Investment, and Growth—Colombia," In: *Development Policy: Theory and Practice*, 97–99. See also Jaroslav Vanek, *Estimating Foreign Resource Needs for Economic Development* (New York, 1967). For Argentina, see Díaz-Alejandro, *Essays*, ch. 7.

37. Leff, "Export Stagnation and Autarkic Development in Brazil," QJE, 81: 286–301 (1967); Little, Scitovsky, and Scott, *Industry and Trade*, ch. 7.

38. One should, of course, take into account the fact that the industrial growth stimulates both direct and indirect employment. Thus, not all employment growth in the service sector can be looked upon as residual; i.e., a sector into which people go if they cannot find employment in industry. Many government financial and commercial services grow in a fashion complementary to industry. It is obvious, however, that the extremely high rates of growth of employment in services in Latin America reflects a large proportion of residual labor absorption. Interesting analyses and data on employment in Latin America can be found in Raúl Prebisch, *Transformación y desarrollo: la gran tarea de América Latina* (Washington, D.C., 1970); also in ILO, *Hacia el pleno empleo: un programa para Colombia* (Geneva, 1970).

39. Little, Scitovsky, and Scott, *Industry and Trade*, ch. 3; Henry J. Bruton, "The Import Substitution Strategy of Economic Development: A Survey of Findings," 17 (Mimeographed Research Memorandum No. 27, Williams College, Williamstown, Mass., 1969); Baer and Michel Hervé, "Employment and Industrialization in Developing Countries," QJE, 80: 88–107 (1966); Benjamin Cohen and Nathaniel Leff, "Employment and Industrialization: Comment," QJE, 81: 162–164 (1967); Baer and Hervé, "Employment and Industrialization: Reply," QJE, 81: 532–533 (1967).

40. Little, Scitovsky, and Scott, *Industry and Trade*, 41–47; W. Baer and Andrea Maneschi, "Import-Substitution, Stagnation and Structural Change: An Interpretation of the Brazilian Case," JDA, 5: 177–192 (1971); King, *Mexico: Industrialization*, 26–32; Naciones Unidas, *El desarrollo económico y la distribución del ingreso en la Argentina* (New York, 1968); ILO, *Hacia el pleno empleo*, ch. 10.

41. Although capacity utilization data are rare because of capacity measurement difficulties, some evidence of underutilization can be found in the following sources: Baer and Maneschi, "Import Substitution," and "Industrial Development in Latin America," *Economic Bulletin for Latin America*, 14: 2: 14–15 (1969); Little, Scitovsky, and Scott, *Industry and Trade*, 93–99; Baer, *The Development of the Brazilian Steel Industry*, 89.

42. For a discussion of regional imbalances in the Brazilian context, see Baer, *Industrialization*, 163–185.

43. For a thorough survey and analysis of the potential effect of income redistribution in Latin America, see William R. Cline, *The Potential Effect of Income Redistribution on Economic Growth in Six Latin American Countries* (mimeographed; Discussion Paper No. 13, Research Program in Economic Development, Princeton, N.J., 1970).

44. Nicholas Georgescu-Roegen first raised this question in an article published in Brazil, "Inflação estrutural e o crescimento economico," RBE, 22: 5–14 (1968); since then he has published an expanded version in English: "Structural Inflation-Lock and Balanced Growth," *Economies et Sociétés*, Cahier de L'I.S.E.A., Tome IV: 3 (Geneva, 1970). An interesting model of growth and stagnation based on Georgescu-Roegen's original idea is contained in Francisco Lopes, "Subsidios a formulação de um modelo de desenvolvimento e estagnação no Brasil," RBE, 23: 59–78 (1969).

45. An alternative might be a change in the demand profile of lower income groups. A good example of this was the boom in automobile sales in Brazil in the late Sixties. This boom was mainly due to the rise of "consorcios." This is an ingenious device which was invented to create credit for buying cars. Under a typical scheme, a group of, say, 24 people get together to buy a Volkswagen. Each member of the consorcio agrees to pay every month 1/24th of the price of a VW into a kitty and every month a VW is bought. Payments are readjustable for inflationary rates. Thus, each month one member gets a VW, but everyone continues to pay for 24 months, until everyone has received his VW. The doubt which can be raised about this scheme is whether the opportunity cost to the economy is not too great. People buying cars will forego buying many other goods (often wage goods) and many will forego saving.

46. It could be claimed that the "structural lock" problem is not important since imbalances between the demand and productive profiles are eliminated over time as investment takes place in shortage areas. However, given the huge amounts of excess productive capacity which was referred to earlier, this problem cannot be disregarded on the basis of long-run adjustments.

47. I would like to thank David Felix for pointing this out. Also see his article "The Dilemma of Import Substitution—Argentina," 65–70.

48. Joel Bergsman and Arthur Candal, "Industrialization: Past Success and Future Problems," In: *The Economy of Brazil*, Howard S. Ellis, ed., 47 (Berkeley and Los Angeles, 1969).

49. Given their many special economic and political circumstances, it is doubtful whether the examples of Taiwan, Korea, or Hong Kong can be taken as proofs that the Latin American economies were not in a dilemma.

50. Erroneous price policies in the late Forties when Brazil still dominated the world coffee market had nothing to do with the argument that agriculture was sacrificed. A valid argument might be that Brazil neglected the use of resources to invest in a new type of agriculture which would diversify agricultural exports. Although this would have been a correct policy to follow, it would not have been a substitute for ISI.

51. Baer, *The Development of the Brazilian Steel Industry*, ch. 2.

52. "Industrial Development in Latin America," *Economic Bulletin for Latin America*, 14: 12 (1969). In an interesting study of Peruvian industries, Christopher Clague found that labor intensive industries are less efficient than capital intensive ones. He finds this discouraging since labor intensive industries produce more easily exportable products. "The Determinants of Efficiency in Manufacturing Industries in an Underdeveloped Country," EDCC, 18: 188–205 (1970).

53. I have developed this point in "Sobre os usos e abusos da teoria economica," RBE, 22: 72–83 (1968).

54. For a discussion of such "complementation agreements" in Latin America, see GATT, *International Trade 1968*, 63–74 (Geneva, 1969).

55. A good critical appraisal of Latin American integration possibilities can be found in Keith Griffin, *Underdevelopment in Spanish America*, ch. VI (Cambridge, Mass., 1970). The best and most extensive empirical work on specialization possibilities within a Latin American common market has been done by a group of Latin American research institutes (collectively known as ECIEL) led by Joseph Grunwald of The Brookings Institution. Results were presented at a Conference on Research in Income and Wealth of the National Bureau of Economic Research by Joseph Grunwald and Jorge Salazar under the title, "Economic Integration, and Price and Value Comparisons in Latin America" and published in *International Comparisons of Prices and Real Income: Studies in Income and Wealth*, D. J. Daley, ed. (N.Y., 1972).

56. In his interesting study, "The Potential Effect of Income Redistribution on Economic Growth in Six Latin American Countries" 95 (mimeographed, Discussion Paper No. 13, Princeton, 1970), William Cline found that "Using the estimated income distributions and consumption function estimates from family budget studies, simulation exercises suggested that for Argentina, Brazil, Mexico and Venezuela income redistributions toward equality of the level found in Britain would cost on the order of 1% annual growth in GNP. . . ."

BIBLIOGRAPHY

BAER, WERNER

1962 The Puerto Rican Economy and U.S. Economic Fluctuations. Río Piedras.

1965 Industrialization and Economic Development in Brazil. Homewood, Ill.

1969 The Development of the Brazilian Steel Industry. Nashville, Tenn.

BAER, WERNER AND I. KERSTENETZKY

1971 The Brazilian Economy in the Sixties. In: Brazil in the Sixties. Riordan Roett, ed. Nashville, Tenn.

BAER, WERNER AND A. MANESCHI

1971 Import-Substitution, Stagnation and Structural Change: An Interpretation of the Brazilian Case. The Journal of Developing Areas (JDE). Jan.

BARANSON, JACK

1969 Automotive Industries in Developing Countries. Baltimore. (Includes analysis of Argentinian, Brazilian, and Mexican Industries.)

BERGSMAN, JOEL

1970 Brazil: Industrialization and Trade Policies. N.Y.

BRUTON, HENRY J.

1967 Productivity Growth in Latin America. American Economic Review (AER). Dec.

1968 Import Substitution and Productivity Growth. Journal of Development Studies (JDS). April.

1968 Export Growth and Import Substitution. Research Memorandum No. 22. Williams College, Center for Development Economics. Williamstown, Mass.

1969 The Import Substitution Strategy of Economic Development: A Survey of Findings. Research Memorandum No. 27. Williamstown. (This is a survey of the findings of Williams College economists studying ISI in various parts of the world, including Latin America. The inclination of this survey and most Williams College researchers is more towards what I have called the "market critics.")

BRODERSOHN, MARIO S., ed.

1970 Estrategias de industrialización para la Argentina. Buenos Aires. (This volume contains articles both on ISI problems of Argentina and also on the general nature of ISI and its related problems.)

CILINGIROGLU, AYHAN

1969 Manufacture of Heavy Electrical Equipment in Developing Countries. Baltimore. (Includes considerable information on Brazil, Argentina, and Mexico.)

CLAGUE, CHRISTOPHER

1970 The Determinants of Efficiency in Manufacturing Industries in an Underdeveloped Country. Economic Development and Cultural Change (EDCC). Jan. (Efficiency in Peruvian industries.)

CLARK, PAUL G.

1967 Brazilian Import Liberalization. Research Memorandum No. 14. Williamstown, Mass. Sept.

1967 Import Demand Functions for Brazil. Research Memorandum No. 15. Williamstown, Mass.

CLARK, PAUL G. AND RICHARD WEISSKOFF

1967 Import Demands and Import Policies in Brazil. Research Memorandum No. 8. Williamstown, Mass. Feb.

CLINE, WILLIAM R.

1970 The Potential Effect of Income Redistribution on Economic Growth in Six Latin American Countries. Mimeographed Discussion Paper No. 13. Princeton.

DEAN, WARREN

1969 The Industrialization of São Paulo, 1880–1945. Austin, Tex.

DEVRIES, BAREND A.

1967 The Export Experience of Developing Countries. Baltimore. (DeVries' statistical analysis also covers most Latin American countries.)

DIAZ-ALEJANDRO, CARLOS F.

1965 On the Import Intensity of Import Substitution. Kyklos. 18: 495–511.

1966–67 An Interpretation of Argentine Economic Growth Since 1930. JDS. Oct. and Jan.

1970 Essays on the Economic History of the Argentine Republic. New Haven.

DORFMAN, ADOLFO

1967 La industrialización en la América Latina y las políticas de fomento. México.

ELLIS, HOWARD S., ed.

1969 The Economy of Brazil. Berkeley and Los Angeles. (See especially articles by Bergsman and Candal, "Industrialization: Past Success and Future Problems"; and by Samuel A. Morley, "Import Demand and Import Substitution in Brazil.")

FELIX, DAVID

1968 The Dilemma of Import Substitution—Argentina. In: Development Policy: Theory and Practice. Cambridge, Mass.

1969 Economic Development: Take Offs into Unsustained Growth. Social Research: 36: 2.

1970 Monetarists, Structuralists, and Import-Substituting Industrialization: A Critical Appraisal. In: Inflation and Growth in Latin America. Baer and Kerstenetzky, eds. Homewood, Ill. New printing, Cambridge, Mass.

FERRER, ALDO

1963 La economía Argentina. México/Buenos Aires.

FURTADO, CELSO

1963 The Economic Growth of Brazil. Berkeley and Los Angeles.

1966 Subdesenvolvimento e estagnação na America Latina. Rio de Janeiro.

1968 Um projeto para o Brasil. Rio de Janeiro.

(For a summary of Furtado's ideas on growth and stagnation in Latin America which are elaborated in various publications of his, see W. Baer, "Furtado on Development: A Review Essay," JDA, Jan. 1969.)

FURTADO, CELSO AND A. MANESCHI

1968 Um modelo de simulação de desenvolvimento e estagnação na America Latina. RBE. June.

GENERAL AGREEMENT ON TARIFFS AND TRADE (GATT)

International Trade. (Annual volumes which contain excellent information on the performance of less developed countries in world markets.)

GEORGESCU-ROEGEN, NICHOLAS
1970 Structural Inflation-Lock and Balanced Growth. Economies e Sociétés. 4: 3. Geneva.

GRIFFIN, KEITH
1970 Underdevelopment in Spanish America. Cambridge, Mass.

GRUNWALD, JOSEPH
1970 Some Reflections on Latin American Industrialization Policies. Journal of Political Economy (JPE). 78: 4: 826–856.

GRUNWALD, JOSEPH AND JORGE SALAZAR
1972 "Economic Integration, and Price and Value Comparisons in Latin America." In: International Comparisons of Prices and Real Income: Studies in Income and Wealth. D. J. Daly, ed. N.Y.

GRUNWALD, JOSEPH AND PHILIP MUSGROVE
1970 Natural Resources in Latin American Development. Baltimore.

HARBERGER, A. C.
1970 Economic Policy Problems in Latin America: A Review. JPE. July/Aug., Part II.

HIRSCHMAN, ALBERT O.
1958 The Strategy of Economic Development. New Haven.
1968 The Political Economy of Import-Substituting Industrialization. QJE. Feb.

HUDDLE, DONNALD
1969 Postwar Brazilian Industrialization: Growth Patterns, Inflation, and Sources of Stagnation. In: The Shaping of Modern Brazil. Eric N. Baklanoff, ed. Baton Rouge.

HUNT, SHANE J.
1969 Distribution, Growth, and Government Economic Behavior in Peru. (Mimeographed). Princeton.

INTERNATIONAL LABOR ORGANIZATION
1970 Hacia el pleno empleo: Un programa para Colombia preparado por una misión internacional organizada por la Oficina Internacional del Trabajo. Geneva.

INTER-AMERICAN DEVELOPMENT BANK
1970 Socio-Economic Progress in Latin America. Ninth Annual Report, 1969. Washington, D.C.
(This issue contains a general review of Latin American economies in the Sixties.)

JOHNSON, LELAND J.
1967 Problems of Import Substitution: The Chilean Automobile Industry. EDCC. Jan.

KAFKA, ALEXANDRE
1961 The Theoretical Interpretation of Latin American Economic Development. In: Economic Development for Latin America. Howard Ellis and Henry Wallich, eds. N.Y.

KING, TIMOTHY
1970 Mexico: Industrialization and Trade Policies Since 1940. N.Y.

LEFF, NATHANIEL
1968 The Brazilian Capital Goods Industry, 1929–1964. Cambridge, Mass.
1967 Export Stagnation and Autarkic Development in Brazil. QJE. May.

LITTLE, IAN, TIBOR SCITOVSKY AND MAURICE SCOTT
1970 Industry Trade in Some Developing Countries. N.Y.

LOPES, FRANCISCO
1969 Subsidios a formulação de um modelo de desenvolvimento e estagnação no Brasil. RBE. June.

MAMALAKIS, MARKOS
Growth and Structure of the Chilean Economy: 1840–1968.
(Mimeographed; soon to be published by Yale University Press).

MAMALAKIS, MARKOS AND CLARK W. REYNOLDS
1965 Essays on the Chilean Economy. Homewood, Ill.

MACARIO, SANTIAGO
1965 Protectionism and Industrialization in Latin America. Economic Bulletin for Latin America. March.
MORLEY, SAMUEL A. AND GORDON W. SMITH
1970 On the Measurement of Import Substitution. AER. Sept.
MOSK, SANFORD A.
1954 Industrial Revolution in Mexico. Berkeley and Los Angeles.
MUÑOZ, OSCAR
1968 An Essay on the Process of Industrialization in Chile Since 1914. Yale Economic Essays. Fall.
PELAEZ, CARLOS M.
1968 The State, the Great Depression and the Industrialization of Brazil. (Unpublished Ph.D. dissertation, Columbia University). N.Y.
1968 A balança comercial, a grande depressão e a industralização Brasileira. RBE. Mar.
1969 Açerca de politica governamental, da grande depressão e da industrialização no Brasil. RBE. Jul./Set.
1970 O desenvolvimento da industria do aço no Brasil. RBE. Abr./Jun.
PREBISCH, RAUL
1970 Transformación y desarrollo: la gran tarea de América Latina. Banco Interamericano de Desarrollo. Washington, D.C.
REYNOLDS, CLARK W.
1970 The Mexican Economy: Twentieth Century Structure and Growth. New Haven.
ROBOCK, STEFAN H.
1970 Industrialization through Import-Substitution or Export Industries: A False Dichotomy. In: Industrial Organization and Economic Development. J. W. Markham and G. F. Papanek, eds. Boston.
SHEAHAN, JOHN
1968 Imports, Investment, and Growth. In: Development Policy: Theory and Practice. Gustav F. Papanek, ed. Cambridge, Mass.
1969 Criteria for Investment Allocation in Colombia. Center for Development Economics Research Memorandum No. 33. Williamstown. Nov.
SCHYDLOWSKY, DANIEL M.
1967 From Import Substitution to Export Promotion for Semi-Grown-Up Industries: A Policy Proposal. JDS. July.
SCITOVSKY, TIBOR
1969 Prospects for Latin American Industrialization within the Framework of Economic Integration: Bases for Analysis. In: The Process of Industrialization in Latin America. Inter-American Development Bank, Washington, D.C.
STEIN, STANLEY AND BARBARA H. STEIN
1970 The Colonial Heritage of Latin America. N.Y.
STRASSMANN, W. Paul.
1968 Technological Change and Economic Development: The Manufacturing Experience of Mexico and Puerto Rico. Ithaca, N.Y.
TAVARES, MARIA CONÇEICÁO
1964 Auge y declinación del proceso de sustitución de importaciones en el Brasil. Boletín Económico de América Latina. Mar.
TENDLER, JUDITH
1968 Electric Power in Brazil: Entrepreneurship in the Public Sector. Cambridge, Mass.
UNITED NATIONS ECONOMIC COMMISSION FOR LATIN AMERICA (ECLA)
1965 The Process of Industrialization in Latin America. N.Y.
1969 Industrial Development in Latin America. Economic Bulletin for Latin America. 14: 2: 1–77.

UNCTAD
1968 Trade Prospects and Capital Needs of Developing Countries. N.Y.
VANEK, JAROSLAV
1967 Estimating Foreign Resource Needs for Economic Development. N.Y. (Case Study of Colombia.)
VERNON, RAYMOND
1963 The Dilemma of Mexico's Development. Cambridge, Mass.
1964 (editor) Public Policy and Private Enterprise in Mexico. Cambridge, Mass.
VILLELA, ANIBAL V.
1971 Fontes de crescimento da economia Brasileira. (Mimeographed.)

THE CENTRAL AMERICAN MODEL OF GROWTH: CRISIS FOR WHOM?

by

*Edelberto Torres-Rivas**

Translated by Margaret Towner

INTRODUCTION

Limited by their short-sighted vision, annual "conjunctures," and sectorial analyses of economic life, many studies of Central American reality yield little understanding either of the model of development that is being applied in the region or to the significance of the ups and downs that the Central American economies experience as a result of its application. Many such analyses and their predictions are based on variations in foreign commerce, resulting in optimistic visions of development that depend on the level of coffee prices that are determined ten thousand kilometers away in the developed countries. Thus, frosts in Brazil are celebrated as brief victories for the local export economy. This apologetic position, an easy one to adopt if one is working with traditional statistical indicators, is unconsciously based on an ideological vision that results in the utilization of a theoretical apparatus that carelessly disregards specific characteristics of dependent societies.

Central America as a region has a Gross Domestic Product (GDP) of more than U.S. $12,000 million (1976), seventh highest[1] in Latin America, and a population of 17.8 million. Central America ranks third in the export of coffee and sugar, second in export of meat, and first in export of bananas to the North American market. The basic common characteristics of Central American economies are defined by the importance of the agrarian sector (25 percent of GDP and about 70 percent of exports) as a source of social wealth and dividends, by a chronic crisis in agricultural production for the internal market, and by the weakness and newness of the industrial structure. At the same time that there are similarities among the countries, there are even more important internal differences in social structures — the locus of results of any development pattern — as well as in the well-known macroeconomic variables such as population, size, GDP, and GDP per capita, etc.

Paradoxically, Costa Rica and Nicaragua are more similar to each other than to the other Central American countries — Guatemala and Honduras being the most dissimilar. The well-known success of birth-control policies in Costa Rica (a decline in births from 45 per thousand to 30 per thousand dur-

* The author, Professor of Sociology, Confederación Universitaria Centroamericana (San José, Costa Rica), specializes in the history of economic development and social structure. The translator received her Masters Degree in Latin American Studies from California State University, Los Angeles. This article was first published in Guatemala by the University of San Carlos in their journal *Alero*, IV, 1 (May-June 1979), 37-57.

[1]After Brazil, Mexico, and Argentina, the three Latin American countries with the highest production are Venezuela, Colombia, and Chile with medium levels of production.

ing the last ten years) contrasts with apparent failures in the other countries (especially El Salvador where, for a similar period, births increased from 28 to 35 per thousand). This clearly shows how, *ceteris paribus*, results of social experiments are totally conditioned by the diverse components of the social and cultural structure of a society. Costa Rica and Nicaragua are the most urbanized societies in a region dominated by small rural agricultural settlements which have recently been affected by migratory movements, resulting in increasing metropolitanization. Among the capital cities in the past ten years, San José, Costa Rica, for example, absorbed 62 percent of the total population that migrated to urban areas within that country; Guatemala City, one half; San Salvador, 40 percent; Managua, 36 percent; and Tegucigalpa, 30 percent.

While illiteracy is generally tending to diminish overall in the region — an indicator of the degree of diffusion of "the basic skills required by a developing society"[2] — the internal qualitative differences (rural/urban, male/female, high income/low income) and interregional differences have been accentuated in the process. Whereas only 10 percent of the Costa Rican population is illiterate (1976), at the other extreme, 51 percent of the Guatemalan population is illiterate (rural women, 74 percent; urban men, 19 percent). Further evidence of these differences can be found in statistics on access to education. Costa Rica and Guatemala again represent the extremes (52 percent and 27 percent of the total school-age population attend school, respectively), while the other countries fall somewhere in between (El Salvador, 36 percent; Nicaragua, 33 percent; and Honduras, 30 percent). Other indicators of similar type appear in Table 1, further illustrating similarities and differences in Central American society.

The still-to-be-completed economic history of Central America has historical landmarks indicative of similarities and differences among its component parts. Transitory forms of productive organization, most at the extractive level (cochineal, indigo, and cacao), predominated during the colonial period and at the beginning of the Republican era. Even bird feathers and "balsams," used in primitive therapy, were exported on occasion. The region began to define its economic structure when the supply and demand created by the European industrial revolution allowed the consolidation of a primary-export economy and an internal market of manufactured luxury goods. Coffee first and then bananas constituted the basis of this export-oriented economic structure which utilized abundant land and labor. The manner by which internal activity was established and its links with international commerce conditioned the entire internal social structure, the nature of political power, and cultural life. The export-oriented economy notably retarded national and social integration and contributed to the extreme rigidity of political and social relations. Since independence, development has been determined by an externally oriented dynamic whose essential nature has remained unchanged in spite of efforts (after the Second World War and especially after 1955) — which we will analyze later on — to implant a new productive base dependent on the growth of an internal market industry. Since about 1955, the efforts of Central American governments, some entrepreneurial sectors, and diverse international organizations have been directed

[2]CEPAL (1976) is a document from which we have obtained the majority of the statistics presented in this section.

toward applying resources, developing programs, and producing studies to further this new direction.

Table 1

Central America — Basic Statistics

	GUATEMALA	EL SALVADOR	HONDURAS	NICARAGUA	COSTA RICA
Indicators of Standard of Living and Social Well-being (a)					
% EAP Under Social Security (1973)	30	8	9	17	49
Life Expectancy	52.9	57.8	53.5	52.9	68.2
Mortality Rate [1-5 years x 1,000 population (1970-1975)]	30.0	14.5	20.0	18.4	4.0
Number Hospital Beds x 100 (1972)	221.0	187.0	159.0	229.0	399.0
Electric Energy (KWH x h.) (1974)	145.0	232.0	155.0	321.0	672.0
Population (Thousands) (b)					
1950	967.1	653.0	457.0	351.0	272.0
1960	1,205.8	791.4	557.0	436.7	362.7
1970	1,465.9	1,252.3	741.1	572.4	520.3
1975	1,603.5	1,598.3	859.2	653.9	633.1
Annual Rates of Growth (%) (b)					
EAP: 1950-1960	2.2	1.9	2.0	2.2	2.9
EAP: 1960-1970	2.0	2.6	2.9	2.7	3.6
Total Population 1950-1960	3.4	2.8	3.0	3.0	4.0
Total Population 1960-1974	2.9	3.5	2.7	2.8	3.4
Employment/Unemployment (Thousands) 1970 (c)					
Economically Active Population (EAP)	1,623	1,081	799	659	535
Employed	1,428	968	753	600	508
Unemployed	195	113	46	59	27
Total	5,179	3,441	2,583	2,222	1,798
New Places Required 1970-75	289.4	190.5	149.2	125.7	119.2
Average Actual New Employment 1970-75	58.1	38.0	30.4	25.3	24.0
Aggregate Industrial Value: (Millions of CA pesos, 1960) (d)					
1960	133.1	82.7	42.1	53.8	67.7
1976	385.9	259.7	86.7	213.5	224.0
Annual Growth Rate (%)	6.9	7.4	4.6	9.0	7.8
Intraregional Trade as a % of Total External Trade, by Country (e)					
Export 1960	6.5	10.8	12.0	5.5	2.2
Import 1960	31.6	29.8	5.6	22.2	20.2
Export 1973	5.5	11.0	7.4	3.9	3.2
Import 1973	20.8	25.0	12.1	27.5	18.2

Sources: (a) CEPAL (1976: Tables 17, 30, 32, 49)
(b) CEPAL (1976: Tables 2 and 5)
(c) CELADE (1968) and CEPAL (1971)
(d) SIECA (1975) and Bancos Centrales (1977-1978)
(e) SIECA (1975)

Because of the way in which it was inserted into the national society — with foreign capital investment and technology — the banana plantation was not linked to the rest of the economy. Capitalism arrived through external demand in the form of commercial capital; export agriculture organized the internal factors which rested on a precarious development of the productive forces and encouraged those social relations of production that would permit higher rates of accumulation. The result of all this, which extends throughout an important part of our history, is a coffee economy that unevenly articulates noncapitalist forms of production and organization with other more developed forms. In some countries like Guatemala and El Salvador, labor was forced and practically unpaid; in others like Costa Rica, there was an extended peasant economy that only marginally contributed labor or productive surplus to coffee production. We are not interested in discussing here the problem of capitalism vs. feudalism in Central American history. When capital appears in agriculture, it does so, in our experience, only to maintain an external relationship and to control, partially and weakly, some stages of production such as the final preparation of beans for exportation. This is a stage of production that can be initiated with a noncapitalist base but which, since it is oriented towards the world market, constitutes an activity that produces profit in its final stage that finishes in and is directed from the exterior.

The history of agrarian development is part of a later history of economic development based on industrial development that is oriented towards the internal market. The export economy constitutes a necessary stage of transition to the capitalist economy; hence, capitalism only appears completely formed with an industrial economy. Following this consolidation, a new stage in agrarian development begins in which capital will gain control of agriculture in a contradictory, unequal, but new manner, modifying its traditional structure and creating new forms of production in the countryside.

In Central America, the crises of the 1930s and the effects of the Second World War discredited the model of development based on monoculture and monoexportation exemplified by the relations between the banana enclave and the local economy. The post-war economic, political, and ideological situation weakened the power of the dominant agrarian classes. The numerous social problems and conflicts that had been frozen for the long period that ended with the 1940s provoked crises (in Guatemala, El Salvador, and Costa Rica) or readjustments (in Nicaragua and Honduras). These were inevitable disequilibriums in the traditional political forms of domination provoked by the rise of new forces and groups formed in the previous period as well as by the need to reorganize the whole society on a new basis.

The period that we can refer to in order to understand this vision began in the decade of the 1950s. In Central America it was characterized more by a political than economic need to find a new basis for the accumulation of capital. It was based on liberal rather than socialist principles: to improve the standard of living of the majority of the population, to adopt a code of law based more on consensus, and to modernize Central American cultural and political life held back by oligarchic dominations.

THE PROCESS OF INDUSTRIALIZATION

In the experience of most agrocommercial societies, the initial stage of industrialization was facilitated by certain internal conditions derived from external demand. The constant growth of production and productivity which resulted from the expansion in the international demand for agricultural products created internal purchasing power for manufactured products supplied first through importation and later less sophisticated types of internal industrial production. The size of the internal market, the volume of population, and, obviously, a certain level of capitalist agricultural development were important in determining the growth of the internal market.

The Central American economy, however, evolved in a different direction. Monoproducing specialization and the total absence of other sources of endogenous growth turned the export sector into the motor for economic growth without the long-range effects of encouraging the development of an internal market. Depending exclusively on international demand, the export sector operated with great independence, with little correspondence to the necessities of the social development of these societies.

Latin American Perspectives, Issues 25 and 26, Spring and Summer 1980, Vol. VII, Nos. 2 and 3

Monoproducing specialization did not favor the formation of an internal demand linked to a beginning manufacturing infrastructure. The export sector was unable to establish an internal market nucleus due to the nature of the organization of production and commercialization of the two basic types of exports (coffee and bananas) and to the geographic and demographic dimensions of these countries. The lack of internal demand is related to the high concentration of property, the result of capitalist development through a "landlord path" and, more importantly, the virtual monopoly of the cultivation and commercialization of coffee. The only sector of the population which created a demand for industrial goods was a minority of people closely linked to foreign capital and who received a part of its benefits. At the other end of the scale was an over-abundant labor force with wage levels so low as to seriously limit the formation of an internal market. In this case the "wage-earner" was not a consumer. The concentration of a relatively better-paid workforce in the banana sector did not significantly increase internal demand due to the organization that the enclave gave to its labor force — a partial consumer of imported products. The rest of the economy consisted of peasants locked in a system of subsistence.

Until 1950, Central American societies had only a tiny manufacturing sector. It was neither strengthened by the crisis of 1929 nor by the Second World War. In other Latin American countries, the industrial sector appeared at first as a by-product or reflection of the expansion of exports and then as an effect of the crisis of these exports. In these societies, therefore, we can refer to a second stage in the process of industrialization, based on the so-called "model" of import substitution. Manufactured goods that were previously imported began to be produced internally. The installation or expansion of these industrial enterprises, generally of cheap consumer goods, was made possible by a pre-existing local demand and productive experience, both resulting from the constant expansion of income that, at the same time, generated the expansion of the export sector.

In Central America export activities produced a contrary effect — that of inhibiting the appearance of an internal, global, diversified demand and by creating a minuscule sector that, upon concentrating income, only increased the pace of importation of luxury and immediate consumption goods or employed coffee profits in an unproductive manner. The consumption of urban workers did not play a significant role because the vast majority of the population was in the countryside. We now know that some of the most important coffee groups in Central America have been investing for some 25 years in the North American market, in other words, behaving in an entrepreneurial fashion, distinguished only by the region in which they chose to invest. Ultimately the limits of the experience were reached, and the internal market endured a long period of economic stagnation (1930-1946), accompanied by a corresponding strengthening of peasant economies and weakening of the monetary economy, before the door would open, erratically and with difficulty, at the end of the 1950s to a new model of growth.

The idea of industrialization in Central America was necessarily linked to the project of regional integration. The goal of regional integration was to establish a new stage of economic growth for the region, based on a form of capital accumulation which would take into account relative losses in the export sector. However, the project was never realized for reasons specific to this experience rather than those in other Latin American countries (balance of payments problems, or crisis, or disorder in the international supply of manufactured goods). In the following discussion we present our view of a summary of the basic characteristics of this process.

1) In the case of Central America, we are talking about an industrial process that took place in the heart of an agrarian society whose traditional exporting structure not only did not weaken but became relatively stronger. Since 1948, agrarian production oriented toward international demand has increased in spite of continual oscillations in prices, arbitrarily determined quotas in buyers' markets, and the internal distortion caused by the indefinite prolongation of ways of life and activity that resisted capitalist modernization. The *rate* of growth in agriculture was significantly less than that of the industrial or service sectors. However, in relation to the international market, the region preserved the dependent commercial profile that it had when it was first incorporated into the same system more than one hundred years ago. Coffee production has tripled since 1948, banana production has doubled but with many ups and downs and with a redistribution of productive forms; the production of cotton, sugar, meat, and other minor products increased after the 1950s, diversifying supply and the productive structure but further strengthening the external orientation of the economy. The five most important farm products have contributed almost 70 percent of the exports in Central America, a percentage that has been virtually constant for the past fifteen years.[3]

The important volume of earnings from agrarian exports means that industrialization has depended not only on the evolution and basic characteristics of the internal market but also on its capacity to export. The availability of dividends was converted into a decisive factor in creating the necessary conditions for extended reproduction of capital. As a result of the historic moment in which this industrial project developed, the export sector had to rely on foreign capital investment and, above all, the transference of technology and imported forms of business organization, promotion, publicity, and marketing systems.

It is possible to see in this process a fundamental difference characteristic of dependent capitalism: when an internal demand appears in these societies, the mechanism that generates this market does not have a functional relationship with the dynamics of accumulation. In so-called endogenous capitalist economies, the creation and growth of the internal market, the basis of production and consumption of manufactured items, comes to be the counterpart of the levels of accumulation, which means that a correspondence or at least an association exists between the rhythmn of accumulation and the growth of demand.

The growth in productivity did not generate accumulation in the export economy in the proportion hoped for; hence, there was no reason why it should transform into corresponding growth in global demand. The fact that the industrial project took place in the context of an export economy that was not in crisis made that project sensitive to and dependent on this economy and, as such, reinforced the tendency — in itself characteristic of export

[3]In 1976, for example, $1,000 million of coffee, $282.7 million of cotton, $231.3 million of sugar, $265.4 million of bananas, and $124.4 million of meat were exported.

economies — toward the separation between internal production and international circulation. It is a fact that industrial production tends to follow this sequence since the growth of this production depends less on the increased demand provoked by nonaccumulated surplus value than on in the relative expansion of the market, stimulated by the creation of a free market zone parallel to the erection of stiff tariff barriers.

This last point will be taken up again later. We now need to construct a general characterization of the industrialization project, one which is closely linked to the growth of the traditional exporting sector and, as a result of its subordination to it, maintains high import levels based on the horizontal growth of the market.

2) The policies of industrial promotion that emerged at the end of the 1950s did not appear in the context of a crisis in the world market manifested as disorganization in foreign commerce in the periphery. Rather, they emerged as a result of a reorganization of the system dictated by the almost total hegemony of the United States, achieved at the price of the Second World War through the policies of economic reconstruction initiated under U.S. protection.

To use the language currently in vogue — more conventional than conceptual — this industrialization process took place according to the import-substitution "model" which is nothing more than the transference of previously imported production to the internal sector, focusing production around consumer goods for immediate consumption. It tried to satisfy a pre-existing demand by substituting some imports for others without significantly diminishing the overall import coefficient. The result of this readjustment of the productive apparatus was the emergence of "final touch industries," in which the imported content (and hence the aggregate external value) of the finished product is qualitatively greater than the utilization of local inputs and/or labor.

This reorientation of supply and its relative growth can only take place with large foreign investments of fixed capital, importation of equipment, technology, and industrial raw materials, which explains the active presence of foreign capital in the process. During this period, the ease of obtaining investment financing for investment in infrastructure and industrial activities was due to the growing availability of foreign capital resources. The reason for the presence of international capital was to create new sources of accumulation different from and more flexible than the traditional forms of investment in agriculture and services.

Industrial activity was reduced to the processing of local raw materials or the finishing of consumer goods partially processed abroad — all with imported capital. Foreign control over the local process left little opportunity for the assimilation of new technologies and for the rise of entrepreneurial projects utilizing the knowledge of these technological processes. The industrial mentality of the bourgeoisie was reduced, in consequence, to a subordinate condition — that of administrator. That explains, for example, the commercial success of institutions like the Instituto Centroamericano de Administración de Empresas (INCAE) with offices in Nicaragua, which trained technical leaders who were in demand as a result of technological renovation and business administrators who often did not understand the technological processes simply because the equipment was imported.

The change in direction of foreign investment, in our case almost totally North American, is a well-known fact. Although the change would probably have taken place anyway since it reflects a new moment in the growth of international capital, there is no doubt that the stimuli created by the state in the framework of the Common Market project favored this change. North American capital, whether associated with local resources or not, has gained control of almost all the branches of industrial activity, especially those with assured profitability and, in so doing, has confirmed the parasitic character of these types of investments.

The available information about foreign investment is fragmented and out of date. Statistics about the quantity of investments by types of industries, for example, or by industrial branches for each of the countries and for different periods are not available. Table 2 is a comparative example of only the quantity of foreign investment in Central America, and it shows some of the regrettable extremes of the problem in terms of the rates of return. As can be observed, the region produced the highest rates of profit in Latin America.

Table 2
Profits from North American Private Investments
(1977, in millions of U.S. dollars)

Country	Total Investment	Growth %	Rate of Return %	Industrial Investment	Growth %	Rate of Return %
Argentina	1,505	10.2	18.1	930	3.6	7.5
Brazil	5,956	10.0	11.4	3,935	7.1	9.2
Mexico	3,175	6.7	9.2	2,328	5.0	7.0
Chile	187	4.5	8.0	52	6.[illegible]	9.6
Colombia	706	8.0	13.0	436	12.4	15.6
Peru	1,409	3.3	5.4	157	6.5	0.0
Central America	734	7.9	13.2	248	8.3	17.3
Others*	1,063	3.8	13.7	171	23.0	14.6

Source: Business Latin America (1978)

In the import-substitution model of growth, the recourse to foreign technology appears as an inevitable fact. Use of this technology does not necessarily result in the substitution of a previous demand but rather in the creation of a supply according to standards of consumption of the most developed countries. What are popular consumer goods in the developed countries become in the underdeveloped structure exclusive objects of an expensive and sophisticated demand. Additionally, this model, as applied in Central America, only resulted in substitution of former imports by newer ones made up of raw materials, partially finished goods, and capital (see Table 3).

As a result on the one hand of the growth of foreign investment and on the other of the persistence of a high import coefficient, one of the key problems of economic modernization appears in the size of the foreign debt. As can be seen from Table 3, the value of imported industrial imputs tended to decline relatively (from 57 percent to 44 percent) during the period under consideration, that of industrial equipment doubled, and the tendency towards the exportation of utilities, royalties, and services of capital was equally high.

Table 3
Value of Industrial Production, Importations of Machinery and Costs by Origin (in millions of U.S. dollars)

	1963	1969
Imported industrial machinery and equipment	45.7	91.5
Imported industrial inputs	220.1	321.1
Industrial inputs produced in Central America	166.3	405.2
% imported inputs	57	44.3
% regional inputs	43	55.7
Gross Value of Industrial Product	1,130.0	1,981.1
Imported inputs, as % of gross value of industrial product	19.5%	16.2%

Source: BID/INTAL (1974, IV: Tables 23 and 30)

The debt appears to be related to externally imposed conditions of this type of international accumulation of capital. In the past, the exporting sector dealt with the sphere of consumer goods, facilitating and expanding the possibilities for importation. Today, it deals with capital goods, raw materials, and semi-industrial products, thus increasing more than before the level of debt for the region.

It is notable, for example, how, in spite of the high prices of export products during certain periods (for example, 1977-1978), the deficit in the current account of the balance of payments continues to grow. Between 1974 and 1978, Central America accumulated a deficit that represents approximately 75 percent of the value of extraordinary exports in 1977. This deficit on current account has made it necessary to rely on growing quantities of foreign capital; in 1977 alone, the new capital investment amounted to more than U.S. $913 million.

In a mono-agricultural exporting situation like that experienced in Central America in the past, an indebtedness (such as reflected in Table 4 above) would have created a crisis for some Central American countries. The situation is certainly critical, but not sufficiently so as to paralyze economic activity. The deficit in the current account of the balance of payments did not originate in the export sector, and the crisis has not impeded the advance of industrialization. Apparent independence was achieved because capital, technology, and so-called material elements of constant capital were not obtained through mere commercial exchange but rather through the mediation of foreign capital in its double role as direct investor and financier of loans. In this manner the highly vulnerable and dependent character of these economies was redefined.

3) An important characteristic of the process that we have been analyzing is that it has not resulted in increasing the concentration of capital because

capital has been highly concentrated from its beginning. This result is based on assumptions that have social and political consequences of primary importance; such concentration would not have been possible without the double complicity of the state and its economic policies on the one hand and those benefits which the state derives from the nature of the foreign investments on the other.

Table 4
Foreign Debt of Central America
(December 1976, in millions of U.S. dollars)

Country	Debt	Gross Industrial Product	Debt. as % of GIP
Guatemala	551	5,541	10
El Salvador	462	2,567	18
Nicaragua	936	1,992	47
Costa Rica	933	2,191	42
Argentina	6,190	44,840	14
Mexico	17.533	63,851	27

Source: Bancos Centrales (1977-1978)

The concentration of capital is explained by the manner in which the industrial enterprises are "imposed," i.e., as a transfer of preexisting production factors from the exterior (when they jump highly protective national barriers) and also by the effect of the type of technology imported, given the physical and demographic limitations of the market. We are dealing with the establishment of manufacturing plants at a rate which exceeds demand; because of this disequilibrium, the establishment of manufacturing is surrounded by potentially explosive conditions. And it is known that these conditions are always political.

The economic "policies" of the Central American governments in favoring industrial investment of any origin consist of the creation of privileges oriented towards assuring profits through increasing the quantity of value [i.e., by simply extending production] and by not elevating the rate of surplus value. Concentration of capital is not only a consequence of the "natural" tendencies of capital but also, in this case, artificial political tendencies.

A result that has not been studied sufficiently, except in the pristine example of El Salvador, is that the concentration of manufacturing has as its base the concentration and centralization of capital in other productive sectors, especially in agriculture and commerce. The constitution of a petty bourgeoisie that is multifunctional, oligopolistic, and relatively powerful is a result of this multiple monopoly. In other words, not only industrial but social wealth is concentrated, and they condition each other.

What has been stated does not negate that the monopolistic character of industrial activity in Central America is a consequence of inequality between supply and demand provoked by a complex of structural, economic, and above all political conditions. Economies of scale only function here if they are guaranteed conditions of almost complete control over the market. As a result, there are not only tariff protections but laws of industrial patronage which favor certain enterprises. The liberal policies are based on ideological assumptions which believe monopolistic practices to be a market condition rather than a result of the process of capitalist accumulation.

Some recent investigations allow us to assess the true dimensions of this process or, at least, give us some insight into its tendencies. In one survey of 320 manufacturing sectors (Rapoport, 1977), it was found that in 160 of these sectors, one company or enterprise was responsible for more than 50 percent of the production. According to this source, there should be a greater concentration of production in Costa Rica and Nicaragua, which suggests that such conditions of monopoly (defined as the participation of the "n" largest firms in a given sector of production, measured by the total value of the same) tend to arise in the newest sectors. This tendency also seems to appear progressively in the most sophisticated industrial activities, that is to say in the levels of production closest to intermediate goods and durable consumer goods — in those which investment is greater and the technology utilized is more expensive.

If it is true that the tendential law of the concentration of capital is inversely related to the size of the market, concentration should be greater moving from the regional to the national level. In fact, the above-mentioned data (Rapoport, 1977) supports this. Utilizing a percentage index (that for the United States in the 1960s, for example, would be 40 percent), the average degree of concentration in the manufacturing sector is 48 percent if the region were considered a single market and 78 percent if the countries are considered separately. (Pakistan, which has one of the most concentrated structures, has an index of 80 percent.)

4) Now we shall analyze an aspect that is more than a specific characteristic of the process of industrialization; it is a generic feature of the model of development of dependent capitalism. The impossibility of absorbing the labor force and the concentration of income are two of the most negative characteristics of the functioning of an exclusive and polarizing model such as the one that capitalism has generated in this region. A related problem is that, technically speaking, these characteristics may significantly limit the dynamics of the accumulation of capital.

Given this reality, there are various interrelated dimensions that require explanation because of the inhumaneness of their results. Permanent unemployment and regressive tendencies in the distribution of income can either be subjects of moral condemnation or simply attributed to the costs of the development of capital. Is it not a fact that capitalism always develops stained by the blood and sweat of the workers?

Another aspect to point out is that structural unemployment appears to be inherent in the development of the productive forces in the periphery of the system instead of constituting a stage in which "marginality" appears as a necessarily transitory process. The concentration of income constitutes, in the same way, a condition for the expansion of capital in relative terms. Thus, we can ask, do both the unemployment and concentration of wealth that appear associated with the new state of industrial development constitute, in the long run, limits to the accumulation of capital? It is worthwhile to examine, briefly, the nature of these problems in the Central American experience.

a) The rate of growth of the Economically Active Population (EAP) between 1950 and 1970 was 2.4 percent for the whole region, whereas population increased an average of 3.2 percent. Even the most superficial comparison of both indicators shows a serious deficiency in the labor market. The 1970 data on open unemployment, utilizing the official technical parameters, are quite conservative: 8.4 percent for the whole region, 12 percent for Guatemala, and 5 percent for Costa Rica. However, a study by the Organización Internacional del Trabajo (OIT) for Costa Rica shows a rate of total unemployment of 15.2 percent,[4] which suggests that behind the former statistics is a hidden and more serious reality.

The previous data reveal a new dimension when separated into rural and urban sectors. The estimated total unemployment for the agricultural sector in 1970 — considering employment as equivalent to 280 days per person per year — was 44.4 percent for Central America as a region, reaching as high as to 58.5 percent for El Salvador and as low as 14.7 percent for Costa Rica.[5] In order to have maintained the present (1975) rates of employment, it would have been necessary to create 874,000 new jobs, and only 175,000 jobs were created (or 20 percent of those needed). In the first five years of this decade, only one out of every five persons entering the labor market obtained work (see Table 1 for figures on employment and unemployment).

The results of almost two decades of encouraging industrial growth reveal a common sense truth — that increases in productivity are incompatible with increases in employment. The basic result is the incapacity of the industrial sector to absorb even normal demographic increases (assuming that, *ceteris paribus*, the countryside was not complying with its fatal job of expelling increasing numbers of workers). Of all the developmentalist theories, the theory that increased industrialization increases employment is the one that has most rapidly revealed itself as profoundly false.

b) Closely associated with the previous problem of employment is the remuneration of labor and, in general, the problem of the distribution of income within the framework of the model of economic growth that we are considering (see Table 5). It is not enough to say that the industrialization mechanism in these societies reinforces the exclusive and polarizing characteristics of an agrarian society supposedly on the way to overcoming its problems. The "oligarchic" style that related peons to the masters of the land changes qualitatively only to take on new dimensions in social and political life.

No one doubts that the accumulation of surpluses in the form of surplus labor forms the basis of the functioning of the system. Every economic system that wants to grow will depend on its capacity for accumulation, but at the same time, it cannot be based indefinitely on the repetition of the same possibilities of capital realization. In order to avoid this blockage which would result in the paralysis of growth, the model inevitably requires the re-

[4]The recognized unemployment is 5 percent; to that should be added the so-called equivalent unemployment which is 10.2 percent. The latter is composed of visible and invisible underemployment.

[5]In the rest of the countries, the statistics are as follows: Guatemala, 52.3 percent; Honduras, 42.5 percent; and Nicaragua 21.5 percent.

inforcement of the tendencies towards the concentration of income. But to what point?

Table 5
Central America: Distribution of Income in Relation to Total Population (1970, in Central American pesos)

Stratum	Annual per capita income	Strata of income (%)	Percentage total pop.	Total pop. (thousands)
HIGH	17,600	31	5	756
MIDDLE	5,680	30	15	2,268
LOW	246	26	30	4,536
VERY LOW	74	13	50	7,560

Source: SIECA (1975: 18)

The available data barely allow us to show, on the one hand, that the tendencies towards the concentration of social wealth (utilizing the income indicator) have increased in the last few years and that this, on the other hand, has been seriously weakened as a result of inflation in the present decade and by the authoritative application of stabilization programs on the part of the ownership sector and the state. In analyzing this problem one must inevitably mention the nature of the state and the role it plays, which is far from that of an impartial arbitrator in the relationship between capital and labor. State protection appears in order to reduce the costs of capital, and police repression grows at the same time in order to maintain low salaries. Though this is generally true, it is less so for Costa Rica and much more so in the cases of Guatemala and El Salvador.

In analyzing the problem of salaries, it is necessary to consider the particular characteristics and direction of working-class organizations. It is this organization that determines, fundamentally, the final conditions of the sale of labor. Structural analysis hides the fact that objective determinations of the market are not sufficient to explain salary levels; we need also to know the subjective conditions of organization, class combativity, and the possibilities of institutional channeling or repression of conflicts. To wait for the growth of the economy before finally offering better wage and living conditions — like the bosses' strategy proposes — does not correspond to the true movement of capital. The political and union power of workers varies; it increases or decreases according to the rate of exploitation of labor power.

This truism has special meaning in Central America where the means for defending the standard of living and income of the popular classes are impeded by the use of direct noneconomic methods: extreme anti-union violence. The final logic of repression is not, hence, the danger of guerrillas but rather the containment of salaries. "Social-democratic" programs obviously have a political price that owners' groups are not always willing to pay. In the same way that these social programs have a limit, the repression of social conflict also has a price, one that the bosses are today finding themselves obliged to pay.

THE CENTRAL AMERICAN ECONOMY AND THE CRISIS OF "REGIONAL INTEGRATION"

Eighteen years after its signing in 1960, the General Treaty of Central American Economic Integration as a project of economic growth exhibits some symptoms of weakness. Reference is frequently made to the "crisis" of the Common Market, and this same crisis is generally associated with the armed conflict between El Salvador and Honduras and the later separation of Honduras from the Common Market, resulting in the abrupt interruption of commercial traffic between both countries. Since this unfortunate incident in 1969, which is in itself evidence of the irresponsibility of governments and their respective armies, the integrationist project has continued advancing where it has been on track. For this reason it is, therefore, appropriate to ask what is meant by the reference to crisis: Is it a crisis provoked by economic growth? Or, is it the project itself and its basic conception that is shipwrecked helplessly?

One thing is certain, assuming our statistics are correct and our analytical focus adequate. The argument which singles out fraticidal "war" between El Salvador and Honduras as the cause and beginning of the crisis is inadequate. The self-exclusion of Honduras from the Common Market was something that had been sought and negotiated for some time by the government of Honduras. Intraregional trade was hurt, but it recuperated within twelve months and since then has continued increasing; in fact the value of this trade has almost doubled. Further evidence can be found in the data for the "Encuesta selectiva de las inversiones Centroamericanas en el subsector manufacturero" (Bobadilla, 1977: 5).

Of a total fixed investment of 456.1 million Central American pesos in the manufacturing sector, corresponding to a sample of 142 important enterprises in 1974, only 139.2 million pesos (30.5 percent) were invested between 1960 and 1969 (i.e., before Hondura's break from the Common Market). After the conflict, between 1969 and 1973, however, 270 million pesos were invested, which corresponds to 59 percent of the total investment in the sample. What is interesting, finally, is that these investments took place in relatively sophisticated sectors of technology.

The so-called crisis of the Common Market has to be analyzed on the basis of the causes or factors which resulted from its specific characteristics. It is true that the rhythm of growth of intraregional trade became more erratic, and there were small decreases in relative growth rates which, correctly interpreted, show one of the critical points of the process: the approaching of the limits for the easy "substitution" of imports (see Table 1, aggregate industrial value).

If the rate of growth of regional trade, apparently for some the only indicator of interest, increases at a slower rate than that of industrial growth, it would indicate that the regional market tends to be displaced by the national market in some countries and/or trade is concentrated in one or two countries. From this point of view, it is certain that the apparent cause of the crisis, the one which is most immediate and which would appear to contribute most decisively to discrediting the present functioning of the integrationist process, is the growing disequilibrium between some countries that sell a lot and others that buy a lot. Over the years some economies have emerged as

Latin American Perspectives, Issues 25 and 26, Spring and Summer 1980, Vol. VII, Nos. 2 and 3 selling economies and others as net buyers, and this in itself detracts from the primary goals of the Common Market project.

During the years since 1960, Guatemala has developed as a major supplier of the region, and El Salvador, which until 1974 had always produced a surplus in its favor, has begun to have growing deficits relative to Guatemala. Between 1960 and 1977, the total accumulated value of exports from Guatemala and El Salvador to Honduras, Nicaragua, and Costa Rica were U.S. $700 million more than the purchases that those two countries made from the rest.[6] Guatemala received over 679 million Central American pesos of this total; the trade deficits were also shared unequally, the greatest part belonging to Nicaragua (40 percent of the total), followed by Honduras (33 percent), and the least amount to Costa Rica (27 percent).

Why does the greatest competition come from the Guatemalan industrial complex? The previous data do not reveal the emergence of an aggressive industrial bourgeoisie of national origin capable of commanding the development of the productive forces in its favor. The rise of the Guatemala/El Salvador axis is the result of preexisting factors that the integrationist program of the Common Market only accentuated. If the indicators of gross capital formation were indirectly related to the volume of accumulation reached, the Salvadorean local bourgeoisie would be the most prepared to divert capital resources towards industrial investment. The high level of concentration of wealth explains the dynamism of the Salvadorean entrepreneurial minority. In Guatemala the volume of accumulation was less, but the manufacturing experience was relatively more important. In both societies the over-supply of labor power is as important as the extreme authoritarian rigidity of their social political relations. Does this last point suggest the hypothesis that the costs of production in both countries may be less than in Nicaragua and Costa Rica because of the differential weight of variable capital? Is the competitiveness of the final product guaranteed by means of payment of lower salaries rather than greater productivity? It is difficult to respond affirmatively because the available data do not permit a valid comparison between real levels of income for the working population of these countries.[7] Later, we will return to this problem.

The disequilibrium in the economic growth of the region, expressed in the imbalance of intraregional commerce, attracted little attention in the 1960s because the amount was small and because traditional exports seemed to mask the importance of such balances. Only Honduras officially recognized its inability to adapt rapidly in face of the exigencies of the integration process. In the 1970s such problems could no longer go unnoticed because they had also produced a trade deficit in relation to the rest of the world. In reality, Central America always had an unfavorable trade balance throughout the entire period, especially with North America.[8]

[6]Data from SIECA, based on CIF imports registered by country.

[7]On the other hand, the simple comparison of average salaries, by economic activity in 1970 and in Central American pesos gives the following results: Guatemala, 88.3 Central American pesos a month; El Salvador, 64.1; Honduras, 63.7; Nicaragua, 93.3; Costa Rica, 78.9.

[8]Cline (1977: 69) on analyzing the benefits from economic integration in terms of "economic well-being" indicates that Honduras, Nicaragua, and Costa Rica have permanent negative balances in intrazonal commerce "which does not signify that they benefit relatively less." The intraregional deficits, he indicates, are always less than those with the rest of the world so that the deficits with the region are more the result of general deficits with international trade.

All of the above demonstrates that the Common Market project never went beyond the first stage of being a free trade zone, and also failed, as well, in its attempt to achieve productive integration. Instead, it created a highly competitive and noncomplementary productive structure. In this way, with the mechanisms of capital unleashed, to use the language of the Regional Organization for Central America and Panama-Agency for International Development (ROCAP-AID), free enterprise and the free market only resulted in a growing inequality in economic growth favoring Guatemala and El Salvador. But it is difficult to point out who the winners and losers are in when the property of enterprises most favored have been of North American origin. In any case, the coefficient of industrialization, one of the most conventional statistics for comparing productive structures, reveals a general average for the region of 17 percent, in which countries are represented in the following order: Costa Rica, 23 percent; Nicaragua and El Salvador, 21 percent; Guatemala, 17 percent; and Honduras, 15 percent.

Table 6

Central America: Index of the Agricultural Industrial Product per Worker (1950=100)

	1960	1965	1970	1975
GUATEMALA				
Agriculture	110	121	154	198
Industry	128	151	195	208
EL SALVADOR				
Agriculture	121	130	141	145
Industry	126	181	205	230
HONDURAS				
Agriculture	89	91	113	102
Industry	211	206	215	119
NICARAGUA				
Agriculture	112	182	192	231
Industry	150	250	318	344
COSTA RICA				
Agriculture	125	146	178	204
Industry	157	200	245	289

Source: CEPAL (1976, Table 12: 79)

The utilization of other measures, such as the mean rates of growth of the Aggregate Industrial Value (see Table 1), or the rate of the growth of the Industrial Product per Worker (see Table 6) calculated for periods of median range, show unmistakable advantages for Nicaragua and Costa Rica, which, however, appear as the big losers in commercial exchange. The previous statement notwithstanding, the gap in the absolute levels of the Aggregate Industrial Value at constant prices between both groups of countries as shown in Table 1 has more than doubled since 1960. An explanation must be found for this apparently contradictory result.

To begin with, the initial advantages of Guatemala and El Salvador come from the absolute size of their economies and their relatively large industrial base and not, as is believed, from a larger or more equal national income per capita. This represents, evidently, a temporary advantage, one in which growth is initially a step ahead of development. Furthermore, one should mention the important degree of interdependence reached between the national economies of Guatemala and El Salvador and the further development of preexisting and growing cultural ties based on a political affinity between economic and military elites. The proximity between both countries is no longer only geographical; it is now based on an unappreciated infrastructural integration and on a cluster of joint investments that increase the interdependence of both bourgeoisies. The opposite occurs with the rest of Central America where the unresolved post-war trauma between the Honduran and Savadorean societies is kept alive by military men with short memories. It is known that the leaders of both armies understand each other better than do the people who follow them. There are also notorious political differences between Nicaragua and Costa Rica that only came to light when the crisis of the Somoza dictatorship was exposed. Finally, Guatemala and El Salvador contain 60 percent of the population and produce more than 50 percent of the Gross Product of the region, which means the enterprises of both countries are guaranteed more than half of the Central American market.

Perhaps because of the initial advantages that this integrated market offered — e.g., some favorable conditions in infrastructure (superior, in any case to those that Honduras and even Nicaragua offered) and the sinister capacity of the military governments of both countries to "discipline" the local workforce — investments have tended to locate in Guatemala and El Salvador. As was pointed out in a recent publication, "the risk that an enterprise runs upon investing with eyes toward a large market and finding itself limited later to a reduced national market is much less if it establishes itself in Guatemala or El Salvador . . . " (Banco de América, 1978: 3) which, if true, would tend to prolong the initial advantages obtained by these countries and consequently increase the imbalances in regional exchange.

Finally, in order to complete the explanation of the seemingly paradoxical situation of Nicaragua and Costa Rica, whose industrial structures grew more rapidly than those of Guatemala and El Salvador but which had increasingly negative balances as a result of Central American trade, it is worthwhile to look at the structures of industrial development in both groups of countries. Guatemala and El Salvador have developed a manufacturing structure clearly oriented towards the regional economic space on the basis of producing and selling competitively priced goods for immediate consumption (foods, textiles, clothing, furniture, leather, etc.) for which there was a preexisting demand which had been locally supplied by traditional industrialists. These artisan industries have been destroyed by the liberalization of trade. The relatively larger size of the internally integrated market of Guatemala and El Salvador probably permits a greater utilization of economies of scale and, allows them to compete with more favorable prices in the rest of the area despite the distances and the growing cost of land transportation. Even counting the inflation of recent years, production in these countries continues to be maintained at competitive levels.

The analysis of the character of the "crisis" is related to that of the nature of the integration process. Is it an irreversible phenomenon which determines that the problems of integration can only be resolved with more integration, or has integration found its limit and the process of "disintegration" set in, expressed in the discrediting of the mechanisms that until now have been functioning and in the loss of confidence in the institutions that direct it? (see Table 1 for intraregional trade . . .).

To the extent that there are some national economies more "integrated" than others, reflected by the importance that intraregional trade acquires in the total structure of foreign trade, and to the extent that there are some economies more dependent on the luck of this process than others, irreversibility is only a part of this problem. If the present process were totally paralyzed, an improbable occurrence given the current productive, commercial, and political structures, those countries that now appear to have advantages would be the most seriously affected. In reality, it would be something like the Pirro War, in which everyone loses.

The strictly econometric analysis of the integrationist process carried out in recent studies by the SIECA-Brookings Institute group reveals that, in 1972, the net benefits of economic integration were 165 million Central American pesos, equivalent to 3 percent of the regional Gross Domestic Product for that year. If the sum total of the net benefits ("annual flows") were taken for the total number of years since 1960, it would give a total of more than $3,000 million that would probably be distributed in the following unequal manner: 39.3 percent Guatemala; 24.1 percent Nicaragua; 21.4 percent El Salvador; and 9 percent Costa Rica and Honduras.

It thus is not possible to maintain an optimistic view even within the technocratic vision. The social costs of the process defy quantification, and, as such, underemployment and low incomes translate into the perpetuation or even deterioration of truly deplorable living conditions. The real results of integration are found in the rates of infant mortality, malnutrition, the extremely slow decline in illiteracy, the accelerated increase in underemployment, deterioration in housing, lack of opportunities for getting ahead, and at times even the actual physical degradation of the population.

It is true that the integrationist model has contributed towards vitalizing and diversifying economic activity, improving distribution and utilization of regional resources, and fomenting Central American cooperation at other levels. However, inasmuch as it has been a model directed and taken advantage of exclusively by North American capital and a small entrepreneurial elite (merchants and industrialists), it has converted itself into a capitalist model of growth with no interest in avoiding the evils that "free" enterprise necessarily produces.

CONCLUDING REMARKS

What appears to be irreversible because of the nature of the interests that it has generated and strengthened can be corrected only at the cost of these same interests within the framework of capitalist development. To rethink the original project in light of present realities would mean that the monopoly bourgeoisie (national and foreign) would have to end the mostly corporative direction of the process that it has been able to maintain until now and, consequently, the role of the state would have to be strengthened. Economic growth depends on the capacity for accumulation that the society has; the decisive factor is to determine who controls this process in order to understand the forms that the accumulation takes. If it is the crisis of integration that is referred to, we must read between the lines to determine that this means the failure of accumulation by means of private enterprise. To strengthen the state would mean to test its capacity to direct capitalist accumulation under new proposals. It would mean political power, for example, capable of returning to the Balanced Regional Industrial Growth project suddenly abandoned, less ideologically than pragmatically, by foreign capital. But it is not just more equal benefits for participant countries that are needed; the classes that live and produce within them must also benefit more equally. All this depends, however, on the character of the national classes, the type of relations and conflicts that they establish, and the political culture that previous history has passed on.

The processes of economic integration are processes of economic growth. Abandoned to the so-called laws of the market, to the anarchic reign of private interests, the results could not be different from those that are presently observed. In fact, the easy substitution of imports and the first increments in intraregional trade cannot serve as a base for social or economic development nor can they provide any optimism for the future. Thus, whatever causes are sought to explain the problems of economic integration, they always have a final goal which defines them. The larger problem is not the regional disequilibrium that has undoubtedly been caused, but the social disequilibrium that underlies all this reality. Trade disequilibrium, expressed as both positive and negative returns, hides the brutal consequences of a process that has repeated an already known and much warned about experience in other countries in Latin America.

Paradoxically, the country that has the most important trade returns in its favor, Guatemala, is the one that has highest unemployment and the most unequal distribution of income; nor is it coincidental that Guatemala is the country with the most anti-union violence. Costa Rica, as is known, maintains net deficits in trade, but the social gap is less, and its political structure is more democratic and tolerant.

In the present crossroads, the crisis of the Common Market can only be resolved on a political level. The decisions that have to be made in order to readjust the process to new realities of economic and social development are profoundly political. No one doubts that in such a crossroad there are many routes to be taken. A strengthening of institutions by means of supra-national decisionmaking was one of them. The treaty framework proposed by SIECA was a well-intentioned project but impossible to carry out. The search for industrial exports to the rest of the world, which Costa Rica now attempts, is another alternative. For that, a highly concentrated and specialized structure would be needed in order to compete internationally; for example, an economy completely oriented towards the producing and selling of underwear internationally. There are also those who give more importance than is merited to the development of agroindustries. Furthermore, some governments are irresponsibly open to the complacency of free zones.

No project that forgets the internal market will be able to function. Back in 1960 this amnesia was perhaps understandable and permissible. Given the degree to which economic growth has advanced, any new strategy of growth should, at least partially, attempt to vitalize internal consumption. We all know that the market is composed of solvent consumers and not citizens. Of eighteen million of the latter, only two million have the option of participating in the market. Under these conditions it is possible to advance, but only very slowly, responding to strictly limited stimuli from the natural growth of demand. The boundaries of the market need to be socially broadened. Until now, the axis of the accumulation of capital has not been based on the broadening of the sphere of circulation, limited by the secular tendency to remunerate work at lower than, or very close to, its real value. The politics of low salaries and regression of income have until today been a condition for the growth of consumption among the higher strata of society, those that "live off of surplus." It is probable that technical progress augments productivity, but it does not broaden demand because at no time has it been translated into a relative decrease in prices. "Produce small expensive quantities in order to earn more," reveals an impeccable but short-term logic. The longer-term project of the bourgeoisie should be an attempt to increase profits through the increase in the rate of surplus value. The crisis of the common market is not, obviously, a crisis in realizing capital, but the search for expansion through the internal market could improve profits.

Situated as we are outside bourgeois rationality, we can only think about this possibility on the condition that neither imperialist capital nor the local bourgeoisie continue commanding the process, or at least that their interests not be the only ones that preside. However, in order for this to succeed, it is necessary that new social forces and new political alliances have a presence in the state and, as a part of the state, finally project economic growth with social development and political democracy.

REFERENCES

Bancos Centrales (de las capitales de Centroamérica)
1977-1978 *Informes Anuales*

Banco de América
1978 *Actividad Económica*, I, 5 (November)

BID/INTAL (Banco Interamericano de Desarrollo e Instituto para la Integración de América Latina)
1974 *El Desarrollo Integrado de Centroamérica en la presente década*, Vol IV, Buenos Aires

Bobadilla, Horacio
1977 "Encuestra selectiva de las inversiones de Centroamérica en el subsector manufacturero," Appendix No. 6 in *Beneficios y costos de la Integración Económica Centroamericana*, Serie Estudios Proyectos SIECA-BROOKINGS, Volume II, Guatemala

Business Latin America
1978 (October 11), information taken from *Actualidad Económica del Perú*, 12 (January-February 1979)

CELADE (Centro Latinoamericano de Demografia — Chile)
1968 *Boletíin Demografico*, I, 2 (October)

CEPAL (Comisión Económica para América Latina)
1971 "Consideraciones sobre la situación del empleo en Centroamérica," Mexico City: CEPAL, mimeographed (April)

1976 "Desarrollo y política social en Centroamerica," Mexico City: CEPAL (August 11), mimeographed

Cline, W.
1977 *Beneficios y costos de la Integración Económica Centroamericana*, Serie Estudios Proyecto SIECA-BROOKINGS, Volume II, Guatemala

Rapoport, A.
1977 "Estructura industrial en centroamérica," chapter II in *Beneficios y costos de la Integración Económica Centroamericana*, Serie Estudios Proyecto SIECA-BROOKINGS, Volume II, Guatemala

SIECA
1975 *La política de desarrollo social dentro de la integración económica*, Guatemala

SIECA-Brookings
1977 "Encuestra selectiva de las inversiones de Centroamérica en el subsector manufacturero," (see Bobadilla)

J. Lat. Amer. Stud. 15, 269–294. *Printed in Great Britain*

Economic Development Over the Long Run – Central America Since 1920

by V. BULMER-THOMAS

1. *Introduction*

The development of Central America in recent decades presents a paradox. As measured by the growth of real Gross Domestic Product (GDP) per head, the region's performance compares favourably with the rest of Latin America and other less developed countries (LDCs). At the same time, political convulsions have become more acute, and in no part of the isthmus – not even in Costa Rica – is political stability assured.

There are several possible responses to this paradox. One is a virulently anti-Marxist response, denying the relevance of any form of historical materialism, in which the evolution of the political system is divorced entirely from its economic substructure. Another is to downgrade the economic achievements of Central America, arguing that conventional measures of performance are a poor indicator of economic health.

Neither response will be adopted in this paper. I do not wish to deny either the achievements of the Central American economies or the connection between the political and economic systems. By taking the long view, however, one may observe how the model of economic development adopted has involved resource shifts which make untenable the old political systems; these shifts, which in the short run can be dismissed as 'marginal', only acquire significance in the long run since their influence takes many years to be felt.

A study of Central American economic development over the long run is hampered by the absence of official statistics. Official national accounts for each country go back, in most cases, only to 1950. As part of my work for a study of Central America in the inter-war years, I have prepared the national accounts back to 1920 (see Bulmer-Thomas, 1982*a*), which together with the official statistics gives a time-series for each country of

63 years (1920–82). While in no sense perfect,[1] a time-series of this length for five republics makes it possible to distinguish between permanent and temporary changes in the economy and to observe the operation of any long-term cyclical forces.

This paper does not attempt a complete overview of the Central American economies since 1920; given the limitations of space, that would be neither possible nor appropriate. Instead, I shall focus primarily on the agricultural sector, which to this day remains dominant in terms of employment, foreign exchange earnings and (at least at world prices) output.

This continuing dominance of agriculture is at first sight surprising in view of the deliberate attempt to foster industrialization through a Customs Union in the late 1950s and 1960s. These attempts, inspired by the U.N. Economic Commission for Latin America and carried through by regional technocrats, led to a wave of optimism that Central America was in transition towards a new model of development in which economic, social and political modernization would occur simultaneously (see Torres Rivas, 1973).

Such optimism can now be seen to be premature. Throughout most of the isthmus, agrarian interests (the traditional oligarchy) exercise preponderant influence over political affairs and have successfully neutralized the efforts of the region's technocrats to breathe new life into the Central American Common Market (CACM).

The formation of CACM was not the first occasion on which the oligarchy survived a challenge to its political hegemony. An earlier crisis had occurred during the depression of the 1930s; on that occasion, however, the oligarchy survived by increasing the power of the state, over which it continued to exercise great influence either directly or indirectly.

This increased state power ensured that the challenge presented by the CACM was potential only. The traditional interests of the oligarchy

[1] Since writing this paper, my attention has been drawn to two studies of national accounts for Central America (ECLA, 1978; Mooney, 1968), in addition to those mentioned in Bulmer-Thomas (1982*a*). The ECLA study pushes back the time-series for each country in Central America to 1945 and is the basic source for figure 1 and tables 1 and 2 in Pérez Brignoli's article in this issue of the *Journal of Latin American Studies*. The paper by Mooney estimates the national accounts for El Salvador from 1945 to 1965.

Regrettably, all of these studies differ slightly in terms of their results (compare, for example, Table 1 in my paper with Table 1 in Pérez Brignoli). The differences arise from the use of alternative concepts, sources and methodologies, which in principle could and should be resolved; until that laborious task has been carried out, however, I prefer to work with my own time-series on the grounds that it is at least internally consistent.

(export agriculture) were safeguarded and the extra resources needed by industrialization and urbanization had to come from elsewhere; furthermore, industry's need for an expanding internal market based on income redistribution was averted through carrying out import-substitution at the regional level. The effort, therefore, to steer Central America towards industrial modernity without generating a political or social crisis must be deemed a failure.

The oligarchy never abandoned the export-led model of growth which had proved so successful in the half century up to the Great Depression. Indeed, during the heyday of the CACM one may observe two models of development co-existing uneasily at the same time. The collapse of the CACM, however, led to further intensification of the traditional export-led model.

It is the implications of this intensification which form the principal focus of this paper; as we shall see, the price which must be paid for the continuing dominance of the oligarchy based on its agricultural export interests is a breakdown of social and economic relations in the rural economy. This breakdown is presenting a third challenge to the oligarchy, which may yet prove to be decisive.

2. *Economic Performance Over the Long Run*

At the economy-wide or aggregate level, the measure of performance most commonly used in country descriptions is provided by the growth of real GDP. These growth rates for each country are reported in Table 1 for various periods;[2] the entry for Central America is an unweighted arithmetic average of the growth rates recorded for the five republics.

Several features of Table 1 are worthy of comment; one may note, first, that the economic depression of the last few years has been intensely severe, surpassing in extent for several countries the drop in real output recorded after the 1929 depression. With the exception of these two periods, real GDP fell only in two cases: Nicaragua from 1974 to 1979 (which was

[2] For the years before 1950, I have used my own estimates of GDP for all republics except Honduras. For the latter, an official estimate exists back to 1925 (see *Banco Central de Honduras*, 1956), although my own estimates were needed for the period 1920–5. For the period after 1950, I have used official statistics, although for the earlier years it has been necessary in some cases to adjust GDP at current prices to constant 1950 prices, using a variety of price information. For the most recent years (1981–2), I have used estimates published in *Inforpress* (1982) together with unpublished figures made available to me by the Economist Intelligence Unit (London). Both the figures for 1981 and 1982 can be expected to be revised in the future.

Table 1. *Rate of Growth of Gross Domestic Product at 1950 prices.* (Rates expressed as geometric annual averages)

Period	Costa Rica	El Salvador	Guatemala	Honduras	Nicaragua	Central America*
1920–4	3.0	4.3	5.4	0.5	1.9	3.0
1924–9	0.2	2.6	3.8	8.3	6.4	4.3
1929–34	0	−0.7	−0.6	−2.4	−4.9	−1.4
1934–9	8.0	3.3	12.5	0.2	2.4	5.3
1939–44	−2.7	3.5	−4.7	2.4	4.6	0.6
1944–9	10.9	6.8	6.9	5.3	6.9	7.3
1949–54	5.1	3.8	3.5	2.0	11.3	5.1
1954–9	4.1	3.2	4.9	5.1	3.1	4.0
1959–64	3.9	7.2	5.0	3.9	6.8	5.3
1964–9	7.8	4.7	5.5	4.5	5.5	5.6
1969–74	7.1	4.9	6.4	3.5	5.4	5.5
1974–9	5.4	3.5	5.3	5.2	−4.7	2.9
1979–82	−1.2	−8.1	0.8	0.5	4.9	−0.6
1920–9	1.4	3.4	4.5	4.8	4.4	3.7
1929–39	3.9	1.3	5.8	−1.1	−1.3	1.7
1939–49	3.9	5.1	0.8	3.9	5.8	3.9
1949–59	4.6	3.5	4.2	3.5	7.1	4.6
1959–69	5.8	5.9	5.2	4.2	6.1	5.5
1969–79	6.3	4.2	5.9	4.4	0.2	4.2
1920–50	3.0	3.1	3.8	2.4	3.2	3.1
1950–82	5.0	3.4	4.6	3.7	4.2	4.2

* Figures for Central America are unweighted arithmetic averages of country rates.
Sources: see note 2.

mainly due to a massive 25% reduction in real GDP during the 1979 civil war year) and Costa Rica during the Second World War.

Secondly, if we ignore the periods of falling real output (1929–34 and 1979–82), the real GDP growth rate for the region comes close to 5% per annum – a respectable performance by international standards. This rate tends only to be surpassed when exceptional conditions prevail (e.g. the period 1944–9, when the productive forces artificially restrained during the Second World War were released, and the period 1949–54 when the Commodity boom triggered off by the Korean war prevailed).

The figures in Table 1 suggest the following periodization:

(*a*) 1920–9. A decade in which the traditional model of export-led growth is consolidated after the dislocations of the First World War. During this period, export specialization reaches its peak, with coffee and bananas accounting for more than 70% of export earnings in all republics and more than 90% in Costa Rica, El Salvador and Guatemala. In the second half of the decade problems of excess supply in world coffee markets start to be felt, causing a reduction in the rate of growth of GDP for Costa Rica,[3] El Salvador and Guatemala. In Nicaragua and Honduras, however, the rate of growth accelerates, as virgin banana lands are opened for production.

(*b*) 1929–34. A quinquennium in which most of the output-reducing impact of the depression is experienced. In one case (Costa Rica) the fall in output begins before 1929 and in several republics (Costa Rica, El Salvador, Guatemala) the turning-point is reached before 1934. In all cases, the fall in output is much more modest than the fall in prices and in two cases (El Salvador, Nicaragua) the fall in output is dwarfed by the fall in recent years.

(*c*) 1934–9. A period of strong recovery in the 'coffee republics' (i.e. those whose principal export was coffee), while the performance of the 'banana republics' (Nicaragua,[4] Honduras) was much less impressive. Recovery was based primarily on import substitution in agriculture (ISA) and only secondarily on import substitution in industry (ISI) and/or increases in the export quantum. The hypothesis suggested by this dichotomy (see Bulmer-Thomas, 1982*a*) is that ISA was easier to achieve in the coffee than banana republics, since in the former the land and labour required for an increase in home output were more readily available.

(*d*) 1939–44. A quinquennium in which economic performance is determined primarily by the impact of the Second World War. On the export front, the requisitioning of the banana fleets by the U.S. navy posed severe problems, but new markets also appeared for war-related products (e.g. quinine), or products whose supply to the U.S. market was interrupted by the Japanese occupation of parts of Asia (e.g. rubber, abacá). The poor growth record of Costa Rica in this period (GDP actually fell) was due to the collapse of banana exports after 1941 caused by transportation problems. Similar problems occurred in Honduras and Nicaragua, but these were more than offset by strong ISA and gold export performances respectively.[5]

(*e*) 1944–9. The exploitation of idle resources in the post-war years

[3] Disease on the banana plantations after 1925 was also responsible for the sharp fall in the rate of growth of GDP in Costa Rica.

[4] In general, coffee has been a more important source of export earnings than bananas in Nicaragua, but this was not true for most of the 1930s. It should be clear that the use of the phrase 'banana republics' is not intended in the pejorative sense used by O'Henry.

[5] On the importance of gold to the Nicaraguan economy in this period, see Cantarero (1949).

caused a boom of almost unparalleled proportions in all republics. The major beneficiary in each case was the export sector, which successfully recaptured markets lost in the war. During this period, exports also became more diversified; timber, cacao and abacá acquired significance in Costa Rica,[6] while sesame and cotton increased in importance in Nicaragua. Cotton also started to make an important contribution to export earnings in El Salvador.

(*f*) 1949–54. Despite high commodity prices caused by the Korean war, the export quantum did not expand rapidly in this period, and the rate of growth decelerated in all republics except Nicaragua.[7] The indirect impact of high commodity prices proved beneficial, however, through its impact on government revenue and expenditure and the relaxation of the foreign exchange constraint. In El Salvador, ISI proved to be important for the first time.

(*g*) 1954–9. Despite the fall in their price, the quantum of traditional exports rose sharply in this period and contributed substantially to the rise of real GDP. Export diversification also continued with cotton and sugar increasing in importance throughout the isthmus, while coffee exports expanded rapidly in Honduras.

(*h*) 1959–69. A decade of rapid growth dominated by the formation of the Central American Common Market (CACM). In all republics, the industrial share of GDP rose, although the rise was least marked in Costa Rica and in Honduras the share fell between 1964 and 1969. The diversion of resources from agriculture, however, was in relative terms only and the agricultural sector continued to grow in all republics, with beef added to the list of major agricultural exports.

(*i*) 1969–74. Although GDP continued to grow rapidly in all the republics, the difficulties facing CACM in the wake of the war between El Salvador and Honduras in 1969[8] began to manifest themselves in the performance of the industrial sector. The deceleration in the latter's rate of growth, however, was compensated for by the rise in world commodity prices after 1971, which favourably influenced the volume of agricultural exports in all republics.

(*j*) 1974–9. Despite the continued weakness of CACM and the world economy, real GDP continued to rise rapidly in all republics except

[6] The export of cacao from Costa Rica began in the late 1930s, when the United Fruit Company turned over idle banana lands for alternative uses (see Seligson, 1980).

[7] The exceptionally high growth of GDP in Nicaragua was due to a boom in social infrastructure developments.

[8] It is now generally accepted that the CACM's present difficulties would have arisen without the 1969 war. See, in particular, Delgado (1978).

Nicaragua.[9] The main stimuli were provided by the extraordinary rise in commodity prices (mainly coffee and sugar) and by the sharp rise in foreign capital inflows.

(*k*) 1979–82. A period in which the economic crisis, which had been threatening for many years, was finally realized. The weaknesses of CACM were brought into the open with the closing of frontiers, the intra-regional payments crisis, the collapse of exchange rate stability and the adoption of unilateral action by partner countries. The fall in commodity prices proved more rapid than anticipated and the drying up of new capital inflows focused attention on the foreign exchange constraint as the major obstacle to future growth.

The growth of real GDP is not intended as a measure of economic welfare. It can be adjusted, however, in a number of ways to approximate the change in welfare; one such adjustment allows for changes in population, another for the difference between the growth of product and home expenditure with or without terms of trade effects. The first adjustment will be presented here, while the second will be left to the next section.

Unlike the case of many other LDCs, rapid population growth in Central America is not exclusively a post-1950 phenomenon. While it is true that the annual rate of growth of population has accelerated in the last three decades, it stood above 2% even in the 1920s for all republics except El Salvador.[10] The rate of growth appears to have fallen slightly in the 1930s (when the unweighted Central American average was 2.05% p.a.) before returning in the 1940s to its 1920s level (2.2% p.a.). Since 1950 the rate of growth of population has regularly exceeded 3% p.a. in all republics except Costa Rica, where the demographic transition began in the late 1960s.[11]

As elsewhere, the cause of the acceleration in the rate of growth of population has been primarily the fall in the death rate. The Crude Death Rate (CDR), which in the 1920s was roughly 20, is now much closer to 10 – a drop which in the absence of any change in the Crude Birth Rate (CBR) is sufficient to add 1% to the rate of growth of population.[12] Several

[9] Even in Nicaragua, GDP increased rapidly up to 1978 when it fell by 8%, falling by a further 25% in 1979.

[10] El Salvador's annual rate of growth of population in the 1920s (1.7%) was held back by high death rates.

[11] The present Costa Rican annual growth rate of population, however, still exceeds 2% – very similar to the rate recorded in the 1920s.

[12] The CBR is measured as the number of live births per thousand of the population; the CDR measures the number of deaths per thousand of the population. The difference between the two measures the net increase in population on the assumption of no international migration.

Table 2. *GDP per head (in 1950 dollars) for selected years.* (figures in brackets refer to home expenditure per head)

Year	Costa Rica	El Salvador	Guatemala	Honduras	Nicaragua
1920	226 (186)	110 (98)	166 (151)	147 (133)	154 (148)
1929	212 (199)	128 (119)	184 (182)	184 (155)	185 (153)
1939	252 (250)	128 (107)	256 (240)	129 (111)	132 (105)
1949	286 (271)	185 (168)	220 (223)	152 (133)	182 (189)
1959	309 (325)	192 (188)	243 (247)	158 (148)	262 (261)
1969	390 (409)	256 (246)	300 (284)	175 (165)	363 (359)
1979	558 (682)	289 (299)	377 (354)	193 (191)	251 (238)
1982	493 N.A.	196 N.A.	353 N.A.	177 N.A.	263 N.A.

Sources: see note 15.

countries, however, noticeably Nicaragua and El Salvador, have also experienced sharp rises in the CBR, giving a further stimulus to population growth.[13]

The results obtained from adjusting GDP growth for population changes are given in Table 2, the most striking feature of which is the ability of the recent crisis to wipe out the gains of decades; Nicaragua and El Salvador, for example, recorded in 1982 much the same GDP per head as in 1959. The stagnation of GDP per head in Honduras over the whole period is also a marked feature of the table; not only has Honduras (since 1940) acquired the dubious status of being the poorest Central American country, it has also not yet recorded the income per head of Costa Rica in 1920.[14]

With the exception of Honduras, income per head more than doubled between 1920 and the beginning of the recent crisis (1978–80). This increase, however, has been very unevenly distributed, with most of it occurring in the second half of the period; from 1944 to 1979, GDP per head grew at more than 2 % p.a. in Costa Rica and Guatemala, while from 1939 until the civil war GDP per head in Nicaragua grew at more than 3 % p.a. El Salvador, by contrast, has experienced periods of rapid growth (1920–9, 1939–49, 1959–69), interspersed with periods of slow or negative growth (1929–39, 1949–59, 1969–82).

[13] In Nicaragua, however, this stimulus has been moderated by the fact that the CDR was already low in the 1930s, varying between 11 and 14 (see Cantarero, 1949, p. 38).

[14] An explanation of Honduras' poor performance would require an article to itself. Much of the explanation, however, has to do with Honduras' heavy dependence on banana exports; production, prices and markets of these exports have, for much of the period, been controlled by multinational fruit companies concerned with the maximization of global, not national, profits. Banana exports have also generated less government revenue than other exports in Central America.

It would be tempting to look only at the figures for 1982 in Table 2 and argue from this that the present crisis results from economic backwardness. This is a temptation which should be resisted; the sharp fall in GDP per head in recent years is as much a consequence of the present crisis as its cause and for much of the period (particularly since the Second World War) the growth in GDP per head has been high by international standards. Furthermore, the poor performer (Honduras) is the exception which proves the rule, since Honduras is not yet in the midst of a social revolution, while the fastest growing country (Nicaragua) was the first in recent years to experience one.

3. *Home Expenditure and Terms of Trade Effects*

In the previous section, economic performance has been measured using Gross Domestic Product (GDP). GDP, however, measures output (net) and includes exports while excluding imports as can be seen very clearly when written as:

$$y = e + x - m \tag{1}$$

where y represents real GDP, e represents real home expenditure, x represents real exports and m real imports.

Real home expenditure (e) includes consumption and investment (both private and public); it therefore represents a better guide to the standard of living than real GDP. In the absence of direct measurements, it can be approximated from equation (1) as

$$e = y - x + m \tag{2}$$

where this time it will be noted that e varies negatively with x and positively with m. Thus real imports – by adding to the resources available for consumption and investment – increase real home expenditure while exports subtract from it.

The data on real home expenditure are given in parentheses in Table 2.[15] A pattern emerges for most republics of a post-war period in which real home expenditure per person has either exceeded or come close to

[15] Real imports and real exports for the 1920–50 period were obtained as a by-product of the national accounts estimates (see the Appendix to Bulmer-Thomas, 1982*a*). For the period after 1950, they were obtained by deflating the value of imports and exports by unit values given in the U.N. *Yearbook of International Statistics*. Where the latter did not report unit values, I have referred instead to national sources to cover most of the gaps. The remaining gaps have been filled as follows: I have used the series for El Salvador to cover lacunae in the series for other countries in the case of import unit values, while I have constructed the missing observations for export unit values using the prices of principal exports and moving weights. Figures for 1982 are not yet available, which accounts for the missing entries in Table 2.

real GDP per person, while falling short of the latter in the pre-war period. The exception seems to be Honduras, where real home expenditure in the representative years has fallen short of real GDP per person in both periods.

Starting from a given year (say 1950), if the external terms of trade improve, then a given volume of exports will permit a higher volume of imports, i.e. real imports and real home expenditure will rise. The opposite will be true if the external terms of trade deteriorate. One possible interpretation, therefore, of Table 2 is that movements in the external terms of trade for Central America since 1920 account for the change in the ratio between home final expenditure and real GDP.

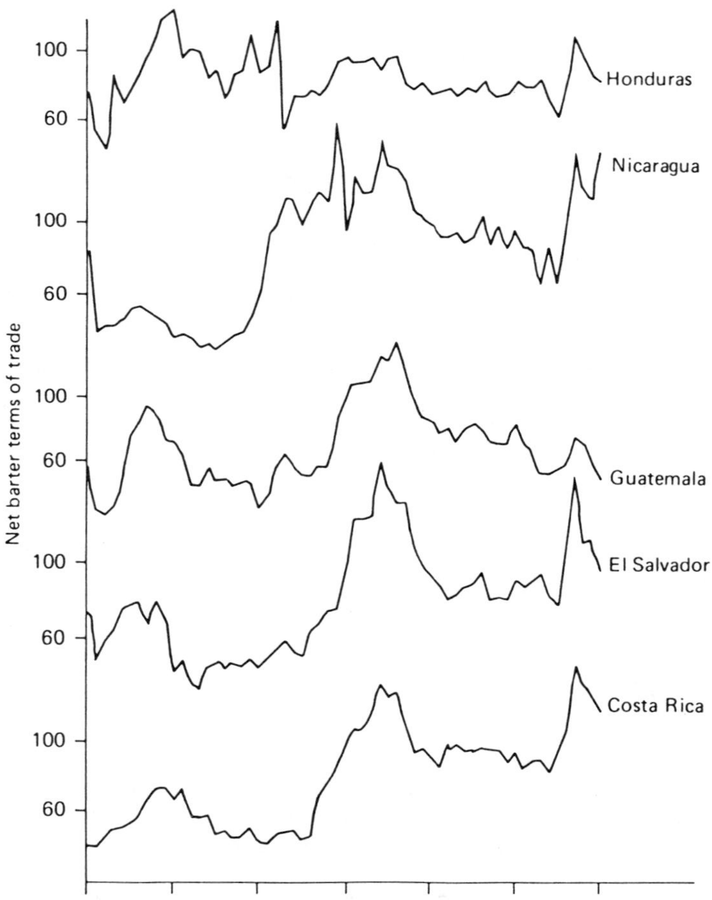

Fig. 1. Net barter terms of trade (1950 = 100). (Sources: see note 16.).

The net barter terms of trade for the Central American republics are presented in Fig. 1.[16] While the terms of trade before 1950 are in almost all cases adverse (i.e. less than 100), the post-1950 picture is much more mixed with periods of sharp improvement at the beginning and end, but a tendency towards 'secular decline' in the intervening years. Honduras, however, is again the exception, since banana prices did not profit from the commodity boom in the Korean war so that most of the post-1950 period is also marked by adverse terms of trade.[17]

Movements in the external terms of trade, therefore, explain much of the gap between real home expenditure and real GDP per person in Table 2, but not all of it. Real imports, however, can grow faster than real exports for reasons other than favourable movements in the barter terms of trade; even with constant prices, a growing deficit on commodity trade is possible if capital inflows are rising, and this certainly did occur in Central America during the 1960s and much of the 1970s.

The adverse terms of trade experienced before 1950 are in part a consequence of using 1950 as the base, since there was a sharp improvement in Central American commodity export prices in the late 1940s. Thus, export prices were close to their peak in 1950 and in consequence much of the 'secular decline' in the post-1950 period is also a reflection of the choice of base year. I have experimented with 1930 as the base year and the position changes dramatically; the 1920–50 period is now one of mixed fortunes, while the 1950–80 period is dominated by positive external terms of trade (i.e. greater than 100), although again Honduras is a sad exception.

The lesson from this experiment in changing the base year is that it is movements in the net barter terms of trade which count rather than the absolute magnitude. From this we can establish the following key periods in the evolution of Central America's external terms of trade; an initial period of decline as a result of the 1921 depression is followed by a sharp improvement which passes its peak in the late 1920s. This is followed by a lengthy period of deterioration which is only reversed in the later stages

[16] For the period after 1950, the price of exports (p_x) and the price of imports (p_m) are simply those corresponding to unit values as described in the previous note. For the period before 1950, the price of imports is assumed to be the same for all republics and was derived from the time-series prepared for Honduras on nominal and real imports (see *Banco Central de Honduras*, 1956). The price of exports was obtained for each republic by deflating the nominal value of exports by the real value as given in my national accounts estimates. The net barter terms of trade have thus been defined as ($p_x/p_m \times 100$) with 1950 = 100.

[17] The relevant banana price is f.o.b. It does not follow that banana retail or auction prices did not rise.

of the Second World War. There follows a spectacular improvement which reaches its peak at the end of the Korean War, leading into nearly two decades of deterioration; the improvement in the early 1970s is almost as dramatic as that thirty years before, but the turning point (1977) is reached more quickly.

What conclusions can be drawn from the evidence on GDP and home expenditure per head in Table 2? In general, the results confirm the picture presented in Table 1 of steady (but not spectacular) economic growth, with the exceptions provided by the long-run stagnation of Honduras and the collapse of the last few years. There is little support here for the notion of Central America as an area locked into traditional methods of production and isolated from advances in the world economy.

On the contrary, the evidence on growth presented in Tables 1 and 2 suggests an economy which over the last sixty years has been subjected to a considerable degree of transformation. As we shall see, the roots of the present crisis lie to a large extent in the tensions and dislocations generated during the course of that transformation; it is change, not stagnation, which lies at the heart of Central America's problems.

The data presented so far, however, are all highly aggregated and do not permit us to establish the exact nature of the economic transformation which has occurred in central America. We must, therefore, turn from aggregate to sectoral performance, beginning with the all-important agricultural sector.

4. *Changes in Agriculture's Relative Share*

Both cross-section and time-series studies (Chenery, 1975) of LCDs suggest that the agricultural sector's share of GDP will decline as income per head rises. The decline is explained in a number of ways (Johnstone, 1975), of which one of the most persuasive is Engel's law; according to the latter, the proportion of income spent on foodstuffs declines as income rises, which suggests that the output of the agricultural sector will rise less rapidly than GDP itself.

The relative decline in agriculture is assumed to be accompanied by rapid urbanization, which attracts rural out-migration and a net capital inflow from the rural economy. The migration of rural labour permits in turn a rise in the productivity of agricultural labour, raising rural real incomes and expanding the market for industrial goods. This accentuates the tendencies towards further urbanization and a virtuous circle is established, leading towards the transformation of a primarily agrarian economy into an industrial one.

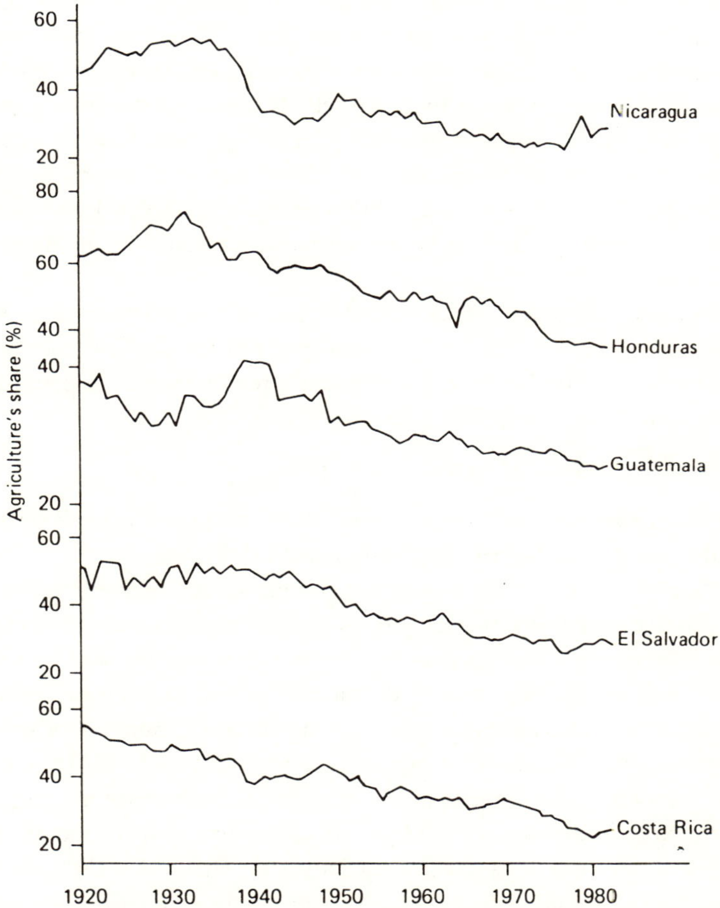

Fig. 2. Agriculture's share of GDP (1920–82) for Central American republics at 1950 prices. (Sources: see note 18.).

The time period dealt with in this paper is long enough to assess the validity of this model for Central America, since GDP per head since 1920 (see Table 2) has risen substantially in all cases except Honduras. We may begin, therefore, by looking at the change in agriculture's share of GDP over time (see Fig. 2).[18]

[18] The source for the data before 1950 in Fig. 2 is my own estimate of agricultural net output (see Bulmer-Thomas, 1982*a*), except in the case of Honduras from 1925 to 1950 where official figures have been used. Attention should be drawn to the 'leap' in Guatemala's agricultural share in 1935/6; there is general agreement (see, for example, Greib, 1979, pp. 349–50) that the apparent increase in agricultural output in that period

When the beginning and end of the period are compared, a sharp decline in the relative importance of agriculture can be observed. However, the rate of decline is by no means constant over time, and there are sub-periods of considerable length when the share either does not decline or in some cases actually rises. Furthermore, the decline is most sharp (when end periods are compared) in the case of Honduras, for whom the rise in GDP per head was the smallest, while the decline is least dramatic in the case of Guatemala, which experienced a substantial rise in income per head.

The model outlined above refers, in any case, to a relationship between agriculture's share of GDP and income per head, and time may be only a poor proxy for the latter. A more precise test is therefore provided by regression analysis using the equation:

$$\log (Va/P)_t = \alpha + \beta \log (y/P)_t + \gamma \log P_t \qquad (3)$$

where Va represents net output (value added) in agriculture, P stands for population and y, as before, represents real GDP.[19]

The use of logarithms in equation (3) means that the parameters (β, γ) can be interpreted as elasticities (growth and size elasticities respectively). *A priori* reasoning suggests that the growth elasticity (β) will be positive but less than unity; this implies that a rise in real income per head (*cet. par.*) will raise value added per head in agriculture, but not in the same proportion; thus the share of agriculture in GDP will fall. By contrast, the size elasticity (γ) is expected to be negative; the increase in population, *cet. par.*, expands market size and permits above proportionate growth in non-agricultural activities, so that agriculture's share of GDP again falls.

The results of equation (3) are given in Table 3 and provide a severe

---

is due in part to the improvement in recording statistics under Ubico's rule; it seemed preferable, however, to live with this error rather than trying to 'smooth' the data.

After 1950, official figures have been used to derive agriculture's share, although in certain cases (e.g. Costa Rica in the 1950s) it was necessary to make an adjustment to data in nominal prices to adjust to 1950 constant prices. Figures for the last two years on agricultural net output have been obtained from the same sources as were used for real GDP (see note 2).

[19] In a classic study, Chenery (1968) used agriculture's share as the dependent variable rather than agricultural value added per head; in this case, *a priori* reasoning suggests that the 'β' coefficient will be negative; I have experimented with this equation and the results confirm those given in Table 3. Many studies on sectoral performance also use the square of real income per head as well as real income per head in order to capture any non-linearities in the relationship between agriculture's share and real income. The omission of this additional variable, however, is much less serious in a time-series study, where the range of observed real incomes is much smaller than in cross-section work.

Table 3. *Agricultural Response Patterns in Central America (1920–82)*

	Regression coefficients in equation (3a)[1] with respect to:				
	Intercept a^*	log (y/P) (β)	log P (γ)	$\bar{R}^2$	Durbin–Watson statistic
Costa Rica	1.74	1.2	−0.48	0.98	1.77
	(5.91)	(14.8)	(8.9)		
El Salvador	2.74	1.09	−0.53	0.94	2.2
	(7.05)	(12.09)	(6.99)		
Guatemala	0.39	1.13	−2.28	0.97	2.19
	(1.22)	(16.99)	(5.87)		
Honduras	1.17	1.24	−0.41	0.97	2.15
	(2.13)	(12.37)	(8.27)		
Nicaragua	1.82	0.82	−2.27	0.92	2.09
	(2.84)	(9.99)	(2.72)		

Note: Figures in brackets are *t*-statistics.

(1) Estimation of equation (3) by Ordinary Least Squares revealed a high degree of serial correlation. The equation was therefore re-estimated using a maximum likelihood iterative technique (see Beach, 1978)

$$\left(\log \frac{Va}{P}\right)_t - \rho\left(\log \frac{Va}{P}\right)_{t-1} = a^* + \beta \log\left(\frac{y}{P}\right)_t - \log\left(\frac{y}{P}\right)_{t-1} + \gamma[\log P_t - \log P_{t-1}] \tag{3a}$$

where $a^* = a(1-\rho)$. The results in Table 3 refer to the parameter estimates in equation (3a), from which it can be seen that the Durbin–Watson statistic is in each case within the acceptance region for no autoregression.

challenge to the model outlined at the beginning of this section. While the size elasticity comes out as negative in all cases (as expected), the growth elasticity is less than one for one country only (Nicaragua). In all the other republics, the β coefficient exceeds unity, which implies that an increase in real income (population unchanged) will raise, not lower, agriculture's share of GDP. Thus the observed long-run decline of agriculture's share only comes about because the share-increasing tendency of the growth elasticity is subdued by the share-reducing tendency of the size elasticity.

A further challenge to the received wisdom on agriculture's declining share and rural out-migration is provided by the figures on urbanization. By 1950, for example, the proportion of the population classified as rural (see Torres Rivas, 1973, Table 16) was over 70% in all republics and over 80% in Honduras. These figures are so high that it is difficult to see how the decline in agriculture's share between 1920 and 1950 (see Fig. 2) could have been accompanied by much rural–urban migration. Indeed, in the case of El Salvador (see Durham, 1979, p. 55) there was only a six-percentage-point drop in the proportion of the population classified as rural between 1892 and 1950.

The validity of Engel's law is not in question among economists; indeed, it is one of the few empirically established laws of economics which have stood the test of time. The problem, therefore, is to explain the performance of the agricultural sector in Central America in a manner which does not contradict Engel's law.

Engel's law, however, refers to the demand for foodstuffs; even if we ignore the fact that much agricultural output does not consist of foodstuffs, it is possible for supply to outstrip home demand if there are favourable export opportunities. We need, therefore, to distinguish between two branches of agriculture: one producing goods for the home market, the other producing goods for the world market. I shall call the first branch Domestic Use Agriculture (DUA) and the second Export Agriculture (EXA).

Many products are sold in both home and world markets; none the less, in the case of Central America, world markets are dominant in the case of coffee and bananas and, to a lesser extent, cotton and sugar. I have therefore defined EXA in tems of these four commodities, so that DUA refers to all other agricultural products.[20]

Engel's law can be said to apply to DUA. It does not, however, apply to EXA unless the country producing the export crop is a dominant supplier to the world market; this is not the case in Central America, with the possible exception of bananas. A shift of resources into EXA can, therefore, move agriculture's share in a perverse direction in terms of the conventional model.

The division of agriculture into two branches has further implications of great social importance. EXA tends to be large-scale, land-extensive, using hired labour and sometimes highly mechanized; DUA, by contrast, tends to be small-scale land- and labour-intensive using family labour. According to the CIDA study of the 1960s (reported in Dorner, 1983, table 3), while 80% of the output of sub-family farms was destined for the home market, only 25% was similarly allocated in the case of the largest size category of farms. A movement from one branch of agriculture to the other

[20] For the period before 1950, I have used my own national accounts estimates to effect the division of agricultural net output into EXA and DUA. For the period after 1950, I have constructed estimates for EXA using the same principles as were applied in the period before 1950 (DUA is then obtained as a residual). This method is not ideal, because each republic prepares unpublished estimates on value added in each branch of agriculture as part of the annual national accounts exercise. So far, I have not been able to check my results against the official (but unpublished) figures.

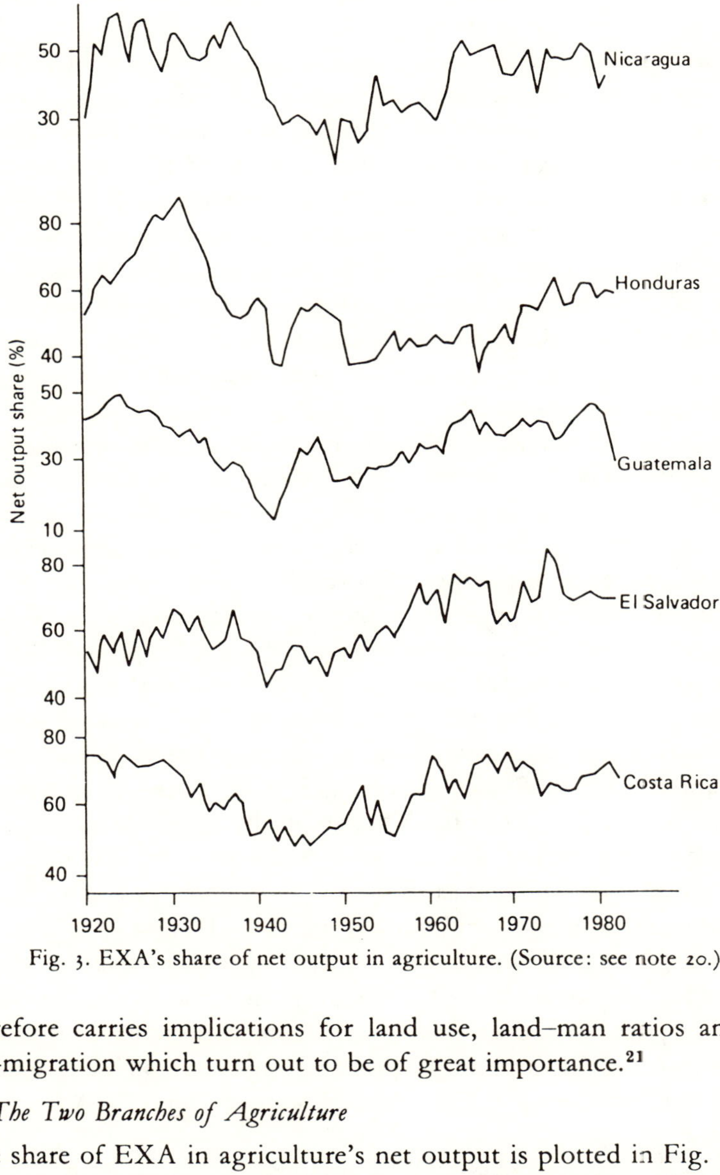

Fig. 3. EXA's share of net output in agriculture. (Source: see note 20.).

therefore carries implications for land use, land–man ratios and rural out-migration which turn out to be of great importance.[21]

5. *The Two Branches of Agriculture*

The share of EXA in agriculture's net output is plotted in Fig. 3 (there is no need to plot DUA's share as this is a residual and can, therefore, be

[21] This description of the two branches of agriculture should not be taken too literally; coffee (part of EXA) is often produced in small-scale, labour-intensive units, while rice (part of DUA) is sometimes the opposite. Despite these qualifications, the contrast remains valid – as can be seen for El Salvador in figure 2.17 and for Honduras in figure 4.9 of Durham (1979).

derived from Fig. 3 very easily). Although the period extends to 1982, the data for the last two years are very provisional.

The first feature to note is the extraordinary importance of EXA. In the late 1920s, for example, when the export-led model reached its peak, EXA accounted for more than 70% of agriculture's net output in Honduras and Costa Rica and more than 50% in a further two republics (El Salvador and Nicaragua). Only in Guatemala does EXA's share fall below 50% in the 1920s and even there the share exceeded 40%.

The ability of several republics (El Salvador, Honduras, Nicaragua) to increase EXA's share in the 1920s helps to explain why in Fig. 2 agriculture's share of GDP for these same countries actually rises during this decade. A rapidly expanding EXA permits agriculture to grow at a rate faster than that implied by the growth of home demand.

A high (and increasing) EXA share also implies specialization in EXA and a neglect of DUA, as resources are reallocated from the latter to the former. This implies an increase in imports of foodstuffs, which Central America certainly experienced in the late 1920s when such imports represented 20% by value of the total import bill.

The presence of food imports, however, means that growth of DUA is no longer determined (at least in the short run) by the growth of home demand. In the 1930s, for example, several republics enjoyed rapid increases in DUA (see Bulmer-Thomas, 1982*a*), which were achieved in part through import substitution. This accounts for the rise in the share of agriculture in GDP in Guatemala and, to a lesser extent, in El Salvador during the 1930s. The fall in EXA's share in the 1930s, therefore, is due not so much to the collapse of export markets (the quantum of exports – but not the value – held up well) as to the rise in importance of DUA.

The second feature to note about Fig. 3 is the substantial rise in EXA's share after the Second World War. Indeed, in several republics export specialization has come close to, if not surpassed, the levels achieved in the 1920s. Significantly, the formation of CACM seems to have made little, if any, impact on this process of specialization, which suggests that the incipient industrial sector did not compete seriously with EXA for scarce resources.[22]

[22] The absence of competition for scarce resources between the industrial sector and EXA is one of the themes of the paper by Reynolds (1978*a*). This lack of competition is surprising, given the initial impact of ISI on the internal terms of trade, until one considers the political economy of Central America in this crucial period. The export agricultural interests were able to influence fiscal, credit and exchange rate policy in a way which neutralized the initial adverse movement in the internal terms of trade. In El Salvador, for example, the proportion of private credit allocated to EXA actually increased between 1961 and 1975 (see Baloyra, 1982, p. 187).

Several republics for part of the post-war period have experienced a constant or even rising share of agriculture in GDP despite rising income per head. Nearly all these observations can be explained by a sharp increase in EXA's share in the same period; thus, favourable world market conditions permit EXA to grow faster than DUA and a rising EXA share permits agriculture to grow faster than GDP.

The decline in EXA's share in the two decades up to 1950 means that DUA's share was rising. DUA, however, is by hypothesis the labour-intensive sector, so that the 'push' factors influencing rural out-migration are likely to be less severe in periods when DUA's share is increasing. This, it is argued, helps to account for the low levels of urbanization in 1950.

By contrast, when EXA's share is rising, the push factors influencing rural out-migration increase substantially; EXA competes with DUA for land and labour (not capital), which in turn either increases landlessness among the peasantry, or reduces the median size of family farms; in both cases the supply of labour for hire (wage labour) increases, since even those with farms must now seek off-farm work to supplement their farm earnings. Wage labour in EXA, however, is highly seasonal so that annual incomes are usually low and often insecure. The gap between labour supply and demand in EXA then exerts downward pressure on real wages, which ensures that a large share of the value of the product consists of economic rent (see Reynolds, 1978*b*). These rents are not eroded through competition, because Central America is a price-taker in international markets, and their size discourages an outflow of capital resources, until comparable rents can be earned elsewhere.[23]

6. *Export Agriculture and the Pressure on Land*

The hypothesis that a rapid expansion of EXA contributes sharply to the push factors influencing rural out-migration assumes that most of the increase in EXA's production occurs through increases in area cultivated rather than through increases in yields. If the increase is achieved through changes in yields, then the demand for hired labour rises sharply (labour is being substituted for land), but the supply of labour is not affected. Far from encouraging rural out-migration, an increase in yield would increase real wages and discourage any outflow.

[23] The difficulty of attracting resources away from EXA, when economic rents are high, helps to account for the high nominal and effective rates of protection offered to industry during the CACM experiment. Indeed, one may generalize from this and argue that the path to industrial development is likely to be very different in a region rich in natural resources (such as Central America) when compared with the path followed in less favourably endowed regions (such as East Asia), precisely because the attraction of agricultural investment is much smaller in the latter.

Before presenting the data on yield/area increases in EXA, the special case of banana production must be mentioned. It has always been the case that bananas are cultivated on only a fraction of the area owned by banana companies (national or multi-national). This is because of the ever-present threat of disease, although it is also designed to forestall competition and reduce alternative occupations for the local labour force.

Within the cultivated fraction (see Ellis, 1978, table C.3) yields have risen substantially; in the period 1947–6, yields increased by some 200 % in Costa Rica and Guatemala and by nearly 100 % in Honduras. At the same time, the cultivated area remains only a small part of the total available for banana production so that it does not serve as a useful guide to changes in man-land ratios.

Table 4. *Increases in Area and Yield for EXA* (%)

Period	Costa Rica	El Salvador	Guatemala	Honduras	Nicaragua
Cotton					
Area (1950–80)	—	289	2307	—	829*
Yield (1950–80)	—	94	349	—	95*
Cane sugar					
Area (1950–80)	130	154	392	279	131
Yield (1950–80)	36	25	83	35	81
Coffee					
Area (1935–80)	73	72	136	340†	103‡
Yield (1935–80)	261	65	54	41†	51‡

* The terminal year is 1978 (3-year average) rather than 1980, because the civil war played havoc with the cotton crop in that year.

† There are no data on area and yield in Honduras for 1935, so the period 1945 (3-year average) to 1980 has been used instead.

‡ Figures for 1935 are based on a single observation rather than a 3-year average.

— Neither Costa Rica nor Honduras can be considered a serious exporter of cotton, so they have been omitted from the table.

Sources: The figures have been obtained from the *F.A.O. Production Yearbook*, with annual data estimated as 3-year averages. Pre-war data are taken from the Institute of Agriculture's *International Yearbook of Agricultural Statistics.*

Figures for the remaining export crops are presented in Table 4. While the increases in yields have not been negligible, they have in general been dwarfed by the increases in area. This is particularly noticeable in the case of cotton where, for example, area sown in Guatemala increased by 2,307 % between 1950 and 1980, but the difference between the increase in area and yield is also very marked in the case of cane sugar.

Coffee provides a qualification to the hypothesis that increases in EXA have been achieved primarily through increases in area cultivated; Costa

Rica, for example, experienced a much sharper rise in yields than area between 1935 and 1980, while the increase was roughly similar over the same period in El Salvador. This is not particularly surprising, as much coffee is still grown in small units where the more intensive use of family labour and/or material inputs is a legitimate alternative to increases in area. It remains true, however, that in the other three republics area increases were much more important than changes in yield.

The expansion of EXA has not been the only source of competition for the land devoted to DUA by the peasantry. The spectacular rise of the livestock industry (the most land-extensive of all branches of agriculture) and its transformation into an export activity in the 1960s has exacerbated the problem of land pressure considerably. In Nicaragua, for example, the area recorded as under permanent pasture at the end of the Second World War was 280,000 hectares and this had risen to 3,420,000 hectares by 1980. Comparable increases have been recorded in the other republics.

In order to determine land pressure quantitatively, it is necessary to deduct from the total land area the area devoted to (i) EXA, (ii) permanent pasture, (iii) forest and woodland, (iv) uncultivated land; this gives the Net Arable Land (NAL) available for production of crops for the home market (including subsistence). Division of NAL by the economically active population (PEA) in agriculture then gives a rough measure of the land–man ratio and, by implication, a measure of land pressure.[24]

The results of this experience are presented in Table 5 for the years for which data could be obtained. They present a very striking picture, in which the pre-1950 relative decline of EXA is accompanied by an improvement in the land–man ratio, while the post-1950 relative increase in EXA is accompanied by a sharp deterioration in the land–man ratio. A comparison between countries reveals the desperate position of El Salvador, since the estimate of NAL available per member of the agricultural PEA has fallen well below that of the other republics.

The data presented in Table 5 suggest a serious deterioration over the last three decades in the land–man ratio. This, in turn, implies a reduction

[24] It could be argued that if Net Arable Land (NAL) is the numerator, then the denominator should be the agricultural labour force net of those employed in EXA. There is a strong argument against this, however, in addition to the more mundane consideration of data available. Employment in EXA is typically neither permanent nor secure; in Guatemala, for example, the *Instituto Guatemalteco de Seguridad Social* reported that agricultural employment had fallen from 412,400 in 1981 to 168,000 in 1982 (see *Central America Report*, 18 March, 1983, p. 82); since nearly all this 'employment' is in EXA, its precarious nature in the wake of a deterioration in world market conditions is made abundantly clear.

Table 5. *Land–Man Ratios in Central America (in hectares): Arable Land and Permanent Crop Area (net of EXA) divided by Agricultural Labour Force*

Year	Costa Rica	El Salvador	Guatemala	Honduras	Nicaragua
1980	1.150	0.558	1.092	*	*
1975	1.328	0.553	1.102	1.133	1.908
1970	1.299	0.663	1.111	1.222	2.092
1965	1.620	0.706	1.159	1.280	2.133
1960	N.A.	0.928	1.341	1.906	2.296
1955	1.084	N.A.	N.A.	2.183	N.A.
1950	0.893	0.961	1.701	2.076	3.327
1945	0.563	0.824	N.A.	1.352	1.845
1940	0.569	N.A.	1.576	N.A.	N.A.
1935	N.A.	N.A.	N.A.	N.A.	N.A.
1930	0.539‡	0.587	0.989	N.A.	N.A.
1925	0.634	N.A.	N.A.	N.A.	N.A.

* Figures on arable land and permanent crops for 1980 were revised drastically by the F.A.O., making them inconsistent with earlier years.
‡ = 1929.
Sources: same as for Table 4. Estimates of the agricultural labour force were not always consistent, however, and where necessary earlier figures were revised to make them consistent with later estimates.

in real incomes among tenant farmers and owner-occupiers not involved in EXA, which prompts a search for additional sources of income. This encourages two types of migration: rural–rural migration (in search of wage labour within the rural economy) and rural–urban migration. Within the context of the model of economic development adopted by Central America, both types of migration have tended to be socially and politically destabilizing. The urban demand for labour has not kept pace with the increase in supply, while the rural demand for hired labour (particularly in EXA) has not provided work of a permanent nature and has frequently required the separation of the head of the household from the rest of the family.

The picture presented in Table 5 is complemented by the more familiar data on concentration of ownership from the agricultural census. By 1979, for example, farms in Guatamala with less than one *manzana* accounted for 41.1 % of all farms compared with 21.3 % in 1950 (see Inforpress, 1982). In El Salvador, farms with less than one hectare accounted for 2.55 % of the total land area (see Montgomery, 1982, p. 29) compared with 4 % in 1971, while the proportion of properties in this category was 37.2 %. In Costa Rica, between 1963 and 1973, the smallest farm size increased in number by 80 % compared with an increase in all farms of 29 % (see Seligson, 1980, p. 147).

Agricultural census data, however, have too often been interpreted as if the increased concentration of land ownership was simply due to rapid population growth. While the latter exacerbates the situation, the relative expansion of EXA (and land for livestock) is also an important contributory factor. While population growth is to a considerable extent beyond the control of the authorities – at least in the short run – the same is not true of the allocation of resources within the agricultural sector. Table 5, therefore, points to the need for explicit recognition of the role of government policy in a way which census data do not.

7. *Conclusions*

With rare exceptions, the source of dynamism is the Central American economy since 1920 has been provided by EXA.[25] The most important exceptions are the periods of import substitution in agriculture (1930s) and import substitution in industry (1960s); specialization in EXA has made possible rapid growth in real GDP and, to a lesser extent, income per head (except in Honduras). The expansion of EXA, however, has disrupted economic and social relations in agriculture to the point where the political model underpinning EXA is called into question.[26] Political and social stability in Central America, therefore, threatens to break down *because* of the success of export-led growth rather than *despite* it.

This interpretation of Central America's economic development is inconsistent with the Prebisch–Singer thesis of a secular decline in the net barter terms of trade of primary producers. As Fig. 1 shows, there has been no long-term tendency for the terms of trade to deteriorate, although there is perhaps a disturbing asymmetry between rapid (but brief) improvements in the terms of trade and slow (but lengthy) declines.

It is quite possible that Central America's external trade exhibits unequal exchange in Emmanuel's sense (see Emmanuel, 1972). However, the strength of the theory of unequal exchange lies in its ability to predict a deterioration in the net barter terms of trade of the periphery irrespective

[25] This remains true despite the increase in importance of industry achieved through CACM. In a recent study of the latter, it was stated (Reynolds, 1978*a*, p. 288 n. 2): 'A striking feature of econometric models of income determination in the region is the evidence of the continuing dominating effect of terms of trade and other export-related fluctuations on the level of domestic income and product. This is so, despite almost two decades of integration policy designed to diversify these economies to reduce their vulnerability to foreign trade cycles.'

[26] Many works have looked at the relationship between EXA and the political system. See, for example, Monteforte Toledo (1972).

of the initial pattern of specialization (see Evans, 1981). Since such a deterioration has not come about, it is not of great interest to establish whether trade between Central America and the rest of the world involves unequal exchange in a static sense.

Nor is it true that Central America's growth has been growth without development. Although social indicators (e.g. literacy, life expectancy) stand at low levels today, they are still much higher than they were sixty years ago and compare reasonably well with other countries with similar levels of income per head. The test of development should not be the performance of advanced countries, but the past record of a country and the present record of comparable countries. If one does not use such a yardstick, the charge of growth without development becomes tautologically true.

The success of the CACM in the 1960s (see Bulmer-Thomas, 1982*b*) led to the illusion that the dominance of the export-led model of growth had ceased. The CACM experiment, however, was incorporated within the very same political model which had spawned export-led growth with only minor modifications. With the benefit of hindsight, we can now see that CACM never really threatened the export-led model and when (in the 1970s) hard choices had to be made, it was the industrial sector which suffered.

The export-led model is justified in terms of the Ricardian theory of comparative advantage: by specializing in those activities (EXA) in which she has a comparative advantage, Central America can increase the level of consumption permitted by its human and physical resources.

There are several problems with the theory, however, two of which are relevant in the context of Central America. First, the theory does not account for the neglect of DUA; if anything, Central America has a comparative advantage in all natural resource-intensive products (EXA and DUA) and a comparative disadvantage in manufactured goods. If export-led growth had taken place on the basis of those crops currently produced under DUA, the implications for factor use, employment, income distribution and so on would have been very different.

Secondly, the theory does not say how the gains from trade will be distributed. Substantial gains from trade can coincide with an increase in inequality in the size distribution of income – something which has quite clearly occurred in Central America.[27] In related theories (e.g the Heckshers–Ohlin theorem), there is a presumption of factor price equalization

[27] See, for example, table 23 in Reynolds (1978*a*).

between different countries; this equalization, however, is stated as a tendency only and is conditional upon a number of restrictive assumptions.

At the present time, the export-led model is in deep crisis. This is not just a matter of falling commodity prices, which have occurred at various stages in the last sixty years; it is much more to do with the breakdown of social relations within the agricultural sector as a result of the specific way in which the export-led model has operated.

If the political system surrounding the export-led model now collapses, it may prompt a search for an alternative and herald a retreat into autarchy. It is not export-led growth, however, which is at fault, so much as the policies which have promoted it and which have encouraged excessive increases in area together with low returns to labour.

Significantly, the revolutionary government in Nicaragua has not turned its back on EXA, much of which remains in private hands; the distribution of the gains from trade, however, is different in Nicaragua from, say, Guatemala, and employment in EXA is becoming much more permanent in character (see Barraclough, 1982).

Nevertheless, even revolutionary governments would be well advised to avoid the extremes of export specialization which Central America has experienced. Sharp changes in the barter terms of trade impose severe strains on very open economies, making macro-economic stability very difficult to achieve. It is one thing to propose the reform of international commodity markets; it is altogether another to act as if they were already reformed.

References

E. Baloyra, *El Salvador in Transition*, (Chapel Hill, University of North Carolina Press, 1982).

Banco Central de Honduras, *Cuentas Nacionales* 1925–55, Tegucigalpa, 1956.

S. Barraclough, *A Preliminary Analysis of the Nicaraguan Food System* (UNRISD, 1982).

C. Beach, and J. MacKinnon, 'A maximum likelihood procedure for regression with auto-correlated errors', *Econometrica*, No. 46 (1978).

V. Bulmer-Thomas, 'Central America in the Inter-War Years'. Queen Mary College, London University, Working Paper No. 85 (1982*a*). Forthcoming in R. Thorp, (ed.), *The Periphery in World Crisis: Latin America in the 1930s.* (Macmillan).

V. Bulmer-Thomas, 'The Central American Common Market', in A. El-Agraa, (ed.), *International Economic Integration*, (London; Macmillan, 1982*b*).

Luis A. Cantarero, 'The Economic Development of Nicaragua, 1920–1947' (Unpublished Ph. D. thesis, University of Iowa, 1949).

H. Chenery, and M. Syrquín, *Patterns of Industrial Growth*, (O.U.P., 1975).

H. Chenery, and L. Taylor. 'Development patterns: among countries and over time', *Review of Economics and Statistics*, No. 50 (1968).

E. Delgado, 'Institutional Evolution of the Central American Common Market and the Principle of Balanced Development', in W. Cline and E. Delgado (eds.), *Economic Integration in Central America*, (Washington, D.C., Brookings Institution, 1978).

P. Dorner, and R. Quiros, 'Institutional dualism in Central America's agricultural development', in Stanford Central American Action Network (ed.), *Revolution in Central America* (Boulder, Colorado, Westview Press, 1983).

W. H. Durham, *Scarcity and Survival in Central America* (Stanford, Stanford University Press, 1979).

ECLA, *Series Historicas del Crecímiento de América Latina*, (Santiago, 1978).

F. Ellis, 'The Banana Export Activity in Central America 1947–1976' (Unpubished Ph.D. Thesis, University of Sussex, 1978).

A. Emmanuel, *Unequal Exchange: An Essay on the Imperialism of Trade*, (Monthly Review Press, 1972).

D. Evans, 'Unequal Exchange and the Neo-Ricardian Theory of Comparative Advantage', in I. Livingstone (ed.), *Readings in Development Studies*, (London, Allen & Unwin, 1981).

K. Greib, *Guatemalan Caudillo*, (Ohio University Press, 1979).

Inforpress, *Centro América 1982: Análisis Económicos y Políticos Sobre La Regioń, Guatemala*, (1982).

B. F. Johnstone and A. Kilby, *Agricultural and Structural Transformation* (Oxford, O.U.P., 1975).

M. Monteforte Toledo, *Centro América: Subdesarrollo y Dependencia* (México, 1972, 2 vols.).

T. S. Montgomery, *Revolution in El Salvador* (Westview Press, 1982).

J. P. Mooney, 'Gross Domestic Product, Gross National Product, and Capital Formation in El Salvador, 1945–65', *Estadística* (1968).

C. Reynolds, 'Employment Problems of Export Economics in a Common Market: The Case of Central America', in W. Cline and E. Delgado (eds.), *Economic Integration in Central America* (Washington, D.C., Brookings Institution, 1978).

C. Reynolds, 'Appendix E – A Model of Employment and Labor Shares in an Export Economy with Import Substituting Industrialisation', in *ibid*,

M. Seligson, *Peasants of Costa Rica and the Development of Agrarian Capitalism* (Madison, University of Wisconsin Press, 1980).

E. Torres Rivas, *Interpretación del Desarrollo Social Centroamericano* (San José, EDUCA, 1973).

Journal of Development Economics 19 (1985) 1–24. North-Holland

GOOD-BYE FINANCIAL REPRESSION, HELLO FINANCIAL CRASH

Carlos DIAZ-ALEJANDRO*

Columbia University, New York, NY 10027, USA

Received December 1983, final version received March 1984

Some unintended consequences of financial liberalization in Latin America are analyzed in this paper. Intrinsic imperfections in financial markets, and the policy dilemmas they pose, are reviewed first. The stylized facts of Southern Cone experiments in financial liberization are then presented. Alternative ways of organizing domestic capital markets under Latin American conditions are discussed, and an eclectic, reform mongering program is proposed.

1. Introduction

This paper seeks to understand why financial reforms carried out in several Latin American countries during the 1970s, aimed at ending 'financial repression', as defined by Ronald McKinnon [see, for example, McKinnon (1980)], and generally seeking to free domestic capital markets from usury laws and other alleged government-induced distortions, yielded by 1983 domestic financial sectors characterized by widespread bankruptcies, massive government interventions or nationalizations of private institutions, and low domestic savings. The clearest example of this paradox is Chile, which has shown the world yet another road to a de facto socialized banking system. Argentina and Uruguay show similar trends, which can be detected less neatly in other developing countries, including Turkey. Indeed, even in the United States some worried observers have warned against the dangers of pell-mell deregulation of commercial banks [see Kareken (1981)].

*A version of this paper was first presented at a conference held in Bogota on November 22 and 23, 1982 — sponsored by the Universidad de Los Andes and the Banco de la República. Visits to CINVES, in Montevideo, and CIEPLAN, in Santiago de Chile, during March 1983, were very helpful for extending that early version. I am grateful to all these institutions and to numerous individuals who shared with me their views of the events narrated and of the issues discussed in the text. Among those who are unlikely to find embarrassing my acknowledgement of their help, I may mention José Pablo Arellano, Edmar L. Bacha, Guillermo Calvo, Jonathan Eaton, Richardo Ffrench-Davis, Arminio Fraga Netto, Jeff Frieden, Eduardo García d'Acuña, Jose Antonio Ocampo, Hugh Patrick, Gustav Ranis, Patricio Meller, Miguel Urrutia and Laurence M. Weiss. My gratitude is no less for the often extraordinarily generous cooperation of those not explicitly named.

The paper will first review dilemmas posed by intrinsic imperfections of any financial market, and will look at legal prerequisities for the reasonably efficient operation of those markets. Then it will examine the stylized facts of some Latin American experiments in financial liberalization, particularly those carried out in Southern Cone countries (Argentina, Chile and Uruguay). Finally, alternative ways of organizing domestic capital markets under Latin American conditions will be discussed; policies regarding the links between domestic and international financial markets will also be considered.

2. Peculiarities and dilemmas found in domestic financial markets

Are banks special, and really all that different from butcher shops? Neither type of firm is *exactly* like the textbook idealization of the atomistic firm operating in a perfectly competitive market, where spot prices summarize all information relevant for buyers and sellers of the product. Customers at a butcher shop will not only look at price , but will also attempt to ascertain quality; in some countries they will be aided by government-established quality categories and certifications. Breakdowns in the trust consumers have in their butchers or in government certification, say because of rumors regarding meat tainted by poisonous substances, could produce a kind of 'run' on butcher shops, and widespread failures among them.

The comparison is surely being forced. Few butcher shops will deliver meat of standard quality out of town to third parties on instruction from a customer. Few externalities could be expected from a 'run' on a butcher shop under suspicion. Furthermore, a butcher will seldom turn down a customer who wants to buy with cash everything in sight at the price announced by the butcher (he will just make sure the cash is not counterfeit); a banker will surely not lend all a customer wants to borrow at the going interest rate. The former is a spot transaction; the latter involves a promise to repay in the future which may or may not be sincere or wholly credible. Enforcing the loan contract or liquidating collateral property will involve costs, and even with speedy enforcement the bank may be unable to get all of its money back. The bank will incur costs to explore the credit-worthiness of borrowers; the butcher will not care much for the reputation of cash-carrying customers. There is no humanly possible way of devising a fail-proof system of finding out the true intentions of borrowers, so lenders are likely to end up rationing credit, i.e., putting a ceiling on what arms-length customers can borrow, regardless of their willingness to pay higher interest rates [see Stiglitz and Weiss (1981)]. Banks share with other financial intermediaries the problem of seeking reliable borrowers, but having liabilities that are payable on demand at par puts a premium on safe and fairly liquid loans for banks. Banks supply a service that is a very close substitute to the bulls and coins supplied by governments; such pretension imposes special limits on banks' portfolios.

Financial intermediaries, including banks, rely on borrowed funds; owners of those institutions typically invest their own capital only in amounts which are a small fraction of their total lending. A depositor in a bank will have preoccupations similar to those a lender has when eyeing a borrower: will I be able to get not only the promised yield but also my money back or delivered to a third party as specified in the legal contract? In a totally unregulated system the rational depositor will attempt to process a great deal of information regarding financial institutions, balancing expected returns versus risks of not being able to dispose of his funds as promised.

One can *imagine* a world in which all financial intermediation, including the payments system, is private and without any direct government regulation. The information imperfections may be partly offset by investments in information gathering by lenders and depositors; with the passing of time reputations would be built up. Balance sheets of financial intermediatries would be widely available and closely analyzed. It is even conceivable that possible economies of scale involved in the processing of information may not be so large as to impede large numbers of financial agents, assuring some competition among them. Unexpected shocks and informational failures in this economy could of course lead to bankrupticies of some financial intermediaries; an informed public presumably would know the source of such events, so there would be no ripple effects contaminating sounder institutions. One would expect to find a rich risk-return menu available to savers in this world, which would also generate an unregulated stock market for those preferring equity arrangements for obtaining or investing funds. Concentration of economic power, in the form of 'economic groups' and conglomerates, would presumably exist only if there are economies of scale to yield social benefits, with free entry checking monopoly behaviour. In this world, the market rate of interest would hover around the natural rate.

Note that even a purely laissez-faire financial system must count with some indirect government inputs in the form of an efficient and fair judiciary and police system to punish fraud and to handle the enforcement of contracts and the settlement of disputes and bankruptcy cases. And behind *that* one must presumably have a polity generating such a judicial and police system, and a body of contract, antitrust and bankruptcy laws which are regarded as fair, efficient and enforceable. Financial agents feeling a temptation to cheat on their contracts or give false information must know that such behavior will have very high costs; they must also know that even if they flee their country the long arm of the law is likely to reach them abroad. Governments in this world must be expected neither to change nor to corrupt these rules; domestic private citizens must not only believe in the stability of this system, but also believe that other citizens also have that belief. Foreign financial agents, when dealing with those of our country, must not expect to have these rules changed when things go wrong for them; foreign financial agents dealing within our economy would presumably be subject to the same rules of the game as our financial agents.

Even among those who find a predominatly laissez-faire financial system not only imaginable but also a desirable goal of policy, there are differences on how to organize the underlying monetary system. Some take for granted that the government will have a monopoly in the supply of cash and coins. Aware of the macroeconomic instability which could be generated by sudden changes in the public preferences between cash and the demand deposits supplied by banks subject to fractional reserves, as during the early 1930s in the United States, these observers would impose 100 percent reserves on banks supplying those deposits, while leaving the rest of the financial system unregulated. [See Friedman (1959).] In this view, a significant difference exists between money (cash plus demand deposits) and other financial assets. Other observers would carry a laissez-faire policy even into cash, eliminating the government monopoly, and leaving individual agents free to choose among all potential suppliers of cash, including foreign governments. In this approach there would be no need to impose reserve requirements on banks, which would be totally free of government regulations. The money supply would presumably adjust to real needs, while price and wage flexibility would maintain macroeconomic balance [see Hall (1982)].

The laissez-faire vision also has (at least) two variants regarding how the unregulated domestic economy should manage its exchange rate. If the country is large enough, those giving the government a monopoly over the money supply advocate a freely fluctuating exchange rate, with no restriction on international trade or on capital flows. If the country is small (with the borderline between large and small left fuzzy), even money monopolists favor some form of fixed exchange rate system. For politically turbulent nations, a variant of the liassez–faire vision in a small country would do away with the local central bank, i.e., no national could be trusted with the money monopoly, which would be turned over to a presumably benign and responsible foreign government, as in the cases of Panama and Puerto Rico.

No industrial country has come close to the laissez-faire vision, at least since the 1930s. The government monopoly over cash has been maintained, while banks have been regulated and subjected to fractional reserve requirements. In the United States, an explicit federal deposit insurance for accounts below a certain size was introduced during the 1930s and maintained since then, eliminating old-fashioned 'runs' on banks. Like any other insurance scheme, deposit insurance is vulnerable to moral hazard consequences, i.e., it induces depositors to think that 'one bank is as good as another', and leads bank managers to undertake riskier loans. To avoid such insurance-induced risk-taking, supervision over bank portfolios has accompanied deposit insurance. Indeed, the Federal Reserve holds impressive discretionary powers regarding the lending policies of commercial banks, and over their liquidation or merger, if banks are found to be in trouble. Those discretionary powers, however, are subject to review by the Treasury, Congress and the courts. Vigilance has been exerted by the Fedral Reserve to keep non-banking companies from owing or controlling banks.

While a trend towards bank deregulation has occured in the United States during the 1970s and early 1980s, removing some archaic populist controls, the view the 'banks are special' has been reaffirmed. The rescue of the Continental Illinois during 1984 in the face of a new type of run by uninsured international depositors, a rescue which extended de-facto insurance to all depositors, showed that *large* banks are quite special. This view is based on the externalities generated by the liquidity, mobility and acceptability of bank-issued transaction accounts, characteristics which take special significance in periods of financial stress [see Federal Reserve Bank of Minneapolis (1982)]. Only banks create and incur liabilities that are payable on demand at par and that are readily transferable to third parties. Your safe payments system is also my safe payments system; it is partly a public good, not only serving individuals, but also providing backup liquidity on which the whole of the financial system rests. The Federal Reserve Bank of Minneapolis concludes:

> '... the case for segregating *essential* banking functions into an identifiable class of institutions is every bit as powerful today as it was in the 1930s. If anything, concerns regarding financial concentration, conflicts of interest, and the fiduciary responsibilities associated with lending depositors' money may be more relevant today than they were 50 years ago' (p. 13).

Other industrial countries, such as Japan and those in Western Europe, are even farther away from the laissez-faire vision for the financial system than the United States. In several of those countries interest rates are also controlled or supervised by monetary authorities, and international capital flows are regulated. None relies on just price and wage flexibility to seek macroeconomic balance. (Note that those advocating a fixed-money-growth rule are typically as skeptical of the speedy workings of price and wage flexibility to maintain macroeconomic balance as Keynesian economists.)

Finally, it is difficult to find small and open countries which have *given up* monetary sovereignty after tasting it. Politically sovereign countries using other countries' moneys, or 'permanently' committed to a fixed exchange rate and unrestricted capital mobility with a monetary 'big brother', usually have come to those arrangements as part of a transition from a colonial status, and it is moot whether the arrangements are regarded as really permanent or only as a step in monetary learning by doing, a step which had to be accepted to placate special internal and external interests rather than taken after a thoughtful consideration of national welfare. During October 1983 there were reports that Israel was about to abandon its monetary sovereignty; the Minister responsible for the proposal resigned shortly afterwards.

3. Notes on the financial history of Latin American and Southern Cone experiments

While the financial history of Latin America remains to be written it appears that by 1920s most countries had succeeded in establishing commercial banks of the (then) traditional sort; several countries carried out banking reforms during those years following the advice of Professor E.W. Kemmerer, of Princeton University, and of visitors from the Bank of England. The banking system of South American countries already included institutions owned by national and provincial governments; Argentina, for example, had an important government-owned mortgage bank and several other public banks. The late 1920s were characterized in most Latin American countries by fixed exchange rates, convertibility and price stability; domestic interest rates were closely linked to those in New York and London. Although there was no 'financial repression', critics pointed to a lack of medium- and long-term credit, particularly to finance industry and non-export agriculture. Within agriculture, those without real estate collateral also complained about non-availability of credit. Domestic stock and bond markets were small; only Argentina seems to have had a promising formal domestic financial market, dominated by mortgage paper.

The 1930s brought exchange controls and the expansion of government financial institutions, which at the height of the crisis proved their usefulness in decreasing the incidence of panics and runs; the massive bank bankruptcies which occured in the United States during the early 1930s were not witnessed in the large Latin American countries, apparently thanks to the presence of state banks plus an activist policy of rescuing most private banks in trouble. By the 1940s many countries had development banks granting medium- and long-term credits to non-traditional agriculture, industry and construction. Those credits, at least during the 1930s and early 1940s, seemed to have been granted at interest rates still ahead of domestic inflation, or at least not too far behind it, and in most cases contributed to an upsurge in capital formation. Public development banks remained, often through the 1950s, relatively small and efficient, as in the case of the Brazilian BNDE. The drying-up of external sources of finance during the 1930s and 1940s encouraged these efforts to mobilize local savings.

By the 1950s, however, it was clear that in South American countries experiencing inflation the development banks created to solve one form of perceived market failure (lack of long-term credit for socially profitable non-traditional activities) had led to another, i.e., a segmented domestic financial market in which some obtained (rationed) credits at very negative real interest rates, while non-favored borrowers had to obtain funds in expensive and unstable informal credit markets. Public controls over the banking system typically led to negative real interest rates for depositors. 'Financial repression' became an obstacle to domestic savings and their efficient allocation, and financial intermediation languished.

In inflation-prone countries, financial reforms were introduced during the 1960s in the form of indexing of some loans and deposits; those involving the housing market were a particularly popular field for these new policies. Post-1964 Brazil is the clearest example of a sustained effort to revive the domestic financial system and domestic savings using a number of indexing devices, but maintaining close government supervision of financial institutions and of interests rates charged in formal markets. The results of the Brazilian reforms have been mixed: domestic financial savings have been encouraged relative to the pre-1964 situation, in spite of continuing inflation, and the new policies supported impressive rates of capital formation. But attempts to encourage a significant stock market have failed, and the financial market remains heavily dominated by public securities. Private agents have shown reluctance to offer indexed securities. Credit to some sectors, such as agriculture, has been heavily subsidized for long periods of time. Brazil has also retained controls over the links between domestic and international financial markets, while following a passive crawling peg exchange rate policy, with sporadic jumps and other innovations.

In Central American countries, with a tradition of price stability and conservative macroeconomic management (before the 1970s), bank concentration and an association of a few private banks with dominant economic groups, historically raised concerns about monopoly power. Galbis (1979, p. 349) noted:

> 'The experience of El Salvador suggests that interest rate freedom cannot be expected to be a panacea and automatically produce interest rate equilibrium in countries that have a relatively concentrated and unsophisticated financial system, which is the typical case in small, less developed countries. Positive policy actions to avoid market distortions might be required.'

This type of concern led to the nationalization of the banking system in Costa Rica in the late 1940s and in El Salvador in 1979. Government regulation, including selective credit allocations, over such oligopolistic structures may make matters worse, consolidating access by a few favored businesses to subsidized credit; post-Second-World-War Greece is said to be an example of inefficient and inequitable regulation of concentrated banking sector.

Southern Cone countries, coming out of sundry populist experiences around the mid-1970s, undertook financial reforms going beyond those of Brazil in a laissez-faire direction. Post-1973 Chile provides the clearest example of this type of financial liberation [for a careful narrative, see Arellano (1983a,b)]. That experiment started with a fully nationalized banking sector; a first task was to return most banks to the private sector. This was done by auctioning them off, with generous credit arrangements, or by returning them to previous owners; apparently little effort was spent on investigating the banking credentials of new entrants. At an early stage interest rates were freed and 'financieras' were allowed to operate with practically no restrictions or supervision; early bankruptcies in December 1976 and January 1977 of the more adventurous and unregulated 'financieras' led to the establishment of minimum capital requirements for entry. Authorities repeatedly warned the public that deposits were *not* guaranteed, beyond very small deposits with banks, and that financial intermediaries, like any other private firm, could go bankrupt; it was explicitly stated that there would not be a 'bailing out' of banks and other financial intermediaries. Since 1974 multi-purpose banking was allowed, on the ground that the Chilean market is too small to sustain specialized financial institutions of efficient size. Reserve requirements were steadily reduced, reaching less than ten percent of deposits by 1980.

During 1977 it became apparent that an important bank (the Banco Osorno) was in serious trouble. The authorities, fearing that its bankruptcy would tarnish external and internal confidence in Chilean financial institutions, intervened, and rescued all depositors and the institution. Apparently, the fear that external loans would decrease if the Osorno had been allowed to go bankrupt was the crucial argument for intervention. Naturally, frech warnings were issued that, from then on, financial intermediaries would not be rescued. At that stage practically no inspection or supervision of bank portfolios existed; only in 1981 were significant regulatory powers given to the Superintendency of Banks. One may conjecture that after this event most depositors felt, de facto, fully insured and foreign lenders felt that their loans to the private Chilean sector were, in fact, guaranteed by the State. After 1977, banks, rather than 'financieras', became predominant in the financial system.

During 1979 the Chilean economic authorities started a process expected to culminate in a pseudo-exchange-rate union [see Corden (1972)] with the United States. The nominal exhange rate between the peso and the U.S. dollar was fixed in July 1979, and restrictions over convertibility and capital movements were relaxed; by 1981 those restrictions had been considerably weakened, and Chile witnessed a massive capital inflow. Presumably the hope was to make lending to Chile subject to no more currency risk than lending to Puerto Rico or Panama; the nominal exchange rate was supposed to last 'for many years'. Some of the economic authorities dreamed of doing away with the national currency altogether, but feared that the military might not wish to go that far.

The theoretical underpinnings of these policies included a special version of the monetary approach to the balance of payments, plus the hypothesis that financial markets, domestic and international, were no different from the market for apples and meat. Voluntary financial transactions between private agents were their own business, and presumably Pareto-optimal. Indeed, the nationality of those private agents was regarded most irrelevant. The then Director of the Western Hemishere Division of the International Monetary Fund put it this way at meeting held in Santiago de Chile during January 1980 [see Robichek (1981, p. 171)]:

> 'In the case of the private sector, I would argue that the difference between domestic and foreign debt is not significant — barring governmental interference with the transfer of service payments or other clearly inappropriate public policies — if it exists at all. The exchange risks associated with foreign borrowing are presumably taken into account as are the other risks associated with borrowing, whether it be from domestic or foreign sources. More generally, private firms can be expected to be careful in assessing the net return to be derived from borrowing funds as compared with the net cost since their survival as enterprises is at stake.'

The same author went on to argue that overborrowing by the private sector, even with official guarantees, was very unlikely, provided official guarantees were given on a selective basis; only public borrowing on international financial markets was regarded as posing more serious debt service risks [see Robichek (1981, p. 172)].

Convergence of domestic inflation and interest rates toward international ones proved to be a slow process, during which the fixed 'permanent' nominal exchange rate yielded great incentives for private capital inflows into Chile: during 1981 the current account deficit reached an astonishing 14 percent of Chilean Gross National Product, with international reserves holding their own, while domestic savings appeared to collapse. The process of financial liberation had also led to a widely noted (by opposition economists) concentration of potential economic power in the hands of a few conglomerates or economic groups, which combined financial and non-financial corporations. Before 1981, the official view seems to have been that those economic groups must reflect some economies of scale, and could be regarded as one special type of butcher shop, disciplined by free entry and other competitive pressures. Their allocation of credit resources, often heavily loaded in favor of companies associated with the group, was presumed to be more efficient than that which government bureaucrats could achieve.

As late as March 1981 international business publications were writing that 'Chile's free-enterprise banking environment' was proving to be a powerful magnet for foreign banks, and that more entrants into the thriving sector were lining up. (See *Business Latin America*, March 11, 1981, p. 79.) By June 1981 the same publications were noting with concern the cessation of payments on local credits by CRAV, a Chilean sugar company, as well as other blemishes on the economic miracle, but argued that 'the problem areas pose no immediate threat to growth' (*Business Latin America*, June 3, 1981, p. 173). Following the CRAV news, the Central Bank supported financial institutions to stem incipient 'runs'. By November 1981 the position of two important private Chilean banks and several 'financieras' became critical: they were 'intervened' by the Central Bank. Further interventions of financial intermediaries occurred during the first half of 1982; rather than harsh bankruptcy proceedings, these actions apparently involved a generous expansion of credit to the private sector. Between the end of December of 1981 and the end of June 1982, domestic credit in Chilean pesos expanded by 41 percent; of the net increase in domestic credit, 92 percent went to the private sector [see International Monetary Fund (1983, pp. 118–119, lines 32 and 32d)].

The massive use of Central Bank credit to 'bail out' private agent raises doubts about the validity of pre-1982 analyses of the fiscal position and debt of the Chilean public sector. The recorded public sector budget deficit was nonexistent or miniscule for several years through 1981, and moderate during 1982. [For evidence on the apparent Chilean fiscal performance, see McKinnon (1982).] The declining importance of ostensible public debt in the national balance sheet was celebrated by some observers; indeed it was argued that public sector assets, such as remaining public corporations, exceeded its liabilities. Ex post it turned out that the public sector, including the Central Bank, had been accumulating an explosive amount of contingent liabilities to both foreign and domestic agents, who held deposits in, or made loans to the rickety domestic financial sector. This hidden public debt could be turned into cash as the financial system threatened to collapse. Eminent students of fiscal and financial systems, who were involved in the Chilean reforms, apparently overlooked this potential debt bomb. (Present at the creation and early development of the new Chilean financial system were experts brought together by the Organization of American States Program for the Development of Capital Markets; together with the Chilean Central Bank, this program sponsored seminars on capital markets in Santiago during 1974, 1976 and 1977.)

By late 1981 and early 1982 Chile was also feeling the full force of the international economic crisis and discovering that it was not a 'small country' in international financial markets, in the sense of being able to borrow, in either public or private account, all it wished at a given interest rate, even including a generous spread. Pressures mounted on the already overvalued nominal exchange rate, fixed with respect to the U.S. dollar since July 1979; in June 1982 the unthinkable devaluation was carried out in haste, initiating a period of experimentation, which has included clean and dirty floating, a crawling peg, multiple rates, and a tightening up of exchange controls.

The official exchange rate rose rapidly from 39 pesos per U.S. dollar to a range of 74–80 pesos by January 1983; the free rate went substantially above official quotation. Those who had dollar debts were placed under stress; financial difficulties contributed to and were aggravated by a drop in real Gross National Product of about 14 percent during 1982. The Central Bank undertook rescue operations of banks and other financial intermediaries during the second half of 1982, to avoid a breakdown of the financial system. In January 1983 a controversial, massive intervention in five banks, the liquidation of another three, and the direct supervision of another two left the government in control of a good share of the Chilean corporate sector, as well as of its domestic and foreign debts. It has been estimated that non-performing assets of banks rose from 11 percent of their capital and reserves at the end of 1980, to 22 percent at the end of 1981, to 47 percent at the end of 1982, and to 113 percent in May 1983 [Arellano (1983a, p. 192)].

Many of those linked to the intervened banks and associated companies, including ex-Ministers of the Pinochet regime, charged that the January 1983 measures by the Central Bank and its now active superintendency of banks were unnecessary, arbitrary and politically motivated, hinting that rival economic groups stood to profit from the measures. General Pinochet himself took the lead in charging the troubled economic groups with a number of sins, including betrayal of the General's good faith. During 1983 and 1984 some well-known financiers and ex-Ministers were jailed, charged with fraud. Specifically, it has been charged that Banco de Chile and three other private Santiago banks set up a new bank in Panama, which was used to circumvent limits on how much a bank could loan to members of its own group, when those measures were belatedly (during 1981) imposed to control 'the conglomerates' rampant self-lending tactics' (*The Wall Street Journal*, March 6, 1984, p. 38)

Whatever the merits of these charges, it was clear that the domestic financial crisis in Chile had questioned not only the future of many existing banks and corporations but also the rules of the game as they had been understood during the years of the 'Chilean miracle'. The opaqueness of the intervention procedures, and of the announced processes to settle the tangled web of inter-company and bank debts even raised questions about the regime's respect for property rights or at least its willingness to provide effective mechanisms for the efficient exercise of those rights. On the other hand, only the depositors with the three liquidated banks underwent any direct losses (up to 30 percent of their deposits); all other depositors were assured that they could get their money back.

The 1982–83 breakdown of rules, and the reliance on discretion by Chilean officials, extended to the handling of private external debts. In contrast with other heavy borrowers, such as Brazil, a large share of the pre-1982 capital inflow into Chile went directly to private banks and corporations, borrowing abroad without government guarantees. Indeed, both private borrowers and lenders were warned by government officials that they were on their own, and that such debt could in no way be regarded as a Chilean *national* debt. In spite of these ex-ante announcements, during early 1983 external debts of private banks were taken over by the government, which announced its intention to continue servicing them. Those private debts have been included in debt rescheduling being negotiated between the Chilean state and the foreign bank advisory committee for Chile. Apparently the Chilean government caved in under pressure from the bank advisory committee, which argued that it would be extremely difficult for the international financial community to focus its attention on the pressing needs of Chile while an increasing number of companies and their associated Chilean banks were experiencing or approaching a suspension of their payments and subsequent bankruptcy. To make their viewpoint absolutely clear, foreign banks apparently tightened up their granting of very short term commercial credits to Chile during the first quarter of 1983, a technique reportedly used with some success ten years earlier vis-à-vis the same country. The International Monetary Fund, also active in the debt rescheduling exercise, has not publicly objected to this threat to the Robichek doctrine.

In sum, the ad hoc actions undertaken during 1982–83 in Chile to handle the domestic and external financial crisis carry with them an enormous potential for arbitrary wealth redistribution. The lessons private agents are likely to draw from these events are unlikely to be compatible with a reconstruction of a domestic financial sector relying on credible threats of bankruptcy to discipline borrowing and lending. In spite of the ex-post government guarantees to peso deposits, private individuals decreased their demand for peso-denominated assets, as domestic inflation picked up, and expectations grew that the clearing up of the domestic debt tangle would involve additional inflation, exchange-rate depreciation and arbitrary controls. Faith in orderly judicial proceedings to clear up debts and claims on assets appeared to be quite low; stories abounded of debtors fleeing the country, and of petty and grand financial chicanery going unpunished.

Argentine and Uruguayan domestic financial experiences offer a number of similarities and some contrasts to the narrated Chilean events [see Frenkel

(1984)]. In those countries domestic financial intermediation also flourished and then collapsed. Major comparative points are the following:

(1) Whether or not deposits are explicitly insured, the public expects governments to intervene to save most depositors from losses when financial intermediaries run into trouble. Warnings that intervention will not be forthcoming appear to be simply not believable. Fernandez (1983) has blamed explicit insurance for financial deposits by Central Bank authorities in explaining the Argentine financial crash of 1980–82. But, as we have seen, explicit insurance was much less used in Chile, where nevertheless many firms and households apparently felt that their deposits were implicitly guaranteed by the Central Bank [see Arellano (1983a,b)].

(2) The Central Banks, either because of a misguided belief that banks are like butcher shops, or because of lack of trained personnel, neglected prudential regulations over financial intermediaries. Not surprisingly, the assets held by Argentine and Chilean banks and 'financieras' around 1980-81 appeared to have substantially riskier relative to those held by similar institutions in the United States or in Western Europe, and relative to plausible counterfactuals of sensibly-regulated financial intermediaries in those countries. It has been argued that in Uruguay the presence of U.S. owned banks, regulated indirectly by the Federal Reserve, reduced the magnitude of risk-taking by banks.

(3) The new financial institutions in the Southern Cone attracted fresh entrepreneurs and stimulated the creation of new conglomerates and economic groups. While new entrepreneurial blood has an attractive aura, experience indicates that such venturesome animal spirits are better channeled toward non-financial endeavors, where the disciplining threat of bankruptcy could be more credible.

(4) In economies characterized by intractable market and informational imperfections, conglomerates and economic groups, even as they may correct government-induced financial repression imperfections, could exacerbate others, particularly via the creation of oligopolistic power. The close association of financial intermediaries with non-financial corporations, frowned upon by United States regulations, can indeed lead to distortions in the allocation of credit, as shown by the Argentine and Chilean experiences. Linkages in both countries between banks and firms, which were hardly arms' length, were responsible for the high use of debt by private firms. In Chile by late 1982 private firms were more indebted than state enterprises; within the private sector, extreme indebtedness was found among those that controlled banks (and that had acquired from CORFO those firms nationalized under the Allende Presidency). Between 1975 and 1982, Chile went from a financially shallow economy, where inflation had wiped out real value of debt, to an excessively financially deep economy where creditors

owned a very large share of real wealth, a clear case of 'too much debt and too little equity'. Interpenetration of economic and financial power appears to have reached extraordinary levels. The two largest business groups in Chile by late 1982 controlled the principal insurance companies, mutual funds, brokerage houses, the largest private company pension funds and the two largest private commercial banks; about half of all private external debt was channelled through the domestic banking system, so control of banks allowed ready access both to domestic and foreign credit. By late 1982 many banks had lent one quarter of more of their resources to affiliates.

(5) The freeing of interest rates and the relaxation of controls over financial intermediation will not necessarily encourage intermediation beyond short-term maturities. The flourishing of private financial intermediaries in the Southern Cone, even at the height of the boom, was limited to deposits and loans of less than six months' duration. Longer-term intermediation via banks or bonds, not to metion via active stock markets, remained very weak. Insofar as the new policies destroy pre-existing government-supported long-term intermediation arrangements, as in the case of the Chilean housing system, SINAP, financial liberation will reduce available long-term financial instruments. Stock markets may witness short booms, but will mobilize very few funds; charges of manipulation and fraud, plus lack of protection for minority stockholders, will reduce public interest in buying stocks in unregulated or badly regulated stock markets. It has been charged in the Chilean case that false stock transactions were an important component in the growth of financial intermediaries during 1977–81. It is argued that market prices of shares owned by large business groups were manipulated upwards, via phony transactions, to increase the value of collateral used to secure loans and to induce fresh inflows into captive mutual funds.

(6) The end of financial repression undoubtedly encouraged many types of financial savings; Arellano (1983a, b) documents the boom in Chilean financial savings and intermediation especially during 1977–82. Paradoxically, however, total domestic savings did *not* increase in the South American experiments in financial liberation, in spite of handsome returns to savings. Chilean Gross National Savings *fell* from an average of 16.3 percent of Gross National Produce during the decade of the 1960s, to 12.4 percent during 1975–81 [Arellano (1983b, p. 12)]. Arellano cogently argues that the expansion in Chilean financial savings came mainly from the foreign capital inflow, the recording on both sides of the ledger of accumulated interest and of capital gains, and a reorientation of saving flows from the public to the private sector [see also Harberger (1982) for a discussion of the poor performance of Chilean savings]. In 1980–81 reforms to the social security system gave a further boost to funds flowing into private financial institutions, by changing the pay-as-you-go government-managed system into a

capitalization scheme, in which pension funds were to be managed by private financial institutions.

(7) Aggregate investment performance showed no clear sign of either improving or becoming more efficient, in the South American countries undergoing financial liberation. In Chile gross fixed investment during the 1960s averaged 20.2 percent of Gross Domestic Product; during 1974–82 it reached only 15.5 percent of GDP [see Arellano (1983a, p. 226)]. Argentine and Uruguayan performance was better on the investment front, partly because public sector capital formation did not shrink as the Chilean case.

(8) Foreign lenders take govenment announcements that it will not rescue local private debtors, especially banks, with non-guaranteed external (or domestic) liabilities even less seriously than depositors take the threat of a loss of their money. The alleged Japanese attitude of not differentiating between the public and private external debt of a developing country appears to have been upheld ex-post as a sounder guide to action than the Robichek doctrine. Foreign banks lending to both the public and private sectors of a country have considerable leverage to convince governments to take over ex-post bad private debts, especially those of financial intermediaries. There appear to be no international referees to keep them from exercising such leverage. The substantive differences between the nationalization of Mexican private banks during 1982 and the intervention in Chilean private banks during 1983 may be less than one would think by reading the editorials of the international financial press. International banks, knowing they are regulated at home, where they also have close political connections with their governments, expect the same in borrowing countries.

While debts of private Chilean banks to foreign banks were fully assumed by the government, other operations by Southern Cone banks carried out abroad do not seem to have received the protective mantle of home-government support. For example, the Argentine authorities declined to accept responsibility for claims on the New York branch of the failing Banco Intercambio Regional, which was taken over by the New York State Banking Department [Johnson and Abrams (1983, p. 23)]. Given this experience, it is unlikely that Southern Cone banks will emerge as important competitiors in international banking in the near future.

(9) The combination of pre-announced or fixed nominal exchange rate, relatively free capital movements, and domestic and external financial systems characterized by the moral hazard and other imperfections discussed above set the stage not only for significant microeconomic misallocation of credit, but also for macroeconomic instability, including the explosive growth of external debt, most of which was incurred by private Chilean banks, followed by abrupt cessation of capital inflows. That macroeconomic instability would occur even assuming tranquil circumstances, but it is of course exacerbated by external shocks hitting economies made particularly

brittle and vulnerable by that combination of policies and institutions. Contrary to some old and new notions, the experiences of Argentina, Chile and Uruguay show that what happens to the *nominal* exchange rate does affect the *real* exchange rate, at least in the short and medium runs, and that changes in the exchange rate can be an important and efficient mechanism of adjusting the balance of payments. Faulty exchange rate policy appears much more important in explaining financial turbulence and the severity of the Chilean 1982–83 depression than the reduction in import barriers. The credibility of the latter was reduced by peso overvaluation, inducing an import binge and reducing local savings.

(10) Short-term real interest rates, plausibly defined, on the whole remained very high in Argentina, Chile and Uruguay, even during periods of massive capital inflow. A number of hypotheses have been offered to explain this phenomenon: macroeconomic policy; expectations of devaluation and inflation, which in the short run did not materialize; a change in the real productivity of capital; and even excessive spreads originating in Central Bank Reserve requirements. As in the case of explanations for the high, but less spectacular, real interest rates recorded in the United States during the early 1980s, none of the hypotheses are fully satisfactory [see Litterman and Weiss (1984)]. From the viewpoint of this paper, the most intriguing hypotheses for explaining extravagant Southern Cone real interest rates, which in Chile reached 32 percent per annum on the average during 1976–82 according to Arellano [Arellano (1983b, p. 31); this is the rate charged for short-term loans], focus on the nature of financial deregulation and imperfections in those markets. It was noted earlier that the high Chilean interest rates were reflected mainly in double-entry bookkeeping. It can be argued that firms and households borrowing at extravagant rates either expected them to last for very brief periods, or, if they did not, borrowers expected the government to bail them out, knowing as they did that many other borrowers were in a similar situation. Such expectations, of course, favored 'distress borrowing': either interest rates fell, or government would 'bail out' everyone. Whatever the validity of these arguments may be, it is clear from the Southern Cone experience that the type of deregulation experience by those countries gives no assurance of stable real interest rates hovering around reasonable estimates of the socially optimal shadow real interest rate. Some observers have argued that the main function of high real interest rates was to transfer the ownership of real enterprise wealth from debtors to creditors, a mechanism doomed to stop when no more shareholders' wealth was left.

(11) As elsewhere in Latin America, the decline in real Gross Domestic Product in Argentina (11 percent between 1980 and 1982), in Chile (15 percent between 1981 and 1983), and in Uruguay (14 percent between 1980 and 1983) may be said to be the reult of unfavorable external circumstances

during the early 1980s, combined with less than optimal domestic policies. As noted earlier, policy-induced stickiness in nominal exchange rates delayed adjustment to changes in external terms of trade and changes in capital flows. The brittle Southern Cone domestic sectors must also bear blame for first exaggerating the boom, then aggravating the recession and finally delaying recovery. The consequences of the Chilean financial crash have been the most spectacular, leading to a massive rearranging of the national balance sheet. Such a rearranging, however, has been a slow and opaque process, leaving many economic entities not knowing who owns what, or who owes what to whom, hardly ideal circumstances for encouraging a revival of private investment.

(12) As with international debt, the sorting out and allocation of losses and blame for 'mistakes' (only clear ex-post) by borrowers and lenders in the domestic financial markets present monumental conceptual and legal problems, especially when 'mistakes' are widespread. Since 1982 Argentina appears to have taken the time-honored route of washing out old financial mistakes via inflation (which is not allowed to be reflected in interest rates); this approach favors borrowers over lenders. As noted earlier, in the Chilean case the path out of the morass remains unclear; inflation accelerated, but 'only' to around 25–30 percent during 1983. There are few precedents and less accepted doctrine regarding financial processes as bizarre as those experienced by Chile during 1975-83. Bankruptcies, financial distress and confusion delay recovery beyond what would be necessary to achieve real adjustment to the new international terms of trade, capital market realities and expectations about growth in the international economy.

4. Options for Latin American domestic financial systems

Southern Cone domestic financial systems of the late 1970s and early 1980s ended up with a pessimum 'middle way': de facto public guarantees to depositors, lenders and borrowers, and no effective supervision and control (until it was too late) of the practices of financial intermediaries. Reform could logically head in two opposite directions: more laissez-faire with binding (constitutional?) commitments against future bail-outs, or toward more public controls, possibly culminating in nationalization of the banking system, as in Costa Rica, El Salvador, India and France. Other Latin American countries outside the Southern Cone, such as Brazil and Colombia, have domestic financial systems that, while showing signs of stress during the last few years, have not undergone Southern-Cone-type of crisis; their experiences (including their post-1981 troubles) could be useful in sketching desirable characteristics of domestic financial arrangements.

As noted earlier, the credibility of a government commitment to a truly laissez-faire domestic financial system is very low. Firstly, as illustrated in the recent Chilean experience, foreign financial agents will not accept a separation of private and public debts when a crisis arrives; financial laissez-faire in one peripheral country does not seem viable. Secondly 'public opinion', including generals and their aunts, simply does not believe that the state would (nor could) allow most depositors to be wiped out by the failure of banks and financial intermediaries. It may be that private financial agents, domestic and foreign, lenders, borrowers and intermediaries, whether or not related to generals, know that the domestic political and judicial systems are not compatible with laissez-faire commitments which a misguided Minister of Finance or Central Bank President may occasionally utter in a moment of dogmatic exaltation. When a crisis hits, agents will reason, bankrupcy courts will break down; when most everyone (who counts) is bankrupt, nobody is! Thus, even if one believed, à la Hayek, that the externalities and public good characteristics of the domestic monetary and financial system are negligible, one may conclude that the political, and social, infrastructure found in many developing (and developed?) countries conspires against the viability of such a pure laissez-faire financial system. The zealot may conclude that the nation does not measure up to the purity of the model.

So should one move back to good old 1950s style financial repression, extensive controls and perhaps full nationalization of the domestic financial system? It can be argued that a *believable* alternative system could be designed, avoiding many of the inefficiencies of financial repression while avoiding those of the Southern Cone experience, and blending both public and private financial agents. What follows sketches some features of that eclectic system.

Negative real rates of interest became common in Latin America during the 1940s and 1950s as inflation gained momentum and many monetary authorities maintained ceilings on nominal interest rates offered and charged by the banking and financial system. At that time most South American countries (but not Mexico, Venezuela, Central America and the Caribbean) also maintained extensive exchange controls. Limited international capital mobility buttressed the taxing of cash balances and financial repression; the then prevalent Keynesian orthodoxy also encouraged these developments. While persistently negative real rates of interest in the formal financial market occured only when the government imposed rate ceilings and exchange controls, it is not obvious that public regulation and participation in the domestic financial market necessarily had to lead to negative rates of interest. The Mexican financial system of the 1950s and 1960s, praised by development scholars, contained both public institutions and substantial government regulations. As already noted, the post-1964 Brazilian indexing and other financial reforms could hardly be described as involving a laissez-faire approach. The celebrated South Korean financial reforms of the 1960s were carried out with a high degree of public ownership and control of the formal financial sector [see Gurley et al. (1965, p. 45)].

Assuming that a country intends to maintain monetary sovereignty but that significant, yet not explosive, inflationary expectations persist, there is a strong case for making sure that firms and households have available a domestic liquid financial asset yielding a real interest rate which is not far below, nor much above, zero. The inflationary tax borne by currency balances may result from the inability of the fiscal system to find non-inflationary sources of revenues, or it may be simply a by-product of an inflationary spiral, whose inertial momentum could only be halted by a severe real contraction. Presumably the transactions convenience provided by domestic currency will be enough to generate some demand for it, even under moderate inflation, an assumption supported by South American experiences. But without a liquid and safe store of value denominated in domestic currency, which at least maintains its purchasing power, a national monetary and financial system will have little long-run credibility, short of draconian controls. It could also be argued that without such an asset the system would not meet the most elementrary tests of social equity.

It should be emphasized that introducing a 'zero-real-rate assets' next to a zero-nominal-rate asset involves a delicate trade-off, which may increase welfare only if the inflation tax on money remains 'reasonable'. The zero-real-rate asset will reduce the demand for money, but may also reduce the demand for assets denominated in foreign currencies. An inflation which accelerated sharply above historical norms, introducing massive currency substitution, could destroy the credibility of all domestic financial assets.

There are many possible ways to supply a zero-real-rate asset. The banking system, for example, could provide indexed savings accounts; depending on practical considerations, they could be used partly as checking accounts. At least that segment of the banking system would have explicit and full deposit insurance, perhaps only for accounts below a certain (generous) limit; insurance for larger accounts could partial. Naturally, the use by banks of funds coming from those accounts would be tightly regulated by a flinty-eyed superintendency of banks. Indeed, practical considerations could lead to the requirement of 100 percent reserves on that type of deposits, to be placed in very safe assets.

Enormous potential power is given by this scheme to the regulatory agencies: it could end up in the total control of credit by the Central Bank. Experiences in Latin America and elsewhere with a public monopoly of credit have not been so encouraging as to make one indifferent to this possibility. Safeguards against the monopoly scenario would include allowance for the supply of alternative financial assets, by either private agents or decentralized public ones, plus an active Congressional supervision of the regulatory agencies and the public banks. The latter point suggests that democracy, whatever its more fundamental virtues, is an important technical input for a healthy domestic financial system.

Suppliers of riskier financial assets would not have available public deposit insurance but would be subject to less regulation. Nevertheless, these would still include minimum capital requirements, strict 'transparency' information rules (regarding both assets and connections with other firms), and clear 'risk-may-be-hazardous-for-your-health' warnings to the general public. After recent experiences it is probably better to proceed cautiously in this segment of the domestic financial market, but not so cautiously as to make it an empty set. Interest rates offered and charged by these intermediaries would be expected to show significant real rates; at least on an experimental basis those rates would not be set by the monetary authorities, but spreads between rates paid to depositiors and those charged to borrowers would be subject to antitrust vigilance (as entry into this sector would not be completely free). Those spreads would depend, inter alia, on possible official reserve requirements; these could be presumed to be quite low for this segment of the market. Both foreign and private institutions would be expected to participate, but entry regulations and antitrust vigilance would be on guard against interlocking directorates among financial and non-financial firms and would lean against the creation of dominating economic groups and conglomerates. Prohibitions against the mingling of financial and non-financial firms, as in the Unites States's Glass–Steagall Act, appear particularly desirable where markets are relatively small.

Latin American experience, and indeed that of Continental Europe last century, makes one skeptical that private markets alone will generate a flow of financial intermediation high enough to support a rate of long-term fixed capital formation which fully exploits available high social rates of return to long-term investments. Private uncertainties and skepticism of all sorts, which will not disappear by freeing interest rates, reduce the scope for private long-term finance and for stock markets; the latter have continued to languish even when encouraged by various subsidies, as in Brazil. It will be recalled that this was the original motivation for the creation of public development banks in Latin America during the 1930s and 1940s. The need remains to close gaps left in long-term capital markets by acute uncertainties found in Latin American societies, and public development banks remain a plausible solution, in spite of the abuses and errors in their management registered over the last 50 years. Not all experiences have been negative; as noted earlier, public mortgage banks obtaining funds by issuing indexed obligations yielding modest real rates of interest and correspondingly pricing their mortgages, have registered important accomplishments in anumber of countries. The crucial lessons remain the avoidance of real interest rates too far from plausible estimates of the shadow opportunity cost of capital, plus political mechanisms to check potential abuses of those public agencies.

Decentralized, efficiently-run public financial intermediaries operating together with private intermediaries could play several important functions, besides merely plugging gaps in the long-term segment of the market. As recent Latin American experiences have shown, confirming the evidence of the early 1930s, during financial crises the public appears to turn to public banks for greater security. ('Flight to quality' in the Latin American context also benefits large, well-known banks.) Public banks could help focus market interst rates around the social opportunity cost of capital, decreasing instability in real interest rates. Those institutions could channel external funds, helping to keep tabs on the foreign debt and improve borrowing terms. Their operating costs would give evidence and provide a yardstick on reasonable spreads between interest rates paid to depositors and those charged to borrowers. By providing long-term credit to new, non-traditional activities, development banks would eliminate one of the excuses frequently given for extravagant protection against imports. Indeed, the valid cases for infant-industry protection or promotion are likely to be most efficiently handled under Latin American conditions using public credit instruments, suitably priced, rather than by barriers agains imports. Needless to say, public banks will not yield these results without a great deal of effort and pressure by those in charge of their management and supervision. Considerable experimentation is also likely to be needed, particularly regarding the establishment of a structure of interest rates compatible with both a vigorous rate of fixed capital formation and a matching flow of voluntary domestic savings.

The real exchange rate, no less than the real interest rate, remains a crucial price for Latin American economies. The southern Cone emphasis on exchange rate management as an instrument to achieve nominal targets, letting market forces settle the real exchange rate, emerges from recent experience as less successful than the Brazilian–Colombian crawling peg practice, which targets the real exchange rate as an explicit objective of policy. As with the real interest rate, the correct real exchange rate is not easy to define and calculate exactly, but grossly over- or under-valued real exchange rates, like giraffes, are not so difficult to recognize on sight. 'The correct real exchange rate' would be that compatible with expected current account deficits, output levels and long-term capital inflows, given commercial and other policies. These are *real* considerations; what about the role of the exchange rate (and of expected changes in *nominal* level) as a crucial link between domestic and international financial markets, and its impact on the capital account of the balance of payments?

Domestic policies targeting real interest rates and real exchange rates will not be compatible with free or untaxed capital movements and unrestricted convertibility, except by fluke (or short of extravagent average levels of reserves). This is not a pleasant conclusion for those familiar with past experiences with exchange controls over international flows in Latin America or elsewhere. Limitations on unconditional capital-account convertibility, however, may have greater or smaller inefficiencies and inequities depending on the context in which they are undertaken. A real exchange rate hovering around its long-run equilibrium level will do much to reduce pressure on convertibility limitation; it would be absolutely essential to avoid the temptation of manipulation convertibility restrictions to buttress overvalued exchange rates, as in the past. The heterodox tool of exchange controls must be managed with orthodox concern for real exchange rate. Note, incidentally, that even without convertibility restictions overvalued exchange rates can be propped by manipulating the capital account of the balance of payments, i.e., high interest rates went along in the Southern Cone with overvaluation.

The prudential regulatory machinery could be used to discourage volatile international financial flows relying primarily on taxes or tax-like requirements, i.e., via special reserve requirements for certain types of unwanted international financial transactions, as is the practice in several Western European countries. Taxes would also be expected to capture arbitrage profits from borrowing abroad and lending domestically, under 'normal' circumstances. Persistent subsidies to encourage foreign borrowing would be a sign that either the real exchange rate or domestic real interest rates have drifted from their equilibrium levels.

Unrestrained convertibility in the capital account is in fact a luxury, desirable in itself, enjoyed only by a handful of countries which have either a very developped or a very underdeveloped domestic financial system. It is neither the ususal practice in OECD countries [see Bertrand (1981)], nor was it the expectation of at least some of the architects of the Bretton Woods system [see Crotty (1983)]. So long as domestic currency balances may be burdened by an inflation tax higher than those levied on foreign currencies, some limitations on convertibility are widely perceived as a necessary part of transitional policy package [see, for example, McKinnon and Mathieson (1981)].

The case for some limitations on free capital account movements rests partly on macroeconomic considerations, partly on the need to correct microeconomic imperfections on domestic and international financial markets. Events during 1982 must have put an end to the notion that there are small countries in international financial markets, in the sense that those countries could borrow all they want at a given interest rate. Currency and sovereign risks will inevitably tilt the supply schedule of foreign funds to any country in an upward-sloping direction, and may even give it a kinkier look, so that there will be a gap between private and social costs of borrowing [see Harberger (1981) for a clear, but apparently unheeded, exposition]. Moral-hazard considerations on both sides of the market, or expectations of bail-outs, reinforce the case for home-country supervision of international financial flows; if home countries do not undertake that supervision others will do it for them.

These considerations also cast doubt on the desirability of allowing the domestic financial system to offer deposits denominated in foreign currencies, either to domestic residents or to foreigners. Such deposits sharply curtail the freedom of maneuver of monetary authorities, for the sake of maintaining the credibility and reputation of the banks offering them. (The point is partly applicable to any contry whose banks have an international scope, even if deposits are denominated in home currency.) The Mexican and Uruguayan experiences suggest that deposits denominated in foreign currencies and insured by the home Central Bank enhance vulnerability to crises, introducing the likehood of sharp discontinuities in the rules of the game. At any rate, in general that type of deposit would not be compatible with limitations on capital account convertibility, limitations which would also rule out the feasibility of totally clean float for the exchange rate, including both spot and future quotations.

5. A final caveat

Recent Chilean experience shows that a balanced budget by itself will prevent neither a serious financial crisis nor acute macroeconomic turbulence. Yet previous Chilean experiences, and those of other Latin American countries, also show that fiscal extravagance is a sure way to bring about not only economic dislocation, but also the weakening and even collapse of fragile democratic institutions. This paper has discussed neither fiscal policy nor strategies on how to eliminate inflation. Implicity, it has assumed that Latin American inflations may be sustained by many sources, not just budgetary laxity, and that in most countries for the foreseeable future 'living with inflation' will be a more credible goal than eliminating it, and that this must be taken into account when designing desirable domestic financial policies, as well as other measure.

Nevertheless, there are inflations (and budget deficits) which no domestic financial system with a minimum of coherence could live with. Examples include inflations which accelerate for more than, say, three years in a row, reaching levels substantially above historical norms, or inflationary rates which fluctuate unpredictably from year to year. Under either circumstances relative prices will become very volatile, and real and financial calculations very difficult. In contrast, the Colombian experience of the last ten years or so provides an example of an inflation which is fairly predictable and relatively easy to live with. Finally, it would be nearly impossible to design reasonable financial systems, in a mixed-economy context, which could be compatible with sustained public expenditures and budget deficits of the magnitude of those registered in Chile during 1971–72, in Argentina during 1974–75, or in Mexico during 1981–82.

References

Arellano, José P., 1983a, El financiamiento del desarrollo, in: CIEPLAN, Reconstruccion economica para la democracia (Editorial Aconcagua, Santiago de Chile) 189–237.

Arellano, José P., 1983b, De la liberalizacion a la intervencion: El mercado de capitales en Chile: 1974-83, in: Estudios CIEPLAN, no. 11, Estudio no. 74. Dec., 5–49.

Bertrand, Raymond, 1981, The liberization of capital movements — An insight, The Three Banks Review, no. 132, Dec.

Corden, W. Max, 1972, Monetary integration, Princeton Essays in International Finance no. 93 (International Finance Section, Princeton University, Princeton, NJ) April.

Crotty, James R., 1983, On Keynes and capital flight, The Journal of Economic Literature XXI, no. 1, 59–65.

Federal Reserve Bank of Minneapolis, 1982, Are banks specials?, Annual report.

Fernandez, Roque B., 1983, La crisis financiera Argentina: 1980–1982, Desarrollo Economico 23, no. 89, 79–98.

Frenkel, Roberto, 1984, Notas para una investigacion sobre el sistema financiero en Argentina, processed (CEDES, Buenos Aires).

Friedman, Milton, 1959, A program for monetary stability (Fordham University Press, New York).

Galbis, Vicente, 1979, Inflation and interest rate policies in Latin America, 1967-76, International Monetary Fund Staff Papers 26, no. 2, 334–366.

Gurley, John G., Hugh T. Patrick and E. S. Shaw, 1965, The financial structure of Korea. Reprinted by Research Department, the Bank of Korea, Seoul.

Hall, Robert E., 1982, Monetary trends in the United States and the United Kingdom: A review from the perspective of new developments in monetary economics, Journal of Economic Literature 20, no. 4, 1552–1556.

Harberger, Arnold C., 1981, Comentarios, in: Banco Central de Chile, Alternativas de politicas financieras en economias pequenas y abiertas al exterior, Estudios Monetarios VII (Banco Central de Chile, Santiago de Chile) Dec., 1981–188.

Harberger, Arnold C., 1982, The Chilean economy in the 1970's: Crisis, stabilization, liberalization, reform, in: Karl Brunner and Allen H. Meltzer, eds., Economic policy in a world of change, Carnegie-Rochester Conference Series on Public Policy 17 (North-Holland, Amsterdam) 115–152.

International Monetary Fund, 1983, International financial statistics (Washington, DC) March.

Johnson, G.C. and Richard L. Abrams, 1983, Aspects of the international banking safety net, International Monetary Fund Occasional Paper no. 17, March.

Kareken, John H., 1981, Deregulating commercial banks: The watchword should be caution, Federal Reserve Bank of Minneapolis Quarterly Review, Spring/Summer, 1–5.

Litterman, Robert B. and Laurence Weiss, 1984, Money, real interest rates and output: A reinterpretation of postwar U.S. data, processed (Federal Reserve Bank of Minneapolis, Minneapolis, MN).

McKinnon, Ronald I., 1980, Financial policies, in: John Cody et al., eds., Policies for industrial progress in developing countries (Oxford University Press, New York) 93–120.

McKinnon, Ronald I., 1982, The order of economic liberalization: Lessons from Chile and Argentina, in: Karl Brunner and Allan H. Meltzer, eds., Economic policy in a world of change, Carnegie-Rochester Conference Series on Public Policy 17 (North-Holland, Amsterdam) 159–184.

McKinnon, Ronald I. and Donald J. Mathieson, 1981, How to manage a repressed economy, Princeton Essays in International Finance no. 145 (International Finance Section, Princeton University, Princeton, NJ) Dec.

Robichek, E. Walter, 1981, Some reflections about external public debt management, in: Banco Central de Chile, Alternativas de políticas financieras en economías pequeñas y abiertas al exterior, Estudios Monetarios VII (Banco Central de Chile, Santiago de Chile) Dec., 171–183.

Stiglitz, J. and A. Weiss, 1981, Credit rationing in markets with imperfect information, The American Economic Review 71, no. 3, 393–410.

Stabilization with Liberalization: An Evaluation of Ten Years of Chile's Experiment with Free-Market Policies, 1973–1983*

Sebastian Edwards
University of California, Los Angeles and National Bureau of Economic Research

Introduction

The recent (post-1973) economic experience of Chile has attracted considerable attention, both from professional economists and from the media.[1] Most observers have been particularly impressed by the sharp contrasts observed in Chile in such a short period of time. For example, in 1973 Chile had one of the highest rates of inflation in the world (over 600%), whereas in 1981 it experienced one of the lowest rates of inflation (9.5%). Also, in 1975 real GNP declined by 12.9%, but during 1977–80 real GNP grew at an average rate of 8.5% per annum. In 1982, however, the country faced a new recession, with real GNP dropping by 14.5%. In 1983 the GNP was reduced further by 2.3%. The fact that these episodes developed while the military government was actively pursuing free-market-oriented policies that greatly liberalized the economy adds considerable interest to the Chilean case.[2]

The year 1973 marked an important turning point in Chile's economic and political history. In September of that year the military took over the government from President Salvador Allende, and a period of dramatic economic changes began. Chile was transformed from an economy isolated from the rest of the world, with strong government intervention, into a liberalized, world-integrated economy where market forces were left free to guide most of the economy's decisions. The period 1973–81 was characterized by important achievements: inflation was greatly reduced; the government deficit was virtually eliminated; the economy went through a dramatic liberalization of its foreign sector: tariffs were reduced to a uniform 10% level, and prices, including interest rates, were full liberalized. Probably one of the most interesting aspects of the Chilean economy during this period is that major stabilization and liberalization attempts were undertaken simultaneously. Moreover, during this period the Chilean economic authorities introduced a novel stabilization program based on the fact that the economy's links with the rest of the world had been greatly increased by the liberalization of trade. In this stabilization strategy the manipulation of the nominal exchange rate replaced monetary control as the central tool of the antiinflationary effort.[3]

The free-market policies implemented by the military regime since 1973 can be viewed as a reaction to a long tradition of government intervention and controls that had characterized the Chilean economy since the 1930s.[4] Between 1940 and 1970 Chile's growth record was modest: real gross domestic product (GDP) grew at an average rate of 3.7% per annum, while real per capita GDP grew at 1.7% per annum. During these 30 years Chile basically followed an import-substitution development strategy, which greatly closed the economy from the rest of the world. In general, available evidence suggests that this inward-looking strategy had some negative effects on Chile's economic growth, by reducing domestic savings, introducing distortions and inefficiencies, and tending to increase capital-labor ratios. This period was also characterized by high government deficits and chronic inflation.[5]

From the perspective of economic growth, 1973–83 has been characterized by a highly variable record. During this period Chile experienced one of the highest rates of growth in its history—9.5% in 1977—and also some of the highest declines in real GDP: −12.9% in 1975 and −14.5% in 1982. Table 1 presents data on real GDP and real per capita GDP between 1970 and 1983. As may be seen, the first 2 years of the military regime (1974–75) were characterized by a decline in real per capita GDP. This reduction in economic activity was especially dramatic in 1975—GDP per capita declined by 14.4%—as a consequence of the stabilization program and the decline in the terms of trade (the fall of the price of copper was especially severe). On the other hand, in the years 1977–80 extraordinarily high rates of growth of GDP, averaging 8.5% per year, were achieved. However, as may be seen from table 1, real per capita GDP reattained its 1971 level only in 1980. A crucial question then, which will be addressed below, is to what extent these high growth rates were due only to a recovery process, starting from a very low initial level of GDP. Finally, in late 1981 Chile entered a deep recession, and real GDP declined dramatically during 1982 and 1983. This crisis had led, in 1983, to a highly unstable and explosive political situation.

The purpose of this paper is to examine in some detail Chile's economic performance during the period since the military coup. The analysis provides an evaluation of 10 years of military regime, placing emphasis in the stabilization and liberalization policies. Special atten-

TABLE 1

REAL GROSS DOMESTIC PRODUCT (GDP) AND REAL GDP PER CAPITA IN CHILE: 1970–83

Year	Real GDP (Billions 1977 US$) (1)	Rate of Growth of Real GDP (%) (2)	Per Capita Real GDP (1977 US$) (3)	Rate of Growth of Per Capita Real GDP (%) (4)
1970	13.1	2.1	1,403	.2
1971	14.3	9.0	1,502	7.1
1972	14.1	− 1.2	1,459	− 2.9
1973	13.4	− 5.6	1,355	− 7.1
1974	13.5	1.0	1,345	− .7
1975	11.7	− 12.9	1,152	− 14.4
1976	12.2	3.5	1,172	1.8
1977	13.4	9.9	1,266	8.0
1978	14.5	8.2	1,347	6.4
1979	15.7	8.3	1,434	6.5
1980	16.8	7.5	1,516	5.7
1981	17.7	5.3	1,568	3.4
1982*	15.1	− 14.5	1,312	− 16.3
1983*	14.7	− 2.3	1,257	− 3.9

SOURCE.—Banco Central de Chile.
*Preliminary.

tion is given to the recent (1982–83) events that have led to one of the worst recessions in the country's history. The paper is organized in the following form: in Section II the stabilization program and the employment problem are discussed and the crucial role played by the exchange rate policy in the antiinflationary program is emphasized. In Section III the liberalization of international trade is discussed. Section IV, on the other hand, presents an analysis of the liberalization of the domestic financial markets and of the capital account of the balance of payments. It is noted that the Chilean economy was characterized during this period by extremely high interest rates and low domestic saving ratios. Section V presents a brief discussion of the sources of growth between 1975 and 1980. Section VI focuses on the 1982–83 recession, including the January 1983 agreement with the IMF. It is argued that this recession was in part the result of policy inconsistencies and mistakes. The end notes contain a fairly comprehensive reading list of works related to Chile's economic development during the recent period.

II. The Stabilization Program and the Employment Problem

In October of 1973 the military government announced that the reduction of inflation—which had exceeded 600% in the previous 12 months—was one of its main economic goals.[6] Other important short-run objectives were reducing government controls, reducing the fiscal deficit, reorganizing the productive sector, and avoiding a major balance-of-payments crisis. During the first 18 months of the regime some of these objectives were (partially) achieved—relative prices were realigned, a unified exchange rate was established, the balance-of-payments crisis was avoided, and government finances were somewhat straitened—but inflation was still out of control. The growth rate of consumer prices reached 370% in 1974.

Until April of 1975 a gradualist antiinflationary approach had been followed. At this time, however, this policy was abandoned and an abrupt stabilization program was implemented. The new program was based on traditional views regarding economic stabilization in a closed economy and called for a drastic reduction in inflation in 1 year. The main characteristics were: (*a*) an across-the-board reduction in government expenditure (between 15% and 25%); (*b*) a 10% temporary hike in income taxes; (*c*) an acceleration of the program of reducing the size of the public sector, which had begun in 1974; and (*d*) a tight monetary policy.[7]

Table 2 presents information about inflation and stabilization during the 1970s and early 1980s. As may be seen from columns B, C, and D, the main feature of the 1975 stabilization package was a major fiscal shock that resulted in 80% real reduction of the fiscal deficit and thus of one of the major sources of inflation. This decline in the deficit level in 1975 was accomplished mainly by the reduction in government-sector expenditures through the reduction of the number of civil servants. It has been estimated that the fiscal crunch resulted in a reduction in government employment by about 100,000 workers, or 2.4% of the labor force.[8]

As table 2 shows, government revenues as a percentage of GDP also increased substantially in 1975. The increase was effected by a comprehensive tax reform that introduced a flat 20% value-added tax, full indexation of the tax system, elimination of most tax exemptions and subsidies, unification of corporate and noncorporate income taxes into a flat-rate business tax, and integration of personal and business income taxes.[9]

The stabilization effort of 1975 relied on a tighter monetary policy as well. Even though Harberger has argued that it cannot be said that there was a monetary crunch,[10] during the initial phase of the stabilization program the control of monetary aggregates was a central aspect of the overall policy.[11]

The 1975 stabilization program had a prompt effect on inflation: the growth rate of prices declined from 69% in the second quarter of 1975 to 26% in the fourth quarter of 1975. Nevertheless, in spite of the virtual elimination of the major source of money creation—the fiscal deficit—the growth rate of prices seemed to be regaining its old pace, as the rate of inflation climbed to 47% in the first quarter of 1976. At this time a major change in the stabilization strategy took place: the

TABLE 2

INFLATION AND STABILIZATION: 1973–82

YEAR	(A) INFLATION RATE (%) (December to December)	(B) GOVERNMENT EXPENDITURE 1977 Millions of US$	(B) GOVERNMENT EXPENDITURE Percentage GDP	(C) GOVERNMENT REVENUE 1977 Millions of US$	(C) GOVERNMENT REVENUE Percentage GDP	(D) FISCAL DEFICIT 1977 Millions of US$	(D) FISCAL DEFICIT Percentage GDP	(E) RATE OF GROWTH OF M1 (%) (December to December)	(F) PROPORTION OF TOTAL CREDIT RECEIVED BY GOVERNMENT	(G) RATE OF DEVALUATION OF PESO (%) (December to December)	(H) BALANCE OF PAYMENTS (Millions US$)
1970	34.9	3,681	28.1	3,301	25.2	380	2.9	...	.56	20.0	...
1971	22.1	4,633	32.4	2,989	21.2	1,644	11.2	110	.69	33.3	...
1972	487.5	4,540	32.2	2,637	18.7	1,903	13.5	157	.77	56.3	...
1973	605.9	5,990	44.7	2,693	20.1	3,297	24.6	317	.88	1,340.0	− 21
1974	369.2	4,374	32.4	2,957	21.9	1,417	10.5	272	.85	419.4	− 55
1975	343.2	3,206	27.4	2,902	24.8	304	2.6	258	.85	354.5	−344
1976	197.9	3,148	25.8	2,867	23.5	281	2.3	194	.75	104.9	414
1977	84.2	3,337	24.9	3,095	23.1	242	1.9	108	.59	60.5	113
1978	37.2	3,451	23.8	3,335	23.0	116	.9	67	.40	21.4	712
1979	38.0	3,627	23.1	3,878	24.7	−251	− 1.7	65	.29	14.9	1,047
1980	31.2	4,200	25.0	4,284	25.5	− 84	− .6	57	.10	0	1,244
1981	9.5	4,195	23.7	4,726	26.7	−531	− 3.0	60	.02	0	70
1982	20.7	4,379	29.0	4,032	26.7	−347	− 2.3	9	.07	88.3	−1,165

SOURCES.—Column A is taken from the Instituto Nacional de Estadísticas (INE) for years 1970–72 and 1979–82, and from René Cortazar and Jorge Marshall "Indice de precios al consumidor en Chile," manuscript (1980), for 1973–78. Columns B through D are taken from *Exposición de la hacienda pública* (Santiago: Ministerio de la Hacienda, 1981); Columns E and F are taken from *International Financial Statistics* (Washington, D.C.: International Monetary Fund, various issues). Columns G and H are taken from *Indicadores económicos y sociales, 1960–1982* (Santiago: Banco Central de Chile, 1983).

NOTE.—A minus sign means deficit. Data for 1970–72 are not available in col. H because in 1980 the Central Bank changed the way balance of payments statistics are recorded.

emphasis shifted from the control of the quantity of money as the major antiinflationary tool, and the manipulation of the nominal exchange rate became the basic stabilization instrument. It was argued that opening the economy to the rest of the world—tariffs had already been reduced from an average of 94% in 1973 to an average of 33%—made a stabilization program designed for a closed economy largely ineffective. It was further argued that since in an open economy there is a close link between the domestic rate of price changes and the rate of devaluation (plus the rate of world inflation), the domestic rate of inflation basically depended on the behavior of the exchange rate.[12] In June of 1976 the government revalued the Chilean peso by 10% as a means of breaking inflationary expectations. In 1977 a new 10% appreciation was implemented, and starting in January 1978 a novel policy of preannouncing changes in the exchange rate (the so-called exchange-rate table) was introduced as a means of further reducing the domestic rate of inflation.

Because the trade reform had reduced most import barriers, it was expected that this system of preannounced devaluations would tend to work in a way similar to a fixed exchange-rate regime, where inflation tends to be, on average, equal to the world rate of inflation *plus* the rate of devaluation. Initially, however, the rate of inflation exceeded the sum of the devaluation and world inflation, resulting in a real appreciation of the Chilean peso.[13] In June of 1979, as a way of further reducing the domestic rate of inflation, the preannounced devaluation system was ended and a fixed exchange rate was adopted, in which the peso was pegged to the U.S. dollar at a rate of 39 pesos per dollar. During the next months the rate of inflation declined substantially but still exceeded the world inflation, generating a further real appreciation of the Chilean peso. Finally, in 1981 the domestic rate of inflation converged to the world level, with an annual change of consumer prices of only 9.5% in that year.

On the production side, the immediate short-run effect of the stabilization program was to generate a large reduction in the level of economic activity in 1975. The fiscal shock plus the sharp decline in Chile's terms of trade resulted in a 12.9% reduction of GDP in 1975 and in a steep increase in the rate of unemployment, to almost 20% in September. Even though the economy began to recover rapidly after 1975, and real GDP regained its 1974 level in 1977, unemployment remained at extraordinarily high levels throughout the period. Table 3 presents data on the labor force, unemployment, the so-called Minimum Employment Program—which is a low-wage public works program designed to cope with the unemployment problem—and real wages. As may be seen from this table, open unemployment (which excludes the Minimum Employment Program) never dropped below 10% and in fact experienced a dramatic jump in 1982. The high rate of

TABLE 3

UNEMPLOYMENT AND WAGES IN CHILE: 1970–82

Year	Total Labor Force (1,000s) (A)	Total Unemployment (1,000s) (B)	Open Unemployment Rate (%) (C)	Minimum Employment Program (1,000s) (D)	Minimum Employment Program as % of Labor Force (E)	Index of Real Wages* (1970 = 100) (F)
1970	2,909.4	100.5	3.5	...	...	100.0
1971	2,967.4	96.6	3.3	...	...	129.0
1972	2,979.9	97.6	3.3	...	...	114.5
1973	n.a.	n.a.	n.a.	...	...	64.4
1974	n.a.	n.a.	n.a.	...	...	60.0
1975	3,114.7	464.6	14.9	118.7	3.8	63.9
1976	3,182.3	405.0	12.7	209.3	6.6	76.5
1977	3,199.0	378.5	11.8	179.6	5.6	81.3
1978	3,476.6	495.3	14.1	124.2	3.6	82.9
1979	3,477.5	474.2	13.6	152.2	4.4	83.7
1980	3,635.5	378.4	10.4	207.2	5.7	96.2
1981	3,688.0	417.0	11.3	171.3	4.6	109.5
1982	3,503.6	679.1	19.4	322.7	9.2	107.9

SOURCES.—Banco Central de Chile and Instituto Nacional de Estadisticas.

NOTE.—The labor force and unemployment figures (cols. A–C) refer to periods September to December for 1970; and October to December for the rest of the years. These are, however, the best data available at a national level. Quarterly data are available for the greater Santiago area. The data on the minimum employment program (col. D) refer to the October-to-December average of each year. n.a. means not available.

*To construct the real-wages index the GDP deflator was used, because the official price index has been manipulated and understates inflation. René Cortazar and Jorge Marshall, "Indice de precios al consumidor en Chile," manuscript (Santiago: Cieplán, 1980).

unemployment during the late 1970s may be traced to a number of causes including the negative effect of the stabilization program on the demand for labor; the reduction of the public sector, which resulted in the elimination of approximately 100,000 jobs; and the liberalization of foreign trade, which generated a major readjustment in the manufacturing sector.[14] In spite of the persistence of a high unemployment rate, real wages and salaries slowly increased between 1976 and 1980, and in 1981 they finally surpassed their 1970 levels.[15]

Two important characteristics of the behavior of the labor market during this period deserve special attention. First, a minimum wage was in effect throughout the period. Between 1975 and 1979 the minimum wage increased in real terms by 20%. There is no doubt that this minimum-wage law should be added to the list of explanations for the persistently high rates of unemployment during the recovery.[16] Second, during this period a backward indexation system was in effect, whereby nominal wages were automatically adjusted by the inflation rate in previous months. This procedure was implicitly established during the first year of the regime and was then formally incorporated into the 1979 labor law. Of course, one of the main features of a backward indexation system is that in a situation characterized by decreasing inflation, real wages will automatically increase as a result of the indexation mechanism. This was indeed the case in Chile, especially in 1980 and 1982, as is illustrated in table 3.[17]

Regarding the evolution of income distribution during the period, the available evidence is quite scarce. However, a study performed by Heskia, using data for the greater Santiago area, suggests that there was no major change in the distribution of personal income (as measured by the Gini and Theil coefficients) between 1970 and 1979.[18] If, however, family earnings are used in the analysis, a small deterioration in the distribution of income is detected between 1970 and 1979. On the other hand, there is little doubt that the distribution of wealth worsened during the period: the privatization of the banking sector and public enterprises resulted in the creation of a small number of conglomerates that controlled a large number of assets.[19]

There is also no doubt that the stabilization policy was largely successful, in the sense that it practically eliminated inflation in a fairly short period of time. However, an important question—one yet to be answered—is to what extent this stabilization program was unnecessarily harsh in terms of reducing output. A definitive answer to this question would require additional research, but there are indications that the costs of reducing inflation may have been unnecessarily high. For example, as Diaz-Alejandro has argued,[20] the reduction in public investment during this period added to the costs of the stabilization program. The 1976 revaluation of the peso, by tending to raise the relative price of nontraded goods, made the adjustment in this sector more difficult. In effect, the revaluation of the peso tended to generate an excess supply in the nontraded goods sector at a time when what was needed was a *reduction* in the excess supply already created by the decline in the rate of growth of domestic credit. In addition, the subsequent use of the exchange rate as the major stabilization tool resulted in an important real apreciation of the peso and a significant loss in the competitiveness of the domestic industries. As will be argued in Section VI, the adoption of a fixed exchange rate—with inflexible real wages—in June of 1979, as the final step of the stabilization process, was a serious policy mistake, which precipitated the 1982–83 recession.

III. The Liberalization of International Trade

The major objective of the military economic program was to transform Chile into a free-market-oriented economy. This was to be achieved through a number of measures, including the privatization of state-owned enterprises, the reduction of the public sector, the liberalization of the foreign sector (both the current and capital accounts of the balance of payments), the liberalization of the domestic financial sector, and the freeing of other key markets. The liberalization of foreign trade is discussed in this section. The next section will be devoted to the analysis of the liberalization of the domestic financial market and of the current account of the balance of payments.

One of the most dramatic policy measures undertaken by the military regime was the opening of international trade. In a 5-year period all quantitative impediments to trade were eliminated and import tariffs were reduced from an average of 100% to a uniform 10% level. This tariff reduction took place in two stages. The first was carried out within the framework of the Andean Common Market (*Pacto Andino*), and tariffs were reduced to between 10% and 55%. The second stage began with Chile's withdrawal from the Andean Pact. In early 1977 the minister of finance announced that the trade liberalization process was to be intensified and that with few exceptions—the most notable being automobiles—import tariffs on all goods were to be equal to 10% by the end of 1979.[21] Table 4 contains information on the evolution of nominal tariffs and effective rates of protection by sectors between 1975 and 1979. As may be seen, while in 1975 the dispersion of nominal sectoral tariffs was moderate—with the exception of basic metals industries, average tariffs ranged from 58% to 74%—the dispersion of effective rates of protection was extremely high. In fact, the standard deviation of nominal tariffs was 13.4% in 1975, while for effective tariffs it was 51%.

During its early phase, the tariff reduction process was complemented by an exchange-rate policy aimed at maintaining or even increasing the real exchange rate. The purpose of this policy was to

TABLE 4

Effective and Nominal Rates of Protection in Some Sectors: 1975 and 1979 (%)

Sector	Effective Tariff in 1975	Nominal Tariff in 1975	Effective Tariff in 1979	Nominal Tariff in 1979
Agriculture, forestry, and fishery	−36	n.a.	10	10
Food, beverages, tobacco, textiles, and leather	72	74	10	10
Timber, furniture, and paper products	11	68	10	10
Nonmetallic mineral products	−38	62	10	10
Basic metals industries	38	38	10	10
Chemicals and derivatives of coal, oil, and rubber	47	58	10	10
Metallic and metallurgical industries*	95	73	10	10

Sources.—First col.: Sebastian Edwards, "Una nota sobre el ahorro, la inversión y el crecimiento económico en Chile," Documento 167 (Santiago: Depto. Estudios BHC, 1977). Other cols.: Molly Pollack, "Fuentes del crecimiento industrial en Child," working paper (Santiago: Depto. Estudios BHC, 1981).

*Excludes the automobile sector.

compensate the loss of competitiveness in the import substitution sectors resulting from the tariff reductions.[22] However, as discussed in the previous section, toward mid-1976 the rate of change of the exchange rate became the major stabilization tool, and the rate of devaluation was deliberately kept below the ongoing domestic inflation. During 1976 the real exchange rate declined by 20% and during 1977 it declined a further 14%. This reduction of the real exchange rate was accentuated after June of 1979, when the nominal exchange rate was fixed to the U.S. dollar.[23]

The tariff reduction process and the accompanying exchange-rate policy greatly affected the structure of production and growth in Chile. Initially, the major beneficiaries of this process were nontraditional (or non-copper) exports, which experienced a sharp increase, growing from 11% of total exports in 1970 to 34% in 1980.[24]

Table 5 presents the rates of growth of GDP at the sectoral level. Surprisingly, the tariff reduction process did not have a very large impact on the manufacturing sector as a whole, whose share in GDP was only reduced from 24.3% in 1965–70 to 21.5% in 1980. However, the structure of production within the manufacturing sector was greatly affected. Industries that had traditionally enjoyed a very high level of protection experienced large output losses, and many firms went into bankruptcy.[25] Seven out of 20 manufacturing subsectors had lower levels of production in 1980 than in 1970.[26] Some of these sectors, especially textiles and leather goods, had traditionally had a high degree of protection. On the other hand, the industries that experienced

TABLE 5

RATE OF GROWTH OF REAL GDP BY SECTORS (%)

Sector	1970	1975	1976	1977	1978	1979	1980	1981	1982*
Agriculture and forestry	3.6	4.8	−2.9	10.4	−4.9	5.6	1.8	2.2	−3.3
Fishery	−5.4	−6.7	33.9	15.4	17.9	14.3	7.5	13.6	8.8
Mining	−3.0	−11.3	12.2	2.7	1.6	5.4	5.9	3.6	5.7
Manufacturing	2.0	−25.5	6.0	8.5	9.3	7.9	6.2	2.6	−21.6
Electricity, gas, and water	5.3	−3.8	5.8	5.8	6.7	6.8	5.9	3.5	−29.0
Construction	5.5	−26.0	−16.5	−.9	8.1	23.9	25.7	16.2	−.2
Commerce	−1.5	−17.1	2.5	24.8	20.0	11.0	10.8	5.7	−17.8
Transport and communication	4.7	−7.7	4.7	10.8	8.4	9.0	11.1	5.4	−9.9
Financial services	15.4	−4.2	9.3	14.5	20.2	28.0	22.1	8.5	n.a.
Services of dwellings	3.7	1.8	.7	.6	.9	.5	1.0	1.7	n.a.
Public administration	1.5	1.9	5.9	1.8	−3.1	−1.2	−3.3	−1.6	n.a.
Education	2.6	1.8	−2.3	2.4	2.2	1.9	−.6	n.a.	n.a.
Health	3.1	−1.7	4.2	2.7	3.2	5.7	3.1	n.a.	n.a.
Other services	1.4	−4.5	3.5	5.7	5.7	6.4	5.6	n.a.	n.a.
GDP	2.1	−12.9	3.5	9.9	8.2	8.3	7.5	5.3	−14.3

SOURCE.—Banco Central de Chile.
NOTE.—n.a. means not available.
*Preliminary.

an increase in production during the 1970s—beverages, paper products, and tobacco, among others—did so by greatly increasing their efficiency, introducing new technologies, and adopting modern management systems. Table 6 presents some data on employment and productivity, by sectors, in 1976 and 1980. As may be seen, the manufacturing sector as a whole experienced an important increase in productivity. Other sectors where efficiency was substantially increased were commerce and financial services.

Trade liberalization had an important impact on agricultural production as well. The traditional negative effective protection suffered by this sector was eliminated, and the fairly high real exchange rate that prevailed during the first years of the experiment helped promote a number of nontraditional agricultural exports. While the share of the agricultural sector in GDP remained basically constant (6.5% in 1965–70 and 7.0% in 1978–81), there were major changes in the composition of production, with resources tending to move away from the so-called traditional products toward export-oriented crops. However, the lack of adequate data makes it particularly difficult to evaluate the overall performance of the agricultural sector during this period.[27]

In general, the change in the structure of production between 1970 and 1980 was due largely to tariff reduction.[28] However, other policy measures, such as the creation of the domestic capital market, also affected the composition of GDP. As revealed in table 5, the commercial and financial sectors grew faster, on average, between 1976 and 1981. The rapid growth of the commercial sector followed the change in orientation of the economy toward an open free-market system. On the other hand, the financial services sector grew as a result of the financial reform that liberalized interest rates, reduced the degree of the banking regulation, and allowed the establishment of foreign banks.

A subject that has been extensively debated in Chile is the extent to which the process of tariff reductions "contributed" to the unemployment problem. Elsewhere,[29] I have developed a model that assumes short-run factor specificity and sticky real wages to analyze the short-run unemployment effects of the tariff reform. The results of this study indicate that an upper bound for the unemployment effect of this reform is 3.5 percentage points of the labor force or 129,000 people, with most of this unemployment located in the food, beverages, tobacco, textiles, and leather products subsectors (57,000 people). This is not a negligible number, but it does indicate that an explanation for the greater part of unemployment should be sought elsewhere.

In summary, it is possible to state that the trade reform had a major impact on growth and on the structure of production in Chile. Resources were reallocated toward competitive sectors and the level of efficiency in the tradable-goods sector improved.[30] Even though this process raised unemployment in the short run, in the medium run there

TABLE 6

EMPLOYMENT AND PRODUCTIVITY BY ECONOMIC SECTOR: 1976 AND 1980

	1976			1980		
	Employment (1,000s)	Employment: Total (%)	Value Added per 1,000 Workers (Millions 1977 US$)	Employment (1,000s)	Employment: Total (%)	Value Added per 1,000 Workers (Millions 1977 US$)
Agriculture	500.3	18.0	2.4	499.9	15.8	2.7
Mining	73.2	2.6	14.3	66.6	2.1	18.3
Manufacturing	467.7	16.8	5.7	511.5	16.1	7.1
Public utilities	28.5	1.0	10.0	24.0	.8	9.3
Construction	103.9	3.7	5.3	142.6	4.5	6.4
Commerce	439.9	15.8	3.8	580.0	18.3	5.3
Transport	172.2	6.2	3.7	199.6	6.3	4.7
Financial services	63.6	2.3	11.6	98.2	3.1	16.1
Communal services	921.2	33.1	n.a.	1,040.8	32.8	n.a.
Other sources	8.7	.3	n.a.	6.3	.2	n.a.
Total	2,779.2	100.0	n.a.	3,169.5	100.0	n.a.

SOURCES.—Banco Central de Chile and Instituto Nacional de Estadisticas.

was a tendency for employment to increase in the expanding sectors.[31] In early 1983, however, as a way of combating the recession, most tariffs were increased to a uniform level of 20%. Even though this represents a partial reversal of the liberalization policy, 10 years after the military coup the Chilean foreign sector is still significantly freer than in most developing countries and fairly close to what economists have generally advocated.[32]

IV. The Liberalization of the Domestic Financial Sector and of the Capital Account of the Balance of Payments

A major policy objective of the military regime was the liberalization and modernization of the financial sector. Until 1973 the domestic capital market had been highly repressed, with most banks being government owned. Real interest rates were negative, and there were quantitative restrictions on credit. The liberalization process began slowly, in early 1974, by selling banks back to the private sector, freeing interest rates, relaxing some restrictions on the banking sector, and allowing the creation of new financial institutions.[33] International capital movements, however, were strictly controlled until mid-1979. In June of that year, the government decided to begin to liberalize the capital account of the balance of payments, and some restrictions on medium- and long-run capital movements were lifted. The final steps in this process were taken in April 1980 when regulations regarding the maximum monthly inflow of foreign capital were lifted.[34] Short-term capital movements, however, were forbidden throughout most of the experiment. Even though only medium- and long-term capital movements were allowed, the opening of the capital account resulted in a massive inflow of foreign capital. In 1980 capital inflows more than doubled those of 1979—US$2,499 million versus US$1,242 million—and in 1981 the level of capital inflows doubled again, to US$4,507 million.[35]

One of the most important consequences of opening of the capital account was a further real appreciation of the peso due to massive capital inflows. To the extent that nontradables are normal goods in demand, lifting existing restrictions on foreign borrowing will result in higher expenditures on these goods (as well as on tradables) and on a real appreciation of the domestic currency. In the particular case of Chile, a high proportion of the funds obtained from abroad were used to finance nontradables, especially the construction sector (see table 5). The effect of capital inflows on the real exchange rate in Chile has been extensively discussed by, among others, McKinnon, Diaz-Alejandro, Muñoz, Corbo, and Edwards and Edwards.[36] Harberger,[37] for example, has estimated that the opening of the capital account can explain up to 25 points of the appreciation of the peso between mid-1979 and early 1982.

One of the most puzzling characteristics of the behavior of the financial sector between 1977 and 1982 has been the extremely high *real* interest rates that prevailed throughout most of the period.[38] The real rates averaged above 30% per annum for long periods of time and remained high despite a major rise in total credit and the massive inflow of foreign capital in late 1980 and 1981. Table 7 presents some summary statistics on the behavior of the financial sector. As may be seen, with the exception of July-September 1979 and August-November 1980, real rates of interest were extremely high. This table also shows the large differential between the domestic nominal interest rates (col. 1) and international nominal rate (col. 4). These differentials, however, can be partially explained by the existence of financial, exchange rate, and country risk premiums.[39]

What is most surprising, however, is that the liberalization of the domestic financial market and the existence of positive real interest

TABLE 7

Interest Rates, Inflation, Money, and Exchange Rates in Chile: Quarterly Data 1977–81

	Nominal Borrowing Interest Annual Rate (%) (1)	Annualized Inflation Rate (%) (2)	Libor Interest Rate (%) (3)	High Powered Money (1978 − I = 100) (4)	Quantity of Money (M3) (1978 − I = 100) (5)
1977:1	124.6	100.0	5.6	46.9	47.5
1972:2	83.6	59.2	6.1	56.0	57.3
1977:3	70.8	54.3	7.2	71.2	66.7
1977:4	99.8	45.4	7.6	88.4	80.7
1978:1	70.7	32.7	7.7	100.0	100.0
1978:2	55.6	30.6	8.5	102.2	108.2
1978:3	55.5	38.2	9.3	106.5	113.2
1978:4	70.0	20.5	12.0	115.2	126.2
1979:1	47.3	30.2	10.7	116.4	147.0
1979:2	44.1	35.1	10.7	112.9	149.6
1979:3	42.7	62.0	12.0	109.5	152.8
1979:4	46.1	30.9	14.6	120.2	163.6
1980:1	52.0	31.4	17.0	107.6	187.6
1980:2	32.7	30.7	11.3	121.4	195.1
1980:3	31.8	28.6	12.2	122.2	208.4
1980:4	34.2	34.4	16.2	126.0	217.9
1981:1	45.0	11.5	16.5	111.0	249.4
1981:2	40.9	11.1	17.2	109.7	273.2
1981:3	38.8	11.6	18.5	105.4	297.9
1981:4	42.5	4.2	14.8	99.3	309.3
1982:1	48.2	7.0	15.6	117.8	367.7
1982:2	49.9	4.2	16.2	133.0	353.3
1982:3	66.5	11.3	12.1	140.8	360.4
1982:4	89.5	20.7	9.5	167.5	379.

Sources.—Banco Central de Chile and IFS.

rates for the first time in many years did not result in an increase in domestic savings, as was widely expected by the economic authorities and others.[40] In fact, domestic savings not only did not increase but stood at one of the lowest levels in history. Gross domestic investment was remarkably low during the period, and public-sector investment fell to one of its lowest levels. As may be seen in table 8, only in 1980 did gross domestic investment surpass 20%. Harberger has suggested that the low level of domestic savings can be explained by the behavior of asset prices during the period.[41] Starting in 1976, asset prices increased dramatically, with the real index of stock prices, for example, increasing by 323% between 1977 and 1980! To the extent that savings decisions depend, in a Metzlerian fashion, on the differential between actual and desired wealth, this dramatic increase in asset prices, and consequently of perceived wealth, could indeed provide an explanation to the poor savings effort during the period.

An alternative explanation for the low level of domestic savings is related to the privatization policy pursued by the government. In 1974, as a way of reducing the importance of the public sector, a process of privatization of government-owned firms was implemented, with firms being auctioned to private (domestic and foreign) bidders. In general, the government used the proceeds from these sales to finance current expenditure. Thus the private savings used to acquire these firms were in effect matched by *negative* government savings.[42]

Since domestic savings were very low, gross capital formation was increasingly financed by foreign savings. In 1980, foreign savings reached 8.5% of GDP, while in 1981 they rose to 14.5% of GDP, representing 66% of total gross domestic investment. The current account deficits associated with these high levels of foreign savings began to generate a serious foreign indebtedness problem in 1981. In that year total foreign debt increased almost 50%—from US$10,987 million to US$15,546 million—reaching 50% of GDP.[43] It was thought at the time by the economic authorities and other observers that since most of the new debt had been contracted by the private sector (without any government guarantee), this increase in foreign indebtedness did not represent a threat for the country as a whole: if a domestic private borrower could not pay its foreign obligations, that was a *private* problem, between him and the foreign creditor, which would be solved through a regular bankruptcy procedure.[44] As events showed later, this distinction between private and public debt was highly artificial, and the Chilean government ended by taking over all of the private-sector foreign debt, independent of the facts that the original borrowers went bankrupt and that there were no previous government guarantees on those loans.[45]

As has been noted by a number of observers, the behavior of interest rates constitutes one of the major puzzles of the recent Chilean

TABLE 8

INVESTMENT AND SAVINGS IN CHILE: 1970–82

Year	Gross Domestic Investment/GDP (%)	Gross Capital Formation on Fixed Capital/GDP (%)	Depreciation/GDP (%)	Net Domestic Savings/GDP (%)	Gross Domestic Savings/GDP (%)	Foreign Savings/GDP (%)
1970	23.4	20.4	11.0	10.6	21.6	1.7
1971	20.8	18.3	11.9	6.0	17.8	2.9
1972	15.2	14.8	10.4	(.1)	10.4	4.8
1973	14.3	14.7	19.2	(9.7)	9.5	4.8
1974	25.8	17.4	11.8	13.5	25.3	.5
1975	14.0	15.4	15.7	(7.2)	8.5	5.6
1976	13.6	12.7	14.1	1.4	15.4	(1.9)
1977	14.4	13.3	11.7	(1.0)	10.7	3.7
1978	16.5	14.5	10.5	1.1	11.6	4.8
1979	19.6	15.6	11.0	2.7	13.7	5.9
1980	23.9	17.8	11.4	4.1	15.5	8.5
1981	22.0	18.5	n.a.	n.a.	7.5	14.5
1982*	9.6	13.8	n.a.	n.a.	n.a.	n.a.

SOURCE.—Banco Central de Chile.
NOTE.—Parentheses mean negative number.
*Preliminary.

experience.[46] At present there does not appear to be an acceptable solution to this puzzle; however, any analysis that attempts to deal with the interest rate behavior during the Chilean experiment should at least recognize the following elements:

a) There was an important increase in the *demand* for credit, triggered by an increase in perceived wealth and permanent income. This higher demand for credit was directed toward both investment projects and increased consumption. Toward the end of 1981 the demand for credit continued to grow. However, at this time it was essentially a demand by firms that expected to avoid bankruptcy.[47]

b) There was a continuous increase in the expectations of devaluation, stemming from the decline in the real exchange rate after June of 1976. The higher current account deficits of 1980 and 1981, the low rate of domestic savings, and the dramatic increase of foreign indebtedness also helped to increase these expectations.

c) An increase in the world interest rate, that affected the effective cost at which Chile could borrow abroad. Between the first quarter of 1979 and the third quarter of 1981 the nominal Libor rate increased from 10.7% to 18.5%.

d) The existence of transaction costs that posed obstacles to arbitrage.[48]

e) An increase in the country risk premium attached by the international financial community to Chile. This increase in the country risk premium was basically the result of the rapid growth of the foreign debt and the extremely low level of investment. Also, the collapse of a major conglomerate (Grupo Crav) and some banks during 1981 forced foreign banks to reassess their risk perception of Chilean borrowers.

In general, it appears that Chile's inability to increase domestic savings and gross domestic investment presaged, from the early years of the military regime, the economy's inability to maintain a consistently high growth rate over a long period.[49]

V. Savings, Investment, and the Sources of Growth

Although capital accumulation is far from the only source of growth, the extremely modest level of investment in 1977–80 makes one wonder how Chile managed to grow so fast during this period. This section presents an analysis of the sources of growth in Chile during 1976–80.[50] Since a thorough study of the sources of growth in Chile during the military regime requires certain data that are not readily available, the results presented here should be considered preliminary estimates.

Any accounting study of the sources of growth in Chile in the recent period must meet two basic requirements. First, it should incorporate the effects on growth of the efficiency gains associated with improved resource reallocation.[51] Second, it should take into account the changes in the degree of capital utilization observed throughout this period.

With respect to the resource-reallocation effect, some studies have attempted to estimate the (static) welfare gains resulting from a reduction or total elimination of distortions in Chile. More than 20 years ago Harberger estimated that the elimination of all distortions would result in a static increase in Chile's national welfare of about 15% of national income.[52] He also indicated that this static effect would result in a higher rate of growth, by 1 to 2 percentage points per year, for a limited period of time. Coeymans has recently estimated that the tariff liberalization process would result in a static improvement of Chile's welfare of around 3% of national income; Schmidt-Hebbel, on the other hand, estimated that the recent liberalizations policies (both trade and others) would result in a static increase in welfare of 10% of income. He also suggests that this welfare improvement would be spread through 10 years, contributing 1 percentage point per annum to the growth rate during this period. Although an exact computation of total welfare gains resulting from the liberalization of Chile's economy is beyond the scope of the present paper, it appears that Schmidt-Hebbel's estimates can be considered an approximate measure for the static efficiency gains from the liberalization reforms.

The second question to be considered in a discussion of the recent sources of growth in Chile is the degree of capital utilization.[53] Schmidt-Hebbel has estimated three alternative series of capital utilization for this period. All of them indicate a sharp decline in the rate of use of capital in 1975—ranging from 6.7% to 13.4%—with a subsequent recovery between 1976 and 1979. Two of his series indicate that in 1979 the degree of capital utilization was still below that of 1974, but the third suggests that already in 1977 the rate of use of the capital stock had reached its 1974 level. These estimates, then, suggest that changes in the rate of capital utilization played an important role during the recent (1977–80) growth process. Furthermore, as will be argued below, this change in capacity utilization constitutes a crucial step in understanding Chile's extraordinarily high rates of growth in the late 1970s.

In order to obtain some orders of magnitude for the importance of some of the sources of growth during this period, I computed the contributions to growth of changes in the stock of physical capital and changes in employment. If it is true that changes in the degree of capital utilization and efficiency improvements made important contributions to growth during the period, we would expect that the residuals obtained from this exercise would be very large—that is, larger than the residuals obtained in these computations for Chile before 1970. Table 9 shows estimates of the stock of capital between 1970 and 1981. These figures were computed using the infinite inventory technique suggested by Harberger[54] and data from the new National Accounts. Table 10, on the other hand, shows the contribution to growth of changes in the quantities of capital and labor between 1975 and 1979

TABLE 9

Stock of Reproducible Capital: 1970–81 (Millions 1977 US$)

Year	Equipment and Machinery	Building and Construction	Inventories	Total
1970	7,551	25,797	1,733	35,081
1971	7,763	26,957	2,885	37,608
1972	7,769	27,750	2,141	37,660
1973	7,846	28,325	2,088	38,259
1974	7,863	29,316	3,220	40,399
1975	7,878	29,749	3,057	40,684
1976	7,830	29,966	3,165	40,961
1977	7,997	30,203	3,312	41,512
1978	8,327	30,568	3,601	42,496
1979	8,774	31,133	4,231	44,138
1980	9,422	31,993	5,268	46,683

Source.—Constructed from National Accounts Data obtained from Banco Central de Chile.

and of imputed contributions to growth of changes in capacity utilization and gains in efficiency generated by the liberalization program. In these computations labor was assigned a share of 52% of GDP, while capital was assigned a 48% share.[55] The data on changes in the stock of capital were taken from table 9, and the data on the evolution of employment were obtained from Edwards.[56]

Column 4 in table 10 shows the "grand residual" obtained after having taken into account the contributions of the quantities of capital and labor to growth. As expected, these residuals are very high—indeed, much higher than those obtained in earlier accounting studies of the sources of growth in Chile—indicating that during the recent period factors other than changes in the quantities of capital and labor played important roles. The most plausible variables to explain this grand residual are efficiency gains and change in the degree of capital utilization. Indeed, if we assume that between 1977 and 1980 the resource reallocation process contributed with 1.5 percentage points to annual growth, and we use Schmidt-Hebbel's estimates of the degree of capital utilization, these residuals are significantly reduced.[57] This is shown in columns 5, 6, and 7 of table 10. However, these residuals are still fairly large—in fact, larger than what can plausibly be attributed to higher "quality" of labor and capital, and "technical progress"—suggesting that there are still some measurement problems and that the full understanding of the growth process in Chile between 1977 and 1982 will require additional research.

TABLE 10

THE SOURCES OF GROWTH IN CHILE: 1975–80

	Actual Rate of Growth of GDP (1)	Contributions of Changes in Physical Capital (2)	Contributions of Changes in the Quantity of Labor (3)	"GRAND" Residual (1 − 2 − 3) (4)	Contribution of Efficiency Gains (5)	Contribution of Change in Capacity Utilization (6)	Residual (1 − 2 − 3 − 5 − 6) (7)
1975	−12.9	−3.7	.3	−9.5	...	−5.4	−4.1
1976	3.5	1.3	.3	1.9	...	1.0	.9
1977	9.9	3.8	.6	5.5	1.5	1.6	2.4
1978	8.2	1.4	1.2	5.6	1.5	.4	3.7
1979	8.3	1.1	1.9	5.3	1.5	.7	3.1
1980	7.5	3.2	2.8	1.5	1.5	...	.0

SOURCES.—Column 1, Banco Central de Chile; col. 2 taken from table 9; col. 3 computed from Edwards, "El problema del empleo en Chile: 1975–1980—un análisis preliminar," manuscript (Santiago: Depto. Estudios BHC, 1980); col. 5 estimated from Klaus Schmidt-Hebbel, "Análisis del cricimiento económico en Chile en el periodo 1960–1979 y proyecciones para 1980–2000," Documento no. 140 (Santiago: Depto. Estudios BHC, 1981); col. 6 computed from data presented in Schmidt-Hebbel.

VI. The 1982–83 Recession

By late 1981 it became apparent that the high rates of growth experienced during the previous years were coming to an end. The fourth quarter of 1981 was characterized by extraordinarily high real interest rates (over 40%); a huge current account deficit, amounting to almost 15% of GDP; rising unemployment; and a reduction of real GDP of 3.3% with respect to the fourth quarter of 1980. On the positive side, inflation was only 9% that year.

In 1982 the economic situation became almost chaotic: GDP declined by 14.3%, open unemployment (excluding the minimum employment program) reached 23.7% in September of that year, the exchange rate was devalued by almost 100%, a major financial crisis developed, and Chile had serious problems servicing its foreign debt. Table 11 presents the behavior of some of the most important macroeconomic variables between the first quarter of 1980 and the second quarter of 1983. As may be seen, the recession showed up quite abruptly during the fourth quarter of 1981. The causes of this extraordinary turn of events in late 1981 will be analyzed below, and some important developments of 1982–83—such as the agreement with the IMF—will be discussed. The main thesis of this section is that the 1982–83 recession was, to a large extent, triggered by policy inconsistencies and mistakes. It is also recognized that the world economic situation had a negative impact on the Chilean economy: the decline in Chile's terms of trade by almost 23% between 1980 and 1982 and the higher world interest rates were particularly harmful. With respect to policy mistakes, the exchange rate policy, which in June of 1979 had fixed the peso to the dollar, and the wage rate policy, which precluded by law any downward adjustment in real wages, became highly inconsistent in mid-1981.[58] In addition to fixing the peso, the choice of the dollar as the currency of reference was unfortunate. During most of the 1980–83 period the dollar appreciated against other major currencies. The appreciation of the dollar explains approximately 10 percentage points of the appreciation of the Chilean peso. Another serious problem during this period, which greatly affected the outcome of the crisis, was the collapse of the banking and financial sector in late 1982. This collapse was the consequence of a very large proportion of bad loans held by banks.[59]

As has been discussed in Section IV above, between the second quarter of 1980—when the last steps toward opening the capital account to medium- and long-term flows were taken—and the third quarter of 1981, Chile was flooded by foreign capital. In 1980 capital inflows (i.e., the surplus of the capital account) amounted to US$3.2 billion, representing 8.5% of GDP. In 1981 this figure climbed to an extraordinary level of US$4.8 billion, or 14.4% of GDP. This increase in the level of capital inflows had a number of consequences, including a

TABLE 11

BEHAVIOR OF SOME KEY MACROECONOMIC VARIABLES IN CHILE: 1980–83

	Real GDP (Millions 1977 pesos) (1)	Δ% Real GDP With Respect to Same Quarter Previous Year (2)	Open Rate of Unemployment (%) (3)	Minimum Employment Program as % Labor Force (4)	Rate of Inflation (Yearly %) (5)	Exchange Rate (Pesos/Dollar) (6)	Real Borrowing Interest Rate (Annualized %) (7)	Foreign Savings (Millions of 1977 US$) (8)
1980:								
1	86,936	n.a.	12.0	4.7	. . .	39.0	. . .	259
2	89,750	n.a.	. . .	. . .	38.7	39.0	. . .	253
3	89,122	n.a.	12.3	5.6	32.9	39.0	. . .	297
4	97,638	n.a.	. . .	. . .	31.3	39.0	5.6	507
1981:								
1	94,274	8.4	11.0	4.7	28.4	39.0	36.5	602
2	96,233	7.2	. . .	. . .	22.8	39.0	35.6	593
3	99,317	11.4	12.4	4.6	18.0	39.0	35.2	973
4	94,408	−3.3	. . .	. . .	11.4	39.0	47.8	780
1982:								
1	85,714	−9.1	18.4	4.2	7.6	39.0	53.1	565
2	84,230	−12.5	. . .	. . .	4.5	46.5	47.3	300
3	81,015	−18.4	23.7	7.0	8.3	67.4	13.0	341
4	78,196	−17.2	. . .	. . .	19.0	73.4	30.7	266
1983:								
1	77,611	−9.5	22.0	9.6	16.1	73.4	29.5	82
2	80,489	−4.4	. . .	. . .	26.3	77.7	13.5	81
3	80,000	−1.2	n.a.	9.6	31.6	82.3	. . .	n.a.
4	83,500	6.8	n.a.	. . .	19.0	87.5	. . .	n.a.

SOURCES.—Columns 3,4 from *Comentario sobre la situación económica: Primer semestre 1983* (Santiago: Universidad de Chile, 1983); cols. 1, 2, 7, 8 from Banco Central de Chile; cols. 5, 6 from International Financial Statistics (Washington, D.C.: International Monetary Fund, various issues).

NOTE.—n.a. means not available.

major real appreciation of the peso (27% between the third quarter of 1979 and the first quarter of 1982), which significantly reduced the degree of competitiveness of Chile's exportable and import-competing industries (see table 12). Also, as a result of this capital inflow the level of the foreign debt (especially private debt) increased dramatically, exceeding 50% of GDP in late 1981.

This level of capital inflows was clearly not sustainable in the long run, and in the second half of 1981 it began to decline. In the fourth quarter of 1981 the capital account surplus dropped to US$800 million, from an average of over US$1.2 billion during the 3 previous quarters. In the first quarter of 1982 the capital account surplus was US$500 million; in the second quarter it was US$295 million; and in the third quarter a capital account deficit of US$170 million was observed. In order for the economy to adjust to this lower inflow of foreign capital, and consequently of expenditure, a *real* devaluation of the peso was

TABLE 12

Real Exchange Rate in Chile: Quarterly Data 1979–83 (1979: III = 100)

	Index of Basket of Nominal Exchange Rates (1)	Chile's CPI (2)	Index of Consumer Prices for Group of Industrial Countries* (3)	Index of Basket Real Exchange Rate (1 × 3 / 2) (4)
1979:				
1	95.1	83.7	99.1	112.7
2	99.4	90.2	105.2	116.0
3	100.0	100.0	100.0	100.0
4	98.8	109.1	110.5	100.0
1980:				
1	95.4	116.4	114.2	93.6
2	100.2	125.1	118.0	94.6
3	100.3	133.1	120.0	90.4
4	99.4	143.3	122.7	85.1
1981:				
1	95.0	149.4	125.3	79.7
2	92.9	153.7	128.2	77.5
3	92.7	157.0	130.9	77.3
4	93.9	159.6	133.1	78.3
1982:				
1	90.3	160.8	134.4	75.5
2	96.8	160.5	136.5	82.4
3	127.6	170.1	138.7	104.0
4	139.5	190.0	139.8	102.6
1983:				
1	138.3	198.3	140.3	97.8
2	143.8	209.8	n.a.	n.a.

*The industrialized countries (shares in parentheses) are the United States (55%), Germany (12%), Italy (5%), France (7%), and Japan (21%).

now required. Since the nominal exchange rate was fixed (at 39 pesos per dollar), this adjustment had to take place through a decline in the nominal price of nontradable goods and of real wages.[60] The problem, however, was that according to the indexation mechanism incorporated into the labor law of 1979, real wages were virtually inflexible downward. At this point it became apparent to most observers that a fixed exchange rate and the real wages policy were highly inconsistent and that their coexistence represented a policy mistake. As Corbo and Edwards, Sjaastad, and Barandiaran et al. have indicated, these policies amounted to imposing two *numeraires* in the economy. As a result of this inflexibility in real wages, relative prices did not adjust. Quantities, however, did, with the resulting reduction in production and employment.

One possible—and traditional—way to have solved the crisis would have been to abandon the fixed parity and to devalue the peso. The purpose of this measure, of course, would have been to generate a real devaluation and an improvement in the degree of competitiveness of the economy. However, again because of the wage rate policy, it is not clear to what extent the nominal devaluation would have succeeded. If wages are 100% indexed, a devaluation will tend to be fully translated into higher wages and prices and thus will be to a large extent self-defeating.[61]

In spite of the crisis, between the second half of 1981 and the first half of 1982 the government followed a passive policy, arguing that the economy would automatically adjust to the new circumstances.[62] In particular, the economic authorities strongly rejected the idea of intervening in the labor and exchange-rate markets, and even stated that to devalue would be equivalent to committing economic suicide. Throughout the period the government followed the so-called neutral monetary policy, where all increases in high-powered money were supposed to be the result of increases in the Central Bank's holdings of international reserves.

Toward mid-1981, as a result of the real appreciation of the peso and the adverse world economic environment, a number of industries in the tradable-goods sector ran into serious financial trouble. Most of these firms responded to hard times by borrowing heavily from the capital market. This situation, however, was complicated by the fact that there were close ownership relations between borrowers (the troubled firms) and lenders (the domestic banks). In fact, during this period domestic banks made a number of large loans to related firms, generating what was later called the "related portfolio" (*cartera relacionada*). The problem was that most of these were bad loans, which eventually could not be repaid.[63] A serious financial crisis resulted: firms could not pay their debts to local banks and local banks could not pay their debts to international banks. In January of 1983 the government decided to act, intervening in four banks and ordering the liquidation of four others. As a result, 10 years after the military coup, the Chilean government controls 70% of the domestic banking sector.[64]

As the economic and financial situation became more serious late in 1981, the public began rapidly to lose confidence in the government policies. The sustainability of the exchange rate was questioned, and in spite of several official statements, a strong speculation against the peso developed. Economic agents readjusted their portfolios toward a higher proportion of assets denominated in foreign exchange. Of course, the higher expectations of devaluation were translated into higher domestic interest rates, further hurting the overall picture. In June of 1982 the government finally decided to abandon the "automatic adjustment" approach and to pursue a more active policy. The peso was devalued by 18%, and the indexation clause of the labor law was amended. However, this was too little and too late. At this point the loss of credibility in the government policies was almost complete, and the devaluation accelerated the speculation against the peso, with a resulting large loss of international reserves in the following weeks. The international financial community reacted negatively to these measures, and the flow of foreign funds to Chile was further reduced. The June devaluation was followed by a brief experiment with flexible rates and by a dual-rate system. In early 1983 the new minister of finance declared the inconvertibility of the peso, imposed severe exchange controls, and implemented a (temporary) hike in import tariffs to a uniform 20% level. In 12 months—between June 1982 and June 1983—the Chilean peso had been devalued by 99%. Since inflation during this period was only 32.7%, a real devaluation had taken place, helping the exportable sectors to regain some of the competitiveness lost during the previous years. There are some observers, however, who believe that the adjustment of the price level had not been completed in June of 1983, and that a tight monetary policy was required to assure the success of the devaluation policy.[65]

In late 1982 the government approached the IMF in order to obtain financial assistance to service the foreign debt. Private banks were also approached, and a rescheduling of the foreign debt was proposed. A standby agreement with the IMF was signed January 10, according to which Chile would receive US$875 million. Private creditors also agreed to renegotiate the debt subject to the fulfillment of the conditions imposed by the IMF. This stabilization program had the traditional IMF conditionality characteristics, and called for a limited increase in domestic credit during 1983 (50 billion pesos), a fiscal deficit below 2.3% of GDP, and a loss of reserves not exceeding US$606 million for the year. In early 1983, and as a complement to the IMF agreement, the government implemented the so-called Emergency Program, whose main points included relief to domestic debtors (especially for debts in foreign currency), the promotion of the construction sector, and the development of public works to reduce unemployment. The so-called POJH program was created.[66] By the end of the first quarter of 1983, however, the limit on credit experience imposed by the IMF had been exceeded, and the Emergency Program was replaced by the Operative Program. The objective of this program was to bring the economy back into line with IMF conditions. This was achieved by September 11, 1983, the tenth anniversary of the military coup.

Notes

* A previous version of this paper was presented at the World Bank Conference "Economic Liberalization: Adjustments during the Transition," October 1983. The opinions expressed in this paper are mine and not those of the National Bureau of Economic Research.

1. For an analysis of the Chilean economy before 1973 see, e.g., Jere Behrman, *Foreign Trade Regimes and Economic Development: Chile* (Cambridge, Mass.: Ballinger Publishing Co., 1976), and *Macroeconomic Policy in a Developing Country: The Chilean Experience* (Amsterdam: North-Holland, 1977); Vittorio Corbo, *Inflation in Developing Countries* (Amsterdam: North-Holland, 1974); Ricardo Ffrench-Davis, *Políticas económicas en Chile 1952–1970* (Santiago: Ediciónes Nueva Universidad, 1973); Vittorio Corbo and Patricio Meller, "Alternative Trade Strategies and Employment Implications," in *Trade and Employment in Developing Countries,* ed. Anne O. Krueger (Chicago: University of Chicago Press, 1982); Pablo Trivelli and Hugo Trivelli, "El crecimiento económico en Chile," in *1940–1975: Treintaycino años de descontinuidad económica* (Santiago: IEH, 1979). For an analysis of the 1970s see Dominique Hachette, "Aspectos macroeconómicos de la economía chilena, 1973–1976," *Documento de trabajo*, no. 55 (Santiago: Universidad Católica, 1978); World Bank, *Chile: An Economy in Transition* (Washington, D.C.: World Bank, 1980); Arnold C. Harberger, "The Chilean Economy in the 1970s: Crisis, Stabilization, Liberalization, Reform," in *Economic Policy in a World of Change,* ed. K. Brunner and A. Metzler, Carnegie-Rochester Conference Series on Public Policy, vol. 17 (New York: Elsevier North-Holland Publishing Co., 1982), and "A Primer on the Chilean Economy: 1973–1983," manuscript (Chicago: University of Chicago, 1983); Alejandro Foxley, "Towards a Market Economy: Chile 1974–1975," *Journal of Development Economics* 10 (February 1982): 3–29; Jose Pablo Arellano et al., *Modelo económico chileno: Trayectoria de una crítica* (Santiago: Editorial Aconcagua, 1982); Vincent Parkin, "Economic Liberalization in Chile 1973–82: A Model of Growth and Development or a Recipe for Stagnation and Impoverishment?" *Cambridge Journal of Economics* 7 (June 1983): 101–24; James Hanson, "What Went Wrong in Chile?" (paper presented at the Conference on Economic Liberalization: Adjustments during the Transition, Washington, D.C., 1983); Bela Balassa, "Policy Experiments in Chile: 1974–83," in "National Economic Policies in Chile," ed. Gary Walton, manuscript (1984); Sebastian Edwards, "Interest Rates and Money in a Semi-open Economy: Chile 1979–1981," mimeographed (Los Angeles: UCLA, Department of Economics, 1982); Gary Walton, ed., "National Economic Policies in Chile," manuscript (1984). Regarding media coverage, see, e.g., *Time* (January 14, 1980); the *Wall Street Journal* (October 5, 1979; January 18, 1980); and the *Economist* (February 2, 1980); see also the *New York Times* (December 8, 1982).

2. The Chilean experience is particularly interesting because for many

years economists have argued that developing countries should follow liberalization processes similar to the one that took place in Chile in the mid- and late 1970s. See, e.g., Ronald J. McKinnon, *Money and Capital in Economic Development* (Washington, D.C.: Brookings Institution, 1973); Ian Little, Tibor Scitovsky, and Maurice Scott, *Industry and Trade in Some Developing Countries* (Oxford: Oxford University Press, 1970); Anne O. Krueger, *Liberalization Attempts and Consequences* (Cambridge, Mass.: Ballinger Publishing Co., 1978), and "The Problem of Liberalization," manuscript (Washington, D.C.: World Bank, 1983); Bela Balassa, ed., *Development Strategies in Semi-industrial Economies* (Oxford: Oxford University Press, 1982).

3. For analytical discussions of the characteristics of this approach to stabilization, see the recent article by Mario I. Blejer and Donald J. Mathieson, "Preannouncement and Exchange Rate Changes as a Stabilization Instrument," *IMF Staff Papers* 28 (December 1981): 760–92; Slobodon Djacij, "Balance of Payments Dynamics and Exchange Rate Management," *Journal of International Money and Finance* 1 (August 1982): 179–92; and Rudiger Dornbusch, "Stabilization Policies in Developing Countries: What Have We Learned?" *World Development* 10 (November 1982): 701–8. This type of anti-inflationary policy was also used in Argentina.

4. These free-market policies were proposed and implemented by a group of economists popularly known as the "Chicago boys."

5. See Behrman, Corbo, Corbo and Meller, and Hachette.

6. See speech by Minister Gotuzzo, pp. 75–82 in Juan Carlos Mendez, *Economic Policy in Chile* (Santiago: Dirección de Presupuestos, 1979).

7. See Mendez.

8. See Sebastian Edwards, "El problema del empleo en Chile: 1975–1980—un análisis preliminar," manuscript (Santiago: Depto. Estudios BHC, 1980).

9. The rigorous process of tax reform began late in 1974. However, only toward mid-1975 was its impact felt in the economy. For an exposition of the main aspects of the reform see Minister Cauas's speech, in Mendez, p. 119.

10. See Harberger, "The Chilean Economy in the 1970s."

11. See also Arnold C. Harberger, "Comment on Foxley," in *Economic Stabilization in Developing Countries* ed. William Cline and S. Weintraub (Washington, D.C.: Brookings Institution, 1981). Other experts agree that there was no monetary crunch in Chile (see Alejandro Foxley, "Comment," in ibid., p. 233). The main reason we observed a reduction in the fiscal deficit in 1975, while the Central Bank continued to create credit (see table 2), rests in the fact that government enterprises—which are not part of the fiscal sector—still ran huge deficits. See Alejandro Foxley, "Stabilization Policies and Their Effects on Employment and Income Distribution: A Latin-American Perspective," in ibid.; Harberger, "The Chilean Economy in the 1970s."

12. To a certain extent this policy was based on the analytical structure provided by the simple version of the monetary approach to the balance of payments. See the extensive discussion in Mario Blejer and Luis Landau, eds., *Economic Liberalization and Stabilization in Argentina, Chile and Uruguay: The Monetary Approach to the Balance of Payments* (Washington, D.C.: World Bank, 1984, in press). See also Ronald I. McKinnon, "The Order of Economic Liberalization: Lessons from Chile and Argentina," in *Economic Policy in a World of Change,* ed. K. Brunner and A. Metzler (New York: Elsevier North-Holland Publishing Co., 1982).

13. Carlos F. Diaz-Alejandro ("Southern Cone Stabilization Plans," in *Economic Stabilization in Developing Countries,* ed. William Cline and S. Weintraub [Washington, D.C.: Brookings Institution, 1981]) has pointed out

that this initial discrepancy between domestic inflation and the sum of world inflation and devaluation rate was a common characteristic of the recent Southern Cone Stabilization Programs. For discussions of the preannounced devaluations system, which was also adopted by Argentina, see Guillermo Calvo, "Devaluation: Levels or Rates," *Journal of International Economics* (May 1981): 165–72; Blejer and Mathieson; Djajic (n. 3 above).

14. See Edwards, "El problema del empleo en Chile"; René Cortazar, "Chile: Distributive Results 1973–1982," in Walton, ed.

15. Guillermo Calvo ("The Chilean Economy in the 1970s," in *Economic Policy in a World of Change,* ed. K. Brunner and A. Metzler [New York: Elsevier North-Holland, 1982]) has suggested that the Chilean unemployment might be of an equilibrium quasi-voluntary type. For an analysis of the recent unemployment problem in Chile see Edwards, "El problema de empleo en Chile"; Tarcisio Castañeda, "La relación entre variables demográficas y el empleo en Chile," working paper (Santiago: Universidad de Chile, 1983); and Cortazar. It is important to notice that the increase in real wages reported in table 3 is lower than the official rate of growth of wages as reported, e.g., in the Banco Central de Chile *Boletín.* The reason is that in table 3 the real-wage index has been computed by using the GDP deflator as the relevant price index instead of the CPI. It is generally accepted that the official CPI underestimates inflation. See René Cortazar and Jorge Marshall, "Indice de precios al consumidor en Chile," manuscript (Santiago: Cieplán, 1980); and Harberger, "The Chilean Economy in the 1970s."

16. See Edwards, "El problema del empleo en Chile"; and Tarcisio Castañeda, "Salarios mínimos y el empleo en el Gran Santiago 1976 y 1978," working paper (Santiago: Universidad de Chile, 1983).

17. See Harberger, "The Chilean Economy in the 70's" and "A primer on the Chilean Economy." See also Balassa, "Policy Experiments in Chile" (n. 1 above).

18. See Isabel Heskia, "Distribución del ingreso en el Gran Santiago: 1957–1979," working paper (Santiago: Universidad de Chile, 1980).

19. See Balassa, "Policy Experiments in Chile"; Cortazar.

20. See Diaz-Alejandro, "Southern Cone Stabilization Plans."

21. Larry Sjaastad ("The Failure of Economic Liberalism in the Southern Cone," *World Trade* 6 [March 1983]: 5–26), has suggested that this second stage of the trade liberalization program—the reduction of tariffs to a uniform 10%—was the result of pressures by some groups in the private sector. For an analysis of the trade liberalization process, see Larry Sjaastad and Hernan Cortez, "La reforma comercial en Chile," *Cuadernos de Economía,* no. 55 (October/December 1981), pp. 317–60. See also Ricardo Ffrench-Davis, *Políticas económicas en Chile 1952–1970*; and Pilar Vergara, "Apertura externa y desarrollo económico," *Estudios Cieplán* 4 (1981): 101–18. However, in 1983 as a way of combating the effects of the recession, tariffs were (temporarily) raised to 20%. There are some exceptions, with higher tariffs applied to milk and other products.

22. On the relation between exchange rates and a tariff reform see Balassa, ed., *Development Strategies in Semi-industrial Economies* (n. 2 above).

23. See Harberger, "Comment on Foxley."

24. The increase in nontraditional exports during the initial stages of a liberalization has been observed in a number of countries. See, e.g., Krueger, *Liberalization Attempts and Consequences* (n. 2 above).

25. See Ricardo Ffrench-Davis, "Liberalización de importaciones," *Estudios Cieplán* 4 (1981): 79–91; and Vergara.

26. For a more detailed discussion, see Sebastian Edwards, "Economic Policy and the Record of Economic Growth in Chile: 1972–1983," in Walton, ed. (n. 1 above).

27. See, e.g., the discussion in Lovell Jarvis, "La distribución de tamaño de las propiedades agrícolas chilenas en 1979," *Estudios de Economía* 17 (1981): 29–61.

28. Notice, however, that theoretically (in a world with more than two goods) it is not possible to know if the increase of effective protection in a particular sector will result in an increase in production in that sector.

29. Sebastian Edwards, "Minimum Wages and Trade Liberalization: Some Reflections Based on the Chilean Experience," Working Paper no. 230 (Los Angeles: UCLA, Department of Economics, 1982).

30. See Juan E. Coeymans, "Liberalización del comercio exterior y sus efectos sobre la asignación de recursos y el empleo," *Cuadernos de Economía* 15 (1978): 183–245; and Klaus Schmidt-Hebbel, "Análisis del cricimiento económico en Chile en el periódo 1960–1979 y proyecciones para 1980–2000," Documento no. 140 (Santiago: Depto. Estudios BHC, 1981).

31. See Coeymans.

32. See Little et al.; Krueger, *Liberalization Attempts and Consequences* and "The Problem of Liberalization"; McKinnon, *Money and Capital in Economic Development* and "The Order of Economic Liberalization"; Balassa, *Development Strategies in Semi-industrial Economies*.

33. However, by international standards, the banking sector was still highly repressed. At the end of 1974, e.g., the effective rate of required bank reserves was 66%!

34. For a detailed analysis of the institutional itinerary of the capital-account liberalization, see Ricardo Ffrench-Davis and Jose P. Arellano, "Apertura financiera externa: Le experiencia chilena in 1973–80," working paper (Santiago: Cieplán, 1981).

35. These figures refer to funds allowed in accordance to Article 14 of the Exchange Law. Most private funds were imported this way. The surplus of the capital account of the balance of payments, on the other hand, increased from US$3.2 billion in 1980 to US$4.8 billion in 1981.

36. McKinnon, *Money and Capital in Economic Development* and "The Order of Economic Liberalization"; Oscar Muñoz, "Crecimiento y desequilibrio en Chile," *Estudios Cieplán* 8 (1982) 128–44; Vittorio Corbo and Sebastian Edwards, "El rol de una devaluación en la economía chilena actual," working paper (Santiago: Depto. Estudios BHC, June 1981); Edwards, "Economic Policy and the Record of Economic Growth in Chile."

37. Harberger, "The Chilean Economy in the 1970s."

38. See Donald Mathieson, "Estimating Models of Financial Market Behavior during Periods of Extensive Structural Reforms: The Experience of Chile," *IMF Staff Papers* 30 (June 1983): 350–93.

39. See Edwards, "Interest Rates and Money in a Semi-open Economy."

40. These expectations were based on the analysis of financially repressed economies by, among others, McKinnon (*Money and Capital in Economic Development*) and Edward Shaw (*Financial Dependency in Economic Development* [Oxford: Oxford University Press, 1983]). For a recent critical discussion on the relationship between savings and the interest rate in developing countries, see Alberto Giovanini, "The Interest Elasticity of Savings in Developing Countries: The Existing Evidence," *World Development* 11 (July 1983): 601–8.

41. Harberger, "The Chilean Economy in the 1970s." See also Edgardo

Barandiaran, Felipe Montt, and Molly Pollack, *Noveno informe de coyuntura* (Santiago: Depto. Estudios BHC, 1982).

42. See several issues of Ministerio de Hacienda, *Exposición de la hacienda pública* (Santiago), for the way in which the fiscal budget was financed.

43. See Sebastian Edwards, "Deuda externa ahorro doméstico y crecimiento económico en Chile," *Estudios Internacionales* 15 (Septiembre 1982): 260–75.

44. See, e.g., Ministerio de Hacienda, *Exposición de la hacienda pública* 1981; and Walter E. Robichek, "Some Reflections about External Public Debt Management," pp. 89–103 in *Estudios Monetarios VII*, ed. Banco Central de Chile (Santiago: Banco Centrale de Chile, 1981).

45. See Carlos Diaz-Alejandro, "Good-Bye Financial Repression, Hello Financial Crash," working paper (New Haven, Conn.: Yale University, 1983).

46. See Harberger, "The Chilean Economy in the 1970s"; Calvo, "The Chilean Economy in the 1970s"; Sjaastad; Dornbush.

47. See Barandiaran et al. (n. 41 above).

48. This point has been stressed by Sjaastad.

49. Sebastian Edwards, "Una nota sobre el ahorro, la inversión y el crecimiento económico en Chile," Documento 167 (Santiago: Depto. Estudios BHC, 1977).

50. There are a number of studies on the sources of growth in Chile before 1970. See, e.g., Arnold Harberger and Marcelo Selowsky, "Las fuentes del crecimiento en Chile: 1940–1962," *Cuadernos de Economía* 10 (1966): 1–16; Victor Elías, "The Sources of Growth in Latin-America," *Review of Economics and Statistics* 60 (1978): 36–70; and Schmidt-Hebbel. Most of these studies suggest that improvement in the quality of labor made important contributions to growth. This evidence is also supported by Marcelo Selowsky, "On the Measurement of Educational Contribution to Growth," *Quarterly Journal of Economics* 83 (1969): 149–63; and Marcelo Selowsky and Lance Taylor, "The Economics of Malnourished Children," *Economic Development and Cultural Change* 22 (October 1973): 17–30. On the relationship between capital accumulation and other sources of growth in accounting-type models, see Sebastian Edwards, "Domestic Policies and Foreign Resource Requirements," *Quarterly Journal of Economics* 99 (February 1984): 201–6.

51. Accounting studies of the sources of growth do not always incorporate this resource reallocation effect. Some exceptions are Sherman Robinson, "Sources of Growth in Less Developed Countries," *Quarterly Journal of Economics* 85 (August 1971): 391–408; and Edward Denison and William Chung, *How Japan's Economy Grew So Fast*. (Washington, D.C.: Brookings Institution, 1976). It is important to note that, from a theoretical point of view, in a second-best world the reduction (or even elimination) of some distortions only may result in welfare losses.

52. See Arnold C. Harberger, "Using the Resources at Hand More Efficiently," *American Economic Review* (May 1959): 134–46.

53. Edwards, "Economic Policy and the Record of Economic Growth in Chile"; Timothy Condon and Jaime de Melo, "A Simulation Analysis of the Macroeconomic Effects of Capital Inflows and Wage Indexation in Chile: 1977–1981," mimeographed (Washington, D.C.: World Bank, 1983).

54. See Arnold C. Harberger, "Perspectives on Capital and Technology in LDC's," in *Contemporary Economic Analysis*, ed. M. J. Artis and A. R. Nobay (London: Croom Helm, 1978).

55. Between 1970 and 1980, labor's share of GDP was 52.9% and capital's 47.1%.

56. See Edwards, "El problema del empleo en Chile."

57. This annual gain in efficiency is somewhat higher than what Schmidt-Hebbel computed.

58. For discussions on the 1982–83 recession in Chile see, e.g., Ricardo Ffrench-Davis, "Una evaluación del modelo económico," *Estudios Públicos* 11 (1983): 41–73; Vittorio Corbo, "Recent Developments in the Chilean Economy" (paper prepared for the conference on National Economic Policies in Chile, 1983); Daniel Wisecarver, "Dogmatismo y pragmatismo: Una década de política económica en Chile," *Estudios Públicos* 11 (1983): 91–134; Sjaastad; Sergio de la Cuadra, "The Chilean Experiment," *Focus*, no. 8 (August 1983), pp. 259–74; Balassa, "Policy Experiments in Chile"; Hanson (n. 1 above); Harberger, "A Primer on the Chilean Economy."

59. See, e.g., Harberger, "A Primer on the Chilean Economy."

60. Rigorously, a world inflation higher than the domestic inflation would also do it. However, this solution would take a very long time.

61. On wage indexation policies in open economies see, e.g., Joshua Aizenman and Jacob Frenkel, "Wage Indexation and the Optimal Exchange Rate Regime," working paper (Chicago: University of Chicago, August 1983).

62. See Ministerio de Hacienda, *Exposición de hacienda pública* (Santiago, 1981).

63. The financial situation became more difficult after June 1982 when the peso was devalued. Agents who had borrowed heavily in foreign exchange suddenly saw their debt doubled.

64. *Comentario sobre la situación económica: Primer semestre 1983* (Santiago: Universidad de Chile, 1983).

65. See ibid.; and Harberger, "A Primer on the Chilean Economy."

66. See *Comentario sobre la situación económica*.

World Development, Vol. 16, No. 8, pp. 867–881, 1988.
Printed in Great Britain.

0305–750X/88 $3.00 + 0.00

High Inflation, Heterodox Stabilization, and Fiscal Policy

MARIO I. BLEJER and ADRIENNE CHEASTY*
International Monetary Fund, Washington, DC

Summary. — In 1985–86, Argentina, Bolivia, Brazil, and Israel introduced stabilization programs aimed at drastic and immediate reductions in inflation. Besides traditional fiscal and monetary policies, the stabilization packages included a number of "heterodox" elements such as wage and price freezes, exchange rate pegging, and deindexation measures. This paper delineates the analytical relationship between the traditional and heterodox policies, discusses the role and impact of the heterodox policies in the programs, and examines in detail the role of traditional fiscal policy when coupled with heterodox policies and applied with the aim of moving quickly from very high to very low inflation.

1. INTRODUCTION

The role of fiscal policy differs, depending on the economic circumstances in which it is undertaken, on the additional policy instruments used, and on the specific objectives it is trying to achieve. This paper examines the stabilization programs introduced by Argentina, Bolivia, Brazil, and Israel between July 1985 and March 1986, when hyperinflation was an imminent threat for each of these economies, so that a primary policy aim had to be the attainment of a quick and drastic reduction in inflation.

These stabilization programs are interesting from a fiscal point of view, not only because the behavior of fiscal variables under very high inflation differs from fiscal responses under a regime of stable prices, but also because the packages contained some innovative elements, which themselves affected the role that fiscal policy was called upon to play.

The programs were considered innovative for two reasons. First, they created major discontinuities in the trends of the main macroeconomic variables, rather than following the gradual adjustment paths of traditional stabilization packages. For this reason, they have usually been referred to as "shock" programs. Second, in most cases they included a number of incomes policy elements such as wage and price freezes, together with exchange rate pegging and deindexation measures. These components have been characterized as "heterodox," compared with the "orthodox" emphasis on demand management through fiscal and monetary instruments. However, in practice, traditional "fundamental" policies, mainly in the monetary and fiscal areas, formed the bulk of each program. In fact, the designers of the shock programs considered the *combination* of heterodox and fundamental (demand management) policies crucial to the success of the programs.

The objective of this paper is to make the analytical aspects of the design of these programs explicit, so that the relationship between the traditional and innovative elements of the programs is highlighted, with particular emphasis on the place of fiscal policy.

The paper contains three main sections. The first substantive section (Section 2) discusses briefly the economic rationale for the policy measures in a representative shock program by putting them in the perspective of recent theories of inflation determination. Section 3 provides a taxonomic description of the aims and measures of the shock programs, and in particular the specific contribution of the heterodox elements; and Section 4 describes in detail the role played by fiscal policy, the interactions between inflation and budgetary policies, and the feedbacks between the heterodox and the fiscal elements of the programs, in order to throw light on the appropriate role of fiscal instruments in the design of a strategy to stem hyperinflationary pressures.[1]

*The authors are grateful to many of their colleagues at the Fund for their helpful comments on earlier versions of this paper. The views expressed are the authors' own and do not necessarily reflect those of the Fund.

2. ANALYTICAL UNDERPINNINGS OF THE SHOCK PROGRAMS

(a) *Inertia, credibility, and the money supply*

Although the designers of the shock programs started with different aims, policy constraints, and country characteristics, their approaches to the inflation problem were similar. The general view was that, once inflation reaches a very high rate, two different kinds of variables become important in its generation and perpetuation. First, as recognized in traditional adjustment programs, demand pressures on domestic prices arising from excess absorption are a crucial determinant of inflation. This implies that fundamental variables must be restricted; demand-management policies, therefore, have a central role to play in the shock programs. Second, and less traditionally, inflation is also considered to be strongly influenced by inertial forces, which are determined mainly by expectational variables. Inflationary expectations (either informal or institutionalized into indexation schemes) tend to be self-fulfilling, as individuals behave consistently with their predictions about inflation. Given a history of high inflation, and the expectation that the inflation pattern will be difficult to break, the existence of inertia in response to an actual change in policy regime greatly reduces the flexibility of economic policy, slows the speed of reaction to policy change, and so increases the costs of adjustment. The heterodox elements of the shock programs were an attempt to break the inertial process by severing the link between yesterday's and today's inflation.

The relationship between inertial forces and demand management policies operates in two directions. On the one hand, it must be recognized that inertial forces cannot be translated into effective price increases unless monetary policy is accommodating. In traditional models of inflation, the money supply is a truly discretionary policy variable and, therefore, inertial inflation cannot play a permanent role. If a government decides to stop increasing the money supply, incipient inflation, arising from expectations or from higher demand, will not be realized, because people will not have the liquidity to bid up the general price level (though relative prices may change as demand shifts).

It is obvious, however, from the many failed attempts of stabilization in Argentina, Bolivia, Brazil, and Israel, that in reality the process of money creation may be subject to many pressures, and may be propelled by the inflationary process itself. The impetus to increase the money supply may come, therefore, from outside the realm of the monetary authorities. In particular, monetary policy is rarely completely independent of fiscal policy. If this is the case, a restrictive monetary policy will be difficult to implement, unless the fiscal forces or other outside influences which affect money creation are controlled. Furthermore, if the monetary authorities attempt to cut the money supply (or reduce its rate of growth) without complementary decisions in other sectors of the economy, the adjustment of these other sectors to less liquidity may be haphazard and painful.

While monetary control can vitiate the influence of inertia on the price level, on the other hand, the presence of inertia may reduce the effectiveness of traditional demand management policies. The argument is as follows: one thesis of the rational expectations school[2] says that inflation can be stopped abruptly, with low transition costs, if the government implements drastic fiscal and monetary policies which are consistent with price stability. However, in order to be effective, these policies must be *credible* — the public must be convinced that fiscal and monetary restraint will be maintained for a long time. Unfortunately, there is no simple way in which the government can convince the public that its policies will be sustained. If, for example, the public does not believe that the government can persist in the enforcement of tight policies, for fear of high unemployment, then their inflationary expectations will remain entrenched. Faced with this situation, the government will not be inclined to adopt tight policies at all, and, since high inflation will persist, the public's expectations will have proved to be self-justifying or "rational."

Among the reasons the public may not accept the government's announced long-term disinflationary targets is that in countries with a long history of inflation and failures of disinflationary policies, there exists a deep-rooted pessimism about the goverment's ability to control inflation. This causes considerable downward rigidity in basic, longer-term, inflationary expectations. These basic inflationary expectations are, in addition to institutional mechanisms, the forces behind the concept of "expectational inflationary inertia" and make the use of a monetary and fiscal squeeze as the basic disinflationary instrument very costly. To avoid the large costs in terms of employment and output that arise from the combination of monetary restraint and inflationary inertia, the "heterodox" stabilization packages augmented demand management with temporary incomes policies including initial price freezes.

The question is, of course, what ensures that

the expectational inertia will be dislodged by the package of wage-price-exchange-rate freezes? Certainly, there is no guarantee that incomes policy will reduce the basic level of inflationary expectations, but there are two considerations which indicate that it could. First, provided that the proper adjustments in the fundamentals (such as the current account of the balance of payments and the budget deficit) have been carried out, the imposition of a price (and exchange rate) freeze can help the government demonstrate that the economy can effectively function without inflation and without any stresses in the strategic areas — such as the current account of the balance of payments or the debt-income ratio. As a result of this demonstration effect, individual agents may come to accept the state of low inflation as a realistic possibility.

Second, as long as the government combines incomes policy with a fixed exchange rate, there is an explicit or implicit commitment not to resort to inflation to achieve other objectives (through, for instance, eroding the real wage to make the economy more competitive). When the fundamentals are consistent, this commitment may be credible and may carry over to the period when controls are lifted.

To summarize, program designers augmented traditional demand management theories by considering that the money supply is usually accommodating and that it might be forced to accommodate not only demand pressures created by an elevated level of absorption but also demand pressures created by individuals who behaved "as if" absorption was high, even when that was not presently the case. Given the added cost that these "inertial" demand pressures implied for the implementation of traditional stabilization programs (a cost which some felt to have explained the failure of traditional stabilization programs in the past), it was important to add "transitional" policies which would change expectational and indexation-induced inflation without a prolonged lagged adjustment period.

(b) *Inflation-tax financing of the fiscal deficit*

Although there are many plausible mechanisms through which monetary expansion is generated by the inflation process itself,[3] one central variable behind money supply growth is the fiscal deficit.[4] One way of describing somewhat simplistically the relationship between inflation, the deficit, and the money supply is in terms of the so-called inflation tax model.

When the desired level of the deficit cannot be financed by debt issue, the government will generally finance it by money creation. The real deficit is thus financed by changes in the real value of the debt and inflation-tax revenue on the holding of real money balances. However, the demand for real money balances falls as inflation rises. In other words, the base of the inflation tax is eroded as the tax rate rises. Hence, if the government wishes to maintain a given real deficit regardless of the inflation rate, it will have to generate the inflation tax necessary to finance that deficit through higher and higher rates of nominal money growth as the inflation rate grows. This model of inflation has the implication that countries may face a maximum sustainable fiscal deficit (indicated by D^* in Figure 1), given their private sectors' willingness to hold other types of government debt. If the government tries to finance a deficit higher than the maximum, the money supply will always exceed money demand, so that the necessary inflation tax revenue will not be forthcoming. If the government persists in printing money, inflation will get higher and higher without the government's control of real resources being increased. In these circumstances, hyperinflation will be a strong possibility.[5]

Under this hypothesis, then, there is an absolute limit to government's deficit financing. This limit is determined by the attainment of a sort of "threshold" inflation rate. If accelerating inflation were then to be observed in the

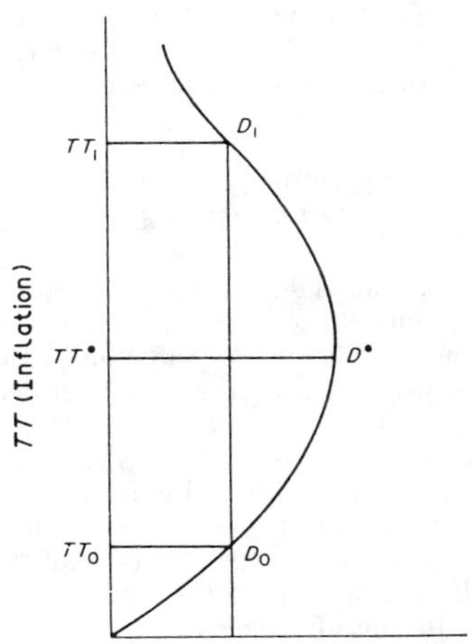

Figure 1. *Limitations to inflation-tax revenue.*

economy, adjusting the money supply would not allow the government to maintain its real deficit.[6]

A second implication of this hypothesis is that, for the more plausible shapes of the money demand schedule, the same deficit could be observed at a high inflation rate as with a low inflation rate.[7] (In Figure 1, the deficit is the same at π_0 (D_0) and π_1 (D_1).) At the high inflation rate, (π_1), the deficit would be financed "inefficiently." Hence, in economies experiencing very high levels of inflation, an effective money-demand increasing policy might allow the government to maintain the size of its present deficit while reducing inflation. Given the dependence of money demand on inflationary expectations and general confidence in the economy, the policy problem is to find the combination of expectation-changing policies sufficient to create the jump from the "high inflation trap" where real money demand is low to the "efficiently" financed deficit where money holdings are higher. If it were indeed possible for the government to maintain its deficit, and hence its real level of absorption, and still bring down the inflation rate through expectational policies, a more general question would then become relevant: might it not be possible to reduce the inflation rate without cutting real output? In the shock program countries, the search for ways to cut inflation while minimizing output loss became very important and gave a rationale for the implementation of policies, such as price freezes and exchange rate fixing, which were considered necessary to insure a transition from one equilibrium level of inflation to another.[8]

3. THE TERMS OF THE SHOCK PROGRAMS

Despite substantial differences in specific policies from country to country, the twin concerns of government credibility and inflationary financing of the fiscal deficit structures described in Section 2 may be seen as the framework within which shock programs were designed. This framework also provides a rationale for the general features which were common to the various programs, and a consistent classification for the different categories of measures adopted as part of the disinflation strategy.

(a) *General features*

The first common feature of the programs was the aim of the authorities to bring down inflation *drastically* and *immediately*. This must be seen in the context of their historical record — the failures of previous attempts to slow inflation gradually and the low degree of credibility given to the announcement of further stabilization schemes.

A second common feature is their high degree of *comprehensiveness*, encompassing policies directed at most of the more important macroeconomic variables. The need perceived for a comprehensive plan was largely dictated by the objective of bringing down inflation immediately. A partial approach could result in serious distortions which might endanger the entire plan in the short term and damage the country's growth potential over the medium term; for example, if wage policy were excluded from the plan, a rise in real wages (in terms of tradable goods) would lead to a balance of payments crisis. However, the need for comprehensiveness was also dictated by the perception of inflation determination. If inflation is generated by both excess absorption and inertial forces, a successful plan cannot confine itself to the adjustment of the key macroeconomic variables such as the current account or public debt ratios but should include nominal policies which address expectations. On the other hand, a successful program cannot deal only with inflationary inertia when the fiscal stance and other fundamental variables are incompatible with low inflation levels and with sustainable growth.

The third common feature of the programs was the attempted *synchronization* of the heterodox policies, especially the synchronization of the exchange rate and of wage policies with the price freeze. Such a precise coordination in the timing of the policy measures when inflation is stopped at a high speed was viewed as essential to avoid serious distortions in relative prices in the initial stages of the program.

(b) *A classification of shock program measures*

The elements of a broadly defined or "representative" shock program can be grouped into three different types: (a) preparatory reforms; (b) expectation-adjusting policies; and (c) demand-management policies. A short account of the type of measures in each category is provided here.

(i) *Preparatory reforms*

These were implemented prior to the formal launching of the plan and included equilibrating adjustments in key relative prices (goods prices, wages, the exchange rate, the interest rate, etc.)

and, in some cases, structural reforms in fiscal, monetary, and other key policy areas.

The need to resort to some pre-equilibration mechanisms arises from the perception that the creation of large discontinuities in inflation through the administrative control of nominal variables, including wage and price freezes, may exacerbate existing disequilibria in one or more markets. If markets are in disequilibrium at the time their prices are frozen, then pressures to equilibrate will be manifested through quantity adjustments, besides continued price pressures. Hence, a logical corollary policy to the freezes contained in the shock programs would be prior attempts to equilibrate goods, factor, and asset markets, so that legislation would merely validate and publicize the underlying economic reality, rather than trying to force an unrealistic alignment of markets.

It should be mentioned that a clear tradeoff was perceived between equilibrating and not equilibrating prices prior to the program. Upward price adjustments at the beginning of the program would indeed hamper the decline of inflation and, thus, erode the credibility of the program. On the other hand, if prior equilibration did not take place, price freezes would soon come under strain as disequilibrium corrective price pressures emerged. In addition, freezing prices out of equilibrium could tend to perpetuate any distortions that might follow disinflation. Moreover, if the disequilibrium price freeze were maintained for a significant length of time, they would create serious damage to the country's ability to grow through response to economic incentives.

(ii) *Expectation-adjusting policies*

Expectation-adjusting policies were "impact" measures — where the effect of the policy was to be felt immediately after the policy announcement was made. Their objective was to attack directly the inertial component of inflation by creating a hiatus between past and present inflation and, in this manner, dampen future expected inflation. Two types of measures in this category could be distinguished:

Temporary "shock" measures. Some shock measures were designed to be transitional. They were to lead a frontal and direct attack on inertia by abrupt changes in expectations. Measures of this sort included freezes of key prices and were designed to create large discontinuities with the previous policy regime and to assault basically all relative prices: (i) domestic prices, (ii) the exchange rate, (iii) wages, (iv) returns to forward contracts, and (v) returns to financial assets. In cases where indexation mechanisms had institutionalized the inflation link, these types of policies could include the direct (e.g., legislated) break in the indexation system. Furthermore, in all of the shock programs, the announcement of the program was itself considered important in affecting expectations. Thus, in each country the policy packages were announced formally and *en bloc* by the authorities.

Impact measures on fundamental variables. Other shock measures were designed to break inertia by adopting policies which would generate a confident and sustained conviction that future government actions would be consistent with lower inflation rates. Since expectations are usually rooted in the actual behavior of fundamental variables, the shock measures included: (i) very large immediate (in some cases one-time or temporary) adjustments in fiscal variables;[9] and (ii) announcements of future radical changes in these variables.

Immediate impact measures differed from traditional demand-management policies because of one or more of the following characteristics: they were expected to have an immediate impact on the fiscal deficit, domestic credit, the trade balance, etc.; they were large in size relative to more permanent, sustainable demand-management policies; and, given their once-and-for-all nature, or the detrimental effects that they could have in the long run, they were expected to be temporary.

Announcements of future reforms were intended to affect fundamental variables in the longer run. Their immediate impact lay in the credibility lent by their announcement of the government's intentions to sustain the changed policy regime.

(iii) *Traditional demand-management policies*

In tandem with the impact measures, more conventional policies were also used to alleviate demand pressures. They included mainly deficit reduction and credit restraint, and were expected to have the traditional gradual impact on the economy.

(c) *Some remarks on the heterodox elements of the programs*

Of the various categories of policies incorporated in the shock programs, the high-visibility impact or expectation-adjusting policies have given rise to most debate. Some impact policies are fiscal in nature and will be discussed in the next section. Others, including direct controls and various deindexation mechanisms, were intended to correct recalcitrant inflationary expectations without having a major effect on traditional fiscal and other demand-management variables. As will be discussed later, even when impact policies are intended to alter expectations rather than the "fundamentals," they are normally associated with budgetary costs and reductions in activity and, therefore, it would be misleading to represent such policies as capable of reducing inflation without cost to the real side of the economy. But, in addition to the indirect cost of impact policies, questions may be asked about the specific role which these policies have actually played. Without an understanding of their mechanisms, it is not feasible to assess the extent to which the shock programs actually departed from traditional stabilization packages.

The assumptions underlying the inclusion of policies to attack inertia in most of the stabilization programs were: (a) that inflationary expectations take time to adjust and may prolong inflation beyond the point where underlying fundamental variables no longer warrant price increases; and (b) that inflationary expectations can only be affected in the short term by impact policies, including price and wage controls. However, even if (a) is a correct description of reality, it is possible that expectations could change rapidly in response to drastic and credible changes in fiscal and monetary variables, without the need to resort to additional impact measures as assumed by (b). Moreover, even when impact policies are deemed to be an essential component of the stabilization package, it is important to consider their costs and the complications involved in their implementation.

(i) *Price controls*

Price controls have been among the more prominent impact policies used. While there is little disagreement with the notion that, without fundamental adjustments, price controls cannot alter the underlying inflationary pressures in the economy, it has become apparent as well that the implementation of price and wage controls *at disequilibrium levels* makes them untenable, increases their distortionary effects, and thus hinders economic growth. Moreover, if the controls are not expected to be sustainable, people will move out of money and nominal assets into goods at an accelerated rate, thus exacerbating the inflationary pressure on the price level and making the expectation of inflation and rupture of the price controls self-fulfilling.

In addition, price controls may be associated with output losses arising from the large discontinuities, the administrative complications, and the uncertainties that wage and price freezes create in the economy, in which case the loss of output will be larger than the output loss to be expected at the outset of a program without incomes policies.

The types of costs that arise from price controls may well have a direct fiscal component. Even if prices are, and remain, at equilibrium, the administrative (and in some cases political) costs to government of controlling prices directly are significant. If prices start from a disequilibrium position, either the government or the private sector will have to bear the cost of the discrepancy between quantities supplied and demanded. When the government bears the cost, through increasing producer subsidies, for example, the price of the good has only been controlled in a very narrow sense and the operation has a clear fiscal cost.

(It should be noted that, no matter how carefully prices are aligned in equilibrium at the beginning of a program, only rarely will that equilibrium remain relevant as soon as the program goes into effect. The idea of setting equilibrium prices in one regime, initiating a program which has as its main aim a drastic, sudden, and complete change in that regime, and expecting prices to be invariant to the change, makes sense only in a world where not only inflation but also any reduction in the government deficit, any change in the exchange and interest rate, any change in the labor and financial markets, are all completely neutral with respect to the structure of relative commodity prices. More generally, the only type of growth that would be compatible with such a policy regime would be completely technologically neutral (a condition more restrictive than most theoretical assumptions about growth and very unlikely to be achievable in practice).)

A specific problem associated with freezing prices out of equilibrium relates to public sector tariffs. If they are fixed at a disequilibrium level at the outset of the program, this implies the emergence of a subsidy on public services. The price freeze not only ensures that this subsidy is perpetuated but may also lead to the gradual substitution out of high-priced goods and into government services. Inasmuch as this takes place, it exacerbates subsidy payments due from the government.

In general, any subsidy element in prices which remains during a freeze will tend to worsen the budget deficit and/or the financial situation of public enterprises. This, in turn, represents an expansionary fiscal policy, and this expansionary policy increases both demand pressures and expected inflation.[10] If, on the other hand, the subsidy is not recognized in the government budget but, instead, must be borne by private sector producers, shortages will occur which will also have detrimental effects on inflationary expectations and the credibility of the government's policy stance. Hence, the use of a disequilibrium set of prices lowers the probability that a price freeze can be sustained, besides substantially raising its cost and its impact on the budget.

When the economy is at full employment, the ability of price controls to suppress inflation may be weakened further. Controls may be more costly and less effective than in conditions of excess capacity because supply constraints become apparent almost straight away and, so, all the extra pressure from increased subsidies and transfers has to be repressed through the price freeze at a high and increasing cost. Relatively slack conditions, therefore, make the price freezes less likely to be broken and less costly to administer.

The contribution of sectoral excess supplies was apparent in both of the seemingly well-managed price freezes in Israel and Argentina, where excess supplies (a) permitted the price freeze to work, and (b) reduced the costs associated with its removal.[11] However, it is possible that the creation of excess supplies may be achieved only at the expense of the program goals of minimum output loss and reactivation of long-term growth. For instance, it has been suggested that the maintenance of a very high interest rate immediately after the introduction of a shock program will encourage the running down of inventories and, thus, alleviate prior supply constraints.[12] The corollary to a policy of interest rates, however, is that investment will be depressed, even to the extent that total production may fall, creating sizable output losses.

In practice, high *ex post* real interest rates appeared in most of the shock program countries, but these arose either because financial risks and expectations did not abate or as a consequence of the restrictions on financing the public sector through credit creation, coupled with the impact of a higher money demand when inflation fell. In other words, given its other policies which affected the interest rate, the government had very limited scope for an independent interest rate policy as a way of controlling the amount of slack in goods markets and, thus, phasing out the price freeze.

(ii) *Deindexation schemes*

Another issue to which the shock programs attached great importance was the removal of formal indexation. According to the theory of inertial inflation, one of the main culprits in prolonging inflation after underlying real causes of price pressure are removed is the widespread indexation of the economy. The indexation mechanisms have two components: a mechanical link between past inflation and present price increases and an expectational component, whereby indexation schemes minimize the variance of expected future incomes in such a way that individuals do not anticipate large discontinuities in their permanent income and in the consumption power that the income provides. Therefore, for a deindexation scheme to be successful it would have to, on the one hand, create an abrupt discontinuity between past and present price increases and, on the other, generate changes in expected permanent income significant enough to make individuals alter their consumption patterns.

The effort to deindex the economy in the context of the programs may be analyzed by looking separately at the labor and capital markets. It can be said, in both cases, that the amount of deindexation which actually took place, despite the prominence accorded to it in the programs, was minimal.

Regarding wages, the so-called "deindexation schemes" did not result in any long-run change in the expectations of individuals about the level of their permanent income which might have changed their consumption and savings patterns, nor did they bring about any structural change in the system and in the mechanics of wage formation. Although wages were frozen in all the countries except Bolivia, the public was, in general, given to understand that the freeze was a short-term measure and that former levels of real wages could be restored, if not by legislation, through the bargaining process. In fact, it could be said that, in some cases, there was a refinement in the protection with which the indexation mechanisms offset the cost of inflation on incomes.[13] In theory, the price freeze itself would have accomplished the same end as the deindexation schemes. If the freeze had succeeded in abruptly cutting inflation, from then on the relevant inflation rate to be taken into account in the indexation equations would have been correspondingly less important. This is, in fact, what happened. The price freeze dampened the inflationary spiral. However, if inflation should increase again, for any exogenous reason, the same inflation growth as before could occur in each country, given that the wage indexation mechanisms, although slightly changed in some cases, essentially remain in place.

Analogously, there was very little deindexation of financial assets. In Argentina, there were no formal deindexation announcements concerning financial assets although the application of the conversion scale to financial contracts was regarded as a deindexation measure, sufficient on its own to accomplish deindexation. In Israel, the indexation of long-term financial assets was not disrupted. The only substantive change was the prohibition of foreign exchange-linked deposits with maturities of less than one year. Likewise, in Brazil, the only deindexation that was enforced was on financial instruments of less than one year's maturity. While a year's standstill was imposed on the indexation of longer-term assets, this pause would be costless to asset holders (unless they tried prematurely to liquidate their assets) because long-term assets could be indexed to a new government bond which, by design, would be fully adjusted for inflation.

Comparable to the case of wages, the most important program element in the treatment of financial assets was the breaking of the link between past inflation and present asset returns. This took place in Argentina and Brazil through the conversion table applied to financial contracts, which attempted to eliminate the expected (but, because of the price freeze, unrealized) inflation component of the contracts. This prevented potentially large real transfers of income from debtors to creditors, thus avoiding dissatisfaction which could have undermined the price freeze in the same way that fulfilling past wage contracts at the expense of profits could have. As in the case of wages, the disruption was a purely temporary though politically important phenomenon, and the crucial characteristic of an indexation scheme, i.e., the ability to index wealth to inflation, remains substantively unchanged.

In summary, wage and asset-return freezes and conversion tables cannot be seen as true deindexation schemes. They did not create any lasting structural change in the ability of the economy to prevent the re-emergence of inflation. In that respect, the importance accorded them by the designers of the shock programs (relative to fiscal and monetary policy) may be considered to have been overstated. On the other hand, given the use of the other "impact" measures, a necessary role did emerge for them in legitimizing the use of incomes policies and price freezes by validating the legislated disruptions in wage and price trends and, thus, in cutting inertia.

4. FISCAL POLICY AND HIGH INFLATION

In the shock programs, by far the greater part of adjustment of fundamental variables was attempted through fiscal policy. Performance under the programs highlighted the fact that high inflation and the implementation of shock stabilization measures have some particular implications for fiscal policy, which are analyzed in this section.

The traditional conclusion that cutting the fiscal deficit leads to reductions in inflation is supported by the inflationary-financing model: as deficits are assumed to be financed by the inflation tax, a smaller deficit will "require" less inflation. However, the optimal fiscal policy to bring down very high inflation may be different from fiscal policy in an economy with a stable price level, because it will be complicated by the interrelationships and feedbacks between fiscal policy and inflation, as well as by the possible existence of inertial inflation, in which the stance of fiscal policy plays a less direct role.

A number of these issues are discussed here, with particular focus on the following five aspects: (1) the size of the deficit may itself be a function of the inflation rate; (2) different fiscal policies may affect inflation in different ways, so that success in reducing inflation through cutting the deficit will be dependent on the specific type of policy used to reduce excess government absorption; (3) different fiscal policies have different effects on aggregate demand and on output, so that the optimal fiscal package should tend to attain the necessary reduction in absorption while minimizing output losses; (4) the composition of economic activity, and specifically the financial system, is not invariant to inflation, which suggests that tax bases may not be inflation-neutral; and (5) even if inflation is not reduced, attempts to do so through impact policies may affect the budget.

(a) *The effects of inflation on the budget*

While the size of the fiscal deficit affects inflation because of inflation-tax requirements, the other methods of financing the deficit are not invariant to inflation. This weakens the neat hypothesized dichotomy between inertial and demand-driven inflation because, if the higher is inflationary financing, the lower are traditional revenues, then reducing the inflation rate may allow a higher level of public spending to be sustained (financed by a recovery in traditional revenues), even if all fiscal policies remain unchanged. As Tanzi (1978) has shown, the *net* gain from inflation-tax revenue, in terms of ability to finance a fiscal deficit, is much lower when the loss in traditional revenues is taken into account than if inflation tax is calculated in isolation. In the long run, the economy's growth potential may be far higher without inflation (as compared with its potential in an inflationary environment) than is usually recognized.

The calculation of the low-inflation budget corresponding to a given set of policies in a country suffering from high inflation is complicated by the fact that almost every element of the budget is affected by inflation, but with different elasticities. If the elasticity of government expenditure with respect to increases in nominal income is greater than the nominal income elasticity of government revenue, then the real deficit will rise with inflation, faster than the simple real money balances model would predict.[14] Likewise, reductions in inflation may generate unexpected gains or losses in revenues and expenditures.

On the expenditure side, the inclusion of nominal government interest payments in the deficit hugely magnifies the percentage increase in interest payments relative to the increase in other expenditure and in revenue as the inflation rate rises. This effect is particularly marked when most of the debt is not indexed and nominal interest rates are flexible.[15]

On the revenue side, it can be shown that the real value of tax collections falls when inflation is high, because of the inevitable lag between the time when the tax legally falls due and its date of collection (and because of other elements of the tax system).[16] Bracket-creep in progressive income tax schedules would offset some of the collection lag-induced decline, but countries with high inflation quickly develop indexed tax systems, which protect taxpayers against the effect of inflation on their real tax obligations. (Besides, income taxes have tended to be less important in the shock program countries than in industrial countries.)

In order to minimize the negative impact of inflation on the budget, revenue buoyancy should be maximized and administrative lags minimized. If taxes and other instruments are to grow in line with nominal income, regressive schedules should be avoided, as should specific tax rates. Negotiated values applied to imports or domestic goods subject to excises can also lead to large losses of buoyancy as inflation increases. The same is true of public sector tariffs, which are often the most difficult prices in the economy to index fully. Furthermore, utility bills are often paid far less frequently than other obligations. Subsidies also tend to emerge on central bank interest rates, and these, too, contribute to the public sector deficit, whether or not the subsidy is made explicit in public sector accounts.

Lags in revenue collected are usually not balanced by lags in expenditure. It has often been said that the government is more efficient in indexing its obligations than its assets. For instance, attempts to lag payment of the public sector wage bill may cut this month's inflation, but probably at the cost of making deindexation much less acceptable to public servants if the government later decides to implement an adjustment program.

In the initial phases of the programs, the "passive" reductions in the deficit as inflation fell were very striking. In Brazil, the drop in inflation reduced the public sector borrowing requirement from 27% of GDP in 1985 to an estimated 10% in 1986,[17] with nearly 18 percentage points of this arising from the reduction in indexed debt service. The Argentine deficit also fell significantly, and while the drop also partly reflected a fall in monetary correction payments, the impact of the automatic effect on revenue recovery associated with the slowdown of inflation was particularly striking in that country.[18]

It is, on the other hand, ironic to note that the revenue gain associated with the slowing down of inflation is less, the more perfectly the fiscal system has adapted to inflation prior to the shock program (by minimizing collection lags, etc.). The Brazilian tax reform of December 1985 provided a good example of the possible post-inflation costs of having succeeded in adapting to inflation. The tax reform included a reduction in withholding to facilitate the indexing of tax liabilities which, in turn, was designed to improve real revenues. However, the reduction in withholding implied that lags in collecting revenue were lengthened. Under high inflation, because of the impact of indexing tax liabilities, apparently the gains from the reduction in withholding had exceeded the losses; under low inflation, only the losses from the longer collection lag remained. Moreover, when inflation is high, it may pay the government to introduce complex administrative systems with much policing and high penalties in order to minimize losses from lagged payments. Once inflation falls to reasonable levels, however, these systems may be inappropriate and cost more than they earn for the government, given that the cost of any delay has dropped.[19]

(b) *Tax rate increases versus cuts in government activity*

In practice, cutting deficits tends very often to affect the level of prices. Hence, restrictive fiscal measures in situations whose price stability is a central goal must be chosen with special care. In inertial systems where inflationary spirals are fueled by formal and informal indexation, deficit cutting through relative price realignments (such as increases in indirect tax rates, the reduction of government subsidies, or the raising of public sector fees and tariffs) may impart an upward push to inflation which more than offsets any gradual alleviation in price pressures through budget contraction. If the government wants to cut the deficit through revenue measures, it will thus be important to remove or relax indexation mechanisms beforehand. On the other hand, while inflation persists, individuals will be wary of permitting the government to remove these "insurance systems" which prevent their wealth from being eroded. Hence, *simultaneous* implementation of tax changes and indexation-removal schemes may be crucial to the success of either policy. This is an additional reason why, in the shock programs, the "synchronization" of policies discussed in the previous section played an important role.

If indexation schemes cannot be cancelled, it is likely that reducing the deficit through reduction in real government activity, such as cuts in expenditure on wages or goods and services, will be more successful in inducing a quick fall in inflation than will tax, tariff, or subsidy adjustments. It is also probable that cuts in transfers affect inflation only with a lag if transfer recipients have slowly adapting expectations or if they perceive the transfer cut as temporary: their demand will not fall immediately by the full extent of the cut in their current income.

However, cuts in government activity may be regarded as undesirable since they may create political difficulties by placing the full burden of adjustment on a few people (civil servants and government suppliers). In addition, governments may not be convinced that the level of absorption is too high or unsustainable.[20] If inflation is inertial (in the sense that it could be reduced without reducing the sustainable deficit), then cuts in government activity could be inappropriate. (This issue is discussed in detail in the next subsection.)

In the recent shock programs, the major instruments for reduction of the fiscal deficit were rate increases and subsidy cuts, rather than reductions in government activity. It was considered that the importance of fiscal contraction in bringing down prices, through whatever method, outweighed any negative impact of the rate increases on the price level. Moreover, it was also claimed that severe rate increases at the outset of a program could actually mitigate inflationary expectations since they reduce the government's need to implement further price shocks in the future, in addition to preempting relative price distortions, as discussed above.

The experience of the shock programs suggests that large rate changes may be undertaken with relatively small effects on the price index.[21] This suggests that, empirically, governments need not be overconcerned with using price-related instruments to cut the fiscal deficit, despite the arguments outlined above.[22]

(c) *Minimizing output losses — fiscal policy implications*

One of the most consuming concerns in the shock programs was the desire to avoid recession during the period of adjustment. As discussed earlier, it was believed that output losses could be avoided inasmuch as inflation was inertial, that is, could be reduced without cuts in aggregate demand. Ideally, expectations would be changed without any change in the government deficit. In reality, however, even if inflation was purely inertial, *temporary* deficit cuts were seen as efficacious ways of changing people's expectations, raising their confidence in economic management and increasing their demand for money.[23] Implicit in this belief was the idea that the improvement in private sector expectations would lead to a surge in activity which would offset the decline in government absorption. In general, tax and price-changing policies have a smaller multiplier effect on aggregate demand than the government direct expenditure multiplier; this would suggest that deficit cuts implemented with the objective of changing expectations rather than purely cutting total absorption should be effected by changes in prices rather than government activity. It is also possible that policies which affect prices are more costlessly reversible than those which involve reductions in staff and in maintenance, so that rate changes are more suited to temporary deficit cuts. Those characteristics of price-realigning fiscal policies, together with evidence from the shock programs that the price adjustments provoke relatively little inflation suggest that, as a general rule, price-realigning fiscal policies are probably more efficient than deficit reduction through cuts in activity. However, though increases in taxes and prices may have a smaller impact on present growth than have cuts in government activity, it has been argued, with respect to minimizing output losses over the longer run, that they will depress long-term future growth by damaging incentives in the economy.[24] If high marginal tax rates are inimical to growth, the tax base may deteriorate (relative to GDP if the high rates lead to shifts out of taxed activities, or in line with a fall in GDP if growth prospects are damaged). In other words, closing the short-run deficit may be done at the cost of increasing pressures on the long-run deficit. If the public perceives an inconsistency, the government's fiscal policy will not be credible, and inflationary expectations will not come down *pari passu* with short-run fiscal restrictions.

The extensive use of *temporary fiscal measures* has been a striking difference between the recent shock programs and more traditional adjustment programs. An explanation for this is that the emphasis in the shock programs on announcement effects and on quick results meant that, if deficit cuts were to be used to reduce inertial inflation, they would have to be large and to generate a very rapid inflow of real resources to the government. The need for an up-front and large collection of revenue is almost by definition too extreme to be sustained without large output losses, and there is usually the presumption that extreme measures will be replaced later by gradual policies on either the revenue or the expenditure side. In other words, the reduction in permanent income is expected to be much smaller than the immediate effect on current income. This presumption itself, however, ensures that the public accepts much larger temporary policies and much larger temporary deficit cuts than it would any permanent change, and therefore allows expectations to be affected more quickly.

Temporary overshooting of fiscal adjustment may also give the government room to implement long-run, growth- (and possibly revenue-) enhancing structural changes which are costly in the short run. An example of this in the context of the programs were the cuts in government employment, which reduced long-run labor costs but necessitated immediate funds for relocation and redundancy payments.

The largest temporary measures in the programs were the forced saving schemes. In conception, these were designed to have no effect whatsoever on permanent incomes. It should be noted in this context that the impact of forced saving schemes on the government's long-run financing gap is more or less invariant to whether or not the government pays back the forced loan. If the loan is repaid, government expenditure will rise by that amount in the year the repayment takes place. On the other hand, repayment creates credibility in the loan as an asset, and permits the government to refinance the loan. If the loan is not repaid, present government expenditure is lower, but the government will find it more difficult to raise revenue through such a scheme again. In both cases, the net impact on the financing gap could be the same.

While temporary fiscal measures have immediate effects which cannot be sustained, *structural fiscal measures* which improve future fiscal management will sustain the long-run fiscal balance but may have no immediate revenue impact. Such measures (such as the announcement of tax reforms in Argentina and Bolivia, and of civil service reform in Israel) are included in shock programs because of the support they supposedly give government credibility — in other words, they have a pure, though temporary, announcement effect. Their value depends on how plausible they are, *ex ante* (so that their announcement will have some impact), and on how soon they actually begin to be carried out. If the policies are not implemented, government credibility is eroded; there is a "reverse announcement effect" in the sense that, because the policy was introduced with much publicity, government failure to implement it will be more noticeable than if it had never been promised, and future promises will be received with less confidence.

A related reason to include announcements of future fiscal policies in a shock program is that they minimize the loss of future output by providing guidelines for long-range private sector decisions. In particular, private investment may depend on future as well as present rates of interest, so that government's projected credit use over the life of a planned investment may affect that investment decision.

(d) *Growth of the financial system under inflation and its tax implications*

A feature of many tax systems in high-inflation countries is their relatively high reliance on financial transactions as a tax base. This occurs for two reasons. First, the financial system tends to grow as a share of GDP as the country adapts successfully to inflation. The financial structure gets larger and more sophisticated as, in order to preserve the national currency as the unit of account, more complicated financial transactions are developed which incorporate indexation mechanisms to capture changes in nominal values more perfectly. Hence, the share of income and profits taxes, etc., from the financial sector may grow disproportionately with inflation.[25] Second, as inflation rises, the government's traditional inflation tax base, money, is shrinking. The logical alternative tax bases are the money substitutes which have become attractive as inflation hedges.

If the volume of financial transactions is indeed affected by the inflationary process, it could also be expected that a fall in the rate of inflation will reduce the relative size of the sector. In particular, the demand for money-substitutes tends to fall drastically as inflation disappears, as their properties as inflation-hedges become less valuable. It is therefore likely that, following rapid disinflation, the financial tax bases will shrink, both on asset transactions and on incomes.[26] Revenue losses on income taxes will be exacerbated if banks may offset losses that they may incur against their tax obligations.

This effect was observed in practice. In the countries which introduced shock programs, the financial sector fell into difficulties as inflation dropped. In Brazil, for example, the private banking system shed 140,000 workers in the first weeks of the program. Brazil also suffered revenue losses in consequence of the tax reform implemented just before the Cruzado Plan. Financial system taxes were adjusted in the reform, with relatively higher rates being placed on inflation-hedging assets and transactions (such as Stock Exchange trading) which helped maintain nominal values, and relatively lower rates on assets that were not so elastic to inflation. These reforms meant that, when inflation fell, the private sector's shift in assets created a permanent revenue loss.

The public financial sector, in particular, may be expected to be vulnerable to the large inflation cut observed during the initial phase of a successful shock program. Public banks will be worse off than their private sector counterparts, if they are not free to shed labor. Also, public bank portfolios tend to be in longer term and less tradable assets (particularly in development banks) so that portfolios can only react with long lags to large changes in inflation. In the interim, the profitability, and indeed the viability, of the public financial sector may be endangered.

While inflation may affect the financial sector, government management and regulation of asset markets may have an effect on the rate of inflation. Given an excess money supply, pressures on the prices of domestic goods will be higher the fewer the domestic and foreign assets in which individuals are permitted to hold wealth. Limitations on the type of assets and on the available composition of private portfolios may arise because capital markets are relatively unsophisticated. However, government regulations such as exchange restrictions and institutionally-set interest rates also shrink portfolio options, and may thereby exacerbate inflation.

(e) *The interrelationship of fiscal and impact policies in the shock programs*

Regardless of the degree of success of impact policies in reducing inflation, they themselves may be expensive for the budget. For instance, the cost of implementing a price freeze may be substantial. If public utility prices are frozen at low rates, the budget will suffer. If prices are frozen with an element of government subsidy in them, the subsidy will be perpetuated, and if they happen to be frozen at low disequilibrium rates relative to other goods, the aggregate subsidy will increase as individuals substitute into the relatively cheaper subsidized good.

Other labor policies of the government may also be expensive. For example, redundancy payments and pension, social security or health scheme pay-offs make the costs of laying off public servants quite high in terms of a single year's deficit.

If successful adjustment generates a sudden improvement in the balance of payments, which leads to a drop in revenue from trade taxes, this loss must also be factored into post-program revenue projections. In Argentina, for example, the shortfall in 1985 revenue due to external restraint was estimated at half a percentage point of GDP.

5. CONCLUSIONS

The experience of Argentina, Bolivia, and Israel under the recent shock programs offers two sets of insights: first, concerning the innovative elements of the packages and, second, about fiscal policy in the presence of high inflation and unorthodox strategies for curbing it. It is certainly true that these programs, and in particular their so-called heterodox components, have succeeded in catching public imagination and mobilizing public support, at least in the short run, for the implementation of policies that usually result in significant costs during the period of adjustment. Public confidence in the government and in its policies is such a crucial element in restoring stability and in attaining a successful level of economic management, recovery, and growth, that the innovations of these programs cannot be dismissed lightly.

However, it is difficult to make stronger claims about the virtues of shock programs based on the recent evidence. Although direct controls and freezes can attain a very dramatic and immediate fall in the rate of inflation, it has not proven possible to reduce inflation for more than a short period of time by impact policies alone. In fact, there are strong indications that the size and quality of adjustment in fundamental variables was the most compelling catalyst to inflation cuts, possibly through their impact on expectations as well as their direct impact on excess absorption. Likewise, it is becoming more and more clear that pure expectational policies cannot play a decisive and independent role in actually changing deep-rooted public perceptions and bring down inflation without imposing real losses to the economy.

Furthermore, freezes, controls, and incomes policies are not costless. They entail administrative and political costs, as well as economic costs in terms of shortages, bottlenecks, losses of efficiency and, possibly, damage to long-run growth potential, particularly when prices are frozen out of equilibrium. Moreover, they may also have a fiscal cost by causing the budget to deteriorate, thus eroding the authorities' ability to adjust successfully the fundamental variables. When evaluating the benefits of these policies, it is important to consider these implicit and explicit costs.

It is not simple to provide a sound operational content to the assumptions on which the use of impact policies has been based, particularly the concept of inertial inflation as an independent source of price pressures. It is, in fact, possible that the inertial component of inflation is not separable from the "real" component, so that, though price freezes are actually working to remove some inertia in inflation, their influence cannot be perceived unless a fundamental adjustment is taking place at the same time. More generally, given their direct and indirect dependence on the reduction of excess absorption, as well as the danger they entail that a country's long-run growth potential will be compromised, the shock programs have not revealed any practical or significant painless way of cutting inflation.

On the other hand, however, we are not left with the result that traditional demand-management policies function exactly as economists had always believed in adjusting the price level. In particular, the conduct and effects of fiscal policy in high-inflation countries, by themselves or in the context of shock programs, may differ from the conventional analysis. Fiscal management becomes more difficult in that policymakers must take into account additional complications arising from the persistence of the inflationary process and from the transition from high to lower inflationary levels. Among these, we have discussed the fact that the high-inflation deficit is not the same as the low-inflation deficit; that the optimal tax base under high inflation may disappear as inflation drops; and that administrative mechanisms which are cost-effective under high inflation may appear too cumbersome under lower inflation rates.

Some of the general intuitions embodied in the shock programs may also provide important lessons for fiscal policy. Large temporary fiscal measures may play a valuable role in adjustment, as may announcements of future changes in fiscal regimes. On the other hand, some accepted beliefs about fiscal policy do not seem to have been supported in practice. For example, deficit reduction through tax and rates increases was not shown to generate significantly higher inflation than deficit adjustment through cuts in activity.

In sum, from the evidence at hand at this point, it could be said that, while shock programs have heightened our awareness that the manipulation of expectations may significantly affect the outcome of an adjustment program, expectation-changing policies are not a substitute for fundamental adjustment through an appropriate fiscal and monetary stance, but may only be successful in conjunction with traditional demand-management policies. The implementation of those policies, unfortunately, is not as straightforward in the presence of expectation-changing policies as in the traditional case; and the success of the policies, when they are called upon to ward off the threat of hyperinflation, is more difficult to ensure than when inflation is not an important determinant of the behavior of fiscal variables.

NOTES

1. In many cases, available data were not specific enough to quantify the issues discussed in this paper. The issues are included, however, both because of their conceptual importance and because of the large body of qualitative evidence which supports their significance in the context of the shock programs.

2. See, for example, Sargent (1982).

3. Monetary policy is quite likely to be accommodating in high inflation because: (i) there may be no formal policy of restricting credit to the private sector, even though the authorities have decided to impose *fiscal* restraint; or (ii) even if the monetary authorities desire to reduce private sector credit concomitantly with public sector credit, they will face strong resistance. Pressures will come, for example, from firms who have granted wage increases consistent with high inflation and who will face difficulties and, ultimately, bankruptcy if they do not get access to the credit which would enable them to pay these increases.

4. There are clearly many other sources of monetary growth that do not originate in fiscal deficits. A detailed examination of the working of monetary policy instruments and of the evolution of monetary and

reserve aggregate is needed to complete a theory of monetary hyperinflation. This, however, goes beyond the scope of this paper. On this subject, see, for example, Calvo and Fernandez (1983). They analyze the possibility of affecting the steady-state level of inflation, at a *given* budget deficit, by means of monetary management, mainly changes in the reserve ratio of commercial banks.

5. In perfect foresight models, a sufficient condition for the emergence of hyperinflation would be an exogenous, non-marginal shock to push it past the threshold level at which the deficit becomes unsustainable. In models which include any element of inertia, either from expectations or from any other structural rigidity in the economy, hyperinflation can be induced without an exogenous shock.

6. This is strictly correct in the steady state. Calvo (1978) and Barro and Gordon (1981) have developed models where the government can continue to extract resources even at very high rates of inflation. In their models, when inflationary expectations, formed rationally in the light of the government's revenue objectives, are given at each date, the government can generate more revenue if it selects a rate of monetary expansion greater than that expected by the public. The public then anticipates this change and revises its expectations, but the government can choose an even higher rate of monetary growth, and so on. Such a process can result in infinite rates of monetary expansion and inflation, and there is no equilibrium.

7. This exposition does not take into account the inverse relationship between normal taxes and inflation-tax financing which has been pointed out by Tanzi (1977). This relationship, and its implications, are discussed in Section 4.

8. Bruno and Fischer (1985) commented that "The existence of a high inflation trap suggests that it may be possible to reduce the inflation rate in a high inflation economy by policies typically regarded as unsound, such as fixing the exchange rate, or freezing nominal wages or prices, in an attempt to make the transition from a high to a low inflation steady-state."

9. The main fundamental impact measures were the introduction of forced savings schemes, which substituted for other tax revenue in the short run. These forced savings schemes became strongly identified with the popular conception of the nature of a shock program.

10. This is shown by Chu and Feltenstein (1978) to have happened in Argentina during the 1970s.

11. See Blejer and Liviatan (1987).

12. See Blejer and Liviatan (1987).

13. In Israel, for example, since October 1985 formal indexation of wages has been restored and its degree has even been enhanced: cost-of-living adjustments of 80% will henceforth be paid after cumulative consumer price index (CPI) increases reach 4%, or every three months.

14. This is one explanation of why countries tend to find themselves at the high-equilibrium inflation trap, rather than at an inflation level corresponding to an efficiently financed deficit. The presence of inflation-endogenous elements in the budget makes the deficit likely to overshoot the low-level equilibrium.

15. It could be argued, however, that because the inflation component of interest is not income but rather amortization, the impact on demand of interest payments that reflect inflation is much lower than the impact of other expenditure components (see Tanzi, Blejer, and Teijeiro, 1987).

16. See Tanzi (1977).

17. Before further fiscal reforms were implemented in November of that year.

18. The characterization of this increase in revenue as "automatic" does not carry the implication that it should not be counted when evaluating the fiscal effort undertaken as part of the programs. The increased real revenue represented a cost to the private sector and, in that sense, is not qualitatively different from an increase in revenue generated by higher tax rates.

19. The tendency of high inflation to generate complex administrative and regulatory structures will damage a country's ability to return to growth after the shock program, unless there is a concomitant liberalization of the system. Such liberalization was ignored in shock programs other than in Bolivia (except for the structural fiscal measures discussed in the next section) but might be important for sustaining the programs' success in the long term.

20. None of the countries discussed was considered to be at full employment and, thus, government demand was viewed as a crucial component of effective aggregate demand.

21. In Brazil, for example, compulsory levies of 25% to 30% on cars, gasoline, and alcohol were introduced in July 1986. Following these steps, the authorities modified the index used to measure official inflation in order to purge the index from the impact of the levies. For July and August, inflation was 5.3% in the "unpurged" version, and 2.9% in the "purged" version of the index. Likewise, at the outset of the program in Bolivia, where the price of gasoline rose by 750% and domestic prices of other publicly provided goods and services were raised to reflect the 93% devaluation, the inflation rate in the month following the start of the program was 56% — 10 percentage points lower than the 66% rate of the month leading into the program. (All the figures represent monthly averages.)

22. This conclusion is probably valid even though part of the explanation for the insignificant impact on prices

could be problems with the way the price indices were constructed.

23. Many economists have suggested that the long-run sustainable deficit would probably have to be overshot during a shock program, not only in order to convince people of the government's determination to switch to conservative fiscal management but also in order to generate excess supplies in the economy which would allow price freezes to be maintained. (See Blejer and Liviatan (1987), and Dornbusch and Fischer (1986).)

24. Liviatan (1986).

25. The growth of the financial sector with the increase in the rate of inflation is likely to reach a limit. If hyperinflation develops, a shift out of the national currency as the unit of account will take place and an extreme shortening in the length of contracts will be observed. The process is generally accompanied by extensive financial disintermediation.

26. The validity of this argument hinges on the type of interest rate policy followed since changes in relative interest rates could affect, in different ways, the relative size of the various segments of the financial system, thus affecting differentially the asset income tax base.

REFERENCES

Barro, R. J., and D. Gordon, "Rules, discretion, and reputation in a model of monetary policy," *Journal of Monetary Economics*, Vol. 12 (July 1983).

Blejer, Mario I., and Nissan Liviatan, "Fighting hyperinflation: Stabilization strategies in Argentina and Israel, 1985–86," *IMF Staff Papers*, Vol. 34 No. 3 (September 1987), pp. 409–438.

Bruno, Michael, and Stanley Fischer, "Expectations and the high inflation trap," Mimeo (September 1985).

Calvo, Guillermo A., "Optimal seignorage from money creation: An analysis in terms of the optimum balance of payments deficit problem," *Journal of Monetary Economics*, Vol. 4 (1978), pp. 503–517.

Calvo, Guillermo A., and R. B. Fernandez, "Competitive banks and the inflation tax," *Economic Letters*, Vol. 12, Nos. 3–4 (1983), pp. 313–317.

Chu, Ke-young, and Andrew Feltenstein, "Relative price distortions and inflation: The case of Argentina, 1963–76," *IMF Staff Papers*, Vol. 25, No. 3, (September 1978), pp. 453–493.

Dornbusch, R., and S. Fischer, "Stopping hyperinflation: Past and present," *Weltwirtschaftliches Archiv* (April 1986).

Liviatan, N., "Inflation and stabilization in Israel — Conceptual issues and interpretation of developments," WP/86/10 (Washington, DC: International Monetary Fund, 4 November 1986).

Tanzi, Vito, "Inflation, lags in collection, and the real value of tax revenue," *IMF Staff Papers*, Vol. 24, No. 1 (March 1977), pp. 154–167.

Tanzi, Vito, "Inflation, real tax revenue, and the case for inflationary finance: Theory with an application to Argentina," *IMF Staff Papers*, Vol. 25, No. 3 (September 1978), pp. 417–451.

Tanzi, Vito, Mario I. Blejer, and Mario O. Teijeiro, "Inflation and the measurement of fiscal deficits," WP/87/17 (Washington, DC: International Monetary Fund, 13 March, 1987).

Sargent, T., "The ends of four big inflations," in R. Hall (Ed.), *Inflation* (Chicago: NBER and University of Chicago Press, 1982).

MACROECONOMIC POPULISM*

Rudiger DORNBUSCH

Massachusetts Institute of Technology, Cambridge, MA 02139, USA
National Bureau of Economic Research, Cambridge MA 02138, USA

Sebastian EDWARDS

University of California, Los Angeles, CA 90024, USA
National Bureau of Economic Research, Cambridge, MA 02138, USA

Macroeconomic populism is an approach to economics that emphasizes growth and income distribution and deemphasizes the risks of inflation and deficit finance, external constraints and the reaction of economic agents to aggressive non-market policies. The purpose of our paper is to show that policy experiences in different countries and periods share common features, from the initial conditions, the motivation for policies, the argument that the country's conditions are different, to the ultimate collapse. Our purpose in setting out these experiences, those of Chile under Allende and of Peru under Garcia, is not a righteous assertion of conservative economics, but rather a warning that populist policies do ultimately fail; and when they fail it is always at a frightening cost to the very groups who were supposed to be favored. Our central thesis is that the *macro*economics of various experiences is very much the same, even if the politics differed greatly.

1. Introduction

The purpose of the study is to develop a paradigm of populist macroeconomics.[1] Macroeconomic populism is a policy perspective on economic management that emphasizes economic growth and income redistribution and deemphasizes the risks of inflation and deficit finance, external constraints and the reaction of economic agents to aggressive non-market policies.

We analyze two populist economic programs, Chile during Allende's Unidad Popular (1970–1973) and Peru under Alan Garcia. We show that policy experiences in different countries and periods share common economic

*This is a much shortened and revised version of a paper presented at the second meeting of the InterAmerican Seminar on Economics, IASE, Bogota, Colombia, March 30–April 1, 1989. The authors are indebted to conference participants, Eliana Cardoso, Vittorio Corbo, Al Fishlow, Javier Iguiniz, Richard Eckaus, Eduardo Engel, Jose de Gregorio, Caterina Nelson, Eva Paus, Andres Solimano, Jose Pablo Arellano, Miguel Savastano, and Andrew Zimbalist for helpful suggestions. The research reported here is part of a project supported by the World Bank. S. Edwards gratefully acknowledges the support of the University of California Pacific Rim Program.

[1]See, also, Sachs (1989) where the same issue is pursued.

features, from the initial conditions, the motivation for policies, the argument that the country's conditions are different, to the ultimate collapse. It is clear that the Unidad Popular of 1970–73 experience in Chile had political goals that were very different from the experience in Peru. Even so, we want to emphasize that the political mobilization strategy had strongly similar elements and that, overall, there are remarkable similarities between the Allende experience and that of Alan Garcia's Peru.

The similarities in approach in Chile and Peru are particularly striking with respect to the way policymakers viewed the objective conditions of their economy, how they proposed that strongly expansionary policies should and could be carried out, and how they rationalized that constraints could be dealt with. Most impressive is the fact that in the end, foreign exchange constraints and extreme inflation forced a program of violent real wage cuts that ended in massive political instability, violence, and in the case of Chile even in a coup. We do not doubt the sincerity of the policymakers who embark on these programs, and we share their conviction that income distribution is unacceptably unequal. The very sincerity of these policymakers convinces us of the usefulness, and indeed the necessity of laying out exactly how and why the programs do go wrong.

External influences (debt crises and economic blockades, among others), domestic structural policies (socialization of firms, banks nationalization), and inconsistent fiscal and exchange rate policies bring about an unsustainable situation; inflation goes out of control, and the foreign exchange constraints force realism on policymakers. Accounts of these experiences often emphasize politics and, especially, external factors as central to the demise. External destabilization can be an important part of the unravelling of an economic program. But we emphasize the extreme vulnerability that makes destabilization possible. By and large this potential results from unsustainable economic policies. We think that only to the extent that the mechanics of the macroeconomics of populist programs are fully understood, will these policies cease to be popular among politicians.

Before embarking on the case studies we emphasize that we do not cover the political issues which surely are equally if not more important in the historical developments in the two countries. We omit politics not because we think they are irrelevant, but because we want to highlight to the clearest extent possible the economic developments. The view we present is therefore possibly biased because it omits the political motivation, on occasions, for economic motives.

2. The populist paradigm

Populism has traditionally been a fuzzy concept. Political scientists have struggled to provide a meaningful and precise definition. Drake (1982), for example, emphasizes three elements of a tentative definition: populism uses 'political mobilization, recurrent rhetoric and symbols designed to inspire the people', it draws on a heterogeneous coalition aimed primarily at the working class, but including and led by significant sectors from the middle and upper strata and, third, populism 'has connoted a reformist set of policies tailored to promote development without explosive class conflict'. He notes [Drake (1982, p. 218)]: '[The programs] normally respond to the problems of underdevelopment by expanding state activism to incorporate the workers in a process of accelerated industrialization through ameliorative redistributive measures'.

Conniff (1982, p. 5) has argued that 'populist programs frequently overlapped with those of socialism'. We emphasize that the redistributive objectives are a central part of the paradigm. Whether they are motivated by a strategy of massive social reform is consequential, but is not central to our own discussion.

Populist economic programs exhibit strong similarities. In this section, we set out in paradigmatic fashion what we see as the critical common factors. In later sections we analyze these for the experiences of Chile and Peru.[2] The intellectual identification of issues is summarized under the following headings:

Initial conditions. Dissatisfaction with the country's growth performance. Most typically, though not always, the country has experienced moderate growth, stagnation or outright depression as a result of previous stabilization attempts. The experience, often – though not necessarily – under an IMF program, has reduced living standards. Serious economic inequality provides economic and political appeal for a radically different economic program. Preceding stabilizations have improved the budget and the external balance sufficiently to provide the room for, though perhaps not the wisdom of, an expansionary program.

No constraints. Policymakers explicitly reject the conservative paradigm. In their view idle productive capacity provides the leeway for expansion. International reserves and the ability to ration foreign exchange give room for expansion without the risk of running into external constraints. The risks of deficit finance are portrayed as exaggerated or altogether unfounded. It is argued that expansion is not inflationary (if there is no devaluation), because spare capacity and decreasing long-run costs contain cost pressures; in any event there is room to squeeze profit margins by price controls.

The policy prescription. Populist programs emphasize three elements: reactivation, redistribution of income and restructuring of the economy. The common thread here is 'reactivation with redistribution'. The recommended

[2]In a larger project we expect to look at a significant number of experiences in Latin America to get a sharper picture of the phases and ultimate breakdown of programs.

policy is to redistribute income, typically by large real wage increases that are not to be passed on into higher prices. Inflation notwithstanding, devaluation is rejected because of the inflationary impact and because it reduces living standards. The economy is to be restructured to save on foreign exchange and support higher levels of real wages and higher growth.

In populist experiments events tend to evolve in four phases or stages:

Phase I. In the first year or so, the policymakers are fully vindicated in their diagnosis and prescription: growth of output, real wages and employment are high, and the *macro*economic policies are nothing short of successful. Controls assure that inflation is not a problem, and shortages are alleviated by imports. The run-down of inventories and the availability of imports (financed by reserve decumulation or suspension of external payments) accommodate the demand expansion with little impact on inflation.
Phase II. Bottlenecks, partly as a result of a strong expansion in demand for domestic goods, and partly because of reactions to the scarcity of foreign exchange, start to appear. Whereas inventory decumulation was an essential feature of the first phase, the low levels of inventories and inventory building are now a source of problems. Price realignments and devaluation, exchange controls, or increased protection become necessary. The government tries to stabilize, but fails to put a check on wage increases and on the growth of government expenditure. Inflation increases significantly, but wages keep up. A massive underground economy emerges. The budget deficit worsens tremendously as a result of pervasive subsidies on wage goods and foreign exchange.
Phase III. Pervasive shortages, extreme acceleration of inflation, and an obvious foreign exchange gap lead to capital flight and demonetization of the economy. The budget deficit deteriorates violently because of a steep decline in tax collection and increasing subsidy costs. The government attempts to stabilize by cutting subsidies and by undertaking a real depreciation. Real wages fall massively, and politics become unstable. It becomes clear that the populist policies have failed.
Phase IV. Orthodox stabilization takes over under a new government. An IMF program will be enacted; and, when everything is said and done, the real wage will have declined abruptly, to a level significantly lower than when the whole episode began! Moreover, that decline will be very persistent, because the politics and economics of the experience will have depressed investment, decapitalized the manufacturing sector, and promoted capital flight. The severity of real wage declines is due to a simple fact: capital is mobile across borders, but labor is not. Capital can flee from poor policies, labor is trapped.

After briefly analyzing the propagation mechanisms of high inflation in populist-type experiences, we turn to the episodes of Peru and Chile to sketch the policymakers' diagnosis and the actual events. We start with the Chilean case, because the facts of the entire experience can now be seen. The results suggest what to look for in the Peruvian experience.

3. The mechanisms of high inflation under populist macroeconomics

In this section we briefly review the relationship between key macroeconomic variables and sketch the propagation mechanisms of high inflation in populist experiments. The emphasis is put on the relationship between real wages, the real exchange rate, real interest rate, the fiscal budget and inflation. We show that policies based on wage increases and deficit expansions face severe tradeoffs. While higher wages will be achieved, inflation will erupt, competitiveness will be eroded and an external crisis will take place. We show in this section that in the short run, while international reserves last, the more severe aspects of this tradeoff can be kept under control.

The starting point is the relation between real wages, w, the real exchange rate, R, and employment. Consider a world where there are exportables, importables and nontraded goods. The consumer price index is

$$P = P_x^x P_m^m P_n^n, \tag{1}$$

where the superindexes x and m are the share of exportables and importables in consumption. The home goods share thus is $n = 1 - x - m$. Home goods are produced using labor and importables:

$$P_n = aWZS, \tag{2}$$

where a is the per-unit requirements of labor and imports, W is the nominal wage, Z represents the profit markup and S the subsidy [i.e., $S = 1/(1+s)$ with s the percentage subsidy rate]. As discussed later, the subsidy may either take the form of direct cash transfers or of negative interest rates on credit.

Exports prices are given in the world market so that the domestic price of exportables is equal to the world price P^* times the exports exchange rate e:

$$P_x = P^* e. \tag{3}$$

On the imports side prices are determined by the given world price, P^*, the imports exchange rate and the tariff, T:

$$P_m = \alpha\beta P^* eT, \tag{4}$$

where α denotes the terms of trade and β, if it differs from unity, measures the differentiation of the exchange rate structure between imports and exports. Define the real exchange rate, R, as the ratio of wages to traded goods prices on a weighted basis for export and import competing industries:

$$R = (W/P_x)^{1-\sigma}(W/P_m)^{\sigma} = (W/eP^*)K^{-\sigma}, \quad K = \alpha\beta T. \tag{5}$$

Eq. (5) indicates, then, that the real exchange rate is given by the nominal wage rate measured in terms of exportables with an adjustment for the terms of trade and for exchange rate or tariff protection.

The real consumption wage, w, is given by the ratio of money wage to the consumer price index:

$$w = W/P = \theta(R, K, ZS). \tag{6}$$

Eq. (6), substituting from (1) to (5) in W/P, highlights that real wages and competitiveness are negatively related. Subsidies or reductions in profit margins play a special role since they increase real wages without a deterioration in competitiveness. Protection increases competitiveness, but it reduces real wages.

On the other hand, assume that employment, L, is demand determined by profitability in the traded goods sector and by the derived demand for labor in the home goods sector. A fraction κ of labor income is spent on home goods, and G represents government spending on home goods. In addition there is credit expansion Q which is made available to state enterprises or the private sector for spending on home goods. We then have

$$L^{d} = \rho(R) + \gamma\kappa(WL + P_n G + Q)/P_n, \quad \rho' > 0 \tag{7}$$

or

$$L = \rho(R)/(1 - \kappa/ZS) = L(R, ZS, G, K/W). \tag{7'}$$

According to (7′) employment is positively affected by subsidies or by a squeeze of profit margins because these raise real wages and hence demand for nontraded goods. Moreover, according to this equation, an increase in government spending and a gain in competitiveness (i.e., a decline in R) will raise the level of employment.

We further assume that there are various sources of *acceleration* of the rate of inflation:

$$\Delta\pi = \cap(L^{d} - L) + \lambda(w' - w) + \delta\Delta R/R - \phi\Delta S/S. \tag{8}$$

It is implicit in this formulation the presence of automatic indexation and hence inertia. According to eq. (8) inflation stays constant unless one of three shocks occur:

- corrective inflation from real depreciation or subsidy removal,
- demand inflation associated with an excess of labor demand over the level of full employment,
- social conflict shocks which arise when the target real wage, w', exceeds actual real wages.

The model is closed by the financing equations: the external balance and the budget. The external deficit depends on competitiveness and the interest differential between domestic and foreign assets adjusted for the anticipated depreciation of the exchange rate, v:

$$b = B(R, v); \qquad b_1 > 0, \quad b_2 > 0. \tag{9}$$

The budget deficit, on the other hand, is assumed to depend on subsidies, on foreign exchange losses and tariff revenues, and, via tax collection, on the level of activity and hence on competitiveness:

$$d = D(S, \beta T, R). \tag{10a}$$

The deficit, in turn, is financed by reserves decumulation and by money creation. Money creation depends on the budget (b), the external balance (d) and credit expansion (q) each measured relative to nominal income:

$$\dot{M} = (d + b - q)PY. \tag{10b}$$

To derive actual time paths of alternative policies and their impact on the path of employment, real wages and inflation the model would have to be simulated. For our purposes, however, it is already instructive in that it highlights the basic tradeoffs that are faced by a policymaker who seeks to expand the level of economic activity (i.e., reducing unemployment) via wage rate and expansionary fiscal policies. The model in fact shows that real wages can be raised either by a real appreciation (i.e., real exchange rate overvaluation) or by subsidies. But real appreciation interferes with the external constraint and subsidies are inflationary. Employment can be expanded by subsidies or by real depreciation. The former is inflationary and the latter hurts real wages. The room for policies that raise real wages *and* employment is therefore severely limited. While there is foreign exchange available the tradeoffs are not apparent, but once reserves run out the tradeoffs will suddenly, and cruelly, appear: inflation will then rapidly accelerate.

The acceleration of inflation, once it takes place, is magnified by adjustments in the financial sector.[3] Velocity rises in response to increased inflation and that implies a decline in the base for the inflation tax. But with a decline in real balances, even higher inflation rates are required to finance a given budget deficit. The increasing inflation, in turn, interferes with the efficiency of revenue collection, leading to a widening of the deficit. Once inflation becomes very high the relation between inflation and the budget becomes dominant. Moreover, because of the sharp rise in velocity the deficits that can be financed at a given inflation fall radically. At this point a vicious circle takes over, and the only way out is by implementing a severe stabilization program that cuts the deficit, generates a major real depreciation and reduces real wages. As will become apparent from our analysis of the Chilean and Peruvian cases in sections 4 and 5, this model captures some of the most important aspects of the mechanics of macroeconomic crises under populist regimes.

4. Economic policies in Allende's Chile

In September of 1970, Salvador Allende, the socialist candidate of the Unidad Popular (UP), was elected President of Chile. A unique political and economic experience evolved in the following three years.[4] The Unidad Popular was a political coalition of left and center-left parties dominated by the Socialist and Communist parties which sought to implement deep institutional, political and economic reforms. Its program called for a democratic 'Chilean road to socialism'.[5] Both communists and socialists initially recognized the multiclass nature of the Unidad Popular and considered the alliance and the politics that sustained it to be a tactical intermediate step that would help set the basis for the transition to socialism [see the discussion in Zammit (1973)]. Vuskovic (1973, p. 50) noted:

> . . . economic policy is subordinate, in its content, shape and form, to the political need for increasing the Popular Unity's support . . . The urgent need to achieve rapid recovery of the economy, and to extend the benefits to the mass of the working population, cannot be undertaken in isolation from the structural changes; they are all necessarily inter-

[3]See Dornbusch and de Pablo (1988) on the inflation dynamics.
[4]See Oppenheim (1989) for a recent review of the literature on this experience.
[5]See Stallings (1978) and de Vlyder (1974) for a discussion of politics and economics in Chile.

dependent. It is not possible to make deeper changes without broadening the Government's political support, and economic reactivation and income redistribution will provide an impulse to these fundamental changes.

4.1. Initial conditions, diagnosis and short-run program

The Unidad Popular faced a somewhat stagnated economy with a rapidly increasing rate of inflation. Between 1967 and 1970, Chile's real GDP per capita grew only at 1.2% – significantly below the Latin American average. Inflation had steadily increased during the last few years of the Frei administration, reaching 35% in 1970. On the positive side, the balance of payments showed substantial surpluses during all but one of the Frei years and the central bank had a significant stock of international reserves of approximately U.S. $400 million or half a year of imports.

The short-run economic objectives of the UP included:

- initiating, at a rapid speed, a whole range of structural economic transformations, including a massive nationalization program;
- raising real wages, especially for the lower classes;
- reducing inflation;
- increasing the rate of output growth;
- increasing consumption, especially among the poorer groups; and
- reducing the economy's dependence on the rest of the world.

The nationalization program was to be achieved by a combination of new legislation, requisitions, and stock purchases from small shareholders. The other goals – output and consumption growth, with rising salaries and declining inflation – were to be accomplished by an increase in aggregate demand, mainly generated by higher government expenditures, accompanied by income redistribution measures and severe administrative controls over prices.

This macroeconomic program, in the structuralist tradition, was based on a number of key assumptions. First, it was believed that there was ample excess capacity in the manufacturing sector. Second, it was thought that this low rate of capacity utilization was closely related to the existing pattern of consumption and income distribution. Third, it was assumed that there was a dualistic manufacturing sector, where firms producing 'luxury' goods had excessively high capital/labor ratios. Fourth, inflation was considered to be a reflection of the economic structure, not of financial or monetary pressures. In what follows, we will analyze these key assumptions in some detail.

Significant excess capacity in the manufacturing sector was at the center of the macroeconomic program and provided the intellectual base for the belief that large fiscal deficits would not necessarily be inflationary. Americo Zorrilla, Allende's first Minister of Finance said:

> The subutilization of installed capacity is another feature of the current economic situation . . . In 1969 it was possible to increase production, due to subutilization, by more than 30 percent . . . [A]ccording to recent studies . . . unutilized capacity has reached, in the last few years, 61 percent in the cloth industry, 50 percent in the baking industry . . . 74 percent in the shoe industry, etc. [As reproduced in Garcia (1972, p. 72).]

An important corollary of the unutilized capacity hypothesis was that firms in many sectors faced decreasing average costs so that, under proper administrative price controls, demand increases would not generate inflationary pressures. Moreover, to the extent that many of the larger firms were indeed nationalized, as called for by the UP program, it was thought that output could be greatly increased even with price reductions. In a document prepared by the Planning Office (ODEPLAN) in 1971, it was stated that by 'combining the increase in production derived from a higher use of installed capacity . . . the former monopolies will be able to absorb, without problems, the required wage increases, while maintaining, *or even reducing*, prices and still generating the same surplus'.

The lack of 'full' utilization was, in turn, attributed to two fundamental factors: The monopolistic nature of the manufacturing industry and the structure of income distribution [Vuskovic (1970)]. Based on this diagnosis, it was thought that if income was redistributed towards the poorer groups through wage increases and prices were properly controlled, there would be a significant expansion of demand and output.

Regarding inflation, the UP program emphasized rigidities, bottlenecks, and the role of monopolistic pricing and played down the role of fiscal pressures and money creation.[6] Very little attention was given to the financial sector. In fact, in his memoirs, the former Allende Minister and Vice President Clodomiro Almeyda relates how, in the first meeting of the economic team after the elections, the CEPAL-oriented technocrats expressly, and convincingly it would seem, argued that monetary and financial management did not deserve too much attention.[7] Alfonso Inostroza, the President of the Central Bank, stated in early 1971 that the main objective of the monetary policy was to 'transform it into a key instrument . . . to achieve the complete mobilization of productive resources, and their allocation to

[6]Of course, this was consistent with the structuralist view on inflation. See Sunkel (1960) and Baer and Kersternetzky (1964).

[7]See, for example, the 1971 CIAP Report reproduced in *Panorama Economico*, no. 260, Feb.–Mar. 1971, p. 36.

those areas that the government gives priority to . . .' [see Inostroza (1971, p. 8)].

As to Chile's external vulnerability, the UP basic program stated that, along with a reduction in import dependence, a priority of the new government would be to 'execute a foreign trade policy tending to expand and diversify our exports . . .' [Unidad Popular (1969, p. 24)]. This objective was to be achieved without providing any price incentives. Quite the contrary, the UP economists thought that changes in the exchange rate had very little, if any, effects on exports or imports. In fact, it was stated that an important goal of the policy was to 'avoid the scandalous devaluations of [the] . . . currency' (p. 24). Indeed, one of the first measures undertaken by the Allende administration was to eliminate the system of crawling peg that had been adopted, with great success, by the Frei administration.

The UP view of the way the economy functioned ignored many of the key principles of traditional economic theory. This was reflected not only in the greatly diminished attention given to monetary policies, but also by the complete disregard for the real exchange rate as a key variable in determining macroeconomic equilibrium. Moreover, the Unidad Popular failed to recognize that their policies would be unsustainable in the medium term and that capacity constraints were going to become an unsurmountable obstacle to rapid growth. Also, the UP technocrats greatly underestimated the role of expectations and the capacity of the public to react to severe inflationary pressures. Bitar (1986, ch. 5) portrays very clearly the government's inability to control events, and to shift the emphasis from redistribution to accumulation.

> It turned out to be very difficult to contain the forces unleashed in 1971. The sequential conception of redistribution followed by accumulation assumed that basic political and social conduct could be altered and popular expectations changed virtually instantaneously. In the next few months [early 1972] it proved impossible to apply this thinking with the facility that had been hoped for.

4.2. Phase I: Rapid growth with repressed inflation

Armed with the intellectual framework analyzed above, the UP rapidly began to implement its program in late 1970. In terms of structural reforms, two basic measures were immediately undertaken: First, the Agrarian Reform was greatly intensified with a very large number of farms being expropriated.[8] Second, a project for a Constitutional Amendment aimed at

[8]The agrarian reform law passed by Congress during the Frei administration provided the necessary tool. See Alaluf et al. (1972).

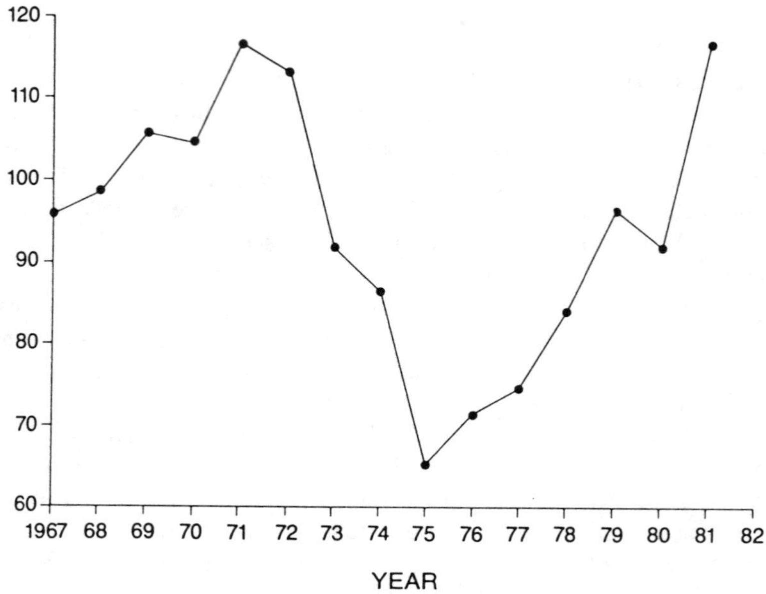

Fig. 1. Chile: The real wage (index 1967–69 = 100).

nationalizing the large copper mines – until then jointly owned by large U.S. firms and the Chilean state – was studied.[9]

In terms of macroeconomic policy, the government rapidly applied measures that were consistent with its program. Government expenditures greatly expanded and in 1971 real salaries and wages in the public sector increased by 48%, on average. Salaries in the private sector grew at approximately the same rate. Fig. 1 shows the gain in real wages during this year. The short-run package was topped by a generalized scheme of price controls.

In the first two quarters of 1971, manufacturing output increased 6.2% and 10.6% compared to the same periods in the previous year. Manufacturing sales grew at even faster rates: 12% during the first quarter and 11% during the second quarter. Overall, the behavior of the economy in 1971 seemed to vindicate the UP economists: real GDP grew at 7.7%, average *real* wages

[9]On June 11, 1971, Congress unanimously approved the constitutional reform that nationalized large copper mines. See Geller and Estevez (1972), and Ffrench-Davis and Tironi (1974). The reforms of the banking system and large manufacturing firms were somewhat more difficult, because the government lacked the institutional channels for implementing the nationalization program. Initially, this obstacle was overcome by purchasing blocks of shares – especially bank shares – at very high prices. These acquisitions were complemented by a process of requisition based on an old, and until then forgotten, decree law promulgated during the short-lived Socialist Republic of 1932.

increased by 17%, aggregate consumption grew at a real rate of 13.2%, and the rate of unemployment dipped below 4%. Not too surprisingly, given the behavior of real wages, there was a significant improvement in income distribution. In 1971 the labor's share of GDP reached 61.7%, almost 10 points higher than its 1970 level of 52.3%; and this happened without an acceleration of inflation. What was even more important for the UP was that the policies rapidly paid off politically. In the municipal elections of 1971, the UP parties saw their share of the vote climb from the 36% they had received in the 1970 presidential election to around 50%.[10]

All of this created a sense of euphoria in the government. The fact that the fiscal deficit had jumped from less than 3% of GDP in 1970 to almost 11% in 1971 did not worry the UP technocrats. Nor did they think much on the fact that the rate of growth of the money supply had surpassed 100% in annual terms in the fourth quarter of 1971, and that the rate of growth of domestic credit to the public sector was approaching 300%. All of this, in fact, was part of the plan [see Lopez (1972)].

Of course, these macro policies were rapidly generating a situation of repressed inflation. The high growth rate of GDP in 1971 rested heavily on an almost 40% increase in the imports of intermediate goods. As a result, the stock of international reserves inherited by the Allende government was reduced by more than one-half in that year alone. A steep reduction of inventories was another important factor contributing to the expansion of consumption. By the end of 1971, the mounting inflationary pressures became evident (see table 1). The supply problem was aggravated by a series of labor disputes in many large establishments that resulted in the takeover of those firms by their workers. In fact, this procedure became the institutionalized way in which the government seized a large number of firms.[11]

4.3. Phase II: Inflation, bottlenecks and failed stabilization programs

During 1972, the macroeconomic problems continued to mount. Table 1 shows that inflation reached 217% and the fiscal deficit surpassed 13% of GDP. Domestic credit to the public sector grew at almost 300%, and international reserves dipped below $77 million. Consumption growth dominated the expansion in demand (see table 2).

The underground economy grew as more and more activities moved out of the official economy, and as a result more and more sources of tax revenues

[10]The strong showing in early municipal or Congressional elections was not uncommon in Chile. In fact, the Frei government had a similar experience in 1965.

[11]See Dornbusch and Edwards (1989) for a more detailed discussion of the nationalization process. See, also, Alaluf et al. (1972).

Table 1

Chile: Main macroeconomic indicators.

	1970	1971	1972	1973
Inflation[a]	34.9	34.5	216.7	605.9
Growth	2.1	9.0	−1.2	−5.6
Real wages (1970: 3 = 100)	98.4	115.1	103.5	70.3
Government revenue[b]	23.7	20.4	18.2	20.2
Government spending[b]	26.4	31.1	31.2	44.9
Budget deficit[b]	2.7	10.7	13.0	24.7
Money growth[a]	52.9	99.3	100.9	264.4
International reserves ($ million)	320	129	95	36
Trade balance ($ million)	246	73	−161	−73
Black market premium (%)	99	358	898	2349

[a]Percent, Dec.–Dec.
[b]Percent GDP.

Sources: Banco Central de Chile; International Monetary Fund; Edwards (1986); Edwards and Cox-Edwards (1987); Solimano (1988).

Table 2

Chile: The growth rate of real GDP and demand (percent per year).

	1970	1971	1972	1973
GDP	2.1	9.0	−1.2	−6.6
Consumption				
Private	−0.5	13.2	7.7	−6.6
Government	5.9	12.4	5.7	1.7
Investment	6.5	−2.0	−20.1	−6.0
Exports	2.1	0.8	−15.1	2.8
Imports	0.9	8.5	3.2	−5.4

Source: Banco Central de Chile, *Indicadores Economicos y Sociales 1960–1985*.

disappeared. A vicious cycle took over; repressed inflation encouraged the informal economy, resulting in reduced taxes, higher deficits, and, thus, in even higher inflation. In 1972, two stabilization programs were implemented, and boith failed.

When evaluating the difficulties, the dominant view among UP economists was that the authorities had failed to impose appropriate controls in implementing the macroeconomic program [Garcia (1972)]. This view guided the first, rather weak, attempt at stabilizing the economy which was launched in February of 1972. No serious measures aimed at correcting the major macroeconomic causes of these problems were undertaken. It simply was not convenient to reduce government expenditures, the policy of granting salary

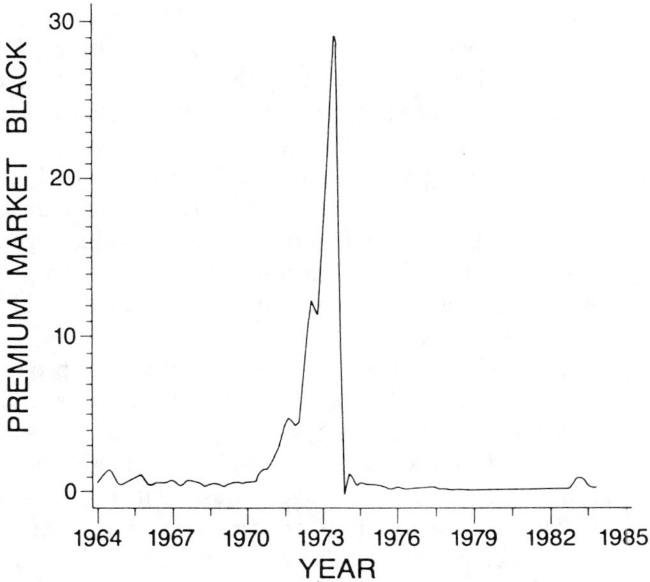

Fig. 2. Chile: The black market for dollars.

increases that exceeded inflation was maintained, and a significant devaluation was ruled out.[12]

The most serious problem was the loss of control over wages. Unions in both nationalized and private firms demanded increasingly higher wage adjustments. The government faced a dilemma. If it refused to grant the wage adjustments, it would help the macroeconomy, but would hurt its political objectives. Under these circumstances, the government chose, every time, to uphold its revolutionary label.[13]

By mid-1972, it became apparent that the February stabilization program was a failure. The underground economy was now generalized, output began to fall, open inflation reached an annual rate of 70% in the second quarter, foreign exchange reserves were only $82 million, and the black market rate was climbing at a very fast pace (see fig. 2). From a political perspective, parliamentary elections scheduled for March of 1973 made the situation particularly difficult. An economic crisis would work against the UP in those elections. In August of that year, and under the political monitoring of the Communists, a new stabilization program was launched.

Unlike the previous plan, the cornerstone of the August program was a massive devaluation of the escudo. It was expected that, as a result, the ever-

[12]In 1971 a small devaluation was followed by the creation of four different exchange rates.

[13]Moreover, a number of economists argued that higher real wages could be sustained as long as the government was able, via increased controls, to extract additional 'surplus' from the private sector. See Bitar (1979).

mounting pressures on the balance of payments would subside. The program also called for two basic measures to contain the fiscal pressures. First, price increases for the nationalized firms were authorized so as to reduce the financing requirements of the newly formed nationalized sector. Second, the program called for a massive increase in production as the major way to close the gap between aggregate supply and aggregate demand. This increase in output was expected to be a response to *political* rather than economic incentives. In fact, at that time, the Communist Party's main slogan became 'Let's win the battle for increased production!'. The devaluation and a large number of price increases resulted in a monthly rate of inflation of 22.7% in August and 22.2% in September.

In spite of the action taken on the exchange rate front, the program failed as no change in the wage rates policy was introduced. In the second week of August, the government announced that it had reached an agreement with the national federation of workers (Central Unica de Trabajadores, CUT) with respect to an across-the-board wage adjustment to be granted on October 1st, except for firms subject to private bargaining. The new wage policy called for an increase in public and private sector wages by a proportion equal to the accumulated rate of inflation between January and September. In addition, the new policy called for more frequent wage adjustments (*Que Pasa*, no. 70, Aug. 17, 1972, p. 14). In this way, by a stroke of the pen, the effects of the devaluation were fully offset.

4.4. Phase III: Acceleration of inflation and chaos

During the first quarter of 1973 Chile's economic problems reached chaotic proportions. Compared to the first quarter of 1972, inflation reached an annual rate of more than 120%; industrial output declined by almost 6%; the real exchange rate was even more overvalued, and foreign exchange held by the Central Bank was barely above $40 million. The black market by then covered an ever widening range of transactions in foreign exchange. The fiscal deficit continued to climb as a result of ever higher expenditures and of rapidly disappearing sources of taxation. In that year, the fiscal deficit exceeded 23% of GDP.

Once more the policymakers faced the options of implementing a major corrective stabilization program or of furthering the extent of controls. And once again they opted, in March of 1973, for the latter. The extent of the economic crisis quickly alienated the middle classes, and the political confrontation with the opposition became increasingly severe.[14]

[14]Of course, it must be remembered that, in the midst of this polarization, the support commanded by Allende actually grew: whereas in 1970 the UP received the votes of 30% of the electorate, in the municipal elections of 1971 it reached 50% and even in 1973 its share still stood at 44%.

In concluding, we must comment on the role of domestic economic opposition and the foreign economic blockade. The strategic use of economic disruption by the opposition, foreign enterprises and foreign governments indeed played a role in the ultimate unravelling of the Allende policies. A more neutral external environment probably would have allowed the Allende experiment to continue for some time. But the uncontrolled side effects of the consumption growth policy (shortages, inflation and related effects) sufficiently weakened the ability to govern.[15] As a result, destabilization by domestic opposition forces and foreign companies and governments could be effective. We advance this view as a hypothesis.

On the 11th of September 1973, the Allende presidency came to a sudden and shocking end. When the military took over, the country was politically divided and the economy was in shambles. Inflation was galloping, relative price distortions – stemming mainly from massive price controls – were generalized; black market activities were rampant; real wages had dropped drastically; the economic prospects of the middle class had been greatly damaged; the external sector was facing a serious crisis; production and investment were falling steeply; and the government finances were completely out of hand. This was the beginning of Phase IV, a stage where frightful real wage cutting (see fig. 1 above) took over.

5. Growth with redistribution in Garcia's Peru

When Alan Garcia assumed the Peruvian Presidency in August 1985, he captured the world's imagination: a dynamic, charismatic leader taking charge of a country desperately in need of social and economic progress. The fact that he adopted a confrontational attitude on external debt did not hurt his image, either in Latin America or in progressive circles in Europe and the United States. On the domestic front, he had an unambiguous message: growth and redistribution. That policy lasted two years before running aground in a catastrophic manner.

In early 1988, Alan Garcia's populist government staged a dramatic turnaround on the policies that had driven the country to bankruptcy: budget cutting, real wage cutting and massive exchange depreciation were the predictable aftermath of three years of reckless mismanagement. But that was not the end of the story, hyperinflation was to follow and the political consequences of economic destruction and pauperization are still to come. Real wage cutting and yet worse poverty, in the Peruvian context, may well

[15]Rosenstein-Rodan [in Orrego Vicuna (1975, pp. 219–220)] notes of the Allende policies, oriented toward consumption: 'This part of Allende's policies was more Populism than Socialism. Even Fidel Castro is supposed to have observed 'Marxist socialism is a revolution of production – this is a revolution of consumption'.

Table 3

Peru: Growth and inflation (percent per year).

	1950–60	1960–70	1970–75	1975–80	1980–85
Growth per capita	2.8	2.6	1.6	−1.0	−4.2
Inflation	8.0	9.3	12.6	50.0	102.1

Source: Kuczynski (1977), Central Bank and Ministry of Finance.

be the opening phase for massive and perhaps violent confrontations.[16] In the rest of this section we analyze in some detail the recent experience with populist policies in Peru. The analysis shows a remarkable similarity between this case and the Chilean episode.

5.1. *From Belaunde to Garcia*

In the 1950s and 1960s Peru experienced significant growth of real per capita income and moderate rates of inflation.[17] Table 3 shows that the problems of declining per capita income and high inflation date from the second half of the 1970s.

In the past 25 years, three major stop-go phases can be discerned. The first was the Belaunde expansion which crashed in 1967–68. The second phase ran until 1974. During this period the extremely favorable world environment permitted a massive expansion until 1974, with an average growth rate of per capita income of 3.7% per year in the 1969–74 period (see fig. 3).

The second Belaunde administration (1980–85) had to cope with extraordinarily adverse conditions. Belaunde inherited an economy with deep social problems: Per capita income had declined since 1974 and, the external balance improvement of the late 1970s notwithstanding, the interventionism of the military government had created pervasive distortions. The possibility of advancing the economy was drastically limited as a result of a combination of shocks: the world recession of 1980–82, terms of trade deterioration, the explosion in world interest rates and the resulting rise in debt service obligations, external credit rationing, and natural disasters. These shocks combined to choke off any room for expansion. In 1982–83, under an IMF program, real GDP per capita declined by 16% and inflation nearly doubled to 112%.

[16]More so than in any other country of Latin America, economic performance is central to maintaining the very precarious social peace in Peru. At issue is not only the possible confrontation between left and right. Far more dangerous is the widening conflict opened by the Maoist *Shining Path* guerrilla. The outcome is wide open because of the divisions between rich and poor, the city and the sierras, white and indios.

[17]See Thorp (1987), Thorp and Bertram (1978), and Kuczynski (1977) for history and extensive references.

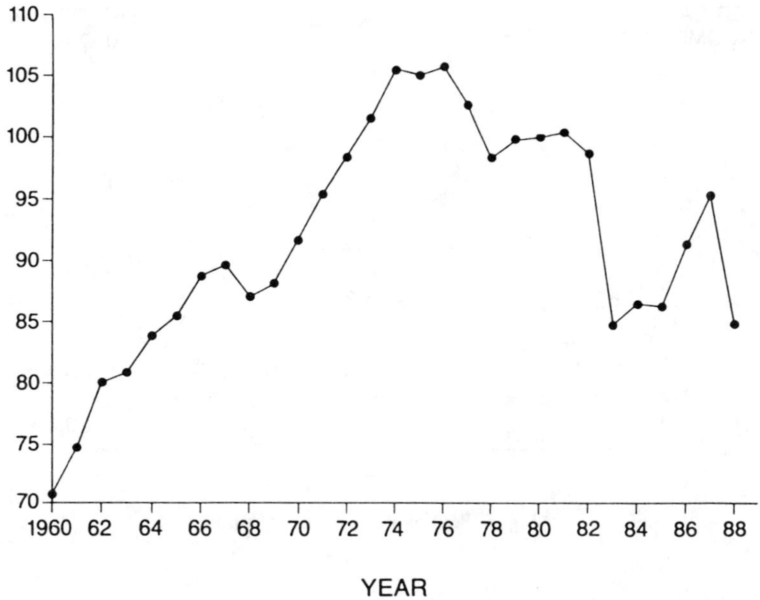

Fig. 3. Peru's real per capita income (index 1980 = 100).

This disastrous economic performance of the Belaunde government led to a total rout in the elections and thus brought Alan Garcia into power in 1985 with 45.8% of the votes.[18] The election which swept Garcia into office in a landslide victory carried one clear message: growth first! [see Ortiz de Zevallos (1989)]. This message, regardless of its feasibility, conditioned the economic policies of the Garcia Administration from the very beginning and is now taking the country to the brink.

5.2. Diagnosis and policies: The heterodox program

In July 1985, the last month of the Belaunde administration, inflation reached 250% at an annual rate. Unemployment was pervasive, idle capacity abounded, and real wages had been reduced in an effort to cope with the external crisis. Against this background, Garcia's government developed a populist project of expansion, entitled 'Growth with Redistribution', which emphasized economic recovery combined with disinflation.

Premises and policies. Three points are central to an understanding of why economic policy took the form it did. The first is the impressively unequal distribution of income. Fig. 4 shows the income distribution in Peru with a

[18]See Wise (1988) and Ortiz de Zevallos (1989) for a review of politics.

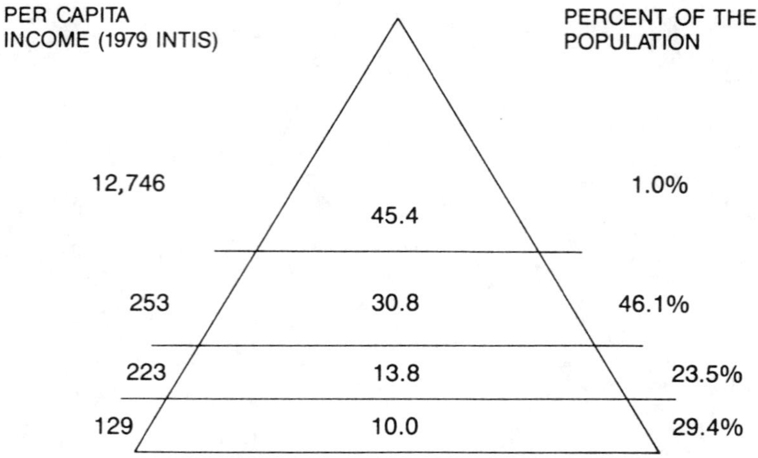

Fig. 4. Peruvian income distribution.

diagram widely used by the authorities. The striking fact is that 1% of the population receives nearly half the national income [see Glewwe (1988)].

The second is that policymakers were impressed with the large gap between actual and perceived potential output. In Carbonetto et al. (1987, p. 41), it is estimated that actual output was only 66% of potential output in 1984, leaving a 34% gap to be made up by the judicious choice of policy.

The third consideration is that Peruvian economists, in company with economists throughout Latin America, were unimpressed with the effectiveness of IMF programs. It should be remembered that at this time Israel and Argentina made their heterodox stabilization efforts, as did Brazil shortly afterwards. The orthodox approach to stabilization had been discredited by the strong recessionary effects and the absence of any success stories. The alternative, heterodoxy, had all the appeal of offering an end to inflation without the attendant costs of unemployment.[19]

Against this background, the general theme of economic policy was summarized in the *Plan Nacional de Desarrollo 1986–90* (p. 63) from which we quote extensively.

> The new economic policy seeks to pass from an economy of conflict and speculation to one of production and consensus. In this economy it is

[19]See Dornbusch (1982, 1988a), Bresser Pereira and Nakano (1987), and Bruno et al. (1988).

> possible to make compatible stability, growth, distribution and development in a context of national planning which finds concrete expression in dialogue and social and economic concertation.
>
> Planning of economic development will be full, decentralized and participatory and concertation will center on the effort to make compatible the generation of savings and productive investment with attention paid to the undelayable priority of attending to social needs. We need to reconcile economic efficiency with social equity in a productive dynamics which is fundamentally sustained by domestic resources.

Specific premises and prescriptions in the national development strategy can be paraphrased as follows [Plan Nacional de Desarrollo 1986–90 (pp. 63–65)]:

- The necessity to redistribute income as a means for sustained growth and the possibility to bring together with the redistribution process the necessary capacity to save and invest.
- Salaries and profitability: The generalized and open-ended restraint on wages reduces profitability because it reduces workers' purchasing power, bringing about recessive effects that reduce demand and thus the benefits of a dynamic economy.
- The fiscal deficit: The fiscal deficit is not necessarily inflationary. It only is so if domestic demand exceeds potential output. With substantial idle capacity there is a need for a certain deficit.
- Money creation: Must increase demand, thus allowing an increase in real liquidity since the opposite would slow growth.
- Interest rates: Increased real interest rates do not raise savings, since the latter depend fundamentally on income, but they discourage productive investment.

The specific targets of the economic program are set out in table 4. The new economic policy was based on four measures [Carbonetto et al. (1987, p. 15)] which in many ways resemble the Allende policies which we discussed above:

- Rapid expansion of effective demand via real wage increases.
- Financial de-strangulation to give firms relief and contain cost pressures by reducing financial costs of enterprises, effective interest rates, indirect taxes and other elements of costs.
- Reestablishment of selective exchange rates and abandonment of the devaluation policy.
- The external accounts were to be kept in balance by the growth in exports, import substitution and limitations on debt service to be compatible with acceptable growth. Of course, many of the foreign exchange and growth

Table 4

The 1986–90 Peruvian economic development plan.

	1985	1986	1987	1988	1989	1990
Growth						
GDP	1.4	6.5	6.2	6.1	6.3	6.2
Consumption	0.1	8.5	6.3	5.7	5.0	5.2
Exports	3.5	−13.6	4.8	5.8	5.9	5.9
Imports	−24.6	5.0	13.7	11.9	5.6	7.4
Investment	−12.3	12.0	14.4	11.8	11.6	10.7
Budget deficit[a]	0.6	2.3	2.3	2.1	1.8	1.6

[a]Percent of GDP.

Source: Presidencia de la Republica (1986).

Table 5

Peruvian macroeconomic indicators.

	1985	1986	1987	1988
Inflation[a]	158	63	115	1722
Growth	2.5	9.5	6.9	−8.4
Real wage[b]	111	126	137	105
Trade balance ($)	1173	−67	−463	−84
Government revenues[c]	42.7	32.1	25.9	23.5

[a]December–December.
[b]Index July, 1985 = 100.
[c]Percent of GDP.

Source: World Bank, Ministry of Finance, National Institute of Planning.

policies on which any success of the plan might have depended never saw the light of day. This is particularly the case for foreign exchange savings strategies.

5.3. *Phase I: The first two years*

The immediate priority for the Garcia administration was to introduce a 'heterodox' program of stabilization: inflation reduction via an incomes policy combined with a massive reactivation of the economy.

In the short term, the heterodox program was immensely successful. Inflation declined sharply (as shown in table 5), employment increased, and the real wage was pushed up substantially (as shown in fig. 5). In the last quarter of 1987, the real wage stood 52% above the level of 1985. Growth, too, had been very substantial. In 1986, the economy grew by 9.5%; and, in 1987, by another 6.9%.

It is important to recognize just how successful the heterodox approach is. Given enough foreign exchange and a depressed economy, expansion of

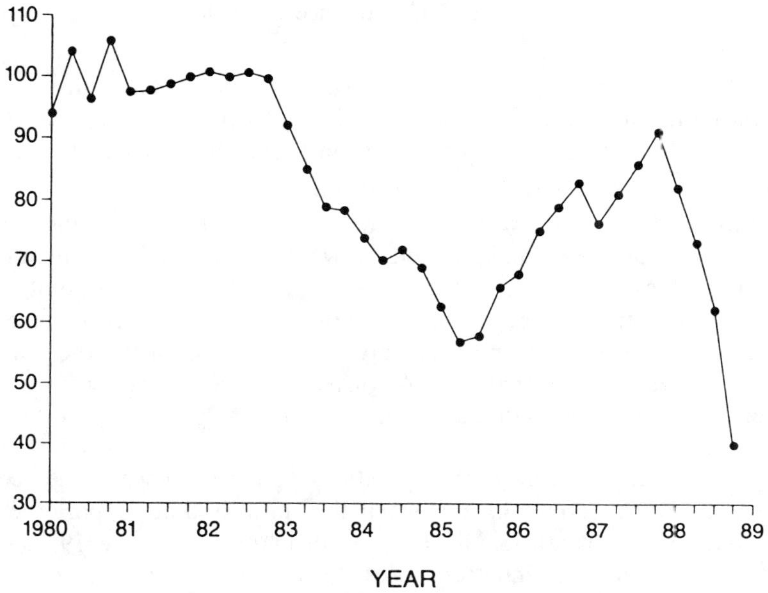

Fig. 5. Peru: The real wage (index 1982:2 = 100).

domestic demand can work. In fact, the success is broadly shared because the recovery of demand can raise firms' profitability by raising capacity utilization. That was indeed the case in Peru. A year after the program started Garcia was celebrated by the business class for the success of his recovery strategy. Private investment increased by 24% in 1986 and another 18.6% in 1987.[20]

By early 1987, the program was at the peak of its success: real GDP had grown cumulatively more than 20% since the third quarter of 1985, while inflation had been reduced from 188% to only 75%. Despite the startling success, the strain was starting to appear in rising cost pressures and a growing loss of foreign exchange. However, as in the case of Allende's Chile, these strains were obvious to economists, but were far from alarming to policymakers or the public.

5.4. Phase III: Inflation and collapse

The turning point came in July 1987, in the form of a political conflict that erupted as a result of a proposal to nationalize the banking system. On July

[20]See Centro de Economia Aplicada (1988) and especially Iguiniz (1988) for an evaluation of the first three years of the program.

27th, 1987, President Garcia declared [see Presidencia de la Republica (1987b, p. 1)]:

> In Peru, today, the financial system is the most powerful instrument of concentration of economic power and thus of political influence; it is the major obstacle to the democratization of production and the accumulation of the surplus.

At this time the right, with public appearances of Vargas Llosa, dramatized the shift in government policies toward socialism. This juncture also represented the end of the recovery policy and the turning point toward inflation and foreign exchange crises. Although the constraints tightened only gradually and bottlenecks emerged only in few places, during the remainder of 1987, it is fair to say that July–August of that year represented a crucial period, after which the continuation of expansionary policies could no longer be defended.

Populist programs such as that practiced in Peru fail when the economy runs out of foreign exchange and when the controls that support the initial redistribution and expansion have to be dismantled. By late 1987, growth was petering out and inflation, brought about by external constraints, bottlenecks and the adjustment of severe price distortions, exploded.

To understand what went wrong it helps to return to the basic philosophy of the program. This is fully documented in *El Peru Heterodoxo: Un Modelo Economico*, a 500-page book published in mid-1987 by the economic architects of the program [see Carbonetto et al. (1987)]. The most striking revelation of this book is the extraordinary extent to which policymakers in the Garcia administration, as had the Allende policymakers before them, diverged from accepted economics. Thus we learn (pp. 75–76) that

> An examination of the Peruvian record reveals that periods of moderate inflation are associated with expansionary fiscal policies. And periods of major inflation are associated with fiscal restraint. Thus, the record shows exactly the opposite of what is predicted by a theory which explains inflation by fiscal deficits.

And, to dispel any doubts (p. 82):

> If it were necessary to summarize in two words the economic strategy adopted by the government starting in August 1985 they are *control* (meaning control of prices and costs and recognizing that this could be done only temporarily for the first twelve months) and *spend*, transferring resources to the poorest so that they increase consumption and create a demand for increased output, thus 'justifying' that idle capacity be put to use.
>
> It is necessary to spend, even at the cost of a fiscal deficit, because, if this deficit transfers public resources to increase consumption of the poorest they demand more goods and this will bring about a reduction

Table 6

Peru: Real levels of controlled prices (July 1985 = 100).

	Dec. 1986	Dec. 1987	Dec. 1988
Average[a]	75	59	58
Rice	73	61	47
Light, electricity	49	40	16
Telephone	84	87	32
Gas	58	33	25

[a]Weighted by expenditure shares.

Source: *Apoyo*.

in unit costs. Thus the deficit is not inflationary, on the contrary! This constitutes without doubt the basic premise on which the economic team acted and the major departure from the earlier strategy that had emphasized adjustment from the demand side.

Peru learned in 1987–88 that there indeed are serious tradeoffs in policy: continued rapid growth and massive real wage increases are incompatible with moderate inflation.[21] In 1986 inflation was only 63%, far below the level at which the program started. But the experience of high growth with moderate inflation, after a while, became an artifact of the controls and subsidies on public sector prices and on foreign exchange. Subsidies and controls were used to avoid price increases in politically sensitive areas. In 1987–88, most petroleum products sold at one-third their July 1985 price. Electricity prices, the price of rice, and bus fares had declined by more than a third, as had the real price of foreign exchange (see table 6).

5.5. Phase III: The hyperinflation

When adjustments in the controlled prices had to be made, inflation accelerated rapidly.[22] Naturally, the massive increase in the budget deficit also contributed to the acceleration of inflation. The deficit, in turn, greatly increased as a consequence of a massive policy of subsidies, and as a result of the extraordinary decline in real tax collection (see table 7). In 1975–86, tax collection had averaged above 12% of GDP, and in 1985, it rose to 13.2%. However, by 1988, and as a result of a sharp decline in compliance, tax collection had fallen to only 7.5% of GDP. Additionally, the Central Bank's policy of multiple exchange rates contributed in an important way to the deficit. This policy alone resulted in losses amounting to 2% of GNP from buying foreign exchange at a high price from exporters and selling it at a low or subsidized price to importers.

[21]This, of course, is exactly what we point out in our model in section 2.
[22]See Dornbusch and Edwards (1989) for further details on this issue.

Table 7

Peru: Public sector financing requirement (percent of GDP).

	1985	1986	1987	1988[a]
Overall public sector deficit	4.4	6.7	9.9	6.1
Budget deficit	2.4	4.9	6.5	5.3
Central Bank losses	1.9	1.8	2.8	0.8
Credit to development banks	0.8	1.4	1.9	0.8
Public sector financing requirement	5.1	8.1	11.2	6.9
Domestic financing	1.2	5.7	9.8	6.9

[a]Estimate.

Source: World Bank, Central Bank and Ministry of Finance.

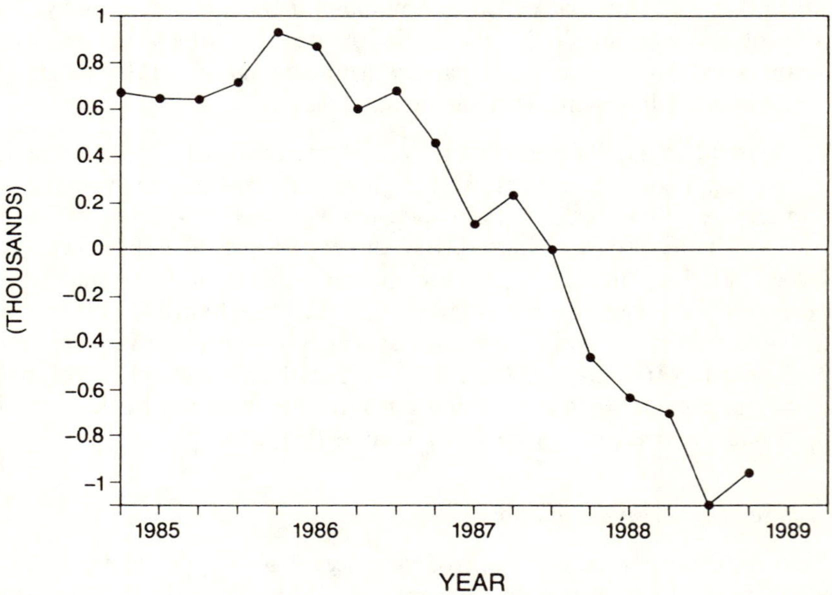

Fig. 6. Peru: Net foreign reserves (billion $U.S.).

The large budget deficit not only contributed to inflation, but also affected the allocation of credit and hence investment. While foreign exchange reserves lasted, the government could sell foreign exchange rather than borrow in the home market or print money. However, with reserves precariously low, there was no room left for further foreign exchange sales to finance the deficit (see fig. 6).[23] The declining reserves forced a more

[23]The net reserves included on the liability side $800 million of arrears to the IMF. The gold position of the central bank had been revalued at various points and amounted to $659 billion in December 1988.

consistent exchange rate policy which immediately raised the inflation rate. Thus external financing of the budget deficit ultimately had an inflationary cost, even though it may have been delayed by a year or two.

As has traditionally been the case in populist experiences, the government also resorted to the banking system to help finance the deficit. High reserve ratios for banks or direct financing requirements effectively achieved this. The counterpart of this policy was a 30% decline in real bank credit to the private sector in three years.

Since September 1987, the World Bank and Peruvian authorities had been discussing stabilization. But the political impetus for major policy changes was missing. The only impetus for change came from the external balance side where a crisis had been building up quite visibly. The trade surplus of above $1 billion in 1985 had become a deficit by 1987. Reserves declined by over $1 billion to the point where net reserves were negative at the beginning of 1988. The response to the looming foreign exchange crisis was a major devaluation in late 1987, which in the short run resulted in a small real depreciation. This helped stem capital flight and the widening trade deficit for some time. However, as in Allende's Chile, shortly after this corrective step, generalized and massive wage increases were granted. In a vicious cycle, then, accelerating wage and price increases eroded the initial gain in competitiveness. The renewed appreciation of the real exchange rate for imports since the end of 1987, and the resulting exchange losses of the central bank, signal the government's inability to force a real depreciation.

5.6. Phase IV: What next?

Economic mismanagement need not be shortlived. If the politics are supportive and external destabilization is not a factor, such a regime can last another year or even more. At the time of this writing there seem to be few avenues open to Peru. One possibility is that Garcia makes time by radicalizing his own position and policies in the direction of socialism and increasing government intervention. A massive program of nationalizations and control, of the type Allende pursued in his last year, would give the government more than a few months of breathing space, except if it were overthrown.

But while there is apparent stability, the extreme reduction in living standards and the growing number of strikes do suggest that surviving to the elections in April 1990, will not be easy.[24] The very depth of the economic collapse in late 1988 caused so sharp a fall in imports that the external constraint, for a while, was lessened. The real exchange rate in the informal

[24]By April 1989 the decline in economic activity and the restrictions of imports had become so massive that an actual reserve recovery had taken place. The reserve gains were sufficient to feed a rumor of another reactivation program.

Table 8

Peru: Real wages and real per capita GDP: 1985–1989 (index July, 1985 = 100).

	Real wages			
	National average	Minimum wage	Government	Per capita GDP[b]
1985	111	120	113	100
1986	126	124	118	107
1987	137	131	136	112
1988	105	118	101	110
1989[a]	56	64	43	81[c]

[a]July 1989.
[b]Index, 1985 = 100.
[c]April 1989.
Source: Peru: Ministry of Economics.

market actually declined to pre-1987 levels. But the collapse of real wages and activity was devastating. In fact, official estimates placed the decline in per capita real income, between 1987 and April 1989, at 25% (see table 8). Just how far the disintegration of the economy has gone is apparent from a survey in January 1989 reported by *Apoyo*, an economic consulting service in Peru. Middle and upper income respondents predominantly indicated that they would buy dollars given extra income. Of the lower income groups, more than half reported that they would spend the extra income on food.

6. Concluding remark

It is clear that the two instances of populism discussed here led to disastrous consequences for those who were meant to be the beneficiaries. The central question then is whether populist policies are outright unsustainable, or whether there is a variant which, properly executed can in fact succeed. We leave to further research the elaboration of the thesis that expansionary policies – somewhat similar in spirit to populist policies – can succeed provided they stay far clear of foreign exchange constraints, emphasize reactivation only for a brief initial period and then shift to growth policies. Most important for success, expansionary policies need to be aware of capacity constraints and have to rely for their financing on an extremely orthodox fiscal policy and rigorous tax administration. Within those restrictions it would appear that there is room left for achieving redistributive objectives in an effective way.[25]

[25]See Dornbusch and Edwards (1989) for a detailed discussion on three alternative future scenarios for Peru. See Edwards (1989) for a discussion on the inability of the Peruvian advisors to learn from the Chilean experience.

When looking forward into the next few years, one cannot avoid wondering whether economic systems have 'memory', and whether the mistakes of past populist regimes have been learned. This question is particularly relevant for the Chilean case where in March 1990 a new government – in all likelihood of centre-left persuasion – will face urgent and immediate pressures to improve the social conditions of the poor. Needless to say it is not possible to answer this question today. However, both the writings of the economic team of the likely new Chilean government, as well as the economic program of the *Concertación*, do suggest that some of the more important lessions regarding the design of economic policy have indeed been absorbed. Only the passing of time will allow us to verify this conjecture.

References

Almeyda, C., 1987, Reecuentro con mi Vida (Ediciones del Ornitorrinco, Santiago).

Alaluf, D. et al., 1972, La Economia Chilena en 1971 (Instituto de Economia, Universidad de Chile, Santiago).

Baer, W. and I. Kersternetzky, 1964, Inflation and growth in Latin America (Yale University Press, New Haven, CT).

Bitar, S., 1979, Transición, Socialismo y Democracia (Siglo XXI, Mexico, D.F.).

Bitar, S., 1986, Chile. Experiment in democracy (Institute for the Study of Human Issues, Philadelphia, PA).

Bresser Pereira, L.C. and Y. Nakano, 1987, Inertial inflation (Westview Press, Boulder, CO).

Boorstein, E., 1988, Allende's Chile (International Publishers, New York).

Bruno, M., G. di Tella, R. Dornbusch and S. Fischer, 1988, Inflation stabilization. The experience of Israel, Argentina, Brazil, Bolivia and Mexico (MIT Press, Cambridge, MA).

Carbonetto, D. et al., 1987, El Peru Heterodoxo: Un Modelo Economico (Instituto Nacional de Planificacion, Lima).

Centro de Economia Aplicada, 1988, Evaluacion de dos años y medio de Gobierno, Julio 1985–Diciembre 1987 (CEA, Lima).

Conniff, M., 1982, Latin American populism in comparative perspective (University of New Mexico Press, Albuquerque, NM).

de Vlyder, S., 1974, Allende's Chile (Cambridge University Press, Cambridge).

Dornbusch, R., 1982, Stabilization policies in developing countries: What have we learned?, World Development 10, no. 9 [reprinted in: Dollars, debts and deficits, MIT Press, Cambridge, MA (1987)].

Dornbusch, R., 1988a, Inflation stabilization: The role of incomes policy and of monetization, in: Exchange rates and inflation (MIT Press, Cambridge, MA).

Dornbusch, 1988b, Peru on the brink, Challenge, Sept./Oct.

Dornbusch, R. and J.C. de Pablo, 1988, Deuda Externa e Inestabilidad Macroeconomica en Argentina (Editorial SudAmericana, Buenos Aires).

Dornbusch, R. and S. Edwards, 1989, Macroeconomic populism in Latin America, Working paper no. 2986 (NBER, Cambridge, MA).

Drake, P., 1982, Conclusion: Requiem for populism?, in: M.L. Conniff, ed., Latin American populism in comparative perspective (University of New Mexico Press, Albuquerque, NM).

Edwards, S., 1986, Stabilization with liberalization: An evaluation of ten years of Chile's experience with free market policies, 1973–1983, in: A. Choksi and D. Papageorgiou, eds., Economic liberalization in developing countries (Basil Blackwell, Oxford).

Edwards, S., 1989, The debt crisis and economic adjustment in Latin America, Latin American Research Review 3, 172–186.

Edwards, S. and A. Cox-Edwards, 1987, Monetarism and liberalization. The Chilean experiment (Ballinger, Cambridge, MA).
Falcoff, M., 1989, Modern Chile 1970–1989 (Transaction Publishers, New Brunswick, NJ).
Ffrench-Davis, R. and E. Tironi, eds., 1974, El Cobre en el Desarrollo Economico Nacional (Ediciones Nueva Universidad, Santiago).
Foxley, A., 1981, Stabilization policies and their effects on employment and income distribution, in: W. Cline and S. Weintraub, eds., Economic stabilization in developing countries (Brookings, Washington, DC).
Foxley, A., 1983, Latin American experiments in neoconservative economics (University of California Press, Los Angeles).
Foxley, A. and O. Munoz, 1974, Income redistribution, economic growth and social structure: The case of Chile, Oxford Bulletin of Economics and Statistics 36, no. 1.
Garcia, Norberto, 1972, Algunos Aspectos de la Politica de Corto Plazo en 1971, in: D. Alaluf et al., eds., La Economia Chilena en 1971 (Instituto de Economia de la Universidad de Chile, Santiago).
Geller, L. and J. Estevez, 1972, La Nacionalizacion del Cobre, in: D. Alaluf et al., eds., La Economia Chilena en 1971 (Instituto de Economia de la Universidad de Chile, Santiago).
Glewwe, P., 1988, The distribution of welfare in Peru 1985–1986, Mimeo. (World Bank).
Herrera, C. et al., 1987, Reactivacion y Politica Economica Heterodoxa 1985–1986 (Fundacion Friedrich Ebert, Lima).
Iguiniz, J., 1988, Evaluacion Critica de la Politica Economica Bajo Garcia: Balance a los Tres Anos de Gobierno, Mimeo. (Fondo de Region Andina, Lima).
Inostroza, A., 1979, El Programa Monetario y la Politica de Comercio Exterior de la Unidad Popular, Panorama Economico, March.
Kuczynski, P.-P., 1977, Peruvian democracy under economic pressure (Princeton University Press, Princeton, NJ).
Lopez, J., 1972, La Economia Politica de la Unidad Popular: Una Evaluacion de su Primer Año de Gobierno, in: D. Alaluf et al., eds., La Economia Chilena en 1971 (Instituto de Economia de la Universidad de Chile, Santiago).
Martner, G., ed., 1971, El Pensamiento Economico del Gobierno de Allende (Editorial Universitaria, Santiago).
Ministerio de Economia, 1987, Programa Trienal 1988–1990 (Ministerio de Economia, Lima).
Nove, A., 1976, The Political economy of the Allende Regime, in: P. O'Brien, ed., Allende's Chile (Praeger, New York).
Novoa, E., 1971, Vias Legales para Avanzar al Socialismo, Revista Mensaje 167.
ODEPLAN, 1971, Objetivos del Plan 1971, in: G. Martner, ed., El Pensamiento Economico del Gobierno de Allende (Editorial Universitaria, Santiago).
Oppenheim, L., 1989, The Chilean road to socialism revisited, Latin American Research Review 24, no. 1, 155–183.
Ortiz de Zevallos, F., 1989, The Peruvian puzzle (Twentieth Century Fund, New York).
Orrego Vicuna, F., ed., 1975, Chile: The balanced view (Institute of International Affairs, University of Chile, Santiago).
Pazos, F., 1972, Chronic inflation in Latin America (Praeger, New York).
Presidencia de la Republica, 1986, Plan Nacional de Desarrollo 1986–1990 (Instituto Nacional de la Republica, Lima).
Presidencia de la Republica, 1987a, Plan Nacional de Desarrollo 1988 (Instituto Nacional de Planificacion, Lima).
Presidencia de la Republica, 1987b, Porque la Estatizacion del Sistema Financiero Peruano (Instituto Nacional de Planificacion, Lima), Aug.
Presidencia de la Republica, 1987c, Diagnostico y Programacion 1987 (Instituto Nacional de Planificacion, Lima).
Ramos, J., 1980, The economics of hyperstagflation, Journal of Economic Development, 467–488.
Ramos, J., 1986, Neoconservative economics in the southern cone of Latin America, 1973–1983 (Johns Hopkins University Press, Baltimore, MD).
Rosenstein-Rodan, P., 1974, Why Allende failed, Challenge, May–June.

Sachs, J., 1989, Social conflict and populist policies in Latin America, Working paper no 2897, March (NBER, Cambridge, MA).
Seers, D., 1964, Inflation and growth: The heart of the controversy, in: W. Baer and I. Kerstenetzky, eds., Inflation and growth in Latin America (Yale University Press, New Haven, CT).
Solimano, A., 1988, Politica de Remuneraciones en Chile: Experiencia Pasada, Instrumentos y Opciones a Futuro, Coleccion Estudios Cieplan, no. 25, Dec. (CIEPLAN, Santiago).
Stallings, B., 1978, Class conflict and economic development in Chile, 1958–73 (Stanford University Press, Stanford, CA).
Stallings, B., 1988, Self-destruction of an auspicious initiative: Peruvian debt policy under Alan Garcia, Mimeo. (University of Wisconsin, Madison, WI).
Sunkel, O., 1960, Inflation in Chile: An unorthodox approach, International Economic Papers, no. 10, 107–131.
Thorp, R., 1987, Trends and cycles in the Peruvian economy, in: P. Bardhan et al., eds., International trade, investment, macro policies and history (North-Holland, Amsterdam).
Thorp, R. and G. Bertram, 1978, Peru 1890–1977 (Columbia University Press, New York).
Unidad Popular, 1969, Programa Basico de Gobierno (Editorial Universitaria, Santiago).
Vuskovic, Pedro, 1970, Distribucion del Ingreso y Opciones de Desarrollo, Cuadernos de la Realidad Nacional, Sept.
Vuskovic, Pedro, 1973, The economic policy of the Popular Unity government, in: J. A. Zammit, ed., The Chilean road to socialism (University of Texas Press, Austin, TX).
Wise, C., 1988, Peru in the 1980s: Political responses to the debt crisis, Mimeo. (Columbia University, New York).
World Bank, 1985, Peru. Country economic memorandum (World Bank, Washington, DC).
World Bank, 1988, Peru: Policies to stop hyperinflation and initiate economic recovery (World Bank, Washington, DC).
Yanez, J., 1978, Una Correccion del Indice de Precios al Consumidor Durante el Periodo 1971–73, in: F. Contreras, ed., Comentarios Sobre la Situacion Economica (Instituto de Economia de la Universidad de Chile, Santiago).
Zammit, J.A., ed., The Chilean road to socialism (University of Texas Press, Austin, TX).

Journal of Economic Perspectives—Volume 4, Number 3—Summer 1990—Pages 61–74

The Latin American State

Albert Fishlow

The role of the state in Latin American economic development is undergoing fundamental reconsideration. Even while political scientists have been bringing the state back in, economists have been busy trying to take it out (Evans, Rueschmeyer and Skocpol, 1985). Reduced government intervention has seemingly been the winning side. Earlier presumptions about the clear benefits of public guidance no longer orient development strategy in most countries in the region. Instead, there is new vitality to the claims for the advantages of market liberalization and privatization of state enterprise. An apparent new consensus regarding a diminished role for the state in Latin America has emerged, reinforced by the rising liberal tendencies in industrialized countries and the precipitate rejection of central planning in the socialist bloc.

This debate is central to development economics as a field, so much so that Deepak Lal (1985, p. 53) identifies its demise with this new recognition of the importance of "policy induced, and thus far from inevitable, distortions created by irrational dirigisme." But this reconsideration takes on a special significance in Latin America for two reasons. First, the model of state-led industrialization through import substitution is identified with the region. Raul Prebisch and the Economic Commission for Latin America (1950) were the most prominent advocates of this new, post-World War II development strategy, and it still is esteemed by many Latin Americans. Second, countries of the region have experienced a sharp break with past growth trends in the 1980s, experiencing a cumulative average decline in per capita income of some 10 percent during the decade. There is strong impetus for a new approach.

■ *Albert Fishlow is Professor of Economics at the University of California, Berkeley, California.*

This essay focuses on the reasons underlying the new commitment to reduced state participation. In particular, I suggest that the impetus comes less from newfound ideological conviction in the virtues of the market than from ineffective macroeconomic policy in the 1980s. The principal problem confronted by the countries of the region is a fiscal shortfall, not massive inefficiency resulting from misallocation of resources. Latin America is not Eastern Europe, where reform translates into elimination of the monopoly of state ownership and the structure of central command. Latin American countries have adhered to market capitalism, but without experiencing its magical effects in recent years. It is the contest between the micro- and macroeconomic explanations that illuminates why surface agreement on a reduced state role conceals a continuing divergence of views within the region.

Visible and Invisible Hands

At least through the early 1970s, development economics largely defined itself as a subfield by its emphasis upon market imperfections and the potential for Pareto-improving government intervention. Attention was especially directed to how government could seek out dynamic externalities and exploit large divergences between private and social rates of return to investment. The belief was that private markets would lead to inferior solutions if left to themselves. After all, historical reliance on markets had not closed the development gap.

The World Bank (1988, p. 49) has labeled such a perspective as the "public interest" view. One can separate out several components. First, there is a problem of providing public goods and infrastructure, where market response leads to inadequate supply or natural monopoly. Second, there are other market failures owing to externalities, imperfect information, and so on. Third, there is a need for state policy to determine appropriate levels of capital accumulation, since future generations are not well represented in private preferences. Finally, and not least, the concentration of private power and wealth constitutes a reason for state correction in the name of social justice and equality. This adds up to an active and positive role for the state through direct production of goods and services, management of revenues and expenditures and regulation of private activity.

In the specific context of Latin America, the theory of industrialization through import substitution enshrined almost all these principles. A pillar of the approach was the belief that static market signals overestimated the returns to primary exports because of potential deterioration of the terms of trade. Prebisch's emphasis upon an inevitably negative trend rang true scant years after the decline in commodity prices during the Great Depression. On the domestic side of the market, private rates of return underestimated the advantages of investment in industry, by neglecting the savings from avoiding costly imports, the benefits of technological and labor skill externalities and the consequences of coordinated production decisions. Individual consumption decisions, especially given the large disparities in income distribution, did not add up to an appropriate savings rate. The policy obligation of government was not only to offer the appropriate shadow prices through trade restrictions and credit and tax subsidies, but also to undertake complementary investment in infrastructure and strategic sectors and increase overall capital accumulation.

For some larger Latin American countries, principally Brazil and Mexico, import substitution policies were compatible with accelerated industrialization and high rates of aggregate growth. From 1953 to 1973, Brazil and Mexico increased their share of regional income from 43 to 54 percent, reflecting their relatively higher rates of growth. For other countries, the results were deficient. The share of regional income going to Argentina and Chile declined from 27 to 19 percent (ECLA, 1978).

But even where a strategy of import substitution worked, it was at the expense of growing disequilibrium in three critical dimensions. First, policy-induced exchange rate overvaluation discriminated against exports, especially non-traditional ones, making the balance of payments and access to essential imports more precarious. Second, an increase in government expenditures was not matched by increased tax revenues, thus giving rise to larger deficits financed primarily by accelerating inflation. Third, the emphasis upon industrialization frequently occurred at the expense of inadequate agricultural development that left significant pockets of rural poverty and hampered development of an ample internal market.

An import substitution strategy was deliberately unbalanced, and hence not permanently viable even where initially favorable. Successful implementation required timely adaptations to stimulate exports, enhance revenues and sustain increases in agricultural productivity. Few countries were so adroit. The first post-1945 development crisis in the region occurred in the early 1960s, as evidenced by an aggravating balance of payments problem and rising inflationary pressures afflicting many countries.

The external constraint and fiscal deficits motivated new efforts to increase inflows of public resources. Through the creation of the Inter-American Development Bank and establishment of the Alliance for Progress, assistance was provided to finance structural reforms. These were still much oriented to the domestic economy and in the spirit of public intervention. Indeed, planning was enshrined as a national requirement, and because of its political origins, the Alliance emphasized land reform and greater income equality.

Only by the mid-1960s, under continuing strains and sometimes under military aegis, did there begin to be wider acceptance of the importance of market signals and the opportunities for greater expansion of exports. Import substitution thus was not a monolithic or unchanging doctrine. By the time that a professional literature critical of the import substitution style of Latin American state intervention began to appear in the late 1960s and 1970s,[1] reality (and local criticism) had already made itself felt.

For Latin America as a whole, economic growth accelerated from 5.2 percent per year in the decade 1953–63 to 6.4 percent in 1963–73; the proportional increase in per capita performance was a much more dramatic 50 percent. The more successful countries were able to sustain a large public presence while also giving greater scope to market signals and the opportunities afforded by continuing expansion of international markets. Export performance, and access to imports, emerged as the most significant determinants of country growth rates during this period (Cardoso and Fishlow, 1989, p. 14).

Even the oil shock could be withstood, but at the expense of increased external indebtedness and deterioration of domestic policy in the more difficult external environment. Regional growth slowed after 1973, but was still higher than the results in other areas. The true precariousness of the Latin American situation only became apparent when the second oil shock coincided with an abrupt rise in real interest rates and OECD recession. Countries had chosen their new style of adjustment via debt rather than blindly following the original import substitution and interventionist model, and the choice was a bad one. Asymmetric integration into the world economy through financial flows instead of exports took a heavy toll. When voluntary capital inflows virtually ceased after 1982, the only immediate possibility was drastic reduction in imports and income. The rest of the decade has been characterized by large resource transfers, accompanied in most countries by high real interest rates, large deficits financed by internal debt, accelerating inflation and economic stagnation (Fishlow, 1986, 1988).

This Great Depression of the 1980s, made more pointed by Asian success, has directed attention to structural deficiency. External agencies, on which almost all countries came to rely, conditioned their money on a greater commitment to liberalization. Plans to assist with the debt burden, whether proposed by Baker or Brady, required evidence of emphasis on the private sector. At the same time, more open politics and a regular electoral calendar in most Latin American countries have assured mounting domestic debate and pressure to redefine the role of the state.

The outcome has been new emphasis upon the virtues of the invisible hand. That commitment has been given greater force by two theoretical amendments to the standard Pareto efficiency argument. First, the rent-seeking literature has emphasized the additional distortion created by "directly unproductive profit-seeking" activity in response to opportunities afforded by government intervention (Bhagwati, 1982; Krueger, 1974). Second, there has been a special emphasis upon outward orientation as the key source of successful economic development. A corollary proposition is also frequently implicitly or

[1]Among the critical literature, Little, Scitovsky, and Scott (1970) was first. But note that back in 1964, ECLA's *Economic Bulletin for Latin America* carried two articles critical of excessive protectionism and recognizing the end of the import substitution model.

explicitly added: liberalized domestic markets as well as freer imports are necessary to guarantee the competitiveness required for export growth.[2]

Despite their prominence, neither of these new criticisms of state intervention is decisive. They do not rule out the existence of externalities and imperfections that justified policy activism in the first place. The focus on rent-seeking correctly highlights the importance of how intervention is implemented, but in many cases only costs of response are reckoned, to the exclusion of positive benefits from public action. Even those costs are often assumed without regard to institutional mechanisms like auctions and performance-related allocation of subsidies that can do much to reduce the deadweight burden. The rent-seeking model posits a static competitive Eden as the counterfactual alternative rather than the reality of powerful private interests and inadequate price signals.

If anything, modern economic theory has reinforced a more skeptical view of laissez-faire. Incomplete markets, imperfect information, strategic interactions, principal-agent problems, transactions costs, and bounded rationality take up a large part of the microeconomic literature. Stiglitz (1988) sees this new theory as the unifying element in tackling development issues. Economies of scale, external economies, and path dependence are now at the heart of the new growth economics (Arthur, 1988; Shleifer, 1989).

The appeal of outward orientation is its empirical basis. The calculations of effective protection and the oft-replicated statistical linkage between export performance and economic growth lend support to the critique of dirigiste policy. Two cautionary notes are in order about these findings. The data do not speak with a single voice with regard to the virtues of outward orientation; and the contribution of liberalization to successful export growth remains a contentious one.

High effective protection levels frequently exaggerate actual productive inefficiency; tariff reforms are not followed by massive failures and significant reallocation of resources. Multiple cross-section studies demonstrating a favorable impact of exports on aggregate performance are not fully satisfying in three ways (Fishlow, 1989). First, causality remains an issue. Improved productivity yields greater international competitiveness as well as the other way around. A majority of countries fail a Sims-Granger causality criterion. Second, the source of improved performance may be excessively attributed to exports by the production function framework utilized; there is strong evidence that access to imports is equally or more important. That means that exports partially count for their earnings of foreign exchange, not their allocative benefits. Third, the favorable impact of export growth will be mediated by its form; export-led industrialization is different from specialization in exports that are resource-based.

[2]For a summary of the arguments concerning outward orientation, and more extensive references, see Krueger (1985) and Balassa (1989).

This is not an argument against fully exploiting international market opportunities. Latin American countries have no doubt exaggerated the benefits of a focus on the internal market. But that does not make an export emphasis the appropriate universal alternative. Export growth of 10 to 15 percent a year may not be feasible. Rather than such an ambitious export-led process of development, the objective for many countries should be an export-adequate strategy where diversifying exports regularly keep up with product growth and earn needed foreign exchange. Unlike the econometric inferences of an elasticity of output growth to export growth of .3, computable general equilibrium models show a much smaller effect of an order of .1 (Chenery, Robinson and Syrquin, 1986, pp. 321–22). Less is at stake.

But a still more critical question is the relationship between market signals and successful export penetration. Overvalued exchange rates are prejudicial. But simply getting them right, without other complementary policies that encourage investment and technological change, may not be enough. The response to the exchange rate depends not only on entrepreneurial capacity but the flexibility of the productive structure. The objective is not to get prices right in isolation, but to follow consistent policies long enough for productive transformation to occur. Liberalization of the financial system and trade may be the consequence of successful industrialization rather than the cause of competitive efficiency.

In sum, no one has yet shown that the failure of government intervention *necessarily* outweighs market failure. On the contrary, effective state action is widely regarded as an underlying feature of successful outward-oriented Asian economic performance. Westphal's paper in this symposium argues, as do many others, that Korea and Taiwan did not succeed in exports because of simple liberalization, but rather as a result of a conscious and state-directed development strategy. In Latin America as well, before this last dismal decade, the steady record of Brazilian and Mexican economic growth was associated with technocratic policy design and implementation.

Even if there has been implementation failure in Latin America, that is an argument for correcting it, not for pursuing a second-best policy of laissez-faire in the presence of externalities that can be exploited to accelerate economic development. Paradoxically, the very array of powerful private interests celebrated by the rent-seeking and related literature requires a strong state to manage successful reform. In the absence of state capacity, concentrated market and political power and other imperfections may make laissez-faire an *n*th-best choice.

From Satisfactory Performance to Stagflation: The Deficit as Cause

The argument in favor of an altered state role in Latin America has to come from the side of macroeconomic failure, not a debilitating sectoral misallocation. Despite a greater public presence in many countries in the 1970s, evidence suggests that there had already been more, not less, attention to market signals and international competitiveness. Despite the eloquence of Hernando de Soto (1989) in chronicling a stifling Peruvian mercantilism, the earlier tide of structuralism has been in retreat. In most of the region, rent-seeking was arguably less prevalent in the 1970s than it had been in the 1950s and 1960s, and export performance improved during the decade. Even in the dismal 1980s, according to the Inter-American Development Bank (1989, p. 4), "[E]xport activity has grown much more rapidly than the rest of the economy. ... [It] increased by 32.3 percent between 1980 and 1987, while the rest of the economy did so by only 7.4 percent."

Rather, the real villain of the piece is fiscal inadequacy.[3] This has made it more difficult for Latin American countries to adjust effectively to the less favorable external economic environment of the 1980s. The rise in world interest rates and an initially high external debt reflected itself in increased public expenditures. For the region, external debt service rose from about 3 percent of GNP in 1977–78 to as much as 8 percent in 1984, before falling to around 6 percent in the late 1980s (World Bank, 1984, 1989). Because much of the debt was public or publicly guaranteed, it helped to elevate interest costs to significant fractions of public expenditures: for large debtors the amounts were a fifth and more. Those countries that successfully managed the export surpluses required to effect the payment thus faced an internal transfer problem: how was the indebted public sector to acquire the foreign exchange?

The stylized answer is through increased domestic finance of an increased deficit. Despite some reduction in non-interest governmental expenditure, principally for investment, no full compensation occurred. Hence countries faced larger deficits and at the same time less access to foreign finance; that is what made it such a crisis. In aggregate, Latin American government deficits (after some correction for the inflation component of interest payments) rose from 4 percent of national product in 1980 to levels of 7 to 8 percent in the period 1981–87 (ECLA, 1989). Longer-term comparable data are available for Brazil, where government deficits (excluding the central bank component) rose from approximate balance in the early 1970s to 5 percent and more in the early 1980s.

The options for financing this deficit were either increases in real internal debt or a tax on financial intermediation: the inflation tax on base money plus indirect effects through reserve requirements and credit controls. For many countries, in the absence of a developed capital market, the only resort was accelerated inflation; for others, principally Brazil and Mexico, increased domestic debt figured prominently. Neither was a viable solution. As private agents protected themselves against the inflation tax, higher rates of inflation

[3]For recent treatment of, and extensive other references to the fiscal problem, see Reisen and von Trotsenburg (1988) and Easterly (1989). There is a considerable difficulty in assembling the comparable comprehensive data on the consolidated public sector needed for analysis.

were required, possibly extending well beyond the point of maximum revenue collection. As internal debt put pressure on domestic interest rates, not only was private investment crowded out, but interest payments themselves grew at faster rates than revenues. In the end, the financeable deficit compatible with stable inflation tended to decrease even while the actual deficit increased. Tax collections were eroded by accelerating inflation, directly through the Tanzi-Olivera effect[4] and indirectly by the increased incentives for evasion to compensate for reductions in wealth. Indexing assured that past inflation rates reproduced themselves.

Under these conditions, the deterioration in economic performance in Latin America is no great puzzle. Investment declined on the supply side, and demand was stifled to try to dampen inflation. Uncertainty was fed by the considerable variability in real magnitudes as inflation levels climbed. Public policy floundered between efforts to stabilize through fixing exchange rates and public sector prices, and price liberalization to reduce subsidies and public enterprise deficits.

By 1985, inflation necessarily became a principal preoccupation in several countries as it exceeded all previous bounds. The array of special circumstances elicited a heterodox response, the first of a series whose most recent manifestation was Brazil's March 1990 program. These plans, in their varying form in different countries, have much to say about the critical fiscal problem and the role of the Latin American state.

The Argentine Plan Austral and the Brazilian Plano Cruzado were the first, launched in 1985 and 1986, respectively. They started from a theory of inertial inflation. Both ended indexing arrangements that institutionalized adjustment to past inflation; wages were set to nominal levels corresponding to their real average over a previous period. Both promised more rigorous monetary and fiscal policy. Both anchored prices to a newly devalued and more realistic exchange rate. Both introduced new monetary units and froze prices and wages to create instantaneous disinflation. Both were launched in an overt political fashion by civilian presidents and gained initial widespread support.

After initial successes, both soon unravelled, as price and wage controls eroded and repressed inflation became overt. Despite a series of new partial programs in the same spirit, inflation soared. In Argentina it was necessary to advance the inauguration of a new president in 1989 as speculation defeated all attempts to stabilize; and in Brazil, inflation exceeded 70 percent a month in early 1990 in the last months of the lame-duck government.

By contrast, the Bolivian stabilization plan put in place in 1985 and the Mexican effort initiated in 1987 have thus far been more successful and enduring. The former, under conditions of hyperinflation and dollarization,

[4]The consequence of inflation in eroding real tax collections through sheer delay in receipt was given prominence, and empirical justification, in Tanzi (1977). The independent and earlier discovery by Julio Olivera, an Argentine economist, is usually given recognition by those steeped in the Latin American tradition.

relied on massive devaluation and a subsequently fixed exchange rate to anchor price stability. The latter was structured around a negotiated incomes policy to restrain inflation to lower levels of price and wage increase with the exchange rate again serving as anchor. In both, import liberalization was also pursued to provide an external check on domestic prices.

What especially characterizes both of these successful stabilization programs are much greater underlying fiscal discipline and restraint on demand than in Argentina or Brazil. In Bolivia, there were significant dismissals in state enterprises (in COMIBOL, the state mining company, from 30,000 to 7000) and a reduction in public sector real wages. Revenues from increased taxes on petroleum rose sharply in the short term, while more wide-ranging reform has proceeded more slowly. In Mexico, in 1987 the primary surplus (exclusive of interest payments) was already close to 5 percent of gross product; in both 1988 and 1989 the surplus continued to increase (CIEMEX-WEFA, 1990).

Rational expectations theory has been a misleading guide in its implication that inflation can be stopped at modest costs, something all too appealing to Latin American ears. There has been too much attention to changing expectations and establishing the credibility of fixed exchange rates and monetary restraint and too little to the need to remedy the underlying fiscal imbalance. The future orientation of the theory works best when there is a memory of earlier stability to which to return. In Latin America, the gold standard was itself less the rule than the exception; postwar inflation at high rates erased any residual memory.

Previous experiments with international monetarism in Chile and Argentina at the end of the 1970s foundered out of misplaced faith in an exchange rate anchor and the automaticity of adaptive international flows. The later heterodoxy in Argentina and Brazil, although more drastic as inflation has mounted to four digits, retained—at least until the latest effort in Brazil—a deep fear of recession as the counterpart of stabilization. What the Bolivian and Mexican experiences suggest is that the check to inflation is far from costless. Instantaneous conversion to belief in future price stability was less important than a soft economy that discouraged wage and price increases. External reserves and even explicit coordination can help, but in the end credibility has been earned the hard way.

The lesson is clear. It requires an effective state, not reliance on the market alone, to establish expenditure priorities and impose restraint. Inflation is symptomatic of a lack of command. Magic formulas don't work. They obscure the underlying lack of consensus within Latin American countries and ineffective mobilization of elite opinion that made it impossible to raise taxes early in the debt crisis or adequately to cope with a deteriorating fiscal balance in the 1950s and 1960s. External finance, and proliferation of the public sector, concealed the real weakness of the state during the 1970s.

Privatization may now be emerging as another panacea. It promises to satisfy the need for larger domestic finance, reduced public expenditure and greater productive efficiency all at the same time. Foreigners and internal interests alike find it easy to criticize overblown bureaucracies and overextension of state enterprises. But a closer look counsels caution.

First, the objectives may be inconsistent. Where the dominant motive is immediate finance, because of the salience of government deficits, it is the best-managed and most efficient enterprises that must go, reducing future net revenues. There is a tradeoff between present and future, not a pure gain. Fire sales of money-losing public enterprises are not likely to bring in much money. Recording the proceeds as revenue rather than as a means of financing the deficit gives too favorable an impression of the benefits.

Second, selling off the perpetual losers will only reduce future claims on public subsidies if macroeconomic policy is conducted better. Favored work rules, controls over prices and high levels of indebtedness help to explain poor bottom line results. Two of these factors do not operate at the enterprise level, and even wages and employment are not set entirely independently by private firms. Change in ownership alone does not make the crucial difference. Moreover, note that restructuring debt to make enterprises more attractive to new owners simply transfers the future interest payments to another part of the government accounts.

Third, promises of how privatization will increase efficiency may be overstated. Measuring productive efficiency in parastatal activities is not easy because cash flow results can distort. The very rapid growth of state enterprises during the 1970s—they multiplied by a factor of 2 and 3 times in several Latin American countries—was associated less with a comprehensive strategy of expansion in key sectors than financing balance of payments gaps. That is, Latin American governments used guaranteed loans for such enterprises as a means of increasing capital flows and access to foreign exchange. State enterprises remained with the specific financial liabilities, increased in real terms through devaluation and higher interest rates, although there was sometimes no counterpart in real investment. This problem is further compounded by the generalized tendency to place controls on public sector prices as a way to check accelerating inflation. New private owners may not be better managers. What may count more than ownership is greater exposure to competitive forces, possibly through import liberalization when the domestic market is small.

Fourth, it matters who buys and how. If credit is extended to finance purchases, the public deficit is reduced but not total demand. If private wealth is further concentrated by the acquisition of the new assets, pressures on public officials for special treatment will be enhanced rather than reduced. It is interesting that holders of the external debt have resisted conversion into equity of public enterprises; they prefer to use swaps for more attractive private assets.

In sum, the deep-seated deficit problem in Latin America and its attendant serious consequences permit no easy solution. The debt crisis of the 1980s has underlined the fragility of the state and its inability to respond to the less favorable external environment. Increasingly, the issue is not merely debt reduction but redesigning the Latin American state. In the last analysis, there is limited gain, both fiscally and in the balance of payments, that is available under the Brady plan to reduce the debt burden of Latin America.

Redesigning the Latin American Developmental State

There are two competing models of redesign. One starts by stripping away public functions and confidently assigning them to the private sector and the market. The other begins by confronting the central challenge of the public deficit and defining a new development strategy. Their partial congruence in some particulars creates not only a false impression of consensus, but leads to inconsistent policy. For where the first gives priority to a reduced state and slashed expenditures, the latter requires a stronger state and command over resources.

Although the multilateral institutions seem to favor immediate and wide-ranging liberalization, in conjunction with aggregate restraint, there is limited evidence to support such an approach, particularly where markets have been working. This shock therapy promises too much too quickly. One has to reduce inflation quickly when it has reached stratospheric levels, but that is only a first step. Initial success can help to restore confidence, but it can also promote a misplaced euphoria that conflicts with the institutional underpinning of fiscal responsibility that is at the heart of effective governance and economic development.

Countries in the region have become committed to change, but most are groping toward the second of these models. They are doing so both because liberalism is still not widely seen as an attractive doctrine, and because there is need to offer a developmental perspective to satisfy an increasingly frustrated populace. Pinochet's "Chilean miracle" is not an ideal that Latin Americans wish to emulate. Vargas Llosa's vision of a Peru radically transformed and democratized by deregulation is the exception that proves the rule, and has not been rewarded at the polls. Salinas's Mexico, even while moving to greater integration in the world economy and closer links to the United States, retains a strong and active public role. Underlying Mexican trade liberalization, moreover, is a powerful macroeconomic logic: imports have dampened inflationary pressures and there is need to attract capital inflows to avert a looming foreign exchange constraint.

The convergence toward a stronger state is independent of political origins and winning campaign slogans. The Argentine Peronist Menem professes Manchester liberalism, while the Brazilian conservative Collor embraces confiscation of wealth. Economic emergency compels strong measures, and increasing recognition that the state is too large and too weak. Not until, and unless, there is an increase in public revenues as well as reduced expenditures, will control of inflation long succeed. One can hope that this lesson is being learned and that external advice will reinforce internal predispositions.

Macroeconomic equilibrium, once achieved, will not by itself guarantee economic development. The length of the crisis has intensified uncertainty and rewarded private sector caution. Restarting and sustaining economic growth is where the public sector has a central and critical role. First, increased public investment is essential to larger private investment; deteriorating infrastructure and lack of adequate public services have reduced private returns. Increased spending also sends the important signal that the fiscal emergency is over. Second, there is need for larger social expenditures for the improvement of education and health as well as expanded programs targeted to the poor. Evidence suggests significant increases in inequality and poverty as a counterpart of the stagnation and accelerating inflation of the 1980s. Political stability requires more than rhetorical recognition of this fact. Third, the public sector must become a better regulator and subsidizer, even as it divests some of its productive activities and liberalizes trade. Natural monopolies in private hands will have to be overseen; financial activity cannot be left unattended; priority private investment will have to be encouraged. Industrial policy in developing countries starts from knowing what has gone before; it does not have to be, and especially for the smaller countries should not be, synonymous with an emphasis on the internal market.

In short, there is still a very constructive role for the state, based upon theory and practice. To perform that role effectively requires a new coalition of political support that is founded on both new and old realities: much reduced external finance and need for larger domestic saving, especially of the public sector itself; an expanded, but more competitive, international market in manufactured products, based upon diffusion of technology and imports of capital goods; limits to the domestic tax base; and unacceptably high income inequality throughout the region. Political transformation is very much a component of redesign of the state; democratization is only a beginning.

Populism, with its primary focus on inequality and its predisposition to a very activist and inward looking state, is not the principal constraint to such transformation in most of Latin America.[5] Raging inflation has weakened its appeal. Opposition to effective policies has not come from mass organization; the poor do not speak with a single, or very loud, voice. Labor unions are divided and less powerful than in the 1960s. Real wages have undergone significant decline in almost all countries.

[5]See Sachs (1989) and Dornbusch and Edwards (1990). Both papers come perilously close to identifying macroeconomic failure with populism tautologically. Nominal wage demands obviously reinforce inflation and impede stabilization. What is needed, however, is careful analysis of the special force of wage demands and their channels of pressure under populist regimes rather than others; and a careful look at whether wages were the decisive causal factor in provoking initial macroeconomic disequilibrium.

The blocking forces have been others. One has been the absence of an effective structure of political parties. Another has been a private sector interested more in guaranteed benefits than risk taking, and comfortable with a state presence that provided transfers and assured order without threat from below. Technocrats were able to satisfy those demands so long as they had abundant resources; as those diminished, so did the quality of their policies.

The technocrats have been blamed for the failure, while the private sector has emerged in some eyes as the future savior. The conversion to a narrow market-oriented view risks discarding a three-decade process of increasing sophistication of Latin American public administration. Bureaucrats do not only wear black hats. Some have contributed to imaginative policies and defended the national interest against powerful private rent seekers. The heart of the matter is not simply taking the state out, but bringing the private sector, and civil society, back in more positively.

The challenge to the countries of the region is formidable. There are no simple blueprints. The Asian developmental state cannot be copied. That brand of corporatism where authority was more centralized, resources readily available to the state and pressures from income inequality less salient proved much more functional than the Latin American style of catering to all. The prospects for economic development in the region during the decade ahead and beyond hinge upon the outcome of the process of redesign of the state that is now under way. The longer it takes to bring this process to successful fruition, the more the accumulated forces of economic erosion of the last decade make success difficult to achieve.

■ *I acknowledge the very helpful substantive and stylistic suggestions of the editors—Carl Shapiro, Joseph Stiglitz and Timothy Taylor—and financial support from the Rockefeller and MacArthur Foundations and from IBER.*

References

Arthur, Brian, "Self-Reinforcing Mechanisms in Economics." In Anderson, P., K. Arrow and D. Pines, eds., *The Economy as an Evolving Complex System*. Redwood City: Addison-Wesley, 1988, pp. 9–31.

Balassa, Bela, "Outward Orientation." In Chenery, Hollis, and T. N. Srinivasan, eds., *Handbook of Development Economics*, vol. 2. Amsterdam: North-Holland, 1989, pp. 1645–1689.

Bhagwati, Jagdish, "Directly Unproductive Profit-Seeking Activities," *Journal of Political Economy*, 1982, *902*, 988–1002.

Cardoso, Eliana, and Albert Fishlow, "Latin American Economic Development: 1950–1980," NBER Working Paper No. 3161, 1989.

Chenery, Hollis, S. Robinson, and M. Syrquin, *Industrialization and Growth: A Comparative Study*. Oxford: Oxford University Press, 1986.

CIEMEX-WEFA, *Mexican Economic Outlook*, March 1990.

DeSoto, Hernando, *The Other Path*. New York: Harper and Row, 1989.

Dornbusch, Rudiger, and S. Edwards, "Economic Crises and the Macroeconomics of Populism in Latin America," *Journal of Development Economics*, 1990, forthcoming.

Easterly, William, "Fiscal Adjustment and Deficit Financing During the Debt Crisis." In Hussain, I., and I. Diwan, eds., *Dealing with the Debt Crisis*. Washington D.C.: The World Bank, 1989. pp. 91–113.

Economic Commission for Latin America, *The Economic Development of Latin America and Its Principal Problems*. New York: United Nations, 1950.

Economic Commission for Latin America, *Economic Bulletin for Latin America*, 1964.

Economic Commission for Latin America, *Series Históricas del Crecimiento de América Latina*, Santiago, 1978.

Economic Commission for Latin America, *América Latina: La Política Fiscal en los Años Ochenta*. Serie Política Fiscal, *2*, Santiago, 1989.

Evans, Peter, D. Rueschmeyer, and T. Skocpol, eds., *Bringing the State Back In*. Cambridge: Cambridge University Press, 1985.

Fishlow, Albert, "Latin American Adjustment to the Oil Shocks of 1973 and 1979." In Hartlyn, J., and S. Morley, eds., *Latin American Political Economy*. Boulder: Westview, 1986. pp. 54–84.

Fishlow, Albert, "From Crisis to Problem: Latin American Debt 1982–87." In Wesson, R., ed., *Coping with the Latin American Debt*. New York: Praeger, 1988, pp. 7–18.

Fishlow, Albert, "Latin American Export Strategy in the 1990s," mimeo, Inter-American Development Bank, 1989.

Inter-American Development Bank, *Economic and Social Progress in Latin America*, 1989.

Krueger, Anne, "The Political Economy of the Rent-Seeking Society," *American Economic Review*, June 1974, *64*, 291–303.

Krueger, Anne, "Import Substitution versus Export Promotion," *Finance and Development*, 1985, *22*, 20–23.

Lal, Deepak, *The Poverty of Development*. Cambridge: Harvard University Press, 1985.

Little, Ian, Tibor Scitovsky, and Maurice Scott, *Industry and Trade in Some Developing Countries: A Comparative Study*. Oxford: Oxford University Press, 1970.

Reisen, Helmut, and Axel von Trotensburg, *Developing Country Debt: The Budgetary and Transfer Problem*. Paris: OECD, 1988.

Sachs, Jeffrey, "Social Conflict and Populist Policies in Latin America," NBER Working Paper No. 2987, 1989.

Shleifer, Andre, "Externalities as an Engine of Growth," mimeo, University of Chicago, 1989.

Stiglitz, Joseph, "Economic Organization, Information, and Development." In Chenery, Hollis, and T. N. Srinivasan, eds., *Handbook of Development Economics*, vol. 1. Amsterdam: North-Holland, 1988, pp. 39–71.

Tanzi, Vito, "Inflation, Lags in Collection and the Real Value of Tax Revenue," *IMF Staff Papers*, 1977, *24*, 154–167.

World Bank, *World Debt Tables, 1983–84*. Washington D.C.: The World Bank, 1984.

World Bank, *World Bank Development Report, 1988*. New York: Oxford University Press, 1988.

World Bank, *World Debt Tables, 1989–90*. Washington D.C.: The World Bank, 1990.

World Development, Vol. 18, No. 6, pp. 861–878, 1990.
Printed in Great Britain.

0305–750X/90 $3.00 + 0.00

The State and Industrial Strategy

HELEN SHAPIRO
Harvard Business School, Boston, Massachusetts

and

LANCE TAYLOR*
Massachusetts Institute of Technology, Cambridge

Summary. — The debate about the role of the state in promoting industrial growth in developing economies is reviewed. We begin with the ideas of the early development economists of the 1950s and 1960s, then take up two waves of neoclassical criticism (respectively emphasizing the primacy of the market and the lack of autonomy and competence of the developmentalist state), and sketch the elements of a countercritique. The fact that all successfully developing economies apply industrial strategies incorporating institutional change is emphasized, and boundary conditions and lessons from experience which delimit sensible strategic choices are pointed out.

1. INTRODUCTION

The debate about industrial strategy in the economic development literature has always been charged. During the past decade, the voltage rose as planners faced a rapidly changing global economy at the same time as their ability to act domestically was curtailed by fiscal constraints. Meanwhile, two neoclassically based attacks against state intervention were vigorously mounted in the 1970s and 1980s, and a reaction is getting underway. These shifts in objective circumstances and intellectual foundations notwithstanding, the fact remains that industrial strategies continue to be pursued — all governments intervene to shape their economies' productive structures by default or design.

The goal of this paper is to set out guidelines not only about how governments should select industrial strategies, but also how they should make the difficult transition from one policy regime to another when that becomes desirable or necessary. We begin our discussion by reviewing "old" views (*circa* 1960) of the role of the state, and the two waves of neoclassical attack. A countercritique is put forth, emphasizing the specificity of each country's industrial experience. "Boundary conditions" to successful policies are addressed, which lead to generalizations about the strategy lines different kinds of economies might pursue.

2. THE ROLE OF THE STATE

Industrial strategy rests upon directed public interventions at the sectoral or firm level, aimed at stimulating particular lines of economic endeavor. Microeconomic "targeting" of policies toward particular sectors is necessarily involved. The state may also undertake economy-wide actions complementary to the sectoral thrusts. *All* governments engage in industrial strategy in this sense. Historically, no country has entered into modern economic growth without the state's targeted intervention or collaboration with large-scale private sector entities.

(a) *Industrial strategy: the development theorists' view*

Alexander Gerschenkron (1962) was among the first to postulate conditions that lead economies to follow different strategy lines. Based on his study of European industrialization, he argued that a

*The arguments in Sections 2 and 3 are presented in more detail in Shapiro (1988) and the ones in Sections 4 and 5 draw on a paper prepared by Taylor for UNU/WIDER conference on medium-term adjustment held in Helsinki, August 8–11, 1988. Comments by George Lodge and Thomas McCraw on a previous draft are gratefully acknowledged.

country's economic position relative to more advanced nations directly influenced the nature of the state's intervention in its development process. In particular, the English industrial revolution was not a model for those that followed. Its own success guaranteed that all subsequent attempts would significantly vary.

Because it came first and embodied relatively unsophisticated technology, England's industrialization was more gradual and less capital intensive than its followers. The rapid pace of technical change and the widening disparities between their actual and potential rates and levels of economic development dictated other paths for countries in the then-periphery. Germany, Italy, and Russia were likely to jump immediately into the most modern industrial sectors, characterized by capital intensity and scale economies. In these economies, however, capital was scarce and diffused, and the entrepreneurial class either risk averse or financially weak.

Different initial conditions engendered diverse institutional forms and sectoral compositions when industrial growth got underway. In the follower countries, Gerschenkron suggested that the state itself had to substitute for the market and "force" industrialization. Whereas the government's role in an "autonomous" development effort was largely restricted to creating a suitable environment for private capital, in the followers the state became more directly involved with the extraction and allocation of resources, and the establishment and management of firms. Greater "relative backwardness' led to more widespread public intervention to overcome economic inertia.

Throughout the 1960s, economists more directly concerned than Gerschenkron with development policy shared a consensus favoring state intervention, based on different but related criteria. The Keynesian revolution, which cast doubt on the market's ability to achieve optimal results, was used to legitimize economic planning. Keynes's emphasis on domestic economic prosperity as opposed to international concerns was extended to support national industrialization strategies in the Third World.

Development economics arose as a separate field of study following these Keynesian precepts. It also incorporated Schumpeter's (1934) distinction between structural economic change (or "development" in his usage) and mere growth. General equilibrium theory, it was argued, could not describe the dynamic heart of the process — long-run development would not automatically flow from decentralized, optimal decision making in the short run. Hirschman (1958) and others saw development as a sequence of punctuated disequilibria. An investment project could create opportunities for others elsewhere, either by raising profits for industries downstream by lowering their costs of production or by making it possible to take advantage of scale economies by expanding the market or inducing greater specialization among firms. An individual investor's profit and loss calculus could not adequately capture such social benefits (or costs). As Allyn Young (1928) had emphasized early on, dynamic externalities arising from investment could move the system away from equilibrium in ways that comparative static analysis could never take into account.

Scitovsky (1954) explained the conditions required for the price mechanism to achieve optimal dynamic allocation: complete and functioning markets, an absence of increasing returns, and complete tradability. Empirical study showed that these conditions did not obtain in less developed countries (LDCs). Those economies were plagued with structural rigidities. Wages and exchange rates were singled out as not reflecting true opportunity costs. Private costs to investors supposedly exceeded social opportunity costs, understating industry's social return. Beginning with the work of Prebisch (1950), the Latin American structuralist school emphasized institutional barriers preventing free factor mobility and productivity growth. Development, therefore, would require creating the conditions under which capitalism could work, i.e., functioning labor and capital markets and national market integration.

From a planning perspective, Chenery (1961) and others showed how optimality of a free trade regime depended on the absence of market imperfections (including economies of scale). Singer (1950) and Prebisch (1959) embellished this work by arguing that static comparative advantage as revealed by current prices could not capture secular trends. Differences in price and income elasticities for primary and manufactured goods meant that raw material exports could not pay for manufactured imports in the long run. The supposed inevitability of future foreign exchange shortages provided an argument for industrialization not easily read from current relative prices.

Distinct viewpoints are evident in the 30-year old literature, but a perception of development as a process of dynamic, nonmarginal change united all the authors. Required investments are lumpy and (in a poor country) large in comparison to savings flows or even the national capital stock. Although it may provide adequate signals for marginal changes, the price mechanism cannot guide "big" industrial decisions, nor can it be relied upon to induce the resource transfer necessary for industrialization. Public interventions are required both to support investors (via protection, subsidies, cheap credits, etc.) and to invest directly to break critical bottlenecks. A greater extent of market failure in less developed as opposed to richer economies provides the basic rationale for expanding the scope of state intervention.

These theoretical arguments also justified import-substitution schemes already in process. Export-led growth was inconceivable to Third World technocrats and politicians who had witnessed (and seen their economies strongly affected by) the collapse of raw material prices and world trade in the 1930s. Trade expansion continued to look bleak in the mid-1950s while Europe was rebuilding and its currencies were still not fully convertible. Confronting foreign exchange constraints, many countries shifted their economic focus to the domestic market. Industrialization was also in the interest of the political coalitions that emerged in newly-formed states. In this environment, development banks, state-owned enterprises, and industrial targeting arose naturally in the developing world.

(b) *Neoclassical reactions*

There were at least two major problems with the literature just reviewed. One is that while it was rich with diagnoses of why backward economies do not develop, it offered limited guidance as to how the government was to intervene to set things right. Planning tools such as social cost-benefit analysis and programming models soon proved unable to blueprint industrial growth. More fundamentally, the development theorists tacitly assumed that the state had unlimited capacity to intervene in the economic system. Its failure to carry out its assigned developmental role(s) became apparent, almost equally quickly. While doubt about the adequacy of the market was the main thrust of the first wave of dissent, the development economists' unstated beliefs about the nature of the state and its capacity to intervene became the target of the second attack.

P. T. Bauer (1972, 1984) was prescient in pointing out these problems. Generalizing from his experience in India, he had articulated most of the 1980s vintage criticisms of an expanded public sector 20 years before. He not only considered government failure, i.e., corruption and mismanagement, more critical than market failure, but reversed the direction of causality: intervention *caused* and did not cure market imperfections. Implicitly, he assumed the market mechanism capable of self-correction. Bauer was especially fearful of the adverse political consequences he thought were associated with concentration of economic power by the state.

Toye (1987) is correct in dubbing Bauer "a pioneer of the counterrevolution," but Bauer was distinctly a lone wolf until the first neoclassical reaction put traditional development economics squarely on the defensive. This initial blow was aimed at the state's capacity to guide structural change. Using new analytical tools from trade theory such as effective rates of protection and domestic resource costs, Little, Scitovsky, and Scott (1970) showed that industrial strategies were inefficient — the incentives they created were highly unequal for different economic actors. These authors and their successors sought (how successfully is taken up below) to correlate "distorted" policy regimes with poor economic performance. Read between the lines, they advocated *laissez faire* as the only viable alternative to an incentive mare's nest.

This neoclassical critique was bolstered by the success of export-oriented countries such as South Korea and Taiwan which at the time were thought to have noninterventionist states. Their rapid growth in comparison to economies which followed import-substitution strategies seemed to provide empirical validation for Harry Johnson's (1967) earlier claims that dynamic gains could be had from free trade. An avid follower, Anne Krueger (1984) later explained that: "From a theory without any evidence in the early 1960's suggesting departures from free trade for dynamic reasons, the tables are turned; empirical evidence strongly suggests dynamic factors that may be associated with export-led growth" (p. 139). Export expansion somehow spurred by market liberalization became the industrialization strategy of choice.

Work around the turn of the decade by Krueger, Balassa (1971), and others was not so much anti-intervention as anti-import substitution. The debate between old-style development economists and more orthodox theorists still centered on market failure. It focused on whether to intervene, and with the exception of Bauer and a few isolated voices from the Left — Galbraith (1964) and Myrdal (1970) — the protagonists stopped well short of denying the state's political and institutional capacity to fulfill its prescribed role. That more radical claim came with the second phase of counterrevolution.

The "neoclassical political economy" of the 1980s explicitly attacks the early development economists' implicit belief in the efficacy of government intervention. Lal (1983) is a representative introduction. Echoing Bauer, he contends that "bureaucratic failure" may be worse than "market failure." Other authors set up formal models of the interaction between state and economy to show how government intervention is likely to produce inefficiencies. State policy is endogenized to the general equilibrium system by depicting it as the outcome of individual optimizing behavior in the political realm. Srinivasan (1985) classifies this effort under three heads: Mancur Olson's collective action framework, Buchanan's public choice school, and related work on trade, development, and economic history.

Olson (1982) argues that due to bargaining costs and the problem of free riders, individuals are unlikely to organize in their collective interest unless they are in small groups and/or can impose selective incentives on group members. Such coalitions of self-interested persons are likely to try to redistribute income toward themselves instead of working to raise efficiency and national income, the full benefits of which they will not receive. In stable (or static) societies, politics will increasingly be organized to cater to these interests. Efficient resource allocation will be inhibited, and by extension there will no incentives for Schumpeterian entrepreneurs to seek out technical innovations that might speed overall growth.

While Olson is primarily concerned with the implications of his coalitions for growth and social change, Buchanan (1980) is specific about the economic losses that result from profit seeking in the presence of the state. The "public choice" school argues that the emergence of monopoly and other distortions from public policy does more than impose a deadweight loss on the economy (as measured by the famous "little triangles" of comparitive statics). Competition for rents which accrue to the winners of government largesse turns into widespread "directly unproductive profit-seeking" (DUP, pronounced dupe) activities, in Bhagwati's (1982) phrase. Examples include lobbying, active politics, bribe paying, etc. Since almost any state intervention opens space for a rent (import quotas, traffic cops, defense contracts — the list is endless), the risk is that seeking government favors will override normal market activity. Rational rent seeking by individuals can produce extreme suboptimality for the economy as a whole.

Krueger's (1974) article on rent seeking and Buchanan's extension of deadweight loss calculations have been widely applied in the trade and development area. Krueger emphasized quantitative restrictions placed on imports. Firms will compete for import licenses and their attached rents: "To the extent that rent-seeking is competitive, the welfare cost of import restrictions is equal to the welfare cost of the tariff equivalent *plus the additional cost of rent-seeking activities.*"

More recent contributions have attributed DUP activity to those seeking to set up particular policies in the first place. Actors within the government itself may enter the fray, as do bureaucrats in Bardhan's (1984) extension of this line of thought to the Indian state. In his view, conflicts between bureaucrats and industrialists over appropriation of rents interact with India's traditional rural-urban disparities to perpetuate stagnation. Like other explanations of the slow "Hindu rate of growth," Bardhan's theory is to an extent belied by the improved performance of the large, distorted, and closed Indian economy after the early 1980s.

With regard to industrial strategy, rent seeking has strong implications. Inward-oriented development, by definition, relies upon market restrictions and state intervention, which supposedly create an environment more congenial to DUP than a more open, export-promoting policy line. The theory thus arrives at another explanation for the relative success of export-promoting strategies: the state is less involved so the economy is less prone to DUP. A generalization is that freer trade and factor mobility reduce rent seeking by restraining the interests and making cartels harder to maintain. The success of South Korea, where everyone now admits that the government has been extremely interventionist, is explained by its use of policy tools associated with external orientation which allowed for greater market play. The pressures of international competition are supposed to mitigate the worst sort of rent seeking observed in countries practicing pure import-substituting industrialization (ISI).

Douglass North's (1981) work on economic history can serve as a final example of the new neoclassical approach. The state, for North, becomes its own "vested interest group," creating a tradeoff between economic efficiency and state power. Paul Kennedy's (1987) subsequent best-selling discourse on military spending twists this line of thought into a vicious circle — the effort to be a great power induces internal economic tensions which make great power status ever harder to sustain.

North argues that specification of property rights is the key explanatory variable for economic performance, subject to technological constraints. He arrives at this view via the well-known Coase (1937) theorem, which shows that if property rights are well-specified and transaction costs are zero, individuals will face correct incentives and free trade will lead to efficient resource allocation among them. North endogenizes institutional change and a theory of the state to account for the persistence of inefficient property rights: economic and political efficiency are equivalent only when this condition coincides with the state's objectives. For example, because of transaction costs such as monitoring, the state may choose to raise its revenue by creation and taxation (or direct management) of a monopoly. The state may marshal ideological arguments to support its ends, but be opposed by nonfavored firms or people who strive for an alternative regime. Tension is inevitable in the presence of a Northian (or Bardhanian) state.

To summarize, there is no question that the DUP school is correct in emphasizing that state intervention, for reasons both intended and unforeseen, does not necessarily lead to efficient outcomes, in either a static or dynamic sense. Moreover, the state's enormous presence means that its actions change the environment in which firms and people operate in unexpected (and unexpectable) ways. Ironically, the early development economists did not perceive these problems because they accepted the traditional neoclassical separation of the economic and political spheres. Basically, they did not contemplate a theory of the state.

Before the new critique surfaced, neoclassical theory at least assumed that markets function, presupposing a minimal "night watchman" role for the government. In contrast, the omission of the state as an explicit actor is a fundamental flaw in the development theorists' argument, since they relied upon the state as an agent of change and presumed that it had the requisite political autonomy and administrative tools to carry out the task. In the presence of widespread market failure, the superior capacity of government functionaries to allocate resources became an article of faith. The state's ability to undertake sectoral targeting and its fiscal capacity for direct intervention were taken for granted.

The question remains, however, whether the neoclassical political economy model is any more relevant than the one it seeks to discredit.

3. ELEMENTS OF A CRITIQUE

The new literature reveals a number of shortcomings. We take up the economics of public intervention first, then go on to criticize the positive theory of the state that the neoclassical authors propose, and finally bring in perspectives on industrial strategy from other social sciences.

(a) *The economics of state interventions*

As we observed in connection with Little, Scitovsky, and Scott's (1970) book, two linked ideas are central to the neoclassical perspective: (1) elimination of distortions will enhance economic efficiency in Pareto's sense, and (2) increased efficiency will in turn lead to better macroeconomic performance, conventionally measured by the rate of growth of GDP. Solid support for either proposition is difficult to find.

With regard to "getting the prices right," a balanced judgment is that such a step frequently may be a necessary condition for enhanced microeconomic supply performance, but is scarcely ever sufficient. For example, such findings appear in 18 country studies of stabilization and adjustment programs organized by the World Institute for Development Economics Research (WIDER), reviewed by Taylor (1988). Several country cases of trade improvements were associated with price reform *in conjunction with* public interventions such as aggregate demand manipulation, export subsidies, public investment, and barter trade deals, but in other countries price reform alone produced poor results.

At issue is Gerschenkron's long-forgotten point about backwardness and inertia: more than a market signal is required to displace the previous "equilibrium" in order to make nontraditional export markets and investment projects attractive. An established rule of thumb among agricultural economists is than an anticipated 30–40% rate of return plus other incentives are required to make farmers switch to a new, untried crop. Similar generalizations no doubt apply in industry; especially in poor countries, the state is (or was, in many parts of the world) the only entity with deep enough pockets to make beyond-market incentives sufficiently sweet. It is also the only entity with broad enough coercive powers to make credible threats to actors throughout the economy when they fail to perform.

Whether enhanced micro efficiency, if attained, significantly raises the growth rate is a methodologically thorny issue to address. Any quantitative judgment requires a counterfactual reference point. Little triangle estimates of the welfare gains from eliminating distortions have remained stubbornly small ever since Harberger (1959) broached the question in a serious way. One side effect of the invention of rent seeking was to increase the welfare gains by widening their base (*vide* the Krueger quotation above) but the Ptolemaic fallacy begins to arise: you add epicycles to the model to get the result you desire. Any moderately clever general equilibrium modeler can also make the triangles shrink.

As discussed in more detail below, econometric results are also not informative. Relating growth performance to increased exports (as a proxy for liberalization?) has become an active cottage industry. However, most regressions of the GDP growth rate on the export growth rate come up with a coefficient about the size of the export share (as would follow from differentiating the national product identity). Raising the coefficient by making export growth "explain" a Solow-Denison technical progress residual à la Feder (1983) is a regression fallacy: one trending variable relates to any other with close but meaningless goodness of fit.

More fundamentally, the neoclassical isomorphisms between absence of distortions, efficiency, and growth are ahistorical and timeless. They fail to account for the experience of the advanced capitalist economies, as Schumpeter with his emphasis on entrepreneurs and innovations recognized long ago. During the industrialization push in all now-rich countries, public interventions were rife. Horowitz (1977) shows that US courts restricted individuals' control over property; decisions came to favor community property over absolute domain. While the court actions served the general welfare, they violated Buchanan's strict conditions for Pareto optimality. The Handlins (1969) and Hartz (1948) demonstrate that although they were constrained by the constitution in their choice of instruments, US state legislatures controlled exports and granted monopoly power to public corporations.

At the federal level, industrial interventions in the United States during the 19th century were huge. The government targeted railroads and farmers with land give-aways (millions of acres to the railway companies and 240 acres to the farm families who avoided speculation), and was highly protectionist until after World War II. Following the Meiji Restoration, the Japanese state set itself up as entrepreneur, financier, and manager in several manufacturing lines. Its activist role continued throughout the militarist period and after World War II in the famous industrial programming of MITI. Although different in form and character, interventionist policies continue in the United States. Despite its pro-market rhetoric, the government continues to direct American production capacity and technical advance to support both military and economic ends. Boeing would not be Boeing, nor would IBM be IBM, in either military or commercial endeavors without Pentagon contracts and civilian research support.

Returning to the developing economies, the key issues is what form the Gerschenkronian challenge to industrialize may take. At present, the international arena presents new opportunities (and constraints) to LDCs, but they can only be seized (and evaded) by timely and versatile policy moves. Dynamic gains from trade may not be available to, nor the export-promotion strategy warranted for, every economy. Fishlow (1986) and Cline (1982) propose a series of counterarguments about the institutional requirements for export-led growth, the nature of traditional exports (the elasticities, and much more important, as argued below, the possibilities of extending industrial activity downstream), and the potential fallacy of composition if all LDCs attempt trade expansion.

The success of an outward-oriented development scheme is contingent on structural conditions that cannot be taken for granted. Boratav's (1988) WIDER study shows that Turkey's export "miracle" in the first part of the 1980s rested upon a preexisting industrial base created by ISI, policies leading to contraction of domestic demand for manufactures, attempts at general price reform, subsidies of up to one-third of export sales plus related incentives, and rapid growth in demand for the products the country could produce by culturally compatible buyers in the region (the Gulf countries and both sides in the Iran-Iraq war). Had any one of these factors been missing, the boom probably would not have occurred.

Turkey's and other experiences with ISI suggest that this strategy need not lead to results as dismal as is often claimed. Fishlow (1986) shows how disaggregation reveals divergent histories in Latin America. During 1965–73, Brazil's GDP grew at 9.8% annually; Mexico's grew at 7.9%. For 1970–80, the rates were 8.4 and 5.2% respectively. Median growth rates for East Asia (South Korea, Taiwan, Indonesia, Malaysia, the Philippines, and Thailand) during these periods were 8.3 and 8.0%. More fundamentally, evaluating performance by comparing growth rates does not make a lot of sense — "fast" or "slow" growth depends on the basis for comparison and the relative stage of development. Brazil is not Korea; in another popular contrast, India is not Korea or even China.

The international environment also complicates the task of neoclassical political theory. In particular, domestic DUP activity is not the only distortion of free markets that occurs. The existence of transnational corporations (TNCs), strong oligopolies in certain world markets, unequal access to technology, and other factors contradict the basic assumptions of free trade. Helleiner (1990) and other exponents of the strategic trade models that have recently appeared show how economic rents need not be competed away in the presence of economies of scale, and how intervention may be Pareto superior to *laissez faire*. Empirical studies demonstrate that these complications affect industrial structure and performance. The ways in which leading sectors develop change with the context, and correspondingly have different macro-level effects. The implications for DUP models are manifold. The need for the state to bargain effectively with the TNCs complicates North's story: the case studies in Newfarmer (1985) give a good feel for the difficulties that can arise. DeVries (1983) points out in criticizing Olson that coalitions may arise to meet challenges during periods of stagnation and not cause them.

The basic problem is again one of counterfactuals: in attacking the government, neoclassical political economy posits an idealized market in its stead. This easily manipulable base for comparisons simply does not exist, as numerous counterexamples show. TNCs may (or may not) enhance efficiency, but they surely carry economic and political clout. Chicago-based literature on regulation stresses that the market itself generates its own rent seeking entities and redistributions of income. There is a peculiar asymmetry in the DUP models, whereby individuals coalesce to force a political redistribution, but do not do the same in the marketplace. The political arena is depicted full of lobbyists and cartel builders, while the economy is presented as being more or less subject to competition. Despite greater putative openness under a liberal trade regime, there is no guarantee that an export-promotion strategy is any less subject to DUP activity than import substitution. So-called fictional exports mushroomed in Turkey during the 1980s, as firms bought up emigrant remittances to turn in the hard currency along with doctored invoices to skim extra profits off the spate of export subsidy flows.

(b) *The absent neoclassical state*

As they reify the market, the neoclassical political economists elide an explicit discussion of the state, despite their claim to making public action an endogenous variable. Their argument presupposes a passive, pluralist state that is acted upon by interest groups with equal access to its largesse. Indeed, the characteristics of the favors that it distributes are often not fully specified, although general equilibrium implications differ. Blomqvist and Mohammad (1986) show how levels of efficiency loss are affected by the line of production in which rent receivers engage, while Barbone (1985) argues that changes in the level of wealth implicit in the claim to an import quota affect aggregate demand.

Besides the nature of the state's favors, the specific groups to whom they are distributed will have economic and political implications. Bowles and Eatwell (1983), Barry (1983), and Cameron (1983) all argue that neoclassical political economy posits a peculiar counterfactual combining a non-politically organized society with an ideal liberal state, completely neutral with regard to distribution. Potential conflicts between universal suffrage and capitalism as well as the importance of liberal, democratic institutions for social (and therefore economic) stability are ignored.

The pluralist model is inapplicable to many developing countries, e.g., Brazil. There, throughout this century the state has never been the passive favor dispenser of the DUP literature. In the 1950s, it attempted to insulate itself from interest group pressure, but also created new interest groups by virtue of its interventions (Shapiro, 1988). If the state has some degree of autonomy, it need not resort to authoritarianism to eliminate DUP activity, as neoclassical authors like Lal (1983) suggest. Stable policy is another tool: if the government establishes credibility in its commitment to a particular policy line (e.g., expansion of the automobile industry in Brazil), DUP activity in that area will be ineffective and tend to wane.

Under certain conditions, the state itself may be able to extract rents from the private sector and shape investment behavior, possibilities that neoclassical political economy does not recognize (see Shapiro, 1988). Its standard assumption that individuals foresee the future perfectly with at most random errors flies in the face of the rigidities and risks of the Third World, where consequences of political and economic change are largely unknown. An important intervention, discussed more fully below, is public investment. Recent evidence suggests that public projects "crowd in" private investment via complementarities, rather than crowding it out by driving up interest rates (a market signal). In another area, one has to explain how both directed incentives and public investment have been orchestrated to transform ISI into export promotion in South Korea and elsewhere. Externalities and the uses of policies to reduce fundamental uncertainty about economic affairs have to be built explicitly into any credible theory of the developing country state.

As mentioned above, neoclassical authors lean toward authoritarianism as a device to preclude special interests from taking over the state. Lal's judgent is famous: "A courageous, ruthless, and perhaps undemocratic government is required to ride roughshod over these newly-created special interest groups" (1983, p. 33). Findlay (1986) blurs the issue but without explicitly discussing the nature of the state; he implies that the emergence of authoritarianism in South Korea and Brazil explained their shift toward export orientation. By contrast, from the field of political science, O'Donnell's (1973) bureaucratic-authoritarian model for Latin America at least tried to explain *why* military regimes were inclined to open their economies to international finance, and why democracy was no longer compatible with economic growth.

The underlying neoclassical suspicion that democracy is not compatible with economic growth unwittingly echoes some Marxist theories of the state. Offe (1974) and Offe and Ronge (1975) have analyzed the inherent contradiction between the capitalist state's primary concerns: accumulation of capital and political legitimacy. Fiscal crises along O'Connor's (1973) lines are brought forth. For example, an argument heard often in Brazil is that keeping up investment and satisfying popular demands under a fiscal constraint may simply be beyond the competence of the state (Weffort, 1978; Malloy, 1987).

The subtle difficulty with both the Marxist and neoclassical frameworks is that recognizing a potential contradiction between democracy and economic expansion in no way implies a logical affinity between authoritarian states and capitalist growth. Nor is democracy necessarily correlated with a poor growth record — there are at least moderately succesful social democracies at all income levels around the world. The combination of dictatorship and outstanding economic performance, when it appears, is due to particular conditions in particular states, which must be specified. In his classic study of dictatorship and democracy, Barrington Moore (1966) saw affinities between the rise of democratic institutions and capitalism. Recent authors find an indeterminate relationship between economic policy and political regime, e.g., Haggard (1985) on the linkages between political regimes and the sorts of economic stabilization programs they apply.

The neoclassical faith in authoritarianism finally proves inconsistent in several ways. Lal (1983) is the first to point out that bureaucrats have no special talent for running an economy, but presumably they would be called upon to do so (at least at second hand) in his authoritarian state. They would have to be nonarbitrary in their use of concentrated power. Authoritarian regimes as actually observed do not behave in such ideal fashion. Latin American military rulers were not notably efficient, and demonstrated that the distribution of spoils is not a civilian monopoly. Olson (1982), predictably, sees the difficulties of Latin American states in exercising control as arising from excessively powerful interest groups seeking industrial protection to the detriment of agriculture. A more plausible view is that despite superficial regime changes, Latin America suffers from too much stability in its class and institutional structure.

(c) *Other perspectives*

Briefly, it is worth noting that the social science literature outside of economics had drawn a whole different set of conclusions from the experience of later industrializers such as Japan (Johnson, 1982) and South Korea. This body of work frequently argues that sensible policy and the institutional means by which to implement it are the keys to a successful industrial strategy. In the tradition of Gerschenkron, effective institutional change is the critical explanatory factor for self-sustaining growth. From this angle, the debate about state intervention becomes sterile when it is waged entirely in market vs. nonmarket terms. Those who credit the invisible hand in all success cases have biased vision: if an economy grows rapidly, they see market forces in action; if it grows slowly, bad public policy is at fault. Those at the other extreme reduce economic development to a problem of domestic institution building. Structural constraints may be posed by the domestic and international economies, but they are ultimately nonbinding.

Such narrow frameworks are reminiscent of the earlier debate on mercantilism. Whether fiscalism built up national states at the expense of economic development was defined by Heckscher as a tradeoff between "power versus plenty." Along North's lines, a conflict of interest between the crown and the merchant class was presumed. But as Wilson (1967) remarks:

> It seems doubtful whether the controversy is a very fruitful one. For it becomes plain as soon as we try to define what "mercantilists" meant by "power" that they were thinking of a political system which rested on an economic base and had certain economic ends. Equally, "plenty" was thought of in relation to politics and strategy. "Wealth" was not merely an economic conception; it had to be of a character that would coincide with and reinforce the strength of the nation and its capacity to defend itself... "Power and Plenty," that is to say, were not mutually exclusive conceptions but complementary conceptions (p. 495).

The question becomes one of what conditions created the "fiscal desperation" (p. 494) of Spain, or the British fiscalism that "seemed to move in parallel with powerful private and public interests and was less evidently damaging to economic development..." (p. 521). What applies to visible fiscalism applies to the invisible hand as well.

4. BOUNDARY CONDITIONS

There are examples of successful industrial strategies in both the developed and developing economies, but many such initiatives have failed for both political and economic reasons. Some of the successes seem to be associated with authoritarian regimes, others with democratic institutions. Institutional responsiveness seems central to success. Can anything more definite be said about sensible strategies in specific contexts in the developing world?

In this section, arguing mainly on economic grounds, we try to describe more concretely the circumstances in which certain industrial policies may (or may not) have a chance for success. The argument is organized in terms of context-dependent "patterns" of industrial change that have been observed, and associated "boundary conditions" delimiting the sort of policies that it makes sense to use in specific national cases. We concentrate on seven sets of conditions, discussed roughly in order of ease of quantification: country size, internal vs. external orientation, labor skills, wages and income distribution, the fiscal and managerial capacity of the state, the economy's industrial heritage, and productivity growth and access to technology. Other factors such as the nature of the bureaucracy also influence the prospects for successful policy implementation, as discussed by Evans (1989).

(a) *Country size*

The size of a country, best measured by population, influences its industrial prospects. This insight is old (dating to Werner Sombart at least) and has been elaborated econometrically by Hollis Chenery and coauthors, e.g., Chenery, Robinson, and Syrquin (1986). Chenery's statistical approach relies on both continuous relationships and sample splits. His most fruitful division has been between "large" and "small" nations, with the frontier at a population of (say) 20 million. The equations fit better for large countries: they seem to follow a more uniform pattern of industrial change. This observation is consistent with the importance of specialized, niche-oriented industrial strategies for small, open economies, as discussed below.

The econometric results for a big country can be summarized as follows: it typically enters earlier into import substitution and has a higher manufacturing share of GDP than does a small country at the same per capita income level; it pursues import substitution further into intermediate and capital goods and producers' services. The statistically "typical" large country's import and export shares of GDP are likely to be around 10% (with a standard deviation of about the same size; Korea is far more open than the norm) while a small country's shares may be more than one-half.

Both the regressions and (more importantly) country histories suggest that big countries exploit import-substitute-then-export (ISTE) strategies in manufacturing. The basic premise is that big, protected markets permit economies of scale and scope. At the same time, they allow the luxury of allocative inefficiency for extended periods of time — high-cost production creates economic loss, but does not represent a binding restriction on inward-oriented growth. In a favorable context, a statically inefficient industrial sector may become the base for breaking into the world trade with import-substituting products, as Turkey's example in the 1980s suggests.

With due regard to our warnings about facile country comparisons, South Korea and Brazil make an interesting contrast. Korea, with its unusually high trade shares, has successfully designed policies to direct the transformation of domestic production for a protected local market into export capability. A highly skilled labor force and rapid growth of a capital stock embodying world-class technology have played a central role. Brazil has historically directed more of its output toward the domestic market and has lower trade shares, e.g., Brazilian commodity exports were about 8% of GDP in the early 1980s, as opposed to South Korea's 38%.

Brazil's industrial strategy has relied on rapid demand growth in the domestic market to generate scale economies and technical change. One disadvantage is that sales prospects at home are more limited than for the world as a whole, and a concentrated income distribution (as discussed below) may be required to support purchases of modern goods. Indeed, there is always a risk that the domestic market will become saturated. Without access to external credit, domestic demand in an ISI strategy cannot grow much faster than exports in the medium to long run, i.e., there are lower bounds on the ratio of imports to GDP. If foreign resource flows decline, the state may be forced to tighten fiscal policy as a "third gap" binds (Bacha, forthcoming; Taylor, 1989); we take up this problem below. Foreign obligations may be especially vexing if (as in Brazil's case) much technology was imported via TNCs.

An advantage of an inward-oriented industrialization strategy is that it may pay off in terms of an autonomous growth path (less subject to external shocks) in the long run, as Hughes and Singh (1987) emphasize in the cases of India and China. When they occur, external shocks can be offset via domestic recessions which force firms to seek export markets abroad, so long as they have enough dynamism to maintain international competitiveness. This is one of several areas in which industrial and macroeconomic policies interact, favorably in the short run but unfavorably in a longer period if continued recession holds down capital formation, making local production facilities increasingly noncompetitive in the world market (as may have happened in the late 1980s to automobile plants in Brazil).

Since small countries are far more open to foreign trade, they are likely to find the ISTE approach less fruitful. Sector-level inefficiencies can easily degenerate into a binding foreign resource constraint. With benefit of hindsight, one can see that now-prosperous small economies earned foreign exchange by exploiting niches in which they could be efficient producers for export trade, e.g., downstream expansion of forest products plus high-skill/high-tech manufacturing in Canada, Sweden, and Finland, shipping in Norway (before oil), high-tech industry and financial services in Switzerland, etc.

Following the Canadian "staple school" of economic historians (Innis, 1962; Watkins, 1963), Hirschman (1977) raised the practically imporant question of the growth potential of the resource base. Timber and oil may favor downstream industrial and marketing expansion more than, say, sugar and bauxite. In the long run, local production of such raw materials can lead to capacity to manufacture the relevant capital goods, e.g., paper machines and components for oil refineries or petrochemical plants with associated engineering skills. The policy issues center around manipulating effective protection for downstream activities so that they can develop in an effective fashion.

Building upon a "staple" service is also an option to be explored. Entrepôt trade can be an extremely productive base, as exemplified recently by Hong Kong, a small economy which skipped much import substitution (in part because the Shanghai textile industry migrated there in the wake of the Chinese revolution) and rapidly attained export capability in many lines. Its experience is hard to replicate, however, since Hong Kong follows a prosperous city-state model of great antiquity which is not open to the overwhelming majority of poor countries in the world. For a large nation, an industrial city selling largely to the internal market is a mixed blessing (because of regional disparities, migration flows, etc.) but it is also an omen for general growth — inward-looking industrialization seems to need an "engine." Hong Kong's metropolitan economic numbers are not more striking than São Paulo's or Bombay's, even though the hinterlands of Brazil and India grow far more slowly than their national city-states.

A special political economy underlies the successful small country approach, as Katzenstein (1985) points out for the prosperous European economies. Historically, the private sector took the lead and absorbed the failures in opening niches, but bankruptcies were cushioned by "oligarchic" politics (close linkages among large industrial firms, labor unions organized from the top down, and a stable state) plus publicly supported safety nets. Small prosperous countries initially practiced protection, but now maintain undistorted trade regimes and adjust to rapid technical change through close cooperation among public, corporate and labor elites. In Switzerland, Sweden, and the Netherlands, nationally based TNCs are the entrepreneurs in international markets, but depend on the rest of the system. These countries exploit niches not only in manufacturing, but also in financial and other services. Very few small developing economies have started such a transition — Singapore and Hong Kong are the recent success cases (entrepôt trade, finance, and low wage manufacturing) and, for internal political reasons, Lebanon appears to have failed.

(b) *Internal vs. external orientation*

The degree of "openness" of an economy has at least two interpretations: the levels of its trade shares (obviously affected by the nation's size), and the comparative absence of interventionist commercial policies. On both definitions, openness has implications for industrial strategy. But, as we have already seen, just how it influences industrialization and growth is a topic of intense debate.

The mainstream view is that high foreign trade shares — especially exports — in GDP help industrialization; hence, policy should be directed toward eliminating barriers to trade. There is also an increasing body of literature supporting the opposite point of view, e.g., papers from WIDER on the topic include Taylor (1987), Chakravarty and Singh (1988), and Helleiner (1990). The best summary so far is that the debate is inconclusive: an *a priori* case for either an open or closed trade policy regime can never be fully proved.

As we observed above, this Scotch verdict also applies to the empirical evidence on the relationship between openness and growth (based largely on cross-sectional regressions and computable general equilibrium models in the absence of comparative historical studies). Chenery, Robinson, and Syrquin (1986) present cross-country regressions showing that within country groups based on population and trade specialization in manufactures and primary products, the yearly GDP growth rates of export-oriented economies were a few tenths of a percent above the overall average during the period 1950–83. Using another grouping based upon per capita GNP and observed growth rates, McCarthy, Taylor, and Talati (1987) show that fast-growing countries did not on average have either high or increasing shares of exports in GDP between 1962 and 1984. Examples are easy to cite: among middle-income countries, Jamaica (12%), Uruguay (5%) and Portugal (16%) have high industrial export shares of GDP and grow slowly; Colombia and Brazil have shares of 2 or 3% and their growth has historically been fast. Poorer countries' growth rates are more subject to the vagaries of capital inflows and primary product trade, but similar observations hold: Cameroon and Egypt have grown fairly rapidly with industrial export shares of about 1%, while slow-growing India (until recently) and Honduras both have shares of 3% or more.

Despite these inconclusive results, the empirical literature does present five boundary conditions that appear to apply fairly widely:

First, and least controversial, the ratios of manufactured to primary products both produced and exported tend to rise as per capita GDP goes up. In a broad sense, industrialization *is* concomitant to economic growth.

Second, trade and output data suggest that at the two-digit level of industrial classification, import substitution usually precedes production for exports, as we have already observed. The lag may be very short as in the case of South Korea (except for automobiles, where the transition took 20 years), but normally one must think in terms of quinquennia or decades. But this sector-average generalization does not rule out the possibility of a country's exporting a particular product the day it begins to be produced.

Third, both production and trade shares vary within narrower ranges in large countries than in small ones, emphasizing the importance of niche-seeking strategies for the great majority of economies in the world. The relatively few large economies that exist shape their industrial structures more in line with domestic demand.

Fourth, countries poor (rich) in natural resources tend to have high (low) shares of industry in both exports and GDP. Japan and Korea on the one hand, and the United States and Brazil on the other are obvious examples.

Finally, Fishlow (1985) raises a useful distinction between "export-led" and "export-adequate" growth. In terms of broad regional distinctions, the labels describe Asian (externally oriented) and Latin American (internally oriented) strategies. The current problem for countries pursuing the latter line is how to regain a viable growth process under fiscal duress.

To summarize, empirical regularities linking country size, observed trade shares, and economic performance help set limits on how policy can affect openness and growth. Boundary conditions suggest that the trade and production patterns of Costa Rica will never resemble Brazil's, for a variety of reasons. The implication is that policy should not be formed in one economy taking a vastly different one as a model. However, if some intervention is effective in (say) Jamaica, it might pay off in Costa Rica as well, since both small, open countries share many of the same limits to growth.

(c) *Labor skills*

There is no question that high skills are required of workers in industrial modes of production — substantial literacy and numeracy are required to produce commodities ranging from Green Revolution wheat to computer codes for microprocessors. Successful industrializers since World War II exemplify the pattern — Korea has virtually complete literacy and world-class ratios of engineers and technically trained persons to the overall population.

The real policy question is how both formal education and on-the-job training can be geared toward industrialization, in a period of tightened budget constraints for most governments in the Third World. Quoting UNESCO data, Schultz (1988) observes that public expenditure on education per child more than doubled during the period 1970–80 in all developing regions, and then decreased in 1982. A fair guess is that educational spending in most poor countries in the late 1980s continued this tendency toward stagnation or decline. Even if industrial jobs can be successfully created, these data suggest that skill constraints may increasingly bind. In a time when most governments are short of cash, policies to encourage the private sector to shoulder a greater share of the national educational effort may be required. Regulatory action supporting on-the-job training and similar activities may partially counteract the state's inability to tax the private sector in this regard.

(d) *Wages and income distribution*

Evidence from the WIDER studies and elsewhere suggests that progressive income redistribution is likely to stimulate aggregate demand (Taylor, 1988). Compositional shifts may also occur, although country-level evidence suggests that the new commodity basket may be either more or less labor intensive (i.e., wealthier segments of the population who lose in the redistribution may bias their consumption toward either labor-intensive services or capital-intensive commodities, depending on context). There is also likely to be a reduction in import intensity of demand.

These compositional shifts are all relatively weak, so that the short-run effect of redistribution on industrial strategy can probably be ignored. The important conjunctural factor is the change in aggregate demand. It suggests that redistribution can only be pursued up to a certain point, beyond which balance of payments and/or inflation problems arise.

Beyond the conjuncture, dynamic feedbacks

become important. Real wages are often central to the distributional process, and their secular growth may be necessary for industrialization in the long run. Now-popular efficiency wage arguments (Bowles and Boyer, 1988, give the radical version) suggest that worker motivation and efficiency depend on good pay. The bulk of demand for advanced products must come from exports or wage income. These linkages mean that which classes gain from productivity increases is an important question. On the one hand, worker motivation and internal demand require real wage increases; on the other, if real wages rise more slowly than productivity, unit labor costs fall, which can help trade. But it is clear that aiming for low wages alone is *not* a viable or sustainable strategy. South Korea would never have shifted its exports from human hair and cheap garments to automobiles and electronics had its wages stayed at the levels of 1955.

(e) *Fiscal and managerial capability of the state*

The WIDER studies emphasized how in many countries public investment stimulates private capital, via complementarities; the same point is also recognized by the International Monetary Fund (Blejer and Khan, 1984). Recent econometric results support the observation, e.g., Chakravarty (1987) estimates that the "crowding-in coefficient" for public on private investment in Indian agriculture lies between one and two, while Ortiz and Noriega (1988) find a Mexican economy-wide coefficient of one. For a 72-country international cross section, Barro (1989) gets a coefficient of one.

Despite the importance of crowding in, many governments currently find public investment impossible because (even with improved tax performance and current spending cuts) they are fiscally constrained. In the major debtor countries, the public sector owes 5% or more of GDP in external obligations each year — new projects are a luxury impossible to afford. In macro models with three or four gaps (investment crowding in and inflationary pressure can be added to the traditional savings and foreign exchange constraints), Bacha (forthcoming) and Taylor (1989) show that reducing state capital formation may be the only plausible response to output losses and inflation stemming from a tightened foreign exchange constraint. The implications for long-term growth are, needless to say, poor.

Besides fiscal problems, an important empirical question is whether the state can in fact handle all the obligations we have discussed. Theories of how it functions aside, finding an existing government capable of making use of the local resource base, utilizing the advantages and avoiding the problems inherent in the country's size, maintaining an intelligent stance between import substitution and export promotion, seeking export niches, hastening skill creation, and dealing effectively with new technologies like microprocessors is not an easy task. Optimal performance in all areas is impossible. The question is whether the state can effectively cope. Its managerial capacity — even to supervise a regime of *laissez faire* — is perhaps the most important boundary condition of all.

Here, we can only flag the issue — Evans (1989) takes up some of the problems it creates. But one observation (especially relevant for Africa) follows naturally from the discussion earlier in this paper: arguments for liberal policies may be based on desperation about the capacity of the state. Since the public sector does so badly, the reasoning goes, an unfettered private sector couldn't possibly do worse. This view ignores the objective difficulties — unfavorable ecological conditions, plummeting export volumes and prices, political turmoil — that African and other poor countries have faced, as well as the historical fact that industrialization does not flourish in a fully free-market regime. However, the fact that the private sector is unlikely to create industrialization on its own does not answer the question about how state capacity can be improved. Even under favorable macroeconomic conditions, a painful learning process is likely to be involved.

(f) *Industrial heritage*

As we have stressed, industrialization is an historical process: each country must be seen as traversing a particular dynamic path. For a poor country, its initial conditions obviously matter. South Korea in the 1950s had a low per capita income and little capital stock. However, there had been a recent, successful land reform, and the population was well educated and had been exposed to industrial culture during the colonial period under the Japanese. Ample human capital, generous foreign aid, privileged access to American and Japanese markets, and other intangible factors set the stage for the Korean industrial miracle. The contrast with African countries which still struggle with relics of a much more exploitative form of colonialism could not be sharper. Their lack of educational infrastructure and even rudimentary industrial experience stand out.

As a country pursues industrialization, transitions continue to occur. Toward the end, fully developed economies enter more or less competitively into world markets with levels of export subsidies, import barriers, and activities like dumping restrained to "normal" levels (with normality being a flexible concept, *vide* Japanese import restrictions and the increasing interest of the United States in "strategic trade"). In the developing world, the import-substitute-then-export strategy means that large economies may hold themselves (or at least many of their products) away from international competition for periods measured in decades. Small countries are necessarily more open to trade, and arguably have fewer opportunities for dynamic gains from distorting prices in the short run. Conceivably, their size deficiencies could be offset by regional production/trading groups, although their record of success so far is bleak. Flexible manufacturing processes as discussed by Piore and Sabel (1984) may also provide opportunities for surmounting problems posed by economies of scale, but they are just beginning to be applied in the developing world.

Neither import substitution nor the return toward international competitiveness is typically led by the invisible hand. Internally, as the small, prosperous, European economies exemplify, an interlocking institutional network allows negotiation among well-organized groups — unionized labor, transnational companies, and big government. *Chaebol* and *zaibatsu* confronted by labor and activist states demonstrate the same tendencies in Korea and Japan. A key long-term result of a successful industrial strategy is a set of institutions conducive to high levels of investment and saving (undertaken, as Keynes observed, by different institutional groups whose actions have to be coordinated), absorption of technical change, and demand control mechanisms through which the government can support a steady pace of output growth.

Externally, an export push may be required to compensate (so to speak) for a period of import substitution. As we have observed, successful newly industrialized countries (NICs) often follow this pattern, although there are historical exceptions — the United States remained quite closed throughout its industrialization and India is now. But would both these economies improve their performance by pushing sales abroad?

The benefits of more exports are easy to enumerate. They can support the current account as imports are liberalized (except when there are negative domestic resource costs), and by simple arithmetic raising a modest export share of GDP toward unity is likely to be a less painful process than further reducing an already low import coefficient toward zero. Also, when world trade is expanding faster than world GDP, exports tap into a rising source of demand. As we have noted, the unknown for countries making the transition over the next decades is whether or not international trade will continue to grow as rapidly in the future as it has in the recent past. As Hobson (1902) observed long ago, progressive income redistribution and creation of a welfare state can also underwrite growth in demand.

Rapid export expansion aside, the "return" involves a transition from noncompetitive to competitive trade, as Chenery (1975) pointed out. On the export side, the emphasis shifts from primary products with a small internal market to manufactures and services sold both abroad and at home. Goods initially produced to substitute for imports (often creating a further dependence on imported intermediates and capital goods) must ultimately find external markets if world-class costs and variety are to be provided to domestic consumers. There is no reason why production for appropriate niches should not initially be supported by import barriers and export subsidies; indeed "opportunity costs" of not trading have to be ignored until learning and scale effects take hold. The point is that full industrialization only occurs after infant firms grow up, and can compete more or less effectively on international terms. The issues raised by DUP theorists are important in this context — why should a firm try to compete with foreigners instead of seeking national rents? Directed public interventions, social consensus, and profit opportunities in world-market competition necessarily must play a role in the difficult transition from noncompetitive to more competitive trade.

(g) *Productivity growth and access to technology*

International competitiveness depends on steadily growing productivity and access to best-practice technology. With regard to productivity, it is useful to distinguish improvements due to better resource allocation and trend increases over time. In the mainstream view, liberalized trade and industrial policy should improve allocation. However, in a recent review article, Pack (1988) concludes that "... to date, there is no clear confirmation of the hypothesis that countries with an external orientation benefit from greater growth of technical efficiency in ... manufacturing. When combined with the relatively small static costs of protection [i.e. small triangles], this finding leaves those with a predilection toward a neutral regime in a quandary" (p. 353). And again, "[c]omparisons of total factor productivity growth among countries pursuing different international trade orientations do not reveal systematic differences in productivity growth in manufacturing, nor do the time-series studies of individual countries that have experienced alternating trade regimes allow strong conclusions in this dimension" (p. 372). Allocative efficiency gains do not seem to result from liberal policy moves.

With respect to sources of productivity growth over time, Pack does observe that there are often large gaps between current LDC and international best-practice technology. Moreover, along Kaldor-Verdoorn lines, Amsden (1988), in her WIDER country study of South Korea, emphasizes that rapid output growth (perhaps coming largely from exports) can feed back positively into new, late vintage capital formation and productivity increases. As we have already observed, one source of Korean cost competitiveness is the fact that labor productivity grows faster than real wages, reducing unit labor costs. The virtuous circle to more exports, additional investment in export industries, and further productivity gains is successfully closed.

After the effects of formal schooling and on-the-job learning are taken into account, it is clear that if productivity is to be raised, new technology must be acquired. Despite isolated exceptions (e.g., Korean and Brazilian design of new models of cars and armored personnel carriers), little technical innovation occurs in the developing world. New technology must be obtained through deals with international suppliers, involving licensing and royalty costs, or via direct foreign investment on the part of transnational firms. Either route involves extensive bargaining between local public and private sector firms and external suppliers, under the aegis of the state.

The conditions of these bargains vary with a country's own industrial history and time. Dealing in the 1980s with Suzuki about setting up an automobile industry, India may have been in a weaker position than was Brazil when it dealt with Ford and Volkswagen 30 years before: the corporations were groping almost as blindly as their potential host at that stage. The main similarity is that a process beginning with assembly and leading toward rising domestic content is one policy goal. The time frame for such a change may be fairly short, since NIC industrial sophistication has by now reached the point at which international productivity levels in greenfield plants can be rapidly acquired, as in production of car engines during the past decade in Mexico.

Even this comfortable generalization breaks down, however, when new technologies like those based on microprocessors are at issue. Stimulating local applications rather than production of hardware has emerged as the relevant policy objective — Sweden, the most computerized economy in the world, does minimal local manufacture. In developing countries, pursuing computer literacy and familiarity emerges as the relevant policy goal. Traditional ISI strategies do not apply, but state and privately supported educational initiatives possibly may.

5. POLICIES IN ACTION

The discussion so far shows that forming industrial strategy (or reforming policies inherited from the past while growth and industrialization proceed apace) is a complex pursuit. Small wonder that practical policy advice in the area boils down to compiling lore about interventions that have (or have not) worked in one context, and trying to extrapolate about the outcomes they might provoke in another. In this spirit, we offer a few suggestions about possible approaches to strategy.

Before turning to specifics, a word about general orientations is in order. Industrial strategies can follow three broad lines — proactive state guidance of the economy, *laissez faire*, and a middle way.

The proactive industrializing state has fallen from fashion in recent years, especially in its traditional central planning attire. With party cadres calling the shots throughout the system under guidance from the top, planning did aid industrialization in big countries with simple economies and strong states — the Soviet Union in the 1930s and China two decades later. However, when production processes become more interlinked and technically harder to organize and consumers grow more sophisticated, absence of personal freedom and room for initiative handicaps adoption of new techniques and products, braking productivity growth. A rule-bound, rent-seeking bureaucracy becomes an additional fetter on change. The current wave of reforms in (ex?) socialist nations is aimed precisely at removing these obstacles to modern economic growth.

Proactive guidance can also take the form of widespread, intense industrial targeting. Such policies have been practiced with some success by the NICs in both their import-substitution and export-promotion phases. However, they fit less well into an economy that is small, open, and lacks industrial sophistication. In such a context, public participation in, but not direction of, the economy runs naturally between the free market and centrally planned extremes. As noted above, this road was taken by small country development "success cases" such as those in East Asia since World War II and in European social democracies after the turn of the century. For the reasons just discussed, elements of the strategies appropriate to large and small countries are best described through empirical generalizations rather than the abstract model used by neoclassical economic theory. They include the following:

(1) Even with successfully interventionist strategies, the government generally guides but does not directly manage decentralized, market-responsive decision making at the firm level. Especially in developing economies where middle-level cadres are weak, highly able people to do the guiding from the top of both the state and key enterprises are essential. There do not have to be large forces of "planners," but they need political backing, which in turn rests upon effective state mediation among interest groups. Guidance takes place through continual consultation among the state and producer, export and labor organizations. It may be centralized as in the famous presidential Blue House export targeting in Korea or in MITI in Japan, or more widely spread as around the development banks, planning ministry, and producers' organizations in Brazil. The point is that flexible, institutionally appropriate channels are created.

(2) Through the consultation process there is feedback from producers to the state, which centralizes information and selectively shares it among firms. National solidarity and an ideology of growth sanction such bureaucratic transgressions of the rules of market game. If such forces do not coalesce behind an industrialization push, it is much more likely to fail.

(3) The state also provides venture capital for new enterprises, often at highly favorable interest rates. This is a form of lending that traditional, garden-variety banks are usually not willing to undertake. Development banks, if aggressive, can play a key role in providing venture capital and long-term investment finance in general. Their project search and identification procedures have to take place at the micro level — among the 20,000 commodities in the seven-digit SITC. Economists' two-digit level computations of effective protection rates and domestic resource costs are not of great use in identifying potentially profitable niches and sources of productivity growth in detail. Market knowledge and intuition are essential to the decision process. A publicly backed private sector is the institution best suited to carry it out.

(4) Targeting is universal, with the state giving support to "thrust industries." However, in success cases, incentives can be (and are) withdrawn if firms do not meet performance criteria such as export expansion or incorporation of best-practice techniques. When scale economies are possible, protection plus barriers to entry through firm licensing may be combined. If too many producers are in an already protected market, cost reductions due to rising output volume at the firm level may never be realized unless the state or a large private sector agent brings about consolidation. For an industry starting *ab initio*, the relative merits of a quota *cum* licensing and a tariff regime have to be weighed; the former may only be essential when an existing sector has to be rationalized.

(5) The most effective incentives depend on context. Some drain and others add revenue to the treasury, and this dimension must be weighed. Some are administratively difficult, provide especially strong incentives for rent seeking, etc. Large countries on an ISTE path may opt for a Brazil-type "law of similars," banning any imports that compete closely with items produced at home; smaller economies might suffocate under such blanket provisions, but then they have to manage detailed import tariffs or quotas. Cheap credit is often an effective, easily administered incentive, but the government has to have the power (and the will) to cut it off if firms do not satisfy performance criteria.

(6) The criteria themselves should be straightforward and transparent — exports and technical advance. More theoretical considerations such as potential economies of scale may be used in selecting industries for targeting, but firms should perform according to simpler rules. "White elephants" grazing happily on state subsidies are not permitted to thrive in a well-run economy. In many cases, the monsters' pale hue is due to poor management, which can be changed. In situations where a bad investment decision was initially made or a good one was overtaken by external competition (e.g., Swedish shipyards), the government accepts an obligation to retrain and reemploy workers discharged in white elephant liquidations. Rapid overall growth lets this sort of transition hurt less.

(7) The issue of who bears the costs of the policies just sketched must be addressed. Vicious DUP circles involving the government and specific social groups can always appear — a successfully industrializing state will cut such knots and with luck compensate the losers from the fruits of productivity growth (e.g., Korean real wages rise less rapidly than productivity, but they do rise). External circumstances may make interventionist strategies more feasible in some contexts than others. A government that is fiscally constrained because it pays interest on external debt has few degrees of freedom; indeed, pushing exports via domestic recession to transfer resources abroad may distort the whole economic system. Successful growth may be impossible in debtor economies without reduced payments, in which case foreign institutions would pay part of the adjustment cost.

(8) There is often division of control, implicit or regulated through licensing, of sectoral production among national public and private enterprises and sometimes transnational corporations (or TNCs). Public enterprises do best in infrastructure, "base"

industries, and sectors like oil and high-tech services in which, largely for social reasons, labor and management come to share a strong ethos of performance. Parastatals become bureaucratized and do poorly in sectors where performance depends on complex product and process changes; private enterprise often does a better job of keeping up.

(9) "Infrastructure" broadly construed includes health and education. As already noted, small European countries specializing in high productivity exports, Korea, and Japan all score high on indicators such as ratios of technical people to the overall population, student scores on international science examinations, and overall well-being of their residents. The educational system in many economically successful nations is geared more toward high average performance than individual brilliance.

(10) In the rich small countries and the NICs, synergy between state and private sector extends to capital formation. As noted above, public investment often does not crowd out private investment from its assigned sectors, but in fact crowds it in. The implication is that state investment programs should be designed to raise productivity in both the public and private sectors. As noted above, a state-directed phase of growth is not likely to end successfully unless private institutions appear to sustain high investment levels and generate and channel savings flows to finance them.

(11) Orthodox economic theory suggests that distortions should just be avoided — in practice this recommendation reduces to little more than common sense. Successful industrializers hold distortions in line, but their efforts in this direction should not be exaggerated. The NICs are not models of *laissez faire*; nor were the generations of successful economies preceding them. Long-term, large divergences from market signals are costly; in a shorter run they may stimulate entrepreneurship and productivity growth. Neoclassical theory mostly gives static allocation rules. They boil down to a list of "don'ts," useful curbs to exuberance in decision making but secondary to dynamic processes of change.

6. SUMMARY AND CONCLUSIONS

The early optimism of development economics was misplaced — in the competence of the state, in the effectiveness of its interventions, in the independence of the national growth project from international trade, technology, and capital markets. In contrast to their predecessors, the legacy of 1980s vintage development economists will be documentation of imperfect policy making. The operating assumption of imperfect markets has been replaced by the presumed inevitability of imperfect states. Many have concluded that the former is the lesser of two evils, the implication being that governments should get out of development altogether.

The difficulty with this largely neoclassical recommendation is that its attempt to frame the question of the role of the state as a choice between evils is fundamentally flawed. This perspective only reinforces the profession's tendency to view economics and politics as distinct spheres. When economists finally discovered the state, they found it wanting and tried to reason it away. In the new neoclassical synthesis, the political and economic sciences are once again divorced.

But the state cannot be dismissed so easily. As we have noted repeatedly, virtually all cases of successful economic development have involved state intervention and improvisation of an industrial strategy. Mainstream economists deny this reality, arguing that no political arrangement can exist under which the state's actions will not be vitiated by DUP. But on the other hand, they want that state to act by disengaging itself from the economy. A much more sophisticated political economy is required, to *explain* and not just postulate the relationship between state and society.

Beyond these theoretical issues, changing conditions also have to be recognized. Constraints on public action have become more binding in recent years. Both foreign debt obligations and policy pressures such as International Monetary Fund and World Bank conditionality impose limits and generate internal political realignments. Fiscal costs of subsidies become more irksome at the same time as globalization of industrial activity makes it harder to attract foreign investment simply to serve an internal, albeit protected, market.

The general lesson to be learned from experience is that there are no bags of policy tricks that work regardless of context. However, that does not mean the policy decisions are contingent only on internal and external political and economic conditions of individual countries. Comparative analysis helps explain *why* particular strategies perform well or poorly in particular contexts. We have seen that successful industrial strategies have respected the boundary conditions limiting economies in which they were applied, and have incorporated the context-dependent structures discussed above. They were also flexible and adaptive. By describing boundaries and institutional dynamics within a consistent framework, we have attempted to move the intellectual debate about the state's role in development toward a synthesis that policy makers can use.

REFERENCES

Amsden, Alice, "Republic of Korea," Stabilization and Adjustment Policies and Programmes Country Study No. 14 (Helsinki: WIDER, 1988).

Bacha, Edmar L., "A three-gap model of foreign transfers and the GDP growth rate in developing countries," *Journal of Development Economics* (forthcoming).

Balassa, Bela, "Trade policies in developing countries," *American Economic Review, Papers and Proceedings*, Vol. 61 (1971), pp. 178–187.

Barbone, Luca, "Essays on trade and macro policy in developing countries," PhD dissertation (Cambridge, MA: Department of Economics, Massachusetts Institute of Technology, 1985).

Bardhan, Pranab K., *The Political Economy of Development in India* (Oxford: Basil Blackwell, 1984).

Barro, Robert, "A cross-country study of growth, saving, and government," NBER Working Paper No. 2885 (Cambridge, MA: National Bureau of Economic Research, 1989).

Barry, Brian, "Some questions about explanation," *International Studies Quarterly*, Vol. 27 (1983), pp. 17–27.

Bauer, P. T., *Reality and Rhetoric: Studies in the Economics of Development* (London: Weidenfeld and Nicolson, 1984).

Bauer, P. T., *Dissent on Development* (London: Weidenfeld and Nicolson, 1972).

Bhagwati, Jagdish N., "Directly unproductive profit seeking (DUP) activities," *Journal of Political Economy*, Vol. 90 (1982), pp. 988–1002.

Blejer, Mario, and Mohsin Khan, "Government policy and private investment in developing countries," *IMF Staff Papers*, Vol. 31 (1984), pp. 379–403.

Blomqvist, Ake, and Sharif Mohammad, "Controls, corruption, and competitive rent-seeking in LDCs," *Journal of Development Economics*, Vol. 21 (1986), pp. 161–180.

Boratav, Korkut, "Turkey," Stabilization and Adjustment Policies and Programmes Country Study No. 5 (Helsinki: WIDER, 1988).

Bowles, Samuel, and Robert Boyer, "A wage-led employment regime: Income distribution, labor discipline, and aggregate demand in welfare capitalism" (Helsinki: WIDER, 1988).

Bowles, Samuel, and John Eatwell, "Between two worlds: Interest groups, class structure, and capitalist growth," in Dennis C. Mueller (Ed.), *The Political Economy of Growth* (New Haven, CT: Yale University Press, 1983).

Buchanan, James, "Rent seeking and profit seeking," in J. M. Buchanan, R. D. Tollison, and G. Tullock (Eds.), *Toward a Theory of Rent-Seeking Society* (College Station, TX: Texas A&M University Press, 1980).

Cameron, David R., "Creating theory in comparative political economy: On Mancur Olson's explanation of growth," Paper presented at the Annual Meeting of the American Political Science Association (Chicago: 1983).

Chakravarty, Sukhamoy, *Development Planning: The Indian Experience* (Oxford: Clarendon Press, 1987).

Chakravarty, Sukhamoy, and Ajit Singh, "The desirable forms of economic openness in the South" (Helsinki: WIDER, 1988).

Chenery, Hollis B., "The structuralist approach to development policy," *American Economic Review, Papers and Proceedings*, Vol. 65 (1975), pp. 310–316.

Chenery, Hollis B., "Comparative advantage and development policy," *American Economic Review*, Vol. 51 (1961), pp. 18–51.

Chenery Hollis B., Sherman Robinson, and Moshe Syrquin, *Industrialization and Growth* (New York: Oxford University Press, 1986).

Cline, William, "Can the East Asian model of development be generalized?" *World Development*, Vol. 10 (1982), pp. 81–90.

Coase, Ronald, "The nature of the firm," *Econometrica*, Vol. 4 (1937), pp. 386–405.

DeVries, Jan, "The rise and decline of nations in historical perspective," *International Studies Quarterly*, Vol. 27 (1983), pp. 11–16.

Evans, Peter, "Predatory, developmental and other apparatuses: A comparative analysis of the Third World state," *Sociological Forum*, Vol. 4, No. 4 (1989).

Feder, Gershon, "On exports and economic growth," *Journal of Development Economics*, Vol. 12 (1983), pp. 59–73.

Findlay, Ronald, "Trade, development, and the state," Paper presented at the 25th Anniversary Symposium on the State of Development Economics (New Haven, CT: Economic Growth Center, Yale University, 1986).

Fishlow, Albert, "Brief comparative reflections on Latin American economic performance and policy" (Helsinki: WIDER, 1986).

Fishlow, Albert, "The state of Latin America economics," in *Economic and Social Progress in Latin America* (Washington, DC: Inter-American Development Bank, 1985).

Galbraith, John Kenneth, *Economic Development in Perspective* (Cambridge, MA: Harvard University Press, 1964).

Gerschenkron, Alexander, *Economic Backwardness in Historical Perspective* (Cambridge, MA: Harvard University Press, 1962).

Handlin, Oscar, and Mary Flug Handlin, *Commonwealth: A Study of the Role of Government in the American Economy: Massachusetts 1774–1861* (revised edition) (Cambridge, MA: Belknap Press of Harvard University Press, 1969).

Haggard, Stephan, "The politics of adjustment," *International Organization*, Vol. 39 (1985), pp. 505–534.

Harberger, Arnold, "Using the resources at hand more effectively," *American Economic Review, Papers and Proceedings*, Vol. 49 (1959), pp. 134–146.

Hartz, Louis, *Economic Policy and Democratic Thought: Pennsylvania 1776–1860* (Cambridge, MA: Harvard University Press, 1948).

Helleiner, G. K., "Trade strategy in medium-term adjustment," *World Development*, Vol. 18, No. 6 (1990) [this issue].

Hirschman, Albert O., "A generalized linkage approach to development, with special reference to staples," *Economic Development and Cultural Change*, Vol. 25, Supplement (1977), pp. 67–98.

Hirschman, Albert O., *The Strategy of Economic Development* (New Haven, CT: Yale University Press, 1958).

Hobson, John, *Imperialism: A Study* (London: J. Nisbet, 1902).

Horowitz, M., *The Transformation of American Law* (Cambridge, MA: Harvard University Press, 1977).

Hughes, Alan, and Ajit Singh, "The world economic slowdown and the Asian and Latin American economies: A comparitive analysis of economic structure, policy and performance" (Helsinki: WIDER, 1987).

Innis, Harold A., *The Fur Trade in Canada* (revised edition) (New Haven, CT: Yale University Press, 1962).

Johnson, Chalmers A., *MITI and the Japanese Miracle* (Stanford, CA: Stanford University Press, 1982).

Johnson, Harry G., *Economic Policies Toward Less Developed Countries* (Washington, DC: The Brookings Institution, 1967).

Katzenstein, Peter, *Small States in World Markets: Industrial Policy in Europe* (Ithaca, NY: Cornell University Press, 1985).

Kennedy, Paul, *The Rise and Fall of the Great Powers* (New York: Random House, 1987).

Krueger, Anne O., "Comparative advantage and development policy 20 years later," in Moshe Syrquin, Lance Taylor, and Larry Westphal (Eds.), *Economic Structure and Performance: Essays in Honor of Hollis B. Chenery* (New York: Academic Press, 1984).

Krueger, Anne O., "The political economy of the rent-seeking society," *American Economic Review*, Vol. 64 (1974), pp. 291–303.

Lal, Deepak, *The Poverty of "Development Economics"* (London: Institute of Economic Affairs, Hobart Paperback No. 16, 1983).

Little, Ian M. D., Tibor Scitovsky, and Maurice Scott, *Industry and Trade in Some Developing Countries: A Comparative Study* (London: Oxford University Press, 1970).

Malloy, James J., "The politics of transition in Latin America," in James M. Malloy and Mitchell A. Seligson (Eds.), *Authoritarians and Democrats: Regime Transition in Latin America* (Pittsburgh: University of Pittsburgh Press, 1987).

McCarthy, F. Desmond, Lance Taylor, and Cyrus Talati, "Trade patterns in developing countries, 1964–82," *Journal of Development Economics*, Vol. 27 (1987), pp. 5–39.

Moore, Jr., Barrington, *Social Origins of Dictatorship and Democracy* (Boston: Beacon Press, 1966).

Myrdal, Gunnar, "The 'soft state' in underdeveloped countries," in Paul Streeten (Ed.), *Unfashionable Economics: Essays in Honor of Lord Balogh* (London: Weidenfeld and Nicolson, 1970).

Newfarmer, Richard (Ed.), *Profits, Progress, and Poverty: Case Studies of International Industries in Latin America* (Notre Dame, IN: University of Notre Dame Press, 1985).

North, Douglass, *Structure and Change in Economic History* (New York: W. W. Norton, 1981).

O'Connor, James, *The Fiscal Crisis of the State* (New York: St. Martin's Press, 1973).

O'Donnell, Guillermo, *Modernization and Bureaucratic-Authoritarianism* (Berkeley, CA: Institute of International Studies, University of California, 1973).

Offe, Claus, "Structural problems of the capitalist state," in K. von Beyme (Ed.), *German Political Studies*, Vol. 1 (London: Sage, 1974).

Offe, Claus, and Volker Ronge, "Theses on the theory of the state," *New German Critique* (1975).

Olson, Mancur, *The Rise and Decline of Nations* (New Haven, CT: Yale University Press, 1982).

Ortiz, Guillermo, and Carlos Noriega, "Investment and growth in Latin America" (Washington, DC: International Monetary Fund, 1988).

Pack, Howard, "Industrialization and trade," in Hollis B. Chenery and T. N. Srinivasan (Eds.), *Handbook of Development Economics*, Vol. 1 (Amsterdam: North-Holland, 1988).

Piore, Michael J., and Charles F. Sabel, *The Second Industrial Divide: Possibilities for Prosperity* (New York: Basic Books, 1984).

Prebisch, Raul, "Commercial policy in the underdeveloped countries," *American Economic Review*, Vol. 49 (1959), pp. 257–269.

Prebish, Raul, *The Economic Development of Latin America and Its Principal Problems* (Lake Success, NY: United Nations Department of Social Affairs, 1950).

Schultz, T. Paul, "Education investment and returns," in Hollis B. Chenery and T. N. Srinivasan (Eds.), *Handbook of Development Economics*, Vol. 1 (Amsterdam: North-Holland, 1988).

Schumpeter, Josef A., *The Theory of Economic Development* (Cambridge, MA: Harvard University Press, 1934).

Scitovsky, Tibor, "Two concepts of external economies," *Journal of Political Economy*, Vol. 62 (1954), pp. 143–151.

Shapiro, Helen, "State intervention and industrialization: The origins of the Brazilian automobile industry," PhD dissertation (New Haven, CT: Department of Economics, Yale University, 1988).

Singer, Hans, "The distribution of gains between investing and borrowing countries," *American Economic Review*, Vol. 40 (1950), pp. 473–485.

Srinivasan, T. N., "Neoclassical political economy: The state and economic development" (New Haven, CT: Economic Growth Center, Yale University, 1985).

Taylor, Lance, "Gap disequilibria: Inflation, investment, saving, and foreign exchange" (Cambridge, MA: Department of Economics, Massachusetts Institute of Technology, 1989).

Taylor, Lance, *Varieties of Stabilization Experience* (Oxford: Clarendon Press, 1988).

Taylor, Lance, "Economic openness: Problems to century's end" (Helsinki: WIDER, 1987).

Toye, John, *Dilemmas of Development* (Oxford: Basil Blackwell, 1987).

Watkins, Melville H., "A staple theory of economic growth," *Canadian Journal of Economics and Political Science*, Vol. 29 (1963), pp. 141–158.

Weffort, Francisco, *O Populismo na Politica Brasileira* (Rio de Janeiro: Paz e Terra, 1978).

Wilson, C. H., "Trade, society, and the state," *Cambridge Economic History of Europe: Part IV* (Cambridge: Cambridge University Press, 1967).

Young, Allyn, "Increasing returns and economic progress," *Economic Journal*, Vol. 38 (1928), pp. 527–542.

Bolivia: Hyperinflation, Stabilisation, and Beyond

*by Manuel Pastor, Jr.**

This article argues that the Bolivian hyperinflation of 1984–85 was fundamentally rooted in problems of external finance and distributional conflict and shows how the New Economic Policy (NEP) addressed these issues with an orthodox approach that attracted the support of international lending institutions and shifted the balance of 'power away from labour. Along the way, I conduct an econometric investigation of the proximate determinants of inflation in both the hyperinflationary and post-inflation periods. I close by considering current and future problems in the Bolivian macroeconomy.

INTRODUCTION

In 1985, a wave of new macroeconomic stabilisation experiments swept through Latin America. Heterodox policies with differing emphases but with a common element of incomes policy and increased government intervention took hold in three Latin American countries: Argentina, Brazil, and Peru. Bolivia, staggering from an inflation rate of over 4,000 per cent in just the first seven months of 1985, bucked this heterodox trend and instead adopted a series of orthodox measures the likes of which had not been seen since the Chilean and Argentine experiences of the late 1970s. Within weeks, the monthly inflation rate fell from over 50 per cent to less than zero; discounting a brief inflationary blip in January, the inflation rate fell to slightly over 30 per cent in 1986 and only ten per cent in 1987. The 'miracle of La Paz' was greeted with enthusiasm by the International Monetary Fund and mainstream economists: in the wilderness of the new heterodoxy, one nation had struck to orthodoxy with what seemed to be tremendous success.

What were the causes of the Bolivian hyperinflation and how did the shift toward orthodoxy end it? I argue below that the Bolivian hyperinflation had two fundamental determinants – the collapse of external finance

*Associate Professor of Economics, Occidental College, Los Angeles, California, USA. The author thanks Samuel Doria Medina, Arthur Mann, Juan Antonio Morales, Herbert Muller, and Jeffrey Sachs for helpful discussions and advice about the Bolivian experience. Thanks also to Jeff Frieden, Keith Griffin, Robby Moore, Jim Whitney, John Williamson, and an anonymous referee for comments on an earlier draft. The author gratefully acknowledges the support of the Fulbright Commission for funding two visits to La Paz in 1987 and 1988 and the research assistance of Mark Marriott and Todd Clark. This article is part of a longer study comparing heterodox and orthodox stabilisation experiences in Peru and Bolivia; the longer work, *Inflation, Stabilization, and Debt: Macroeconomic Experiments in Peru and Bolivia* will be published by Westview Press.

and distributional conflict over burden-sharing – and two proximate determinants – a steadily depreciating peso and excessive monetary growth. A policy shift toward orthodoxy helped end the inflation both because it attracted the foreign financial support needed to stabilise the exchange rate and because it was associated with a resolution of the distributional conflicts in favour of capitalist interests. The results were predictably similar to those achieved by Bolivia's orthodox precursors in the 1970s: an overvalued exchange rate and an unsustainable import boom, extraordinarily high real interest rates and increasing fragility in the financial system, an enhanced dependence on foreign capital flows and orthodox international institutions, and a regressive redistribution which increased social tension and eventually eroded support for the stabilising government.

The paper has the following order. In the first major section, I review the reasons for hyperinflation in Bolivia, a task which involves both a political/historical analysis and some modest econometrics. In the second major section, I analyse the basic elements of Bolivia's 'New Economic Policy' and explore how the policy package – and its 'credibility-gaining' political strategy of suppressing the labour movement and winning the hearts and dollars of international financial institutions – helped cool inflation to its present level. In the final section, I offer some reflections on the future of the Bolivian macroeconomy.

THE BOLIVIAN HYPERINFLATION

The Bolivia hyperinflation raged from early in 1984 until the implementation of the New Economic Policy in August, 1985; the peak was reached in February 1985 when *monthly* inflation topped 180 per cent.[1] While such inflation levels are shocking, the 1984 slide into hyperinflation was not unexpected; Bolivia had been plagued by inflation of around 300 per cent in the two preceding years, GDP had fallen by 11 per cent since 1981, the consolidated public sector deficit had reached nearly 20 per cent of GDP, and the government had lost the support of almost every sector of Bolivian society (see Table 1; all data sources detailed in the Appendix).

In his early and wide-ranging study of the Bolivia hyperinflation, Sachs remarks that 'the Bolivian inflation is apparently unique in the annals of hyperinflations, in that it is the only hyperinflation in the twentieth century that did not come in the aftermath of a foreign war, a civil war, or a political revolution' [*Sachs, 1986:6*]. The hyperinflation was, however, less unique than Sachs contends. First, like the German inflation following the First World War, it was provoked by 'reparations payments' in the form of debt service outflows. Second, while the inflationary period did not see a civil war with open armed conflict, the inflation was partly a result of intense distributional conflict; moreover, the New Economic Programme achieved its anti-inflation victory partly through suppressing working class demands and organisations. I deal with these points below.

TABLE 1.*

MACROECONOMIC DATA FOR BOLIVIA, 1980–88

	inflation rate	rate of growth of money (M1)	rate of depreciation (official rate)	rate of depreciation (parallel rate)
1980	23.9%	41.2%	0.0%	—
1981	25.1%	20.5%	0.0%	68.3%
1982	296.5%	229.7%	701.3%	586.1%
1983	328.6%	209.6%	154.6%	339.6%
1984	2,175.5%	1,781.8%	1,650.2%	1,678.5%
1985	8,168.6%	5,928.7%	18,053.5%	7,655.7%
1986	66.0%	82.9%	21.1%	14.5%
1987	10.7%	38.3%	14.9%	15.1%
1988	18.0%	31.5%	11.8%	—

	GDP growth	public sector deficit as % GDP	private investment as % GDP	public investment as % GDP
1980	−0.5%	9.1%	7.2%	7.1%
1981	0.9%	7.6%	6.1%	7.6%
1982	−4.4%	15.9%	2.8%	9.8%
1983	−6.5%	17.1%	4.7%	8.1%
1984	−0.3%	24.0%	5.4%	6.5%
1985	−0.2%	10.0%	7.2%	4.7%
1986	−2.9%	4.0%	6.2%	6.4%
1987	2.2%	9.7%	—	—
1988	2.8%	6.0%	—	—

	exports (FOB)	imports (CIF)	trade balance	total external debt	
	(US$ mil)	(US$ mil)	(US$ mil)	(US$ mil)	(as % GNP)
1980	942.2	−678.4	263.8	2,700	93.3%
1981	912.4	−975.0	−62.6	3,219	104.3%
1982	827.7	−577.3	250.4	3,328	106.4%
1983	755.1	−589.2	165.9	4,069	147.8%
1984	724.5	−491.5	233.0	4,286	176.7%
1985	623.4	−552.1	71.3	4,805	184.9%
1986	545.5	−711.0	−165.5	5,580	167.8%
1987	518.7	−770.4	−251.7	5,631	151.5%
1988	542.5	−583.6	−41.1	5,456	135.6%

*'—' indicates missing data. Data sources for various series reported in the Appendix. The inflation rates, money growth, and depreciation are all end-of-period (that is, from December of the previous year to December of the current year).

Sources: Carriaga [1989], *International Financial Statistics*, Muller [1988a], UDAPE [1986], and *World Debt Tables, 1988-89*. See Appendix.

Economic Structure and External Shocks

With a 1987 per capita GNP below $600, Bolivia is one of the poorest and least developed countries in Latin America. Prior to the hyperinflation (in 1980), the economy was characterised by three key economic sectors: (1) a domestically oriented sector, consisting of manufacturing (15 per cent of

GDP), agriculture (19 per cent), and public administration (11 per cent); (2) an export-oriented sector in which only two dominant activities (mining at 11 per cent of GDP and petroleum at six per cent) provided 90 per cent of export revenues over the 1980–85 period; and (3) a service sector, including construction (four per cent) and services (35 per cent), which were largely derivative of output and income in the first two sectors.

For analysing the roots of hyperinflation, the most salient features of the Bolivian economy were its nearly monocultural export structure and the public sector's heavy reliance on external finance. The former feature meant that falling mineral prices in the 1980s had an especially serious impact on both GDP and inflation; the inflationary pressures resulted from both the exchange rate effects of a dollar shortfall and the fiscal impact of losses in government-owned mines.

As for the public sector and foreign finance, it is important to note heavy government external borrowing to finance deficits in late 1970s and 1980–81; over the period 1973–81, public long-term external debt rose from $640.4 million to $2.7 billion. This left the economy quite vulnerable to a 'capital shock' in which a reversal in net external resource flows forces both a deterioration in the exchange rate and a shift to 'internal finance', that is, monetisation of the government deficit. Such a 'capital shock' occurred when lending fell in the wake of the regional debt crisis and this played the same role as reparation payments in German case: inflationary stresses were placed on international reserves and government finance.

Political Context and Policy Response

While the hyperinflation may be ultimately rooted in Bolivia's export structure and public reliance on external finance, the take-off to a true hyperinflation also reflects the political and policy paralysis of administration of Hernan Siles Zuazo (1982–85). Zuazo had a rocky road to power; after long-time military dictator Hugo Banzer stepped down, Zuazo's leftist coalition won the plurality in elections in 1978, 1979, and 1980 only to see military coups or parliamentary maneuvers prevent its accession to power. The final coup in 1980 was one of the bloodiest in Bolivian history and put in power a faction of the military with strong ties to the drug trade. Finally embarrassed by having drug dealers run the country and chagrined by the economic crisis detailed below, a new military regime restored the Congress elected in 1980. The Congress, in turn, duly awarded the Presidency to Siles Zuazo.

As in much of the rest of Latin America, the return to the barracks was preceded by a complete disorganisation of the economy. In 1980–81, government authorities had permitted capital flight of nearly $600 million (as measured by net errors and omissions). Helped along by a drop in tin prices, 1982 saw a nearly ten per cent decline in export revenues and a nearly five per cent drop in GDP. With capital flows also collapsing, net international reserves declined to -$265.7 million by mid-1982 [*Morales, 1987 a: 22*]. The military responded to the reserve crisis with a dual exchange rate system that produced expectations of future devaluation and thus attacks on the Bolivia peso. Meanwhile, the deficit for the consolidated public sector passed from 7.6 per cent of GDP in 1981 to 15.9 per cent in 1982 (see Table 2). While net external finance had financed over 50 per cent of the deficit in 1980 and actually exceeded the deficit in 1981, 1982 external financing was essentially zero, a shift which drove internal financing (or monetary emission) to nearly 16 per cent of GDP (see Table 2). In the name of democracy, this economic mess was handed to the new President.

Siles Zuazo sought to deal with the crisis while simultaneously avoiding measures that would hurt his own constituency in the working and popular classes. His first programme (in November 1982) attempted to: (1) establish control over foreign exchange by requiring exporters to turn over 100 per cent of dollar earnings (at the official exchange rate) and restricting imports directly or via differential tariffs and exchange rationing; (2) address the fiscal difficulties by raising export taxes; (3) protect real wages by instituting a trigger mechanism that would fully adjust the minimum wage after a 40 per cent rise in the price level; and (4) 'dedollarise' the economy by converting all dollar-denominated contracts into peso terms. This last measure proved to be the Achilles heel of the programme. Ostensibly designed to delink the economy from exchange rate-driven inflation, the dedollarisation provoked yet another run on the peso, driving up the parallel market exchange rate and inflationary expectations, and thus added to the inflationary impetus coming from the government's monetisation of large deficits.

Exchange problems, government deficits, and inflation were further aggravated by the government's early efforts to partially meet its debt obligations, a strategy which did not promote new lending and thus drained the country of resources even as it worsened the fiscal situation. In retrospect, it seems curious that a seemingly leftist government would honour international obligations at the cost of its own economy and working-class constituents. In 1982–84, however, no Latin American government had yet attempted to openly (that is, as a policy matter rather than as temporary exigency) restrict debt service; as a result, the penalties for non-service were perceived to be extremely high. Moreover, the new Bolivian leaders naively thought that steering the country from a narcotics-ridden dictatorship to a fresh democracy would be sufficient to attract substantial aid from Western nations. As is now well known, the advanced capitalist democracies instead responded to Latin American democratisation by insisting that the new regimes service debts contracted by their military predecessors.

Siles Zuazo thus inherited a structural crisis of debt and export dependence, an immediate context of political and economic chaos, and a recent policy history which included dramatic errors by the previous military regime (particularly the establishment of a dual exchange rate system and the failure to correct budget problems). None the less, Zuazo's first moves, especially the 'dedollarisation' and the decision to service debt, deepened the crisis – and, as I suggest below, the 'civil war' embodied in Bolivia's unequal social structure made it impossible to resolve the problems once they began.

TABLE 2

FISCAL OPERATIONS IN BOLIVIA, 1980–87
(all figures in percentage of GDP)

CENTRAL AMINISTRATION OPERATIONS	1980	1981	1982	1983	1984	1985	1986	1987
current revenue	10.2%	11.4%	5.8%	3.2%	2.6%	7.3%	13.5%	11.8%
tax revenue	8.8%	8.7%	5.0%	2.5%	2.4%	7.1%	13.2%	11.3%
of which transfers from non-financial public firms	3.2%	3.4%	1.8%	0.7%	0.7%	5.1%	9.5%	6.7%
— firm transfers as % of current revenue	30.9%	29.6%	31.3%	21.2%	27.0%	69.5%	70.4%	56.5%
current expenditure	14.8%	15.6%	20.8%	21.8%	19.2%	13.1%	14.2%	14.2%
current account	-4.5%	-4.2%	-15.0%	-18.5%	-16.6%	-5.8%	-0.7%	-2.4%

OPERATIONS OF NON-FINANCIAL PUBLIC FIRMS	1980	1981	1982	1983	1984	1985	1986	1987
pre-transfer current account	5.9%	6.4%	7.0%	3.3%	0.1%	7.4%	11.2%	4.5%
net transfers to general govt.	-4.6%	-4.8%	-4.2%	-2.1%	-2.1%	-6.2%	-11.5%	-7.7%
current account	1.2%	2.0%	2.8%	1.1%	-2.0%	1.1%	-0.3%	-3.2%
capital revenue	0.3%	0.5%	0.1%	0.2%	0.1%	0.1%	0.0%	0.0%
capital exp.	3.6%	3.1%	4.7%	2.8%	2.1%	1.2%	1.6%	3.4%
overall surplus	-2.2%	-0.8%	-1.8%	-1.5%	-4.0%	-0.1%	-1.9%	-6.6%

CONSOLIDATED PUBLIC SECTOR	1980	1981	1982	1983	1984	1985	1986	1987
overall surplus	-9.1%	-7.6%	-16.3%	-17.7%	-24.0%	-10.0%	-4.0%	-9.7%
financing	9.1%	7.6%	16.3%	17.7%	24.0%	10.0%	4.0%	9.7%
external	4.9%	12.4%	0.1%	-0.7%	5.0%	3.9%	5.3%	5.2%
internal	4.0%	-4.7%	17.1%	18.4%	19.0%	6.1%	-1.3%	4.5%
short-term foreign loans	0.2%	-0.1%	-0.9%	0.0%	0.0%	0.0%	0.0%	0.0%

Source: See the Appendix. 1984 figures are preliminary; figures for 1985–87 are estimates; detailed 1988 figures were unavailable.

Inflation and Hyperinflation

Many analysts see inflation as partly the result of unresolved social conflict [*Rowthorn, 1980; Taylor 1983*]. In this view, a wage-price spiral can occur when workers and capitalists are unable to arrive at some explicit agreement about the distribution of income and instead struggle for an increased income share by continually raising nominal claims. While less explored by such proponents of 'class-conflict' inflation, widening government deficits and their monetisation can also be understood in distributional terms: generally, workers clamour for more social spending while capitalists resist surrendering the social surplus (in the form of tax revenues) that will fund these expenditures. If external financing is available, the inflationary impact of such social conflict can be dampened; if such financing is not available, monetisation is required and inflation can result.

The hyperinflation of the Siles Zuazo period reflects both wage-price and deficit dynamics. The persistence of the Bolivian wage-price spiral, particularly surprising in light of the rising unemployment and general market slack of these years, was partly a result of extensive state intervention in labour markets. As noted before, Zuazo's early policies included a 100 per cent indexation of the minimum wage, with adjustments to be made with each 40 per cent increase in the price level. This led other workers to demand similar treatment and by April 1984, the government promulgated a policy of 100 per cent indexation for *all* wages; while adjustment was scheduled every four months, the period between wage hikes was eventually reduced to a month. A wage-price spiral, in short, was codified by government action; union struggles to raise various sectors' wages gave a further impetus to the dynamic.

The pressure to maintain and even raise real wages must be seen in the light of stagnant wages in the 1970s and a dramatic decline in labour's share of income during 1980–82.[2] The labour movement had supported Siles Zuazo and viewed his presidency as an opportunity to make up for those past losses. This attempt at 'catch-up' is shown in Figure 1 in which I plot the movement of real wages and per capita GDP on a quarterly basis from the beginning of 1982 to the middle of 1986; both indices are normalised at 100 for the first quarter of 1982 and the quarterly GDP growth rates are extrapolated from yearly data. With oscillations around the trend the real wage more or less tracks per capita GDP (with a brief surge right after Siles took power in fourth quarter, 1982) until the fourth quarter of 1984; after this, there is a dramatic and short-lived increase in real wages which is subsequently eroded by the hyperinflation, then severely reduced by the 1985 adjustment program (with some recuperation in 1986).[3] The pattern suggests several stylised facts. First, until late 1984, workers were not that successful at catch-up efforts and seem to have been fighting a mostly defensive battle against inflation. Second, after late 1984, unions resorted to clearly unsustainable wage demands, a trend which was surely a factor in pushing inflation up to its highest level in the hyperinflationary period – a monthly inflation rate averaging over 100 per cent between December 1984 and February 1985.[4]

Late 1984 also marks a turning point in government-labour relations. Labour had initially been supportive of Zuazo and offered only moderate protest to early stabilisation efforts. In April 1984, however, the major labour federation, the Central Obrero Boliviano (COB), staged a national strike to protest a new stabilisation package that came on the heels of the visit to La Paz of an IMF mission. The conflict produced one positive result: in May, the government met the COB's demand to finally stop servicing external debt, a move which unfortunately could not erase the damage that debt service had already done to public finances. Mostly, however, the conflict yielded negative consequences: the government was shown to have no control over the labour sector, the unions seized the opportunity to pursue unrealistic and inflationary wage increases, and any possibility of

FIGURE 1

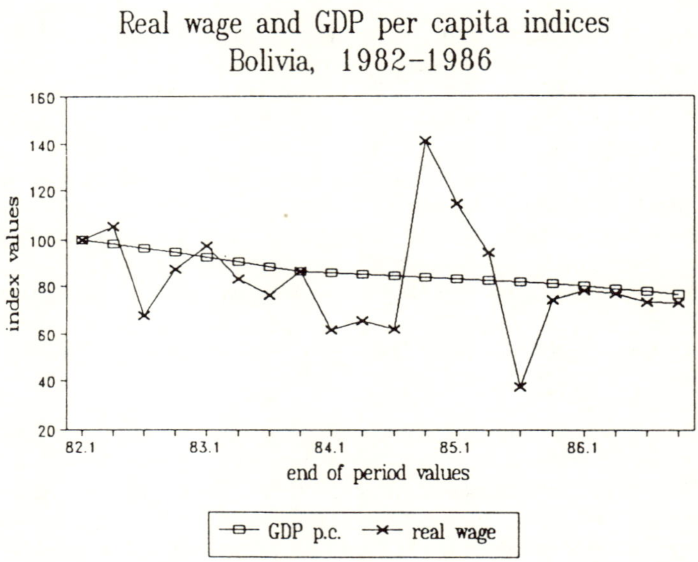

a 'social pact' to restrain inflation evaporated. With political support for his government virtually non-existent, Siles Zuazo called in November 1982 for elections to be held in July 1985 rather than the scheduled July 1986; in the meantime, the government gave up any pretense of restraining the deficit, wages, or any other inflationary pressures.

Bolivia's profound distributional conflicts were also evidenced in the steady deterioration in the country's fiscal position between 1982 and 1985. Workers generally pressed for continued subsidies, other social expenditures, and increases in public employment and salaries.[5] Meanwhile, inflation steadily eroded the value of nominal tax payments while a relatively strong Congressional right was able to resist the implementation of new taxes that might reduce the growing deficit. Returning to Table 2, we can see the results: tax revenues fell from 8.7 per cent of GDP in 1981 to less than three per cent in 1984 while in the same period central government expenditures actually rose slightly as a percentage of GDP (although they fell in real terms). What little restraint there was on the expenditure side was achieved by cuts in government investment; capital expenditures for the consolidated public sector (including central government, local government, and parastatals) fell from 7.3 per cent of GDP in 1981 to three per cent in 1985. The future of the country was being sacrificed to the distributional struggle.

Thus, the Bolivian experience of hyperinflation does indeed mirror other experiences. On the one hand, 'reparations payments' in the form of debt service strained the balance of payments and placed pressure on both the exchange rate and government finance. On the other, class and social conflict pushed the inflationary cycle along, partly through the wage-price dynamic and partly through the inability to saddle some party with the burden of financing government spending once international credit flows ceased.[6]

Intermediate Causes: Money and the Exchange Rate

The discussion above suggests two fundamental requirements for ending the hyperinflation: an improvement in net external flows and some resolution of the underlying social conflict driving both the wage-price spiral and the widening government deficit. There were, however, several intermediate causal factors – particularly monetary growth and exchange depreciation – which had to be addressed.

Table 3 presents data on monetary behaviour from 1980 to 1988 using December-to-December figures. The bottom half of the table documents the dramatic increases in the nominal monetary base between 1982 and 1985; to the right-hand side of this data, I calculate the percentage of the nominal increase accounted for by nominal increases in the various components of the base. We should remember that such 'accounting' for monetary growth does *not* necessarily explain inflation: the 'contribution' of net international reserves to changes in the monetary base reported in Table 3, for example, does not capture the more complex argument that a general foreign exchange shortage forced an exchaneg rate deterioration in the black market and hence domestic price adjustment regardless of what was occuring in the official monetary accounts. In addition, the December-to-December figures are slightly misleading, particularly for 1985 when domestic credit growth was curtailed mid-year as part of the anti-inflation strategy. Despite these limitations, the data do suggest that credit expansion to finance the government deficit played a crucial role in monetary expansion both before and after 1982.

TABLE 3

MONETARY GROWTH AND ITS COMPONENTS

(thousands of Bolivianos 1980–84, millions of Bolivianos 1985–88)

(* indicates the break in the series)

	monetary base	equals the sum of:	net int'l reserves	net credit to public sector	credit to banks	other accounts
1980	13.7		-2.4	13.2	4.0	-1.0
1981	16.2		-5.7	16.7	4.8	0.4
1982	63.7		-63.6	86.7	21.0	19.6
1983	194.8		-24.1	275.8	54.0	-110.9
1984	3345.0		840.0	2926.0	970.0	-1391.0
1985	201.0*		159.0*	-205.0*	130.0	117.0*
1986	380.0		596.0	-538.0	360.0	-38.0
1987	475.0		373.0	-510.0	608.0	4.0
1988	770.0		359.0	-632.0	910.0	140.0

	per cent increase in monetary base		percentage of monetary base growth attributable to changes in: net int'l reserves	net credit to public sector	credit to banks	other accounts
1980	39.8&		-62.0%	135.0%	27.0%	0.1%
1981	17.9%		-136.3%	144.8%	32.2%	59.3%
1982	293.3%		-121.8%	147.3%	34.2%	40.3%
1983	205.8%		30.1%	144.2%	25.2%	-99.5%
1984	1616.1%		27.4%	84.1%	29.1%	-40.6%
1985	5909.0%		80.0%	-105.2%	65.3%	59.9%
1986	89.1%		244.1%	-186.0%	128.5%	-86.6%
1987	25.0%		-234.7%	29.5%	261.1%	44.2%
1988	63.6%		-4.6%	-40.4%	100.0%	45.0%

All reported figures are year-end (that is, December); the components of the base may not exactly add to the reported base due to rounding. The contribution to monetary gwoth of a particular component is calculated by dividing the nominal increase in that component by the nominal increase in the overall monetary base.

Source: *International Financial Statistics*. See Appendix.

Did this monetary expansion play a causal role in the inflation? While the immediate temptation is to conclude that it did, several studies have suggested that hyperinflations are accompanied by a reversal in the traditional causality from money to prices (see, for example, Sargent and Wallace [*1981*]). The specific mechanism by which money 'chases' prices has been modelled in different ways but a simple story may be constructed as follows: (1) given political constraints, the government seeks to maintain some real level of spending, (2) as inflation proceeds, the real value of nominal tax payments declines, and (3) as a result, the government deficit widens and monetary growth accelerates. Sargent and Wallace [*1981*] offer formal tests supporting the notion that prices 'led' money during the hyperinflationary experiences of post-First World War Europe. Morales [*1987b*] conducts such 'causality' tests for the Bolivian experience and finds a similar pattern.

In other research on the Bolivian inflation, Sachs [*1986*] suggests that as the inflation accelerated, economic agents sought to protect the value of both goods and assets in terms of dollars and so adjusted domestic prices according to changes in the exchange rate. In this view, then, the exchange rate 'led' prices; Sachs presents some limited econometric evidence for his position by regressing inflation on the exchange rate and finding a positive relation (which, of course, does not directly test causality but rather assumes it).

To explore these issues further, I conducted Granger-Sims causality tests on inflation, monetary growth, and exchange depreciation. In such tests, prices, for example, are regressed on the lags and leads of a monetary variable. An F-test is then performed on the explanatory power of the leads (or future values) of money; if the F-value is significant, this indicates that the future predicts the past, a phenomenon likely only when the causality is actually running the other way, for example, from prices to money.

The actual details of such causality tests are more complex and vary slightly between applications. For this article, I followed Sargent and Wallace [*1981*]: I calculated the rate of change of the relevant variables, X and Y, by taking the natural log of the current value divided by its immediate lag; I then regressed the resulting X' on Y' in order to obtain an estimate of the autoregressive parameter, $\hat{p}$; I used this parameter to 'quasi-difference' both variables according to the formula, $(X'(1\text{-}\hat{p}L))$ where L is the first order lag operator; and finally regressed the resulting X'' on Y'' in order to obtain the relevant coefficient estimates and F-statistics [*Sargent and Wallace, 1981: 417–18*].

Causality tests using four lags, the current value, and two leads of the independent were conducted for both the longer period of both high and hyperinflation and the shorter period of 'true' hyperinflation. The longer period begins in July 1982 because this is the first month for which I could compute a useable fourth lag (the raw data begin in January 1982, giving a starting inflation rate in February, and a starting 'quasi-differenced' rate in March). The shorter period begins in April 1984 because this is the first month identified by Morales [*1987a: 50*] as involving 'true' hyperinflation, that is, monthly inflation in excess of 50 per cent. The end for both tests is June 1985 since the last month of hyperinflation was August and the tests require two leads.

Table 4 presents the results of this exercise. For reasons of space, I report only the results of the F-test (and not all the various coefficients); for simplicity, I list the results under the alternative hypothesis (for example, price 'leads' money). For the money variable, I follow Morales in choosing the 'monetary base' (bank reserves and currency in the public's hands) as the appropriate measure;[7] the results on money, however, are contrary to

Morales' and suggest that monetary growth leads (or 'causes') inflation, even during the period of 'true' hyperinflation (after the monthly inflation rate topped 50 per cent). As for the relationship between the exchange rate and prices, the results square with Sachs' prior: the parallel or 'free-market' exchange rate led prices through the whole period.

Why the difference with Morales on the role of money? While Morales also follows the Sargent and Wallace method detailed above, he first deseasonalises his data [*Morales, 1987b; 21*]. Such a procedure is theoretically suspect for at least two reasons: (1) if seasonal peaks in inflation result from similarly seasonal increases in the monetary base, this relationship should not be eliminated in a causality determination, and (2) over the short two and a half year period tested here, a seemingly seasonal phenomena (occurring in, say, two of the three years) may simply be a random event and 'correcting' in this case would yield inaccurate estimates. For these reasons, I (and an anonymous referee) believe deseasonalisation to be inappropriate; I therefore stick with the causality results of Table 4.[8]

Relying on these results, I ran regressions on inflation as a function of past inflation, monetary growth (and its lag), and changes in the exchange rate (and its lag); once again, these rates of change are calculated as

TABLE 4

RESULTS FOR GRANGER-SIMS CAUSALITY TESTS ON PRICES, MONEY, AND THE EXCHANGE RATE.

	P 'leads' M	M 'leads' P
July, 1982–June, 1985 (2,27)	3.265 *	9.856 ***
April, 1984–June, 1985 (2,6)	3.363 #	7.474 **
	P 'leads' E	**E 'leads' P**
July, 1982–June, 1985 (2, 27)	0.654	6.226 ***
April, 1984–June, 1985 (2,6)	0.239	3.597 *

*** Significant at 1 %
** Significant at 5 %
* Significant at 10 %
# Significant at 20%

All regressions include four lags, a current value, and two leads; the numbers in parantheses report the degrees of freedom used in calculating the significance of the reported F-values. The figures in the tables are F-values testing the explantory power of the leads; the significance of each value is indicated below the reported F-value.

As indicated in the text, all variables (X) are calculated as rates of change using the formula $\{\log[(X^t)/(X^{t-1})]\}$. Regressions are first 'quasi-differenced' and include a time trend. P is taken from the consumer price index, M from the monetary base, and E from the parallel exchange rate. All data from Morales [*1987a*] and Muller [*1988b*].

$\{\log(X^t/X^{t-1})\}$ but here no 'quasi-differencing' is necessary. Once again, I tested for both the longer period of high and hyperinflation and the shorter period of true hyperinflation; since the data are not 'quasi-differenced' and there is only one lag, the starting and ending points for each regression are slightly different than those used in the Granger-Sims tests. For both the long and short periods, I present both the full model and then a somewhat reduced model focusing on the most significant variables. Starting with column (1) of Table 5, note the anaemic performance of past inflation and monetary growth rates; dropping those two variables (as in column (2)) yields a regression with roughly the same explanatory power (as measured by the adjusted R^2) as when the variables are included). For the shorter time period of true hyperinflation, the results are especially interesting. For the full model (see column (3)), only the lagged exchange rate is significant at traditional levels with the current exchange rate next in order of significance. Dropping the monetary variables and the past inflation rate in column (4) actually yields a regression with higher explanatory power.

TABLE 5

THE DETERMINANTS OF HYPERINFLATION IN BOLIVIA

Dependent = inflation

Variables	March 1982 to August 1985 (1)	(2)	April 1984 to August 1985 (3)	(4)
Growth of Monetary Base	0.331 (2.132)**	0.381 (2.897)***	0.190 (0.680)	
Growth of Lagged Monetary Base	−0.118 (−0.534)		−0.220 (−0.527)	
Change in Parallel Exchange Rate	0.264 (2.398)**	0.221 (2.717)***	0.291 (1.221)	0.199 (1.394)#
Lagged Change in Parallel Exchange Rate	0.373 (4.242)***	0.421 (5.191)***	0.523 (2.947)**	0.553 (3.879)***
Lagged Inflation	0.194 (1.442)#		0.074 (0.326)	
Constant	−0.010 (−0.284)	−0.001 (−0.038)	0.067 (0.481)	0.111 (1.458)#
Degrees of Freedom	(36)	(38)	(11)	(14)
Adjusted R-squared	0.605	0.604	0.432	0.526
Durbin Watson	1.743	1.486	1.357	1.305
F-test	13.545***	21.835***	3.435**	9.876***

*** Significant at 1% (two-tail)
** Significant at 5% (two-tail)
* Significant at 10% (two-tail)
# Significant at 20% (two-tail)

As indicated in the text, inflation is calculated as log (P^t/P^{t-1}); the other variables (growth of monetary base and change in the parallel exchange rate are calculated similarly. For each variable, the coefficient is reported; beneath it (in parantheses) is the T-statistic accompanied by a mark indicating the significance level. Data from Morales [*1987a*] and Muller [*1988a*].

The general insignificance of past inflation (particularly in the shorter time period) indicates that inertial inflation – inflation resulting from the formal or informal indexation of wages or other prices to past inflation – ceased to play much of a role during the hyperinflationary period. While monetary growth is significant over the longer time period, its effects are swamped by the exchange rate during the true hyperinflation. In terms of immediate policy, then, hyperinflation had to be addressed primarily (or at least initially) by stabilising the 'leading price' – the exchange rate. Slowing monetary growth (that is, reducing deficits) was also necessary but secondary in immediate importance to exchange rate stabilisation.

THE NEW ECONOMIC PROGRAMME

The New Economic Program (NEP), launched by the administration of President Victor Paz Estenssoro in August 1985, addressed the political and technical determinants of inflation with five essential policies: (1) stabilisation of the exchange rate, (2) liberalisation of trade and capital accounts, (3) the reduction of government deficit and monetary emission, (4) the resolution of the distributional and political conflicts in favour of capital, and (5) the achievement of new external resources, mostly because the orthodoxy of the programme allowed a *rapprochement* with official creditors. For the longer-run, the government also promised to abandon the state-led development model that had ruled in Bolivia since the 1952 revolution that Paz had helped lead [*Wilkie, 1987*].

Before reviewing the NEP's stabilisation policies in detail, we should note a rather paradoxical point: hyperinflations may be easier to end than the sort of high inflation that was experienced in Bolivia between 1982 and 1984 and in many other Latin American countries in the last several years. Hyperinflation destroys the sort of long-term contracts that embody inflationary expectations and thus continue to force prices up even in a new policy regime (recall the extremely low significance of past inflation in the previous section's regressions). Hyperinflation also breeds a sort of social exhaustion that opens the way for an explicit or implicit consensus in favour of harsh anti-inflationary measures (particularly if the measures, as in Bolivia, are accompanied by repression of those labour leaders that might resist austerity).

The Policies of the NEP

The first goal of the NEP was exchange rate stability. The government began by dramatically devaluing the peso, taking the official rate from 75,000 pesos to the dollar to the parallel rate of 1,000,000 overnight. The government then adopted a 'dirty float' system and attempted to meet most demand in order to prevent a recurrence of the sharp divergence between official and parallel rates. Three months of stability resulted, with only a slight depreciation of the peso between September and November 1985.

In December 1985 and January 1986, however, the exchange rate nearly doubled, reflecting both a shortage of dollar inflows due to the collapse of tin prices and increased inflationary expectations (and thus a flight to dollars) due to a 45 per cent increase in monetary emission in December 1985 [*Morales, 1987a: 84*]. Both the peso depreciation and a 33 per cent monthly inflation in January of 1985 created a debate among policy-makers: some analysts – including IMF officials – argued for wage adjustments and more depreciation while others – including US adviser Jeffrey Sachs – argued that stabilising the exchange rate was key to eliminating the vestiges of hyperinflation. The government followed Sachs and dumped international reserves; the peso appreciated by around ten per cent and monthly inflation quickly fell to zero by March. The events of January and February 1985 thus mark a turning point in policy; from that date, Bolivian policy-makers embraced the view that the exchange rate was the *key* instrument for controlling inflation and the government subsequently resisted any rapid depreciation to correct growing trade problems.[9]

The second component of the NEP was the liberalisation of trade and capital accounts, including the elimination of import prohibitions and the adoption of a uniform tariff.[10] Import competition, coupled with exchange rate stability, essentially played the role price controls served in the heterodox programme of Bolivia's Latin American neighbours: domestic producers were constrained from raising prices beyond the exchange rate times the relevant dollar price. In addition, the uniformity of tariffs served as a signal of orthodoxy that was key in attracting support from international creditors.

The third major thrust of the NEP involved curtailing government deficits and monetary emission. The government immediately froze public sector salaries, spending and investment; as a result, real wages of public employees fell, leading the way in the general reduction of worker income. New revenues were raised by increasing the price of gasoline to international levels and subsequently indexing it to movements in the exchange rate. This increased the *defacto* 'gasoline tax' from 0.4 per cent of GDP in 1984 to 5.6 per cent in 1985 and 7.1 per cent in 1986 [*Morales, 1987a: 79; Mann, 1988:9*].

These immediate measures were soon accompanied by a longer-term strategy to control expenditures and enhance tax revenues. The former was accomplished by reducing public sector employment, particularly in the government mining corporation, COMIBOL. COMIBOL's labour force fell by over 75 per cent between 1985 and 1987, a trend which reflected the government's goals of reducing public sector spending, adjusting to collapsing tin prices, and weakening the backbone of Bolivian labour, the miner's union. On the revenue side, the government struggled with Congress to put in place a new tax system, eventually achieving a victory in the form of a regressive value-added tax.[11]

The regressive nature of the tax reform points to the fourth key aspect of the stabilisation programme: its political and class character. Paz Estenssoro struck a political truce with the major right-wing opposition party of ex-dictator Hugo Banzer and was thus able to avoid the disastrous party conflicts that had prevented Siles Zuazo from getting any serious legislation through Congress. More important than this direct political manoeuvring, however, was the anti-worker and anti-popular tone of the new government. Morales and Sachs are mild on this point: Morales describes the treatment of labour as 'energetic' [*Morales, 1987a: 80*] while Sachs compares Paz's labour policies to Reagan's actions against PATCO [*Sachs, 1986: 30*]. The anti-labour strategy was, however, more profound: when the government's freeze of public sector wages and elimination of wage indexation produced labour protest, the government detained 30 union leaders and confined 145 to remote river ports. As the programme progressed, the government engaged in the wholesale sacking of tin miners, effectively destroying the country's most powerful labour union; instituted legislation which made it easier to fire workers and then allowed unemployment to rise from 15.5 per cent in 1984 to 20 per cent in 1986 [*Muller, 1988a: 33*]; resolved the distributional conflict over government finance with a new regressive tax structure; and continued to harshly respond to workers' protests even several years after inflation has subsided.[12]

The distributional character of the NEP, in short, was no accident and cannot be subsumed under a general discussion of the 'social costs of adjustment'. Reducing labour's power was important both in its own right and as a signal: like the more technical measures on exchange rates and monetary emission, the anti-labour thrust evidenced the seriousness of the new government and thus enhanced its 'credibility' to both domestic capital and orthodox international institutions.

The final key aspect of Paz's programme involved measures to restore net external flows of credit, a requirement for exchange rate stability given the continuing fall in export revenues and the liberalisation-induced import boom. The repatriation of capital flight was encouraged by both the government's legalisation of dollar deposits and its failure to remonetise when the end of the hyperinflation raised the demand for local currency; the resulting liquidity crisis drove real interest rates to an average of ten per cent *monthly* (active or lending rate) between October 1986 and March 1987, enough to encourage the repatriation of flight capital but also enough to choke domestic productive investment. The government also allowed dollar deposits to be made without proof of origin, a thinly disguised ploy to put coca dollars into the financial system.

Finally, the government reestablished cordial relations with official international creditors, particularly the IMF, World Bank, and the Club of Paris. In 1986, Bolivia signed its first Stand-by agreement with the Fund since 1980; agreement on longer-term structural adjustment assistance and rescheduling with the Club of Paris was reached before the end of the same year. In 1987, Bolivian authorities were allowed to indirectly enter into the secondary market for LDC debt (using money deposited by friendly nations in an IMF escrow account) and repurchase their own loans at 11 cents on the dollar, a highly unusual arrangement given the usual restrictions against such repurchases and the fact that the action was coordinated through the IMF.[13] Bolivia's favourable treatment by international financial institutions reflected both Bolivia's inflation success and its decision to stick with orthodox measures. With Argentina,

Brazil, and Peru turning to heterodox stabilisation policies, Bolivia had become the 'good boy' of an increasingly 'bad' group of Latin American debtors.

The Results and Problems of the NEP

The NEP managed to dramatically lower inflation, bringing the annual rate down to around 11 per cent by 1987. Meanwhile GDP, basically stagnant during 1984 and 1985, fell by nearly three per cent in 1986 and recuperated slightly in 1987. Real investment, after rising (surprisingly) throughout the years of the hyperinflation, fell by around 16 per cent in 1986, the first year of stabilisation and the last year for which I have data. The trade balance slipped from a hard-earned surplus of $233 million in 1984 to a deficit of $252 million by 1987, largely the result of liberalisation, the export collapse, and Argentina's refusal to make timely payments on gas purchases. While net external capital flows rose to finance the growing deficit, these eventually proved insufficient and by 1987 net international reserves declined for the first time since 1982 [*Muller, 1988a: 57*].

By mid-1987, frustration with the continuing stagnation of the Bolivian economy led to political pressure on the government to move from stabilisation to 'reactivation'. Reactivation, however, was constrained by the sort of problems experienced by Argentina and Chile during their own orthodox experiments in the late 1970s: an overvalued exchange rate which, coupled with liberalisation, had produced a sharp rise in imports; high interest rates and financial fragility; and a slippage of the government's deficit-reduction success.

The overvaluation problem was made apparent to Bolivian policy makers by the import surge of 1986 and 1987 (see Table 1). Finally 1988 brought some import restraint but not enough for Bolivia to recapture the surplus position it had enjoyed throughout most of the decade. While trade liberalisation was clearly important in the trade deterioration, the 1986–87 import boom was also due to the appreciating peso and 1988's trade improvement was partly driven by depreciation (see Table 6). The NEP had produced a more rational exchange rate policy – as Table 6 makes clear, the large gap between official and parallel rates during the hyperinflation was nearly eliminated in 1987 – but economists both in and out of the government insisted that the government's strategy of fighting inflation by supporting the peso had resulted in an overvaluation of at least 10 to 20 per cent.[14] Such overvaluation worked against the longer-term need to shift resources toward the export sector and gave new momentum to the shift away from the production of goods and toward the commercialisation of imported articles.[15] Moreover, the government's project of effectively 'fixing' the exchange rate made it reliant on both official foreign finance and incoming 'hot money'.

A strategy of resisting depreciation to curtail inflation might have been worthwhile if the exchange rate was indeed still a prime mover of price increases. To test this, I conducted causality tests for post-hyperinflation period. As in the tests for the hyperinflationary period, the regressions

TABLE 6

REAL EXCHANGE RATE FOR BOLIVIA, 1982–88

	official rate	parallel rate
1982–1985	68.8	177.2
1986	103.3	106.0
1987	100.0	101.1
1988	102.5	—

The real exchange rate (e^r) is calculated relative to the US dollar according to the formula, e^r equals $[eP_{US}/P_{BOL})$ where e is the peso/dollar period average exchange rate, P_{US} is the US consumer price index and P_{BOL} is the Bolivian price index. The official rate is normalized at 100 for 1987. The parallel rate is also normalized for 1987 but at a value reflecting the divergence between parallel and official rates for that year, a procedure which allows us to more accurately assess the divergence in the 1982–85 period of high and hyperinflation. 1988 data on the parallel rate was not available. Data sources are detailed in the Appendix.

include two leads, the current value, and four lags for the independent; the data are monthly and start after the January–February 1985 inflationary burst (when policy clearly shifted to supporting the peso). Given this starting point, the first appropriate lagged value is March; after 'using up' an additional observation in the 'quasi-differencing' procedure, the first month for a current observation is August 1986. Data were available on the monetary base and the *official* exchange rate up to December 1988, setting a last useable month at October 1988; observations of the *parallel* exchange rate were only available up to December 1987. In this section, I use the official rate both because more observations were available and because the parallel and official rates are roughly similar throughout the period. Regressions using the parallel rate (as in the earlier tests) require a different procedure due to the small number of available observations but yield a pattern similar to that reported below.[16]

Table 7 reports the results of these causality tests in the stabilisation period. As can be noted, the evidence on either the money-price or the exchange rate-price relation is inconclusive. To pursue the issue further, I ran regressions on the determinants of inflation using the same general model employed for the hyperinflationary period; both a shorter period (using all available data on the parallel rate) and a longer period (using the official rate) were covered. The results, reported in Table 8, are dismal: explanatory power is low (as evidenced by the adjusted R^2s) and while the exchange rate variables are sometimes significant, signs here (and on the monetary variables) are sometimes the opposite of both expectations and our previous results. The best we can say here is that the world has changed: the model that worked relatively well in the hyperinflationary period fell apart in the post-inflation era. On the policy side, this suggests that the policies that worked to end the inflation may have eventually become inappropriate for the post-stabilisation period. By 1988, there may have been room for currency devaluation without a passage into accelerating inflation.

By 1988, several problems besides overvaluation had also become evident, particularly in the monetary realm. The top half of Table 9 shows the pattern of selected real monetary variables since 1980. There is a dramatic decrease in monetary base, M1, and M2 over the hyperinflationary period, a trend which reflects the efforts of economic agents to economise on steadily eroding cash assets; the most dramatic example of this is the decline of M1 *below* the monetary base, a trend which indicates that non-interest bearing deposits had actually fallen below bank reserves (which are also used to 'back' the time and savings deposits represented in M2). The end of the hyperinflation brought about a large increase in the demand for suddenly useful domestic currency; however, fearful of reigniting inflation, however, the NEP's architects allowed only a slow expansion in the real money supply: not that by 1987 the real levels of the monetary base and M1 were still lower than in 1984 while M2 had staged a recovery only by a dramatic increase in foreign currency deposits. This slow remonetisation and the need to retain mobile dollar deposits produced extraordinarily high real interest rates: in 1987, the real savings rate was around 20.1 per cent (on an annual basis) while the ral lending rate was 45.1 per cent. By the end of 1988, the real savings rate had fallen to around ten per cent and the real lending rate to around 20 per cent, an improvement' that reflected some

TABLE 7

RESULTS FOR GRANGER-SIMS CAUSALITY TESTS ON PRICES, MONEY, AND THE EXCHANGE RATE IN THE POST-HYPERINFLATIONARY PERIOD

	P 'leads' M	M 'leads' P
August, 1986–October, 1988 (2,18)	1.029	0.693
	P 'leads' E	E 'leads' P
August, 1986–October, 1988 (2,18)	0.002	0.305

*** Significant at 1%
** Significant at 5%
* Significant at 10%
# Significant at 20%

All regressions include four lags, a current value, and two leads; the numbers in parantheses report the degrees of freedom used in calculating the significance of the reported F-values. The figures in the tables are F-values testing the explanatory power of the leads; the significance of each value is indicated below the reported F-value. As indicated in the text, all variables (X) in all regressions are calculated as rates of change using the formula $\{\log[(X^t)/(X^{t-1})]\}$. The regressions are first 'quasi-differenced' and include a time trend. P is taken from the consumer price index, M from the monetary base, and E from the *official* exchange rate. Data from Morales [*1987a*], Muller [*1988b*], and *International Financial Statistics*; see the Appendix for details.

TABLE 8

THE DETERMINANTS OF INFLATION IN THE POST-HYPERINFLATIONARY PERIOD

	Dependent = inflation			
	April 1986 to December 1987		April 1986 to December 1988	
Variables	(1)	(2)	(3)	(4)
Growth of Monetary Base	0.008 (0.269)		−0.028 (−0.952)	
Growth of Lagged Monetary Base	0.001 (0.043)		−0.026 (−0.819)	
Change in Parallel Exchange Rate	−0.498 (−2.329)**	−0.511 (−2.702)**		
Lagged Change in Parallel Exchange Rate	0.214 (0.804)			
Change in Official Exchange Rate			−0.619 (−1.865)*	−0.586 (−1.840)*
Lagged Change in Official Exchange Rate			−0.666 (2.066)**	−0.610 (2.044)**
Lagged inflation	0.003 (0.010)		−0.011 (−0.065)	
Constant	0.014 (2.417)**	0.015 (5.848)***	0.015 (2.851)***	0.013 (3.563)***
Degrees of Freedom	(15)	(19)	(27)	(30)
Adjusted R-squared	0.103	0.240	0.044	0.102
Durbin-Watson	1.695	1.954	1.784	1.826
F-test	1.461	7.302**	1.295	2.812*

*** Significant at 1% (two-tail)
** Significant at 5% (two-tail)
* significant at 10% (two-tail)
# Significant at 20% (two-tail)

As indicated in the text, inflation is calculated as $\log(P^t/P^{t-1})$; the other variables (growth of monetary base and change in the parallel exchange rate) are calculated similarly. For each variable, the coefficient is reported; beneath it (in parentheses) is the T-statistic accompanied by a mark indicating the significance level. Data from Morales [*1987a*], Muller [*1988a*], and *International Financial Statistics*; see the Appendix for details.

remonetisation (see Table 9) but still constituted a significant obstacle to domestic investment.

Overall, the financial system was also quite fragile. Bolivian bankers had profited from the hyperinflation by serving as channels for capital flight, acquiring fixed assets, and paying negative real interest rates on deposits; indeed, many banks expanded employment, opened new branches, and purchased new capital goods during the Siles Zuazo debacle. With the 'success' of disinflation, fixed assets became less desirable and real interest rates skyrocketed. Both phenomena threatened the asset side of banks' balance sheets, the former directly and the latter by creating debt servicing

TABLE 9
REAL MONETARY AGGREGATES AND THE COMPOSITION OF QUASI-MONEY

	monetary base	M1	M2 (includes quasi-money)	money multiplier (M2/base)
1980	100.0	106.9	168.3	1.7
1981	94.2	102.3	171.1	1.8
1982	93.5	84.8	142.6	1.5
1983	66.7	60.8	90.8	1.4
1984	50.3	50.7	61.0	1.2
1985	36.6	36.0	52.2	1.4
1986	41.6	39.8	88.9	2.1
1987	47.0	49.7	117.1	2.5
1988	65.2	55.5	141.0	2.2

Quasi-money (time and savings deposits)

	percentage of deposits in national currency	percentage of deposits in foreign currency
1980	67.7%	32.2%
1981	72.9%	27.0%
1982	97.5%	2.0%
1983	99.2%	0.8%
1984	98.7%	1.3%
1985	59.6%	40.4%
1986	37.1%	62.9%
1987	21.6%	78.4%
1988	16.9%	83.1%

The real level of the monetary variables is derived by dividing year-end nominal values by the year-end CPI; the base was normalised at 100 for 1980 and M1 and M2 were normalised for 1980 at values reflecting their nominal relation to the base.

Source: *International Financial Statistics.*

difficulties for borrowers. By April 1988, 30 per cent of bank portfolios were in arrears, a figure which understated the problem by not taking into account banks' use of internal refinance to avoid declaring domestic borrowers out of compliance [*Muller, 1988b: 29*].[17] Meanwhile, high rates and the legalisation of dollar deposits had produced a domestic banking system in which roughly two-thirds of total deposits in the domestic banking system were in dollars and nearly all of these deposits were short-term, that is with a maturity of less than 90 days [*Muller, 1988b: 7; Mercado, 1988: 58*]. Thus, the 'success' at repatriating capital had also contributed to fragility: any 'bad news' and this capital would rapidly exit, shattering the financial system and the exchange rate policy in its wake.

By 1988, government finance was also a source of concern. The NEP's impressive performance at reducing the central government's deficit had been largely accomplished by raising transfers from public enterprises to the central administration from 0.7 per cent of GDP in 1984 to 9.5

per cent in 1986 and 6.7 per cent in 1987. This strategy starved public enterprises of new investment, especially the hard-hit state oil company, and threatened long-term growth.[18] Meanwhile, the deficit success seemed to be fading: the overall deficit for the consolidated public sector rose sharply from four per cent of GDP in 1986 to nearly ten per cent in 1987. The continued shortfall triggered policy conflict between the Bolivian government and the IMF: the Fund's traditional austerity ran against the Bolivian government's desire to step up public investment, raise growth rates, and thus 'preserve the economic model' through a victory in the 1989 Presidential elections.[19]

The Fund won that battle – and lost the war. The government scaled back its plans, reduced the 1988 overall public sector deficit to around six per cent of GDP, and went on to lose the elections. The government's candidate, NEP architect and Paz's Planning Minister Gonzalo Sanchez de Losada, did manage to capture a plurality but the main parties on the right and left struck a deal in Congress that awarded the Presidency to the left's candidate, Jaime Paz Zamora, and Cabinet positions to rightists. This political defeat and the events surrounding the election carry important lessons for both policy-makers in general and the new Bolivian government in particular.

Stabilisation programs have an important distributional or class character, a feature especially clear in the case of the NEP. The populace may (and did) tolerate both general austerity and regressive redistribution as long as the memory of hyperinflation is fresh; as the memory fades, however, so does the relative complacency of the popular sectors [*Mann and Pastor, 1989*]. As Sachs [*1987*] noted in his study of 'growth-oriented adjustment', the more equitable income distribution of East Asian LDCs allowed them the distributional 'space' to reduce real wages, consumption, and currency values is the face of macroeconomic difficulties. Bolivia's NEP quickly used up such 'space' and the government lost its political basis.

The policy options for the new government are, however, quite limited by both the problems wrought by the NEP and its own politically unstable coalition. Bolivia's financial fragility, for example, was made quite clear when general uncertainty and the particular fears of a sharp devaluation produced the withdrawal of one-fourth of local bank deposits prior to the elections; the new government eventually assuaged depositors by promising to continue most of the past policy but this promise will soon run against the need to solidify the support of popular groups.[20] Bolivia's options are also constrained by its need for the financial support of international institutions and the United States. The IMF and the World Bank will likely insist that orthodox policy be maintained while the US, involved in a general anti-drug initiative, will push for coca eradication despite the damage this will do to Bolivia's supply of foreign exchange and its ability to absorb those unemployed by the previous stabilisation policy. Meanwhile, the government is tugged by rightists seeking further market liberalisation and by a moderate left hoping to use interventionist policy to raise both wages and economic activity. Sharp policy conflicts and tough policy choices loom in the future.

CONCLUSIONS

Hyperinflations take place in the monetary sphere but their causes may be found in the economic and political disintegration of the real sector. The Bolivian experience reflects such disintegration: the pressure of debt payments eroded public finance while distributional conflict produced both a wage-price spiral and an inability to resolve exactly which social sector would bear the brunt of the budget adjustments necessary to close the public sector deficit.

The New Economic Programme (NEP) attacked these fundamental problems by adopting an orthodoxy that attracted new funds and pushed the burden of adjustment on to lower income groups. The proximate causes of inflation – exchange rate deterioration, large public deficits, and excessive monetary growth – received equal attention: the exchange rate was supported by dumping scarce reserves, borrowing abroad, and raising real interest rates to attract capital flight home; deficits were reduced by raising gasoline prices and then installing a new regressive tax system; and monetary growth was curtailed dramatically, triggering a liquidity crisis that has weakened the domestic financial system. The strategy ended the hyperinflation but left a series of problems in its wake: an overvalued exchange rate, a significant trade deficit, high real interest rates, dependence on short-term flight capital, curtailed private investment, stagnant growth, and a regressive distribution of income that eventually provided the political ammunition for the removal of the NEP's architects.

Was there an alternative to the NEP policies? Despite the apparent costs of the NEP, there may have been little else for Bolivia to do. The heterodox strategies of its neighbors have not only been unsuccessful at ending inflation but also require a far stronger state than existed in Bolivia in 1985. Paz Estenssoro essentially recognised that the state had lost control over most economic variables and thus focused government action on a few key tasks: slashing the budget, suppressing the labour movement, and defending only one price, the exchange rate. Meanwhile, the potential proponents of a more distributionally progressive alternative, the left and labour unions, squandered their political capital during the Siles Zuazo regime and thus lost their best chance to demonstrate that such a progressive anti-inflation strategy was feasible.

With inflation low by Latin American standards and under pressure from working and popular sectors, the new government of Jaime Paz Zamora is likely to attempt some alternative policies. Deviations from the NEP's orthodoxy are, however, constrained by the need for foreign exchange: any distributionally progressive programme could be derailed by either capital flight or the loss of support from conservative international financial institutions such as the IMF. For Bolivia, barely recovered from the hyperinflationary damage of the early 1980s, the present is fragile and the future is uncertain.

final version received February 1990

NOTES

1. For lack of more precise definitions, most economists have adopted Cagan's classification of hyperinflation as beginning when the monthly inflation rate exceeds 50 per cent [*Cagan, 1956*]. By this standard, Bolivia began its passage into hyperinflation in April 1984 despite a brief dip in June and July of that year into single-digit monthly inflation.
2. Between 1973 and 1979, real wages fell by nearly seven per cent even while GDP per capita rose by nearly ten per cent; the divergence suggests a distributional shift away from workers. Over the years 1980–82, real wages dropped nearly 40 per cent (from the 1979 level) while GDP declined by only 12 per cent; again, the data suggest a shift away from workers. More direct evidence of this distributional pattern is offered in Lupo and Larrazabal [*1986:95*]: by one of their measures, the wage share of national output fell from 43 per cent in 1980 to 26 per cent in 1982.
3. Like other sorts of data in the Bolivian case, real wage series are of relatively poor quality and different series report slightly different trends. This series, taken from an UDAPE report as explained in the Appendix on data sources, reflects a compromise between several other series and is especially questionable for the second half of 1986.
4. It would be interesting to submit the wage-price relationship to causality tests similarly to those used below in testing the money-price and exchange rate–price relationships. Unfortunately, consistent wage series are available only on a quarterly basis and this does not afford sufficient observations for the econometric techniques used with the other variables.
5. Central government wages and salaries, for example, actually rose from 5.6 per cent of GDP in 1982 to 7.3 per cent in 1985 [*Morales, 1987a: 76*].
6. The apparent partial recuperation of external finance in 1984 (to five per cent of GDP, about one-fifth of total financing needs) mostly stems from the moratorium on debt service and thus represents accumulating arrears and not new external credit.
7. Morales [*1987b: 21–2*] also suggests that M1 could be appropriate but dismisses M2 as 'unsuitable' because of the high proportion of dollar-denominated deposits included in the latter measure. Both the causality tests detailed below and the subsequent regression analysis would yield quite similar results if we used M1 instead of the monetary base, suggesting that the results are robust to the choice of a monetary variable.
8. On a more practical level, Morales's results are nearly impossible to replicate because his method of deseasonalisation – 'a ratio-to-moving average method with geometric weights' – is noted without any further comment as to how many observations are 'averaged' or what weights are employed. I employed more standard methods to deseasonalise the raw data (an exponential smoothing technique and a detrending procedure that uses standard OLS and monthly dummies) and discovered that causality tests with such deseasonalised data do indeed reverse the monetary causality – prices 'lead' money as in Morales – while leaving the 'leading' role of the exchange rate unchanged. Because of the theoretical problems mentioned in the text, however, these results are problematic and my exercise in deseasonalisation was mostly an investigation of *how* Morales obtained his results.
9. Morales contends that 'exchange stability was a *result* and not the principal *instrument* of the anti-inflation fight . . .' [*Morales, 1987a: 80*]. My own opposing view is given in the text and, I think, is supported by the history, the econometric evidence, and Bolivian policy-makers' continual reluctance to depreciate through the 1985–88 period.
10. Tariffs were immediately set at ten per cent plus ten per cent of the previous tariff; in August 1986, tariffs were set at a flat 20 per cent on all imports [*Mann, 1988: 8*]. In March 1988, this strictly uniform approach was altered slightly by a reduction to ten per cent for tariffs of capital goods. The policy shift reflects Bolivia's investment difficulties and the government's effort to encourage some reactivation.
11. The new tax system was enacted into legislation in mid-1986 but did not become operational until a year later.
12. In July, 1987, for example, the government reacted to the threat of a petroleum workers' strike by inviting labour leaders to negotiations in La Paz, then arresting them and

declaring the oil fields a military zone, an action which implied that strikers would be arrested for being 'absent without leave'.

13. Such repurchases are usually restricted by covenants in loan agreement for somewhat obvious reasons: the right to repurchase provides an incentive for debtors to restrict service, an action which will drive down the value of the debt to levels which might make it economically feasible to simply buy back the debt at steep discounts.
14. This assessment was offered during conversations with government and academic economists and foreign advisors in June 1988.
15. Despite the apparent overvaluation in the post-stabilisation period, non-traditional exports did grow. This pattern, however, may reflect the effect of lower export taxes and the thinness of domestic markets due to the continuing slow domestic growth and low real wages. As for the shift in production, goods output as a percentage of GDP fell from an average 50.7 per cent in 1983–5 to 47.7 per cent in 1987 while services rose from 49.3 per cent to 52.3 per cent.
16. Following Sargent and Wallace [*1981*], I dealt with the shortage of observations by regressing the dependent against its lagged value and the two future values of the independent. Given the need for a lag and the 'quasi-differencing' implicit in the required Hildreth-Lu procedure, the starting current value is May 1986; the ending observation is October 1987. The F-statistic for the hypothesis that the price leads the parallel rate is 1.021 while the F-statistic for the alternative causal pattern is 1.377; neither is significant at any traditional level.
17. Given these problems in the financial system, a 1987 US–AID study calculated that banks had to charge 11–13 per cent above their own cost of funds simply to break even. This partially explains the large spreads between savings and lending rates observed in 1987 and 1988.
18. The increasing reliance on such transfers is further evidenced by the ratio of such transfers to total central administration current revenues: from an average of 28 per cent for the period 1980–85, transfers as a per cent of current revenues rose to an average of 65 per cent for 1985–87 (see Table 2). Table 2 also show the sharp drop in public enterprise investment in the NEP period: capital expenditures in this sector fell from an average of 3.5 per cent of GDP in the years 1980–84 to an average of 1.4 per cent of GDP for 1985–86 (with an increase back to the 1980–84 average estimated for 1987).
19. Details on Fund-Bolivia negotiations are offered in Muller [1988b].
20. Reported in 'Bolivian "Miracle" is at Risk,' in *Latin American Weekly Report*, 3 Aug. 1989.

REFERENCES

Cagan, P., 1956, 'The Monetary Dynamics of Hyperinflation', in M. Friedman (ed.), *Studies in the Quantity Theory of Money*, Chicago, IL: University of Chicago Press.

Carriaga, J., 1989, 'Bolivia's Structural Adjustment Program (1985–89): Its Effect on the National Consensus and the Washington Consensus', paper prepared for the Institute of International Economics conference on 'Latin American Adjustment: How Much Has Happened?', Nov. 1989.

Doria Medina, S., 1987, *1987: La Quimera de la Reactivacion*, La Paz, Bolivia: EDOBOL.

Krugman, P. and L. Taylor, 1978, 'Contractionary Effects of Devaluation', *Journal of International Economics*, No.8, pp.445–6.

Lupo, J.L. and E. Larrazabal, 1986, 'Una Medicion Funcional de la Distribution del Ingreso en Bolivia: 1970–85', in *Analisis Economico*, published by Unidad de Analisis de Politicas Economicas, La Paz, Dec.

Mann, A.J., 1988, 'The Role of Tax Reform in Bolivia Under Economic Liberalization and Stabilization', paper presented at the HIID Conference on Development Reforms, Marrakech, Morocco, Oct. 1988.

Mann, A.J., and M. Pastor, Jr., 1989, 'Orthodox and Heterodox Stabilization Policies in Bolivia and Peru, 1985–88', in *Journal of InterAmerican Studies and World Affairs*, Vol.31, No.4, Winter, pp.163–92.

Mercado, R., 1988, 'El Sistema Bancario y el Proceso de Reactivacion Economica en Bolivia', in C. Toranzo Roca (ed.), *La Reactivacion Economica (Aspectos Financieros)*, La Paz, Bolivia: Instituto Latinoamericano de Investigaciones Sociales, report No.5 from the Taller de Investigaciones Socio-Economicas.

Morales, J.A., 1987a, *Precios, Salarios, y Politica Economica Durante la Alta Inflacion Boliviana de 1982 a 1985*, La Paz, Bolivia: Instituto Latinoamericano de Investigaciones Sociales.

Morales, J.A, 1987b, 'Money Creation and the Demand for Money During the Bolivian High Inflation of 1982–85', mimeo, Universidad Catolica Boliviana.

Morales, J.A. and J. Sachs, 1988, 'Bolivia's Economic Crisis', NBER Working Paper No.2620.

Muller, H. and Associates, 1988a, *Estadisticas Economicas 1988*, La Paz, Bolivia: Instituto Latinoamericano de Investigaciones Sociales.

Muller, H. and Associates, 1988b, 'El Comportamiento Economico del Primer Cuatrimestre', Informe Confidencial, Boletin No.33, Mayo, La Paz.

Rowthorn, B. 1980, *Capitalism, Conflict, and Inflation*, London: Lawrence Wishart.

Sargent, T. and N. Wallace, 1981, 'Rational Expectations and the Dynamics of Hyperinflation,' in R.E. Lucas, Jr. and T.J. Sargent, *Rational Expectations and Econometric Practice*, Minneapolis, Minnesota, University of Minnesota Press.

Sachs, J., 1987, 'Trade and Exchange Rate Policies in Growth-Oriented Adjustment Programs', in V. Corbo, M. Goldstein and M. Khan, *Growth Oriented Adjustment Programs*, Washington, DC: International Monetary Fund and World Bank.

Sachs, J., 1986, 'The Bolivian Hyperinflation and Stabilisation', NBER Working Paper No.2073.

Schuldt Lange, J., 1988, 'Hacia La Hiperinflacion en el Peru?' part of the Guadernos de Investigacion series, Centro de Investigacion, Universidad del Pacifico, Lima, Peru.

Taylor, L., 1983, *Structuralist Macroeconomics*, New York: Basic Books.

Wilkie, J.W., 1987, 'Bolivia: Ironies in the National Revolutionary Process, 1952–86', in J.W. Wilkie and D. Lorey, (eds.), *Statistical Abstract of Latin America*, Vol.25, Los Angeles: UCLA Latin American Center Publications, University of California, pp.911–28.

APPENDIX: DATA SOURCES

Throughout this study, I have used a variety of different sources in constructing the various tables and figures.

In Table 1, the 1980–87 data on inflation, GDP growth, and private and public investment come from Muller [*1988a*]; the 1988 figures on inflation and growth come from Carriaga. Exports and imports come from *International Financial Statistics* (IFS), with CIF imports figured using the *IFS* CIF/FOB factor. External debt figures are from the *World Debt Tables, 1989–90*; the 1973 figure for total external debt in the text comes from the World Bank's *World Tables, 1987*. The growth rate of M1 is calculated from data in IFS while the rates of depreciation are calculated using 1979–81 data from Unidad de Analisis de Politicas Economicas (UDAPE), 'Annexo Estadistico', *Analisis Economico* [*1986*], 1982–87 data from Muller [*1988a*], and 1988 data from *IFS*.

The fiscal figures in both Table 1 and 2 are World Bank estimates generated using a combination of data from the Bolivian Central Bank and estimates by IMF staff. Fiscal data in Bolivia are of extremely poor quality, partly owing to the disorganisation of the public sector during the hyperinflation, and the estimates of Tables 1 and 2 may not square with other sources; they were, however, the most recent and most detailed available. Where I use different sources to point out some subfeature of public finances, this is clearly cited. Since Carriaga's [*1989*] fiscal measures for 1981–87 are more or less the same as those I use in this study, I used his 1988 estimate of the public sector deficit for Table 1.

In the regressions of Tables 3, 4, 6 and 7, I used monthly figures mostly drawn from Morales [*1987a*] and Muller [*1988a*]. I updated the monetary base from December 1986 to December 1988 using *IFS* data; the price and official exchange rate data for 1988 also came from *IFS*.

The real exchange rate (against the dollar) from 1982–87 in Table 5 was calculated as an average of monthly real rates using Bolivian price levels and exchange rates from Muller [*1988a*] and the US, CPI from various issues of the IMF's *International Financial Statistics*; I obtained the 1988 real exchange rate just using period average *IFS* data, calculating earlier years as well to make sure this procedure was consistent.

The quarterly real wage from 1982–86 used in Figure 1 is taken from 'La Economia Boliviana Durante el Ano 1986' released by UDAPE in February 1987 and squares closely with the real wage series offered in Morales [*1987a*]. Data on real wage behavior during 1973–82 (used in discussing the distributional pressures on Siles Zuazo) is taken from a 1988 report 'Empleo, Recursos Humano e Ingresos en Bolivia: Una Propuesta para la Accion' released by the Unidad de Analisis de Politicas Economicas (UDAPE). The real interest rate for 1986 and 1987 is calculated using data from Mercado [*1988: 84*] and Doria Medina [*1987: 67*]; the 1988 figure is calculated using nominal rates from Carriaga [*1989*] and the monthly inflation rate from *IFS*. GDP composition, mentioned in a footnote, is taken from Muller [*1988a*].

Journal of Economic Perspectives—Volume 6, Number 1—Winter 1992—Pages 69–85

The Case for Trade Liberalization in Developing Countries

Rudiger Dornbusch

In a broad swing of the pendulum, developing countries have been shifting from severe and destructive protection to free trade fever. Many of the notable examples are in Latin America. Mexico, after a major unilateral trade liberalization, is now negotiating a free trade agreement with Canada and the United States; Chile, traditionally a highly protected country, is a leading example of reducing trade barriers; Argentina and Brazil have entered free trade agreements. A free trade area for the Americas is becoming a serious possibility. The enthusiasm for more openness of the economy is not limited to Latin America; for example, Korea and Turkey are cases of highly successful liberalization. There are also cases in Africa—for example, Ghana and Botswana—to demonstrate the possibility and the benefits of opening up.

This new enthusiasm for freer trade stems from four overlapping sources:

Anti-statism. The world has seen a broad intellectual swing away from emphasizing the beneficial role of the state in the 1980s, and protection is seen as one of the manifestations of an overly intrusive state. Of course, a shift to a liberal trade regime has not always been the by-product of a more democratic society: Chile under Pinochet or Korea in its liberalizing phase were under authoritarian rule. "Two cheers for the market, but not three," the saying goes; today the market gets at least three cheers, which may be at least one too many.

Poor economic performance. Many developing countries have suffered dismal economic performance and declining productive potential. Much of the reason can be traced to populist macroeconomic policies that engendered debt crises and hyperinflation. Of course, part of the reason was also a very adverse external environment. But since the days of plentiful external credit are gone,

■ *Rudiger Dornbusch is Ford International Professor of Economics, Massachusetts Institute of Technology, and Research Associate, the National Bureau of Economic Research, both in Cambridge, Massachusetts.*

attention must shift to productivity gains as the source of growth. Trade may offer part of the solution.

Information. Citizens worldwide are exposed to more information about the opportunities available in other countries. It is no longer possible to conceal that goods in a country cost three or four times the world price or that they are not available. The elite want their BMWs, almost as a civil right; and the poor want cheap food and low cost consumer durables that are available in world markets; firms know what technologies and inputs their competitors abroad can use and insist on the same access. It is no longer possible to assert that liberal trade policy must immiserize a country; on the contrary, many economic actors now see access to imports as a way of stretching their buying power.

World Bank pressure and evidence of success. Major research projects under the auspices of the NBER and the World Bank have documented the problems of inward-looking trade strategies and discerned the lessons from successful trade strategies (Balassa, 1989; Bhagwati, 1978; Bruton, 1989; Krueger, 1978, 1990; Pack, 1988; Michaely et al. 1991; Thomas and Nash, 1991a, b). The research helped diffuse the black-and-white debate—free trade versus protection—to reach a more differentiated judgment involving the importance of neutral trade regimes as opposed to regimes that are biased against exports. The favorable performance of countries which adopted outward-oriented policies served to make trade liberalization, broadly understood, a central condition for World Bank lending.[1]

This paper next reviews the actual situation of protection in developing countries, to set the stage for a discussion of the prospective gains from liberalization. Three experiences with liberalization are then briefly sketched and the question is raised as to what can go wrong. The paper concludes by taking up two directions in which liberalization is now moving, regional free trade zones and liberalization of trade in services.

Protection in Developing Countries

Protection became the mode for most developing countries during the 1930s. During the Depression, industrial countries adopted restrictive trade policies and commodity prices—a major source of earnings for developing countries—collapsed. Debt service problems loomed, as discussed by Eichengreen in the Spring 1991 issue of this journal. The pursuit of a policy of

[1]These factors apply even more forcefully to Eastern Europe and the Soviet Union. As these economies shed central planning, a wide-open trade regime is seen as a critical measure. Nothing could more dramatize the belief in the promises of openness than the advice to drop from one day to the next all and any obstacles to international trade (Sachs, 1991; Dornbusch, 1991). Nor could any policy have a more drastic immediate effect; when East Germany liberalized totally in its union with West Germany, industrial production fell within a year by 50 percent and unemployment skyrocketed.

industrialization behind protective walls of tariffs and import quotas took hold first as a means of saving foreign exchange for debt payments, and then became viewed as a development strategy. The strategy was predicated on the assumption that primary producing countries would face inevitably a deterioration of the terms of trade; growth in demand for primary commodities was believed to be small because of low income elasticities for commodities and ongoing substitution toward alternative materials. At the same time, high rates of technical progress on the supply side would create a situation of excess supply and declining relative prices.

Trade policy changed little in the period immediately after World War II. Industrial countries continued for some time with highly restrictive trade policies, while many developing countries did not face foreign exchange problems due to their accumulation of foreign exchange reserves during wartime and a subsequent boom in commodity prices during the Korean war. But then commodity prices collapsed again, and developing countries faced stark questions of the appropriate trade and exchange policies. As industrial countries moved gradually in the direction of trade liberalization and currency convertibility, should the developing world follow?

The prevailing view, especially in Latin America, was the doctrine from the United Nations Economic Commission for Latin America, more commonly known as ECLA. In this view, developing countries should pursue an import substitution industrialization strategy to avoid the problem of secularly deteriorating terms of trade (Prebisch, 1959, 1984). Import substitution meant the development of domestic industry behind a high protective barrier of tariffs, quotas and licences. That policy was pursued vigorously. Direct foreign investment helped industrialization proceed, in some cases with extraordinary success, as in Brazil.

There was an intellectual counter-current supporting the classical case for free trade, notably in Jacob Viner's (1952) Rio de Janeiro Lectures and Gottfried Haberler's (1959) Cairo lectures (Meier, 1963). The debate carried into the 1960s when the protection doctrine became the main fare in the newly formed UN Conference on Trade and Development (UNCTAD), the intellectual forum in which developing countries shaped their views on trade and development strategy. Interestingly, while major progress was made in trade liberalization among industrial countries under the GATT, that same GATT allows developing countries substantial leeway in maintaining trade protection (Finger, 1991). This seems peculiar today, since poor countries especially ought to focus on making the best of their resources, but it fit the prevailing ECLA doctrine that protection was a pathway to development.

In the late 1960s and 1970s, protection in developing countries softened in at least one direction. Many countries recognized that protection by tariffs and quotas did keep imports out, but that the resulting decline in demand for foreign exchange also led to an appreciation of the currency and hence a severe tax on exports of both traditional commodities and emerging industrial goods.

Unstable real exchange rates added to the hazards of export activities. Moreover, duties on imported intermediate goods first implied a tax on export activities using these goods, and then helped cause a currency overvaluation which hurt export competitiveness of these products.

From an industrialization standpoint it made sense to avoid the anti-export implications of protectionist policies by reducing duties and pursing policies for stable exchange rates. The NBER studies mentioned earlier document that countries which adopted outward-oriented policies, at least to the extent of neutralizing anti-export bias, performed better than countries who failed to recognize the adverse effects of restrictions on their export potential.

It would be natural at this stage to offer a measure of the restrictiveness of the trade regime of various countries, and perhaps a time series portraying a protectionism index for developing countries. But even with great heroism, it is at best possible to create subjective, qualitative indices for individual countries.

Difficulties emerge from at least five sources. First, even if only tariffs were used, rates of duty differ widely across commodities. Hence one could measure at best weighted averages, but these may give a poor idea of the marginal protective effect of a tariff structure. Because of differing elasticities of demand and supply across goods, aggregate duty rates or total tariff revenue as a percent of sales are a poor measure of restrictiveness. Second, in the presence of intermediate goods the protective effect of a tariff structure depends on tariff rates on final goods relative to those on intermediate inputs. When intermediate goods enjoy lower tariff rates than final goods, as is usually the case, effective rates of protection can exceed statutory rates by a multiple.

Third, tariffs are not the only intervention by which trade might be hampered. The flora of common nontariff trade barriers include restrictive licenses; quotas; outright prohibitions; impediments to foreign exchange transactions (including required advance deposits for such transactions); customs valuation impediments, and more. Quantifying the effects of such restrictions on a common scale is even more difficult.

Fourth, the welfare cost of tariff rates and other impediments to trade depends on general equilibrium effects and market structure. For example, if substitution possibilities are moderate, then the welfare costs of distortions will be small. Similarly, restricted trade leads to imperfect competition, which may impose substantial economic costs.

Finally, restrictions on imports of one kind or another limit the quality, variety and the availability of technology.

While it is impossible to find a single representative number characterizing the restrictiveness of a trade regime, it is still possible to get an impression. An attempt to measure effective tariff rates, making appropriate adjustments for nontariff duties, has been made for the mid-1980s by Erzan and Kuwahara (1989). Table 1 presents some of their results. The first two columns show the effective tariff rates for various regions of the world on all sectors and on manufactures, while the third column shows that nontariff barriers are

Table 1
Protection in a Sample of 50 Developing Countries

	Tariff Rate[a]		*Non-Tariff*
	All Sectors	*Manufactures*	*Measures*[b]
Caribbean	17	20	23
C. America	66	71	100
S. America	51	55	60
N. Africa	39	45	85
Other Africa	36	37	86
W. Asia	5	6	11
Other Asia	25	27	21

Source: Erzan and Kuwahara (1989)
[a] Percent ad valorem tariff
[b] Percent of tariff positions covered by nontariff barriers

sometimes responsible for at least half of the protectionism impact. The table brings out that South and Central America and North Africa have had particularly high average tariff rates, and even more so in manufacturing. Within manufacturing, Erzan and Kuwahara also found that machinery and equipment receives significantly lower tariff rates than other manufactured goods.

More recently, many developing countries have gone beyond compensation for anti-export bias to more radical reform. Quotas are being turned into tariffs, tariffs are being more tightly focused, and tariff rates are being reduced. Invariably, trade policy reform has also been part of a much broader program of policy reform including domestic stabilization and deregulation. Readers interested in the diverse experiences of many nations with such reforms might consult Papageorgiou, Choksi and Michaely (1990), Michaely, Choksi and Papageorgiou (1991), Thomas and Nash (1991b), Shepherd and Langoni (1991), Whalley (1989) and World Bank (1987, 1988).

Gains from Liberalization

Measuring the benefits of trade reform has been a frustrating endeavor. Although the discussion of trade policy at times gives the impression that a liberal trade regime can do wonders for a country's economy, and most observers believe firmly that trade reform is beneficial, yet systematic attempts at quantification fail to single out trade policy as a major factor in economic growth. But then, of course, growth accounting has not come up with a satisfactory explanation for the residual which may be as much as 30 to 50 percent of growth. The channels through which trade liberalization could bring benefits are broadly these: improved resource allocation in line with social marginal costs and benefits; access to better technologies, inputs and intermediate goods; an economy better able to take advantage of economies of scale and scope; greater domestic competition; availability of favorable growth externalities, like the transfer of know-how; and a shakeup of industry that may create a Schumpeterian environment especially conducive to growth. This section will comment on each of these factors.

The static gains from improved resource allocation are the classical source of a gain from freer trade. Under perfect competition a small, price-taking country will gain by eliminating tariffs. Consumers are better off because their incomes stretch further, and resources are used more efficiently because they are no longer used to produce goods that could be imported at a lower price. As one early example of measuring these potential gains, Harberger (1959) estimated the welfare cost of protection in Chile to amount to 2.5 percent of GNP, as opposed to 10 percent for domestic distortions.[2]

While the traditional discussion often focuses on final, homogeneous goods, the case for freer trade is enriched by including the facts that trade liberalization increases the variety of goods, and raises productivity by providing less expensive or higher quality intermediate goods. This aspect has been explored in some recent models of growth; for example, Romer (1989) emphasizes both the productivity of specialized resources and the limitations given by the size of the market. In a restricted economy, only a narrow range of specialized intermediate goods or capital goods can be profitably produced and therefore the full range of technological possibilities, which rely on a potentially broader range of inputs, cannot be exploited effectively. In this model, a greater variety of inputs does more for production than a greater quantity of a narrow range of inputs. Thus, access to a variety of foreign inputs at a lower cost shifts the economy-wide production function outward, which illustrates a concrete link between productivity and the trade regime.

The availability of imported intermediate goods and of technology, whether licensed or embodied in imported capital goods, is an important additional source of gain in shedding a restrictive trade system. If foreign exchange restrictions, for example, make it impossible to use a superior process, resources are wasted. They are similarly wasted if duties or prohibitions foreclose the import of key intermediate goods that may be extravagantly expensive or impossible to produce locally. If appropriate intermediate goods can be imported, a country may easily become an exporter of labor intensive tasks such as assembly services; without such imports, that value-added opportunity is lost, along with the opportunity to graduate over time from assembly to tasks with higher value-added.

It is a well-known proposition that reducing certain tariffs, as opposed to eliminating all of them, is a more delicate issue. A partial tariff reduction is a second-best exercise, so welfare need not necessarily improve. However, it will

[2]These are the famous Harberger "triangles." See Harberger (1959).

generally be true that an equiproportionate cut in tariff rates will raise welfare. For more complicated situations of partial liberalization, computable general equilibrium models can (at least in principle) offer an answer as to the welfare effects.

Free trade leads to a more economically rational market structure. Gains from liberalization also result from scale economies and economies of scope that arise in wider markets. Moreover, markets in protected economies are narrow and lack of competitors from the rest of the world fosters oligopoly and inefficiency. Protectionism can create market power for domestic firms, where under free trade there would be none.[3] The casual evidence of these effects is striking. For example, when Mexico liberalized, firms put under pressure by import competition rationalized their activities to the point that they became export competitive. In fact, they looked to export markets to achieve a scale that would allow them to be competitive. Particularly in small countries where imports are restricted, quality is exceptionally low and variety falls far short of what is available in the world market. And prices are, of course, far above the world market, the more so the smaller and more protected the country.

An open trading environment is also associated with a transfer of know-how. Much is made, rightly, of the transfer of knowledge virtually by osmosis. Haberler (1988, p. 29) made the point this way:

> What J. S. Mill said 100 years ago is still substantially true. "It is hardly possible to overrate the value in the present low state of human improvement, of placing human beings in contact with persons dissimilar to themselves, and with modes of thought and action unlike those with which they are familiar. Such communication has always been, peculiarly in the present age, one of the primary sources of progress."

A similar argument underlies the discussion of the convergence of growth rates among countries in the world economy, as in Baumol et al. (1989) and the literature reviewed in Edwards (1991). However, the force of the Mill-Haberler argument is lessened once protectionism is taken into account. Multinationals can bring direct foreign investment, technology and knowledge, but under the cover of tariffs and quotas they may not do their best. Thus, today in Argentina, the 1964 Ford Falcon is still being produced with the U.S. machinery of that time, without model change, as if the clock had stopped.

Beyond the general benefit of exposure to an advanced, competitive world market, the act of trade liberalization also carries the potential of dynamic benefits. In their systematic study of industrialization and development, Chenery et al. (1986) focused on the sources of growth in total factor productivity. Their work suggests that periods of trade liberalization also tend to be

[3]See Helpman (1989) and Helpman and Krugman (1989) for a broad analysis of the many issues emerging under imperfect competition. See, too, Baumol and Lee (1991).

periods where total factor productivity growth is unusually high. Harrison (1991) and Salvatore and Hatcher (1991) discuss supportive evidence. The 1991 *World Development Report* (p. 100) shows for a large group of countries a positive association between trade liberalization and the residual in GDP growth after accounting for the growth in inputs. An aggressive trade opening may well qualify as a Schumpeterian change that triggers growth. As Schumpeter wrote (1934 [1983], pp. 64–66): "Development in our sense is a distinct phenomenon. ... [I]t is spontaneous and discontinuous change in the channels of the flow, disturbance of equilibrium, which forever alters and displaces the equilibrium state previously existing. ... Development in our sense then is defined by the carrying out of new combinations."

In Schumpeter's analysis, the discontinuity of events and opportunities is the critical ingredient in promoting a new growth environment, it is *change* that is the source of increased productivity. Such a discontinuity involves, specifically, the introduction of a new good; the introduction of a new method of production; the opening of a new market; the conquest of a new source of supply of raw materials or half-manufactured goods; and the carrying out of the new organization of any industry. Together, deregulation and trade reform can shake an economy out of a slow-growth trap, toward an acceleration of growth which then develops its own dynamics and financing. Of course, there is no basis here for a *sustained* increase in growth. Rather, the model suggests a temporary acceleration of growth that need not be sustained indefinitely but will have shifted the economy to a higher growth path.

The Schumpeterian model has substantial theoretical support. For example, firms may well have available better techniques and good ideas, but they are unwilling to implement them except in the favorable setting of economy-wide, major and irreversible change. Once a program of liberalization is put in place, adaptation must take place and that is the occasion to implement major productivity improvements that had been on the shelves. The coordinated response to the change both acts to trigger externalities and it assures thereby that a reversal becomes far less likely. High rates of investment and the associated increase in productivity are a natural by-product of a successful break away from a trapped slow growth economy. Trade liberalization is also a time when opportunities open up, because access to cheap inputs creates export opportunities, which carry rents and profits that can be invested in capital goods, which in turn yield further productivity gains. Although case studies of liberalization paint this picture, it is hard to capture in systematic measurements and cross-country comparisons.

It would be helpful at this stage to offer summary evidence on the proposition that outward orientation is beneficial, whatever the channels. But even though the case for these productivity gains is highly plausible, it has been hard to document in a clear-cut way. The comprehensive survey by Havrylishyn (1990) does identify systematic evidence in support of the theory, but it is not overwhelming. The most plausible evidence comes from case studies. The other important source of quasi-evidence is the more novel work of modelling imperfectly competitive economies in computable general equilibrium models (for example, Norman, 1990). These models highlight that in specific market structures or with specific scale economies, the gains from liberalized trade can be substantial. In fact, in some examples the gains are far larger than the static resource reallocation affects and come to more than 10 percent of GNP.

Recently, a number of studies have tried to investigate the link between growth performance and trade regime. The hypothesis, in line with the arguments brought above, would suggest that more open economies experience higher growth. Of course, without a satisfactory single and internationally comparable measure of openness and with so many other critical factors, investigations of this hypothesis start with a major handicap. The difficulty, of course, is in standardizing for all the factors impinging on growth performance. Edwards (1991) investigates the link to growth performance of a broad range of indicators of openness proposed in the literature and concludes that the sum of the evidence (though few individual pieces) amounts to persuasive evidence of the beneficial effects of an outward trade orientation.

Three Examples: Turkey, Korea and Mexico

In this section we sketch three examples of trade liberalization from three different parts of the world: Turkey, Korea and Mexico.

Following an earlier attempt, Turkish liberalization took place in the early 1980s. Compared to Latin America, Turkey had come early to face a debt crisis. Growth based on borrowing from abroad had been strong, but when financing disappeared, an adjustment of the economy became necessary (Sareacoglu, 1987; Celasun and Rodrik, 1989; Michaely et al., 1991; Papageorgiou et al., 1990). In the 1980–84 period, quotas were substantially eliminated, the exchange rate was depreciated, and the foreign exchange regime was liberalized. By the classification of a comparative World Bank study, the Turkish program was "major, strong and sustained."

The results of Turkish opening (and of accompanying domestic political and economic stabilization and reform) are altogether striking. Figure 1 shows the large increase in the import ratio, illustrating the radical change of trade orientation. During the late 1970s, Turkish imports had been growing about 2 percent per year, while exports were declining at 1 percent per year. But from 1979 to 1989, although Turkish imports grew by 10.4 percent per year, exports grew by 19.2 percent per year. Since overall growth in GDP was about 5 percent per year, this implies that trade became substantially more important to the Turkish economy. Interestingly, as Turkish imports and exports increases, manufacturing also grew from 22 percent of GDP in 1980 to 27 percent of GDP in 1989.

Figure 1
Turkey: Import / GNP Ratio
(percent)

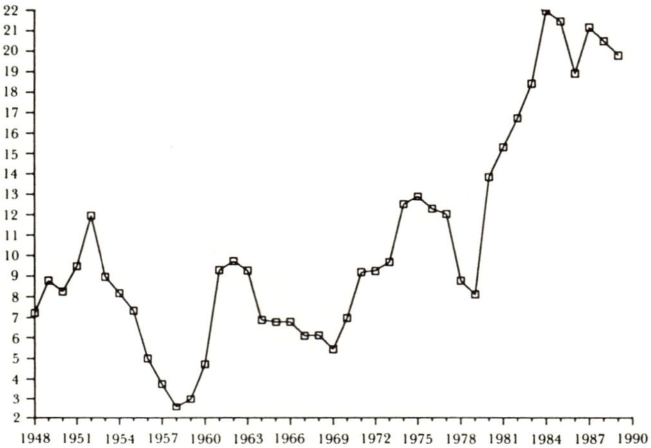

A second example is Korea, where trade reform occurred steadily in the 1970s. Here, the trade liberalization was selective. Major sectors of the economy were excluded, but the selection was accomplished in a manner that apparently did not interfere with productivity and growth. Korea made a point, in particular, of allowing capital goods and intermediate goods to be imported. For example, automobile engines were first imported, then produced under licence and now under Korean design. By 1983, of some 10,000 product classes, 19.6 percent still contained import restrictions. By 1989 the fraction had declined to only 5.3 percent and most of these were primary commodities. Only 46 industrial products continue with import licensing or prohibition. The average tariff has been brought down from 24 percent to 11 percent for industrial products with the prospect under a new tariff law to lower them to 5 percent by 1993 (Young, 1989).

Even though Korea liberalized only selectively, liberalization did take place. Korea's non-oil import/GDP ratio back in 1960 was less than 10 percent, similar to the figure today in Brazil or Argentina. But since 1975 or so, the figure has been in excess of 25 percent. With the help of a selectively liberal import strategy, Korea has been able to develop a highly competitive manufacturing sector that offers its own brand-name manufactures of increasing sophistication, ranging from cars to TV and now high technology goods. Interestingly, even though trade had been substantially liberalized in the 1980s, of the 12 percent import ratio for finished manufacturing, 1.3 percent was in

Table 2
Mexican Trade Restrictions
(percent)

	1982	*1990*
Import License Coverage	100.0	14.1
Tariff Categories	16	5
Maximum Tariff	100.0	20.0
Average Tariff	27.0	13.1
Weighted Average Tariff	16.4	10.4

Source: USITC (1990) and Banco de Mexico

consumer goods. Thus, liberalization was conspicuously concentrated on capital goods.

A third example of liberalization is Mexico. Until 1985 Mexico was totally protected: tariffs, quotas on top and licences in addition, just in case. Table 2 gives an impression of the closeness of the Mexican economy. The result was a very poor productivity performance and an extraordinary degree of monopoly, which was strongly reinforced by domestic restrictions on entry and external restrictions on direct investment.

Starting in 1985, the economy was opened. The scheme first envisaged was a gradual opening, but as political pressures for delays and exemptions built up, the Mexican administration reacted by pushing ahead the timetable and opening radically. Although some areas like chemicals and automobiles have been substantially exempted so far, a great deal of liberalization has been accomplished. Import penetration increased already from an average of 11.3 percent in 1980–85 to 14.5 in 1986–90. By 1990 import penetration had already reached 17 percent. This sharp growth in imports, unaccompanied by an offsetting immediate gain in exports, gave rise to the free trade initiative with the United States which now is under discussion.

In the three countries considered here, the trade liberalization strategy is not being questioned. Trade liberalization was part of a wider strategy of achieving stability and efficient resource allocation. As such, modernization and growth (and the resulting seeds for improved welfare) cannot be attributed uniquely to the trade strategy. But liberalized trade has so fundamentally shaken up the production structure, that more liberal trade is invariably credited with a good share of the performance. In Mexico's case, for example, output growth by 1989–90 was rising to above 4 percent, far exceeding the levels of the past five years. Even if there is no direct measure of the success of liberalization, indirect support comes from the fact that rolling back trade liberalization is simply not on the economic or political agenda.

What Remains of the Case for Protection?

The case for protection rests on one of two pillars: externalities or learning effects. Externalities are, of course, the last recourse of scoundrels; they are invariably invoked as the case for intervention even though documenting them (as opposed to modelling them) is notoriously difficult. Externalities associated with a protection strategy would arise if the physical capital formation associated with industrialization or the formation of human capital carries spillover effects, pecuniary or real, that cannot be appropriated by the individual firm and industry. Learning-by-doing as an argument for protection, by contrast, does not rely on externalities but rather on capital market imperfections that make firms reluctant to engage in the development of the productivity bonus even though from the social point of view it is warranted. Labor market imperfections may also stand in the way of a warranted industrialization if the training of labor that yields the productivity benefits cannot be captured by the investing firm and cannot be borne (for capital market or information reasons) by the workers who will be vested with the benefits. In either case, it is clear that protection is never the first-best strategy. Targeted subsidies are always better, although considerations of feasibility and political economy will always be brought in favor of protection.

Against the massive evidence that small countries will wither behind protective barriers, there is some evidence that protection can also yield success. Korea, Brazil and Japan would be the parade cases. These countries are among those with the highest growth rates of GDP and total factor productivity in the 1965–80 period and none of them is a free trader. Brazilian growth averaged 7.7 percent over the period and that of Korea was 6.7 percent per year; industry grew at 10 and 16 percent per year respectively.

Essential ingredients of the strong performance were three. First, that exchange rate policy was carefully designed to avoid overvaluation and with it macroeconomic bottlenecks. Second, that external credit played a key role as did foreign investment and foreign technology. Third, that the trade regime was sufficiently selective so that intermediate goods and capital goods were not excluded. Care was taken in particular not to tax exports implicitly.

Even though we portray the experience as a success, the interpretation might be open to challenge. Brazil did crash in the 1980s and is now seeking trade liberalization as a means to growth. In Korea, the massive investment in the heavy industry was seen in the early 1980s as a major blunder. Today, with lower oil prices, even that judgment is no longer true. While the discussion remains open, the fact is that under the cover of significant (though porous) protection both countries developed in the 1960s and '70s a world-class manufacturing sector. It remains to discern exactly what makes the difference between an Argentine experience where protection was a disaster and these very positive cases.

It is perhaps the experience of Korea and Brazil where industrialization under the cover of protection led ultimately to highly competitive export industries that accounts for the interest in the export sector as an engine of growth and the locus of government intervention. One direction is to focus on targeted liberalization that does not interfere with the nurturing of infant industries; infants have to grow up at home, they cannot start off as exporters. Another is to shift the focus to export strategies. For example, de Melo and Robinson (1990) develop a model of such a process and find that export externalities, in a computable general equilibrium model calibrated to the typical developing country experiencing export-led growth, that policies that support export externalities yield significant growth effects.[4]

The potential gains from liberalization strategy and the successful nurturing of infant industries by selective protection and subsequent export policies must be qualified in one important dimension. If developing countries as a group open up, there is every reason to believe that their terms of trade will be adversely affected. Flooding the world market with their manufactures, while their market access to industrialized countries remains the same, cannot fail to reduce the prices at which they will export (Faini et al., 1990). But for the individual country, that is not a reason to shy away from liberalization. Even for developing countries as a group, the benefits from the various sources discussed above are likely to outweigh substantially the costs of worsened terms of trade.

Even when there is a case for protection, the Korean experience suggests that the strategy works best when used selectively. In this manner the country will not devote resources to accomplishing the impossible and as a result lower productivity economy-wide. Rather, selective protection (even on a wide basis) serves to capture the learning benefits while minimizing the resource cost. That involves inevitably guessing where the areas of learning and externalities are likely to lie, it involves the risk of double-guessing markets, and it often fails. But in Korea and a handful of other cases, it has helped improve growth or at the least it seems to have done no harm to a stellar performance.

What Can Go Wrong?

One problem for trade reform is political. Too long a phase-in period with too many safeguards for those who might be adversely affected is an invitation to disruption and reversal. The other risk comes from the exchange rate. The elimination of obstacles to trade invariably creates an immediate increase in

[4]Going beyond liberalization, de Melo and Robinson (1990, pp. 30–31) conclude: "If there are externalities to be exploited, policy makers should pursue them aggressively and not worry overmuch about getting the instruments just right . . . [W]hen there are rectangles to be gained, an economy can easily afford some triangles along the way."

imports. But although inputs become more readily available and technology improves, the beneficial rise in exports does not happen immediately, even if a real depreciation is undertaken. For example, when Chile first liberalized imports almost fully in the late 1970s (but overvalued its managed exchange rate) import levels exploded and the exchange rate collapsed. Another stabilization had to be undertaken. Without a real depreciation, exports will scarcely help pay for the higher imports.

Because of balance of payments problems, comprehensive trade reform requires one of two conditions: either the country must be politically in a position to have a major real depreciation of the exchange rate (to help boost exports) or else it must have access to foreign exchange for a substantial period of time. Real depreciation is a problem because it means a fall in real wages unless offset by the improvement in the standard of living that stems from reduced protection. If reserves are not available and depreciation is impractical, the only realistic option for trade policy is to approach liberalization more gradually.

A gradual path to trade liberalization should occur in two steps. In a first round, the country should move from quotas and licences and other nontariff barriers to a uniform, high tariff of (say) 50 percent. Later, as the economy grows and the external balance can support liberalization without the risk of a foreign exchange crisis, tariffs can be taken down to (say) 10 percent. This more moderate policy still opens the economy, because even tariffs at high rates allow competition at the margin, while quotas and licenses are there to prevent it. But at the same time it avoids the grave risk of an exchange crisis.

A drastic example of liberalization at the wrong exchange rate comes from the recent unification of Germany. Prior to unification East Germany had traded mostly with the Soviet Union, and little with nonsocialist economies. When consumers faced unification and free trade with West Germany, they turned overnight from domestic goods toward West German merchandise. In economies left out of world progress, "opening up" translates into a situation where domestic goods become lemons that cannot be sold virtually at any price. The result in East Germany was a decline of industrial production of 50 percent and, for a time, mass unemployment. Joint ventures and western brand names on improved eastern products are seen as the answer.

Of course, the East German experience is special in that the exchange rate conversion made West German goods expensive, but not astronomically so. However, even in a situation where exchange rates are set so that foreign goods are clearly far more expensive than domestic brands, say by a factor of two or three, rapid and pervasive import penetration is likely to occur. Liberalization in Chile and Mexico has made that clear.

The East German experience will be repeated, although on a lesser scale, as other countries open up, whether in Eastern Europe or in the third world. One response is to try and avoid such disruptions by continuing protectionism or traditional trade agreements. But the right answer is to recognize that the adjustment ought to happen, because consumers and producers do want better and more varied goods. Countries should bite the bullet by adopting highly competitive exchange rates, even if that means that imports are relatively quite expensive. Only when there is massive support from abroad and coordinated direct investment (as in the case of East and West Germany) can there be an expectation of avoiding a sharp real depreciation.

New Directions in Trade Strategy

In concluding this essay, we draw attention briefly to two new directions in trade strategy: service trade liberalization and regional free trade agreements.

Most of the discussion of trade liberalization in the past has focused on merchandise trade and until recently almost no attention and certainly no empirical work has paid attention to trade in services. The Uruguay Round of trade negotiations now underway changes that. Trade in services is a major issue for developed countries who see themselves as exporters, but also for developing countries who expect some export opportunities, but also recognize the role of services in promoting productivity.

Most of the recent attention has focused on financial services (banking, underwriting, insurance) where there are obvious gains from scale economies and competition. Financial markets in developing countries (and in Europe) operate far less competitively and with far larger spreads and fees than in the United States. Hence the case for liberalizing financial service trade. But the interest in service trade liberalization extends to other areas: accounting, consulting, legal services, construction planning, design, telecommunications and others. It is clear that the case for liberalized trade in services is no different from that for trade in merchandise. The fact that services have not been much traded in the past draws attention to a stark omission in the traditional assessments of the cost of protection.

The second new direction is even more sweeping: developing countries are looking for free trade arrangements with developed countries. Previously, the issue of market access and preferential access to the markets of developed countries had been a chief item on the agenda of UNCTAD. The General System of Preferences, under which industrial countries gave developing countries privileged market access for a broad range of goods, was a way of implementing that objective. What is new is the willingness to practice free trade as a two-way street. Mexico has taken that route in asking for free trade negotiations with the United States and Canada and, following an acrimonious debate before the U.S. Congress, negotiations are now under way. The United States may take the NAFTA (North American Free Trade Agreement) as a blueprint to allow other countries to adhere on a conditional most-favored-nation basis. If that turns out to be the case, the Americas may become a free trade area in the next decade or two.

■ *I am indebted to Brian Aitken for valuable assistance and to the National Science Foundation for research support. The editors provided abundant, generous and thoughtful comments.*

References

Balassa, B., "Outward Orientation." In Chenery, H. and T. N. Srinivasan, eds., *Handbook of Development Economics.* New York: North Holland, *2*, 1989, 1645–1690.

Baumol, W., S. A. Batey Blackman and E. Wolf, *Productivity and American Leadership: The Long View.* Cambridge: MIT Press, 1989.

Baumol, W. and L. S. Lee, "Contestable Markets, Trade and Development," *World Bank Research Observer,* January 1991, *6*:1, 1–18.

Bhagwati, J., *Foreign Trade Regimes and Economic Development. Anatomy and Consequences of Exchange Control Regimes.* Cambridge: Ballinger, 1978.

Bruton, H., "Import Substitution." In Chenery, H. and T. N. Srinivasan, eds., *Handbook of Development Economics.* New York: North Holland, *2*, 1989, 1601–1644.

Celasun, M. and D. Rodrik, "Debt, Adjustment and Growth: Turkey." In Sachs J. and S. Collins, eds., *Developing Country Debt and Economic Performance, 3,* Chicago: University of Chicago Press, 1989, 615–808.

Chenery, H., S. Robinson and M. Syrquin, *Industrialization and Growth.* Oxford: Oxford University Press, 1986.

de Melo, J. and S. Robinson, "Productivity and Externalities. Models of Export-Led Growth." Working Papers WPS 387, World Bank, 1990.

Dornbusch, R., "Priorities of Economic Reform in Eastern Europe and the Soviet Union." Centre for Economic Policy Research, Policy Paper No. 6, London, 1991.

Edwards, S., "Trade Orientation, Distortions and Growth in Developing Countries," mimeo, University of California, Los Angeles, 1991.

Eichengreen, Barry, "Historical Research on International Lending and Debt," *Journal of Economic Perspectives,* Spring 1991, *5*:2, 149–169.

Erzan, R. and K. Kuwahara, "The Profile of Protection in Developing Countries," *UNCTAD Review,* 1989, *1*:1, 29–49.

Faini, R., F. Clavijo and A. Senhadji-Semiali, "The Fallacy of Composition Argument: Does Demand Matter for LDC Manufacturing Exports?" Center for Economic Policy Research, Discussion Paper No. 499, December 1990.

Finger, M., "Development Economics and the General Agreement on Tariffs and Trade." In de Melo, J. and A. Sapir, eds., *Trade Theory and Economic Reform. Essays in Honor of Bela Balassa.* Cambridge: Basil Blackwell, 1991, 203–223.

Haberler, G., "International Trade and Economic Development." (The Cairo Lectures, 1959). Reprinted in *International Trade and Economic Development.* Washington DC: American Enterprise Institute, 1988, 17–54.

Harberger, A., "Using Resources at Hand More Effectively," *American Economic Review,* May 1959, *49*:1, 134–146.

Harrison, A., "Openness and Growth: A Time-Series, Cross-Country Analysis of Developing Countries," mimeo, World Bank, 1991.

Havrylyshyn, O., "Trade Policy and Productivity Gains in Developing Countries: A Survey of the Literature." *World Bank Research Observer,* January 1990, 5:1, 1–24.

Helpman, E., "The Noncompetitive Theory of International Trade and Trade Policy," *Proceedings of the World Bank Annual Conference on Development Economics,* 1989, 193–216.

Helpman, E. and P. Krugman, *Trade Policy and Market Structure.* Cambridge: MIT Press, 1989.

Krueger, A., *Foreign Trade Regimes and Economic Development. Liberalization Attempts and Consequences.* Cambridge: Ballinger, 1978.

Krueger, A., "Comparative Advantage and Development Policy Twenty Years Laster." In Krueger, A., ed., *Perspectives on Trade and Development.* New York: Harvester Wheatsheaf, 1990, 49–70.

Meier, G., *International Trade and Development*. New York: Harper and Row, 1963.

Michaely, M., A. Choksi and D. Papageorgiou, *Liberalizing Foreign Trade. Lessons of Experience in the Developing World*. Cambridge: Basil Blackwell, 1991.

Norman, V., "Assessing Trade and Welfare Effects of Trade Liberalization," *European Economic Review*, June 1990, *34*:4, 725–745.

Pack, H., "Industrialization and Trade." In Chenery, H. and T. N. Srinivasan, eds., *Handbook of Development Economics*. New York: North Holland, *1*, 1988, 333–380.

Papageorgiu, D., A. Choksi and M. Michaely, *Liberalizing Foreign Trade in Developing Countries. The Lessons of Experience*. Washington, D.C.: The World Bank, 1990.

Prebisch, R., "Commercial Policy in the Underdeveloped Countries," *American Economic Review*, (Papers and Proceedings), May 1959, *40*, 261–264.

Prebisch, R., "Five Stages in My Thinking on Development." In Meier, G. and D. Seers, eds., *Pioneers in Development*. Oxford: Oxford University Press, 1984, 175–191.

Romer, P., "Capital Accumulation in the Theory of Long Run Growth." In Barro, R., ed., *Modern Business Cycle Theory*. Cambridge: Harvard University Press, 1989, 51–127.

Sachs, J., "Sachs on Poland," *The Economist*, January 19th, 1991.

Salvatore, D., and T. Hatcher, "Inward Oriented and Outward Oriented Trade Strategies," *The Journal of Development Studies*, April 1991, *27*:3, 7–25.

Sareacoglu, R., "Economic Stabilization and Structural Adjustment. The Case of Turkey." In Corbo, V., M. Goldstein and M. Khan, eds., *Growth-Oriented Adjustment Programs*, IMF and World Bank, 1987, 119–139.

Schumpeter, J., *The Theory of Economic Development*, [1934]. Reprinted by Transactions Books, New Brunswick, 1983.

Sheperd, G. and C. Langoni, *Trade Reform Lessons from Eight Countries*. San Francisco: ICS Press, 1991.

Thomas, V. and J. Nash, "Reform of Trade Policy," *World Bank Research Observer*, July 1991a, *6*:2, 153–172.

Thomas, V. and J. Nash, eds., *Best Picture in Trade Policy Reform*, Oxford: Oxford University Press, 1991b, forthcoming.

United States International Trade Commission. *Review of Trade and Investment Liberalization Measures by Mexico*. USITC Publication 2275, Washington DC, 1990.

Viner, J., *International Trade and Economic Development*. Glencoe: The Free Press, 1952.

Whalley, J., "Recent Trade Liberalization in the Developing World: What is Behind it and Where is It Headed?," NBER Working Paper, No. 3057. August 1989.

World Bank, *Adjustment Lending. An Evaluation of Ten Years of Experience*, Policy and Research Series No. 1, 1988.

World Development Report, published for the World Bank. New York: Oxford University Press, June 1987.

World Development Report, published for the World Bank. New York: Oxford University Press, June 1991.

Acknowledgments

Harberger, Arnold C. "The Fundamentals of Economic Progress in Underdeveloped Countries: Using the Resources at Hand More Effectively." *American Economic Review* 49 (1959): 134–46. Courtesy of Yale University Law Library.

Prebisch, Raúl. "International Trade and Payments in an Era of Coexistence: Commercial Policy in the Underdeveloped Countries." *American Economic Review* 49 (1959): 251–73. Courtesy of Yale University Law Library.

Seers, Dudley. "A Theory of Inflation and Growth in Under-Developed Economies Based on the Experience of Latin America." *Oxford Economic Papers* 14 (1962): 173–95. Courtesy of Yale University Sterling Memorial Library.

Felix, David. "Monetarists, Structuralists, and Import-Substituting Industrialization: A Critical Appraisal." *Studies in Comparative International Development* 1 (1965): 137–53. Reprinted with the permission of Transaction Publishers. Courtesy of Yale University Seeley G. Mudd Library.

Leff, Nathaniel H. and Antonio Delfim Netto. "Import Substitution, Foreign Investment, and International Disequilibrium in Brazil." *Journal of Development Studies* 2 (1966): 218–33. Reprinted with the permission of Frank Cass & Co., Ltd. Courtesy of Yale University Sterling Memorial Library.

Hirschman, Albert O. "The Political Economy of Import-Substituting Industrialization in Latin America." *Quarterly Journal of Economics* 82 (1968): 1–32. Reprinted with the permission of MIT Press. Courtesy of Yale University Law Library.

Baer, Werner. "Import Substitution and Industrialization in Latin America: Experiences and Interpretations." *Latin American Research Review* 7 (1972): 95–122. Reprinted with the permission of the *Latin American Research Review*. Courtesy of Yale University Sterling Memorial Library.

Torres-Rivas, Edelberto. "The Central American Model of Growth: Crisis for Whom?" *Latin American Perspectives* 7 (1980): 24–

44. Reprinted with the permission of Sage Publications, Inc. Courtesy of Yale University Sterling Memorial Library.

Bulmer-Thomas, V. "Economic Development Over the Long Run—Central America Since 1920." *Journal of Latin American Studies* 15 (1983): 269–94. Reprinted with the permission of Cambridge University Press. Courtesy of Yale University Sterling Memorial Library.

Diaz-Alejandro, Carlos. "Good-bye Financial Repression, Hello Financial Crash." *Journal of Development Economics* 19 (1985): 1–24. Reprinted with the permission of Elsevier Science Publishers B.V. Courtesy of Yale University Social Science Library.

Edwards, Sebastian. "Stabilization with Liberalization: An Evaluation of Ten Years of Chile's Experiment with Free-Market Policies, 1973–1983." *Economic Development and Cultural Change* 33 (1985): 223–54. Reprinted with the permission of the University of Chicago Press. Courtesy of Yale University Sterling Memorial Library.

Blejer, Mario I. and Adrienne Cheasty. "High Inflation, Heterodox Stabilization, and Fiscal Policy." *World Development* 16 (1988): 867–81. Reprinted with the permission of Pergamon Press. Courtesy of Yale Unversity Social Science Library.

Dornbusch, Rudiger and Sebastian Edwards. "Macroeconomic Populism." *Journal of Development Economics* 32 (1990): 247–77. Reprinted with the permission of Elsevier Science Publishers B.V. Courtesy of Yale University Social Science Library.

Fishlow, Albert. "The Latin American State." *Journal of Economic Perspectives* 4 (1990): 61–74. Reprinted with the permission of the American Economic Association. Courtesy of Yale University Law Library.

Shapiro, Helen and Lance Taylor. "The State and Industrial Strategy." *World Development* 18 (1990): 861–78. Reprinted with the permission of Pergamon Press. Courtesy of Yale University Social Science Library.

Pastor, Manuel, Jr. "Bolivia: Hyperinflation, Stabilisation, and Beyond." *Journal of Development Studies* 27 (1991): 211–37. Reprinted with the permission of Frank Cass & Co., Ltd. Courtesy of Yale University Sterling Memorial Library.

Dornbusch, Rudiger. "The Case for Trade Liberalization in Developing Countries." *Journal of Economic Perspectives* 6 (1992): 69–85. Reprinted with the permission of the American Economic Association. Courtesy of Yale University Law Library.